Literary Study of the Bible

Literary Study of the Bible

An Introduction

Christopher Hodgkins

WILEY Blackwell

Registered Offices
John Wiley & Sons, Inc., 111 River Street, Hoboken, NJ 07030, USA
John Wiley & Sons Ltd., The Atrium, Southern Gate, Chichester, West Sussex, PO19 8SQ, UK

Editorial Office
The Atrium, Southern Gate, Chichester, West Sussex, PO19 8SQ, UK

For details of our global editorial offices, customer services, and more information about Wiley products visit us at www.wiley.com.

Wiley also publishes its books in a variety of electronic formats and by print-on-demand. Some content that appears in standard print versions of this book may not be available in other formats.

Library of Congress Cataloging-in-Publication Data

Names: Hodgkins, Christopher, 1958– author.
Title: Literary study of the Bible : an introduction / by Christopher Hodgkins.
Description: 1 [edition]. | Hoboken : Wiley, 2020. | Includes bibliographical
    references and index. |
Identifiers: LCCN 2018049406 (print) | LCCN 2019002179 (ebook) | ISBN 9781118604502
    (AdobePDF) | ISBN 9781118604496 (ePub) | ISBN 9781444334951 (paperback)
Subjects: LCSH: Bible–Criticism, interpretation, etc.
Classification: LCC BS511.3 (ebook) | LCC BS511.3 .H63 2020 (print) | DDC 220.6/6–dc23
LC record available at https://lccn.loc.gov/2018049406

Cover Design: Wiley
Cover Image: © The William Blake Archive/Wikimedia Commons—"Jacob's Ladder"

Set in 10/12pt Warnock by SPi Global, Pondicherry, India

10 9 8 7 6 5 4 3 2 1

To George

Tolle lege

Contents

Acknowledgments

Since this book is the fruit of a quarter-century of teaching, many of my most prominent debts are to colleagues and students. James E. Evans, my first Head in the English Department of the University of North Carolina at Greensboro, invited me in 1994 to develop a course in Literary Study of the Bible, and after my initial trepidation passed, I discovered that English 371 stirred the liveliest and widest-ranging discussions of all my classes – which is saying a great deal, since my other courses engage the most splendid works of the Renaissance, from Thomas More and Philip Sidney and William Shakespeare through the metaphysical poets and John Milton and Andrew Marvell. Indeed, while I have benefited from a number of other texts and textbooks treating "The Bible as Literature" (see Suggestions for Further Reading), my roots in the English Renaissance inspired my book's unique design, for I begin all of my courses with a unit on lyric poetry – whether Shakespeare's *Sonnets*, John Donne's *Songs and Sonnets* and *Divine Poems*, George Herbert's *Temple*, or Milton's *Poems*. So I elect to begin this book in the middle of the Bible, and of biblical literary history, with the Psalms. Each psalm is a "little world made cunningly," and all of them nevertheless model many of the chief devices, characteristics, and themes of Hebrew literature. I have found that starting *in medias res* like the epic poets of old, by unpacking a few representative short lyric poems, is the quickest and most exciting way into the heart of the biblical imagination, and hope that the reader will too.

I also wish I could thank my late colleague Russ McDonald, "Shakespeare god" and unparalleled academic *yenta*, for first suggesting my course's potential as a textbook, and for putting me in touch with Wiley-Blackwell Acquisitions Editor Emma Bennett, who over the course of the book's long gestation was joined or succeeded by Isobel Bainton, Ben Thatcher, Annie Rose, Sarah Wightman, Deirdre Ilkson, Manish Luthra, Jake Opie, Viniprammia Premkumar, and Camille Bramall. As to that gestation, many other projects have delayed the progress of this book – two monographs, four essay collections, one journal special issue, two National Endowment for the Humanities (NEH) grants leading to two born-digital editions, and about a dozen conferences and symposia organized and presented – making my task feel at times, as Marvell said, "vaster than empires, and more slow." I console myself that Moses took fifteen more years than I to arrive in the Promised Land.

But this gradual ripening has meant that virtually every concept, lesson, or example in the finished book has been tested and refined dozens of times in collaboration with the thousands of students who have explored the Bible with me over the decades. These students have come from virtually every religious persuasion, including "none"; from every continent except Antarctica; from scores of academic disciplines across the natural and social sciences, arts and humanities; and they have ranged from Sunday School and Hebrew School stars to biblical neophytes, and from the most enthusiastic *literati* to inveterate poetophobes. This very long "road test" means that while there are some great questions that this textbook does not presume to answer – usually questions of a metaphysical variety – there are very few questions and challenges that this author has not heard or addressed. Thus, my debt of gratitude to my students is practically infinite – hardly a page of this book would exist without them.

Special thanks are also due to some special mentors, colleagues, students, correspondents, and friends who have influenced or discussed or read this work in progress and thus have helped me to improve it (in alphabetical order): Brian Augustine, Beatrice Batson, Anthony Brogan, Neal Buck, Jason Crawford, Anthony Cuda, Sam Fornecker, Kathleen Fowler, John Gabel, Sidney Gottlieb, Malcolm Guite, Hannibal Hamlin, Andrew Harvey, Russell Hillier, Alice Irby, Bill Kellogg, Nathan Kline, Gail McDonald, Charles McKnight, Jeff Miller, Matt Mullins, Kenneth Oliver, Harrison Phipps, Stephen Prickett, Leland Ryken, Joseph Sterrett, Richard Strier, Louis Surprenant, Matt Wallace, Robert Whalen, Joan Whitcomb, and Helen Wilcox.

Many in my family have lived with and responded to this undertaking: my children, Mary, Alice, and George, for much of their lives; my father Royce and late mother Eleanor, in their repeated visits to my classrooms; my brothers Craig and Charles; and my wife Hope – my best friend and best editor. *Consummatum est*!

Preface

Literary Study of the Bible: And the Word Became Text

What is "literary study of the Bible"? More to the point, what is "literary study"? First and foremost, it means attention to form and imagination; that is, a focus on the shapes that we give to our written songs and annals, our arguments and tales – and on the images that animate them. Thus "literary study" means observing the types and traditions of writing; noting the changes that writers and their word-pictures ring on these traditions; listening to the figures and sounds of language; and scrutinizing the effects of these variations on hearers and readers. Add to these elements the storytelling devices of characterization and plot, the atmospheric considerations of tone and mood, and the perennial questions of subject matter and theme, and one has a reasonable sense of what literary study entails. It explores the mysterious space between imaginative adoption and adaptation, and thus it is not an exact science.

Speaking of science, the oldest recorded use of the word "literary" occurs in 1605, in Francis Bacon's *Advancement of Learning*, the first programmatic description and defense of what he called "natural philosophy" and what we now call "the scientific method." This means that the terminology of the specifically "literary" is twin-born with the great empirical project that distinguishes between the imaginary and the factual, the humane and the technical, the fantastic and the real. Yet in 1605, Bacon sees the literary and empirical not as conflicting but as complementary, as two deeply important kinds of *scientia*, or "science" – that is, of knowledge. Indeed, for the father of empiricism, the "literary," far from being an illusion destined to be dispelled by the long march of science, is instead the summation and goal of science itself, virtually synonymous with all "knowing": for, he says, the "literary" is that "which doth most show the spirit, and life of the person." As much as empirical experiment may expose and describe the splendid machinery of life, says Bacon, the point of this machinery is to support human personality. So if we are to know persons, to know spirits – to know souls – we must look to the literary. Without it, Bacon writes, natural and civil history are effectively blind, like "*Polyphemus* with his eye out" – and a Cyclops has no eye to spare.[1] To leap from Homer to Jesus, "If therefore the light that is in you is darkness, how great is that darkness!" (Matthew 6:23).

Having invoked the New Testament, what then do we say about "literary study *of the Bible*"? If we moderns (and now post-moderns) often hear the comparison of the literary and the scientific as an opposition between fancy and fact, we also sometimes hear "the Bible as literature" as either a rejection or as a stratagem – that is, either as a pretext for dismissing or ignoring the Bible's pervasive truth claims and religious content, or as an excuse for proselytizing on their behalf. In other words, in the ears of many, "the Bible as literature" registers as "the Bible as *mere* literature," with "literature" meaning fantasy or legend rather than reality; or, on the other hand, as "the Bible treated as *great* literature for stealth evangelism."

What both of these rather jaded responses have in common is their despair of any way in which people with truly diverse beliefs and backgrounds can approach an open, respectful, responsible study of the Judeo-Christian scriptures – either the secularists fear that the evangelists will try to hijack the discussion, or the religious folk worry that the Word of God will be disrespected and dissected as just another "text." It's not difficult to understand either reaction, for the Bible is both uniquely beloved and highly alarming. No other ancient book is so continuously contemporary in the modern world as the Bible, a runaway best-seller for centuries; no other old book is so intimately familiar, or so excessively strange, often to the same readers; and readers bring to this book, more than to any other set of literary writings, their strong preconceptions about what the text says and how to understand it. Furthermore, even in our supposedly secular age, presidents and jurors are not sworn in on *Moby-Dick*, and people generally have not been willing to die (or to live) for *Pride and Prejudice*. Thus, for many the Bible is a culturally threatening and frightening book, too often used as a weapon; while for many the Bible contains the authoritative Word of God, the fountain of joy, the waters of Life itself for many others, perhaps most, the Bible is a little of both. Thus, few who open a Bible are indifferent to it.

So what, after all, does it mean when the Word becomes "text"? That is, what happens when the professed words of God Almighty come down and dwell among us where they can be put to the question, like words in a play or poem or story? The answer is that, with the right combination of contextual knowledge, ideological humility, and interpretive care, much richer understanding can emerge. While it is worthwhile to approach the Bible with many other devotional and academic methods, our approach in this textbook will be to ask consciously "literary" questions about form, language, characterization, poetic craft, and imaginative tradition – and to contextualize these questions with what can be solidly known (rather than speculatively guessed) about the texts' composition and history. Some devout Bible readers may be concerned that such a focus on human means may obscure the divine ends of these sacred writings; more secular readers may be unsettled that we will find a good deal more textual integrity and complementarity in and among the Bible's books than do many current theorists. Some believers will be disturbed that I don't endorse any one doctrinal system for interpretation, while some skeptics will worry that I decline to refute or criticize the obvious supernaturalism of nearly all the biblical writers.

My response to all such concerns is that the first responsibility of literary interpretation is to interrogate the text as we have it, and to give the original writers and audiences the basic human courtesy of consulting their points of view before imposing our own. No doubt there will be time to correct, to doubt, or to disagree, just as there will be time to endorse, to affirm, or to embrace. But first we need to know, fully and fairly, just what we are choosing to dismiss or to believe. As for the concern that we murder the text to dissect it: anatomy is not merely or necessarily the dismembering of the dead. Indeed, the best and most revealing kind of anatomical study "re-members" the interrelations of vital organs in sustaining the growth and movement of an animate organism – very much alive on the hoof or on foot or on the wing. Similarly, to note that a psalm is made of words and rhythms and parallels and figures and stanzas isn't to leave it flayed like a disarticulated bird, but to re-experience wonder every time the living poem takes flight anew in the reader's eye and ear.

How, then, can literary study of the Bible advance our learning? First, of course, as one of the world's foundational cultural texts, the Bible is an imaginative source book for countless references to come, from *Fiat Lux* and Noah's dove, through "let my people go" and Goliath's head, to the Moneychangers and the Prodigal Son and the City Foursquare. We will trace the Bible's literary influences on confessional writing and Dante's cosmology, Arthurian chronicle and *King Lear*, metaphysical poetry and Goethe's *Faust*. We will draw lines connecting Genesis and Jefferson, Moses and Martin Luther King, Gideon and Churchill, Samson and *Shane*, Job and George Bailey, David and Dylan. We'll attend to Founding Mothers, Warrior Women, Domestic Heroines, Seductresses, and Redeemed Courtesans from Eve, Sarah, Rahab, and Deborah, to Ruth, Jezebel, the Magdelene, and Mary – not forgetting the Whore of Babylon and the Bride of Christ.

Second, we'll consider the Bible's many books as embedded in a network of pan-Mediterranean and Afro-Eurasian cultures stretching back 7000 years, finding echoes of the *Enuma Elish* and *Gilgamesh* in Genesis, drawing comparisons between Hammurabi and Exodus and Akhenaten, hearing anticipations of the Psalms and Canticles in Egyptian love lyrics, and foreshadowings of Homer in the Davidic epic of 1 and 2 Samuel; and we'll discover the roots of Gospel narrative in Hebrew chronicle, of New Testament theological letters in workaday Greco-Latin epistles, and of Revelation's famed symbology in Old Testament apocalyptic prophecy.

But third, we'll advance our learning by not only attending to Bible legacies and sources, but also to the Bible's unparalleled range of characterization, setting, style, and theme. Far from being a monotonous monotheistic monologue, this great book of divinity is a humanistic education in itself, presenting a dizzying diversity of voices, outlooks, and circumstances far surpassing Shakespeare and Dickens. This range begins in the opening chapters of Genesis, with its doubled creation accounts, and appears in the line-by-line variety of Hebrew parallel poetry, and in the famed reticence of biblical narrative style, which portrays different motives and outcomes with shockingly little judgment – so that, as Mark Twain puts it, the story "seems to tell itself." No ancient book, or anthology of books, invites us to consider such varied ethical and personal perspectives, and yet no book is better known for its ultimate moral and cosmic certainty. If by "literary" we mean, with Bacon, that "which doth most show the spirit, and life of the person," then the Bible is "literature" *par excellence*.

Perhaps this is partly why that founding empiricist held an opinion of biblical authority probably shocking to our contemporary ears. Like the next generations of experimental researchers to come after him, from William Harvey through the Royal Society's founders and Isaac Newton, Bacon saw the Bible both as the foundation and the ultimate goal of this accumulation of "literary," humane learning. Trusting in the design and ordained laws of the Creator, Bacon and his disciples sought to think God's thoughts after him, confident that discovery was also a kind of "recovery" of forgotten truth, a rolling back of sin's curse and an advancement of human flourishing that would, paradoxically, take humanity back to the future in a kind of Paradise regained.

It is now, of course, common to hear the Bible spoken of as superseded and even replaced by the research machinery that Bacon wrought. Humanity still seeks some kind of Paradise, but we are told that it will be regained, or gained, by cumulative human means; indeed, in this view, true Paradise can only come when humans fully rely on their own rigorously tested insight, end a childish dependence on the gods, and stand forth to "know good and evil" on their own, and thus merit the optimistic self-imposed title "*Homo sapiens*," "wise men." Yet that very language should bring us up with a start, for the Bible writers anticipated it thousands of years ago, whether in Genesis ("you shall be as gods") or in Ecclesiastes ("adding one thing to another to find out the reason") or in Romans ("professing to be wise"). Somehow, even when we would escape biblical ideas, we find ourselves repeating them, even if many follow these themes to different conclusions.

Perhaps ironically, while many reject the relevance of biblical "divinity" on scientific grounds, others question the worth of the "humanities," as well. Certain ardent advocates of the empirical project see their work not as complementary to the literary, but rather as essentially competitive with it, increasingly dismissing "the humanities" as at best a passing amusement, and at worst a wasteful distraction – useful not as ends in themselves, but only to be admitted on utilitarian terms, as promoters and handmaids of technological and material progress. Newspaper opinion pages and online response sites regularly teem with debates over the relative value to society of projects empirical and humanistic, some arguing that just as God (or the concept of God) "died" in the 1960s, so "humanity" (or the concept of humanity) is dying now, in order to make room for some new human–technological hybridity that will own the future. Ironically, a devaluation of "humanistic" learning, once primarily the theme of religious fundamentalists, has now become a goal of some atheist materialists.

While the full range of these philosophical and theological arguments is beyond the scope of this literary textbook, I would say two things in drawing this preface to a close: first, that, whatever we believe about the Bible's claims for itself, biblical images and categories of thought are more relevant than ever, as we all seem to be drawn irresistibly to language of "knowing the end from the beginning," of seeking a new "Genesis" of "redemption" and even "salvation" by remaking the world "in our image" in order to prevent the "Apocalypse" and somehow return to the "Garden." But second, we will remember Bacon's warning: if the "empirical" is one eye and the "literary" the other, we should beware lest in putting out the "unnecessary" eye we make ourselves as blind as Polyphemus. For really, there are no unnecessary eyes, if we are to see deep and whole.

Such a multiplicity of perspective informs this textbook's very structure. First, the reader will find a kind of "peripheral vision" represented by a series of boxes that periodically illuminate particular linguistic, historical, geographical, or cultural details in order to enrich the main flow of discussion without disrupting it. Second, each chapter ends with "hindsight," raising a series of questions for further exploration and discussion, reflecting back on the main terms and points made in that chapter, and pressing the reader to consider larger implications and consequences.

And third, our literary approach means that our chapter sequence will follow central concepts and a variety of genres more than strict biblical book order. Thus, while Chapter 1 begins with Genesis, it quickly moves into a more general discussion of ancient reading practices, then itemizes inherited literary types as they appear throughout the Bible. This wide-ranging overview segues into Chapter 2 on other preliminary questions of composition and canonicity, touching on varied hypotheses about the Bible's documentary origins. Full-on discussion of specific Old Testament books doesn't begin until Chapter 3, on the most quintessential of Hebrew genres, the lyric poetry of the Psalms and Canticles, followed by Chapter 4 on the wisdom writing of Proverbs and Ecclesiastes. Having started in the middle of the Bible, it is only in Chapter 5 that we return to the beginning, taking up Genesis in depth by dealing with the elements of biblical narrative style, and with its highly condensed and multi-faceted creation accounts, followed in Chapter 6 by discussion of patriarchy and its discontents in the rest of Genesis, and by the book's unfolding succession of divine–human contracts or "covenants."

Chapter 7 takes up epic heroism as developed and modified in the life of Moses throughout the remainder of the Pentateuch, with Chapter 8 considering how the heroic ideal is further remade in the shorter hero stories of Joshua, Judges, and Ruth. Chapter 9 returns to the epic genre with the sweeping sagas of Kings Saul and David in 1 and 2 Samuel, then Chapter 10 turns to the more episodic (and often tragic) national narratives found in the books of Kings, Chronicles, Ezra-Nehemiah, and Esther. Chapter 11 pauses from prose narrative to consider the poetic and tragicomic drama in the ancient Book of Job, while Chapter 12 asks "who speaks for God?" and surveys the wide range of prophetic callings, modes, and literary forms evident in the "Former Prophets" Elijah and Elisha, and in all of the "Latter Prophets," including the "Major Prophets" Isaiah, Jeremiah, Ezekiel, and Daniel, and the "Minor Prophets" from Hosea to Malachi.

Moving from the Old Testament to the briefer books and letters of the New, Chapter 13 examines the political, cultural, and religious developments of the "Intertestamental" period, applying these contexts to the conventions of remade heroic prose narrative in the four canonical Gospels and the Book of Acts; Chapter 14 contextualizes the New Testament epistles, sampling and analyzing a representative variety of divine–human correspondence from the letters of Paul, James, Peter, John, and Jude; and Chapter 15 casts an eye on the dazzling difficulties of Revelation, measuring the fearful symmetry that structures its mighty vision; we scan the bewildering assortment of interpretive schools, but finally circle back, like the Apocalypse itself, to a tree by a river in a garden, where Genesis began.

With this end that is also a beginning, the Bible seems built to remind us that, in a world of partial sight and fragmentary experience, once is not enough. When the Word becomes text, truth takes "more shapes than one," as Milton wrote, and it takes diverse vision – a kind of literary and textual empiricism – to "re-member" these shapes and to see truth plain. So as our first chapter will show, "Reading Like a Hebrew" means learning to look from multiple angles. As old Solomon said, "two are better than one."

Unless otherwise indicated, all biblical quotations are from the New King James Version.

Note

1 *Oxford English Dictionary*, "Literary," def. 1. Bacon, *Advancement of Learning*, 2Bb3v.

Part I

Beginning

1

"The Dream Was Doubled": Reading Like a Hebrew

There probably is no more famous beginning than "In the beginning." The Bible starts with a great and apparently cosmic claim: that there actually was a beginning; that the world and time don't just go around in circles or go on forever in all directions. But to open the Bible at its first book and to read with even moderate attention is to confront an inevitable question: at which beginning do we begin? Even the most rudimentary examination of Genesis quickly discovers not one but two beginnings; or is that two versions of the same beginning?

In Genesis 1 verse 1 we read: "In the beginning, God created the heavens and the earth," an opening assertion followed by the famous six days of creation, culminating in the apparently simultaneous creation of male and female humanity, and followed by the *Shabbat*, God's Sabbath day of rest. Then, turn the page, and in Genesis 2 verse 4 we read: "In the day that the LORD God made the earth and the heavens." This "second start" is followed by the apparently sequential fashioning first of the Man from the earth and then of the Woman from the Man, in all of their naked, unashamed glory – and all in a "day."

So naturally, a few questions arise, especially for the modern, uninitiated reader. First, why do we find the story of creation told twice? Isn't once enough? And second, why do these double accounts of the beginning appear to differ in apparently significant ways? If it's a question of multiple viewpoints, then how do we understand their relation to each other? Is this a case of seeing wall-eyed through conflicting lenses, like a pair of poorly made glasses? Or is it a case of seeing stereoscopically through complementary lenses, with depth of field, for roundness, solidity, and perspective? In other words, in Genesis 1 and 2, are we seeing double, or are we seeing whole?

1.1 Seeing Deep and Whole: Stereoscopic Vision

In the Preface we noted the unique value of approaching the Bible through the conscious study of literary forms – with questions that focus on genre, characterization, figurative language, poetic and narrative structure, and the varied imaginative traditions that provided the contexts for composing its many books. In Chapters 2 and 5 we will discuss this perennial question of narrative doubling in Genesis more fully, but here such doubling can serve to illustrate the practical value of a specifically literary approach to reading the Bible. For what literary study attempts to do, first of all, is to discover a text on something like its own terms, and in the case of the Hebrew Bible, that means learning something about the imaginative equipment of an ancient Hebrew. "Reading like a Hebrew" means asking how the Bible's writers and editors chose structural and figurative devices to address their audiences' expectations and cultural habits of mind.

Literary Study of the Bible: An Introduction, First Edition. Christopher Hodgkins.
© 2020 John Wiley & Sons Ltd. Published 2020 by John Wiley & Sons Ltd.

So, for instance, a literary approach to the twice-told opening of Genesis seeks useful context by turning to instances of doubling elsewhere, and nowhere is such doubling more frequent than in the lyric poetry of the Psalms. The Psalms, for all of their apparently absolute proclamations, also display a high degree of deliberate repetition, contrast, and embellishment. No doubt the Psalms begin with a passage expressing a single, unequivocal viewpoint, without complication or qualification:

> "Blessed is the man," writes the anonymous composer of Psalm 1,
> Who walks not in the counsel of the ungodly,
> Nor stands in the path of sinners,
> Nor sits in the seat of the scornful;
> But his delight is in the law of the LORD,
> And in His law he meditates day and night. (1–2)

Here is one hallmark of the ancient Hebrew imagination emphatically on display – that is, the inclination to draw bright lines between right and wrong, good and evil, and especially between the righteous and the ungodly, and then to sanction these judgments in the name of one almighty God.

In fact, after the psalmist continues for a few more verses elaborating the rewards of the righteous and the miseries of the wicked, he sums up their likely futures in starkly absolute terms: "For the LORD knows the way of the righteous, / But the way of the ungodly shall perish" (6). Very clearly here, the way of blessing is the way of the Law, of walking according to the revealed will of a covenant God. To depart from that way – to "stand in the path of sinners," or to "sit in the seat of the scornful" – is the way to destruction. So the one righteous way would appear to be single rather than double: keep the Sabbath holy, avoid forbidden foods like pork and shellfish, commit no murder, and touch not your neighbor's wife – nor shall you look at her. Keep the Law, in all points great and small, or bid your blessing goodbye.

So far, you may well ask what light this passage sheds on the contrasting perspectives of Genesis 1 and 2. The light is this: while Psalm 1, like Genesis 1, would seem to settle matters, it doesn't. In fact, we soon discover that there's plenty of room in the Psalms for other angles and for second opinions. If it's quintessentially Hebrew to lay down the Law once and for all, it's also quintessentially Hebrew to say, with Tevye the Jewish dairyman from the popular musical *Fiddler on the Roof*, "On the other hand ..." And the other hand for Psalm 1 is found, for instance, in Psalm 32, which is attributed to a formerly righteous man, King David, who now has killed his neighbor in order to take his neighbor's wife, and is starting to groan for it: "Blessed is the man," David also begins – but how differently Blessed than the straight arrow of Psalm 1:

> Blessed is the man whose transgression is forgiven,
> Whose sin is covered.
> Blessed is the man to whom the LORD does not impute iniquity,
> And in whose spirit there is no deceit. (1–2)

Like Johnny Cash's inmate in Folsom Prison, who "shot a man in Reno / Just to watch him die," David the psalmist had known better, had known the Law, but broke it anyway.

Yet in Psalm 32 David imagines the possibility that the Lawgiver God still has a soft spot for lawbreakers, and that the "ex-righteous" can somehow become righteous again. So he ends this psalm by celebrating his recovered righteousness, as if it were a kind of recovered virginity.

Here then we see a second hallmark of the ancient Hebrew imagination clearly on display: if the Hebrews were inclined to draw bright lines separating the sheep from the goats, they also often crossed those lines and identified with the goats. If the Hebrew scriptures proclaim the absolute laws of an unchanging God, they also portray a God of second thoughts and second opinions, a Deity capable not only of monologue but of dialogue, and of compassion. In Chapter 3, we will consider the Psalms in greater depth, but even a quick look at the Psalms shows that the Hebrew desire for a second opinion, for alternate viewpoints and other hands, appears not only among and between poems, but is woven into the very fabric of Hebrew poetry itself, in the pervasive device of parallelism.

It's here that the Psalms' usefulness as context for the doubling in Genesis becomes clearer. Modern readers naturally ask, "Why can't the psalmists say anything just once? Why do they always have to repeat themselves?" And, true enough, the most distinguishing mark of biblical poetry, the genius of its structure, is its insistent line-by-line repetition, its parallelism. Parallelism is a kind of doubling, and is defined by *Webster's Dictionary* as "recurrent syntactical similarities introduced for dramatic or rhetorical effect." Put more simply, Hebrew poetry doesn't rhyme words, as English or French or Italian poets often do; Hebrew poetry rhymes ideas. Sometimes this "idea rhyming" is simply for emphasis, sometimes for contrast, and sometimes for development and embellishment. To put it another way, the biblical poets knew that there's only so much you can see with one eye, so they prefer two; and, perhaps paradoxically, when we look at the world through two eyes, we can see life in three dimensions.

One need only poke a random finger into the Psalms to find a dozen examples of such "three-dimensional" poetry on every page. For instance, there's Psalm 19 (here in the *New Revised Standard* translation), which echoes the cosmic creation language of Genesis 1, and appropriately glitters with varied parallelisms:

> The heavens are telling the glory of God;
> And the firmament proclaims his handiwork.
> Day to day pours forth speech,
> And night to night declares knowledge.
> There is no speech, nor are there words;
> Their voice is not heard;
> Yet their voice goes out through all the earth,
> And their words to the end of the world. (1–4)

To analyze these verses is to see how the parallelisms work to deepen, enrich, challenge, and complement each other: "The heavens are telling the glory of God" – this is the opening statement, which personifies the heavens as praising the Creator –

"And the firmament proclaims his handiwork" – this is the synonymous parallel statement, repeated for emphasis. "Day to day pours forth speech" – again, opening statement – "And night to night declares knowledge" – this is an antithetical statement, made for contrast. "There is no speech, nor are there words; / Their voice is not heard" – this opening statement, a triple parallelism, creates added emphasis, and dramatically contradicts all that has gone before, pointing out that one can't literally hear the stars. "Yet their voice goes out through all the earth, / And their words to the end of the world" – this too is an antithetical statement, deliberately contradicting the previous antithetical statement, in order to heighten the poetic paradox of God's voice heard clearly in the silence of the stars.

So far, then, we've noted that the two opening chapters of Genesis both duplicate and contrast with each other. We've also noted that the poems in the Book of Psalms employ the literary device of doubling, both among poems (as with the contrasting kinds of blessedness and righteousness portrayed in Psalms 1 and 32) and within poems, through the distinctive and pervasive use of parallelism (as in Psalm 19). Scholars generally agree that within individual

Psalms doubling devices like parallelism work as deliberate literary art, so that the contrasts and apparent contradictions within a poem like Psalm 19 exist not just accidentally but intentionally, to produce particular poetic effects. In the case of Psalm 19, the parallelisms seem designed to induce wonder at God's mysterious silent language of the stars. The Book of Psalms contains the work of many different poets, writing over as much as a thousand years, and finally compiled by editors sometime after the Jewish return from the Babylonian Exile in the sixth and fifth centuries BCE. At that time the Psalms were gathered and grouped together thematically into five books, imitating the five books of the Hebrew Law or *Torah* – a conscious and significant artistic arrangement. Scholars may disagree over whether Moses or David or Solomon wrote particular psalms, but they agree that Psalms is a composite book, a purposeful unit carefully crafted from quite varied sources.

Turning back to Genesis 1 and 2, we can apply some of the insights from our preliminary look at the Psalms to the more general question of "reading like a Hebrew." First, an ancient Israelite would see and hear frequent duplication, contrast, and even divergent details as consistent with a high degree of intentional design; in fact such duplication indicated deeper certainty. Outside the realm of lyric poetry, later in Genesis, the prophetic patriarch Joseph speaks to Pharaoh about his repeated contrasting dreams of cattle and corn: "Pharaoh's dreams are one and the same ... the doubling of Pharaoh's dream means that the thing is fixed by God" (Gen. 41:25, 32, *New Revised Standard Version*). Despite the obvious differences in detail between the cows and grain, Joseph announces that Pharaoh's dream was doubled to stress its unified truth. As with parallelistic poetry or musical harmony and melody, difference here is complementary.

The second insight from the Psalms that will help to shape our "Hebraic" reading has to do with the diversity of source material. Despite disagreements about the dating of Genesis, nearly all scholars agree that, like the Psalms, the first book of the Bible was composed using a number of earlier documents. A detailed discussion of this documentary hypothesis will have to wait for Chapter 2, but, to summarize briefly, the dominant academic theory holds that the five books of the *Torah* or Pentateuch – in other words Genesis, Exodus, Leviticus, Numbers, and Deuteronomy – were constructed largely out of four older documents and put in their present form, like the Psalms, sometime soon after return from the Babylonian Exile. Many other scholars hold that there were as many as ten original source documents or histories (the Hebrew word is *Toledoth*), and that these were edited and combined about 900 years before the Exile – that is, soon after the Exodus – although the text was updated and stylistically tweaked over the succeeding centuries.

However, from an artistic and literary standpoint, the question isn't only one of when Genesis was composed, and by whom, but even more importantly why, and to what effects? To use some non-biblical examples, it's possible to be moved by King Priam's begging of Hector's body from Achilles in *The Iliad*, or gripped by Odysseus' dramatic vengeance on Penelope's suitors in *The Odyssey*, although we know little about the poet Homer. Similarly, it's possible for two people to laugh out loud at the antics in *A Midsummer Night's Dream* or weep with *King Lear* while disagreeing over who wrote these two plays (though the evidence is very strong for Will Shakespeare of Stratford). In fact, it's precisely because these epics and plays are so intrinsically and enduringly powerful that we care about who wrote them.

In the same way with Genesis, questions of authorship and original documents aside, the book's double opening has proven to be an intrinsically and enduringly powerful combination – so powerful that for millennia it has inspired in its hearers and readers not only strong emotion and sharp controversy but unfathomable devotion. The unique majesty of this opening derives significantly from its stereoscopic form – its two-eyed, three-dimensional vision. To put it simply, then, what are Genesis 1 and 2 *together* designed to make us think and feel, and how does the passage work?

To answer these questions, let's consider the main differences and the important similarities between creation as imagined in Genesis 1 and in Genesis 2. (For the sake of convenience, we will refer to Genesis 1:1–2:4a as "Genesis 1" and Genesis 2:4b–25 as "Genesis 2.") First, the main differences:

1) Quite famously, Genesis 1 and 2 use significantly different divine names – that is, ways of referring to the Creator God.
2) Each chapter has a distinctive spatial perspective and center of focus.
3) The two accounts differ obviously in how much and what kinds of detail they report.
4) Genesis 1 and 2 have strikingly diverse chronological scales, and in some cases, apparently different sequences of creation.
5) Genesis 1 and 2 portray God creating with different methods and means.

If we elaborate on these differences we can begin to ask what they may mean. The original hearers and readers would immediately recognize the difference in divine names as important. Genesis 1 uses the generic Hebrew name for God, *Elohim*. In contrast, Genesis 2 refers throughout to **Yahweh Elohim**, often rendered "LORD God" or "Jehovah God" in English Bibles, to designate God's covenant name with the Hebrew people. In other words, the generic divine name *Elohim* instantly cues to the Hebrew reader Genesis 1's emphasis on the Creator's universal power over all peoples and nations, while *Yahweh Elohim* cues Genesis 2's stress on the Creator's particular relations with chosen persons and chosen nations.

In a similar way, the opening phrase of each creation account signals to the attentive reader a unique spatial perspective and center of focus for each chapter. "In the beginning, God created *the heavens and the earth*" (1); this italicized phrase puts us in the heavens first, and suggests a panoramic vista, a transcendent and lofty point of view – as if we were hovering high with the Spirit of God looking down over the swelling scene. In contrast, when the second creation account begins with Genesis 2:4b "In the day when the LORD God made *the earth and the heavens*," the earth-first ordering in italics puts our feet on the ground, and hints at a smaller-scale world of close-up personalities, intimate exchanges and conversations, an immanent point of view looking from a sheltered garden upward into the lofty skies.

It follows, then, from these contrasting divine names and spatial relations that the two accounts would differ in how much and what kinds of detail that they report, though not in ways that would necessarily indicate contradiction to a Hebrew reader. Genesis 1, with its transcendent outlook, provides a symmetrical schema of harmonious design, as the six creative days unfold like a pageant. First we encounter the form and setting, and then the creatures to fill the form: light, sky, and landscape on the first three days; heavenly bodies, sky and sea creatures, and land animals on the next three days. All of these creations are "very good" (31), we are told, and all crowned with a seventh day of rest. On the other hand, Genesis 2, in keeping with its close-up and personal perspective, provides not a panoramic schema but instead the intimate details of warm human life. So we observe the names of local rivers, the yearnings of a lonely young man, a fascinating tree with a warning, and the outcry of love at first sight: "This at last is bone of my bones and flesh of my flesh!" (23).

This mention of the human creatures points out yet another divergence, evident to readers both in English and in Hebrew: the apparent chronological and sequential differences between the two accounts. Most obviously, Genesis 1 speaks of multiple "days," while Genesis 2 speaks of one "day in which the LORD God made the earth and the heavens" (4b – the same Hebrew word, *yowm*, being used throughout). But even more importantly, the multiple days in Genesis 1 provide a crescendo that prepares the reader for the crowning climax of the creation: humanity. The human pair, male and female, are created together on "the sixth day" in God's image, placed in the midst of the creation, and given dominion over everything in heaven, earth, and sea.

In contrast, on the single creative "day" mentioned in Genesis 2, the order of creation doesn't seem as important. That is, it's hard to tell whether the man is made before the plants and animals, or after them. Also, the human "dominion" of Genesis 1 is expressed here in humbler terms: the Man (*adam/iysh*) and Woman (*ishshah*) of Genesis 2 are seen as caretakers, placed "in the garden of Eden to till it and keep it" (15) more like happy sharecroppers than imperial viceroys.

However, despite the general indifference to sequence and status in Genesis 2, even a moderately attentive reader will see that one sequential detail is stressed: in contrast to Genesis 1, the LORD God clearly makes the Woman after he makes the Man, and He makes the Woman out of the Man – out of his side, it says, or more famously, out of Adam's "rib." What does this coming last mean? Does it give Adam's rib – the Woman – dominion over Adam, as the climactic creation of humanity gives them dominion over all creation in Genesis 1? Does it imply inferiority to Adam? Or does it suggest that Woman is the completion of all things, neither from his head to rule him nor from his foot to be ruled, as the old saying goes, but from his side, as his partner? Thereby hangs a tale, to be taken up in Chapter 5.

This picture of the LORD God pulling a rib out of Adam's side and molding the bloody mass into a marriage partner stands in rather bold contrast to the more serene means of creation used by God in Genesis 1: that is, mere speech. In fact, the last of the main distinctions between Genesis 1 and 2 is in how they imagine divine creative power. Put simply, *Yahweh Elohim*, the covenant God of Genesis 2, is a God who gets his hands dirty in the red clay that becomes Adam (*adam* being Hebrew for red clay), while the exalted *Elohim* of Genesis 1 doesn't need to dirty his hands because he simply speaks, and it is. To put it another way, the Maker of Genesis 2 is a manual artisan, while the Creator of Genesis 1 is an artist of the Word, a poet or storyteller.

Which of these two creators is better? Which do you prefer? Theological questions aside, which kind of art is superior: a beautiful poem, or a beautiful vase?

And which is more important (to quote W. B. Yeats): "the dancer or the dance"?

And if you had to choose one eye to be put out, which eye would you choose? If these last questions sound increasingly silly to you, then you need to remember that well-educated people have in fact been debating these biblical differences for centuries, especially during the past three centuries, as Greco-Roman ideals of Reason, and Anglo-Scottish ideals of Common Sense, and scientific ideals of Non-Contradiction have been applied to the composite text of Genesis and have found it wanting.

Many analysts of the Bible will point to the different divine names, or the differences in spatial perspective, or the divergences in the details and sequence of creation, or the contrast between verbal and manual creation. They will speak as if they have discovered something truly shocking that the ancient Hebrew writers, editors, and redactors of the *Torah* somehow did not know. There must be some kind of accident here, it is said, because there's more than one creation story, and these stories are different!

So, before I turn to the similarities between Genesis 1 and 2, and then to my conclusions, I'm going to stick my neck out a bit and say this: No, the ancient Hebrews could not drive cars, or type. No, they could not do triple bypass surgery, or download a music file, or microwave their meals. And no, they could not fly to Manchester or Glasgow or Cleveland or Pittsburgh. Yet I will venture that they probably could tell when two creation stories were different, which means that whoever composed and combined Genesis 1 and Genesis 2 probably did so for a reason. And that reason, which should not be too surprising by now, is probably that these ancient Hebrews believed that the two creation stories together gave a deeper, richer, and truer picture of their God than either story could alone.

They believed in a God who kept his promises to everyone on the earth, and who kept covenant with special chosen people; a God of transcendent might and power, a supreme architect and designer, a commander of heavenly armies, who also liked to drop in for informal visits with his creatures and shoot the breeze in the Garden of Eden in the cool of the day. They believed that their God orchestrated creation to honor humanity as his representatives and to give them dominion, and that he expected them to exercise their dominion with the humility of hired hands. And they believed in a God who could make or unmake everything with his Word, yet who also loved to lay his hands on the earth and on Adam, to fashion him and fill him with longings for love and friendship – and then to fulfill his longings by giving him a lover and friend. In short, the composers of Genesis believed that when looking into deep and complex things, it's better to use both eyes and to see all sides.

I've been giving what amounts to a defense, not of a particular religious creed or of a specific biblical interpretation, but of a distinct state of mind, that of stereoscopic, three-dimensional reading. Such a literary approach values the truth, but it knows, as John Milton wrote in *Areopagitica*, that truth comes "in more shapes than one." If textual difference and complexity are not necessarily embarrassments but are often enrichments, it might seem almost unnecessary to note the many ways in which Genesis 1 and Genesis 2 resemble each other:

1) Although the *Yahweh Elohim* of Genesis 2 is God's covenant name in dealing with the Hebrews, the more universal *Elohim* of Genesis 1 is a maker and keeper of covenants as well, including the very Hebrew-sounding covenant of seventh day "Sabbath" rest with all creation.

2) Although Genesis 1 and 2 vary in their heavenly or earthly focus, both chapters imagine God's creation as comprehensive, encompassing both the heavens and the earth, both the earth and the heavens.

3) Both creation accounts portray the Creator as concerned with the "goodness" – the wholeness and fullness – of his creation; in the case of Genesis 1, he expresses this concern positively through the repeated refrain, "and he saw that it was good" (12, 18, 25, 31), and in the case of Genesis 2, he expresses this concern negatively when he says of Adam's single state, "It is not good that the man should be alone" (18).

4) Although the Genesis 1 language of "having dominion" differs from the Genesis 2 language of "tilling and keeping," both creation stories agree that the Creator intends humans to manage the earth under divine authority, and both agree that work was part of the originally good order of things.

5) As to gender hierarchy, while the simultaneous creation of male and female in Genesis 1 may seem more egalitarian, Genesis 2 portrays Woman as being taken from Man's side (not from his foot or his head), and as being made by the LORD God to be man's *Ezer* or "Strong Partner" (20) – a word used regularly elsewhere to describe God himself (see Psalm 33:20, Psalm 70:5, Psalm 115:9, etc.).

6) However human or hands-on or "anthropomorphic" *Yahweh Elohim* may seem in Genesis 2, there is also something quite human-like in the speaking Creator of Genesis 1, as well.

7) In the same way, however limited *Yahweh Elohim* may seem at points in Chapter 2, he's portrayed not just as a maker of breathing clay statues, but also of the high heavens.

8) It's also worth noting that in both Genesis 1 and 2, the Creator achieves his creation quietly, without warfare or violence – the opposite of the very bloody battle in the ancient Babylonian creation myth, the *Enuma Elish*, between the god Marduk and the serpent-monster Tiamat.

Both creation stories seem designed to refute the common ancient notion that the gods created through violence and that bloodshed and conquest are foundational to reality. It's as if someone were to pick up the Genesis scroll expecting a bone-crushing Babylonian version of *Clash of the Titans* or *Godzilla* and find himself instead ushered into the serene presence of a benevolent poetic potentate whose quiet word is as good as his deed. To recognize that the ancient audience of Genesis probably expected a "creation story" that reveled in gory confrontation and cosmic combat is to register their likely surprise at the deliberate anticlimax.

So, in learning to "read like a Hebrew," we may see these stories about beginnings in a new light. If we've been inclined to dismiss Genesis 1 and 2 as textually incoherent because of their duplication and their apparently different details, our brief look at the Psalms, and at these opening chapters of Genesis themselves, has suggested otherwise. At least in Hebrew literature, the presence of repetition and even of apparent conflict isn't evidence of artistic incompetence or poor editing, but rather expresses the very essence of the Hebrew literary ideal – the ideal of duplicating and complicating in order to confirm, to enrich, and to deepen.

On the other hand (to quote Tevye again), if we've been inclined to read Genesis with only one eye open – that is, if we've tended to ignore the very striking variations between the two versions – our close attention to the divergent details of the two chapters can help to open our other eye, and so open our eyes, to the rich depth and complex wisdom of these old words. And perhaps a too-familiar text has become somewhat less familiar, and fresher.

So when we bring this kind of stereoscopic vision to bear on the frequent repetitive devices in Hebrew literature, we'll be less likely to misread and more likely to enjoy and understand biblical texts on something like their own terms. In fact, as we continue in our literary study of the Hebrew Bible together, we will see larger implications as we read doubling and contrasting stories about the origins of sin and evil, about the calling of the patriarchs and the giving of the Law, about bad and good King Saul, and about good and bad King David, indeed about all the bad and the good kings, not to mention the entire "duplicate" books of Deuteronomy and Chronicles.

As we continue on together into the New Testament, which also was largely written by Jews, we will find not merely double or triple but quadruple Gospel narratives, rife with repetition and filled with surprising variety. Beyond the Gospels, the Book of Acts repeats Luke's opening dedication to Theophilus; Paul's letters duplicate and overlap each other frequently; and Paul, once called Saul, tells the story of his conversion many times, and in about as many ways. The New Testament pervasively revisits and repeats the Old, but usually with a difference. And in an end that is also a beginning, the final chapters of Revelation deliberately return us to the scene that opens Genesis: a Tree by a River – but now in a City; and the light of God shining, without need of Sun or Moon – as repetition becomes renewal, and the Last Days lead to Day One.

1.2 Tabernacles for the Sun: Biblical Genres

Much as we need to understand that doubling is both intentional and essential in biblical literature, so learning to "read like a Hebrew" also requires that we know something about the major literary genres and subgenres of the Bible. A literary genre is a type or kind of writing, characterized by certain pre-existing formal expectations and conventions; every writer both adopts and to varying degrees adapts these pre-existing conditions to a present purpose, with a present audience in mind. Accustomed as we are to thinking of the Bible as a very ancient book – its texts having been first written between 3500 and 2000 years ago – we nevertheless must realize that it stands in relation to much more ancient literary and cultural traditions, some originating at least as long before Bible times as Bible times came before our own. Keep in mind, for instance, that the earliest traditional date for the Hebrew Exodus from Egypt – 1440 BCE – places the event during the Eighteenth Dynasty of the Egyptian Pharaohs, more than sixteen centuries after the generally accepted date for the First Dynasty in 3100 BCE. Sixteen centuries is 1600 years. Now consider that 1600 years before our own day, the English language did not yet exist!

What this means is that even the earliest biblical writers and editors inherited many long-standing traditions of composition for such literary forms as **lyric poetry**, **wisdom discourse**, **origin narrative**, **heroic epic**, **hero story**, **national narrative**, **drama**, **prophecy**, and **epistle**. Although the earliest Hebrew compositions in some of these genres may have been oral, and intended originally for spoken or sung performance, eventually these oral compositions were put into writing and thus became, in the most basic sense, literature – that is, written down in letters. While it is not always possible to reconstruct the exact circumstances in which various biblical books were composed and written, it often is possible to determine the compositional traditions – that is, the genres – that helped to shape their creation. But these genres only helped; for a text's larger meanings and effects frequently depend not only on how a writer adopts and enacts a generic form, but also on how he or she adapts that form, indeed, transforms and even transgresses it.

Genres, then, while preconceived and structured, are by nature also flexible and expansive. They may direct, deflect, channel, and reflect their subject matter, but they cannot completely confine it, especially when their subjects are divine power and human passion. To borrow a phrase from Psalm 19:4, generic forms are like "tabernacles for the sun"; though they may give a local habitation and a name to radiant bursts of grief or glory, they cannot contain or constrain the spirit for long. To shift biblical metaphors slightly, if a genre is designed as a tent of meeting, nevertheless the tent must move to follow its master, its pillar of fire. Or consider some more contemporary examples of genre: what do you expect, for instance, when you switch on a television cricket match or basketball game; or when you pick up a detective novel; or when you watch the latest action film, romantic comedy, or screen biography? You expect a mixture of familiar forms with (if successful) some meaningful surprises.

To read like a Hebrew, then, is also to read generically, with an eye for the interplay between cultural form and authorial re-form, between expectation and surprise. As with the stereoscopic devices in the Psalms or in Genesis, this interplay is not necessarily oppositional, but potentially complementary and dynamic. Paying close attention to this interplay can refresh our experience of the biblical text by bringing its interior dramas to life – for in doing so we re-imagine the conditions that the original readers and hearers mainly took for granted.

So the biblical psalmists and the Song of Solomon take up the already very ancient genre of **lyric poetry**, associated with brief outbursts of intimate feeling toward a beloved, whether divine or human; the writers and editors of Proverbs, Ecclesiastes, and Job engage the equally ancient form of **wisdom discourse**, with its tradition of terse, riddling maxims and prudent reverence; while Genesis, as we've already seen, begins by evoking the **origin narrative** of the Babylonian *Enuma Elish*, and then goes on in the story of Noah closely to parallel the Flood of Enlil from *Gilgamesh*. In 1 and 2 Samuel, the account of Saul and David specifically mirrors the elements of the pan-Mediterranean **national warrior epic**; the **national narratives** of Kings and Chronicles display the summary tags and genealogical narrative structure found in the Near Eastern royal and holy history tradition; Job and the Song of Solomon stage their portrayals of unearned suffering and uneasy sexual passion using the conventions of **dramatic dialogue** first developed in the religious theater of Egypt's Middle Kingdom; and prophets from Moses to Malachi speak in the name of *Yahweh* in ways that resemble the **prophecies** of anthropomorphic deities from the western Mediterranean region to Central Asia.

Yet in each of these cases, the Hebrew writers make unconventional use of these conventions, changing what they inherit into something often rich and strange to the eyes and ears of their times – and perhaps to ours. Many of the psalms transmute the formal flattery of the local god-as-tyrant into awestruck praise of a universal Creator who is as good as he is mighty, while many more psalms engage in heart-searching dramas of self-examination and psychological discovery. The Book of Proverbs not only locates true wisdom in prudent self-preservation, but personifies Wisdom herself as present at the Creation, directing the benevolent design of heaven and earth, while Job and Ecclesiastes increasingly complicate the more optimistic wisdom of Proverbs with a counter-wisdom of disillusioned humility – acknowledging that life "under the sun" may never make sense, but that the living presence of God (even an angry God) is worth more than many explanations. We've already noted how the first chapters of Genesis seem deliberately designed to overthrow the expectation that the gods created through bloody, cosmic single combat, instead portraying the Creator first as a serene poet speaking heaven and earth into being, and then as an artisan forming his creatures by hand and breathing them into life. Similarly, the many striking resemblances between the *Gilgamesh* and Genesis floods finally serve to highlight what for the Hebrews was the crucial difference: the Flood of Enlil is caused by one among many squabbling gods who has an arbitrary grudge against the world, while Noah's Flood comes after the long-suffering Creator decides to cleanse the earth of pervasive human corruption and violence.

Likewise, although 1 and 2 Samuel employ many of the narrative devices common to Mediterranean national warrior epics – divine interventions, warrior catalogues, underworld visits, for instance – the story of Saul's fall and David's rise cuts deliberately against ancient Near Eastern notions of kingship: a Hebrew king is not a divine avatar on earth or a law unto himself, but instead a public servant accountable to God's written Law and to his brethren, and who rules "justly … in the fear of God" (2 Samuel 23:3). Even the famous story of young David against the giant Goliath breaks the mold: instead of diverting the reader with lengthy descriptions of single combat, as when Homer's almost evenly matched Achilles and Hector meet before the walls of Troy, David's battle is over almost before it begins; the long odds and the intentional anticlimax show that "the battle is the LORD's" (1 Samuel 17:47). Following this pattern of downsizing monarchs and monarchy, the Books of 1 and 2 Kings and 1 and 2 Chronicles mimic the genealogical structure of Near Eastern royal court narratives only to feature, not the god-kings' terrific greatness ("Look on my works, ye mighty, and despair!" boasts P. B. Shelley's Ozymandias), but instead the mortal follies and failings, as well as the occasional successes, of Judah's and Israel's rulers.

Although no evidence exists that either Job or the Song of Solomon was performed theatrically in Bible times, both books show a resemblance, if not a debt, to the religious dramas of Eleventh- and Tenth-Dynasty Egypt – with their spoken dialogue, their frank, sometimes passionate realism, and their inquiries into divine justice. Yet where these Egyptian sacred dramas seem to have featured the actual bloodshed and sacrificial deaths of some actors, these biblical texts artfully create sympathy for their human subjects, whether for the passionate fears of erotic abandonment expressed by Solomon's latest bride, or for Job's agonizing humiliation and rejection.

In turning, finally, to prophecy, it may seem harder to distinguish by means of genre or literary convention between various divine oracles; after all, the words "Thus says Baal" and "Thus says *Yahweh*" share the common anthropomorphic assumption that these deities speak in human terms and issue their commands through prophets, as kings do through their ministers. As we will see, the biblical prophets claim – and an audacious claim it is – that the proof of their words comes not in the artful speaking, but in the fulfillment, in the demonstrated power of their God. So Moses is shown predicting that Pharaoh will be forced by terrible plagues to "let my people go" (Exodus 9:13); so Elijah challenges the prophets of Baal to a showdown demonstrating that "the god who answers by fire is indeed God" (1 Kings 18:24); so Isaiah mocks the handmade gods of the nations, asserts that *Yahweh* "confirms the word of his servant," and predicts the return of the Jews from exile under a king who will be called Cyrus – 160 years hence (Isaiah 44:26–28).

Of course, many modern interpreters of the Bible doubt or deny the historical truth of these stories and claims; indeed, in the minds of many, such skepticism or denial is a condition of modernity itself. Moses and Elijah may be sacred fictions; Isaiah, though historical, was not only a man, many say, but a later textual tradition, so that these predictions of Cyrus may be the post-dated words of a "Deutero-Isaiah," composed after Persia under Cyrus ended the exile, and then canonized retroactively. We will come to these and related textual theories in due course; the present point is that, to read like a Hebrew, one assumes that the power of the biblical text does not begin or end with the text but depends on something, indeed Someone, outside the text. A contemporary reader may or may not believe in such a Someone, but in order to make literary sense of the biblical text as it presently exists – not as one or another educated guess says that it might or should have existed – one needs to recognize that its writers and earliest readers believed in a divine Author above and outside the words.

In this sense, the Bible is indeed primarily and inescapably a religious text. We might say that the belief in an originating God is the starting-point for practically all biblical literature: such an extra-textual belief is the binding of the book, the overarching assumption. If a reader cannot at least imaginatively entertain such a belief, or temporarily suspend disbelief as one does in reading fantasy or science fiction, that reader will continue to find much of the Bible alien, puzzling, and off-putting.

After the above brief survey of biblical genres – with much more detail to come in later chapters – we should note in conclusion that in some sense the entire Bible (both the Hebrew Bible and the Christian New Testament) presents itself to us as prophecy; not in the narrower sense of the particular genre in which a human messenger takes dictation verbatim from God or a god, as in the Book of Jeremiah or the Qur'an, but in the broader sense that its books claim to be somehow underwritten by divine authorship, authority, creation. To read like a Hebrew is to assume that, while one cannot fully express the inexpressible, one still must try – with every human form, with every genre or plot or figurative device or word within one's reach. All of these are temporary tabernacles to be sure, but are necessary "tents of meeting." And one must read with both eyes open, both for detail and for depth, for complication and irony and perspective, and also in the hope that multiple angles can still combine into one multi-faceted whole.

Common sense naturally looks at all of the Bible's burgeoning variety of genres and also its apparently redundant repetitions and quite reasonably asks: "Well, which version is it? Is God over us or with us?" "Yes," says the Hebrew. "Is God angry or tender? And David – was he an ideal or a failure?" "Yes," the Hebrew answers. "And are Jews separatists or universalists? Is the Messiah a conqueror or a victim? Is the Creator a Poet or a Sculptor?" "Oh, most certainly Yes," comes the reply. For to read like a Hebrew is to respect common sense but, when common sense reaches its limits, to try uncommon sense; and uncommon sense has a response to such questions, when reality outstrips reason: the "Yes" of the multi-faceted text that refuses the one-handed, one-eyed answer.

Questions for Discussion

1   What are some typical modern responses to the opening of the Book of **Genesis** and its two accounts of creation?

2   What are some examples of intentional **doubling** and **repetition** in the Hebrew Bible, and how might they cast light on the doubled creation accounts of Genesis 1–2?

3   What, briefly, might it mean to engage in "reading like a Hebrew"?

4   What is the definition of the word "**genre**"?

5   What are the main **genres** of the Hebrew Bible, and what were some of their origins?

6   What expectations and assumptions would an ancient Hebrew reader have brought to each of the main genres of the Bible?

7   How would some specific biblical books have fulfilled their ancient readers' generic expectations? How would some specific biblical books have surprised their ancient readers by modifying or even transgressing their generic expectations?

2

"In the Scroll of the Book": Composition and Canonicity

How did the Bible come to be? What do we know – and not know – about the people who created its parts, and the individuals, forces, and movements that have delivered the Bible to us over four millennia in its current form? Who decided – and how – which scrolls and passages would be included and which excluded? And what role can literary study play, both in understanding the Bible's origins and interpreting its cherished and often contested books?

In our first chapter, we observed that "reading like a Hebrew" means reading with an eye for intentional doubling, repetition, complexity, and irony. We also saw that a good reader will keep an eye out for how writers adopt and adapt inherited genres in new settings. And we observed that both of these concerns are mainly *literary* ones. That is, the richest reading of the Bible, as of any foreign, ancient, or long-lived writing, requires some contextual knowledge of and imaginative sympathy with its creators and the historic literary forms that shaped them.

So, on the one hand, if we are people of faith, we must suspend, if not our belief in the text, at least any familiar, pre-packaged sense of what the text must mean, and of how it means. The Bible may feel like home to some of us, but it is a very large, very old home, with what are for most readers many unexplored rooms and even wings, stranger and more alien than we know. On the other hand, if we are skeptics, we must suspend, if not our disbelief, at least our modern Western chronological snobbery. Antiquity doesn't equal stupidity; we shouldn't assume, like narrow-minded visitors to a distant country, that difference denotes ignorance, that complexity denotes incoherence, or that paradox masks confusion or falsehood. In certain cases they all may, of course, but a generous mind must learn to distinguish. In this chapter we will explore how competing accounts of the Bible's origins have, during the past few centuries, presented a telling interplay between our better impulses as readers – toward patient "stereoscopic" discernment – and our worse impulses – toward simplistic "one-eyed" reductionism.

2.1   The Documentary Hypothesis: Its Origins, Assumptions, and Evolution

How have these competing interpretive impulses – discernment versus reductionism – played out in modern times? Probably the most representative example of this interplay is found in competing approaches to the composition of the Pentateuch – the five "Books of Moses" that begin the Bible. Well into the nineteenth century, the predominant view of the Pentateuch, both among Jews and among Christians, was still what might be called the "Unitary Hypothesis" – the view that God directly and without mediation dictated to Moses the contents of the *Torah*, much as Muslims believe Allah dictated the entire Qur'an to Muhammad through Jibrail (the archangel Gabriel). In this view, Moses was not so much author or editor as scribe

Literary Study of the Bible: An Introduction, First Edition. Christopher Hodgkins.
© 2020 John Wiley & Sons Ltd. Published 2020 by John Wiley & Sons Ltd.

or secretary; any questions of textual sources, or of the artistic construction of the text out of such sources, were widely viewed with suspicion, as threats to the inspiration and authority of the divine Word.

And yet, questions arose from varied quarters, as readers responded to new intellectual trends and to the actual details of the Mosaic text. These questions led eventually to the formulation in the 1870s and 1880s by the German Bible scholar Julius Wellhausen of an alternative "Documentary Hypothesis." Wellhausen denied Mosaic authorship of the *Torah* and proposed instead a theory of composition by a much later "Redactor," or editor, combining four different and often incompatible "documents" or sources written well after Moses. But long before Wellhausen, elements of his hypothesis were being proposed and developed by others.

In Baruch Spinoza's *Tractatus Theologico-Politicus* (1670), the Dutch-Jewish philosopher argued that reason rather than religious doctrine should guide biblical study, and that God allowed the Bible to develop by ordinary human means, not miraculous ones. He speculated that the Pentateuch, while likely containing in Genesis and Exodus material written in the 1400s BCE by Moses, was mainly compiled from sources spliced together nearly a millennium after Moses – indeed by Ezra following the Jews' return from Babylonian Exile in the sixth century BCE. While Spinoza's views were condemned in his day by Jewish, Catholic, and Protestant leaders alike, they were adopted and developed in the eighteenth century by French physician Jean Astruc, whose 1753 book title proclaims his controversial thesis: *Conjectures on The Original Sources, Which It Seems that Moses Used to Compose the Book of the Genesis*. Astruc claimed to distinguish between Moses' sources according to the divine names used for God: as we already have observed above, *Elohim* in Genesis 1, and *Yahweh Elohim* in Genesis 2. While Astruc recognized Moses as the editor of these sources, he, like Spinoza, doubted Moses' hand in most of Exodus, Leviticus, Numbers, and Deuteronomy.

Twenty years later, in 1773, the young Johann Wolfgang von Goethe – later to be famed for *Faust* – published a paper entitled "Two Important Previously Undiscussed Biblical Questions" in which he cast further doubt on the "Unitary Hypothesis." Goethe argued that the Pentateuch, as a very particularly local and tribal creation, lacked the kind of universal application sought by enlightened, rational thinking, and he devalued the text as a conglomeration of varied sources assembled long after their composition. He also cast mild aspersions on the primitive Jewishness of the entire Old Testament, arguing that only the universal philosophy of Jesus in the New Testament makes the Hebrew scriptures worth reading at all. Finally, in *The Historical Books of the Old Testament* (1866), Karl Heinrich Graf struck another blow against traditional Mosaic chronology, asserting that the ritual and "priestly" Laws of Exodus, Leviticus, and Numbers originated after Deuteronomy – though Graf still maintained that some parts of Genesis were more ancient than the remainder of the Pentateuch.

These accumulating challenges to traditional biblical scholarship represented important gains in interpretive discernment. First, these critics often were responding to actual details in the text that were ignored or discounted by the reductionism of the dominant Unitary Hypothesis. These details included multiple divine names, repeated narrative material (two Creation accounts, multiple stories of patriarchal deception), varied thematic clusters (priestly ritual here, universal ethics there), and, of course, Moses's supposed description of his own death and burial at the end of the book of Deuteronomy. Furthermore, these non-traditional critics also raised the crucial and increasingly unavoidable question: how could holy books composed for ancient Near Eastern wanderers, herdsmen, and bronze-age warriors continue speaking to a rationalist, mechanist, secularizing West? It was left to Wellhausen, Professor of Biblical Studies and Oriental Literature at the University of Göttingen, to provide the most influential explanations and answers.

2.1.1 Hypothetical Documents: Divine Names, Disputed Dates, and the "Polychrome Bible"

As we have seen, many elements of Wellhausen's famed Documentary Hypothesis were already in place well before he began publishing his work in the 1870s. Yet it was Wellhausen who adapted those elements, added other important supporting claims, and, most importantly, provided an ambitious theoretical overview that enabled his revolutionary hypothesis to connect powerfully with other nineteenth-century trends in the natural sciences and literary studies and so to sweep the field. In other words, while Wellhausen did not originate some of his signature claims, he was highly effective at synthesizing, augmenting, and above all advocating his ideas.

In his *Prolegomena to the History of Ancient Israel* (1878; 1882), Wellhausen started from earlier suggestions of composite authorship and post-exilic chronology, added Astruc's and especially Graf's ideas about differing divine names, and engrafted Goethe's assumptions about primitive and conflicting Hebrew tribalism. This combination supported him as he struck the final blow against the traditional "Unitary Hypothesis." Wellhausen denied the existence of *any* original fifteenth-century BCE texts by Moses; he argued instead that the five "Books of Moses" and the Book of Joshua comprised a "Hexateuch" (Greek for "Six Volumes") made up of four main source "documents" composed from the tenth through the sixth centuries BCE and combined by an anonymous "Redactor" in post-exilic Judea. Wellhausen famously distinguished and named these four hypothetical documents according either to the divine name used or to the main subject matter: "J" for "Jahvist" or "Yahwist" (from *Jehovah* or *Yahweh*, 950 BCE); "E" for "Elohist" (from *Elohim* or *Elohe*, 850–600 BCE); "D" for "Deuteronomist" (following the universal ethical focus of the book of Deuteronomy, 600–500 BCE); and "P" for "Priestly" (following a focus on cultic ritual, 500 BCE). So the Documentary Hypothesis also has come to be known, more simply, as "JEDP," or if we include the anonymous post-exilic Redactor, "JEDPR."

The Documentary Hypothesis/JEDPR			
Jahvist (Yahwist)	**Elohist**	**Deuteronomist**	**Priestly**
Yahweh Elohim	*Elohim*	*Yahweh*	*Elohim*
LORD God	*Elohe*	Ethical Focus	Ritual focus
950 BCE	850–600 BCE	600–500 BCE	500 BCE
Genesis 2–3	Genesis 1	Deuteronomy	Genesis-Numbers

Thus, for instance, we read in Genesis 12 and then again in Genesis 20 that Abram/Abraham sojourned in a foreign land and foisted his beautiful wife Sarai/Sarah on its king (first Pharaoh of Egypt and then Abimelech of Gerar) as his marriageable "sister." Wellhausen understands these stories not as two sequential incidents in a unified narrative, but instead as two conflicting versions of the same tale combined by a much later Redactor; and Isaac's similar deception of Abimelech in Genesis 26 is to Wellhausen yet one more conflicting version. And as we noted in our introductory chapter above, the two accounts of Creation in Genesis 1 and 2, with their differing divine names, become for Wellhausen not just alternative angles of vision on the same origin event but mutually exclusive versions with competing visions: the later "Elohist" presents God as an ethically more advanced and transcendent Creator, and the earlier "Yahwist" presents God as a more primitive, limited, and anthropomorphic maker. As different as these two instances of narrative doubling are, Wellhausen's treatments of them have two things in common: he assumes the fragmentary and contradictory nature of the text, and a chronological development from more "primitive" to more "advanced" forms.

When Wellhausen made these claims for discontinuity and contradiction in the 1870s and 1880s, they were bolstered by evidence – or more correctly a lack of evidence – which suggested that the Pentateuch was a creation not of the second millennium BCE, but of the first. Since no system of Hebrew writing was then known to exist before the tenth century BCE, it appeared impossible for an illiterate Moses (if he existed at all) to have written anything. Furthermore, there was little independent archeological or textual evidence to verify the persons and events found from Exodus through Joshua, and for the even earlier persons and events described in the Book of Genesis, there seemed to be virtually no evidence at all.

However, probably the greatest factor in the triumph of the Documentary Hypothesis was its powerful connection to the rising evolutionary spirit of the times, augmenting Charles Darwin's *On the Origin of Species* (1859) and *The Descent of Man, and Selection in Relation to Sex* (1871) by paralleling his theory of biological ascent with a theory of religious evolution. Foundational to this theory is Darwin's understanding of human nature as derived and developed from earlier animal natures. In a similar way, said Darwin's disciples in regard to religion, as humans evolved a brain capable of self-consciousness and symbolic thought, and as they banded together into tribes and primitive societies, they projected their self-consciousness out onto the natural world and imagined a supernatural world behind and beyond it.

According to Wellhausen's contemporary Sir Edward Tylor, in his 1871 book *Primitive Culture*, first came **animism**, a belief that the heavens above, the landmarks, plants, and animals around, and the earth beneath possessed souls or spirits that should be treated with respect and, in the cases of especially powerful entities, fear and reverence. Next came **polytheism**, a belief in many gods, as humans offered increasingly formal worship to the most powerful of these natural forces (sun, moon, mountains, rivers, food sources, sexual drives), and to increasingly anthropomorphic pantheons of often-competing deities. Then, according to Max Müller in *Lectures on the Origin and Growth of Religion* (1878), came **henotheism**, the worship of one god among many, as a tribe or a nation found unity and its rulers authority under the name of a single powerful deity – while they still assumed the reality of the gods worshiped by other peoples and nations.

Finally, said Müller and Wellhausen, sometime between the tenth and seventh centuries BCE in Israel and Judah, came **monotheism**, a belief that there is only one God, and that all other supposed gods are "idols" to be rejected. This narrative of upward progress toward monotheism was a double-edged sword for the Christian West in the later Victorian era: on the one hand, it fit with a widespread Western belief that monotheistic Christian civilization – whether in Germany, Britain, or the United States – was the highest point yet reached in a long process of human social and ethical development; on the other hand, it undercut the metaphysical authority of that monotheism by treating it not as the eternal truth from God the Creator, but rather as the material product of natural selection. "Time and chance happen to them all," said Ecclesiastes; apparently even to God, said Müller and Wellhausen. Now even God had a biography, with a beginning, and, perhaps, a coming end.

The triumph of the Documentary Hypothesis in the late nineteenth century set off an explosion of scholarly and academic activity. Whole departments and schools of Biblical Studies and Oriental Studies (study of the ancient Near East) were founded at universities and colleges in Europe, Britain, and North America, dedicated to the developing project of "Higher Criticism": "higher" than mere sectarian interpretation, and dedicated to identifying and reinterpreting all of the textual sources and particles that were now believed to have made up, not only the *Torah*, but the entire Hebrew Bible. This was the golden age of the textual article and the footnote about the history of a particular word or phrase. Soon the "source criticism" method was applied not only to the "Hexateuch" of Genesis through Joshua, but also to the historical books of Judges, Samuel, Kings, and Chronicles, to the major and minor prophets, and to other such canonical writings as Psalms, Proverbs, Ecclesiastes, and the Song of Solomon. Traditional attributions of authorship to Samuel, Isaiah, Daniel, David, and Solomon were called into question, and as the twentieth century dawned, source criticism (German *Quellekritik*) turned its attentions to the New Testament as well.

However, the same move toward Oriental Studies, with its speculative reconstructions of many-layered textual history, also inspired a new wave of Near Eastern archeology intended to dig through actual earthen layers and provide solid historical evidence as context for these reconstructions. William Wright dug for and discovered the remains of the Hittite Empire, shedding light on Abraham's purchase of Sarah's tomb from Hittite neighbors in Genesis 23, and on the structure of the Sinai covenant in Exodus 19, 20, and 24; James Henry Breasted deciphered and interpreted the tombs of post-Mosaic Pharaohs Akhenaton and Tutankhamun, and discovered King Solomon's stables at Megiddo; William F. Albright excavated Saul's Gibeah, established the reign of Solomon's enemy Pharaoh Shishaq, and helped to authenticate the Dead Sea Scrolls; and H. Dunscomb Colt unearthed ancient Lachish, the major fortified center in Judah that was destroyed by the Assyrian army under Sennacherib. Moreover Giovanni Pettinato, an excavator of Ebla in Syria, found in the site's cuneiform tablets many ancient Hebraic names not formerly found in other Near Eastern languages: Adamu, H'à-wa (Eve), Ebrium (Eber? Hebrews?), Jabal, Abarama, Bilhah, Ishma-el, Isûra-el, Esau, Mika-el, Mikaya, Saul, and David. A large number of biblical locations also occur in the Ebla tablets: for example, Ashtaroth, Sinai, Jerusalem (Ye-ru-sa-lu-um), Hazor, Lachish, Gezer, Dor, Megiddo, Joppa, Ur – and, perhaps, even the infamous Dead Sea "cities of the plain," Admah (Ad-mu-ut), Sodom (Si-da-mu) and Gomorrah (I-ma-ar).

The discovery of these personal and place names, appearing in clay documents dating back to the late third and middle second millennia BCE, followed two other crucial discoveries of the nineteenth century. First, paleographers found and deciphered the Proto-Sinaitic, Proto-Canaanite, and Phoenician alphabets dating back as early as the nineteenth century BCE; and second, others unearthed and read the Creation and Flood accounts of Babylon and Sumeria. In the first case, the existence of these ancient Semitic alphabets, all likely ancestors of Paleo-Hebrew, established that the peoples of Canaan possessed writing systems independent of both Egyptian hieroglyphic and of Near Eastern cuneiform scripts. Thus Hebrews living at the time of the traditional Exodus – 1500–1400 BCE – probably already possessed a system of literacy capable of recording any number of the source texts for the Pentateuch.

Furthermore, some of the likely Babylonian and Sumerian sources of the Pentateuch were coming to light. The *Epic of Gilgamesh*, with its account of "The Flood of Enlil," presents the story of a catastrophic deluge that destroys the earth and its inhabitants, with the exception of one man and his family – they are warned to build a great boat, stock it with food and animals, and ride out the storm. This flood story, recorded sometime between 2000 and 1800 BCE, provides obvious context for the story of Noah and the ark in Genesis 6–9 – but context a millennium older than Wellhausen's dating between 950 and 650 BCE. Moreover, the *Enuma Elish*, a Babylonian Creation epic recorded between 1750 and 1400 BCE, contains important vocabulary echoed in the Creation story told in Genesis 1 – again suggesting a context for the initial composition of Genesis in the second millennium BCE rather than the first.[1]

No doubt, these Babylonian origin tales present a starkly different vision of the cosmos from that found in Genesis: here the lazy gods create humans to do the field-work for them; the earth-god Enki outsmarts the angry storm-god Enlil by warning his human favorite Utnapishtim of the coming flood; and, above all, the earth and seas are originally created by Marduk's tremendously violent combat with the sea-monster Tiamat (related to the Hebrew *tehom* for "sea" used in Genesis). But that is just the point: in this second-millennium Babylonian context, Genesis comes into new focus as a polemical counter to the polytheistic conflicts of a warring Near Eastern pantheon. Genesis pictures instead a serene, generous, diligent, and just Creator speaking the world into being, and then much later regretfully flooding the earth to cleanse it of flourishing human evil, while mercifully sparing one faithful man as a fresh start.

In the light of such discoveries about artifacts, literacy, and background documents, by the mid-twentieth century some scholars began to question and challenge certain conclusions and even the basic assumptions of Wellhausen's hypothesis. If much of the Pentateuch and the following "historical books" contained a good deal of archeologically verifiable cultural data, if the second-millennium Hebrews lived in an age of Semitic literacy, and if even the earliest chapters of Genesis made best sense in a second-millennium context, then it was time to reconsider whether at least part of the Pentateuch was composed in the middle second millennium also. And if that earlier context suggested a surprising coherence to the text, might not biblical criticism turn its attentions more to literary criticism proper – that is, to explaining what the text means, *in its present form*, rather than mainly speculating about its supposed – and unknown – past forms? Indeed, shouldn't practitioners of something called the "Documentary Hypothesis" be wary of making confident "source" pronouncements in the absence of any of the actual JEDP source documents?

So Umberto Cassuto observed that the repetition of material in ancient Hebrew and Near Eastern writing is not usually an editorial accident, but a deliberate *literary* device, whether at the level of parallelism and refrain in poetry, or at the level of doubling and reiteration in longer prose narrative. Similarly, he argued, the variation in divine names is also meaningfully intentional rather than textually accidental; as we saw in the previous chapter, the use of *Elohim* stressing God's transcendent universality, and the use of *Yahweh* or *Yahweh Elohim* stressing his personal, promise-keeping nearness. In addition, asked R. N. Whybray, why would Wellhausen exempt the original J, E, D, and P source documents from such duplication and ascribe it only to the "cut-and-paste" work of the later Redactor? And ultimately, from a strictly narrative and psychological point of view, why can't a character like Abraham be allowed to make the same moral error more than once? And why can't Isaac repeat his father's mistakes? In fact, if we read these repeated patriarchal deceptions simply as human narrative (whether fictional or not) they make perfect thematic sense – as sinful and fallible men (and women) are nevertheless employed and blessed by a gracious covenant God, who tests and purifies his servants in the end.

So, ironically, although "Higher Criticism" was born in the nineteenth century to correct the reductionism of the traditional Unitary Hypothesis, by the early twentieth century it had developed a reductionism of its own, needing correction by the new archeological evidence and explorations of literary form noted above. Furthermore, by the mid-twentieth century the cultural and ideological landscape surrounding Biblical Studies had undergone a dramatic shift. Wellhausen and his early disciples had relied on a rising well of optimism about scientific human progress along German lines, and could assume among many of their avant-garde readers a certain condescension about primitive, tribal texts – especially if the texts were Jewish. (Wellhausen's follower Friedrich Delitzch delivered his 1902 lecture *Babel und Bibel*, arguing that the Hebrew Bible has no historical or moral value, and was praised by German Kaiser Wilhelm for doing his part "to dissipate the nimbus of the Chosen People.") However, by mid-century, the prestige of German "higher thought" had been much diminished by the two world wars, and references to the Old Testament as a mere "Hebrew fable" ran aground on a good deal of archeological bedrock. Some Higher Critical certainties had come to look rather quaint;

scholarly ideas born with the telephone, the gramophone, and the light bulb – and in an era of Anglo-Saxon imperial self-confidence – were beginning to show their age.

The high-water mark of Higher Critical confidence had come at the very end of the nineteenth century in a publishing project that attempted to capture the latest conclusions of source criticism by printing a separate new translation of every Old Testament book, representing each of the many source documents in a different color and making instantly apparent even to the casual reader the varied and highly complex compositional work of the anonymous post-exilic "Redactor." Popularly called the "Polychrome Bible" and published between 1895 and 1899, its editor Paul Haupt commissioned the leaders of the Higher Critical movement – Wellhausen included – to translate and edit particular books. W. H. Bennett's edition of the Book of Joshua gives a good idea of the speculative confidence of the method: in the following passage from Joshua 7 about the stoning of the thief Achan, the words in plain roman are assigned by Bennett to the "Yahwist" writing around 950 BCE, the words in *italics* are assigned by Bennett to a writer/ Redactor working in 500 BCE, and the words in **boldface** to one working in 550 BCE:

> [25] And Joshua said, Why hast thou troubled us? the LORD shall trouble thee this day. *And all Israel stoned him with stones*, and burned them with fire, after they had stoned them with stones.

> [26] And they raised over him a great heap of stones unto this day. **So the LORD turned from the fierceness of his anger**. Wherefore the name of that place was called, The valley of Achor, unto this day.[2]

Even a passage this brief forces us to reflect that Bennett reached his conclusions without access to any of the original source documents, because these documents and their dates were, after all, speculative rather than actual. So we will naturally ask the question, "How does he know?" We wonder how anyone can be so confident about minute subdivisions in even a much more recent text – say, the breakdown of William Shakespeare's and John Fletcher's relative contributions to the play *Henry VIII* (1613). In the case of the far more ancient text of Joshua, with some paragraphs in its "Polychrome" edition subdivided into as many as five colors, such confidence approaches the incredible. Ironically, in the case of the "Polychrome Bible," the prohibitive price of printing in eight colors put an end to the project; only six books – Leviticus, Joshua, Judges, Isaiah, Ezekiel, and Psalms – were produced. (Perhaps also ironically, the editor, Paul Haupt, turned his attentions to the New Testament, becoming an advocate in the 1920s for the idea of an "Aryan Jesus.")

Since the Documentary Hypothesis had as a founding grandfather the poet Goethe, perhaps it is appropriate to end our discussion of the achievements and excesses of this method with the following words of Walter Kaufmann:

> Imagine a Higher Critic analyzing Goethe's *Faust*, which was written by a single human being in the course of sixty years. The scenes in which the heroine of Part One is called Gretchen would be relegated to one author; the conflicting conceptions of the role of Mephistopheles would be taken to call for further divisions, and the Prologue in Heaven would be ascribed to a later editor, while the prelude on the stage would be referred to yet a different author. Our critic would have no doubt whatsoever that Part Two belongs to a different age and must be assigned to a great many writers with widely different ideas. The end of Act IV, for example, points to an anti-Catholic author who lampoons the Church, while the end of Act V was written by a man, we should be told, who, though probably no orthodox Catholic, was deeply sympathetic to Catholicism. Where do we find more inconsistencies in style and thought and plan: in Goethe's *Faust* or in the Five Books of Moses?[3]

It is at present clear that scholarly unanimity surrounding Wellhausen's hypothesis is no more. Some critics, on the evidence noted above, have pushed the initial composition dates well back into the second millennium and into the time of the traditional Moses, while others, taking Wellhausen's speculative method well beyond what even its founder imagined, have subdivided J, E, D, and P into many smaller sources, and in some cases have come to doubt the existence of any coherent biblical text at all until the Hasmonean era – indeed virtually into the era of Roman Judea.

2.1.2   *Toledoth*: Generations of Genesis and Torah

Yet one thing still seems clear amid the diminishing consensus about Higher Criticism: that contrary to the old "Unitary Hypothesis," the current text of Genesis is in fact composed of multiple documents, combined and edited into its current form. Indeed, an alternate "documentary" theory has been developed by P. J. Wiseman in *New Discoveries in Babylonia About Genesis* (1936) and by Donald Wiseman in *Ancient Records and the Structure of Genesis: A Case for Literary Unity* (1985). Their theory is based on a textual fact that is a good deal more evident even than multiple divine names: the fact of the ten *Toledoth* (plural for Hebrew *Toledah* – a **colophon** or genealogical record of ancestors or descendants), which constitute the book as we have it. Significantly, the word *Toledoth*, literally meaning "generations," almost certainly inspired the book's title "Genesis," a title given by the translators of the Hebrew Bible into the Greek Septuagint in 280 BCE (the Hebrew title is *Barashith* – "In the beginning"). These translators seem to have recognized the key to the book's structure: it was composed from genealogies plus narrative elaborations. So we see that ten times[4] Genesis announces the beginning of a section or scroll with the phrase "these are the generations":

1) 2:4 "These are the generations of the heavens and the earth"
2) 5:1 "This is the book of the generations of Adam"
3) 6:9 "These are the generations of Noah"
4) 10:1 "These are the generations of the sons of Noah"
5) 11:10 "These are the generations of Shem"
6) 11:27 "These are the generations of Terah"
7) 25:12 "These are the generations of Ishmael"
8) 25:19 "These are the generations of Isaac"
9) 36:1,9 "These are the generations of Esau"
10) 37:2 "These are the generations of Jacob"

Significantly, these natural divisions of the text – very likely based on earlier genealogical tables, tablets, or scrolls in the editor's possession – show some deeper patterning around the sacred numbers three, seven, and two. The first three *Toledoth* (a number of completion) portray the world before the Flood, while the last seven (a number of perfection) treat the world after. Also, each of the first three tables is paired – for emphasis and confirmation – in a parallel relationship with each of the next three: table 1 (the spread of life and evil after Creation) with table 4 (the spread of life and evil after the Flood); table 2 (the godly line of Seth) with table 5 (the godly line of Shem); and table 3 (the universal covenant of Noah) with table 6 (the particular covenant of Abraham). Finally, each of the last four *Toledoth* matches – for contrast – with another in that group: table 7 (the rejected line of Ishmael, the elder brother) with table 8 (the chosen line of Isaac, his younger brother); and table 9 (the rejected line of Esau/Edom, the elder brother) with table 10 (the chosen line of Jacob/Israel, his younger brother).

Such thematically important patterning – virtually ignored by the Wellhausen school – not only fits the overall literary design of Genesis, but also hearkens back to the sources that probably preceded and produced it. For other ancient genealogies and origin stories were preserved in a similar form; for instance, in the Babylonian *Enuma Elish* of 1750–1400 BCE, seven individual cuneiform tables or tablets were distinguished one from another by an opening phrase or concluding "colophon" briefly describing the document's contents – like a modern title page. These taglines would then be used to organize and sequence the individual component texts into a larger whole. So in the *Toledoth* we discern what is probably the key to the larger design of Genesis, a Documentary Hypothesis indeed: a design that depends on previous documents, and on artful arrangement of these sources that reflects Near Eastern literary practice in the second millennium BCE – making these documents notably less hypothetical than those of the Higher Criticism, and plausibly centuries older.

2.2 New Testament Sources: "Q" and A

We will discuss the origins of the New Testament texts in more detail in the upcoming chapters devoted to them; however, we should note that just as later nineteenth-century scholars of the Old Testament developed their theories of documentary sources, so in the early twentieth century other scholars developed a kind of "source criticism" for the New. Led by the German textual critic Johannes Weiss, they proposed that behind the gospels of Matthew and Luke lay a common source, which contained a rough outline of Jesus's ministry and which served as scaffolding for the elaborations of Matthew and Luke, who were also thought to have consulted Mark. This common outline, called "Q" from German *Quelle* or "wellspring"/"source," was thought to account for many substantial resemblances among the first three gospels, called "Synoptic" gospels, from the Greek for "having the same point of view."

Along with "Q" source criticism came the "demythologization" project of Rudolph Bultmann and Ernst Kasemann, who sought to reconcile the gospels with modern ideas of scientific possibility by distinguishing between "the Jesus of history" (the first-century Palestinian Jew from Nazareth) and "the Christ of faith" (the mythical and symbolic object of spiritual hope). Some proposed that "Q" presented a bare-bones outline about "the Jesus of history," and that the gospels elaborated and "mythologized" that outline for the benefit of the faithful. Bultmann argued that these mythical stories of healings, wonders, and resurrections were never intended to be read literally, and that to survive in the modern world, Christianity must drop its claims to historical truth and instead embrace its rich range of metaphorical and mythic meaning. Opponents of demythologization responded by noting how often the New Testament writers, both of gospels and epistles, claim to follow eyewitness testimony, and link Jesus to clearly historical figures, like Pontius Pilate, and events, like the destruction of the Second Temple.

As to the "Q" theory, it is clear by now that, like the Old Testament's "J," "E," "D," and "P," "Q" has never been found, only inferred; in fact, some have suggested that Mark's gospel might itself be the main or only source for the substantially longer Matthew and Luke, while internal evidence makes it clear that the "Synoptics" differ both in chronology and content from John's gospel. As we will see in a later chapter, whether those differences are to be read as contradictory or complementary has been the topic of much debate.

2.3 "In His Hand Was a Measuring Rod": Community, Councils, and Canons

If the composition of Genesis, the Pentateuch, and the gospels has been hotly and widely contested over the past two centuries, establishing the approved and authorized texts that make up what we call "the Bible" has been the controversial work of millennia. Any collection of authoritative "required reading" is called a "canon," from the Greek word *kanon*, for "straight rod" or "carpenter's ruler"; so a canon gives the rule, the measure, or the standard. Biblical canons claim to represent a standard of religious or spiritual truth, not a standard of literary quality such as, for instance, *The Blackwell Anthology of Renaissance Literature* or some other collection of aesthetically important writing. Yet the Judeo-Christian scriptures contain much famously great writing, and have at times served as a canon of literary style for writers as diverse as the Pearl Poet, Philip and Mary Sidney, John Donne, George Herbert, Anne Bradstreet, John Bunyan, William Blake, Goethe, Lord Byron, Leo Tolstoy, Mark Twain, Ernest Hemingway, Shusaku Endo, Simone Weil, Saul Bellow, and Bob Dylan.

Establishing a canon implies both controversy and consensus: controversy because canons – especially religious and doctrinal canons – necessarily exclude some texts as either false or at least uninspired; consensus because for a canon to exist and to endure, it must speak to the past experiences, present needs, and future hopes of a faith community. Also, canons generally have been made by councils or assemblies that represent these faith communities, so there is always an important element of human discernment and deliberation in deciding what counts as divine truth. This human role makes some believers worry, and many skeptics claim, that revelation can be reduced to mere political or social negotiation. So debates over "canonicity" often resemble debates over composition: either the sacred canon springs, whole as if by dictation, from the mouth of God, or it is only a human construction lacking any divine authority.

2.3.1 *Tanakh*, Old Testament, the Deutero-Canonicals, and New Testament Apocrypha

Whatever we may believe personally about a conflict between human agency and divine revelation, the ancient and early modern councils that created the biblical canons did not think in these terms. In fact, it is inaccurate to speak of them "creating" or "making" a canon: both Jews and Christians saw themselves as *recognizing* a pre-existing reality that had in their view proven itself in multiple ways. From the post-exilic Jerusalem Council of the Jews at the time of Ezra around 450 BCE to the Septuagint translation from Hebrew to Greek in Alexandria in 280 BCE; and from the Christian Council of Carthage in 397 CE to the Roman Catholic Council of Trent in 1570 and the Presbyterian Westminster Assembly in 1645, the criteria for endorsing the "canonicity" of a biblical book were generally threefold: (i) widespread acceptance and use by believers; (ii) association with holy teachers, prophets, priests, or apostles; and/or (iii) the perceived fulfillment or confirmation of prophetically predicted events. Typically, if a council believed that at least two of these conditions were met, the book entered the canon.

Thus, for instance, the Book of Genesis was canonized because the Jerusalem Council believed that (i) it or its sources had long been in use by the Jewish people; (ii) it was the work (at least at its core) of Moses; and (iii) it presented true predictions, such as those of Joseph's rise and of the eventual return of the Israelites from Egypt to Canaan. The Book of Jeremiah was canonized because (i) it had been widely read among the Babylonian exiles for whom it was written; (ii) it was attributed to the Prophet Jeremiah; and (iii) its dire predictions of Jerusalem's fall, and its hopeful prophecies of return seventy years later, were seen as having come to pass. Certain other books – Proverbs, Ecclesiastes, and Song of Solomon – lacked the prophetic confirmation of Genesis or Jeremiah but found acceptance through their association with King Solomon; the anonymous book of Job was canonized because it had been in use for nearly a thousand years and the figure of Job was considered as a kind of seer; and the book of Jonah, however fictional or satiric, was associated with the prophet who ministered in the later decades of the Northern Kingdom of Israel (2 Kings 14:25).

The Canon of the Hebrew Bible/*Tanakh*

"Tanakh" is an acronym for the three main sections of the Hebrew Bible: *Torah/Nevi'im/ Khetuvim* – see below.

- Written between **1500** and **150 BC** in Hebrew and Aramaic.
- First established by Ezra in about **450 BC** (according to ancient Jewish tradition).
- Finalized by about **150 BC** under the Jewish Maccabean kings.

The Hebrew Bible/*Tanakh* contains the same books at the Greek/Russian Orthodox and Protestant Old Testament, although in a somewhat different order:

TORAH – "Law" (Greek "Pentateuch" – "Πεντατεύχος," "five volume[s]")	**Latter prophets (cont.)**
Genesis	Minor prophets (cont.)
Exodus	Habakkuk
Leviticus	Zephaniah
Numbers	Haggai
Deuteronomy	Zechariah
	Malachi
NEVI'IM – "Prophets"	
Former prophets	
Joshua	
Judges	
Samuel (1 and 2)	
Kings (1 and 2)	*KHETUVIM* – "Writings"
Latter prophets	Psalms
Major prophets	Proverbs
Isaiah	Job
Jeremiah	**Five rolls**
Ezekiel	Song of Solomon
Minor prophets	Ruth
Hosea	Lamentations
Joel	Ecclesiastes
Amos	Esther
Obadiah	Daniel
Jonah	Ezra
Micah	Nehemiah
Nahum (cont.)	Chronicles (1 and 2)

Thus, the Hebrew canon makes room for the heroism of Exodus and the anti-heroism of Jonah, the many-voiced lyric power of Psalms and the plodding genealogies of Chronicles, the wisdom of Proverbs and the counter-wisdom of Ecclesiastes and Job, the chaste domesticity of Ruth and the frank eroticism of Solomon's Song.

In a similar way, the Council of Carthage in 397 CE sought to recognize rather than create the New Testament canon.

For instance, Mark's gospel (i) had been in wide use for well over 300 years; (ii) it was associated with John Mark, companion in his youth to the Apostle Peter; and (iii) its prediction of Jerusalem's second destruction (Mark 13) was regarded as having been fulfilled in 70 CE. The Gospel According to Luke (i) had been, like Mark's, in long and wide use; (ii) it was, like the Acts of the Apostles, the work of the Apostle Paul's traveling companion, the Greek physician Luke (Acts 16:6, Col. 4:14), who claims to have interviewed many eyewitnesses of Jesus's life (Luke 1:1–4); and (iii) was almost certainly completed before the fall of Jerusalem, which it too

---

The Canon of the New Testament/New Covenant

- Composed and compiled between **40** CE **and 130** CE in "koiné" ("κοινή") or "common" Greek
- Canonized by the Third Council of Carthage in **397** CE

Matthew
Mark
Luke
John
Acts
Romans
1 Corinthians
2 Corinthians
Galatians
Ephesians
Philippians
Colossians
1 Thessalonians
2 Thessalonians
1 Timothy
2 Timothy
Titus
Philemon
Hebrews
James
1 Peter
2 Peter
1 John
2 John
3 John
Jude
Revelation

---

predicts. And so it goes: Matthew's and John's gospels were attributed to a pair of Jesus's original twelve apostles, and John's gospel especially stresses the writer's eyewitness experience (John 1:14, 19:35, 21:24); the letters of Paul (nearly half the New Testament) claim to be from the apostle to the Gentiles, the former "Pharisee of Pharisees" who sought to exterminate the Church but became its most famous convert; while the letters of James, Peter, John, and Jude, and the Revelation to John, had been widely regarded for three centuries or more as authored by apostles.

But what of the many books excluded from these canons? Usually called the "Apocrypha" (Greek for "hidden things"), they fall into two main categories: those that have been treated as non-canonical but are still recommended as "further reading," and those forbidden by religious authorities as heretical. Roughly speaking, the Old Testament Apocrypha, while canonical for Roman Catholic and Orthodox believers, have been regarded by Jews and Protestants as non-inspired though (often) worthwhile, but the New Testament Apocrypha have been rejected by all the historic Christian traditions, whether Roman Catholic, Orthodox, or Protestant.

The case of the Old Testament Apocrypha presents the largest canonical disagreement within the Judeo-Christian scriptural tradition.

Old Testament Apocrypha – Roman Catholic Bible

From Greek "Αποκρυφα," "hidden things" – called "Deutero-Canonical books" by Roman Catholics.

- All written before the beginning of the Christian Era, but excluded from Hebrew canon.
- Used intermittently over the centuries, but canonized by the Roman Catholic Church at the Council of Trent in **1570** CE in response to Protestant challenges.
- Recommended by Jewish and Protestant authorities, but not canonized by them, and not binding on Church teaching; recognized as canonical by Greek/Russian Orthodox Churches.

---

1 Esdras (Orthodox canon only)   Maccabees (1 and 2)
Tobit
Judith
Rest of Esther
Wisdom of Solomon
Ecclesiasticus (Wisdom of Jesus son of Sirach)
Baruch
Song of the Three Holy Children
Susanna
Bel and the Dragon
Prayer of Manasseh

Called the "Deutero-Canonical" books (for "secondary canon") by Catholics and the Orthodox, they were all composed before the beginning of the Christian Era, excluded by Jewish leaders, though used intermittently in the medieval Church, until they were officially canonized by Rome at the Council of Trent in 1570 in response to Protestant challenges. The Protestant reformers had explicitly followed the Jewish canon for the Hebrew Bible, and these Protestant leaders, like the Jews before them, found these apocryphal books lacking in widespread acceptance, inspired authorship, and prophetic fulfillment.

On the other hand, Catholic and Orthodox authorities hold that these books supplement and in some cases actually complete canonical Old Testament books like 2 Kings (the Prayer of Manasseh), Jeremiah (Baruch), and Esther (The Rest of Esther). Some of their stories have become justly famous for their storytelling brio and their sometimes racy edge: the beautiful and virtuous Judith excites the lust of the drunken heathen general Holofernes so that he loses his head – figuratively and literally! – and the naked but upright Susanna is spied out in her bath by the corrupt elders, who then are exposed in their lechery. And the books of the Maccabees tell the thrilling tale of the Hasmonean revolt that liberates the oppressed Jews from blasphemous foreign tyranny and establishes a new dynasty in the Intertestamental Period. Nevertheless, the relatively late appearance of these Apocrypha in Jewish history, their more limited use among Jews and Christians, and (in some cases) their composition in Greek rather than in Hebrew – all of these factors have kept them, if not actually "hidden," at least as a kind of afterthought in biblical history.

However much Christians have disagreed over including the Old Testament Apocrypha in the canon, they have been historically unanimous in excluding, and usually unanimous in condemning, the apocryphal writings associated with the New Testament.

The New Testament Apocrypha

- Written between **150 and 400** CE.
- Non-canonical for all Roman Catholic, Greek/Russian Orthodox, and Protestant traditions.
- Some recommended, some not – often "forbidden" by historic Church councils.

Apocalypse of Peter	Gospel of Thomas
Barnabas	Hermas
Gospel of the Ebionites	Logia Jesu (Words of Jesus)
Gospel according to the Egyptians	Preaching of Peter
Gospel according to the Hebrews	Gospel of the Lord
Gospel of the Naassenes	Gospel of Truth
Gospel of Nicodemus	Gospel of Mary
Gospel of Peter	Gospel of Judas

It's clear that even by the time of Luke's and John's gospels in the later first century, multiple accounts already had been written of Jesus's life, probably quite a few more than the canonical four gospels (see Luke 1:1–2, John 21:24–25). So why would Christians have rejected these so-called Apocrypha with virtually one voice? These books' failure to meet the traditional criteria of canonicity certainly played an important part, but a crucial factor in many cases was the books' content. The traditional criteria first: the books of the canonical New Testament were mostly complete by the final third of the first century, and finished by century's end, so that they could plausibly claim (if not prove) the eyewitness authority of Jesus's original disciples and apostles, and their widespread use by the early Church, but the New Testament Apocrypha probably were written between the years 150 and 400 of the Common Era. So titles like the Apocalypse of Peter, the Gospel of Nicodemus, the Gospel of Peter, the Gospel of Thomas, and the Preaching of Peter were inherently implausible or patently false, coming between 100 and 350 years after the deaths of their supposed authors or sources. With no evidence of apostolic authority or widespread acceptance by many churches, and with little predictive prophecy to speak of, these books had little to recommend them to the canon-forming Carthage Council.

But it is the books' content that best accounts for the churches' strong condemnation. Many of these Apocrypha also can be classified as Gnostic Gospels, with pictures of Jesus's personal nature, character, and mission that differ strikingly from those in the canonical gospels and epistles. For even at their most divergent, the four New Testament gospels all portray Jesus as a loyal and exemplary Jew who reached out compassionately to Gentiles, and also as the fully human Son of God who came to sacrifice his life on a Roman cross for Jewish and Gentile sin, and then rise bodily from the dead as the sign of God's forgiveness. In contrast, the alternate vision of the Gnostic documents portray Jesus as a divine spiritual master who merely seemed to have mortal flesh but who actually came to liberate a few chosen souls from the limits of material existence by imparting secret knowledge – i.e. *gnosis*, hence "Gnostic" – and who, far from dying on a cross, either bypasses death entirely or is spared crucifixion by the suffering of a substitute.

If the canonical gospels are Passion narratives that stress Jesus's physical humanity and suffering as the atoning Savior, the Gnostic Gospels are more typically collections of sayings that treat humanity's chief problem not as sinful rebellion but as innocent ignorance of mystical truth. And where the four New Testament gospels treat Jesus as fulfilling the righteousness of the Mosaic Law in his obedient life and death, the alternative gospels generally dismiss the Old Testament as a collection of Jewish fantasies and illusions that Jesus came to discredit. It may seem strange to modern skeptics (and some modern believers) who commonly struggle with the idea that Jesus was *divine*, but in the first centuries of the Christian Church, it was much more common to doubt or deny that Jesus was *human*.

There is, we should note, some overlap between the non-canonical and canonical gospels: for instance, the Gospel of Thomas, like the Gospel of Luke, quotes Jesus as saying that "the Kingdom is within you" (Thomas, Saying 3; Luke 17:21), and many of the Gnostic documents, like the Gospel of Mark, report Jesus as giving "secret" teaching to his chosen disciples (Mark 4:11). But for the Gospel of Thomas, salvation comes by mystically realizing the "inner Kingdom," not by Jesus' death, while the "secret" of Mark's gospel turns out to be that "the Son of Man came not to be served, but to serve, and to give his life as a ransom for many" (10:45).

Of course, there is no longer anything "secret" or "hidden" about either the Old or New Testament Apocrypha: the former can be found in any Roman Catholic or Orthodox Bible, and the latter are now widely available in modern translations with extensive scholarly commentary. In a modern era that is frequently skeptical of religious authority, the Gnostic writings naturally attract interest due to their having been "forbidden books," and because they offer an alternative to the more familiar outlook of the canonical New Testament. As we develop our literary analysis of the Testaments Old and New, we will mention these secondary and sometimes unorthodox writings insofar as they help to provide context for (and contrasts with) the canonical texts; in fact, a literary approach will shed more light on how the Apocrypha both complement and contradict the "official" version – and how the once "forbidden books" of outcast, exiled and marginal sects became the official canon in the first place.

2.4 Literary Study of the Bible: A Way Forward

So we have seen that "Source Critics" of the Bible are at something of an impasse – and are increasingly aware that speculative textual reconstruction in the absence of actual source documents can yield no certain results. Thus, Bible scholars have turned increasingly over the past generation to literary study of the texts, not as they once might have been, but as we have them now. As we observed in the Preface and at the beginning of this chapter, literary analysis means reading with an eye for textual art: for intentional doubling, repetition, complexity, and irony; for plot and character development; and for a range of figurative language that imagines and describes one thing in terms of another. We also observed that a good "literary" reader will keep an eye out for how writers adopt and adapt inherited genres in new settings. In other words, the richest reading of the Bible, as of any book from long ago or far away, requires knowing something of its original contexts of and sympathizing imaginatively with its writers and with the traditions that shaped them. So literary analysis attends to what can be best known from the past to understand a text in the present.

Therefore, in the succeeding chapters, we will use all the tools of contextual discovery – archeology, the history of language, past literary models and contemporary sources – as we set the stage for reading a whole range of forms: from lyric, erotic pastoral, proverbial and wisdom discourse, origin narrative, heroic epic, and short story to chronicle history, prophecy, gospel, parable, epistle, and apocalypse. Along the way we will consider the varied theories of composition that have been applied to individual books, and say what can be known about the history of each text, but always with the purpose of experiencing something of their intended meanings and effects, whether appealing or strange to modern eyes and ears. We will begin at the heart of Hebrew literary art: its poetry, and particularly the Book of Psalms.

Questions for Discussion

1 What assumptions underlie the traditional **Unitary Hypothesis** of the Pentateuch's composition by Moses?

2 Who were the important figures in developing the **Documentary Hypothesis**? What observations and questions caused them to question and challenge the "Unitary Hypothesis"?

3 What assumptions underlie the Documentary Hypothesis? According to Julius Wellhausen, what were the different "documents" used to construct the **Hexateuch**, when were they produced, how can they be distinguished, and when were they "**redacted**" into their current form?

4 How have nineteenth- and twentieth-century discoveries in **archeology** and **paleography**, and the translation and study of pre-biblical sources like the *Enuma Elish* and the *Epic of Gilgamesh*, confirmed, challenged, and even modified the Documentary Hypothesis? What was **The Polychrome Bible**, and what does it suggest about the success and the limits of the **Higher Criticism**?

5 What are the ten *Toledoth*, and how do they contribute to the name, the structure, and the meaning of the Book of Genesis?

6 What assumptions underlie Johannes Weiss's *Quelle* or "**Q**" hypothesis of New Testament Gospel composition? What are some arguments for and against these assumptions?

7 What is a **canon** and what are the standards that ancient Jewish and Christian councils used to establish the "canonicity" of Old and New Testament books?

8 What are the **Apocrypha** or **Deutero-Canonical** books of the Old Testament? Which religious traditions accept these books as Holy Scripture, and which do not? In both cases, why?

9 What are the books of the **New Testament Apocrypha**, what distinguishes them from the traditional New Testament, and how are they regarded by the historical Christian Churches? Why?

Notes

1 *Gilgamesh* and the *Enuma Elish* were first translated into English in 1872 and 1876, but not until the middle and later twentieth century did scholars propose that the Flood and Creation stories in Genesis are best understood as polemical responses to these polytheistic traditions. See Conrad Hyers, *The Meaning of Creation* (Philadelphia, PA: Westminster John Knox, 1984).

2 W. H. Bennett, *The Book of Joshua: A Critical Edition of the Hebrew Text Printed in Colors, Exhibiting the Composite Structure of the Book* (Baltimore, MD: Johns Hopkins University Press, 1895).

3 W. Kaufmann, *Critique of Religion and Philosophy* (Princeton, NJ: Princeton University Press, 1978), 377.

4 The descendants of Esau are overviewed in Genesis 36:1–8 and elaborated in Genesis 36:9–43.

Part II

The Old Testament/Hebrew Bible/*Tanakh*

3

Hebrew Poetry: Deep Calls to Deep

We have begun by observing that the special genius of Hebrew biblical literature is its "stereoscopic" quality, its surprising multiplicity of outlook – surprising because it complicates our common sense of the Bible as a book that speaks with one authoritative, if not authoritarian, voice. Many people, believers and skeptics alike, think of the Bible as a one-way text: one God, one chosen people, one truth, one Law, one right, one wrong, one faith, one judgment. Yet built into this supposedly unitary collection of scripture is a rich – perhaps bewildering – variety: repeated and alternative origin accounts and patriarchal stories, diverse genres and forms, varied figurative and structural devices, and many, many different voices spanning twenty centuries. Although the Bible excels in multiple types of narrative and even in certain kinds of prophetic and dramatic form, the heart of Hebrew literary art is found in its lyric poetry, and especially in the Psalms.

3.1 "In the Great Congregation": The Many Voices of Psalms

If one part of the Hebrew Bible can be called the most indestructibly popular, and almost infinitely influential, it would be the Psalms. They are beloved of Jews and Christians alike; they are sung, recited, and repeated at innumerable worship services every week on every continent; they are cherished by readers of many faiths and none. The Psalms also cross over successfully into both high and popular culture, from the choral settings of Hildegard and Bach and Britten, to the poetic lines of Dante and Herbert and Dickinson, to the fictional pages of Dickens and Joyce and Fitzgerald, to the song lyrics of Bob Marley and Bob Dylan and U2.

How do we account for such boundary-breaking popularity? First, biblical poetry is, in the words of the seventeenth-century British metaphysical poet George Herbert, "Heart-deep." Its profound range and depth of emotion speak to practically all conditions of the human soul, from serene trust to jagged doubt, from ecstatic joy to shattered desolation, from tender gratitude to vengeful rage, and from heartbroken penitence to (if we include Solomon's Song) sensuous eroticism. For French reformer Jean Cauvin (better known to English-speakers as John Calvin) the Psalms present "an Anatomy of all the Parts of the Soul" that "has drawn to the life all the griefs, sorrows, fears, doubts, hopes, cares, perplexities, in short, all the distracting emotions" that humans feel.[1] Commentators often speak conventionally of particular types: Psalms of Wisdom, Praise, Lamentation, Penitence, Assurance, Messianic Hope, Ascents, and (most fearsomely) of Imprecation or Cursing.

Literary Study of the Bible: An Introduction, First Edition. Christopher Hodgkins.
© 2020 John Wiley & Sons Ltd. Published 2020 by John Wiley & Sons Ltd.

Psalm Types

Some examples of particular psalm types are as follows (note that types sometimes overlap):
Wisdom – 1, 127, 128
Praise – 8, 9, 33, 100, 117, 122, 126, 148, 150
Lamentation – 22, 39, 73, 88, 89, 90, 120, 137
Penitence – 32, 51, 130
Assurance – 22, 23, 46, 63, 121, 123, 124, 125, 131, 139
Messianic Hope – 22, 110, 132
Ascents – 120–134 (sequence)
Imprecation/Curse – 129, 137

While these are useful categories, it's really rather rare to find a psalm that fits just one of them, so it's just as useful to think of varied psalmic *voices*. If you are listening for your own voice in the Psalms, you are surprisingly likely to hear it; the Psalms make up a kind of literary congregation, whose membership includes not only contented "church folk" but also worriers, skeptics, strident complainers, crestfallen doubters, and, all in all, some pretty spectacular sinners.

A second reason for the remarkably wide appeal of Hebrew poetry is related to its emotional depth and variety: that is, its dynamic sense of psychological discovery. If we are used to thinking of religious poetry simply as doctrine or dogma repeated in verse, we're likely to be intrigued, perhaps even shocked, by the drama that unfolds in many of these lyrics. Far from being mere static statements of settled belief, the Psalms frequently change course partway through, sometimes more than once, as mourning turns to dancing, grief to wrath, complaint to calm assurance, or (occasionally) confident litany to angry lament. Also, these transformations sometimes involve a dramatic change of voice or speaker: a psalm may begin with a human voice full of praise or complaint, only to be abruptly interrupted by the Lord, as it were, "talking back." These divine interventions can have the effect either of a comforting embrace or a slap in the face. In short, many of the Psalms model a spiritual experience that is highly interactive and transformational.

Finally, a third reason for the broad popularity and 3000-year staying power of the Psalms is the highly translatable art of their figure and form.

Terms of Art: Mizmor, Tehillah, Shir, Maskil, Michtam, and Shiggaion

The post-exilic editorial notes to the Psalms use a number of different "terms of art" to describe particular poems or groups of poems in the collection. In modern translations these terms are often left untranslated and include Mizmor ("Psalm," "Melody of Praise," "Lyric Ode" – fifty-eight Psalms), Tehillah ("Praise" or "Hymn"), Shir ("Spiritual Song" – thirteen Psalms), Maskil ("Contemplation," "Instruction" – thirteen Psalms), Michtam ("Golden," "Treasure" – six Psalms), and Shiggaion ("Reeling," "Passion" – one Psalm). As the Eskimo have many words for snow, so the Hebrews had many for song.

As we have already observed and will see in more detail, these Hebrew lyrics, like all poetry, consist of intensive figurative language presented in meaningful structures. However, what makes the Psalms especially translatable between languages and cultures is their dominant structural device of parallelism. Unlike meter and rhyme, which are generally lost in translation, this "rhyming of ideas" can be reproduced faithfully whatever the vocabulary or writing system – from Greek and Latin and English to Arabic and Urdu and Chinese, one line can be tracked by the next, whether for emphasis, contrast, or elaboration.

3.1.1 A Pentateuch of Poems: The Five Books of the Psalter

Before we discuss specific features of Hebrew poetry or particular psalms in more detail, we'll first consider how the Psalms came to be, both as individual poems and as a book.

Psalms: Naming and Numbering

The title "Psalms" comes from Greek *Psalmoi*, or "Songs," the Septuagint's title for what is called in the Hebrew Bible *Sepher Tehillim*, "The Book of Praises."

Individual psalm numbers derive from the Masoretic Text (ninth century CE) of the Hebrew Bible followed by Jews and Protestants and will be used throughout this book:

- The Septuagint Greek translation of the Bible (third century BCE) uses slightly different numbers for the Psalms – adopted by the Latin Vulgate (fourth century CE) and by Roman Catholic and Orthodox Bibles in English.
- Septuagint follows the same essential order of 150 total psalms but differently divides a few psalms, thus:
  - Overall, Septuagint numbering is *one less* throughout most of the Psalter from Ps. 10 through Ps. 147. More specifically:
    - Masoretic Pss. 9 and 10 are separate, but in the Septuagint *combined* as Ps. 9;
    - Masoretic Pss. 114 and 115 are separate, but are *combined* as Septuagint Ps. 113;
    - Masoretic Ps. 116 is *divided* into Septuagint Pss. 114 and 115;
    - Masoretic Ps. 147 is *divided* into Septuagint Pss. 146 and 147.

It is obvious to all biblical scholars, as it is even to the casual reader, that this is a composite book, with individual lyrics attributed to many writers over a period spanning nearly 1000 years – or roughly from 1440 to 450 BCE. The poets who are invoked range from the anonymous composers of the Tabernacle and Temple, sometimes identified as "the Sons of Korah" and "the Sons of Asaph," to the occasional contributors Heman and Ethan the Ezrahite, to other famed figures, including Moses, Solomon, and above all, David. In fact, 71 of the 150 psalms are credited to David, so the book is commonly called "the Psalms of David" by Jewish and Christian commentators. In the absence of any original manuscripts it is impossible to prove that particular psalms were actually the work of these traditional figures, though the demonstrated existence of Semitic literacy and Paleo-Hebrew in the second and early first millennia BCE makes such authorship quite possible. In fact, a significant level of Davidic authorship is particularly likely, given the repeated scriptural mention of his musical and poetic gifts (e.g. 1 Samuel 16:14–23, 2 Samuel 1:17–27, 22:1–51, 23:1–7) and the large number of psalms that bear his name.

The Psalms also successfully straddle the gap between private and public expression, and between individual and corporate worship. They constitute what one might call "the hymnbook of the Hebrews," and give corporate voice to the congregation, yet they often express their praise or complaint in intimate, "I–Thou" terms. As the liturgy of a whole people, the Psalms were artfully arranged, probably by Ezra and other editors in the post-exilic period, and in many cases introduced with brief head-notes explaining their traditional authorship and circumstances. It's also important to note that these editors arranged the Psalms to correspond with that other set of defining volumes, the Five Books of Moses, or the Pentateuch.

Psalm Subdivisions and Headings

The Jewish Talmud (200–500 CE) – the ancient Rabbinical commentary on the *Torah* – holds that the Psalms are arranged in five books after the pattern of the Five Books of Moses, and this five-book structure is internally evident as well:

- An "Amen" or "Double Amen" concludes Pss. 41, 72, 89, and 106, and a "Hallel" ("Praise the LORD") concludes 106 and 150 – the final psalms in each of the five respective books.
- The "Davidic Golden Age" segment of Books I and II (Pss. 1–72) concludes with its own special tagline, "The prayers of David the son of Jesse are ended."
- Psalm headings are notes of post-exilic editors, 450 BCE.

Thus, there are five different "books" within the Book of Psalms, featuring different emphases as the post-exilic generation sought to recover and redefine its national identity by recalling past glories and disasters, returning to spiritual roots, and anticipating restoration and deliverance.

Book I (1–41) and Book II (42–72) of the Psalms thrust the reader into what we might call "the Davidic Golden Age," remembered as the high point of Hebrew civilization, empire, and spiritual blessing. These sections contain the densest concentration of "David's songs": specifically, Psalms 3–9, 11–41, 51–65, and 68–70 are directly attributed to the "Shepherd King." After beginning with Psalm 1, a purpose-made introductory psalm laying out blessings of the "righteous" and the punishments of the "wicked," Book I turns immediately in Psalm 2 to celebrating the victory of God's "Anointed." This kingly figure has historical resonance, since David was "the Lord's Anointed," who had subdued the surrounding nations to Israelite rule, but this figure also has prophetic meaning, since the post-exilic Jews had come increasingly to hope for the future return of David's "Anointed" descendant ("Messiah" means "Anointed" in Hebrew) to whom God would give "the ends of the earth for your possession" (2:8). What follows in the rest of Book I is poetry that vividly imagines varied phases and moments in David's private and public lives, from the enthusiasm of dewy youth (8, 27) and the agonies of personal betrayal and persecution (e.g. 12, 18, 22), to the ecstasies of deliverance and triumph (23, 24) and the sharp variations of sin and restoration (32, 38). Significantly this section, which starts with the blessedness of the unwaveringly righteous (1) and turns to the blessedness of the unrighteous who repent (32), ends with the blessedness of those who humbly consider and help the poor (41). The glories of David's kingdom are seen not only in its conquests, but also in its penitent responses to failure and in its concern for justice.

Book II of the Psalms continues with this Davidic Golden Age theme, presenting another cycle of poems that recall high and low points in David's career. Opening with a lyrical yearning for God in the midst of distress (42:1 – "As the deer pants for the water brooks, so pants my soul for you, O God"), they turn to meditate on kingly marriage (45), divine rescue from siege (46), and David's remorse after his terrible sins of adultery and murder (51); then they turn time back to revisit many episodes of persecution by mad, bad King Saul and his henchmen (52, 54, 55–59, 63). After further reflections on David's personal and Israel's national trials, and on

God's mighty works, Book II concludes in a crescendo of glory with a psalm credited to David's brilliant son and heir, King Solomon – celebrating not only the crowning of the son of David but also the coming universal reign of God's "Anointed" in perfect justice (72:8, 12 – "He shall have dominion also from sea to sea… For he will deliver the needy when he cries …"). As noted earlier, what makes this remembered Davidic Age "golden" is that even its depths lead to renewed heights, and its powers are used to help the weak.

If Books I and II recall an age of gold, then the much briefer Book III (73–89) turns abruptly to portray an age of iron, or even lead – that is, the times of spiritual decline and loss that, the Jews believed, had cast them into exile. This section begins with the seventy-third psalm, which lodges an extensive and nearly despairing complaint about how much the wicked prosper, before its despondent speaker recovers a sense that God inevitably will restore justice. This psalm also begins a series attributed to a set of exilic or post-exilic poets: Asaph (73–83), the sons of Korah (84–85, 87), Heman the Ezrahite (88), and Ethan the Ezrahite (89). The burden of their message – often a very heavy burden – is that Israel's spiritual infidelity, rebellion, and idolatry finally exhausted *Yahweh's* patience and kindled his wrath, so that he utterly destroyed both Northern and Southern Kingdoms, leaving the Temple a smoking ruin and the crown of David rolling in the dust. The pathos and horror of these memories is increased by a few interspersed psalms that recall the glory of God's righteous deeds (75, 77, 78), his Tabernacle or Temple (84), and the just peace in David's city of "Zion" – i.e. Jerusalem (87). Indeed, a single "prayer of David" for mercy is inserted into this sad series as a reminder of lost blessing – and of possible restoration (86). Still, Book III ends on the darkest of notes, as Psalm 88 offers only despairing complaint to God, void of any praise, while Psalm 89 recalls in excruciating detail the fall of Jerusalem and the apparent extinction of David's throne.

The abruptly tragic turn of Book III is answered by a powerfully hopeful turn in Book IV (90–106). This brief series responds to loss and exile with a return to Israel's spiritual roots and heritage. Psalm 90 casts the mind back before the beginning of the Israelite kingdom to the nation's political "founding father," the author of the Law that amounts to the Hebrew "constitution" – Moses. And even Moses is rendered looking back further and deeper to the people's roots: "LORD, you have been our dwelling place in all generations" (1). The exiled, homeless, and wandering Jews are reminded that their God is their original and ultimate "homeland," and that any future earthly re-establishment of the nation will depend on their returning themselves to his spiritual foundations. These foundations are made more explicit in the following psalms, which are mainly anonymous. These poems reflect on the unshakeable character of *Yahweh* – his sovereignty, mercy, justice, and fidelity – as the basis of Israel's future hope, with a couple of cameo appearances by David (101, 103) as reminders of the spiritual passion that made him the nation's most successful monarch. Significantly, as an antidote to Book III's crushing conclusion, Book IV ends with the assurance in Psalm 106 that God has forgiven his wandering people, and with a joyful call for their return to their earthly homeland: "Save us, O LORD our God, and gather us from among the Gentiles, to give thanks to your holy name, to triumph in your praise" (47). As sin and rebellion led to national exile, so spiritual restoration will precede and cause national return.

The final and longest book of the Psalms, Book V (107–150), celebrates both this imminent restoration to Abraham's "land of Canaan" and a more distant future age of messianic rule and heavenly justice. The post-exilic editors of the Psalter wanted to "finish strong"; they saved some of the most exquisite lyrics in their songbook for this concluding section, which also includes an acrostic masterpiece (119) and the Psalms' most artfully arranged sequence, the Songs of Ascents (120–134).

Play Skillfully: The Intricate Acrostic

A Hebrew acrostic poem is one in which each half-verse, verse, or section/stanza begins with a different successive letter of the 22-character Hebrew alphabet. This form tends to highlight the poem's comprehensive vision, an "A-to-Z" survey of a subject. According to A. J. Motyer in *The New International Dictionary of the Bible*, "[a]crostics occur in Psalms 111 and 112, where each letter begins a line; in Psalms 25, 34, and 145, where each letter begins a half-verse; in Psalm 37, Proverbs 31:10–31, and Lamentations 1, 2, and 4, where each letter begins a whole verse; and in Lamentations 3, where each letter begins three verses. Psalm 119 is the most elaborate demonstration of the acrostic method where, in each section of eight verses, the same opening letter is used, and the twenty-two sections of the psalm move through the Hebrew alphabet, letter after letter," celebrating the wisdom and beauty of God's Law. See fuller discussion of Psalm 119 in the next section.

Abounding in poems of assurance, and in a last burst of Davidic glory (108–110, 122, 124, 131, 133, 138–145), Book V is not without its laments (Psalm 137, "By the rivers of Babylon," is particularly heart-rending), but these are mainly included as contrasting foils to the climactic mood of expectancy and exaltation. Psalm 107 begins this theme of restoration by evoking varied scenes of danger and despair – "They wandered in the wilderness ... [Those] bound in affliction and irons... Those who go down to the sea in ships" (4, 10, 23) – only to exult in God's dramatic power to deliver the lost out of their self-inflicted troubles. The next three, all "psalms of David," praise the Lord for his justice and culminate with Psalm 110's promise that Messiah will have the power to make that justice real. Then comes a group of short psalms, culminating in the very shortest of all the Psalms, 117, whose mere two verses make the bracingly universal claim that not only Israel but "all nations" should praise the Lord. This micro-psalm is followed almost immediately by Psalm 119, the longest of the psalms and an acrostic tour-de-force, which unfolds the excellencies of the written Law of God in 22 stanzas, each verse in each successive stanza beginning with the next letter of the Hebrew alphabet from Aleph to Tau – the Jewish equivalent of Greek "Alpha to Omega" or English "A to Z."

At the heart of Book V is a carefully designed **lyric sequence** that amounts to a "book-within-a-book-within-a-book" – the Songs of Ascents. These short lyrics were traditionally recited or sung in this order by post-exilic Jews as they made the yearly journey "up" to Jerusalem for the "Pilgrim Feasts" of Passover, Weeks, and Booths – Jerusalem being generally uphill from all the surrounding territories of Palestine. So the repeated title "A Song of Ascents" (or "A Song of Degrees") refers to the change of *geographical elevation* undergone by the pilgrims as they traveled to Mount Zion – but also to the *devotional elevation* acquired as pilgrims moved from constant conflict "among the tents of Kedar" (120:5) in the Gentile-dominated hinterlands to the tranquility of the Temple or "house of the LORD" in Jerusalem (134:1). The many ups and downs encountered along the way ("When the LORD brought back the captivity of Zion, we were like those who dream" – 126:1; "Out of the depths I have cried to you, O LORD" – 130:1) also can be read as internal spiritual states and are finally resolved in the idealized peace and unity represented by the sacred precincts of the Sanctuary.

After these "Ascents" are done, Book V comes to a climax in a final crescendo of Davidic memory (138–145), followed by the fivefold praises of the concluding "Hallel" psalms (146–150), each beginning "Praise the LORD!" (Hebrew *"Hallelu-Yah," "Yah"* being short for

"*Yahweh*"). Yet there are some clashing notes amidst the dominant concord of this conclusion: Psalm 137 modulates from the pathos of the oppressed exiles' grief ("How shall we sing the LORD's song in a foreign land?" – v. 4) to voicing their terrifying, vengeful bloodlust ("[O Babylon,] [h]appy the one who takes and dashes your little ones against the rock!" – v. 9). And David professes to hate the wicked "with perfect hatred" (139:22) – a curse which he nevertheless instantly softens by including himself among the potentially wicked needing divine grace (139:23–24). Like the dissonance deliberately orchestrated by a composer to heighten the sweetness of the ultimate chord, these parting moments of discord accentuate the *fortissimo* harmonies that ring in the ear and in the memory as the Psalms end. In the last of these lyrics, it is difficult if not impossible to tell whether the kingly court celebrated is that of the restored Messiah on Mount Zion or that of the Almighty Creator seated above the heavens. This is probably by design: as we will see, the messianic deliverer and the divine LORD came to merge in the hopeful Hebrew imagination.

3.1.2 "Create in Me a Clean Heart": Interior Drama and Psychological Discovery

We have seen that each of the five books within the larger Book of Psalms has its own focus or theme: the Davidic Golden Age (I and II), loss and exile (III), return to roots (IV), and messianic hope and restoration (V). Remarkably, despite the Psalms having been assembled – and in many cases deliberately composed – as liturgy for group worship, they are nevertheless characterized throughout by a profound lyric intimacy and frequently dramatic psychological discovery. It is as if the deeps of the psalmist's soul call to the deeps of the reader's, in ways that have evoked powerful responses down the millennia. We'll turn now to a few representative psalms that exhibit the literary devices and techniques which dramatize these spiritual depths.

Psalm 8 might initially seem an unlikely poem to associate with discovery, for in one sense it begins and ends in the same way – with the full-on exultation, "O LORD, our Lord, how excellent is your name in all the earth!" (1a, 9). Nevertheless, this joyous refrain makes a surprising claim: that a supposedly local covenant deity (*YHWH* or *Yahweh*, conventionally transliterated "LORD" in English Bibles), who is the "Adonai" or "Lord" of a relatively small tribe near the western edge of the ancient Near East, actually rules somehow over "all the earth." Furthermore, if we're inclined to read "all the earth" more minimally – that is, as "the surrounding region" or "to the edge of the horizon" – then the psalmist proceeds to surprise us more, and to amaze himself, for "our Lord" has "set [his] glory above the heavens" (1b). He is not just an earth deity, then, but a Lord of the skies, in fact beyond the skies, as well. And who certifies *Yahweh's* greatness? What mighty human lords, what warriors and armed multitudes, endorse his excellence?

> Out of the mouths of babes and nursing infants
> You have ordained strength,
> Because of your enemies,
> That you may silence the enemy and the avenger. (2)

This verse presents an arresting, even shocking, paradox. *Yahweh's* honor guard is made up of babies – the smallest, weakest, most vulnerable of humans, creatures that remain useless far longer than any animal cub or kid – these babies gurgle his praise, "ordaining" the Lord's power over strong evil. Even to our modern minds this infant chorus may seem strange; in the ancient Near East, with its vast military empires built on ruthless strength, it would have seemed an embarrassingly silly retinue for a mighty deity.

And more surprises are in store, for *Yahweh* seems weirdly concerned not only about babies but about other insignificant and marginal beings – like the speaker himself, and the entire human race:

> When I consider your heavens, the work of your fingers,
> The moon and the stars, which you have ordained,
> What is man that you are mindful of him,
> And the son of man that you visit him?
> For you have made him a little lower than the angels,
> And you have crowned him with glory and honor. (3–5)

The speaker's awe at the stars as *Yahweh's* handiwork, and his sense of human limitations ("man" here in Hebrew is *enowsh* or "mortal" and "son of man" is *ben adam* or "offspring of red clay"), only serve to magnify his wonder at the Lord's extravagant generosity in promoting lowly beings to such high position. These references back to the creation in Genesis 1–2 become more explicit in verse 6:

> You have made him to have dominion over the works of your hands;
> You have put all things under his feet …

Humanity is God's image or *tselem* – made male and female, his visible, local representative on earth – and humanity has the power and the responsibility of "dominion" or *maschal* over all the varied creation, from middle earth, to highest skies, to deepest waters:

> All sheep and oxen –
> Even the beasts of the field,
> The birds of the air,
> And the fish of the sea
> That pass through the paths of the seas.

Through both figurative metonymy and synthetic parallelism, the poet drives home the astonishingly universal extent of this Lord's creative power, and also of his authority delegated to his human creatures – creatures who nevertheless share low and earthly origins with the beasts of the field. The surprise is complete – not only is this tribal deity the cosmic Lord, but he stoops to protect and raise the lowly to the highest degree.

So when we return to the psalm's refrain in the last verse – "O, LORD, our Lord, how excellent is your name in all the earth!" – these repeated words now mean something much more, because both the name of the deity and his power have been defined as universal, and because his power, while potentially lethal to his "enemies," has been portrayed as protective and generous to the smallest and the least. So, in repeating that refrain, the psalmist isn't merely saying the same thing twice, but rather is making a discovery and saying something new.

If Psalm 8 presents a degree of surprise and psychological discovery by portraying *Yahweh* as showing a universality and kindness unexpected of the gods, Psalm 22 surprises with a shocking interior drama about unearned agony and stunning redemption. From its unforgettably gripping start – "My God, my God, why have you forsaken me?" – to its exultant conclusion – "They will come and declare his righteousness to a people who will be born, that he has done this" (31) – the psalm oscillates, sometimes jaggedly, between past happiness, present anguish, and future joy so often as to be a very picture of life's paradoxes, its wrenching juxtapositions.

The paradoxical changes of direction on this torturous inner journey are pointed out most frequently by one road sign: the little word "but." "O My God, I cry in the daytime, *but* you do not hear" (2) – the paradox of divine deafness; "*But* you are holy ... our fathers trusted in you ... and you delivered them" (3, 4) – the paradox of a good and strong God who delivered in the past but delivers not in the moment; "*But* I am a worm, and no man" (6) – the paradox of the speaker's apparently sub-human state as a laughing-stock; "*But* you are he who took me out of the womb" (9) – the paradox of God's past maternal tenderness, drowned out in present mockery and agony: "Many bulls have surrounded me ... I am poured out like water ... you have brought me to the dust of death ... they pierced my hands and my feet ... and for my clothing they cast lots" (12, 14, 15, 16, 18). These rapid reversals rack the speaker spiritually in ways that magnify his suffering physically, and that represent more than individual pain, but also the trials of the entire Israelite nation.

Then, just as abruptly, these sharp and frequent juxtapositions and urgent calls for help give way to a serene future hope based on a suddenly complete deliverance: "I will declare your name to my brethren... For ... when [I] cried to him, he heard" (22, 24). In fact, the speaker's hopeful sense of triumph grows increasingly expansive, taking in wider and wider circles of life: "My praise shall be of you in the great assembly... All the ends of the world shall remember and turn to the LORD... They shall come, and shall declare his righteousness to a people that shall be born, that he has done this" (25, 27, 31). "Done what?" we may ask. The speaker has been taken beyond the bounds of human endurance, abandoned by his God, scapegoated and cursed by his own people, tormented by his memories of former blessing, and apparently taken past the gates of death itself – only to be revived and rewarded beyond imagining, and indeed far beyond the bounds of his homeland and of his own generation. This poem not only describes the speaker's trials, but *enacts* them through its oppositions and juxtapositions.

This same kind of interior lyric drama plays out through the juxtapositions and refrains of Psalm 46 – though in this case the poem doesn't contrast present suffering with past and future joy, but rather contrasts an impending cataclysm with inevitable divine deliverance. Combining the horrors of siege warfare with the terrors of natural disaster, the psalm nevertheless registers perhaps the deepest sense of supernatural serenity anywhere in the Psalter. "God is our refuge and strength, / A very present help in trouble," it begins.

> Therefore we will not fear,
> Even though the earth be removed,
> And though the mountains be carried into the midst of the sea;
> Though its waters roar and be troubled,
> Though the mountains shake with its swelling. (2–3)

Conjuring the worst imaginable convergence of geological and sea-borne destruction, these lines crescendo from earthquake to floodtide to something like cosmic dissolution, building toward a climax that threatens to create universal pandemonium – only to fade suddenly to tranquil assurance with the juxtaposition of verses 4–5:

> There is a river whose streams shall make glad the city of God,
> The holy place of the tabernacle of the Most High.
> God is in the midst of her, she shall not be moved;
> God shall help her, just at the break of dawn.

This shift in tone matches a shift in metaphor, as seismic and oceanic images give way to a picture from a city under siege, and yet assured of its survival because of an inexhaustible water source and an overwhelming power within: "a river" and a God who is himself a fortress and a help. When enemies surrounded an ancient walled city, a spring or well within meant life itself;

and if the citadel also held a mighty host – in this case "the LORD of hosts" – then the siege would be outlasted and even turned to victory.

And victory is just what the next verse promises – a victory more absolute than any human army could produce: "The nations raged, the kingdoms were moved; / He uttered his voice, the earth melted" (6). All the invading nations have met their match; in a sudden shift from the defensive to the offensive, it is as if the voice that made heaven and earth in Genesis 1 speaks to unmake it here, or at least unmake everything outside the "city," with a single word.

This stunning reversal – from overwhelming external threats to calm assurance that answers with its own apocalypse – stirs an awestruck assertion: "The LORD of hosts is with us; / The God of Jacob is our refuge" (7). *Yahweh*, now imagined as a general of heavenly armies, has chosen to stand with the sons of Jacob, and to surround them. And the extent of God's pacifying power is elaborated in the following lines:

> Come, behold the works of the LORD,
> Who has made desolations in the earth.
> He makes wars cease to the end of the earth;
> He breaks the bow and cuts the spear in two;
> He burns the chariot in the fire. (8–9)

As if surveying a field of smoking ruin from a victorious battlement, the speaker's vision abruptly expands to embrace "the end of the earth," and what he sees, paradoxically, are the "desolations" that make for peace: divine obliteration of war's weaponry, followed by an intervening command from the LORD himself:

> Be still, and know that I am God;
> I will be exalted among the nations,
> I will be exalted in the earth! (10)

As it turns out, the placid assurance at the heart of the besieged city has as its twin the awestruck stillness in the presence of a divine protector who can make, unmake, and then remake the earth, and who promises peace through absolute victory.

The happy dramatic irony of victims turned to victors is compounded by the repeated declaration, now a refrain: "The LORD of hosts is with us; / The God of Jacob is our refuge" (11). For these sons of Jacob, there may be more than a little trepidation in their voices as they consider the extent of the self-contained but uncontainable power that is "with" them. Far from being a piece of jingoistic nationalism, this psalm combines hope for the besieged and embattled with a sobering reflection on the coming universal and impartial judgment of God.

If the drama of Psalm 46 turns on the arresting contrast between peril and trust, others re-enact renewed anguish and anger. Perhaps the most moving and alarming of these so-called "imprecatory" psalms (psalms of cursing) is Psalm 137, famed for the piercing pathos of its opening lines:

> By the rivers of Babylon,
> There we sat down, yea, we wept,
> When we remembered Zion. (1)

As an exiles' lament, this poem is unsurpassed, with its powerful evocation of opposed places (Babylon vs. Zion) and its association of the exiles' tears with flowing alien waters – a tearful association only increased by the next lines:

> On the willows there we hung up our lyres,
> For our captors there required of us songs,
> And our tormentors mirth,
> Saying, "Sing us one of the songs of Zion." (2–3, RSV)

Willows, which in the poetry of many nations "weep" by the riverside, are imagined as hung with Hebrew harps, abandoned to protest the captors' mocking demand for some Jewish minstrelsy, converting their holy songs into slavish entertainment. To this demand, the psalmist replies with a withering question: "How shall we sing the LORD's song / In a foreign land?" (4).

Many musical settings of this psalm – including not only liturgical versions but also popular folk and reggae renditions by Stephen Schwartz and Bob Marley – end with this pathetic inquiry. And it is a painful, searching question for the Jews, a people whose millennia of wandering and exile well outnumber their centuries of landed nationhood. It is the question confronted in Genesis by the patriarch Joseph when sold into Egyptian slavery, and of many nations and peoples enslaved or dislocated by history's empires, wars, and pogroms: How can we keep our ways and traditions alive in a strange country? How far do the powers of our gods and our laws extend? And when will our enemies pay? When will *they* suffer?

It is this last part of the question, and the psalmist's increasingly vengeful answer, that makes the rest of the psalm – the part often omitted – so hard to read, let alone to sing as a hymn. And yet this gathering curse is no less artful, and in its way no less powerful than the more sympathetic opening. It commences with a solemn vow, understood by any wronged people: Remember!

> If I forget you, O Jerusalem,
> Let my right hand forget its skill!
> If I do not remember you,
> Let my tongue cling to the roof of my mouth –
> If I do not exalt Jerusalem above my chief joy. (5–6)

The leading edge of imprecation is self-directed, or at least directed at any self who fails to raise national loyalty and identity above all others.

But the sharpest curse is reserved not for the forgetful self but for the cruel enemy, as the victim's rage for justice rises to a shrill crescendo:

> Remember, O LORD, against the sons of Edom
> The day of Jerusalem,
> Who said, "Raze it, raze it,
> To its very foundation!"
> O daughter of Babylon, who are to be destroyed,
> Happy the one who repays you as you have served us!
> Happy the one who takes and dashes
> Your little ones against the rock! (7–9)

Calling *Yahweh* both to witness and to action, the anonymous exile calls out against the ancient, intimate enemy, Edom – the tribe of Jacob's brother Esau, settled just east of Judah – which cheered the devastations done by the invading newcomer, Babylon. Invoking and extending the *lex talionis* – the stern Law of "eye for eye" – with savage irony, the psalmist twists a blood-thirsty curse from the language of blessing: "Happy the one" is usually a formula for benediction, but here the chief joy is reserved for those who pay back the Babylonians not merely eye for eye but child for child, indeed skull for skull. With this pitiless picture of new-born heads spattered on stones, the psalm ends, its initial harp music drowned by the jagged screams of dying infants.

If these verses are the antithesis of the infant chorus praising the LORD in Psalm 8, they also remind us that the Psalms are a many-voiced literary congregation in a truly inclusive sense, giving voice not only to the righteously contented and the blessedly merciful, but also at times to more frightening, but also deeply human, feeling. Even as we recoil from such a bloody curse, we must remember the horrors that provoked it, and ask ourselves how we would respond to similar atrocities against our own.

Only two poems later, Psalm 139 revisits the theme of righteous imprecation, only to redirect the speaker's judgment, in a marvelous turn of psychological discovery, toward his own soul. In fact, this Psalm of David begins by celebrating the wondrous penetration of God's insightful eye: "O LORD, you have searched me and known me!" (1). *Yahweh* sees him near and far, day and night, rising and sleeping, in heaven and in Sheol.

> If I take the wings of the morning,
> And dwell in the uttermost parts of the sea,
> Even there your hand shall lead me,
> And your right hand shall hold me. (9–10)

Such an excellent God deserves universal praise, says David, and he turns passionately to denounce any wicked person who is behind in offering it, calling down a mortal curse, and vowing his immortal hate:

> Oh, that you would slay the wicked, O God! ...
> Do I not hate them, O LORD, who hate you?
> Do I not loathe those who rise up against you?
> I hate them with perfect hatred;
> I count them my enemies. (19, 21–22)

The phrase "perfect hatred" may jar ironically on our ears, as a type of dreadful religious zeal, eager to destroy others for their sins but blind to its own. And apparently it jars on David's as well, because having denounced the wicked so fiercely, he can't help asking whether after all he might be counted among them:

> Search me, O God, and know my heart;
> Try me, and know my anxieties;
> And see if there is any wicked way in me,
> And lead me in the way everlasting. (23–24)

In these self-examining words, which end the psalm, we see again how "deep calls to deep," and how the spiritual purpose and the literary genius of the psalms coincide: because the Hebrew God calls all human wisdom finite and fallible, there's always need for another eye or angle of view, a deeper look, a glance at the other hand. This stereoscopic vision helps to account, as we have already observed, for the Psalms' tremendous staying power and wide popularity: both many-voiced and heart-deep, their range and depth of emotion speak to practically all conditions of the human soul, allowing a surprisingly fair say not only to grateful saints, but also to skeptics and doubters, and even to zealots and avengers, while insisting that all must search out and put down their own particular kinds of wickedness – or be found out by the Almighty.

3.1.3 "Play Skillfully": Figure and Form

3.1.3.1 Figurative Language

Having seen how the Psalms offer frequent dramatic reversals and surprises as they portray the dynamic dialogue between heaven and earth, we need to make a few observations about the particular figurative and formal devices that complement these dramatic turns to give Hebrew poetry its peculiar power to move. Figurative language is the very essence of poetry; or rather *intensive* figurative language. For figurative speech – that is, speaking of one thing in terms of another – is in a deeper sense at the heart of all communication. Take for instance the previous, quite ordinary sentence: "For figurative speech ... is in a deeper sense at the heart of all communication." "Figurative" assumes the mental picture of a "figure" or "shape," some image or object that stands for another object; "speech" represents by extension not only oral talk but also written language; "deeper sense" relies on a surface/depth metaphor; "heart" symbolizes a central, vital reality; and even the seemingly abstract "communication" is a compound of Latin roots meaning "a sharing with." So we see that it is virtually impossible to make oneself understood without constant recourse to some form of comparative figure. In this broad sense, all language is "poetic."

However, as already noted, it is the signature quality of poetry to be *intensively* figurative. A density of comparative devices in a relatively compact space is the hallmark of poetry, even more than are meter and line structure, and certainly far more than is rhyme (very rare in ancient poetry). Since it was the Greeks who first itemized and analyzed these various figures, most have Greek names, some familiar, some less so: **metaphor**, a comparison using "is," "are," or other forms of "to be" and asserting an identity not literally observable, such as "I *am* a worm, and no man"; **simile**, a comparison using "like" or "as," for instance "he shall be *like* a tree planted by the rivers of water"; **personification**, speaking of an inanimate object as a person, as in "Lift up your heads, O you gates!"; **anthropomorphism**, speaking of a divinity in human terms, as in "the LORD is my shepherd"[2]; **litotes**, understatement, as in "my word ... shall not return unto me void," meaning "my word ... will accomplish great things"; and **hyperbole**, overstatement, as in "let the bones that you have broken rejoice," when no literal bones have been broken.

Other frequent biblical figurative devices include **symbol**, an image or object with implied representation or comparison, as in "the LORD has raised up a horn of salvation," with "horn" symbolizing strength and independence; **synecdoche**, a part that represents the whole, as in "break the teeth of the wicked, O LORD," with "teeth" standing for all the body's powers of violence; **metonymy**, one thing that represents another by association, as in "rebuild the walls of Jerusalem, O LORD," with "walls" representing the security and peace of the city, and the city representing the entire nation; **paradox**, an apparent contradiction expressing a deeper truth, such as "by his wounds we are healed"; and **allegory**, an extended symbolic narrative, in which characters represent historical, spiritual, or philosophical entities, as in the biblical Song of Solomon.

Most of these examples are drawn from the Psalms themselves, and all from the Hebrew Bible. Once we recognize these devices and go searching for them in the Psalms and in other biblical poetry, we find them interwoven throughout practically every line, and we find ourselves grasping in new ways these poems' meanings, and freshly experiencing their power. Of course, recognizing the Bible's often poetic nature is not to dismiss it as "merely poetic" or "only symbolic" – as if all languages were not at root "poetic" and "symbolic," including the more prosaic languages of journalism or scholarship, or even the more precise language of science.[3] For, as we've already seen, figurative speech is at the heart of all communication.

3.1.3.2 Form: Parallelism – Synonymous, Antithetic, Synthetic

Turning to Hebrew poetic form, we are in a realm more unique and specific to ancient Semitic culture and consciousness. We've already seen in our opening chapters that the structural device of doubling – its distinctive rhyming of ideas – animates Hebrew thought from the line-by-line, back-and-forth parallelism of the Psalms to the larger stereoscopic blocks of doubled prose narrative. For instance, having noted in our first chapter that Psalm 1 begins the Psalter by drawing bright lines between the "righteous" and the "ungodly," let's see how its use of varied parallelisms heightens this effect.

> Blessed is the man
> > Who walks not in the counsel of the ungodly,
> > > Nor stands in the path of sinners,
> > > Nor sits in the seat of the scornful;
> > But his delight is in the law of the LORD,
> > > And in His law he meditates day and night…
> > Therefore the ungodly shall not stand in the judgment,
> > > Nor sinners in the congregation of the righteous.
> > For the LORD knows the way of the righteous,
> > > But the way of the ungodly shall perish. (1–2, 5–6)

In these few lines we see the three main types of parallelism well represented. The most basic form is **synonymous**; it repeats the same idea for emphasis, in somewhat different words but generally with the same syntax. "Therefore the ungodly shall not stand in the judgment, Nor sinners in the congregation of the righteous," gives us grammatically symmetrical statements, with "ungodly" echoed by "sinners," and "judgment" by "the congregation of the righteous" – that is, those who are exonerated by God's justice.

A more complex form of parallelism is **antithetical**; it makes an opposing statement for contrast, again usually with similar syntax, and with mainly similar words to stress the crucial distinction. "For the LORD knows the way of the righteous, / But the way of the ungodly shall perish," is a form that perfectly suits the sharp difference that the psalmist wishes to demonstrate between the "two ways," one of which is connected to the intimate and friendly knowledge of God, while the other is the way to oblivion.

The most complex form of parallelism is called **synthetic**; it works not merely by one-time repetition but by progression and multiple addition, and often has its own tale to tell. In Psalm 1, the opening lines show an immediate narrative thrust, though in this case a negative one: "Blessed is the man who walks not … nor stands … nor sits," as if moving to, then loitering in, and finally resting at, a place of danger, and that danger has a narrative too, with bad "counsel" leading to a sinful "path" and finally to a scornful "seat." Some instances of synthetic parallelism are even more extended: for instance, in Psalm 19, the Davidic speaker enumerates six-fold his praise of the LORD's written Law, in a progression from how the *Torah* converts the soul, makes the "simple" wise, and makes the heart rejoice, to how it enlightens the eyes, endures forever, and is "righteous altogether" (vv. 7–9). This little narrative of the soul's entry through scripture into the covenant, and its growth in the covenant, ends with the scripture connecting the purified soul to eternity – a progressive journey indeed.

3.1.3.3 Form: Refrain and Litany

Another kind of artful doubling is the rhythmic or at least periodic repetition of the exact same words. When this repetition occurs at wider intervals in a poem or song, it is called a **refrain**. When this repetition occurs very frequently, it is called a **litany**, and is often used as a form of insistent supplication or ecstatic praise. We already have noted two examples of refrain in our discussions above of Psalms 8 and 46: "O LORD, our Lord, how excellent is your name in all the earth!" (8:1, 9); and "The LORD of hosts is with us; / The God of Jacob is our refuge" (46:7, 11). These repetitions, we have seen, while repeating the same words, take on different nuances due to the intervening developments within each psalm – and, like the "chorus" in a popular contemporary song, each also provides a kind of pleasant conceptual "backbeat" driving home central themes.

Litany, on the other hand, may initially strike the uninitiated reader as excessive and even tedious, but it is to be understood very much as a public and participatory form, and in this context can approach to ecstasy as the worshiper, like a lover, warms to the adoration of God:

> Oh, give thanks to the LORD, for He is good!
> For His mercy endures forever.
> Oh, give thanks to the God of gods!
> For His mercy endures forever.
> Oh, give thanks to the Lord of lords!
> For His mercy endures forever:
> To Him who alone does great wonders,
> For His mercy endures forever;
> To Him who by wisdom made the heavens,
> For His mercy endures forever;
> To Him who laid out the earth above the waters,
> For His mercy endures forever;
> To Him who made great lights,
> For His mercy endures forever –
> The sun to rule by day,
> For His mercy endures forever;
> The moon and stars to rule by night,
> For His mercy endures forever... (Psalm 36:1–9)

As Psalm 36 proceeds through details of the Genesis creation and Exodus deliverance for its full 26 verses, the dynamic of congregational "call and response" intensifies – and appropriately, the one constant phrase undergirds the message of the LORD's enduring *chesed*, his "mercy" or "steadfast love." Anyone who has ever delighted to hear the words "O thank you thank you thank you thank you!" for a holiday gift, or "I love you I love you I love you I love you!" called from a train platform or a jetway, will admit that, in the right setting and with the right beloved, "litany" can be beautiful indeed.

3.1.3.4 Form: Juxtaposition

Another structural device common to both Hebrew poetry and prose is **juxtaposition**: the placing of two seemingly unrelated passages or elements together without transition in order to suggest a relationship. We've noted that Psalm 19 shows a fine instance of synthetic parallelism. So it also provides a striking example of juxtaposition as its famous opening lines (vv. 1–6) celebrate the splendid beauty of the heavenly bodies – "[t]he heavens declare the glory of God" – but then turn suddenly to praise the written Law (vv. 7–11).

Some modern readers may find this transition abrupt and uncongenial; indeed some critics have even suggested that these were originally two separate, unrelated psalms that somehow arbitrarily became combined. There is no manuscript evidence for such an ancient separation, but the more important question is this: what connection would an ancient Hebrew see between the stars and the scriptures? Genesis 1 gives us the key – just as the creative word from God makes the world, and upholds creation by his Law, so that same word and will are written in the holy scrolls. Thus, for the Hebrews – and for Christians since – the Book of God's Works is both echoed and interpreted in the Book(s) of God's Word. And, as we've already observed, this psalm portrays the scriptures not only as connecting the believer profoundly to the creation, but also as connecting the purified soul to eternity.

We'll conclude by noting two other instances of juxtaposition, already mentioned above as staging the powerful interior dramas of Psalms 22 and 46. In the first of these we observed the wrenching movement back and forth between happy past and agonized present, and then the sudden transition to future joy and glory. And in the second of these we saw the abrupt shifts from impending cataclysm to serene confidence to divine intervention to awestruck worship. It is as if these psalmists – not to mention other biblical poets and prose writers – had anticipated the technique of cinematic "cross-cutting" by about 3000 years!

If ancient Hebrew poetry can anticipate modern screen technology, then we have come full circle to how the Psalms still speak with such power to so many in a modern, more secular age. We began by calling the Psalter a congregation of varied voices, but we might as well call it a skillful arrangement of miniature portraits or even snapshots of the soul. The psychologically probing art of these brief lyrics – their figurative richness, their vivid "rhyming of ideas," their structural variety – has proven itself to be of practically universal appeal. What the Psalms do in their more miniature and intimate ways, the rest of the Bible does writ large – sometimes with less poetic concentration, but usually with the same eye toward the discovery of the soul. We now turn from the Bible's achievement in the individual lyric to a more extended lyric sequence in the Song of Solomon.

3.2 Love Strong as Death: The Song of Solomon

The Bible presents us with practically numberless surprises and paradoxes. We've observed that the One Book of the One God is actually experienced as many books animated by very many varied perspectives on the nature of that God; we've seen that the Psalms frequently work dramatic reversals that leave the speaker – and maybe the reader – transformed; and as we proceed we'll continue to see plenty of mysteries and miracles presenting sometimes wildly unexpected outcomes. But one of the Bible's greatest surprises remains the Song of Solomon. At only 117 verses, it is among the shortest books in the Hebrew Bible and yet has generated more interpretive commentary than nearly any biblical book, New Testament or Old. Traditionally attributed to King Solomon – 1 Kings 4:32 says that "his songs were one thousand and five," and internal evidence points to initial composition during Solomon's reign[4] – it is a book greatly beloved. It is read every Passover by Ashkenazic Jews, every Sabbath by Sephardic Jews, and has inspired both medieval monastic meditation and widespread Protestant reflection. Yet this book, whose language is woven into the prayers and sacred liturgies of Jew and Christian alike, never mentions God and presents itself – literally, at least – as the sensuous erotic yearnings of Solomon's sixty-first wife!

3.2.1 Lyric Sequence or Dramatic Narrative: Whose Story?

Certainly the Song of Solomon proves that interpretive difficulty is no bar to widespread popularity. Canonized both because of its attribution to the great son of David himself, and because of its wide use among Jewish and Christian congregations, the book has an ancient pedigree as sacred scripture, yet its text presents us with many puzzles: Is it merely a **lyric sequence** of poems loosely connected by a love theme, or is it a more clearly connected lyric-dramatic narrative telling a love story? If it is such a narrative, who are the characters who speak and act throughout? And perhaps most importantly, is it to be read figuratively or literally – and what is the function in the biblical canon of a poem that discusses sex pervasively but does not name God?

As befits a book that has inspired many ingenious readings, it also has borne many titles: in addition to the Song of Solomon, it has been called the *Shir ha-Shirim* (Hebrew "Song of Songs," meaning "Best of Songs"), translated *Asma Aismaton* (Greek Septuagint Bible), *Canticum Canticorum* (Latin Vulgate Bible), and Canticle of Canticles (Roman Catholic Bibles in English), and *Das Hohelied* (German for "The High Song"). A close look at its text reveals a number of exquisite individual lyrics that can easily stand on their own among the best of the world's romantic love poetry. Here are a few examples:

> Rise up, my love, my fair one,
> And come away.
> For lo, the winter is past,
> The rain is over and gone.
> The flowers appear on the earth;
> The time of singing has come,
> And the voice of the turtledove
> Is heard in our land.
> The fig tree puts forth her green figs,
> And the vines with the tender grapes
> Give a good smell.
> Rise up, my love, my fair one,
> And come away! (2:10–13)

> You have ravished my heart,
> My sister, my spouse;
> You have ravished my heart
> With one look of your eyes,
> With one link of your necklace.
> How fair is your love,
> My sister, my spouse!
> How much better than wine is your love,
> And the scent of your perfumes
> Than all spices!
> Your lips, O my spouse,
> Drip as the honeycomb;
> Honey and milk are under your tongue;
> And the fragrance of your garments
> Is like the fragrance of Lebanon. (4:9–11):

> Set me as a seal upon your heart,
> As a seal upon your arm;
> For love is as strong as death,
> Jealousy as cruel as the grave;

> Its flames are flames of fire,
> A most vehement flame.
> Many waters cannot quench love,
> Nor can the floods drown it.
> If a man would give for love
> All the wealth of his house,
> It would be utterly despised. (8:6–7)

These are indeed among the "best of songs," anticipating love-lines by Petrarch and Marlowe and Shakespeare and Donne, Bradstreet and Byron and Yeats and Thomas. Its vivid examples of *wasf* or erotic anatomy of the beloved (which the French call *blason de la beauté* – 4:1ff, 5:10ff, 6:4ff, 7:1ff); its dramatic dream sequences; and its evocative refrains ("I am my beloved's and he is mine," "he pastures his flock among the lilies," "Do not awaken love until it please") all rank it with the world's great love poetry, in the tradition of the Greek *epithalamion*, or "songs upon the marriage bed."

The Epithalamion Tradition

While the word *epithalamion* is Greek, the tradition stretches back at least as far as ancient Egypt, with its sensual celebrations of conjugal love. The English Renaissance produced some masterpieces of the form: Edmund Spenser's "Epithalamion" (1595) memorializes the poet's own 1594 wedding night, while Shakespeare's famous sonnet "My Mistress' Eyes Are Nothing Like the Sun" plays ironically with the *blason* tradition, itemizing the mistress' supposed faults before reversing course to praise her as unique and beyond such "false compare."

However, they are not merely separate songs, for they are strung together like beads on a thread, connected by something like a story. It is the story of a dark-tanned country girl come to the city as the newest consort to the great king; who grows enraptured and then sick with erotic desire; who feels the sting of other women's scorn and then the first dread of abandonment; who seeks her lover and lord and finds him only to lose, seek, and lose him again; who casts her mind back to her troubled past and then looks forward to love's future ecstatic consummations. At least, that is the shadow of a story that emerges from the tissue of context that links the many lyric high points of the book – context too persistent for merely unconnected vignettes, but too tenuous for a clear and certain narrative. In other words, the book has undeniable narrative elements – a cast of characters, the emotive ups and downs of a romantic plot, with its dreams, flashbacks, and structural repetitions – but if we turn the magnification up too high, that narrative tends to dissolve in a blur.

For instance, who are the story's characters? There is, certainly, the female lover, perhaps a Lebanese beauty from outside the nation of Israel, but her name is uncertain. Is it **Shulamit/ Shulamith** (still a popular Hebrew women's name in our own day, the feminine of *Shalom*, or "Peace"), or is she "the Shulamite," a woman from the village of Shulem? And, certainly, there is **King Solomon**, *Shlomo ha Melech* in Hebrew, whose name quite famously also means "Peace" – but is Solomon the true love of Shulamit? Or is there an unnamed **rival suitor**, perhaps a loyal shepherd lad from her home village, who seeks to win her back from Solomon's harem? There are, no doubt, "**Daughters of Jerusalem**," who act as a female chorus to Shulamit, questioning, cajoling, advising, and sometimes overtly mocking her. And then, in minor roles, there is **Pharaoh's daughter** – Solomon's *next* and far more important wife? – and there are

Shulamit's brothers, remembered for their possessive and rather harsh distrust of their (formerly) virgin sister. So, while we can't seriously doubt that Solomon's Song presents us with a cast of characters, beyond a certain point we can't be precise about literally who they are.

3.2.1.1 Allegory?

But while the literal meaning of Solomon's Song presents some bewildering questions about whose story it is, there can be no doubt that throughout its reception history, interpreters have almost always preferred an approach not literal, but rather, figurative. Taking their cue from many other biblical passages celebrating the "marriage" of *Yahweh* to Israel or of Jesus Christ to the Church, commentators both Jewish and Christian, and whether Catholic or Orthodox or Protestant, have usually read this Song of Songs as an **allegory** – an extended symbolic narrative – representing the soul's intimate relations with her Lord and Savior.

The Biblical Bridegroom Motif

Biblical writers often speak of God as husband and his people as wife (whether faithful or unfaithful), for instance in Psalm 45, Ezekiel 23, Hosea 2:12–40, Matthew 9:15, Ephesians 5:21–33, and Revelation 21:9–10.

This allegorical approach seems to have appealed so strongly because it offers a plausible answer to that puzzling question: what is the function in the biblical canon of a "Godless" book drenched in sexuality? As we'll see in succeeding chapters, ancient Hebrew and New Testament attitudes toward sexual desire and pleasure largely contradict the stereotypical prudery of the popular imagination; nevertheless, well into the twentieth century, Jewish and Christian interpreters of this book sought to solve both problems at once by reading King Solomon as the Lord of Hosts, or as Christ the King, and Shulamit as his passionate but erring Bride. Thus, in one hermeneutical stroke, the book comes into focus as a story entirely about God – and not in the least about literal sex.

For instance, we might compare the following passage, sensuously describing the anatomy of the "prince's daughter" – perhaps a daughter of Pharaoh? – to the interpretation from the great medieval Rabbi Rashi (1040–1105) and Puritan leader John Winthrop (1587–1649). First the passage:

> How beautiful are your feet in sandals,
> O prince's daughter!
> The curves of your thighs are like jewels,
> The work of the hands of a skillful workman.
> Your navel is a rounded goblet;
> It lacks no blended beverage.
> Your waist is a heap of wheat
> Set about with lilies.
> Your two breasts are like two fawns,
> Twins of a gazelle…
> How fair and how pleasant you are,
> O love, with your delights!
> This stature of yours is like a palm tree,
> And your breasts like its clusters.
> I said, "I will go up to the palm tree,

I will take hold of its branches."
Let now your breasts be like clusters of the vine,
The fragrance of your breath like apples,
And the roof of your mouth like the best wine. (7:1–3, 6–9)

In contrast, Rashi's allegorical reading presents the speaker as "Ha Shem" (God) and the bride as Israel personified. As in most other allegories, every physical or personal detail takes on a corresponding spiritual meaning – the bride's navel and belly become the "Sanhedrin site" and "national center" (Jerusalem), her two breasts become "twin sustainers, the Tablets of the Law," and passionate phrases about sexual contact are redirected to a desire for the holy words of the wise.[5]

Similarly, a Puritan writer like John Winthrop – founder of the Massachusetts Bay Colony in 1630 – meditates deeply on Christ's "sweet Oders," and "the kisses of [his] mouth," and portrays his own sins and spiritual wanderings in terms of the bride's sad experience of turning her bridegroom away and finding herself forlorn (5:2–8). From such allegorical perspectives, the narrative thread that we noted earlier becomes a theological storyline: it is the story of a soul, darkened with dust and sin, come into the spiritual presence of the heavenly King; a soul who grows enraptured and then sick with spiritual desire; who feels the sting of the world's scorn and then her first dread of spiritual abandonment; who seeks her Lover and Lord and finds him only to lose, seek, and lose him again; who casts her mind back to her troubled unregenerate past and then looks forward to love's future ecstatic heavenly consummations. Yet the figurative was not everything for such allegorizers – Rashi considered the *peshat* (the "natural" or literal reading) as foundational to *derash* (the figurative reading), while Winthrop also wrote affectionately to his wife in the language of the Song of Solomon, applying its words to their marital – and physical – union.[6]

3.2.1.2 Literal Love Story?

Significantly, that "natural" level of interpretation has reasserted itself since the middle of the twentieth century, as Jewish, Christian, and secular interpreters have turned their attentions to the literal human loves portrayed by the writer but usually overlooked by spiritualizing readers. This return to the literal has re-engaged with many of the puzzles noted above, particularly about the cast of characters, and has produced a variety of alternate theories: of an **Ideal Love**, a **Romantic Dream**, a **Forbidden Love**, and – most tragically – a **Betrayed Love**. The **Ideal Love** theory is the sunniest and most optimistic – and perhaps the most appealing to many Western religious believers in our more sexually frank era. In this view, Solomon's Song portrays the tender devotion of a young King Solomon and the favorite wife of his youth. Usually stressing Solomon's as-yet-unspoiled ardor, and the eager sensuality of his bride, this theory foregrounds the God-given goodness and joy of marital sex – certainly, as we'll see, an important biblical theme elsewhere – and at times treats the book as a kind of sacred sex manual, a Hebrew or Christian *Kama Sutra*. This theory, while not ignoring the spectacularly polygamous context of Solomon's larger marital career, definitely marginalizes it, treating Shulamit as his one true mate, body and soul.

The **Romantic Dream** theory also treats Solomon as a romantic ideal while building on one of the book's most striking features – its psychologically dramatic dream sequences. In Song of Solomon 3 and 5, Shulamit dreams of her lover, in one case happily ("I found the one I love" – 3:4), and in the other case not ("If you find my beloved … tell him I *am* lovesick!" – 5:8). This theory extends this dream state to most or all of the book: Shulamit is imagined as speaking of her village lover in kingly terms, as if he were the glorious King Solomon himself. In this view, Solomon never literally enters the story, but his example of male beauty, passion, and desirability informs all the talk of love – moving the young village swain to speak to Shulamit in return as if she were a princess.

While these Ideal Love and Romantic Dream theories treat Solomon as a model romantic male, the other two theories see him in darker shades. The **Forbidden Love** theory (or Shepherd Hypothesis) treats Solomonic polygamy more seriously, seeing Shulamit as the latest find in a yearly search for young virgins to freshen the king's bed. Compelled from her family and home, she is also separated from her true love, a "rival suitor" or young shepherd from her home village, who follows her to the capital and attempts to win her back from the king's sensual grasp. This theory ascribes the sweetest and most pastoral passages to this loyal youth – "Rise up, my love, my fair one, / And come away" (2:10) – and offers hope that in the end she is reunited with him back home in "the house of my mother" (8:2). Still, while these pastoral interludes undoubtedly exist in the text, they are not explicitly ascribed to a rival suitor, and can instead be read as the words of the king himself – son, after all, of a shepherd named David.

Finally, the **Betrayed Love** theory attempts to come fully to grips with the realities of life in an ancient Near Eastern harem, as Solomon weds and beds wife number sixty-one – out of 1000 (1 Kings 11:3)! In this view, Solomon is very much the *roué* described in Ecclesiastes 2:1–11, and he has mastered the arts of seduction and sensual pleasure, which he exercises on a naïve young rural beauty, who takes him at his word when he tells her that

> Your hair is like a flock of goats,
> Going down from Mount Gilead.
> Your teeth are like a flock of shorn sheep
> Which have come up from the washing,
> Every one of which bears twins,
> And none is barren among them.[7] (4:1–2)

Swept off her feet by the dashing king, she boasts of her special beloved status to the other women of the harem – the "Daughters of Jerusalem" – whose mockery plants seeds of doubt that grow into increasingly desolate dreams and finally into a full-blown confrontation. Ironically, after he repeats the same blandishments as above, he comes up short, and then tries to break the truth to her gently:

> There are sixty queens
> And eighty concubines,
> And virgins without number.
> My dove, my perfect one,
> Is the only one … (6:8–9)

As if to say, "Yes, there are many others, and there will be many more, but you will always be special to me, precious." Shulamit, having yielded her heart and her virginity to the King, and having been introduced to the ways of multiple marriage, nevertheless still longs poignantly for the kind of exclusive commitment that will "[s]et me as a seal upon your heart" (8:6) – the kind of love which promises that "a man shall leave his father and mother and be joined to his wife, and they shall become one flesh" (Genesis 2:24). But as the book ends, she has only a lifetime of well-heeled sexual exploitation ahead of her.

Clearly, these four theories revive and answer in different ways the question about the book's canonicity. For the Ideal Love and Romantic Dream theories, the Song of Songs belongs in the sacred canon because it celebrates that God-ordained wonder, "the way of a man with a maiden"

(Proverbs 30:19), while for the Forbidden Love and Betrayed Love theories, the book is canonical because it affirms the goodness of monogamous fidelity to "the wife of your youth" (Proverbs 5:18) against the dark backdrop of polygamous lechery – and in the latter case entirely by negative example.

3.2.1.3 Earthly Desire and Heavenly Longing

These alternatives to allegory make clear that a "natural" approach to this famously mysterious book generates many interpretive possibilities, but that both figurative and literal can account for its place in the scriptures – whether as a shadow-play of the soul's divine courtship, or as a story of love in the flesh, happy or tragic. As we will see in our succeeding chapters on Wisdom Literature and on the book of Genesis, mortal erotics often represent the immortal longings of the soul; this is because the powerful concept of humankind as *tselem* – an "image" or representation of God the Creator – means that in the ancient Hebrew imagination, all human stories tell some divine story, simply because all human actions necessarily represent or misrepresent God, sexual actions no less than others. So, in these terms, if the allegorists err, they err not by seeking divine meaning in a carnal story, but by ignoring the divine meaning in each literal, carnal embrace. In other words, if all acts of earthly desire, however misdirected or perverted, are expressions of heavenly longing, then even the erotic dreams of a harem bride (and even a heartbroken yearning for fidelity) are divine revelations of a kind – that love is as strong as death.

We began this chapter by noting that the lyric poetry of the Bible is intimate and dramatic, expressing both individual passion and congregational devotion. We also observed the remarkable stereoscopic vision of this poetry, which is of a piece with the depth of field provided by multiple viewpoints throughout the scriptures. Now, having considered the poetic heart of Hebrew literature, let us turn – both for contrast and for continuity – to its proverbial head.

Questions for Discussion

1 Over what range of time were the **Psalms** likely composed? When, probably, were they assembled into their current form, and by whom? To what writers are the individual psalms traditionally attributed? To whom are the most credited? What do these attributions mean in Hebrew and Christian tradition?

2 Thematically, what are some common **psalm types**? In what ways does this variety of types resemble a congregation? How might the Psalms have been used in congregational worship?

3 What is the significance of the Psalms' **five-book** structure? What qualities characterize each of these five books? What possible sequencing is to be observed *among* these books? *Within* them?

4 What are some instances of what we might call "**interior drama**" and "**psychological discovery**" in the Psalms?

5 What are the effects of **figurative language**, and what are some kinds commonly found in the Psalms? What are examples of each kind?

6 What are the effects of **parallelism** in the Psalms, and what are the kinds of parallelism that we observe? What are examples of each kind?

7 What are **refrain** and **litany**? How do they differ? What functions do they serve? What are examples of each?

8 What is **juxtaposition**, and what are its effects in the Psalms? What are some examples?

9 What are the possible origins of the **Song of Solomon**? By what other names is it sometimes called? When was it written? To whom attributed? How did it come to be canonized?

10 What qualities does the Song of Solomon share with the **lyric sequences** of the Psalms, and with the Bible's dramatic narratives? What is its "cast of characters"?

11 What are the book's main interpretive difficulties? How has it been read **allegorically**, and by whom? What are the main ways that it has been read as a **literal love story**, and by whom?

Notes

1 *Commentary on the Book of Psalms*, tr. James Anderson, Calvin Translation Society (1843–1855; rpt. Grand Rapids, 1963), I, xxxvi–xxxvii.
2 Another form of **anthropomorphism**, less common in the Bible but common in fables such as Aesop's, speaks of animals and other sub-human animate creatures in human terms.
3 Even scientific nomenclature translates from its Latin and Greek roots down to images and sensory perceptions; for instance, among fungi and algae *myxomycophyta* means "the slimy growth," and *cyanophyta* means "the blue-green growth."
4 Song of Solomon 6:4 mentions the fortress of Tirzah as if still in the hands of the Israelites, who lost the city in 950 BCE, midway through Solomon's reign (971–931).
5 Nosson Scherman, R., *The Chumash*, ArtScroll Series, Stone Edition, Mesorah, Brooklyn, 1998, pp. 1263–1267.
6 http://realiajudaica.blogspot.com/2011/04/on-reading-and-translating-shir-ha.html; Winthrop, John, *The Life and Letters of John Winthrop*, ed. Robert Charles Winthrop (Boston: Little, Brown, 1869), 135–36.
7 What sounds insulting to modern ears is actually an extravagant compliment: since most wealth was counted in livestock, and since a great flock of goats would glisten like onyx on a distant mountainside – without the stench – he is saying that she "looks like a million dollars," and observing that that she still has all of her very white teeth!

4

Wisdom Literature: Understanding Their Riddles

We ended the previous chapter with the suggestion that lyric poetry forms the heart of Hebrew literature, while collections of proverbial and wise sayings might be said to make up its "head." As with most supposed polarities – "head and heart," "sense and sensibility," "prose and poetry," not to mention "male and female" – we must be careful neither to understate nor overstate the oppositions. The differences between the Psalms and Proverbs are many and important: devoted passion versus prudent reverence; hymns versus maxims; song versus discourse; and liturgy versus meditation and instruction.

Above all, though, are the differences between what we might call the Davidic and Solomonic personae. These iconic figures include not only the diversities just mentioned, but also two contrasting life narratives: on the one hand, David's humble beginnings, his underdog victories and Saul's persecution, his triumph in forging a unified kingdom, his fall from virtue and then from power, and his eventual repentance and restoration; on the other hand, Solomon's early wisdom and wealth, his royal glory and imperial sway, his sensual indulgence, his idolatry, and the terrible anticlimactic division of the kingdom. In the Hebrew imagination, the shorthand for David's life was the phrase, "a man after God's own heart" (1 Samuel 13:14); for Solomon's life, the shorthand phrase would have been "the wisest of men – who turned to folly" (1 Kings 3:12, 11:1–13). Thus, David's story is an affair of the heart, and Solomon's of the head – with the blessings and dangers attending on each.

Yet these differences in genre between lyric poetry and proverb, and in overarching master narrative, are not absolute: for instance, as we've seen, the poetry of the Psalms begins by celebrating wisdom, and continues by recommending wisdom frequently, while the Book of Proverbs is written in parallel poetry with many striking flights of eloquence and some occasionally tender – and sensuous – sexual scenarios analogous to those in the Song of Songs. Indeed the Solomonic persona is itself expansive enough to include not only the prudent life manager of Proverbs but also the Song of Solomon's passionate lyricist and – as we'll see later in this chapter – the chastened, disillusioned greybeard of Ecclesiastes. In other words, much as Psalms are surprisingly many-voiced, so also does the Bible's wisdom come in more shapes than one, yielding stereoscopic insight. (Our discussion of that other great piece of contrarian wisdom literature, the Book of Job, will wait until a later chapter dealing with the genre of biblical drama.)

Furthermore, the Proverbs, like the Psalms, are clearly another composite book. They are attributed, in large part, to King Solomon (1:1, 10:1), and Proverbs 25 through 29 are presented as "proverbs of Solomon which the men of Hezekiah king of Judah copied" (25:1); while the brief discourses and numerical proverbs of Proverbs 30 are credited to one Agur son of Jakeh (30:1); and the famous final chapter, on kingly duty and the qualities of the "good wife," is

Literary Study of the Bible: An Introduction, First Edition. Christopher Hodgkins.
© 2020 John Wiley & Sons Ltd. Published 2020 by John Wiley & Sons Ltd.

introduced as "The words of King Lemuel, the utterance which his mother taught him" (31:1). It is written that Solomon "spoke three thousand proverbs" (1 Kings 4:32), and though the very nature of proverbs as inherited folk wisdom makes it likely that many sayings were collected rather than created by the king, there is still no reason to doubt an extensive personal contribution to the collection by the son of David. Who then were Agur and Lemuel? Agur is mentioned in the Bible only in Proverbs 30, and may have been a Gentile sage – perhaps an Ishmaelite from Massa in the Fertile Crescent – a possibility consistent with the portrayal of other God-fearing Gentiles like Melchizedek, Jethro, Job, and Job's friends elsewhere in the *Tanakh*. As to Lemuel, some modern commentators have suggested an otherwise unknown Gentile king (though it would be strange for one of the *goyim* to have a Hebrew name), while Jewish tradition holds that this is a pet name ("Devoted to God") given to Solomon by his mother, which if true ascribes the famous discourses on kingly and wifely virtue to none other than David's notorious (and favorite) wife, Bathsheba.

Thus, the Book of Proverbs – so concerned with moral clarity and transparent living – presents us with a few of its own mysteries and riddles. These puzzles include not only the attribution of certain passages, but also some thematic paradoxes: Why would Bathsheba, famous (or infamous) for her disastrous adultery with polygamous King David, be the woman to speak about the joys and glories of monogamous wifely righteousness? And why would the prodigiously oversexed King Solomon preach so tirelessly throughout Proverbs on sexual self-restraint and fidelity to one wife? Many modern interpreters thus doubt these attributions, and propose later, post-exilic dates for the book's composition, during a time when monogamy had become the Jewish norm and Solomon's reputation for debauchery could serve as a powerful object lesson. But while a post-exilic redaction of Proverbs, as with Psalms, seems likely, it is also likely that there would have been much older material to redact, and who would have been more qualified to drive home such moral lessons than the one-time offenders themselves? The books of 2 Samuel and 1 Kings present Bathsheba and Solomon as experiencing the bitter consequences of their transgressions, and, as we will see later in this chapter, Ecclesiastes narrates the sobering lessons of its disillusioned hedonist speaker. So this riddle of attribution may answer itself.

In any case, whether or not the historical Solomon is speaking, the Solomonic persona pervades the Book of Proverbs, voicing its sometimes puzzling expressions – "the words of the wise, and their riddles" (1:6) – and challenging "the simple" to put in the hard mental and ethical work necessary to "get understanding." Perhaps surprisingly – at least to those who associate wisdom with austere asceticism – the Solomonic narrator presents multiple scenes resembling the erotic settings in his Song of Songs.

4.1 "Take Hold of Her": Wisdom and Desire in Proverbs

Commentators on Proverbs generally agree that the book's primary audience seems to be adolescent males, with its advice often addressed parentally to "my son." So, without excluding the older or female audiences with whom the book has always been popular, its focus (especially in the introductory Proverbs 1–9) is on the typical temptations of the young male: what we now call "peer pressure," but also greed, rebellion, and especially sexual lust. Although, as with the Psalms, the book is an artful assembly of some pre-existing parts, the introductory discourse reads very much like a purpose-made opening designed to establish the principles that will define and guide the reader's search for wisdom, and struggle against "folly." In fact, like the wisdom writings of many ancient cultures – from Sumer to Egypt to Greece – Proverbs seeks to manage adolescent passion not by denying or suppressing it, but rather by tapping the power of the male libido to generate dramatic interest and to channel desire toward appropriate fulfillment. So while the book uses many figurative and structural devices to sharpen its impact, it makes especially liberal use of personification, portraying both Wisdom and Folly as attractively female, first as allegorical figures and eventually as flesh-and-blood women that a man can embrace and know – for evil or for good.

Wisdom as Female

Given their dominant patriarchy, one commonplace of ancient Eurasian and Mediterranean civilizations that may surprise the modern imagination is the frequency of female figures personifying Wisdom. From goddesses like the Egyptian Seshat, the Hindu Saraswati, the Persian Anahita, and the Armenian Nane, to others such as the Greek Metris and Athena, the Etruscan Menvra, and the Roman Egeria and Minerva, classical pantheons usually imagined Wisdom as powerfully and attractively female. While the Hebrew Hokmot personifies wisdom, understanding, and insight in similar terms, yet biblical Wisdom acts not as an independent deity but as the servant and expression of *Yahweh*.

The "Wise Fool" Tradition

Although Folly is a negative figure in the Book of Proverbs, elsewhere in the Bible, and in Judeo-Christian tradition, the Fool and Folly serve as figures of ironic wisdom. From David's impersonation of a madman (1 Samuel 21:13–15), the counter-wisdom of Ecclesiastes (see below), and Paul's claim to be "a fool for Christ's sake" (1 Corinthians 4:10), to literary classics such as Erasmus's *In Praise of Folly*, More's *Utopia*, Shakespeare's *King Lear*, and Dostoyevsky's *The Idiot*, outspoken fools and madmen confront the problem of moral inversion: that in a fallen and corrupted age, to be wise in the sight of God is to be a fool in the eyes of the world.

4.1.1 "She Calls Aloud in the Streets": Wisdom and Folly Personified

She does not stay at home, quietly practicing her domestic arts. Instead, she is outspoken, she is public, she "calls aloud in the streets; / She raises her voice in the open squares" (1:20); "she cries out from the highest places in the city," inviting everyone to share her abundant food and her "mixed wine" (9:3). Who is this unreserved woman, offering her company and her rich and intoxicating hospitality to all comers? Surprisingly enough, she is Wisdom, and to be with her is to share in her luxurious feast – and in her drinking party. No doubt, this generous lady has a polemical edge, and her cornucopia comes with a message:

> How long, you simple ones, will you love simplicity?
> For scorners delight in their scorning,
> And fools hate knowledge.
> Turn at my rebuke;
> Surely I will pour out my spirit on you;
> I will make my words known to you…
> Come, eat of my bread
> And drink of the wine I have mixed.
> Forsake foolishness and live,
> And go in the way of understanding. (1:22–23, 9:5–6)

Yet this preacher-woman is also presented as sweetly desirable, and, in a word, embraceable:

> She is more precious than rubies,
> And all the things you may desire cannot compare with her...
> Her ways are ways of pleasantness,
> And all her paths are peace.
> She is a tree of life to those who take hold of her... (3:15, 17–18)

"Take hold of her" – words not usually associated with the unattainably chaste and virtuous female. She is of course an allegorical figure, but three things are particularly remarkable about Lady Wisdom as presented in Proverbs: first, she was, as it were, "present at the Creation," participating in *Yahweh's* founding of the earth and the heavens (3:19, 8:22–31); second, her promises, while spiritual, are not otherworldly, since they point to joy and abundance in this life (as in the passages above); third – and most strangely – she has a good deal in common with her spiritual rival.

For Folly also is an outspoken woman, and public; she too "sits at the door of her house, / On a seat by the highest places of the city"; she also "call[s] to those who pass by, / Who go straight on their way: / 'Whoever is simple, let him turn in here,'" inviting everyone to share her food and her drink (9:14–16). This reads as a careful and deliberate refrain of Wisdom's words, and yet it is obviously antithetical, intended somehow to steal Wisdom's audience and her glory – but with the opposite effect. For what Folly actually has in mind is not a fine meal, but theft: "Stolen water is sweet, / And bread eaten in secret is pleasant," she says – thus admitting that the real thrill in her "feast" is not in the quality of the inferior food (bread and water rather than Wisdom's meat and mixed wine), but instead in the act of transgression itself (9:17). In an ironically perverse sense, sin is its own (and only) reward; in a passage that mocks the stupidity of giving up God's plenty for the world's leavings, sin is a futile, self-inflicted act punished not only by the Law of Moses but also by the Law of Diminishing Returns. Then the narrator closes with the final blow: Folly's dinner companion "does not know that the dead are there, / That her guests are in the depths of Sheol" – the pit of the grave (9:18). Or, as Wisdom puts it even more pointedly elsewhere, "All those who hate me love death" (8:36).

Why make Wisdom and Folly so parallel and at least so superficially similar? First, these comparisons stress that Folly, like all forms of sin, is unoriginal, derivative, and indeed parasitic on goodness – a cheap distracting imitation of the Real Thing. Second, the antithetic parallel between the two "women" points up the solid, wholesome, lasting pleasures of Wisdom in terms that even a gourmet or a hedonist can understand: Why not enjoy the best? Why be the dupe who settles for less – or for nothing? Third, the very resemblances between Wisdom and Folly point up the need for virtue to be more forward and outspoken in promoting its way, not conceding the public square to charlatans and hawkers of stolen goods. And finally, this competition between attractive, outspoken female voices prepares, as we will see, for a surprising redefinition of feminine virtue as anything but shy and retiring.

4.1.2 Folly Made Flesh: The Loose Woman

So the Book of Proverbs personifies the abstractions of Wisdom and Folly in order to increase their vividness, especially for the adolescent male imagination. But Proverbs also moves beyond allegory to the more literal world in which the young man finds himself beset by urgent desires and temptations: the call of sometimes dangerous companions, the lure of quick wealth, the impulse to overthrow true authority, and the siren-song of sex. Though bad company, greed, and rebellion come in for substantial warnings in the opening discourse of Proverbs 1–9 and elsewhere, the parental voice of the narrator returns almost obsessively to the warning against carnal indulgence, and more specifically, against the "loose woman." It is one thing to recognize temptation in the abstract; it is quite another to resist it in the form of warm, enticing flesh. The argument for self-control and restraint is, as noted above, largely prudential and practical: extramarital sex is treated as an exceptionally bad transaction, as trading a few minutes' pleasure for worlds of woe. If this view of sex as sacred to marriage seems silly and restrictive to many today, so it did to many in ancient Israel, which is why the Solomonic narrator presents his case against fornication with special verve and dramatic skill.

Enticements to extramarital sex come in a realistic variety of shapes and settings in Proverbs: a single man's fornication with prostitutes (5:1–14, 6:26), and with married women (2:16–19), and the married man's adultery with women single or wed (6:23–35). Sometimes the categories blur – for instance, the prostitute may be nominally married (2:17, 7:19). But the man who dallies sexually is consistently portrayed not only as immoral, but as an idiot on the road to ruin.

> For the lips of an immoral woman drip honey,
> And her mouth is smoother than oil;
> But in the end she is bitter as wormwood,
> Sharp as a two-edged sword.
> Her feet go down to death,
> Her steps lay hold of Sheol. (5:3–5)

The fatherly narrator attempts to stir the young man's instinct for self-preservation – and his gag reflex – by comparing the enjoyment of prostitutes to the drinking of sewage: "Should your fountains be dispersed abroad, / Streams of water in the streets?" (5:16). In keeping with this prudential theme, the Solomonic narrator presents fornication with an adulteress as doubly dangerous because of her husband's wrath:

> For jealousy is a husband's fury;
> Therefore he will not spare in the day of vengeance.
> He will accept no recompense,
> Nor will he be appeased though you give many gifts. (6:34–35)

Thus, the sweet-talking adventuress becomes the bait in a deadly trap: for a man who offers a bribe in repayment for a wife's "services" will only add insult to the husband's injury, and quite likely to his murderous rage.

The most vivid account of "Folly made flesh" appears in Proverbs 7, in an elaborate and atmospheric scenario of seduction:

> For at the window of my house
> I looked through my lattice,
> And saw among the simple,
> I perceived among the youths,
> A young man devoid of understanding,
> Passing along the street near her corner;
> And he took the path to her house
> In the twilight, in the evening,
> In the black and dark night. (7:6–9)

Foreboding, dusk, gloom, a street corner – all these elements of modern film noir are completed by the appearance of the femme fatale:

> And there a woman met him,
> With the attire of a harlot, and a crafty heart...
> So she caught him and kissed him;
> With an impudent face she said to him:
> "I have peace offerings with me;
> Today I have paid my vows.
> So I came out to meet you,
> Diligently to seek your face,
> And I have found you...
> I have perfumed my bed
> With myrrh, aloes, and cinnamon.
> Come, let us take our fill of love until morning;
> Let us delight ourselves with love..." (7:10, 13–15, 17–18)

With understated irony, we're told that this lady of the evening has spent some daylight hours fulfilling her religious obligations at the Temple, and likely has meat left over from the sacrifice for a night-time feast with her chosen "mark." This wayward worshiper has prepared her bedchamber voluptuously, and there is no need to fear discovery because

> "...my husband is not at home;
> He has gone on a long journey;
> He has taken a bag of money with him,
> And will come home on the appointed day." (7:19–20)

Brazenly admitting to religious and marital hypocrisy, she presents the promise of no-fault gratification: a willing, available, unsupervised, experienced woman! Who could ask for anything more?

> Immediately he went after her, as an ox goes to the slaughter,...
> Till an arrow struck his liver.
> As a bird hastens to the snare,
> He did not know it would cost his life. (7:22–23)

The narrator leaves the climax and conclusion unspecified, pulling his lattice curtain closed while inviting our imaginations to supply any number of dire undoings for this latest victim – whether drunkenness followed by theft, or discovery followed by public shame, or outright death at the hands of the woman or her man, we don't know. But we are warned soberly of Folly's great strength: "For she has cast down many wounded, / And all who were slain by her were strong men" (7:26). Samsons seem to attract their Delilahs, and the Proverbs suggest that the only force stronger than Folly seems to be Wisdom herself – and marriage to a wise woman.

4.1.3 Wisdom Incarnate: The Good Wife

We've already seen that in her outspoken and public recruitment of followers, Wisdom is surprisingly like Folly – or actually, the other way around, because, significantly, Wisdom is presented as the genuine and full-bodied original, while Folly is only her shoddy imitator.

In this way the central persuasive strategy of Proverbs derives from the central assertion of Genesis: that God and his good works are always previous, and that all sin and evil can do is bend, warp, or steal the originals, and pass off these stolen, diluted and contaminated goods to the gullible. So the Solomonic father who narrates Proverbs 1–9 takes pains to remind his young hearers that God is no spoilsport, and that to follow the LORD's ways is to enjoy the best that Creation can offer, including the joys of sexual fulfillment. And so the Solomonic mother (perhaps literally Solomon's mother, Bathsheba) who narrates the book's climax in chapter 31, incarnates all of Wisdom's benefits in the strong, enterprising and fruitful form of "the Good Wife."

In fact, the narrator's earlier visceral warning against the gutter sex of prostitution actually belongs to a much more positive – and equally frank – celebration of marital sexuality:

> Drink water from your own cistern,
> And running water from your own well.
> Should your fountains be dispersed abroad,
> Streams of water in the streets?
> Let them be only your own,
> And not for strangers with you.
> Let your fountain be blessed,
> And rejoice with the wife of your youth.
> As a loving deer and a graceful doe,
> Let her breasts satisfy you at all times;
> And always be enraptured with her love. (5:16–19)

The images of flowing streams and fountains and deer – and of breasts and rapture – remind us of Solomon's Song, but now with an unambiguously monogamous intent: this love lyric is designed to stir a young man's desire, as well as his good sense and his loyalty in relatively equal measure. Taking for granted that young men will naturally desire feminine charms where they can find them, the Solomonic narrator reminds these young men of two things: first, that the husband of a loving wife will usually enjoy enthusiastic intercourse a good deal more often than the young rake who must find his used goods where he can, and for high rent; second, that a man who has enjoyed his wife's youthful bloom owes her his lifelong fidelity, and his tenderness. The passage's somewhat paradoxical language of everyday passion and enduring ecstasy show that this lifelong love in the flesh is sustained by the love of the soul.

And finally it is qualities of soul and mind that the Book of Proverbs praises in the best of women. Having given sexual attraction its substantial due, the book concludes by describing the consummation of that desire in something higher: in the goodness and greatness of character that the ancients usually called "virtue," or in the literal Hebrew, "valor." "Who can find a virtuous wife?" asks "King Lemuel," in the words his mother taught him; "[f]or her worth is far above rubies" (31:10). What follows is a famous catalogue of wifely valor whose surprises increase the closer we look; for these womanly virtues sometimes sound rather manly, and they make no hard distinction between what we have come to call "domestic" and "civic" virtue, that is, between the life of the family and the life of the city. In other words, it is the wife's "private" work of home-making that builds and sustains the "public" world.

To be more specific: the virtuous wife, in providing for her family, necessarily involves herself in the supposedly male spheres of manufacture and trade, labor management, real estate, and agriculture:

> She seeks wool and flax,
> And willingly works with her hands.
> She is like the merchant ships,
> She brings her food from afar.
> She also rises while it is yet night,
> And provides food for her household,
> And tasks for her maidservants.
> She considers a field and buys it;
> From her profits she plants a vineyard. (31:13–16)

Hardly the "domestic angel" of Victorian imagination, or the leisurely suburban housewife of idealized 1950s America, she is firm of body and sharp of mind, especially in seeking a profit for her well-made goods:

> She girds herself with strength,
> And strengthens her arms.
> She perceives that her merchandise is profitable,
> And her lamp does not go out by night…
> She makes linen garments and sells them,
> And supplies sashes for the merchants. (31:17–18, 24)

Yet this hardiness and sharpness have an ultimately kind and tender purpose: "She extends her hand to the poor, / Yes, she reaches out her hands to the needy" (31:20). And in the midst of her generosity and compassion, she doesn't neglect some of the finer things, including quality clothing both for her family and for herself:

> She is not afraid of snow for her household,
> For all her household is clothed with scarlet.
> She makes tapestry for herself;
> Her clothing is fine linen and purple. (31:21–22)

Yet she is, above all, covered in her own goodness, and takes in hand the moral education of her own children:

> Strength and honor are her clothing;
> She shall rejoice in time to come.
> She opens her mouth with wisdom,
> And on her tongue is the law of kindness. (31:25–26)

What should be the rewards for such a life of labor and service? Partly, we may assume, the life itself is its own reward – a life full of meaningful and profitable work, and the satisfactions of children well raised and a husband well-known, are the payments sought by such motherly and wifely love.

But significantly, says "Lemuel's mother," while these private rewards may satisfy her, they should not satisfy her family or her city or her people, who are eager to honor her publicly:

> Her children rise up and call her blessed;
> Her husband also, and he praises her:
> "Many daughters have done well,
> But you excel them all."
> Charm is deceitful and beauty is passing,
> But a woman who fears the LORD, she shall be praised.

> Give her of the fruit of her hands,
> And let her own works praise her in the gates. (31:28–31)

Perhaps it takes a woman to see and to say it, but attention must be paid; excellence must be praised, not only for its own sake but also to encourage it in others. For to be a "good wife" in this biblical sense is to be first and foremost a loving bride and an abundant mother – but also (to use modern terms) a successful CEO, a factory foreman, a land agent, a community benefactor, and an invaluable public servant; indeed Wisdom made flesh. So it is not enough even to thank her; she has earned "the fruit of her hands" (that is, her share of the profits) and she is owed a hero's public honor, as "her own works praise her in the gates" – in the council chambers of the mighty. Again using contemporary terms, such "women of valor" deserve a monument in the Capitol Rotunda, or in Westminster Abbey, or in the Panthéon. If there is no "Tomb of the Unknown Wife" in any of our national capitals, the Book of Proverbs provides something even better: a climactic monument in words, a memorial that has outlived all the great men in their ancient city gates, and is likely to outlive all the other gardens of stone.

Of course, this all may seem a bit much, coming at the end of a book attributed mainly to a king who even in his earlier years had "sixty wives, and eighty concubines, and maidens without number," and in a speech that may trace back to that king's fatally beautiful and notorious mother. And at least as many women who are inspired by the "Virtuous Wife" tribute will be exhausted by the very idea of it! But the Proverbs hold – to paraphrase Robert Browning – that a woman's reach should exceed her grasp, and her reach in this case is from her base in the domestic sphere out into every corner of the public square. If this is a species of ancient feminism, it is a feminism thoroughly at home with the making of homes, while also quietly assured that a "man's world" is a woman's too. As we've seen, there are various Solomonic riddles here: the jaded polygamist rhapsodizing about monogamy, and patriarchal religion creating imaginative space for outspoken feminine power. But in the end, the riddle of Wisdom and desire, like so many other biblical riddles, is answered not by theoretical reason but by practical action and virtuous character. We turn now from the extended discourse of Wisdom and Folly to the multiplicity of riddles and short sayings that make up most of the book.

4.1.4 "The Beginning of Wisdom": How to Read a Proverb

Except for the opening discourse of chapters 1–9 and the closing discourses of chapters 30–31, Proverbs is composed mainly of just that, proverbs and brief sayings, "the words of the wise and their riddles" (1:6). Contemporary culture has analogous short forms based on the notion that brevity is the soul of wit, whether we call them sound bites, slogans, jingles, mottos, or even bumper stickers. But, as the book's introduction warns, its proverbs are to some degree intentionally difficult – hence the words "riddle" and "enigma" – and that built-in difficulty is an important part of their meaning. For "The fear of the LORD is the beginning of knowledge, / But fools despise wisdom and instruction" (1:7). By advertising the challenge immediately, the Solomonic narrator warns the reader that understanding the book requires a certain God-centered receptivity and a willingness to work a bit – that if you don't want to understand, you probably won't, and that if you do desire wisdom and are willing to make the effort, then the Proverbs are for you. The United States Marines practice this same strategy of recruitment by exclusion, announcing in their famous slogan that they "are looking for a few good men." So, we might say, is Solomon – or at least for a few who want to be good.

How then to read the short form of the proverb? First, assume that it's not supposed to be easy, that there may be a puzzle involved to test your interest and commitment, and to train your mind in "knowledge and discretion" (1:4). Second, pay close attention to figures of speech, and to the use of structural devices like parallelism and refrain, which frequently set the terms of comparison or contrast. And third, bear in mind that some proverbs are not merely puzzles, but deliberate provocations, particularly of their favorite target, "the fool." Keeping these caveats in mind, we can look more closely at a few representative examples.

Of course, some proverbs are not particularly puzzling, but simply make their moral point with what is probably the proverbialist's favorite figure, that of vivid simile. For instance, consider 25:26: "A righteous man who falters before the wicked / Is like a murky spring and a polluted well." Imagine a thirsty day in an arid landscape, and then the heart-sinking disappointment when the expectation of clear cool clean water at a long-familiar fountain gives way to disgust at mud or, worse, filth. The crucial elements here are the reader's visceral knowledge of life in a dry country, and the terrible letdown of hope when a good person "sells out." Similarly, one of the more durably amusing proverbs trades on our knowledge of quintessentially canine behavior: "As a dog returns to his own vomit, / So a fool repeats his folly" (26:11). If insanity is defined as repeating the same mistake while expecting different results, the point here is that repetitive moral stupidity simply stinks.

Many other proverbs present a somewhat higher interpretive threshold. Take 26:8: "Like one who binds a stone in a sling / Is he who gives honor to a fool." Obviously, this is one of the myriad proverbs critiquing the disciples and lovers of Folly, in this case advising against the praise of ethical idiocy, but what is the force of the simile itself? As with any comparison, we need to know something of the literal object in the likeness, and if we consult our knowledge of biblical "slings" we may recall the humble but effective weapon that David used against Goliath; that is, a small shallow leather pouch attached to two long leather thongs, made for wide centrifugal spinning and high-speed release. So imagine a person who puts his smooth killer stone in the pouch and then – go figure – ties that stone securely in place with a string. What happens when our would-be David spins his sling and releases the loose thong at his target? With brute physical irony, he becomes his own Goliath. Pause for a moment in the privacy of your home, imitate the action, and imagine the sling wrapped around your neck and the stone crashing into the back of your skull. Moral: reward the bad behavior of others, and it will come back to hurt you.

Some proverbs rely a good deal on juxtaposition and antithesis. One set of sayings in particular presents an apparent contradiction, and seems to invite mockery in return. How to make sense of these sequenced couplets?

> Do not answer a fool according to his folly,
> Lest you also be like him.
> Answer a fool according to his folly,
> Lest he be wise in his own eyes. (26:4–5)

Either this is very bad editing – placing two categorically opposite statements next to each other by accident – or this juxtaposition amounts to a form of deliberate paradox, hiding a deeper coherence. The argument is strong for coherent literary paradox over accidental contradiction; these verses are embedded in a longer series (26:3–12) itemizing the consequences and punishments due to fools and building to an ironic climax in verse 12.[1] So we must ask, is there more than one kind of "according" in view? And the answer is, yes: in verse 4, "according to" means "in the same manner as," while in verse 5, "according to" means "in the way that he deserves." In other words, these two verses can be paraphrased as "Don't answer a fool in his own rude, blustering, ignorant way, or people will think you're a fool too. Instead, answer a fool with clear, temperate, appropriate counter-arguments, so that he won't continue to deceive himself – and perhaps others." These verses call out the fool in a special way – perhaps he is inclined to catch out the scripture as self-contradictory, but he is himself caught out being "simple" and literal-minded.

Numerical Patterns

One distinctive way of organizing distinct proverbs toward a thematic climax is to impose a progressive numerical pattern, as in 30:18–19:

There are three things which are too wonderful for me,
Yes, four which I do not understand:
The way of an eagle in the air,
The way of a serpent on a rock,
The way of a ship in the midst of the sea,
And the way of a man with a maiden.

Note that the pattern generally includes a factor of "plus one" or a "topper" for emphasis, and sometimes a touch of wry humor. For other examples, see 6:16–19 and 30:15–31.

No doubt, such bracing pushback from a riddling text can be irritating, even alarming, as any little proverb might explode right in the reader's hand with shards of sharp implication. And what has been said about these examples can be said about the collection as a whole: despite the proverbialists' winning arts of personification and scenario, their riddles and numerical patterns, the wisdom writers always have designs upon us – openly announced designs, designs for our good (as their writers see good), but demanding and interactive expectations that call us out and expect a response. Yet, as it is with the Bible's stereoscopic vision throughout, so it is particularly with the words of the wise – that wisdom comes in more shapes than one, and calls for a different angle for depth of understanding. So just when we may begin to tire of the Book of Proverbs presenting us with its optimistic program of prudent life management, sanctioned by clear rewards and punishments, there comes yet another "book of Solomon" to blur those lines, looking at life askance and askew with its counter-wisdom.

4.2 "Enjoy Your Toil": The Counter-Wisdom of Ecclesiastes

In one of his best-loved sayings, Jesus tells his disciples to "[c]onsider the lilies of the field, how they grow: they neither toil nor spin; and yet I say to you that even Solomon in all his glory was not arrayed like one of these" (Matthew 6:28–29). In making this famous comparison, Jesus assumes that his Jewish audience knows the story of Solomon's glory: how he decked Jerusalem, and the LORD's Temple, and himself, in great splendor; and presumably how for all that, despite his wisdom and his glamor, Solomon fell far short of the glory of God. In fact, by contrasting Solomon's magnificence with the simple beauty of a field flower, Jesus joins implicitly in the biblical critique of his ancestor as the golden child who squandered God's gifts on lust and luxury (1 Kings 11:1–13). Thus, Ecclesiastes completes the great Solomonic trilogy: Proverbs is his book of sound prudence, the Song of Songs is his book of hot passion, and Ecclesiastes is his book of cool and chastened disillusion.[2] One measure of the tonal distance among the three books: Proverbs ends with its warm tribute to "the virtuous wife"; Solomon's Song sings the erotic praises of "my sister, my bride"; while Ecclesiastes, in one of its most repellant statements, asserts: "One [good] man among a thousand I have found, / But a woman among all these I have not found" (7:28). Thus, the misogynist edges out the general misanthrope, but only very slightly, if one does the math.

Or so, at least, it may seem. For unlike the sayings in Proverbs, which show an internally consistent (and dogmatic) moral viewpoint, the sayings of Ecclesiastes often sound provisional, experimental, random – and at times deliberately confused and provocative. In other words, they sound like what they probably are: the occasional observations of an aging grandee recorded in a journal or commonplace book, and then artfully arranged for emotive and dramatic effect. And in a drama, even a dramatic monologue like Ecclesiastes, we should not conclude too much too soon about any one isolated or particular statement, but reserve judgment. As Solomon might have said if Yogi Berra hadn't, it's not over until it's over.

Was that grandee Solomon himself? Ecclesiastes opens with its attribution to "the son of David … King over Israel in Jerusalem" (1:1,12), which points to the brief period of the United Kingdom under Solomon (971–931 BCE), since all succeeding Jerusalem kings reigned over Judah alone, with Israel as a separate kingdom ruled from Shechem and then Samaria. As in the cases of Proverbs and the Song of Solomon, some modern scholars have doubted this attribution, and indeed in the case of Ecclesiastes the name "Solomon" never actually appears – the author/compiler being referred to throughout as *Qoheleth*, "Preacher," "Teacher," or literally, "Gatherer" – hence the Septuagint Greek title *Ekklesiastes*. We have already noted Solomon's reputation as a wise man and a lyricist, a proverbialist and an exponential polygamist; the Book of Ecclesiastes echoes other reputed aspects of his character as an ancient natural scientist (1 Kings 4:33, Ecclesiastes 2:4–6), and especially as the man who gathered all Israel together at the dedication of the Jerusalem Temple, preached a famed sermon, and taught them a great prayer for the nation (1 Kings 8:14–61). So gathering, preaching, and teaching also belong to the great king's scriptural portfolio. Clearly, the book had a later editor – perhaps in the post-exilic era like Psalms and Proverbs – who attached the opening attribution (1:1) and the final comment (12:9–12). But while Solomonic authorship remains beyond complete proof, it is likely that at least a significant part of *Qoheleth's* text was contributed by the disenchanted old "son of David."

Beyond dispute is that Ecclesiastes contrasts strikingly with the Book of Proverbs. Where Proverbs makes its case for cautious self-management toward a prosperous life, Ecclesiastes instead proposes disillusioned humility in the face of life's inevitable disappointments. Where Proverbs attacks greed, lust, and folly in the name of exalted wisdom, Ecclesiastes laments the difficulty of telling wisdom from folly, and attacks ethical overconfidence as "vanity." Where Proverbs is optimistic about the possibility of earthly human happiness for the righteous, Ecclesiastes is pessimistic about any kind of stable happiness "under the sun." It is also significant that while the Proverbs usually employ God's more intimate covenant name *Yahweh* (transliterated "the LORD" in most English Bibles), Ecclesiastes speaks of God as the more distant, more generic *Elohim*.

Much has been said about these differences, and about the question of which perspective is primary, or more advanced, or more "modern." If "modernism" is the test, then Ecclesiastes would seem the winner: two great literary novels of the early twentieth century take their titles from the book (*The Golden Bowl*, by Henry James, and *The Sun Also Rises*, by Ernest Hemingway), not to mention a popular murder mystery (*Evil Under the Sun*, by Agatha Christie), a science fiction classic (*Earth Abides*, by George R. Stewart), and a rock anthem of the 1960s that recasts Ecclesiastes 3:1–8, one of the book's most famous passages ("Turn! Turn! Turn!" by Pete Seeger and the Byrds). Even more importantly, Ecclesiastes seems to anticipate the Existentialist philosophies of Søren Kierkegaard, Jean-Paul Sartre, and Albert Camus, and the outlooks and attitudes of our more secular, disenchanted age, with its suspicion of authority, its skepticism about moral absolutes, and its reflexively ironic turn of mind.

But these overlaps with our own times shouldn't lead us to reduce the book to contemporary terms, nor to over-read its contrasts with Proverbs. Its remarkable differences mark *Qoheleth's* book not as a direct opposition to Proverbs, but as a distinctively independent-minded life experiment: what can "the wisest of men" – the classic "man who has everything" – learn about life's value by living only on his own vast resources and relying only on his own insight, without reference to divine revelation? What literary form should this counter-wisdom take? And how will its discoveries speak back to the wisdom in Proverbs that begins with "fear of the LORD?"

4.2.1 "Under the Sun": Living by Mortal Light

Few books have a more distinctive opening, or make a more sweeping statement about the meaning of life:

> "Vanity of vanities," says the Preacher;
> "Vanity of vanities, all is vanity!"
> What profit has a man from all his labor
> In which he toils under the sun? (1:2–3)

Beginning with his conclusion (the same pessimistic outcry that will end his discourse in 12:8), the Preacher asserts the emptiness of all things, and asks, rhetorically, what anyone really gains from life "under the sun" – a phrase that he will repeat twenty-nine times in the course of the book. It's a phrase that invokes the sun, usually seen more positively as the highest point in the heavens, as a kind of boundary separating God's heaven above it from the earth beneath it; and the phrase also evokes the unique weight of the sun felt in arid and desert lands, where the landscape becomes the sun's anvil at noon.

Thus, "under the sun" is, for the Preacher, figurative shorthand for a more complex statement of context: "in this present weary world, burdened and confined beneath the sun's arc, and lit by merely mortal light." Hamlet captures the essence of this outlook – he may have been reading Ecclesiastes at Wittenberg! – in his answer to Rosencrantz and Guildenstern about his mental state:

> I have of late – but wherefore I know not – lost all my mirth, forgone all custom of exercises; and indeed it goes so heavily with my disposition that this goodly frame, the earth, seems to me a sterile promontory, this most excellent canopy, the air, look you, this brave o'erhanging firmament, this majestical roof fretted with golden fire, why, it appears no other thing to me than a foul and pestilent congregation of vapors. (Hamlet 2.2.296–304)[3]

In this frame of mind, the world itself seems a close and musty prison (so says Hamlet too), a place of confinement that provides no rewards which can be taken away beyond its walls. So also the Preacher's words "labor" and "toil" (both from the Hebrew *amal*), portray all work "under the sun" as mixed with irksome frustration and void of any lasting fruit.

The most obvious question about the Preacher's complaint is this: What can the great King Solomon – or for that matter, Prince Hamlet – possibly know about toil? How can a monarch, especially a bon vivant like the son of David, understand the plight of a laborer, or feel the weight of frustrated, backbreaking effort? Isn't it laughable that a man with a thousand wives, the lord of imperial revenues, not to mention those gifts from the Queen of Sheba (1 Kings 10:1–13), has the chutzpah to complain about a lack of profit? Yet the Preacher's response to this question is powerful and disarming in its very audacity. Who better to know the worthlessness of wealth than the rich? Who better to know the futility of knowledge than the wisest of men? Who better to know the vanity of human wishes than someone who has indulged every heart's desire?

And the Preacher has indeed taken advantage of every opportunity to "know," in every sense of the word:

> I said of laughter, "It is mad," and of pleasure, "What use is it?" I searched with my heart how to cheer my body with wine – my heart still guiding me with wisdom – and how to lay hold on folly, till I might see what was good for the children of men to do under heaven during the few days of their life. I made great works. I built houses and planted vineyards for myself. I made myself gardens and parks, and planted in them all kinds of fruit trees. I made myself pools from which to water the forest of growing trees. I bought male and female slaves, and had slaves who were born in my house. I had also great possessions of herds and flocks, more than any who had been before me in Jerusalem. I also gathered for myself silver and gold and the treasure of kings and provinces. I got singers, both men and women, and many concubines, the delight of the sons of men. (2:2–8)

If Solomon were founding a university, he would be the Head and Principal Investigator and chief funder of every department: Humor Studies, Practical Oenology, Architecture, Viticulture, Horticulture, Arboriculture, Water Reclamation, Slave Economics, Animal Husbandry, Metallurgy, Finance, Museum Studies, Vocal Music, Applied Concubine Studies – not to mention his endowed chairs in Philosophy, and in Sacred and Erotic Poetry. Admittedly, a few of these departments would and should be illegal nowadays, but the restless, inquiring spirit of his larger project anticipates the ambitions of the European "Renaissance Man" or of great modern research institutions like the University of Chicago, with its Latin motto, *Crescat scientia, vita excolatur* ("As knowledge increases, so life is enriched").

Yet what are the findings of Solomon's investigation into all these ways of knowing? What is his research report?

> Then I looked on all the works that my hands had done
> And on the labor in which I had toiled;
> And indeed all was vanity and grasping for the wind.
> There was no profit under the sun. (2:11)

In fact, if *Qoheleth* University were to have its own Latin motto, it would dissent significantly from the modern notion of intellectual progress: *Qui addit scientiam addat et laborem* ("He who increases knowledge increases sorrow" – 1:18). Imagine those words on the front of a college library – next to *frequensque meditatio carnis adflictio est* ("and much study is weariness of the flesh" – 12:12). What the insatiably curious Solomon claims to have learned is that knowledge, like money, can't buy happiness; quite the opposite.

4.2.2 "The Wind Whirls About": Cycles and Cynicism

What else has the Preacher learned from his long life experiment in seeing only what appears by the mortal light of the sun, and knowing only by his senses? He has observed that, to his extreme frustration,

> One generation passes away, and another generation comes;
> But the earth abides forever.

The sun also rises, and the sun goes down,
And hastens to the place where it arose.
The wind goes toward the south,
And turns around to the north;
The wind whirls about continually,
And comes again on its circuit.
All the rivers run into the sea,
Yet the sea is not full;
To the place from which the rivers come,
There they return again.
All things are full of labor;
Man cannot express it.
The eye is not satisfied with seeing,
Nor the ear filled with hearing.
That which has been is what will be,
That which is done is what will be done,
And there is nothing new under the sun. (1:4–9)

The earth and all its forces are cyclical, and therefore, says the world-weary Preacher, there can be no real gains. Ideas of progress and of novelty are illusions, he says: "Is there anything of which it may be said, 'See, this is new'? / It has already been in ancient times before us" (1:10). If transported to our own time, shown the latest smart phone, and told that he can use it to call an unknown land named "Australia" or view moving pictures sent from a place called "America," he might ask what the calls and pictures would be about. "Love. Death. Beauty. Money. Power," we might reply. "See," he would answer, returning the phone, "there is nothing new under the sun."

Yet, as hard as the Preacher is on the idea of progress, he also dismisses conservative nostalgia with a wave: "Say not, 'Why were the former days better than these?' / For it is not from wisdom that you ask this" (7:10). The closest he gets to an idealized past is his brief concession that in the beginning, "God made man upright," but he adds immediately that "they have sought out many schemes" (7:29). Since Eden was lost, the Preacher assumes, all has been deviation and cycle and flux.

So it is strikingly appropriate that the Preacher's book is built around circles and cycles and repetitions, to a degree remarkable even for Hebrew poetry. Just as the wind whirls about, so do his themes: the cycles of life (1:2–11), the vanity of wisdom (1:12–18, 2:12–23, 4:13–16), the grief brought by pleasure (2:1–11), the seasons of life (3:1–8), the goodness of labor (3:9–15, 11:1–6), the persistence of injustice (3:16–22, 5:8–9), the emptiness of labor (4:1–8), the need for friendship (4:9–12), the place of reverence (5:1–7), the absurdity of wealth and fame (5:10–20), the absurdity of death and appetite (6:1–12), the value of wisdom (7:1–22, 9:13–18, 10:1–20), the folly of women and men (7:23–29), the power of kings (8:1–9), the mysteries of God (8:10–17), the randomness of life (9:1–12), the folly of youth (11:7–10), the tragedy of old age (12:1–12). The question that naturally arises when reading around in these cycles: Do they enact the Preacher's overall conclusion – the vanity of all earthly life – by being vain and meaningless themselves? In other words, if wisdom and achievement and wealth and pleasure don't bring happiness in this world, is there anything that does?

One possible answer is found in the signature phrases that cycle through the book along with its themes: not only "vanity of vanities" and "under the sun," but also "what does it profit," "chasing after wind," "I looked and I saw," "I said to myself/in my heart," "there is an evil that I have seen," and "so that no man can find out." All of these phrases stress the futility of seeking ultimate answers through empirical observation, since the everyday details of life tend to contradict human hopes that life will treat us fairly or explain itself to us.

Yet one particular phrase does suggest that there is after all a secret to some happiness "under the sun": the phrase "enjoy your toil" and its variants, especially when it is paired with the phrase "this is the gift of God." For instance, having declared in chapter 2 the disappointed grief that results from pursuing empirical knowledge and hedonistic pleasure, the Preacher turns to announce, "There is nothing better for a person than that he should eat and drink and find enjoyment in his toil. This also, I saw, is from the hand of God" (2:24). Again, after the famous poem of life's turning seasons in chapter 3, the Preacher adds that "everyone should eat and drink and take pleasure in all his toil – this is God's gift to man" (3:13). And again, "everyone also to whom God has given wealth and possessions and power to enjoy them, and to accept his lot and rejoice in his toil – this is the gift of God" (5:19). These words might seem to appeal naturally to the modern, Western ear. After all, we may ask, "If there is a God, doesn't he want me to be happy? And what will make me happier than a lucrative and satisfying career?" Yet of course the word used is not "career" with its implications of self-definition, security, steady income, and peer recognition; rather, the word is "toil," which as we've noted translates Hebrew *amal*, with its strong connotations of misery, frustration, weariness, and pain. With its echoes of the Genesis curse – more on this in our next chapter – it presents us with a paradox: "learn to find pleasure amid the thorns and burdens of work after Eden." Or, to put that curse more colloquially, "Enjoy your damn job! And knock back a beer and a big meal after work. Take the little pleasures when you can – the big ones are a letdown."

Finally, after numerous repetitions, the Preacher reaches his climactic statement on the topic of "toil":

> Enjoy life with the wife whom you love, all the days of your vain life that he has given you under the sun, because that is your portion in life and in your toil at which you toil under the sun. Whatever your hand finds to do, do it with your might, for there is no work or thought or knowledge or wisdom in the grave, where you are going. (9:9–10)

Imagine these words on a wedding card – the sardonic addition of "vain" into the celebration of marital bliss, the reminder of the grave slipped into its call to hard work. Certainly this is a call to live "in the moment," to seize the day; yet if this is carpe diem, it is a strangely domestic and responsible kind, seizing not the girl of the moment or a roll of the dice, but the wife of one's youth and the tools of one's trade. Here we seem to intersect briefly with the world of Proverbs, but with a striking difference in tone and in context, for what follows immediately is one of the most famously cynical passages among all the cycles in Ecclesiastes:

> I returned and saw under the sun that –
> The race is not to the swift,
> Nor the battle to the strong,
> Nor bread to the wise,
> Nor riches to men of understanding,
> Nor favor to men of skill;
> But time and chance happen to them all. (9:11)

These words are "cynical" in both the modern and the ancient senses of the term: in the modern sense, because the Preacher disbelieves in the innate sincerity or goodness of human motives and actions, and in the ancient sense of the Greek "Cynic" philosophers because he rejects wealth, fame and power as measures of human success.

Ecclesiastes and Classical Philosophy

Many modern scholars have noticed resemblances not only between Ecclesiastes and the Cynic philosophers of ancient Greece and Rome, but also between the books and the ideas of both the Epicureans and the Stoics. Like *Qoheleth*, the Cynics also rejected riches, worldly glory and power as the marks of human value; the Stoics also recognized the vanity of life's pleasures and pains; while the Epicureans also taught that the search for human pleasure and happiness is the purpose of being.

Yet Ecclesiastes's outlook differs from each of these in important ways. Unlike the Cynics, the Preacher never recommends asceticism or withdrawal from the social order; unlike the Stoics, he cannot and does not remain indifferent to the pleasures or the pains of life; and unlike the Epicureans, he treats pleasure not as the highest good, but (like pain) as a message from God.

Was Ecclesiastes influenced by or responding to the Greco-Roman classics? While not completely impossible – assuming that the book was not completed until the fourth or third centuries BCE – neither hypothesis is likely or necessary. Human nature and experience are sufficiently similar in widely different places and times to account for Greeks in the fourth century BCE sounding like a Hebrew long before in the tenth. As the Preacher says, "there is nothing new under the sun."

4.2.3 "Remember Your Creator": The End and the Beginning

Yet what distinguishes the Preacher from cynicisms both ancient and modern is his assertion, against the grain of all the world's demonstrated vanity, evil, and randomness, that love and work are still somehow intrinsically good, because they are the gifts of God. As far as daily practical living is concerned, *Qoheleth* is certain that the disillusioned life is the best (or least bad) mode of existence simply because he believes the happiest people to be those who "enjoy their toil," who don't expect much from life and so are sometimes pleasantly surprised. Here then is the outcome of the Preacher's life experiment: his failed quest for lasting happiness and meaning "under the sun" actually succeeds, he says, in discovering some spiritual bedrock amid the flux – in the experience of domestic happiness, and in life's small pleasures. Human love and the glimmers of joy enduring through earth's cycles and seasons form *Qoheleth's* evidence that human beings are ultimately not designed to live by mortal light alone, but are made to yearn for a life beyond the sun. "I have seen the God-given task with which the sons of men are to be occupied," says the Preacher. "God has made everything beautiful in its time. Also he has put eternity in their hearts, except that no one can find out the work that God does from beginning to end" (3:10–11).

"Eternity in their hearts" is a remarkable expression from a speaker who puts little stock in an afterlife (3:18–21, but 12:7), who sometimes talks of the grave as final (9:10), and who recommends against chatty intimacy with God: "for God is in heaven and you are on earth. Therefore let your words be few" (5:2). But while the Book of Ecclesiastes certainly provides an antidote to any neat creeds of positive thinking or prosperity gospels of pie in the sky, it grows from the same root as the Bible's sunnier book of wisdom – the root of "remember your Creator." When all in Ecclesiastes has been said and done (frequently more than once), the Preacher ends at the beginning, by returning to the Creation, warning the old, and especially the young, to recall who made them: "Remember also your Creator in the days of your youth, before the evil days come and the years draw near of which you will say, 'I have no pleasure in them'" (12:1). What follows is a figurative description of advancing bodily decline, with its moving final exhortation to trust the Creator "before the silver cord is snapped, or the golden bowl is broken, or the pitcher is shattered at the fountain, or the wheel broken at the cistern, and the dust returns to the earth as it was, and the spirit returns to God who gave it. Vanity of vanities, says the Preacher; all is vanity" (12:6–8).

Yet even here Ecclesiastes shows a double motion: while returning to the foundational genesis of all things, the book also reverts back to its own initial outburst, refusing finally to rest, concluding in restlessness. But it is a restlessness whose dissatisfaction and disillusion with earth serve ultimately to draw the reader's attention upwards to heaven. In the end, old King Solomon is rich and weary in all of his faded glory, and his sober but bracing, persistently restless book is both a farewell and a call for a new beginning.

However, after *Qoheleth's* ending, the book's later editor (or editors) thought that another conclusion was necessary, and so added a coda commenting briefly on the Preacher's content and summarizing his message. Like the concluding passage in the Book of Job, the coda of Ecclesiastes has been regarded by some modern commentators as an uneasy attempt to contain or deny the book's heretical potential. No doubt this editorial coda does attempt to relieve or resolve the book's signature restlessness, and to reconcile it with larger biblical themes of obedience and coming judgment. Yet this postscript's summary of the Preacher's message reiterates points repeated throughout the book and stressed in his final two chapters: "Fear God and keep his commandments, for this is the whole duty of man. For God will bring every deed into judgment, with every secret thing, whether good or evil" (12:13–24). Thus, the editors' ending is more a matter of taste than of doctrine, and our reaction may be as well. Do we like our wisdom neat or more unkempt? Do we prefer riddles or solutions? Journeys or arrivals? Or do we love everything "in its season"? We have asked such questions before, and we will ask them again. Perhaps, once more, the Bible is reading us.

Questions for Discussion

1   Over what range of time were the **Proverbs** likely composed? When, probably, were they assembled into their current form, and by whom? To what writers are the differing sections of Proverbs traditionally attributed? To whom are the most proverbs credited? What do these attributions mean in Hebrew and Christian tradition?

2   What, according to the Book of Proverbs, is **wisdom**? How is it defined, where does it come from, and how is it discovered or discerned? What are the results and rewards of wisdom?

3   With what audience or audiences do the Proverbs seem chiefly concerned, particularly in chapters 1–9? How might the **personifications** of **Wisdom** and **Folly** be designed to address these audiences' special interests and problems? How, particularly, are wisdom and desire related?

4   How do **Folly and Wisdom** resemble each other? What are their crucial differences that account for their opposing identities? What do these similarities and differences mean?

5   What do the **sayings of Lemuel** in chapter 31 seem to assume about the places and roles of **women in Hebrew society**?

6   Why were so many individual Proverbs apparently composed to be **riddling** and somewhat obscure? How might a reader go about opening up and interpreting a proverb? A thematic group or cluster of proverbs?

7 Over what range of time was the Book of **Ecclesiastes** likely composed? When, probably, was it assembled into their current form, and by whom? To whom is most of the book traditionally credited? What do these attributions mean in Hebrew and Christian tradition?

8 In what ways does Ecclesiastes function as a statement of **counter-wisdom** in relation to Proverbs? According to *Qoheleth*, the Preacher, what is wisdom? How is it defined, where does it come from, and how is it discovered or discerned? What are the results and rewards of wisdom? What are its disappointments and limits?

9 How does the phrase **"under the sun"** serve to define the extent and the limits of the book's wisdom? What might Ecclesiastes deliberately "not know" because of this perspective?

10 How does the **cyclical** structure of Ecclesiastes relate to and even enact its seemingly jaded and cynical attitude about the "**vanity**" of life "under the sun"?

11 In the world of chance and flux imagined by *Qoheleth*, what are the constants, and how can the young, and the old, discover and experience what lasts? What further comment does the **editorial coda** at the book's end make back on the meditations of the Preacher?

Notes

1 "Do you see a man wise in his own eyes? / There is more hope for a fool than for him."
2 In the Hebrew Bible, all three of the traditionally Solomonic books appear in this order among the *Khetuvim* or "Writings" notable for their art and beauty, though interspersed with Job, Ruth, and Lamentations; in the Christian Old Testament, these same three Solomonic texts appear at the end of a similar Poetical and Wisdom group ordered as Job, Psalms, Proverbs, Ecclesiastes, and the Song of Solomon.
3 *Hamlet, Prince of Denmark*, in *The Complete Works of Shakespeare*, edited by David Bevington (New York: Harper Collins, 1992), 1082.

5

Origin Narrative I: Divine Images in Genesis

It has been this textbook's plan to follow the example of classical epic – and many a modern thriller – by starting *in medias res*, "in the middle of things." So, after discussing Hebrew reading practices and theories of biblical composition, we began by featuring biblical books associated with the Davidic and Solomonic "Golden Age," long after the traditional dates of the Patriarchs and the Exodus. These books appear not at the beginning but in the middle of the Old Testament: Psalms, Proverbs, Ecclesiastes, the Song of Solomon. This focus on the literature of the "midway" period in Israelite history has introduced us to some central features of the ancient Hebrew imagination: its special excellence at poetry; its aesthetic of self-examination and psychological discovery; its reliance on doubling devices such as parallelism and refrain; its development of historically layered texts out of multiple documents; and, resulting from all these factors, a "stereoscopic vision," which insists that seeing deep and whole requires more than one point of view.

Along the way we have already made substantial reference to the Bible's first book, Genesis. We have seen how it illustrates ancient Hebrew habits of mind with its "deep doubling" of Creation and patriarchal stories, and have asked how it came to be composed and canonized. Genesis provides essential contexts for everything from the Psalms' visions of cosmic divine power, to Ecclesiastes' struggle with sin-cursed toil, to the Proverbs' picture of Lady Wisdom present at the Creation. Now we turn to a fuller and closer look at Genesis. A literary study like this will not pretend to answer fully the myriad historical and theological questions that this book has raised over the millennia. Instead, we will focus on the artistry of its form and on its unique system of imagery. More specifically, we will consider its distinct narrative style; its alternate angles of vision on the creation of the cosmos; its portrait of humanity "in God's image"; that divine image in relation to human worth, gender difference, sexual relations, and marriage; and its story about the origin of sin and death. In the following chapter, we'll examine its other foundational stories about the patriarchal system, and the covenants that define the children of Adam, Noah, and Abraham. Finally, we'll analyze the crowning narrative of Joseph and his brothers, a book-within-a-book that ends these beginnings with Israel's transition from being the name of an individual father, to that of a family, a tribe, and a nation.

5.1 Biblical Narrative Style: The Elements

5.1.1 Minimalism

It is not difficult to find literary critics and famed authors writing in praise of the Bible's style, and generally what they admire above all is its remarkable quality of **minimalism** or understatement. In his classic study *The Art of Biblical Narrative*, Robert Alter asks, in a chapter entitled "Characterization and the Art of Reticence,"

Literary Study of the Bible: An Introduction, First Edition. Christopher Hodgkins.
© 2020 John Wiley & Sons Ltd. Published 2020 by John Wiley & Sons Ltd.

> How does the Bible manage to evoke such a sense of depth and complexity in its representation of character with what would seem to be such sparse, even rudimentary means?… In what way … is one to explain how, from these laconic texts, figures like Rebekah, Jacob, Joseph, Judah, Tamar, Moses, Saul, David, and Ruth emerge, characters who, beyond any archetypal role they may play as bearers of a divine mandate, have been etched as indelibly vivid individuals in the imagination of a hundred generations?[1]

Alter is awed by the uncanny ability of biblical narrators to write in the way that successful sketch artists draw: by leaving out everything except the lines that matter, the details that tell by showing. Some great novelists are, if anything, even more impressed with the biblical style. Mark Twain – hardly a model of religious sentiment or piety – writes with undisguised wonder in *The Innocents Abroad*:

> Who taught those ancient writers their simplicity of language, their felicity of expression, their pathos, and above all, their faculty of sinking themselves entirely out of sight of the reader and making the narrative stand out alone and seem to tell itself? Shakespeare is always present when one reads his book; Macaulay is present when we follow the march of his stately sentences; but the Old Testament writers are hidden from view.[2]

And as a special kind of amplified compliment, note the example of Ernest Hemingway, who always claimed that his famous stripped-down prose was modeled on none other than Mark Twain, the style sheet of *The Kansas City Star*, and the Bible. Somehow, thousands of years before the invention of terms like "modernist," "minimalist," or "functionalist," the writers of the Pentateuch, the books of Joshua, Judges, Ruth, Samuel, and Kings, discovered what *not* to say, and learned to render – in Hemingway's words – "the sequence of motion and fact which made the emotion."[3] Obviously, the admirers of this reticent prose style are anything but reticent about it – but are moved precisely by what it leaves to the imagination. And "moved" is the right word: for these writers and critics, it is the Bible's very lack of sentimentalism that actually stirs their feelings.

Examples of narrative minimalism in Genesis, as in other Old Testament prose books, are beyond counting, though we will have cause to glance at quite a few in this chapter. For now, one instance will be enough. Consider the notorious interlude of Judah and Tamar in Genesis 38, which interrupts the story of Joseph's betrayal and sale by his brothers and his enslavement in Egypt. Commenting on this passage, Robert Alter notes that the story of Judah's marriage and fatherhood

> is recorded at a breathless pace… [N]othing is allowed to detract our focused attention from the primary, problematic subject of the proper channel for the [chosen] seed [of Jacob]. In a triad of verbs … Judah sees, takes, and lies with a woman; and she … conceives, bears, and … gives the son a name. Then, with no narrative indication of any events at all in the intervening time, we move ahead an entire generation…[4]

Then, again in rapid succession, Judah marries his oldest son Er to Tamar, God kills Er (without explanation), Onan takes Er's place in the marriage bed but – in a shocking and telling detail – Onan "emitted on the ground" rather than impregnate Tamar in his brother's name, so that the LORD kills Onan too. It is only then that the narrator slows to a pace that allows for the back-and-forth of dialogue, and for time to pass in days and weeks rather than in decades.

In other words, however many fascinated questions we have about the characters' feelings and motives over these two generations, these omitted details are all subordinate to the main event.

That event is the wry tale in the rest of the chapter about how, by impersonating a prostitute, Tamar fools the wily, lecherous Judah into "raising up seed" for her (she has twins!), and publicly exposes her hypocritical father-in-law to boot. As we will see confirmed many times, none of these biblical narratives claims to be an exhaustive record of its subjects' lives; instead, each is sparsely selective and carefully shaped to the master-narrative of human redemption through God's covenant people.

5.1.2 Wordplay

A second pervasive element of biblical narrative style is its **wordplay** – much of which, however, is usually overlooked due to conversion from Hebrew to other languages. "Reading the Bible in translation," said the modern Jewish poet Hayim Nahman Bialik, "is like kissing your new bride through a veil."[5] However good the vernacular version, the full intimacy and texture of the Hebrew is obscured or lost – and nowhere is this truer than with literary wordplay. Like any language, biblical Hebrew is alive with homonyms, assonances, consonances, and rhymes – all rich material for the literary artist who wishes to heighten the impact of his composition through sound effects and double entendres, nearly all of which evaporate when the original is rendered into another tongue. A close look at about any page of the original Hebrew text will reward close examination with fresh and even startling insight.

For instance, in the Genesis 37–39 passage just mentioned above, where a scandalous story from Judah's life interrupts the harrowing account of Joseph sold by his brothers down to Egypt, attention paid to the Hebrew phrasing sharpens our sense of character and intensifies the passage's moral implications. While oldest brother Reuben responds to the news of Joseph's enslavement by rending his garments and speaking a couple laconic words of grief, father Jacob responds with a more elaborate, self-dramatizing ritual and speech, complete with poetic rhythms and a pun: *hayáh ra'ha 'akhaláthu/tárof toráf Yoséf.*[6] None of these nuances comes through in even that most poetic of English translations, the King James Version: "Joseph is without doubt rent in pieces" (37:33). Significantly, these Hebrew verbal effects augment our sense of character: Reuben, something of a rotter up to this point, appears in a surprisingly sympathetic light; Jacob, on the other hand, has not yet broken free of his self-centered focus.

So, while moderns tend to associate puns with jokes and clumsy humor, we see that in the Bible – as in Shakespeare – this kind of wordplay often comments in subtle ways on very serious action. While the truest delights of Hebrew wordplay are for those who have mastered the language for themselves, we will note and explain many examples of such wordplay as they add to our understanding of particular representative stories.

5.1.3 Doubling and Repetition

Far more translatable is that distinctive feature of Hebrew literary style: its constant **doubling and repetition**. Our previous discussions of "Reading Like a Hebrew," and of the Psalms, have observed how in poetry, we see plentiful varieties of parallelism, refrain, and litany. Turning now to the narrative mode, we see these doubling devices sometimes working alongside those devices of wordplay just described above. Key terms and phrases are repeated in altered contexts to highlight changes in characters' feelings, ideas, circumstances, and their moral or spiritual positions. In other cases more obvious in translation, doubling operates at the macro-textual level, as the same or similar speeches, dreams, incidents, and whole accounts are repeated, sometimes exactly, sometimes with meaningful variations.

So, to take varied examples of artful repetition from Genesis alone, chapters 1 and 2 describe the Creation from very different angles; God makes humanity "in his image" in 1:28, while Adam bears a son "in his ... image" in 5:3; the LORD covenants with Abraham three separate times (12, 15, 17); Abraham and Isaac on three occasions deceive a foreign king by passing a wife off as a "sister" (12, 20, 26); and Sarah angrily exiles Hagar from the camp twice (16, 21). So Abraham's faithful servant confirms his divine mission by repeating to Laban the story of how he found the beautiful Rebekah at the well (24); Jacob swindles Esau twice and then finds the beautiful Rachel at the same well (25, 27, 29); while Abraham and Jacob both father sons by their wives' maids (16, 30). Furthermore, God twice meets Jacob at Bethel (28, 35); two of Joseph's fellow prisoners dream, and Pharaoh dreams twice (40, 41); and God repeatedly favors the younger over the firstborn (4, 21, 25, 48, 49). Bear in mind that this extensive list is nowhere near exhaustive. It is as if, to contrast with the generally minimalist style of biblical prose, strategic bursts of language and narration stress central themes – like fountains of words springing from a beautiful but arid landscape of understatement.

5.1.4 Juxtaposition

Another stylistic element common to both Hebrew poetry and prose is **juxtaposition**, the placing of two seemingly unrelated passages or elements together without transition in order to suggest a relationship. We've already observed that this device, when used in the Psalms, intriguingly anticipates quick cinematic cross-cutting. In prose, its use also suggests the effects of certain films – grand visions like *Citizen Kane*, *The Godfather*, and *Amadeus* come to mind – in which profound comparisons and contrasts can be suggested simply by the splicing of two sequences or sets of elements: the burning of an old sled named "Rosebud" followed by the close-up of a sign that warns "NO TRESPASSING"; the baptism of an infant interspersed with the assassinations of the heads of five crime "families"; the mournful glory of Mozart's *Requiem Mass* soaring over the image of the composer's corpse dumped into a mass paupers' grave and dusted with lime.

The juxtapositions of Genesis also carry thematic weight: the theft of Eden's fruit followed by the murder of Abel (chapters 3, 4); Noah's deliverance from the Flood on Mount Ararat followed by the story of his drunken shame (9); the sudden brief appearance of the mysterious Melchizedek to accept Abram's tithe (14); and the joyous birth of Isaac to Sarah followed by Sarah's angry exile of Hagar and Ishmael – and then by God's command to sacrifice Isaac (21, 22). Also, Jacob's terrified preparation to meet Esau is followed by Esau's warm welcome – followed then by the grotesque story of the rape of Dinah and the massacre of the Shechemites (32, 33, 34); the selling of Joseph by Judah and the brothers is followed by the story of Judah's relations with Tamar, followed by Joseph's refusal of Potiphar's wife (37, 38, 39); and Joseph's triumph in Egypt is followed by his mistaken request that Jacob bless his firstborn (48). Again, this list is nowhere near exhaustive; each instance comes as a narrative surprise, and it is such surprises that spur much textual insight. So if when reading Genesis we trip over that stubborn oddball passage or incident that interrupts what we think is the smooth flow of the storyline, we should stop, stoop, and give it a good close look – we may have found a key to its truest sense.

5.1.5 Deferred Judgment

Perhaps the most unexpected element of biblical narrative style, especially in Genesis, is its quality of **deferred judgment** – that is, the narrator's surprising reluctance to pronounce on the morality of characters' actions. We may see this reticence as related to narrative minimalism, but for many readers, whether believing or skeptical, it is surprising because we expect the Bible to be the most moral, or at least moralistic, of books. Why then do so many biblical characters, many of them founding fathers and mothers of faith, behave so badly so often and for so long with so little said about it? Abraham and Jacob in particular accumulate disturbingly long lists of wrongdoing with scarcely a word of narrative condemnation.

We've already glanced at some examples, and can add others: Abraham virtually prostitutes his wife Sarah in the courts of two Gentile kings to protect his own life (chapters 12, 20); he impregnates Sarah's maid Hagar – at Sarah's urging; and he casts the pregnant Hagar out of the camp – also at Sarah's urging (15). Abraham's grandson Jacob more than fulfills his birth-name (literally "heel-grabber," that is "supplanter" or "deceiver"), swindling his brother Esau out of both birthright and blessing (25, 27), in the second case by taking advantage of his aged father Isaac's blindness; he is maneuvered into a polygamous relationship with two wives and two concubines (29); and he fails to take action when his daughter Dinah is raped by a princeling in Canaan (34). Jacob's sons – namesakes of the eventual tribes of Israel – are even worse: Simeon engineers a horrific massacre as grotesque vengeance for Dinah's rape (34); Reuben "lies with" his father's concubine Bilhah (the mother of his half-brothers Dan and Naphtali – 35:22); and Judah leads his brothers in selling Joseph into slavery, while engaging in risky recreational sex when traveling on business (37, 38). Even a relatively straight arrow like Isaac repeats Abraham's "she's-my-sister" act (26).

Also, the women of the family are no ordinary schemers themselves: Sarah, Rachel, and Leah exploit their slave women's wombs (15, 29, 30); Rebekah hoodwinks her visually handicapped husband to secure Jacob's blessing (27); and Leah entraps Jacob into marriage, after which she and her sister Rachel maneuver for conjugal rights on any given night (29, 30). And need I mention that patriarchal family life is well-nigh poisoned by favoritism – favorite spouses and children and siblings?

Meanwhile, what does the narrator have to say? The voice is straightforward, reportorial, and as already noted, strikingly understated. But if we are paying attention to the events described, our response is likely to be anything but dispassionate. To quote Hemingway again, if the narrator's purpose is to reproduce "the sequence of motion and fact which made the emotion," then the emotion made is often shock, bordering on dismay – especially if we were expecting from this great religious book something like ideal saints. So occasional readers who merely dip casually into episodes out of context – or certain higher critics who already regard the text as a historically accidental melange – may well come away disenchanted, even repulsed, by the biblical text. After all, it portrays some undeniably repulsive behavior, frequently without comment.

However, to revise a popular slogan, judgment deferred is not necessarily judgment denied. In fact, there is a profound link between style and substance on this point, so that in some sense the medium really *is* the message. For as we look both backward and forward from the central arc of the patriarchal narrative in Genesis we begin to recognize two textual facts: first, that from the very beginning of human sin in Chapter 3, deferred judgment is a sign not of God's neglect, but of his patience and mercy; and second, that invariably in the course of the book, judgment does come, not usually in the form of the narrator's pronouncement, but rather in the form of an event in the story that usually we would call "poetic justice." That is, each crime finds its own fitting punishment, which often is paid out with interest, but also with grace.

As to the first of these points, even in the early chapters of Genesis, where the Deity intervenes directly to punish sin, the punishment is always to some degree delayed or softened. For eating the forbidden fruit, Adam and Eve had been told "in the day that you eat of it you shall surely die" (2:15), but it is a very long "day," stretching, according to biblical chronology, nearly a thousand years before Adam's death (5:5). When Cain murders Abel, he frets that others – not

God! – will take his life, but the LORD instead puts a special protective "mark" on Cain to ward off attackers (4:15).[7] As the generations and centuries pass from murderous Cain, and humanity grows ever more wicked, God defers judgment so long that finally evil is pervasive and "the earth is filled with violence" (6:13), necessitating a worldwide punishment in the form of a flood – which is itself ameliorated by the survival of Noah. And after the builders of Babel provoke the LORD by claiming a "name" or authority equal to his (11:4), he responds not with more death, but simply decides to "confuse their language, that they may not understand one another's speech" (11:7), thus non-violently dispersing them over the earth.

So by the time the patriarch Abram enters the story, *Yahweh* has been well established in the text as, in the later words of Exodus, "merciful and gracious, longsuffering" – indeed a strangely patient and compassionate deity compared to the thunder-and-lightning gods of the age (34:6). This context is crucial for understanding the second main textual fact about deferred judgment in Genesis: that it will come in due time, that it will emerge from the course of events themselves, and that it will be fitting, often exquisitely so.

Abraham's misdeeds leave us waiting quite some time (decades, in fact) "for the other shoe to drop." We see signs of initial payback, perhaps, in his marital conflicts: Sarah may resent his past failure to protect her virtue in Egypt, and she goads him into the surrogate motherhood arrangement with slave girl Hagar, and when the gloriously pregnant Hagar grows haughty toward her mistress, Sarah bitterly blames Abraham. Furthermore, the child born to Hagar, while blessed and protected by God, does not bode well for the future of the Hebrews – Ishmael will be a stubborn adversary (16:7–12).

But the greatest payback to Abraham comes after the birth of the miracle child Isaac: having allowed the patriarch to flourish despite his sometimes underhanded dealings, and having given him the legitimate son that his heart desires, God commands the unthinkable: "Take now your son, your only son Isaac, whom you love, and go to the land of Moriah, and offer him there as a burnt offering on one of the mountains of which I shall tell you" (22:2). All of Abraham's wealth, and all the spiritual promises of the covenant, are personified in Isaac – and everything that Abraham has hoped and worked and sometimes connived for must now be given up in one stroke of a knife, along with the child of his heart. Of course, as the story famously turns out, on the downstroke of Abraham's knife God intervenes to substitute a sacrificial ram for Isaac, and confirm all the covenant blessings to Isaac's offspring. But the point here is that God requires at Abraham's hand the willingness to yield up all of his gains, both well- and ill-gotten.

The delayed judgment on Jacob is even more complex and at times darkly amusing. After swindling his father and his brother, he flees east to his mother Rebekah's family, and there he more than meets his match. His uncle Laban exploits Jacob's passion for his younger daughter Rachel, and in the dark (and perhaps inebriation) of the wedding night substitutes the older and presumably plainer Leah in the bridal bed (chapter 29). Maneuvered into polygamy and fourteen years of bride-price indenture to Laban, Jacob is constantly vexed by the warring sister-wives as each at different times struggles with barrenness and foists her slave girl on him for surrogate motherhood, with results that exponentially multiply Abraham's trials with Sarah. We witness spiteful family factions, quasi-incest, eventual mass murder, and the most heartbreaking betrayal: the enslavement of a brother by his brothers. Indeed, as we've already noted, Judah's plot to fool Jacob with the blood of a kid on Joseph's "many-colored" coat pays Jacob out (intentionally or not) for his similar hoodwinking of Isaac decades before. Though Jacob has been blessed with a burgeoning tribe of descendants and a great covenant promise, in his old age, the crippled, blind, and chastened patriarch sounds as dyspeptic as Ecclesiastes: "few and evil have been the days of the years of my life" (47:9). Clearly, Jacob's life has turned out both better and worse than he possibly could have imagined.

5.1.6   Irony – Sad, Happy, Complex

This difference between expectation and outcome brings us to the element of biblical narrative style that is the fruit of all the others: **irony**. Whether appearing as incidental sarcasm, as an episodic dissonance between appearance and reality, or as the epic distance between what's expected and what actually happens, irony consistently delivers the most powerful emotional effects throughout Genesis and the other narrative books. It is irony that, in Mark Twain's words, makes "the narrative stand out alone and seem to tell itself." And, contrary to much contemporary usage, irony, while often sad or grim, need not be so: reality can be far better and happier than appearances, and outcomes much more complex.

With a literary device this pervasive, a few examples will have to suffice. There is no shortage of **sad irony** in Genesis, which after all tells the story of how all human sadness began. Compare expectation and outcome in chapter 3: the serpent promises the woman (and her husband who is with her) that if they eat the forbidden fruit, "your eyes will be opened, and you will be like God [*Elohim*], knowing good and evil" (3:4). Interpreting the Hebrew idiom, the promise is that they will come into a new level of understanding; that they will be like gods, possessing comprehensive, independent knowledge – and so no longer need to rely on *Yahweh's* commands. Yet instead, when they take their first bites, "the eyes of both of them were opened, and they knew *that they were naked*" (3:7, my italics) – that is, they certainly came into a new level of understanding, but only as painful experience of how vulnerable and dependent they are in comparison to their almighty Creator. We will have more to say below about the wordplay in this lynchpin passage, but there could be no darker irony than the distance between omniscient Godhood and trembling exposure.

Other instances of sad or dark irony shadow the narrative: Lot chooses the beautiful "cities of the plain," Sodom and Gomorrah, an appearance that conceals a harsh reality, eventually making him a war refugee, a post-apocalyptic survivor, and the drunken father of bastard sons by his incestuous daughters (chapter 19). Jacob, having schemed for the sacred covenant birthright and blessing, sees his sons exploit the covenant sign of circumcision to incapacitate the men of Shechem and engineer their mass murder (34). Sometimes we force the door to heaven, and all hell breaks loose.

In vivid contrast to such grim turns are the answering instances of **happy irony** that brighten the narrative. Like photographic negatives of a night-time scene, these episodes shine with unexpected light. Among the happiest is the story of Isaac's birth: Sarah, long barren, eavesdrops from her tent when a divine visitor tells Abraham that, in her old age, she soon will bear a son. She laughs derisively at the promise, and when the LORD gently calls her out on it, she denies having laughed (18). Jump forward about a year, and Sarah is holding an infant, celebrating the gladdest surprise in her life: "God has made me laugh, and all who hear will laugh with me" (21:6), she says on the day of the boy's circumcision. And they name him Isaac – Hebrew *itzhak*, for "laughter." Sarah is happy that the joke is on her – or rather, on their gloomy pessimism. Similarly, when Jacob returns to Canaan with his huge family decades after his theft of the blessing, he expects to be massacred by Esau, but instead is embraced by him (33); and when Judah offers himself in Benjamin's place as a slave to the mysterious *Zaphnath-Paaneah*, Prime Minister of Egypt, he finds himself embraced and forgiven by his long-lost brother Joseph (44, 45). Sometimes we face our doom, and all heaven breaks loose.

But just as often as either of these sad or happy surprises, the narrative yields **mixed irony**, blending hope and fear, tears and happiness. In biblical narrative, there's usually a fly in the ointment, but there's also usually a silver lining to the cloud. We saw that the sordid story of Judah and Tamar ends with Judah's humiliation – and begins such a transformation of his character that by the end of Genesis he is willing to sacrifice his freedom to release his youngest brother.

And the ill-begotten sons of Judah and Tamar will have bright futures, especially Perez, the first son in a line that eventually will inherit the royal scepter (49:8–12). Yet it's a good wind indeed that blows no one any ill: while Joseph interprets the dream of Pharaoh's chief butler to predict his imminent release from prison, he interprets the chief baker's dream to predict imminent separation from his head – and from this life (40). Doubling the complexity of this irony is the fact that after his release "the chief butler did not remember Joseph, but forgot him" (40:23). And the triple irony is that the chief butler's memory of Joseph suddenly revives when the Pharaoh has a puzzling dream and the butler is eager to recommend "the young Hebrew" as an interpreter (41:9).

So irony plays a potent role from Genesis on. We have seen that it culminates the other signature devices of biblical narrative: minimalism makes every word tell while leaving room for mystery and imagination; wordplay capitalizes on especially loaded terms and phrases to pack them for maximum impact; doubling, repetition, and juxtaposition cue us that something rich and strange is brewing, without telling us what in full; deferred judgment raises the ethical and emotional stakes and heightens narrative tension; and well-executed irony releases these stored imaginative energies, in tragedy, in joy, and at times in bittersweet, wondering bafflement. In the best sense, style suits substance; the writers are hidden from view, the story tells itself, and the motions of the tale stir emotions that point us past the art itself toward a divine Artist.

5.2   Day of Days: Creation in Stereoscope

We already have said and seen a good deal about the composition and the structure of the opening chapters in Genesis, which tell and then retell how the world came to be. We observed that these two tellings, with their important differences and similarities, seem intended in their present form to be taken in together, rather than separately, and to be viewed as complementary, by analogy with our ordinary stereoscopic vision that enables us to see depth and roundness.

Furthermore, we've seen that while the present text of Genesis seems to have been assembled from some earlier individual documents, none that we know has survived, so that many late Victorian theories about their original nature – and about how they were spliced and combined – were largely or entirely speculative. Conversely, we have seen that those theories' complete rejection of second millennium composition, so confident a century ago, has grown increasingly uncertain as archeology, paleolinguistics, and other ancient documentary discoveries have made the case for a Genesis – and a Pentateuch – that were embedded in the contexts of Mesopotamia, Egypt and Canaan 2000–1400 BCE, though no doubt with some editing and redaction continuing over the next 1000 years.

In short, we are finally, in the early twenty-first century, positioned to read Genesis neither through the selective lens of one or another theological system, nor through the shattered lens of hyper-fragmentary documentary speculation, but to read *the text as we have it*, as a work of coherent literary art.[8] And the text as we have it asks us to view the act of creation from two stereoscopic angles, and portrays the Creator as practicing two kinds of creation: verbal and sculptural, or, if you like, poetry and pottery. In Chapter 1, we already discussed in some detail the many stereoscopic effects of reading these richly juxtaposed Creation accounts. We've seen how in Genesis 1 God speaks the world into being with the quiet authority of a bard, proclaiming light into the darkness, order into the chaos, then calling forth all breathing life – and finally humanity – to displace the void. We've seen how in Genesis 2 the LORD God like an artisan molds a man out of red clay, breathes him to life, and then molds a woman out of the man's side, from near his heart, to be his "strong partner" and ("at last!") the object of his desire. Thus, we've seen the creative "Day of Days": the multiple "days" of Genesis 1, with their grand epic symmetry, and the summary "day" of Genesis 2, with its intimate domestic unity.

Since I've said much already about differences and similarities in Genesis 1 and 2, and about what's known (and not known) regarding their composition, I'll turn now to some "creational" themes that are deepened and enriched by their stereoscopic treatment. We'll consider the Creation accounts' quiet polemic against the gaudy violence of contemporary Near Eastern origin stories; their treatment of humanity as the very "image" and breath of God; that divine image gendered as both male and female; the divine genesis and meaning of companionship and of erotic desire; and finally the consummation, completion, and multiplication of this desire in marriage.

5.2.1 "And It Was Good": The Quiet Polemic Against Creative Violence

No summer seems complete without any number of blockbuster films, powered by increasingly realistic animated or digital effects and overwhelming sound technologies, portraying some variation on the epic theme of primordial violence. A hero – not infrequently a god or demi-god from ancient mythology – faces a beastly enemy so mighty that even the gods fear defeat, and the fate of the cosmos hangs in the balance. The hero, relying on his own brute strength, hard-won skill, and clever weaponry, stands alone against the monster and the monster's minions. This is the sort of action that follows, as the hero calls out his enemy:

> "And against the gods my fathers thou hast contrived thy wicked plan.
> Let then thy host be equipped, let thy weapons be girded on!
> Stand! I and thou, let us join battle!"...
> To the fight they came on, to the battle they drew nigh.
> The lord spread out his net and caught her,
> And the evil wind that was behind him he let loose in her face...
> He seized the spear and burst her belly,
> He severed her inward parts, he pierced her heart.
> He overcame her and cut off her life;
> He cast down her body and stood upon it.[9]

This scenario, so common in contemporary action films, also would be familiar to audiences in Babylonian courts and councils in the middle of the second millennium BCE. It is excerpted from the *Enuma Elish*, which narrates in seven cuneiform tablets of poetry the death struggle between the rising hero-god Marduk and the chaos-bringing sea-serpent goddess Tiamat, and the regenerative aftermath of their battle.[10] These words describe the climactic moment of Tiamat's defeat – and provide both a telling parallel to and a stark contrast with the biblical Creation.

For victory over the gods' enemy is not Marduk's only purpose. This story is also a **theogony** – an account of the origin or birth of the gods themselves, and then of the world order – and Marduk's first purpose is his own advancement to supreme godhead through the demonstration of his power, followed by his making of a new cosmos. Before agreeing to fight Tiamat, he had already struck a steep bargain with the council of the gods:

> "If I, your avenger,
> Conquer Tiamat and give you life,
> Appoint an assembly, make my fate preeminent and proclaim it...
> With my word in place of you will I decree fate." (Third Tablet)

The gods' reply?

> "May thy fate, O lord, be supreme among the gods,
> To destroy and to create; speak thou the word, and thy command shall be fulfilled."
>
> (Fourth Tablet)

"To destroy and to create" – note the order. Marduk, a third-generation deity fighting against Tiamat, the primordial goddess of the deep, craves pre-eminence, but he knows that before he can rule and create, he must destroy and kill to prove his power.

So, once his conquest is complete and he has planted his foot on his defeated foe, he sets out to make a world – from her monstrous carcass:

> And the lord stood upon Tiamat's hinder parts,
> And with his merciless club he smashed her skull.
> He cut through the channels of her blood...
> Then the lord rested, gazing upon her dead body,
> While he divided the flesh ... and devised a cunning plan.
> He split her up like a flat fish into two halves;
> One half of her he established as a [firmament] for heaven.
> He fixed a [lock], he stationed a watchman,
> And bade them not to let her waters come forth.
> He passed through the heavens, he surveyed the regions thereof,
> And [with her other half] over against the Deep he set the dwelling of [the Earth]...
>
> (Fourth Tablet)

Finally, having established heaven and earth from the repurposed divine corpse, the new supreme deity devises another "cunning plan" to create a new class of workers who will relieve the gods of their labor: extracting blood from Tiamat's dead consort Kingu, Marduk declares,

> ...blood will I take and bone will I fashion ...
> I will create man who shall inhabit the earth,
> That the service of the gods may be established, and that their shrines may be built.
>
> (Sixth Tablet)

So in seven action-packed episodes, the *Enuma Elish* establishes a **theogony** (the origin of the gods), a **cosmology** (the origin of the world order), and a **political ideology** (a justification of current power relations). Ultimate reality is this: the gods are at war in a fundamentally amoral universe; revolt against the elder gods by younger gods is normative; bone-crushing, blood-drenched force is essential to the act of creation; and therefore we live under a regime of conquest, wrought by creative violence, and slavery is as fundamental to the human order as it is to the divine.

Creative Violence in Other Ancient Eurasian Mythologies

Babylonian theogony and cosmology are not unique in treating pervasive violence as essential to the process of creation. The Greeks, like the Romans after them, present a theogony of inter-generational war among the gods, with Cronos/Saturn attempting to devour his children, and his son Zeus/Jupiter overthrowing him instead. In Norse mythology, the *Æsir* make war on the *Vanir* and *Jotuns*, while even in the relatively gentler theogonies of Egypt, each god struggles to generate him- or herself from the primordial chaotic waters called *Nu*.

Such, then, is the context to which the Book of Genesis responds cosmologically, cultur-ally, and politically. The written form of the *Enuma Elish* dates back probably to the eighteenth century BCE, and its language and imagery provided the dominant understand-ing of divine nature and action, and of natural and human origins, for the Hebrew Patriarchal age through the time of the Exodus and beyond – much as Genesis itself has provided the dominant cosmological contexts for Christendom from late antiquity well into the twentieth century.

So the following famous words from Genesis would certainly be heard differently by a listener in the Egypt or Canaan of the fifteenth century BCE than they would be heard in the Christian or post-Christian West:

> In the beginning God created the heavens and the earth. The earth was without form, and void; and darkness was on the face of the deep. And the Spirit of God was hovering over the face of the waters. (1:1–2)

Most of the phrases in these two sentences would trigger recognitions in the ancient Near Eastern imagination, associations that are clearer if we rephrase the passage more literally (bearing in mind that the Hebrew for "deep" and "waters" is *tehom*, a variant of Tiamat):

> When *Elohim* was beginning to create the heavens and the earth, the earth did not bear any form, and was empty, and the face of *tehom/Tiamat* was dark. And the wind from *Elohim* blew into the face of *tehom/Tiamat*.

These first sentences clearly refer back to the *Enuma Elish's* opening – "When in the height heaven was not named, / And the earth beneath did not yet bear a name" – and strongly echo Marduk's attack on Tiamat – "And the evil wind that was behind him he let loose in her face." Thus, they raise immediate high expectations of a coming battle, a Babylonian-style bloodbath of creative mayhem. Even the name *Elohim* (literally "gods") suggests a polytheistic context. So verse 3 seems to lay down a challenge to a cosmic duel: "Then God said, "Let there be light" – to which the expected answer would be a taunt from the Darkness, or from Tiamat herself, saying "How dare you enter our domain? Will not Darkness swallow your feeble Light, O foolish ones?" – or words to that effect.

However, what follows is no duel, for there is so far but one actor – and here would begin the surprise for the ancient Near Eastern audience with the anticlimactic words "...and there was light" (1:3b). Instead of having to make his word good with destructive force, *Elohim's* word already carries its own good creative force. Verses 4–5 continue this tone of understated control: "And God saw the light, that it was good; and God divided the light from the darkness. God called the light Day, and the darkness He called Night. So the evening and the morning were the first day." Not only is *Elohim's* spoken word powerful; it's also morally authoritative, pronouncing his creation somehow profoundly *right*, not just ethically neutral. In addition, God exercises one of the chief prerogatives of true authority: naming the domain, in this case "Day" and "Night." And finally (this would strike ancient readers as especially strange) he creates light without reference to the sun or any sun-god, such as the Egyptian *Ra* or the Babylonian *Shamash*.

However, an ancient hearer might still expect the real action to begin soon, because in verse 6 *Elohim* proclaims, "Let there be a firmament in the midst of the waters, and let it divide the waters from the waters." The mention of "firmament" probably would stir memo-ries of Marduk's fight with Tiamat, and his rending of her in two in order to separate the heavens and the earth – indeed the climactic struggle in the *Enuma Elish*. But again, these expectations of a slaughtered and fileted sea-serpent are soon disappointed: we're told that God's word "made the firmament, and divided the waters which were under the firmament from the waters which were above the firmament; and it was so" (1:7). "And it was so," like "and he saw that it was good," is another phrase expressing the sort of modest majesty that is the opposite of saber-rattling, chest-thumping warrior bombast. And then again the naming: "God called the firmament Heaven. So the evening and the morning were the second day" (1:8).

And so it goes: the dry land and green things on the third day, the lights and stars on the fourth, the sea creatures and flying things on the fifth day, the cattle and creeping things and beasts of the earth on the sixth. "And it was so ... and it was good ..." are the regular refrains, as *Elohim* calls forth each successive creature with increasing satisfaction. Other elements of this quiet polemic against primordial violence unfold along the way: not only is the sun unnecessary for the creation of light, but the very Sumerian/Babylonian names of "Sun" and "Moon" (*Shamash* and *Sin*) are left out of the text, as these great gods of the ancient pantheons are demoted to merely good and useful creations, "the greater light" and "the lesser light," obediently running their courses. And, as a kind of afterthought, we read that "He made the stars also" – with no further comment (1:16). God spangles the firmament with stars – the stars that the ancients believed governed the fates of heaven and earth, gods and men, and for which were built the great towers and ziggurats. These stars are hung at the last like decorative holiday lights.

Just as the heavenly deities of ancient mythology appear as *Elohim's* obedient impersonal creatures, and Tiamat is de-personified as *tehom* or "the deep," so also do the "sea-monsters" reappear in minor roles, recast as the "great sea creatures" with which "the seas abounded," rather than as rivals to divine power: not only Tiamat, but also Rahab, the ancient feminine serpent slain by the Canaanite storm-god Baal. Rather than the sea creatures being female villains in Genesis, they simply demonstrate the mighty power of their Creator; and *Elohim* "saw that it was good" (1:21).

Ordinary parents often experience the impotence of mere words: as the father's or mother's instructions are repeatedly ignored, every raising of the voice, every escalation of threatened punishment is a reminder of how little power he or she has. "Don't make me come down there!" the parent finally shouts, exasperated by all the ruckus downstairs, and by his or her inability to set things right simply by speaking. God's voice will indeed grow frustrated, and almost humanly angry and weary, later in Genesis – he does "come down there"! – but here in Genesis 1, that divine voice has a serene power deeper than magic, a power that needs no spells or incantations (let alone swords and spears and arrows) but that speaks with calm majesty from its mighty heart. Indeed, along with demoting divine heavenly bodies and monstrous sea-goddesses, this quiet polemic subverts the foundational concept of polytheism itself; for somewhere along the way, the ancient listener would begin to note that, strangely enough, the plural *Elohim* takes a singular verb. This Creator speaks and acts as one – though, as we will now see, he loves difference and variety.

5.2.2 "In Our Image": Man or Manikin?

If Genesis 1 is designed to undermine the Babylonian belief in an amoral polytheistic cosmos created through original violence, Genesis 1 and 2 together are designed to overthrow the social and political implications of that cosmology: that conquest, creative violence, and slavery are original and natural to the human order, as well. In other words, because Genesis portrays a good and beautiful monotheistic cosmos created in harmony and peace, it portrays the creation of a humanity designed for godlike dignity, creative work, and fruitful cooperation.

For we left off our discussion of *Elohim's* six creative days just at their climactic moment, the making of the culminating creature, called *adam*, meaning "of the earth" or "earthling." Usually translated "man" or "humanity," these beings are portrayed as glorious hybrids:

> Then God said, "Let Us make man in Our image, according to Our likeness; let them have dominion over the fish of the sea, over the birds of the air, and over the cattle, over all the earth and over every creeping thing that creeps on the earth." (1:26)

Though fashioned "of the earth," humanity bears *Elohim's* distinctive "image" or *tselem* – showing that there is a touch of the sculptor or potter to Genesis 1's divine Poet after all. Significantly, the term *tselem* is most commonly used in the Hebrew Bible to designate a "graven image" or "idol" set up by humans for false worship, a practice strictly forbidden in the Mosaic covenant and since then foreign to Israelite religion. So it is only *Elohim*, the true Creator, who has the authority to set up "images" of himself. Why? An explanatory example can be found in the book of Daniel, when King Nebuchadnezzar

> made an image [*tselem*] of gold, whose height was sixty cubits and its width six cubits. He set it up in the plain of Dura, in the province of Babylon... Then a herald cried aloud: "To you it is commanded, O peoples, nations, and languages, that at the time you hear the sound of ... music, you shall fall down and worship the gold image that King Nebuchadnezzar has set up... (Daniel 3:1–5)

In ancient Near Eastern cultures, it was common to erect statues of the king or emperor in the capital and throughout the provinces, and subjects were expected to bow before the statues on special occasions to demonstrate their submission to the king's divine dominion. In Genesis 1, we see *Elohim* portrayed as the true and only God-king who sets up images of himself at the center of his newly created earthly "province" so that all creation can show their allegiance to him by submitting to their godlike dominion, or *maschal*.

But what wonderful images! Unlike the mute gold manikins of Babylonian or Assyrian power, everything about these living, breathing likenesses – body, soul, mind, and heart – represents the character and nature of *Elohim* and equips them for responsible rule over all the varied creation, from middle earth, to highest skies, to deepest waters. Sharing earthy origins with their vegetable and animal subjects, these earthlings nevertheless are upright, conscious, creative, clever, and like the creation that they crown, they're *very good* (1:31). Also, remarkably, they reflect the diversity and plurality of being made "in Our image, after Our likeness," for there are two of them, "male and female" (1:27), equally bearing the divine *tselem*. Neither is adequate to represent the Creator alone, but both together constitute a fuller likeness. Cooperation and complementarity are built into the originally *double* divine image, and it is from that original diversity, when unified as "one flesh" through sexual intercourse (2:24), that all human society will spring. We'll turn now to the role of gender in engendering the Maker's plan.

5.2.3 "Male and Female": Gendering Genesis

Speaking of gender in connection to the Book of Genesis is a touchy issue in our time – with many, many millions of religious believers grounding convictions about sexual identity in these pages, and many, many self-described skeptics, and particularly feminists, laying the blame here for centuries of patriarchal misogyny. But while these opening chapters do indeed cut athwart certain contemporary ideas about gender and sex, they also – and perhaps even more so – would have cut against the grain of ancient Near Eastern assumptions about male–female relations.

Indeed, as we've already begun to see, the overall import of Genesis 1 and 2 is surprisingly egalitarian – surprising, that is, if we come to the text expecting a hatred of women and an assertion of intrinsic male superiority. And for those steeped in the worldview of the *Enuma Elish*, the treatment of gender in Genesis would have come as quite a shock.

Put simply, the Babylonian origin story presents us with an overwhelmingly masculine cosmos. It shouldn't escape our notice that the story's battling deities are specifically gendered, and that, in effect, the divine male Marduk must destroy the divine female Tiamat before he can create the world from her dismembered corpse. The carnage-as-creation theme gives the phrase "over my dead body" a drastic new meaning, as the serpentine, flowing feminine is chopped and channeled to suit emphatically male designs. The battle of the sexes is foundational to reality, and the male must win for our world to be born.

So to hearers in this frame of mind, the treatment of masculine and feminine in the opening chapters of Genesis would seem nothing short of bizarre. A God who not only endows his human creatures with the dignity of the divine image, but who also displays that image as equally male and female? A first man and a first woman who share equally in representing *Elohim* in the world, and exercising dominion over it (1:27–28)? While we're at it, why not crown our slaves?

Furthermore, the second chapter of Genesis, which often is spoken of by modern interpreters as the less egalitarian of the two, is from this Babylonian perspective no better. First, according to the latter Creation account, the male is incomplete within himself for happiness ("It is not good that man should be alone"), so that he needs the aid of a suitable, strong ally ("I will make him a helper comparable to him").

"Helpmeet"

Though the old King James Bible's rendering of this phrase – "an help meet for him" – has come to mean something like "the little woman" or "the ladies' auxiliary" in popular usage, it was actually a fine rendering in seventeenth-century English of the Hebrew *ezer*, meaning "fitting partner" or "deliverer." In the Pentateuch, this word is applied not infrequently to God, as in Genesis 49:25 ("By the God of your father who will help you") and in Exodus 18:4 ("[Moses] said, 'The God of my father was my help, and delivered me from the sword of Pharaoh'"). Common male names such as Eliezer ("God is my help") and Ezra ("having been helped") reflect this meaning.

Second, if as in Genesis 1 the last of the creatures – humans – crown the Creation, then in Genesis 2, the latter of the humans – woman – is the crowning perfection of humankind. Third, the woman is created out of the man's side, indicating essential unity and parity.

"Adam's Rib"

As the seventeenth- and eighteenth-century commentator Matthew Henry writes, following the medieval rabbis, "The woman was made of a rib out of the side of Adam; not made out of his head to rule over him, nor out of his feet to be trampled upon by him, but out of his side to be equal with him, under his arm to be protected, and near his heart to be beloved."

Finally – and perhaps most egregiously to the worshiper of Marduk – "a man shall leave his father and mother and be joined to his wife, and they shall become one flesh" (2:24). Can it be that this *Yahweh Elohim* limits a man to only one wife? And that a man's first loyalty is to her, not to his patriarchal home? Who would take such restrictions upon himself? Who would dishonor his father so?

In other words, for such a famously patriarchal text, Genesis 1–2 carries some strikingly – one might almost say pervasively – egalitarian implications where gender is concerned. One can rightly observe that these implications often have been slighted, overlooked, or ignored in Judeo-Christian tradition, but when placed in their original cultural context, these chapters stand out strangely for a quiet insistence on full human dignity for "male and female" that we might call millennia ahead of its time. Of course, the picture of gender relations drawn here will not satisfy all in our time. Those who see gender as entirely socially constructed will disagree with the idea that there is an essential masculinity and femininity fixed or "built in," as it were, to the foundations of creation. Also, those who – male or female – object to binding oneself to a lifetime of exclusive fidelity in monogamous marriage will take issue with its being treated as a fundamental creation ordinance. Devotees of goddess spirituality will perhaps object that the woman in Genesis is no goddess, being clearly created by the Deity, and indeed in Genesis 2 being actually drawn out of the male – a humbling reminder of mutual dependence, that just as men now depend on women for their birth, so woman once depended on the man for hers. And finally, those for whom equality can mean only identity – that is, mathematical sameness – then Genesis, with its idea of mutually complementary and equivalent *difference*, will disappoint. But the Hebrew scripture, with or without a Gallic shrug, says simply *vive la difference!*

5.2.4 "Flesh of My Flesh": Biblical Erotics and Marriage

That famous French phrase about difference between the sexes is spoken most often in contexts that celebrate the expression of erotic admiration and desire, and Genesis 2 gives us the "original" call of sexual longing in Adam's exclamation: "This *at last* is bone of my bones / and flesh of my flesh" (2:23 – English Standard Version, italics mine). There may be some understated humor in the preceding verses 19–20, in which the man has just witnessed a parade of the animals that the LORD God has fashioned for him as potential mates – and Adam's outcry at the sight of the woman shows how relieved he is that *Yahweh Elohim* has made something more fitting, and far more desirable for him, than just a dog or an elephant. Some*one*, of course – the *ezer*, the partner, the soul-mate, the sister-bride taken from his own side, but she is also the exquisitely beautiful object that draws him to her as a magnet draws metal.

Much has been said in our time against the male gaze and the objectification of women, and since ancient times by followers of Moses and Jesus against covetous sexual lust – and no sensible person would want to be treated entirely or even mainly as an object, even an object of art. However, while "beauty is vain, and charm is deceitful" (Proverbs 31:30), nevertheless, "he has made everything beautiful in its time" (Ecclesiastes 3:11). Take it all around, beauty will have its day, and have its due; and in biblical terms, a world in which men simply stopped noticing feminine loveliness is both unimaginable, and even, by most women, undesirable. And the Bible also gives its due to female desire for male beauty – witness the Israelite daughters mad for the striking young David, or Sheba's breathless admiration of Solomon, or Shulamit's heated praise of her lover's sculpted body – not to mention Potiphar's wife pursuing the handsome slave Joseph. Fear drives men to faith, said Martin Luther, and lust to the marriage bed.

But properly speaking, in Genesis 2 there is no lust yet in Eden; that is, no greedy, illicit, ungoverned appetite, sexual or otherwise. The man's spontaneous desire for the woman, and hers for him, are here to be understood as a kind of divine message, a reminder that just as the Creator somehow enjoys company within himself, so his highest creatures are made to long for completion by and union with another. In our discussions of the Song of Solomon and the Book of Proverbs, we've already seen both celebrations of sexual pleasure and warnings against sexual excess; here in Genesis we see the origins of that pleasure and of the limits upon it defined by the created purposes of erotic desire itself, and of erotic expression. In this view of things, two great sexes animate the world, now incarnated as male and female images of God, and their carnal knowledge of each other is above all the seal of an enduring and exclusive covenant love. The Hebrew word for erotic love is *ahab* (yes, the namesake of King Ahab – and Captain Ahab!) and the Hebrew for steadfast covenant love is *chesed*; thus, we might say that *ahab* seals *chesed.* In other words, sex is not primarily for pleasure, or for offspring, or even for the relief of loneliness; primarily, sex is the sign of a permanent, divinely sanctioned love between husband and wife.

And in the ancient Hebrew imagination, a proper understanding of first things makes important but secondary things fall into place. Thus, the covenant-making God, *Yahweh*, creates a covenant-making man and woman, and the sexual sealing of their marriage brings a whole range of blessed byproducts. First, there is a deep companionship based on intimate trust and understanding; it's not for nothing that in Hebrew the sexual act is often called "knowing," both as a physical and as a spiritual relief of loneliness.[11] Second, out of this act of deep intimacy springs society itself, as two becoming one soon brings three and four and many, many more. Third, to this Hebraic way of thinking, in desiring the opposite sex, the couple not only procreates, but also participates in the full diversity of God's likeness, loving the Other, not merely a narcissistic mirror image of oneself. And the fourth byproduct of sex will probably escape no one – the sheer pleasure of it, both as a divine gift and as a solace.

Significantly, these emphases reverse ancient Near Eastern attitudes toward sex as expressed in literature, custom, and law. We have already observed that theirs was a dominantly masculinist world, and in a culture that revered male power, monogamy was rejected as too restrictive on men, and the different functions of sex were divided among various settings to suit the powerful. For those with the means to choose, the sexual economy put erotic pleasure first, and great men built great harems and pleasure-palaces, often without restriction to gender or age – both young girls and boys being highly favored for sexual use. Indulgent men might have affectionate attachments to particular wives, but for recreational intercourse, they generally would prefer any number of expert concubines and catamites. Obviously, an important second priority was the begetting of offspring, on very many wives for the mighty and on multiple wives even for the ordinary man. As to companionship, most ancient cultures – from Sumer to Babylon to Greece to Rome – exalted male friendship far above attachment to females, and while some men no doubt found comradeship with women, for a man to speak of being "best friends" with a wife would have seemed strange indeed, if not ludicrous. After all, a woman owed her all to her lord, while the man owed the woman nothing, any more than he would owe his slave. And a spoiled wife, like a spoiled slave, could breed not children but disorder.

Of course, many ancient men did better by women than these cultural attitudes would suggest, but when they did so they probably either congratulated themselves for their magnanimity, or more likely, felt a kind of shame for their lenience or foolishness. In such a world, Genesis strikes like lightning from the clear blue. Who taught its writers to celebrate the equal worth and dignity of male and female? Who taught them that sex is for covenant love, that a man's first loyalty is to his wife as partner and friend – not to his father – and that our neighbors bear the stamp of God's image? For that matter, where did these writers learn to distrust the power of the spear and the bow; to imagine creation as an act of generosity, not war; to value responsible self-government; to give a higher and limiting law to all human governments and regimes? And who taught them to marry heaven and earth in their own spirited flesh? Who taught them these things? As the ancients might ask, "what is his name, and the name of his son?" (Proverbs 30:4)

However we understand the origin of their origin stories, those who created Genesis 1 and 2 conclude those stories by looking forward to limitless possibilities. At the end of the first Creation account, the man and the woman are poised for a glorious expansion – to "fill the earth and subdue it" (1:28) – and so is God, who pauses on the seventh day to rest from his labors.

Ironically, of Marduk we are told in the *Enuma Elish* that "the lord rested" from the bloody labor of killing Tiamat before undertaking the act of creative butchery that begins the world. But when *Elohim* rests from speaking creation into being, he hasn't really even broken a sweat.

And the second Creation account also ends with the man and his wife poised, "naked … and unashamed," to make the Garden fruitful. Given what we've seen about biblical erotics, it's notable that the Hebrew *arom/erom* for "naked" refers not to sexual nakedness, but instead to the nakedness of dependence, vulnerability, exposure, and limitation – that is, the nakedness of the infant or the weaponless man. When Job, at the height of his grief, cries out "Naked I came from my mother's womb, / And naked shall I return" (Job 1:20), he's not feeling the least bit sexy. And when Adam and his wife stand "naked … and unashamed" at the end of Genesis 2, the primary meaning is not that they are proud of their sexuality – though their erotic attraction is part of their being "very good" – but that, as we might say, they are unarmed and unworried. What have they to fear? They are immortal; they live in the midst of beauty and abundance; and they are protected by the Creator. In short, they are clothed by the Garden, and by the LORD God, and need no other garments. What could ever expose them to danger?

5.3   Nakedness and Knowledge: Deception, Folly, Fall, and Curse

But there is one danger, in the form of two trees, or rather, one in particular: "The tree of life was also in the midst of the garden, and the tree of the knowledge of good and evil… And the LORD God commanded the man, saying, 'Of every tree of the garden you may freely eat; but of the tree of the knowledge of good and evil you shall not eat, for in the day that you eat of it you shall surely die'" (2:9, 16–17). Here, it would seem, is a test, in the literary form of *metonymy* – that is, an expression that describes something indirectly by referring to things around it or associated with it, or by its outer limits. Much as God's Creation of "heaven and earth" indicates "everything from highest to lowest," so the phrase "the knowledge of good and evil" would seem to indicate "knowledge of everything from the best to the worst" – in other words, Godlike omniscience. Thus, "the tree of the knowledge of good and evil" would appear to mean either "the tree that *confers* Godlike omniscience," or "the tree that *tests the desire for* Godlike omniscience" – briefly, "the tree of all-knowing power." The name of the tree and the divine prohibition against eating its fruit (the only prohibition in the entire Creation) together constitute a test of love, loyalty, humility, and allegiance. Add one other element: a tempter.

"Now the serpent was more cunning than any beast of the field which the LORD God had made" (3:1). Enter the villain of the piece – described by a pun so striking in the original Hebrew as to knock our understanding of the passage sideways with surprise. We had last left the first couple "naked … and unashamed," and the Hebrew word here translated "cunning" or "crafty" is *arowm*, which comes from the same root as *arom/erom* – "naked." In other words, we see a figurative contrast between the naked harmlessness of the first couple and what we might call the "naked aggression" of their tempter. At issue then as well are two kinds of shamelessness: that of innocence – needing no shame – and of bare-faced brazenness – feeling no shame.

Here the famed narrative minimalism of the text achieves a maximum level of fascination – and frustration. For surely we might expect some fuller explanation of the origin of evil in God's "very good" world? Who is this "serpent"? How did he get so "cunning"? How, especially, can he speak? And why does he baldly question the promises and commands of *Elohim*? (Note that the chapter moves back and forth between the narrator's *Yahweh Elohim* and the serpent's *Elohim* – a real puzzler under JEPDR theory.) But it's soon apparent that none of these momentous philosophical and metaphysical questions is going to be answered. Instead, the story moves briskly ahead into the serpent's assertions and counter-promises. He begins with an astonishing suggestion, asking "Has God indeed said, 'You shall not eat of every tree of the garden'?" (3:1) – insinuating that in God's garden, *all* fruits are forbidden.

When the woman corrects the serpent, repeating God's single prohibition of the one tree and its dire penalty, he contradicts even more boldly: "You will not surely die. For God knows that in the day you eat of it your eyes will be opened, and you will be like God, knowing good and evil" (3:4–5). It is as if the serpent were to repeat sarcastically those memorable words of the Great and Powerful Oz: "Pay no attention to the man behind the curtain!" This contradiction asserts that in some sense *Elohim* is impersonating a deity, and that to preserve his precarious hold on power, he needs to keep his supposed creatures in the dark about his limits and their true divine potential. And this contradiction comes with a promise: that by eating the fruit their eyes truly will be opened, and that they will indeed be as omniscient as God and so independent of his pretended authority.

At this crucial juncture it is vital to note something both obvious and yet controversial: that the serpent is wrong, indeed that he is telling fat porky whoppers. This is not necessarily to make any particular religious claim. It is only to recognize that by this point in the narrative, we, the readers, know better. First, we know that, in the world of this story, the character called *Elohim* and *Yahweh Elohim* has already established himself as serenely powerful and overflowingly creative and intimately generous, and indeed not only great but good. That he is being stingy or tyrannical, or that he fears a loss of his almighty power, should seem laughable. The serpent might as well shout up at him "Who do you think you are, God?" "Well, actually, *I AM*," *Yahweh* would answer. Second, we know that the serpent misrepresents *Yahweh's* words in a way that any person would find grossly offensive were he or she the one slandered – one rule grotesquely inflated to a universal prohibition. And third – well, the serpent's lies, like his victims, are soon fully exposed.

But back we go to the story. "So when the woman saw that the tree was good for food, that it was pleasant to the eyes, and a tree desirable to make one wise, she took of its fruit and ate. She also gave to her husband with her, and he ate" (3:6). Note that in a pregnant double entendre, the tree is "desirable to make one wise"; thus, the text delays for a moment the discovery that hers is magical thinking, that the woman is following desire rather than wisdom in lusting for Godhood. Note also that "her husband" is very much "with her" in all of this, complicit and cooperative in a shared act of folly.

Milton's Eden

In the most famous retelling of Genesis 1–3, John Milton's Christian epic poem *Paradise Lost (1667, 1674),* the poet goes to great lengths in Book 9 to ensure that Eve is alone and unchaperoned by Adam when tempted by Satan, in the form of the serpent. While tremendously effective as drama, and psychologically rich in characterization, Milton's revision transforms the dynamics of the encounter from one of shared rebellion in quest of Godhood to one of Eve's longing for intellectual parity with Adam, and Adam's overfond erotic attachment to Eve.

For immediately, in a deliberate piece of ironic doubling, the folly, and the fools, are exposed. "Then the eyes of both of them were opened, and they knew ..." we are teasingly told, recapitulating the formula of the serpent's promise – but with a fatal sting in the tail: "they knew that they were naked" (3:7). To stress the point that this nakedness is not the *arom* of "cunning" or cleverness but of shame, the narrator adds that, with pathetic embarrassment and inadequacy, "they sewed fig leaves together and made themselves coverings." Their genitals, once innocent reminders of their creaturely genesis and their kinship with beasts as well as with God, are for the first time sources of humiliation.

What, then, of the serpent's promise? Can anything be said to have been gained by eating forbidden fruit? In one sense, the man and woman are, as the saying goes, "wised up": expecting omniscience, they experience confusion; expecting deity, they experience dependence; expecting to rise above all rules, those rules soon come crashing down on them. Like children told not to touch a hot stove, they now know to their pain that the stove is hot. It may be shocking to our postromantic, postmodern eyes, so used to identifying with the rebel against authority, that the serpent here actually is the villain of the piece, not the complex, semi-sympathetic anti-hero. The theft of the fruit is not portrayed here (as in some later Christian traditions, from medieval liturgy and song to Milton's *Paradise Lost*) as a "fortunate fall." It does not bring any kind of compensatory new blessing or knowledge, but only inflicts the excruciating awareness of having been disastrously stupid – and of being swindled. To put it in contemporary terms, if losing your life savings to an online financial scam is your idea of empowerment, then this is the deal you've been waiting for.

The Fortunate Fall

"O felix culpa quae talem et tantum meruit habere redemptorem," "O happy fault that merited such and so great a Redeemer." So says the *Exultet* of the yearly Latin Easter Vigil, celebrating the Fall of Man as the necessary price for bringing Jesus Christ to redeem the world. Similarly, but with a difference, the anonymous medieval Christmas lyric "Adam lay ybounden" asserts, gratefully, that the Fall made possible the reign of the Blessed Virgin Mary:

> Ne had the apple taken been
> The apple taken been,
> Ne had never our ladie,
> Abeen heav'ne queen.
> Blessed be the time
> That apple taken was,
> Therefore we moun singen.
> Deo gracias!

An English Puritan like Milton could join in this theme, as after the Fall Adam marvels, having been told in advance the story of Christ's sacrifice:

> O goodness infinite, goodness immense!
> That all this good of evil shall produce,
> And evil turn to good … (*Paradise Lost* 12:469–471)

While Genesis 3 does not rule out divine grace and forgiveness in response to sin – far from it – this passage puts the emphasis squarely on the catastrophic loss in this "Paradise lost." Also precluded are Kabbalistic, Gnostic, and occult readings of the Fall that portray it as the beginning of true enlightenment for the initiated and the illuminated. The first sinners are portrayed here as very much in the dark.

It certainly has become common in the study of "canonical" literature to read "against the text" (and especially this text) in ways that turn the tables, sympathize with the rebels, and implicate the authorities. Indeed, such a disposition seems to be the mental precondition for what is often called "modernity." But before reading against the text – an often necessary exercise, no doubt – we need in fairness to know something of how the text *intends* to be read. As it stands, this story seems eerily designed to frustrate our many common reasons for blaming authority, and for extenuating our own or others' transgressions. Was one sole restriction in Paradise really too much? Did Adam and his wife have difficult childhoods in bad family backgrounds? Did they suffer poverty or hunger or abandonment? Were they afflicted with racial, political, or economic oppression, or held down by physical handicap? Were they products of a greedy and hypocritical and violent society or haunted by fear of death? Or may we say that "It's just human nature to break the rules"? Now, perhaps, but then? Isn't the point of the story that in Eden sin was not *yet* the inclination of human nature? Indeed, isn't the point that, in any ordinary sense, the first sin makes no sense, because it is essentially irrational, delusional, and unjustified? Naturally, we read against the text because it reads against us.

Thus, when *Yahweh's* punishment falls on the disobedient couple, the actual sentence seems surprisingly lenient – at least relative to the divine death threat of 2:17 and 3:3 – as well as measured and just. There's a kind of grim farce in how the man and woman think that they can elude God's notice by putting on fig leaves and hiding in the bushes, and even more so in their ignominious buck-passing and blame-shifting. "Who told you that you were naked?" the LORD God demands. "Have you eaten from the tree of which I commanded you that you should not eat?" (3:11). Violation leads to painful exposure, *Yahweh's* question confirms – not the divine omniscience promised by the serpent. Adam's visceral reaction is to evade responsibility by projecting it elsewhere: "The *woman*" – the ignoble accusation comes first from his mouth – "whom *You* gave to be with me" – implicating God in the crime – "*she* gave me of the tree, and I ate" (3:12). So is misogyny born. God's gaze shifts to the woman, and her reply is similarly evasive: "The *serpent* deceived me, and I ate" (3:13).

And at first these evasions seem to work, as the LORD God's initial curse falls on the tempter, who will now be compelled to crawl in the dust and to suffer some kind of devastating and perhaps fatal blow to his "head" from the woman's "seed," or offspring.

The Seed of the Woman

Most readings of this passage agree that it indicates some future conflict between the serpent and the offspring of the woman. Jewish interpretations generally read this as referring to a natural antipathy between humans and snakes as a witness to the sin in the garden; Christians, while acknowledging this literal antipathy, traditionally read the words as a prophecy of how the Son of the Virgin Mary, Jesus Christ, the "seed of the woman" though not of a man, will be "bruised" by Satan in death, but by rising from the dead will destroy Satan's power – and thus will "bruise his head."

Because the serpent lifted himself up proudly to compete with God, he will be constantly prostrate. But the LORD's judgment is not exhausted; he turns immediately to the woman and delivers a sentence that afflicts her with intimate, domestic suffering:

> I will greatly multiply your sorrow and your conception;
> In pain you shall bring forth children;
> Your desire shall be for your husband,
> And he shall rule over you. (3:16)

Childbearing, the uniquely female power of conceiving life, will be shot through with discomfort and sadness; birth will be a sharp agony; and domestic life will be an ongoing battle for mastery. Indeed the very phrase "Your desire shall be for" refers not primarily to the woman's strong emotional attachment to her husband – the "clinging vine" of the dependent wife – but rather is a unique Hebrew idiom (*teshuqah*) for the will to power, as in the next chapter when the LORD warns the jealous Cain that "sin lies at the door. And *its desire is for you, but you should rule over it*" (4:7, my italics). In other words, the woman will seek to control and dominate her man by all the means that she possesses, and the man will respond with overbearing harshness. The battle of the sexes is presented as a curse on male and female alike for their mutual grab at Godhood, and everyone is a loser.

Just as the curse on the woman hits her where, traditionally, it matters to women most – the realm of motherhood and family life – so the LORD's climactic curse on the man impacts his areas of greatest hope and aspiration: the work of his hands, the earth itself, and his immortal longings.

> Cursed is the ground for your sake;
> In toil you shall eat of it
> All the days of your life.
> Both thorns and thistles it shall bring forth for you,
> And you shall eat the herb of the field.
> In the sweat of your face you shall eat bread
> Till you return to the ground,
> For out of it you were taken;
> For dust you are,
> And to dust you shall return. (3:17–19)

Created to create, designed for fulfillment in meaningful effort, and made for a deathless future, Adam will instead see his work transformed to frustrating "toil," with frequent failure dogging his labors, and the weeds often winning out over his crops. And in the ultimate irony, the *adam* raised from the clay by the divine sculptor will be returned to the earth in death – and yet long for eternal life as the amputee feels a lost, phantom limb. Where the breath of God will go that first gave Adam life it will take much of the Hebrew Bible to explain.

All of these curses are, in the purest sense, forms of "poetic justice," both because the punishments suit the offenses in metaphorically significant ways, and because it is the supreme and original Poet himself who is the judge. In this way the medium is indeed the message: the divine Maker (Septuagint Greek *Poietes*, also the root for "Poet") fits his penalties to the crimes with a kind of ironic perfection – tempered with measures of both sarcasm and mercy. So as the LORD God casts Adam and Eve from the garden, his speech drips irony: "Behold, the man has become like one of Us, to know good and evil" (3:22). In other words, "My, my – there's a new God among Us! Look at how all-knowing and almighty the naked little fellow has become! I am SO frightened!" And then a further sarcastic precaution: "And now, lest he put out his hand and take also of the tree of life, and eat, and live forever"; as if to say, "We'd better be careful, or this new little God will steal again, this time from the tree of life, and then actually become immortal – and there'll be no living with him!"

Such divine sarcasm may fall harshly on the modern ear – and not for the last time – but it is tempered by some acts and words of kindness. "Also for Adam and his wife the LORD God made tunics of skin, and clothed them" (3:21), we're told, in a sign of continuing divine care; and note that, unlike many later interpreters, *Yahweh* does not treat Eve as the source of trouble, instead speaking of "the man" as the chief wrongdoer. Indeed, having tried to place the blame on his wife, Adam seems to relent, bestowing on her a surprisingly hopeful name, *Hawwah*, or Eve, "the mother of all living" (3:20). Rather than branding her "mother of sins," or "thief-in-chief," Adam endows her with an honorific, forward-looking title, indicating their intent still to "fill the earth" according to divine command. Significantly, "mother of all living" was also a title of Tiamat, the serpent goddess from whose butchered flesh and blood and bone the Babylonian Marduk fashioned the cosmos; here, even in lost paradise, motherhood means the giving of life by ordinary reproductive means, not the losing of it through cosmic mayhem.

As the beginning of beginnings, these few opening chapters of Genesis warrant far more space than even the substantial consideration that we've given them. Here in this small space we see plentifully exemplified the Bible's distinctive stylistic minimalism, pregnant wordplay, significant repetition, vivid juxtaposition, dramatically deferred judgment, and explosive irony. Some may be shocked that this famous origin story was in some ways not original – that it shows a crucial debt to earlier sources, even if they are adversarial ones. But of course the biblical writers speak as if they are restoring the true version of events, not merely inventing a new version of recycled materials; for to believe in the Hebrew God is to believe, above all, that he is always previous.

We also see in these opening chapters many splendid gifts of the Jews to the world. Whatever we may believe about the God of Israel, if we believe in such principles as intrinsic human value, strict limits on the coercive powers of kings and states, suspicion of militarism, respect for creative work and others' property, responsibilities of self-control and self-government, compassion for the weak and poor, celebration of male and female dignity and harmony, and the rejection of greed and envy – if we believe that these principles apply to all humans regardless of race, nation, tribe, or sex, however young or however old, then directly or indirectly our ideas come from this book.

So we turn now in quicker time to these same literary devices and root themes outworking in the lives and trials of the patriarchs. But I'll conclude this chapter with one last question: many readers may wonder why I have spent this chapter discussing the origins of all things without a single mention of the name now most associated with origins – Charles Darwin? The answer is simple: those who composed Genesis had never heard of him.

Questions for Discussion

1   The elements of narrative style in the Book of **Genesis**, and throughout the major prose books of the Hebrew Bible, are often identified as **minimalism**, **wordplay**, **doubling and repetition**, **juxtaposition**, **deferred judgment**, and **irony**. How would you define these elements, and what examples might you give for each?

2   In what ways might these elements have a cumulative effect in creating the conditions for irony? How would you distinguish between **sad**, **happy**, and **complex irony**, and what might be an example of each?

3   What is the *Enuma Elish*, what were its likely dates of composition, and what basic assumptions about the origins of the gods and of humanity underlie its narrative?

4   In what significant ways – vocabulary, structure, action – do the Creation narratives of **Genesis 1–2 resemble the *Enuma Elish***? How do Genesis 1–2 differ from this Babylonian Creation story? What are the meanings of these similarities and differences, taken together?

5   What does it mean, in Genesis 1, to be made in "the **image** of God"? Who bears this "image," and to what purposes? What other passages in the Hebrew Bible help to define the word "image" (***tselem***) and illustrate its functions?

6   Why, according to Genesis 1–2, does God create humans "**male and female**"? What do these gender distinctions suggest about the Creator? What do they mean for human relations?

7   In Genesis 1 and especially Genesis 2, how does the experience of sexual or **erotic desire** appear? What does this desire represent? What practical functions does it perform? What is its proper goal?

8   In Genesis 2 and 3, what does the "**nakedness**" of the man and woman mean at first, and what does it come to mean? How does that "nakedness" relate to the serpent's tempting approach?

9   In Genesis 2 and 3, what does the **tree of the knowledge of good and evil** represent? What does the **serpent** promise that the woman and man will know if they eat its fruit? After they bite, what do they actually know? How do the LORD God, the man, the woman, and the serpent react to these results? What are the consequences for each?

Notes

1   Robert Alter, *The Art of Biblical Narrative, Revised Edition* (New York: Basic Books, 2011), 114.
2   Mark Twain, *The Innocents Abroad: or, The New Pilgrim's Progress* (New York: Harper and Brothers, 1906), 2:245.
3   Ernest Hemingway, *Death in the Afternoon* (New York: Scribners Classics, 1999), 12.
4   Alter, ibid., 6.
5   Mark Abley, *Travels Among Threatened Languages* (New York: Houghton Mifflin, 2003), 208.
6   Alter, ibid., 4–5.
7   There is no textual basis for racist notions that Cain's "mark" has to do with dark skin color.
8   See Alter, ibid., 12–13, on the "infancy" and the great promise of specifically stylistic literary study applied to the Bible.
9   *Enuma Elish: The Epic of Creation*, tr. L.W. King (London 1902), Fourth Tablet. All further references will be to tablet number.
10   These tablets are still to be seen in the British Museum.
11   Strangely but amusingly to a modern ear, this Hebrew word for "to know" is *yada* – though in contemporary English to say "yada, yada, yada" means something quite different from "know, know, know" – or does it?

6

Origin Narrative II: Patriarchy and Its Discontents in Genesis

We began the previous chapter by recognizing the remarkable level of aesthetic design that the Genesis text displays from its very first chapters through its conclusion. In *The Art of Biblical Narrative*, Robert Alter observes that this design is especially apparent to anyone reading the original Hebrew text. This art determines, he says, "the minute choice of words and reported details, the pace of narration, the small movements of dialogue, and a whole network of ... interconnections within the text."[1] Alter notes that modern critical emphasis on speculative source study has distracted interpreters from recognizing the extraordinary coherence of the biblical stories and their subtlety in using devices such as repetition, juxtaposition, and irony to drive home its central lesson: *Yahweh's* covenant faithfulness despite human fallibility.[2]

In Genesis, as elsewhere in the Hebrew Bible, the LORD's covenant faithfulness is thematized first and foremost through families, and in families mainly through fathers; so to speak of this central covenant theme in Genesis inevitably means speaking of great Hebrew "Founding Fathers," or patriarchs. Through most of the Bible's reception history, the word "patriarch" has had largely positive associations for its readers, but in the past two generations this term has become increasingly controversial, with strong negative connotations for many contemporary people, particularly in the developed West, and especially when one adds a "y" to the end. In a literary study such as this, we needn't resolve all cultural or theological dissonance that this ancient book produces in the modern and postmodern mind. Nevertheless, two opening observations about biblical patriarchy may help some contemporary readers past obstacles to their imaginative engagement with the text. The first observation is that the biblical writers, by assuming and asserting the authority of heavenly and earthly fathers, are no different from most religious and secular authorities of their own and of nearly all eras – at least until ours. If the Bible is to be called a "sexist" book, then most known cultures and civilizations have been more or less sexist too.

But the second and more important observation is that the biblical portrayal of fatherly rule – particularly in Genesis – is persistently and strangely critical of what usually passes for patriarchy, then and now. As we've already seen in the earlier chapters of this book, when *Elohim* chooses to create humanity "in our own image," that image is represented equally by male and female; and in a shock to the Near Eastern patriarchal system, we are told that a man's first loyalty is not to his patriarch but to his spouse; that he shall leave his father (and mother) and cleave to his wife – and his one wife, at that (2:24). And besides this early jab at polygamy, there is the sustained assault in Genesis on the chief guarantee of patriarchal power, primogeniture: repeatedly, fathers are told, not that the eldest will inherit, but that "the older shall serve the younger" (25:23). Combine this preference for the younger with the repeated insistence that the LORD favors the widow, the barren wife, the outcast, the orphan – in other words, the weak and perennial losers in the great game of life – and we see the tide running strong against the cult of masculine privilege and the worship of power. We'll detail below the thematic outworking of both

Literary Study of the Bible: An Introduction, First Edition. Christopher Hodgkins.
© 2020 John Wiley & Sons Ltd. Published 2020 by John Wiley & Sons Ltd.

biblical patriarchy and its discontents, but for the moment two questions immediately arise: First, why is the covenant God of Israel so critical of absolute Near Eastern fatherhood? And second, how do the distinctive techniques of biblical narrative serve this surprising critique? In order to answer both of these questions, we'll need to explore the foundational Hebrew concept of "the covenant," and its central role in the entire biblical storyline.

6.1 "Arc" of the Covenant: The Story of God's Contracts

Since the advent of the multi-season, long-form episodic television drama – think *The Sopranos*, *Mad Men*, *Breaking Bad*, *House of Cards*, *Game of Thrones*, and *Orange is the New Black* – viewers have become accustomed to speaking casually of a "story arc." This "arc" is a pattern of complex development that treats particular actions and plotlines in specific episodes as interesting (and entertaining) not only in themselves but also as parts of a larger over-story, a master narrative that in the end makes large sense of small things – like those great composite portraits of a person or place made from hundreds of tiny headshots, artfully arranged. As *au courant* as this ambitious style of storytelling may seem, and as fresh and rich as it often is, there's nothing new about it: from Tolkien's three-part *Lord of the Rings* and Dickens' and Trollope's episodically published novels, back through Shakespeare's history tetralogies, Spenser's *Faerie Queene*, Dante's *Divine Comedy*, and the medieval mystery plays, to the dramatic trilogies of Euripides, Sophocles, and Aeschylus, and the *Iliad* and *Odyssey* of Homer, the long episodic narrative is a very ancient form. But for sheer size and chronological scope, the biblical arc is in a class of its own. From the first words of Genesis to the final lines of Revelation, in scores of books across as many as fifteen centuries, a single through-line emerges: the story of God's contracts with humanity – the long story of human promises broken, and divine promises kept.

Now contracts are, as the teens like to say, "relatable"; whether we're queens or congressmen, or just ordinary Jacks and Jills, nearly all adults make and live under contracts. A mortgage or lease, a car loan, a credit card agreement, a statement of employment conditions, a marriage – all of these are legal instruments designed to bind the co-signing parties to mutual responsibilities, and to promise mutual benefits. At the national and international levels, governments sign treaties both to empower and to limit power, to promise cooperation and to assure mutual protection in peace and in war. Similarly, in the ages before us, including the Bible's "patriarchal" ages, people bound themselves and others in strong contractual promises. Such a promise the Hebrews called **berith** – related to words for binding and for cutting – and this word is usually translated "covenant." Some of their human covenants strike us as wise, just, and provident, others not: Abraham uprightly buys the cave of Machpelah from the Hittites to bury Sarah, and to start a family tomb (Genesis 23); but the sons of Jacob wrongly negotiate a marriage covenant with the Shechemites only as a ruse to slaughter them in vengeance for the rape of their sister Dinah (34); and Judah foolishly contracts for sex with an unknown prostitute, promising her a young goat and giving his personal identification in pledge – unaware that he is being "taken in" by his wronged daughter-in-law Tamar (38). All these are covenants, of a sort, and all involve patriarchal figures, yet none rises to the level of divine contract.

6.1.1 Kinds of Covenant: Bilateral and Unilateral

To understand the difference between most of the covenants in our own experience and the central divine covenants of the Hebrew Bible, we need to understand the differences between **bilateral** and **unilateral** contracts. All of the covenants just noted above (both the contemporary and the biblical examples) are bilateral – that is, negotiated by both parties, with rights of refusal on each side. However, the divine covenants of the Hebrew God are unilateral – that is, dictated by one more powerful party. Human history is filled with unilateral covenants (generally known as surrender terms) in which the weak are told how they will be disposed of by the strong. It's a generally unedifying, often horrifying genre: Nebuchadnezzar casts down the walls and Temple of Jerusalem, slaughters all resisters, and deports the best and brightest to Babylon for forced assimilation; Rome grinds Carthage to powder and sows its fields with salt; Muhammad gives the Jews of Medinah the choice of conversion or death; the Aztec demand of their Tlaxcalan vassals a steady stream of young sacrificial victims, whose hearts are ceremoniously ripped from their chests in Tenochtitlán; the Spanish *Requerimiento* threatens forced Christian conversion, or extermination, to all who refuse submission to Carlos V throughout the Americas. Other examples are legion, practically regardless of race, color, or creed – and particularly in the ancient Near East, where the conquering king routinely demanded that the vanquished worship his own pantheon and, usually, himself.

So the unilateral covenant, with its myriad instances of self-serving tyranny, would seem to be an unenviable analogy for *Yahweh's* major patriarchal covenants. Yet, as we saw with the parallels between the Creation in Genesis 1–2 and the Babylonian *Enuma Elish*, similarities highlight drastic difference. The God who speaks forth each patriarchal *berith* is, by ancient Near Eastern standards of sovereignty, strikingly magnanimous and gracious: he concerns himself primarily with the ongoing good, happiness, and blessing of his subjects; his conditions, be they few or many, are more formative than punitive; and, most surprisingly of all, the Almighty voluntarily binds himself in multiple, and often infinite, ways. Many Roman and Moorish conquests were notable for the substantial benefits guaranteed by new membership in their respective empires, and in modern times, the closest human analogy to *Yahweh's* unilateral covenants probably would be that of the end to World War II. Unlike the disastrously punitive Treaty of Versailles that ended World War I in 1919, the Allied terms of unconditional surrender imposed on Japan in 1945 began one of the most effective programs of positive nation-building in history. The terms dictated by the force of Allied arms established the basis of a Japan much freer, more prosperous, and more peaceful than would have existed otherwise. No doubt, this analogy is limited. No merely human acts of benevolence, mixed as they are with motives of selfish national interest and emerging Cold War rivalry – not to mention the terror of the atomic bomb – can stand in for the perfect wisdom, justice, and grace attributed by the Hebrew writers to *Yahweh Elohim*. But if postwar Allied policy toward Japan (and West Germany) stands out as a rare bright spot in the long history of conquest, so much more do "the covenants of the LORD" stand in bold contrast to the one-sided dictates typical of god-kings and king-gods in patriarchal Mesopotamia, Egypt, and Canaan. "Therefore know that the LORD your God, He is God, the faithful God who keeps covenant and mercy for a thousand generations with those who love Him and keep His commandments" (Deuteronomy 7:9). Whatever one believes about the existence of such a God, the very idea of this God – faithful, merciful, and steadfast in his covenant love – is a stunning turn in human history.

6.1.2 Keeping Covenant: Promises, Conditions, Signs

How, then, do *Yahweh's* unilateral covenants work? They are, in their constituent parts, not unlike ordinary bilateral, human covenants: contracts that stipulate certain **promises** and **conditions** binding on the parties, and specify some **sign or signs** to endorse and witness the contract – like the etymologically related form of a sign that we call a "signature." The first and most remarkable quality of the divine covenants in Genesis and elsewhere is that there are any promises at all, that the Almighty, speaking from the position of absolute sovereignty, would unilaterally choose to limit, constrain, or obligate himself in any way. This is not the usual way of Pharaoh Thutmose, nor of Kings Abimelech, Shalmaneser, Baal-Hanan, Ashurbanipal, and Nebuchadnezzar – and certainly not the way of the gods for whom these mighty kings were named: Thoth, Moloch, Shulmanu, Baal, Ashur, and Nebo. The second covenantal feature, the conditions, sometimes vary a good deal, depending upon the circumstances of the covenant and the condition of the divine–human relationship to which the contract speaks, but as we will see, these conditions are usually notable for their strong ethical content. The third feature, the sign or signs, also bears a unique and often figurative, even poetic, relation to the promises and conditions. Usually vivid, visceral, or pictorial, covenant signs appeal powerfully to the imagination as representative icons, radiating connotation and meaning. But above all, these divine contracts share one quality in common: they are profoundly personal, linking a conscious, willing, active deity to particular human persons and their many relations. To those persons, the first patriarchs, we now turn.

6.1.3 Specific Covenants: Adamic, Noahic, Abrahamic

6.1.3.1 Adamic Covenant

To the objects of the first covenant, Adam and Eve, we've already given a good deal of attention, as divine image-bearers, as gendered beings, as sexual subjects, and as original sinners. So we needn't belabor the details of this founding divine contract. The promises are staggering: the first man and woman get everything – well, nearly everything – and they get it forever. Genesis 1 promises God's "images" that they will have "dominion … over all the earth" and "every herb that yields seed which is on the face of all the earth, and every tree whose fruit yields seed; to you it shall be for food" (1:26, 29). Genesis 2 repeats the promise of provision – "Of every tree of the garden you may freely eat" (2:16) – and also promises blissful, eternal companionship in giving the woman to the man, and ever after in the man giving himself to the woman (2:18–25).

Yet there are stipulations and limits to this otherwise infinite gift – and here begin the conditions of the Adamic Covenant. In Genesis 1, the first couple is commanded to "Be fruitful and multiply; fill the earth and subdue it; have dominion over the fish of the sea, over the birds of the air, and over every living thing that moves on the earth" (1:28). This is presumably a pleasant duty, involving affectionate and monogamous sexual love, painless childbirth, rapid and exponential population growth, far-reaching cultivation of the unspoiled earth, and harmonious existence with a rich diversity of animate creatures who would be treated as animal companions rather than as food – for yes, Adam and his wife are the original vegetarians. In Genesis 2, these conditions for beneficial human dominion are localized as commands to a pair of happy garden caretakers placed in Eden "to tend and keep it" (2:15), to keep watch over the menagerie of animals (2:19–20), and, fatefully, to keep their distance from the tree of testing, "the tree of the knowledge of good and evil" (2:17). The very presence of this tree (with its reminder of divine command, its title probing the motives of its beholders, and the fearsome threat of death) constitutes the sign of Adam's covenant, the LORD's "signature," as it were.

We've already seen how the breaking of this covenant brings the reality of shame, exile, and death crashing down on the first sinners – abrogating, one would think, all of the divine promises made before the rebellion. But surprisingly, that is not so. There is eventual death – after nine centuries, but it is not immediate. There is naked shame, but it is ameliorated with God-made clothing. There is expulsion from the garden, and the pain of childbirth and the battle of the sexes and the curse on the soil, but even outside the garden, Adam and Eve are still equally divine "images" (5:1–2), still the bearers of offspring and of life itself, and their descendants are still given the earth to fill and make fruitful (9:1). There does come, with horrible swiftness, the first murder by their firstborn child of their second, but *Yahweh's* advance warning and subsequent punishment of Cain for Abel's death seem strangely lenient – not life for life, as we might expect, but a mark of divine protection on the killer wherever his exile shall take him (4:10–15).

Cain and Abel

Debates over whether *Yahweh* prefers shepherds like Abel over farmers like Cain miss the point of this passage. The phrase "firstborn of his flock" (4:3) provides a better clue: Abel gives of his first-born, while Cain *is* the firstborn who, in the first of many divine pronouncements, should not presume on his elder status because, as made explicit later, "the older will serve the younger" (25:23). Cain fails this test of his arrogant, jealous soul and, despite explicit divine warning, murders his brother – a sin to which Claudius alludes in *Hamlet*: fratricide "hath the primal eldest curse upon it."

The Mark of Cain

This phrase has been the occasion of terrible though accidental mischief. As some European Christians sought a biblical warrant for enslaving and oppressing Africans, there grew up the textually unsupported notion that black skin was "the Mark of Cain," which therefore made slavery and segregation an inherited punishment. Any reasonable reading of the passage makes it clear that (i) the mark is not specified, and (ii) it is a protection rather than an excuse for abuse. The real question – why does God protect a murderer? – fits into a larger narrative pattern, already noted, of delayed divine judgment. Cain is the prototype of bloody-minded mankind who finally perish in Noah's Flood. Significant re-workings and allusions to the curse of Cain include *Beowulf* (Grendel is Cain's descendant), *Hamlet* (a brother's murder), and throughout John Steinbeck's *East of Eden*. Films like *The Caine Mutiny*, *High Noon* (Marshall Kane) and the *Bourne* series also build on the alienated wanderer theme.

Compounding the strange sense of leniency in God's ongoing covenant with Adam is the subsequent story of Cain's descendant Lamech. He is the first man to overthrow Adamic monogamy, which promised marital parity, and in its place inaugurate polygamy to display his power. Lamech's bloated sense of sexual entitlement is mirrored by his outsized self-regard; indeed he thuggishly threatens death to anyone who inflicts on him any injury. So Lamech harangues his two wives with exponential arrogance:

> Adah and Zillah, hear my voice;
> Wives of Lamech, listen to my speech!
> For I have killed a man for wounding me,
> Even a young man for hurting me.
> If Cain shall be avenged sevenfold,
> Then Lamech seventy-sevenfold. (4:23–24)

Lamech would rather be feared than loved, and rules with brutally disproportionate shows of violence that demonstrate how far human virtue has already fallen since the Garden, and that point forward to a grim and bloody future. Still, God does not intervene to pass judgment on this increasingly monstrous patriarchal misrule – yet.

These narratives of the first seven human generations end with what appears to be the reminder of a fresh start for Adam's covenant line: "And Adam knew his wife again, and she bore a son and named him Seth, 'For God has appointed another seed for me instead of Abel, whom Cain killed.' And as for Seth, to him also a son was born; and he named him Enosh. Then men began to call on the name of the LORD" (4:25–26). This replacement son, and his offspring, stand at the head of the first major fork in the genealogical road, as the rebellious line of Cain opens out onto a terrible prospect of increasing sexual iniquity, gender inequity, and general havoc, while the more humble line of Seth seeks a restoration of divine favor.

Yet that divine favor is never far to find; the fifth chapter recites the prospering of Adam's descendants through Seth over ten more generations, beginning the genealogy by repeating the original blessings bestowed at Creation and still in effect: "In the day that God created man, He made him in the likeness of God. He created them male and female, and blessed them and called them Mankind in the day they were created" (5:1–2). And the "Sethites" seem to bear out this renewed hope. No specific wickedness is named about them, their longevity remains high, and among them are two men of special note: Enoch, who "walked with God, and he was not, for God took him" (5:23), and at the end, Noah, whose father, another and better Lamech, names Noah from the Hebrew word for "rest" or "comfort," and predicts that "[t]his one will comfort us concerning our work and the toil of our hands, because of the ground which the LORD has cursed" (5:29). Yet there are darker reminders too: we're told that Adam's son Seth, the father of this improved line, is still "a son in his own [Adam's] likeness, after his image" (5:3) – thus bearing Adam's more frail nature, and the mentions of "toil" and the "cursed" ground provide a grimmer ending frame to this more hopeful section, and a foreboding of the change in covenant that will follow.

Genealogies and the Covenants

Certainly tedious for most modern readers are the genealogical passages that frequently take up whole chapters, and sometimes (as in Numbers and Chronicles) large sections of whole books. Why, we wonder, break up the otherwise lively narratives with these monotonous ancestral lists? The answer is that, for the original audiences, these genealogies were of primary interest, with the narrative material being supplemental. In other words, much as each section of Genesis begins, "these are the generations," so the whole Book of Genesis, with ten of these *Toledoth* (family scrolls) should be understood as an integrated set of genealogies supplemented with narrative commentary.

Similarly, in the ancient epics of Homer and Virgil (and in those of their later imitators), the least compelling parts for modern readers are often the lengthy catalogues of warriors (or in Milton's *Paradise Lost*, demons and angels) that seemingly disrupt the flow of the tale.

But surely this is only a matter of perspective – that is, as to whose are the ancestors? Consider the old family album on the living room coffee table. To a person outside the family circle, an invitation to scan the faces of the tribal elders will be of rather limited interest, but to a descendant whose own face and height and stance and manner were mysteriously formed by those elders, the family album will be filled with shocks of recognition, not always pleasant perhaps, but often fascinating.

Patriarchal Longevity

"Methuselah ate what he found on his plate / And never, as people do now, / Did he note the amount or the calory count; / He just ate it because it was chow" – Ogden Nash. The long lives of the Adamic era – Methuselah made it to 969 despite his supposedly unselective eating habits – are short compared to the lifespans of Babylonian kings in the pre-flood era of the *Gilgamesh* epic, which reach into tens of thousands of years. Many ancient origin-myths, including those of Greece and Rome, assume a "devolutionary" and "regressive" direction to history, with human life originally being far longer and stronger at the beginning and then declining in successively weaker generations down to the feeble present, from the Golden Age to the Age of Iron. In Genesis, this sense of a falling off from ancient strength appears in the near-1000-year lifespans of the patriarchs before the Flood with lifespans dropping off dramatically from Noah to Abraham as a sign of human decline. Remarkably, however, the biblical decline into terrible sin is quite abrupt – with fratricide in the second generation and all manner of violence among the long-lived sons of Cain. Again, the Adamic age is characterized by divine slowness to wrath – as God's punishment (shorter lives) lags far behind growing human wickedness.

6.1.3.2 Noahic Covenant

The story of the patriarch Noah is introduced to us in a context of steep moral and spiritual decline.

> Now it came to pass, when men began to multiply on the face of the earth, and daughters were born to them, that the sons of God saw the daughters of men, that they were beautiful; and they took wives for themselves of all whom they chose... There were giants on the earth in those days, and also afterward, when the sons of God came in to the daughters of men and they bore children to them. (6:1–2, 4)

Some have said that "the sons of God" refers to a race of interbreeding angelic or demonic beings, but in context it is more likely that they are the sons of the supposedly "godly" line of Seth, now also following the bent of carnal desire and adopting the polygamous ways of the sons of Cain. The results are impressive – a race of "giants" – but also deadly, as

> the LORD saw that the wickedness of man was great in the earth, and that every intent of the thoughts of his heart was only evil continually. And the LORD was sorry that He had made man on the earth, and He was grieved in His heart. (6:5–6)

The generous covenant with Adam, with its long-delayed punishments and its lenient treatment of mortal crime, has been exploited by a succession of increasingly depraved and remorseless generations, yielding ever more pervasive mayhem: "The earth also was corrupt before God, and the earth was filled with violence" (6:11). And the thrill of transgression has resulted inevitably in a culture of violence, of violating others' borders, their property, their bodies, their very lives. *Yahweh's* dismay and disgust at such a world without enforced consequences leads him to a regretful but drastic conclusion: "I will destroy man whom I have created from the face of the earth, both man and beast, creeping thing and birds of the air, for I am sorry that I have made them" (6:7). Everything and everyone must go – that is, almost everyone; for "Noah found grace in the eyes of the LORD ... 'I will establish My covenant with you'" (6:8, 18).

Those who know Noah's story apart from reading the Bible itself know it mainly in one of two ways: either as the children's tale of "Noah's Ark," complete with a cozy big boat and friendly animals two by two and an impromptu high-sea voyage with a rainbow at the end; or as the Bible's first great outburst of deadly divine wrath. (Theatrical and film portrayals range from the clownish animal lover of the medieval Chester play *Noah's Flood* and John Huston's *The Bible: In the Beginning* from 1966, to the sincerely fanatical anti-human environmentalist played by Russell Crowe in the 2014 *Noah*.) The anthropomorphism of the passage itself is striking, as God is remorseful for his creation of man, as if he has made a mistake and allowed it to grow worse. But while the actual account is far darker than the usual bowdlerized children's version, neither is it the portrait of a vain and capricious heavenly tyrant. Indeed, as we've observed, what's most striking about *Yahweh's* intervention is how tardy it seems, how slow is the kindling of God's wrath. What earthly lord would stand by while his commands are disobeyed, his will is flouted, and his realm is laid waste by renegade subjects – for centuries? Even for days? When we compare the Genesis Flood to the Flood of Enlil described in the *Epic of Gilgamesh*, this tardiness is even more striking, since the Babylonian version lays the blame for the flood not on human sin but on the gods in conflict, executing a petty power play against innocent human victims.

The Flood of *Yahweh* vs. The Flood of *Enlil*

In the Sumerian flood story found in the *Epic of Gilgamesh* (2700–1500 BCE) – clearly a source for Genesis – not only is humanity portrayed as the innocent victim of divine caprice, but there are two gods, Enlil and Enki, who divide the roles of judge and deliverer taken by the one Hebrew God in Genesis. Enlil, the storm god, is outraged by the spread of humanity – whom other gods had created to do their work for them, and who enjoyed life too much and made excessive noise. So Enlil announces to the divine council his plan to exterminate all the brutes with a great flood, and forbids anyone to warn them. But Enki, the earth god, is fond of the man Utnapishtim (also called Astrahasis) and, under the guise of talking to a wall, warns Utnapishtim that the flood is coming and that he and his family must make a large floating cube to protect themselves and the world's animals. After the flood comes and Utnapishtim survives, he celebrates by sacrificing to all the gods, including Enlil, who are hungry for meat. Enlil, pleased, blesses Utnapishtim and his wife with immortality.

The patience of God is magnified further if we assume the viewpoint of the narrator from Genesis 1–2 onward – that *Yahweh Elohim* has any creator's prerogative over his own creation, or an author's right over her own text. That is, just as a human artist or poet has the absolute right to destroy a new but flawed canvas or a corrupted manuscript that bears his name – or as a programmer deletes corrupt software – so the divine Artist has the absolute right to undo the works of his own hands. In fact, thinking of the Creator's power as something like an artist's prerogative will give us a clearer idea of how central is God's identity as Creator to the understanding of his Deity: that his powers of violence are not violent in the usual "legal" sense, since "violence" involves violating an independent entity, and in the Hebraic cosmos, all entities are ultimately dependent on their Maker for their very being. One can't steal one's own property or transgress one's own boundaries. As the old rule of English common law has it, "he that may make, may mar." We may of course doubt the existence of such a God with such rights, but to understand how he behaves in the story we must at least temporarily give him the benefit of these doubts.

Compounding these implications of divine patience and prerogative in the text is the sense of corrupt humanity as a terrible contagion that must somehow be washed away. Thus, the Flood seems a frighteningly appropriate means of judgment, as a universal flushing clean of the polluted earth. And what would seem to be a case of towering misanthropy on God's part is undercut, not only by the egregious human evil described, and by the Maker's right to undo his making, but also by the repeated statements of divine regret, and by the bright exception of Noah. The LORD's judgment is portrayed not as an angry, vindictive plan to exterminate humanity, but rather as an almost infinitely reluctant decision that humanity must be re-begun or, in computer terms, "re-booted." And so come God's warnings to Noah of the approaching cataclysm, and his new covenant for a fresh start.

Remarkably, given his rueful amazement at general human wickedness, God takes Noah very fully into his confidence, explaining his moral rationale for the coming destruction, providing a carefully detailed set of rescue instructions, and promising a renewed covenant that makes Noah, in effect, like another Adam. We needn't belabor the famous divine plan for deliverance (Noah is to build his ark of gopher wood sealed with pitch, bring on board his family and all animals two by two, and seven by seven in the case of sacrificially clean animals); nor need we detail the course of events (forty days and nights of rain, 150 days of total earth immersion, then a touchdown on Mount Ararat and the return of a dove with olive branch to confirm dry land after a year on board) (6:13–8:19). These specifics all confirm the careful concern of God for Noah, but the two crucial moments for patriarchal covenant history come after the return to solid earth.

First comes the Noahic Covenant itself, which renews central features of the Adamic Covenant with certain crucial changes. On the side of continuity, Noah and his sons are told, as in Genesis 1:28, "Be fruitful and multiply, and fill the earth" (9:1), with the promises that the cycle of the seasons will now remain unchanged while the earth itself lasts, and that no more will God bring worldwide floods (8:21–22). But the old Adamic days of easier relations with nature, and of leniency with human sin, are passing away into an era of harsher circumstances:

> And the fear of you and the dread of you shall be on every beast of the earth, on every bird of the air, on all that move on the earth, and on all the fish of the sea. They are given into your hand. Every moving thing that lives shall be food for you. (9:2–3)

Noah learns that humanity is to become both a pariah and a predator, interrupting creation's original harmonies, though now with meat on the menu for compensation. But, in conditions even more grim, bloodthirsty man cannot quench that thirst with real blood – none may be eaten (9:4) – and Cain's original fratricide must now receive the ultimate punishment: "From the hand of every man's brother I will require the life of man. Whoever sheds man's blood, by man his blood shall be shed; for in the image of God He made man" (9:5–6). God seems to have hoped for centuries that humanity might come to its senses under a more permissive regime. But now, after the cleansing Flood he has resigned himself to the idea that even the best of men need a strong dose of fear and coercion to restrain their evil bent. And yet, even capital punishment has its roots in a heavenly principle: that the divine image in every person renders their blood precious in the sight of God.

With these promises (the end of worldwide floods, the continuance of seasonal order, the allowance of eating meat) and these conditions (the command to fill the earth, the prohibition of blood, the institution of a death penalty for murder) comes one great confirming sign, beloved of Hebrew and Sunday School nurseries: the rainbow. And yet, this is no mere infantile symbol: to have seen a real rainbow appear over a storm-washed landscape is to have known the awe of something beautiful both in its perfect symmetry and iridescent colors, and exalted in the loftiness that draws the eye irresistibly upward. The rainbow, associated with the dark edges of receding storms and shot through with light arching to heaven, powerfully represents both divine relenting and human aspiration.

But the dark edges remain, and if God seems resigned to the failings of even the best men, the account of Noah concludes with just such a dispiriting anticlimax. In a story usually left out of the children's Bibles, Noah's return to agriculture leads him to plant grapes, and then to make wine, and then to get drunk – and he "became uncovered in his tent" (9:21). Ironically, the new "Adam," in a new garden of sorts, is also found shamefully naked, and humanity's "fresh start" is already soiled. If Noah is not the first biblical patriarch with feet of clay, he certainly won't be the last – but it is the aftermath of the story that connects most clearly to the continuing covenantal theme. Noah's middle son, Ham, sees his father's exposed condition and reports it, perhaps with some glee, to his brothers Shem and Japheth. The oldest and youngest sons have the decency to cover their father while looking away, but when Noah comes to himself and learns that he has been made sport of by Ham, he pronounces a curse – on Ham's son Canaan! "'Cursed be Canaan; a servant of servants he shall be to his brethren.' And he said: 'Blessed be the LORD, the God of Shem, and may Canaan be his servant'" (9:25–26). Here a great divide seems to open between our times and Bible times.

There are three forebodings in this frightening codicil to the Noahic Covenant. First – and this is one of the hardest concepts for modern Western readers – patriarchal blessings and curses are thought to be binding from father to son and beyond, "even to the tenth generation" (Deuteronomy 23:2). Second, these blessings and curses obviously predate any actual good or bad deeds by their inheritors. And third, this particular prediction seems to foreshadow and indeed authorize later Hebrew conquest of the "land of Canaan," which will become the land of Israel. We will encounter this imaginative trope of intergenerational guilt and grace many times in subsequent chapters and books of the Bible, but at this point we must observe three things: first, that it is central not only to Jewish but also to Christian thinking, in the forms of the Christian doctrines of Original Sin and of the New Covenant; second, that most non-Western cultures still think intergenerationally and collectively about their relationship to good and evil; and third, that contemporary secular discourses of social justice rely heavily on this idea of inherited guilt as well.

The Curse of Canaan: Inherited Guilt and Blessing

The patriarchal idea of an extended "family curse" seems to many like a motif from classical tragedy or the gothic horror genre. Yet as we've noted, its ancient power, while much softened by both Rabbinical Judaism and by Christian ideas of atonement, is surprisingly persistent and contemporary, even in the secular realm. When we discuss the Major Prophets in Chapter 12, we'll see how both Jeremiah and Ezekiel – without denying inherited evil – emphasize God's willingness to forgive each new generation, and also stress the individual's responsibility to choose good in the present (Jer. 31:29, Ezek. 18:2). And when we turn to the New Testament, we'll see how Paul both points back to Adam to show that humanity inherits Adam's curse (Rom. 3:23–24, Eph. 2:5–6, I Cor. 15:22), and in the same passages argues that the death and resurrection of Jesus have freed everyone from inherited guilt.

6.1.3.3 Abrahamic Covenant

With Abraham's covenant, we turn from the "**Universal**" covenants with Adam and Noah – which the LORD makes with the founding and re-founding fathers of the entire human race – to "**Particular**" covenants with Abraham, Moses, and David, which the LORD makes with patriarchs of a specific family or nation. The Universal covenants have traditionally been read – both by Jews and by Christians – as applying inclusively to all humanity, while the Particular covenants have been read as applying exclusively to the people specially chosen. Yet each of these latter three Particular covenants also contains within it an ultimate promise of wide inclusion – of a specific group set apart (and increasingly kept apart) to achieve a mission that will, in the fullness of time, embrace all nations.

Like the Noahic Covenant, the Abrahamic Covenant is introduced in the context of further moral and spiritual decline. After Noah's curse on Canaan at the end of Genesis 9, the next two chapters consist largely of genealogies of which three things mainly can be said: first, that while Noah's descendants are fruitfully multiplying, they are not initially obeying God's command to spread out over the face of the earth; second, that they are accelerating the "devolution" of humanity's longevity after the Flood with ever-decreasing lifespans, from Noah's near-record 950 years to Terah's paltry 148; and third, that nearly all of Noah's offspring inherit his feet of clay rather than his righteousness.

The most noted story in this genealogical passage, about the famous Tower of Babel, strikingly echoes the story of Eden. Instead of obeying a prime directive of the Adamic and Noahic Covenants – "fill the earth" – the over-reaching sons of Ham and Cush apparently led by Nimrod (10:8–10) rally together on the plains of Shinar to build "a tower with a top in the heavens" as they strive to "make a name for ourselves lest we be scattered abroad" (11:4). They create the brick technology later associated in Exodus with Pharaonic slavery, and with these bricks they construct a man-made mountain – which suggests both a platform for viewing the stars (commonly worshiped in Sumer and Babylon) and the Near Eastern mountain-top shrines. In so doing they also anticipate that modern monument to human striving, the skyscraper.

"Make a Name"

The word here is *shem*, which not only means "name" in Hebrew, but also is the name of Noah's first son, as well as a common reverential substitute among Jews for the divine names *Elohim* and *Yahweh*, who is frequently referred to by the devout as *Ha Shem* – "The Name." Thus, the usage here indicates not only an arrogant rivalry with Shem's more godly line, but also suggests a competition with God himself.

The LORD sees and is displeased, not only because of their disobedience, but because of their arrogant hunger for God-like power and omniscience. The dream of self-sufficient "knowing" that led to the first sin in Eden is now organized and on the march. It is not so much that they wish to build that angers *Yahweh*, but what: a symbol of their own over-reaching greatness – like, in modern times, the mammoth works of a Soviet Five-Year Plan, or the vaunting architecture of the Third Reich. These modern analogies, and the often heinous behavior of humanity from Adam to Noah, may help us to hear the special urgency in the LORD's words "now nothing that they propose to do will be withheld from them" (11:6). What new monstrosities does Babel's regime have in store? Given this threat, and the insult it offers to God, it is remarkable that, as in Eden, *Yahweh's* punishments are so lenient, yet effective: "Come, let Us go down and confuse their language," he says (11:7). Rather than sending another killing flood, or "the fire next time," his elegant and bloodless solution is to scramble their communications; because linguistic unity is a great accelerator of totalizing effort, divided languages naturally weaken such projects and whole governments. And this gentler form of judgment succeeds finally in scattering the people abroad (11:8).

So, as we come to meet "father Abraham," it is clear that the "Golden Age" and the "Silver Age" are past; that the heroic era of "giants in the earth" is over; and that, even among the more loyal line of Shem, *Yahweh*-worship has declined to mere glowing embers. By the end of the Genesis 11 genealogy, human life has descended to patterns more recognizable by the modern eye: dense urban settlement in the early cities of the Fertile Crescent; marrying, begetting, and the dispersal of the nations; peoples separated off into distinct language groups and religious cultures worshiping varied gods; and a general ordinariness settling over daily affairs as the generations go about their business while crawling between earth and heaven, cradle and grave.

Ancient Mesopotamia and the Fertile Crescent in the Time of the Patriarchs

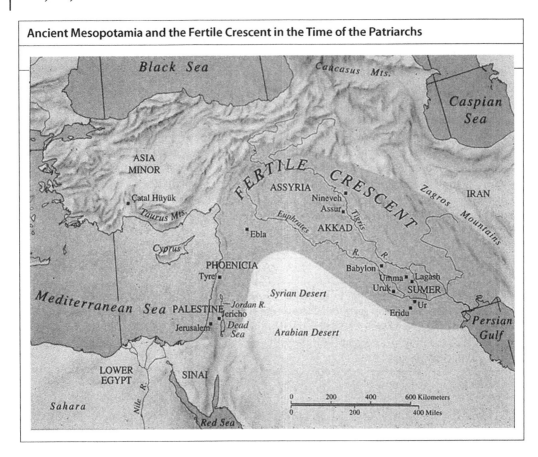

It is out of this urban Near Eastern network that Abram, whose name means "high father," first emerges – specifically, from the city of Ur in Chaldea. He is migrating, with his father Terah, northwest and then southwest along the Fertile Crescent. Married to the beautiful but barren Sarai, committed to caring for his nephew Lot, and bound for the land of Canaan, Abram is leaving behind the comforts and security of his father's country, separating himself from the gods and practices of that country, and setting out to a land of promise. And indeed the covenant that will bear his name makes "land" the first promise:

> Get out of your country,
> From your family
> And from your father's house,
> To a land that I will show you.
> I will make you a great nation;
> I will bless you
> And make your name great;
> And you shall be a blessing.
> I will bless those who bless you,
> And I will curse him who curses you;
> And in you all the families of the earth shall be blessed. (12:1–3)

The LORD promises to bless his descendants with land and – strangely for a man with an infertile wife – vast offspring, and to protect him from his enemies. Significantly, in addition to promising that Abram will be blessed, the LORD also promises that Abram will be a blessing, not merely to his region or country, but to "all the families of the earth." Here, even as *Yahweh* is separating Abram out from the rest of humanity for a special mission, it's clear that somehow this mission eventually will embrace all peoples. From their beginnings, the Hebrews will live with the paradox that their divinely mandated exclusivity has an ultimately inclusive purpose.

The conditions placed on Abram for receiving these promises are few – but in no way easy. First, as already noted, he must leave his homeland and extended family network and, site unseen, emigrate to a new world. This act of obedience is also an act of profound trust, making it clear that under this covenant, belief will be confirmed by action, and that action will fortify faith. "And he believed in the LORD, and He accounted it to him for righteousness," we're told (15:6); and later, "'I am Almighty God; walk before Me and be blameless'" (17:1). Instead of the hundreds of commands that will constitute the later Mosaic Covenant, this covenant stresses Abram's intimate relationship to God as a personal guide whose companionship will direct the patriarch's daily steps. For the Hebrew, faith will be indistinguishable from faithfulness, and deeds inseparable from belief.

Given this emphasis on faithful action, the signs of this covenant resemble conditions as well. The LORD's command to cut loose from familiar surroundings and cultural ways is intensified by more drastic forms of active cutting: the "cutting of the covenant" and, most famously, male circumcision. By "cutting a covenant" with Abram in Genesis 15:9–19, *Yahweh* unilaterally adapts a common ancient Near Eastern ceremony for sealing bilateral human contracts: the two parties would bring varied sacrificial animals to the "signing ceremony," slaughter and divide each in two, and then walk together down the aisle made of divided carcasses reciting the formula of a binding curse that anyone who breaks the covenant will be divided like these animals. Similarly, the LORD commands Abram to bring his sacrifices, kill and split them, and lay them out. But the actual procession takes place in a dream, while Abram is passive and unconscious, stressing his complete dependence on God while God renews his promise to give Abram's descendants all the land "from the river of Egypt to the great river, the River Euphrates" (15:18).

The other covenantal "cutting," more often noted and still very much in practice, is circumcision – the removal of the infant boy's foreskin on the eighth day of his life (17:10–14). Circumcision may seem a strange and even ironic sign for a patriarchal covenant; and indeed it's worth mentioning that in many non-Western patriarchal cultures, the objects of circumcision have been, and still are, the female genitalia. But that has never been so among the Hebrews. Not only are females spared a "cutting," but all males must undergo it as the defining covenant sign. It is as if God's intent is to cut away at the organ most symbolic of patriarchal power and pride, and to claim divine ownership of all the offspring that it will produce. Indeed, that's precisely what it seems to mean – since there is plenty of archeological evidence that in the ancient Near East, statuary images of the erect phallus were common objects of worship, so here the "divine penis" is being cut down to size. And because it is the male member that, in the fullest sense, passes on the "seed" of sin-corrupted human nature, that member must bear a sanctifying mark.

Purification After Childbirth

Because female Hebrew infants were not circumcised, the period of the mother's purification after female childbirth – two weeks – is twice as long as that for male childbirth – one week. See Leviticus 12:1–5.

Besides these signs, the Abrahamic Covenant – as even the title implies – involves the changing of names. "No longer shall your name be called Abram ['High Father'], but your name shall be Abraham ['Father of a Multitude']; for I have made you a father of many nations. I will make you exceedingly fruitful; and I will make nations of you, and kings shall come from you" (17:5–6). "As for Sarai your wife, you shall not call her name Sarai ['Princess'], but Sarah ['Princess of *Yah*'] shall be her name. And I will bless her and also give you a son by her; then I will bless her, and she shall be a mother of nations; kings of peoples shall be from her" (17:15–16). We have spoken above about biblical irony, and one of the most insistent and penetrating ironies in the Genesis narrative is that this father and mother of multitudes are childless – more specifically, that "Sarai, Abram's wife, had borne him no children" (16:1). And, in the book's most pervasive irony, we will trace the many twistings and turnings by which the scheming patriarch and infertile matriarch come to fruitfulness, and the often dubious light that the narrative casts on patriarchy itself.

6.2 Warts and All: Abraham and Anti-Patriarchal Patriarchy

We've already seen how, from the Creation stories onward, Genesis complicates and undercuts conventional Near Eastern notions of patriarchal power and privilege: the almighty yet non-violent and nurturing Creator; the strikingly egalitarian first couple; the curse for the first sin meted out not only to the woman but to the man; Cain the murderous firstborn son; the thuggish and polygamous Lamech; even the drunken Noah. Each of these portrayals appeals, whether by positive or negative example, to an ideal of fatherly authority that practices generosity and self-restraint, and that serves rather than domineers. And a remarkable number of the examples are negative, as if the ultimate fairness of these portraits depended on the patriarchs being painted not as plaster saints, but warts and all.

With Abram and Sarai, there's not long to wait for their narrative of anti-patriarchal patriarchy to begin, as they undulate regularly between model and reprehensible behavior. In Genesis 12, no sooner have they answered God's call to leave their home for a far country than (as we've noted repeatedly above) Abram concocts the self-protective cover story that he is traveling with his very attractive sister, thus fooling Pharaoh and his entire court – and, at least for the time being, getting lucrative rewards for it (12:10–20). The next two chapters return Abram to a more favorable light. In Genesis 13, in order to end a conflict with his nephew Lot over grazing rights in Canaan, he offers to separate from Lot and allows him to choose whatever pastures he prefers (Lot fatefully selects the rich green country near Sodom and Gomorrah), while Abram settles for what is left. In chapter 14, Lot's choice begins to haunt him as he is taken hostage when King Chedorlaomer defeats the Kings of Sodom and Gomorrah, while Abram gathers a force of over 300, rescues Lot and all the goods looted from Sodom and Gomorrah, and even refuses to be rewarded by their kings with any booty, except a day's food for his men. Here Abram's behavior shows the patriarch to be peaceable, generous, clever, courageous, and driven by godly faith and family loyalty rather than by a supposedly "patriarchal" hunger for land, power, or wealth.

Melchizedek

One strong sign of Abram's faithfulness is his blessing by "Melchizedek king of Salem [who] brought out bread and wine; he was the priest of God Most High" (v. 18), and Abram's gift of a tithe (a tenth) of all his possessions to this mysterious priest-king whose name means "king of righteousness." Note that like a number of important righteous figures in the Hebrew Bible (including Job, Jethro, and Hiram of Tyre), Melchizedek is a Gentile whose relation to "God Most High" does not require his becoming a Jew.

Yet Genesis 15 finds Abram, after his bravery and his bypassing of the battle's spoils, complaining anxiously to the LORD that his wealth and inheritance will pass out of his family due to his childless state – for which he blames God. Still, God replies not with rebuke but with a deeper renewal of his promise, vowing that Abram's offspring will outnumber the stars and graphically "cutting" the covenant (see discussion in section 6.1.3.3) with Abram in a dream to guarantee him the land of Canaan. Even in the midst of doubt and some bad behavior, Abram is rewarded for his undergirding faith: "And he believed in the LORD, and He accounted it to him for righteousness" (15:6). However, despite this rather rare narrative endorsement, chapter 16 shows Abram at his lowest ebb yet: at the urging of Sarai, who has despaired of bearing her own child, he resorts to surrogacy with Sarai's Egyptian slave girl Hagar.

Ironically, Hagar flaunts her pregnancy to torment her mistress, and Sarai angrily blames Abram for increasing her shame! "My wrong be upon you! I gave my maid into your embrace; and when she saw that she had conceived, I became despised in her eyes. The LORD judge between you and me" (16:5). With a passive shrug, Abram abdicates any moral responsibility for his compromise, his concubine, or her unborn child: "'Indeed your maid is in your hand; do to her as you please.' And when Sarai dealt harshly with her, she fled from her presence" (16:6). Like Adam and Eve when confronted for eating the forbidden fruit, Abram and Sarai seem to vie for the crown of ignobility, with Hagar herself a close third. The patriarchal line appears doomed by the founding father and mother either to extinction or to bastardy, and the LORD's intervention to save the pregnant Hagar – though a sign of divine mercy to Gentiles – foreshadows a long history of enmity between the offspring of expediency and of promise:

Biblical and Quranic Accounts of Abraham

The Quranic account of these patriarchal characters and events, while overlapping the biblical, differs in crucial details. For in the Qur'an, it is not Ishaq (Isaac) who is the divinely preferred son of Ibrahim (Abraham) in his old age, but Ismail (Ishmael) – whom Ibrahim must offer up as a sacrifice in a test imposed by Allah, a test that Allah halts once Ibrahim's faithful intent is clear. Thus, in this alternate Islamic sacred history – admittedly, composed nearly 2000 years after the description in Genesis – it is not the Jewish descendants of Ishaq who are the chosen of Allah, but the Arabic descendants of Ismail. See the Qur'an, Suras 11 and 37, and compare also Genesis 22.

> You shall call his name Ishmael ["God hears"],
> Because the LORD has heard your affliction.
> He shall be a wild man;
> His hand shall be against every man,
> And every man's hand against him. (16:11–12)

There are many laws written in the Books of Moses, but an unwritten law that is pervasively enforced by circumstance is the Law of Unintended Consequences.

Yet despite Abram's ill-advised emergency measures, chapter 17 finds God intervening yet again to reaffirm his original reproductive plan with two further covenant signs: as already noted above, the changing of names and the additional "cutting" of circumcision. Abram becomes "Abraham," Sarai "Sarah," and the Almighty raises the ante by promising the fruitless couple that they shall breed "many nations" once the patriarchal penis has been modified according to divine command (17:5). (Note the use of the generic divine name *Elohim* throughout this chapter suggesting the Deity's, and the couple's, universal mission to bless all humanity.) The newly renamed Father of Multitudes displays paradoxically mixed responses: falling on his face in awe, he nevertheless "laughed in his heart" with derision, saying to himself,

"Shall a child be born to a man who is one hundred years old? And shall Sarah, who is ninety years old, bear a child?" (17:17). Abraham then makes so bold as to suggest a more "realistic" course to God: "Oh, that Ishmael might live before you!" (18). Remarkably, the divine response is not anger at this reminder of Abraham's past unfaithful behavior, but a patient insistence that while Ishmael shall indeed be blessed, "My covenant I will establish with Isaac, whom Sarah will bear to you at this set time next year" (17:20–21). The name Isaac – *itzhak* or "laughter" in Hebrew – even implies a glint of divine amusement and suggests that ultimately the joke will, happily, be on the patriarch.

This suggestion of happy divine irony is even stronger in the next chapter, when Abraham greets three unexpected visitors with generous and ceremonious hospitality, which is a common sign of virtue in the ancient world. He is rewarded with the revelation that the visitors are angels and that the LORD himself is among them, promising yet again that "Sarah your wife shall have a son" (18:10). This time it is Sarah (eavesdropping from inside their tent) who laughs sardonically: "After I have grown old, shall I have pleasure, my lord being old also?" (18:12). The divine visitor catches her out with a good-natured but alarming question, leading to the sort of exchange one has with a child exposed in a silly lie:

> "Why did Sarah laugh, saying, 'Shall I surely bear a child, since I am old?' Is anything too hard for the LORD? ..."
> But Sarah denied it, saying, "I did not laugh," for she was afraid.
> And He said, "No, but you did laugh!" (18:13–15)

This suggestion of a divine paternal chuckle at childish ways is all the more remarkable given the larger context of the visit; for the visitors are on the road to Sodom and Gomorrah to "see whether they have done altogether according to the outcry against it that has come to me; and if not, I will know" (18:21). Will the LORD's indulgence to his chosen ones, even in their doubts and disobedience, extend even to the *goyim* whose "sin is very grave" (18:20)? How far will God's fatherly patience go in forestalling heavenly wrath?

The Sins of Sodom

The "Cities of the Plain" are closely linked in the Judeo-Christian imagination with particular kinds of sexual sin, most notably the sin of homosexual intercourse, or "sodomy." While same-sex relations are indeed forbidden to Jews and Christians as counter to the Creation norm of heterosexual monogamy established in Genesis 1–2 — see especially Leviticus 18:22 and Romans 1:26–27 — the sins of Sodom include not only forms of forbidden sexuality, but also aggravated assault and a grotesque violation of the ancient laws of hospitality to strangers.

The next incident appears to be the most striking piece of human–divine bargaining found anywhere in the Bible. The anthropomorphism of the passage is high: Abraham speaks to the LORD as if He needs restraining – indeed as if He needs to be kept back from acting unjustly out of irrational rage.

> Suppose there were fifty righteous within the city; would You also destroy the place and not spare it for the fifty righteous that were in it? Far be it from You to do such a thing as this, to slay the righteous with the wicked...! Shall not the Judge of all the earth do right? (18:24–25)

Yahweh assents: "If I find in Sodom fifty righteous within the city, then I will spare all the place for their sakes" (18:26). What follows then is a process of dickering worthy of the Near Eastern souq, and sprinkled with such flattering and at times wheedling language:

> Indeed now, I who am but dust and ashes have taken it upon myself to speak to the Lord: Suppose there were five less than the fifty righteous; … Suppose there should be forty found there?… Let not the Lord be angry, and I will speak: Suppose thirty should be found there?… Indeed now, I have taken it upon myself to speak to the Lord: Suppose twenty should be found there?… I will speak but once more: Suppose ten should be found there? (18:27–32)

At each turn in the exchange, "the Judge of all the earth" promises in straightforward, affectless words to spare the wicked for the sakes of fewer and fewer righteous, down to ten – interestingly a *minyan* or minimum number for a Hebrew congregation, and also within Abraham's unspoken margin of safety: for living in Sodom are his nephew Lot, Lot's wife, two daughters, and their husbands. Is Father Abraham testing the LORD to discover the extent of his mercy? Or, after all, is the LORD actually testing the patriarch – to discover how well Abraham understands both the patience of the Almighty, and its limits? As in the devolution of human virtue from Adam to Noah in Genesis 4–6, this passage stresses the longsuffering nature of true patriarchal justice, whether divine or human; and yet that longsuffering – well past all ordinary human endurance – eventually has an end, whether in a flood or in fire and brimstone.

As the following chapter makes clear through dramatic juxtaposition, the consequences of patriarchal choice can be exponential. Abraham, despite his many failings and flaws, has chosen the way of patience and faith, and reaps blessing. On the other hand, Lot, despite some early advantages, reaps the whirlwind. When given the choice by Uncle Abram, he had seized on the best land, the ease of city life, and praise in the gates of Sodom – and already he has suffered invasion, pillage, and captivity before his uncle came to the rescue. Now, the results of his choosing the Cities of the Plain are far more dire, as two angelic visitors arrive at the gates to discover these cities' wicked ways. Lot is the picture of shameful moral compromise: sitting as a city elder in the gate, enjoying many of Sodom's benefits, he nevertheless recoils from the full results of its corruption, and tries to shield the strangers from the worst of it – or rather, perhaps, to shield the city from their investigation? "'[W]e will spend the night in the open square,'" they tell Lot; "but he insisted strongly, so they turned into him, and entered his house" (19:2–3).

Yet even Lot's nervous efforts at righteous hospitality are shot through with dark, sickening irony. When his fellow citizens learn of the fresh new visitors and all of them mob his house to demand that he "[b]ring them out to us so that we may know them carnally," the would-be patriarch feebly attempts moral persuasion ("Please, my brethren, do not do so wickedly!") and then offers up his own married daughters so that "you may do to them as you wish" (19:5, 7–8). In his heinous confusion, he displays more family feeling ("my brethren") for a crowd of Sodomite rapists than for his own flesh and blood, and in his grotesque misogyny, he would rather see his daughters ravished than fight his reprobate "brethren" to protect his (presumably) male guests.

Of course, fortunately for Lot, these guests are not properly men at all, but angels, and in a rare biblical show of angelic "superpowers," the heavenly agents blind the mob, cast them back, and sternly warn Lot to get his family out of the doomed city immediately before they call in the biblical equivalent of a nuclear strike. Having tried to prostitute his daughters, Lot has so little authority with his sons-in-law that they ignore his warning because to them "he seemed to be joking." Astonishingly, Lot and his family "linger" so long in Sodom that the angels must take them by the hands and force them out of the gates. The angels exhort them, "Do not look behind you nor stay anywhere in the plain," but Lot's civic loyalty is so truly bizarre that he begs to remain in the nearby small city of Zoar (Hebrew for "little") to wait out the coming apocalypse. Indulged even in this by the angel, Lot saves his life but loses his wife, who looks longingly back to Sodom and Gomorrah as they go up in flames, and is changed "into a pillar of salt" – a monument to the sterility and desolation worked by the sins of the fathers (and mothers) (19:12–26).

Fittingly, the aftermath to this account of Sodom's ruin juxtaposes the failed patriarch Lot with the flawed but faithful patriarch Abraham, who stands again "in the place where he had stood before the LORD" when he first separated from Lot in chapter 13 and chose the way of humility, trust, and patience. From there, Abraham looks "toward Sodom and Gomorrah, and toward all the land of the plain, and he saw … the smoke of the land which went up like the smoke of a furnace." He looks not gloatingly, but with some grief at its loss, and with fear and gratitude that "God remembered Abraham, and sent Lot out of the midst of the overthrow" (19:27–29). Lot, on the other hand, though escaped, is still overthrown. Having chosen the way of excess, power, and instant abundance, he is reduced to the sickliest irony of all: without a city, a wife, a fortune, or the respect of his now-widowed daughters, he loses the last shreds of his dignity in their plan for drunken incest that will, in their words, "preserve the lineage of our father" (19:34). At the last, Lot's attempt at patriarchy has rendered his fatherhood as nothing but mere "seed" and his lineage as abominable bastardy; lacking inner fatherly wisdom, courage, faith, or self-restraint, he ends his tale stripped of all outer fatherly trappings, raped by his daughters, in naked shame. Yet his offspring, we are told, will be many: the Moabites and the Ammonites (19:37–38), who, along with the Ishmaelites, will plague the sons of Abraham, Isaac, and Jacob for generations to come.

For the sake of further juxtaposing patriarchal successes and failures, chapter 20 of Genesis gives us the story of Abraham's dubious doings with King Abimelech of Gerar. While many higher critics of the *Torah* have treated this story as simply an alternate version of Abram's deception of Pharaoh in Genesis 12, there's good reason both thematically and structurally to read Genesis 20 as a separate episode. Once we grasp the "warts and all," anti-hagiographic intent of these patriarchal narratives, then it makes perfectly good storytelling sense that even the great patriarch could be so foolish or so conniving as to repeat the same "sister act" twice – simply in a different kingdom. Yet there is a further difference, for here in Genesis 20 we learn that Sarah actually is Abraham's sister – "the daughter of my father but not the daughter of my mother" (20:12) – so the half-sister is the occasion for another patriarchal half-truth, and another undulation before the consummation of God's promise – and not for the last time.

It is at this juncture that the dissonance between patriarchal behavior and divine reward reaches one of its sharpest crescendos, and that the narrator's – and God's – deferred judgment seems particularly troubling. Abraham and Sarah, who have deceived Abimelech with what amounts to a well-tried confidence trick, nevertheless walk away far wealthier from Gerar than when they came, and (stranger still) it is again – as with Pharaoh earlier – the heathen king who apologizes for his moral failing. Meanwhile (strangest of all) Abraham the successful confidence man prays that God will lift his curse of barrenness from the house of Abimelech. God seems more an accomplice than a judge here. And then, on the heels of this apparent moral inversion, comes the greatest blessing of all: the birth of Isaac, the promised heir. The sense of divine favoritism is palpable as the patriarch's sharp dealings are juxtaposed with his greatest hopes fulfilled.

Still, taken on its own, the story of Isaac's conception and birth in 21:1–7 is a joyous and even miraculous one. Although in the past both Abraham and Sarah had laughed cynically at divine promises of elderly parenthood, here they greet their late-life child with gratitude and gaiety. The happy irony of Isaac's name is clear in Sarah's certainty that "all who hear will laugh with me" – and significantly, not "at me." God is credited with keeping his apparently impossible promise, and Sarah's wifely affection seems renewed in her pleasure at having borne a son for Abraham.

Indeed, the crescendo of goodwill seems to grow further as we're told that Abraham will give "a great feast" on the day of Isaac's weaning – traditionally at two years old. Were Genesis a simple piece of optimistic fiction about a saintly ancestor, this would be a good place for the happy ending, or if it were a "family film," for the credits to roll. However, the story instead takes a turn toward family dysfunction as dispiriting as anything in a modern novel or play. Ishmael seems to have inherited his mother Hagar's haughty spirit, and when Sarah sees the sixteen-year-old mocking her little boy Isaac, hope for a family reconciliation is shattered as she demands that Abraham banish the slave-woman and her son. Thickening the plot and complicating the characters even further, Abraham is displeased this time with Sarah's banishment order, but God endorses it; yet God then rescues the outcast mother and son in the wilderness and renews his promise to make Ishmael a great nation – the Arab nation (21:9–21).

As if to round out this portrait of lopsided divine favoritism toward the patriarch, Abimelech himself (the king whom Abraham had deceived into recruiting Sarah for his harem) now seeks out an alliance on the eminently pragmatic grounds that "God is with you in all that you do" (21:22). And that seems precisely true: whether Abraham behaves with courage, grace, and honesty, or whether he behaves like a swindler and a pimp, the patriarchal blessings keep coming – that is, until suddenly all seems lost.

The sacrifice of Isaac in chapter 22 is, in both Jewish and Christian readings of Genesis, the crucial event in Abraham's life; it is central to his identity as the test that confirms the patriarch's absolute commitment to the Hebrew covenant. But in literary terms, it is above all the climax of his story, where every narrative thread is tied and every element of biblical narrative style is on superb display: minimalism, wordplay, doubling, juxtaposition, deferred judgment, and irony. Note, for instance, the exquisite understatement of the opening exchange:

> Now it came to pass after these things that God tested Abraham, and said to him, "Abraham!" And he said, "Here I am." Then He said, "Take now your son, your only son Isaac, whom you love, and go to the land of Moriah, and offer him there as a burnt offering on one of the mountains of which I shall tell you." So Abraham rose early in the morning and saddled his donkey, and took two of his young men with him, and Isaac his son; and he split the wood for the burnt offering, and arose and went to the place of which God had told him. (22:1–3)

With a timed explosion of ironic wordplay on Abraham's name, God calls out to "Father-of-a-Multitude" and tells him to sacrifice not just his son, but his very fatherhood – his affection and pride and joy ("your only son Laughter, whom you love"), his hope of lands and flocks and innumerable descendants, and a great name that will fill all the earth. The patriarch will lay not only his boy on the altar, but patriarchy itself. His reply is wordless, but his action is eloquent: he simply ups and goes, leaving to our imaginations his thoughts, feelings, and expressions.

This narrative reticence and the characters' understatement continues, heightened by intensifying repetition of Abraham's laconic response, "Here I am": first to God's initial summons, then to Isaac's nervous questions, and finally to the angel of the LORD, who speaks urgently and climactically to halt Abraham's plunging knife at the very last moment: "Abraham, Abraham!" (22:11). Significantly, this phrase "Here I am," while seemingly static and passive, actually indicates Abraham's active waiting, his receptivity to God's commands, and his readiness to obey. But what a command – and how awful to obey it! Apart from the irony of cutting off the means of the patriarch's promised offspring, killing an innocent victim would seem to violate the Adamic and Noahic commands about respecting the divine image, while child sacrifice is the signature abomination associated with the Canaanite worshipers of Baal and Moloch. How much is Abraham willing to trust the divine voice? How far is he willing to go?

The answer is, all the way. "[W]here is the lamb for a burnt offering?" asks Isaac, understandably puzzled at the absence of a sacrificial animal. Abraham replies, "My son, God will provide for Himself the lamb for a burnt offering." And so, we're told, "the two of them went together" (22:7–8). Remarkably, Abraham's quiet trust in God is mirrored by Isaac's quiet trust in Abraham – a trust so great that, though he is by now an adolescent, Isaac offers no struggle when his elderly father binds him, lays him out on the wood of the altar, and reaches for his knife (22:9–10).

Juxtaposed with two previous chapters showing Abraham behaving badly and being blessed nonetheless, Genesis 22 may strike the reader as a vivid example of the patriarch finally reaping what he has sown. Phrases that spring to mind may include "pay the piper," "the other shoe drops," and "what goes around comes around." But the irony here is more complex than some sort of delayed karmic balance or exact retribution. For if a death is owed by Abraham, then it is only God the giver of life who can order it taken; yet the puzzle of the passage is that it is not the guilty father's but the innocent son's life in question – and the wonder is that God doesn't take the life. By calling off the sacrifice, the LORD distinguishes himself indelibly from local gods like Baal and Moloch, whose statues dripped with the blood of children offered by their parents. And the deepest lesson is that from the start, this sacrifice has been a "test" (22:1): because the cruel-to-be-kind logic of biblical "testing" assumes that in a world where even the best people are deeply flawed, demonstrated trust will have to stand in for perfect behavior: "now I know that you fear God, since you have not withheld your son, your only son, from Me" (22:12).

The "onliness" of Isaac is, of course, not literally numerical (we can't forget Ishmael), but instead spiritual, and in a real sense anti-patriarchal. The "son of the promise" is not the firstborn of Abraham's youth or strength or stratagems, but a younger son born of waiting, and deferral, and old age, an heir whose very existence testifies to divine power providing in the place of human weakness. And in a final twist, Genesis 22 ends by contrasting Abraham's chastened patriarchy with the more traditional kind: for if God had wanted to choose a merely natural "father of a multitude," he needn't have looked farther than Abraham's brother Nahor, who has already and rather effortlessly fathered a quiverful of children, but not the children of the promise (22:20–24). Here is narrative art of the highest order; this is how the story seems "to tell itself."

6.3 "The Older Shall Serve the Younger": Against Primogeniture

After the climactic test on Mount Moriah, the scroll of Abraham's history winds up with a few summary and transitional chapters – transitional to the succeeding patriarchal narratives of the heir Isaac, his sons Esau and Jacob, and their "generations." While these narratives are no less committed to the "warts and all" recounting of both light and dark passages in the Fathers' lives, they nevertheless focus their anti-patriarchal critiques on the particular mechanism most effective in perpetuating unchecked fatherly power: **primogeniture**, or the inheritance of the firstborn. On the contrary, if there is any watchword that most unites all these stories of chosen sons, it is that "the older shall serve the younger" (25:23). In fact, these are God's own words, revealed in a dream – significantly, not to a patriarch but to a matriarch, Rebekah. As in the earlier chapters of Genesis, both patriarchs and matriarchs are portrayed as consequential people even in spite of themselves; their deeds will live on as blessings or blights to the latest generation.

With the inheritance and succession of the chosen "younger" son Isaac made secure, his mother Sarah lives nearly forty more years, then dies at the age of 137 and is mourned by her husband, who not only weeps for her but seeks to purchase from the neighboring Hittites a permanent burial site in "the cave of Machpelah," rather than accepting it as a gift from the Hittite leader Ephron. As with the spoil offered by the King of Sodom in chapter 14, Abraham will be beholden to no one, particularly not to a Gentile, and his purchase of this burial site is his "down payment" on his descendants' eventual possession of all Canaan. Indeed, most of his successors will find their final rest in this family tomb – including Isaac, Jacob, Leah, and Joseph.

Abraham and the Hittites

Abraham's negotiations for the cave of Machpelah constitute most of Genesis 23, and the prominent mention here of Ephron and his fellow "sons of Heth" has generated much discussion among archeologists, whose discoveries of Hittite artifacts and written tablets over the past century have confirmed that this Anatolian people did in fact inhabit these parts of Canaan during the patriarchal period – that is, between 2000 and 1200 BCE. There is, not surprisingly, a courtly and ritual quality to Abraham's negotiations with Ephron. The friendly Hittite initially offers the land for free only to yield rather cheerfully to the patriarch's repeated insistence on paying full price – a formula that may reflect actual Hittite negotiation customs.

Abraham's business in chapter 24 is about insuring that these covenantal successors will actually come into being – that is, by insuring a proper bride for Isaac. Isaac is strikingly passive in this process: forty years old, devoted to the memory of his mother, and still unmarried, he awaits the life partner who will be found for him by Abraham, or more correctly by Abraham's trusty servant, usually thought to be the Eliezer of Damascus mentioned in Genesis 15. For both Abraham and his servant, marrying Isaac to a worshiper of *Yahweh* is imperative, however stressful the search. Again, through long travel and trial, *Yahweh* helps and provides – and indeed appropriately the name Eliezer means "God is my help." This servant makes the long journey back along the Fertile Crescent to the Mesopotamian "city of Nahor," where he providentially encounters a beautiful young woman who offers water both to him and to his camels – the very sign that he had asked of the LORD (24:14, 19). When Rebekah takes the servant to her brother Laban, the servant repeats in detail his mission, his journey, and his miraculous meeting with Rebekah – more narrative doubling that confirms God's providential hand (24:34–49). And the rich golden nose ring and bracelets given by Eliezer to Rebekah confirm this servant's "blessedness" in the glittering, acquisitive eyes of her brother Laban. Laban's sharp eye for jewelry is matched by his family gift for sharp bargaining, as he and his father Bethuel attempt to lengthen the visitor's stay in a likely effort to drive up the bride price, but Abraham's servant slips the trap and brings home the bride to Isaac. Though a union contracted by proxy at a great distance, the marriage is a love-match. We're told evocatively that "Isaac brought her into his mother Sarah's tent; and he took Rebekah and she became his wife, and he loved her. So Isaac was comforted after his mother's death" (24:67).

The Faithful Servant

Abraham's servant is the sort of man frequently praised in the Bible as representing the believer in relation to God: the trusty, persistent, loyal household retainer who puts his master's interests ahead of his own. If this servant is actually the Eliezer of Damascus named in chapter 15, then his service here in chapter 24 is especially noteworthy, for Eliezer had been Abraham's designated heir, only to be displaced finally by the birth of none other than Isaac. Thus, for him to set out diligently to seek out a wife for Isaac is a remarkably generous and devoted act. Abraham's reliance on him is so great that he asks of him the most binding of oaths: "Please, place your hand under my thigh" – probably a euphemism for "grasp me by my genitals" – "and I will make you swear by the LORD, the God of heaven and the God of the earth, that you will not take a wife for my son from the daughters of the Canaanites, among whom I dwell" (24:3).

If Isaac is comforted after Sarah's death, so, in a different fashion, is his father. Genesis 25 gives us the last of Abraham, yet it is no slow fade, but more of a late flare, as there is still plenty of life in the old man. Once he has been bereaved of Sarah, he consoles himself by fathering six more children on his second wife, Keturah – not to mention the children of the concubines. He makes sure that all of these late offspring are well provided for, but he sends them away to the east, far from the chosen son Isaac. Then, after this lively patriarchal postscript, Father Abraham dies at the age of 175 and is buried next to Sarah in the family tomb at Machpelah – attended in death not only by Isaac but also by Ishmael. With typical reticence, the narrative leaves to our imaginations any conversation between the half-brothers whose descendants often remain such intimate enemies to this day.

The focus turns rather briefly now to Isaac. It is perhaps fitting that after thirteen chapters devoted to Abraham, Isaac is central to less than four, for he appears mainly as a transitional and derivative figure, a little dense, but decent; in more modern terms, something of a "mama's boy" – or perhaps a "daddy's boy." He is notably devoted to his one wife (there are no other women mentioned in the entire course of his life) and his faith and loyalty have powerful effects. When Rebekah, like Sarah, is discovered to be barren, Isaac learns from Abraham's and Sarah's mistake: he "pleads" with the LORD for conception, and wonderfully, Rebekah conceives – twins! But even in this affectionate, devout, monogamous marriage, Adam's curse makes itself felt in family conflict – a conflict that upends the patriarchal norm.

For, as we're told:

the children struggled together within her; and she said, "If all is well, why am I like this?" So she went to inquire of the LORD.
And the LORD said to her:
"Two nations are in your womb,
Two peoples shall be separated from your body;
One people shall be stronger than the other,
And the older shall serve the younger." (25:22–23)

"The older shall serve the younger." It is hard to imagine how strange this would sound to the original hearers and readers, steeped in the ancient Near Eastern and Egyptian tradition of primogeniture – a tradition that, within our own living memory, has recently been normative not only in Asia and Africa, but also in Latin America, Britain, and Europe. Many would regard such a reversal of power relations as a curse, and in a way it is; not in the sense of cursing the undone deeds of as-yet-unborn children, but in the sense of resulting from the firstborn Adam's covenant-breaking grab in the garden, reminding the would-be mighty fathers to submit to the Almighty Father. But more than a curse, this prophecy is above all a test: for how will the twins' parents, and the twins themselves, respond to this prophetic dream? We find out immediately about the twins:

So when her days were fulfilled for her to give birth, indeed there were twins in her womb. And the first came out red. He was like a hairy garment all over; so they called his name Esau. Afterward his brother came out, and his hand took hold of Esau's heel; so his name was called Jacob. Isaac was sixty years old when she bore them. (25:24–26)

Marking the pre-natal rivalry, here are some of the most vivid names in the Bible, hovering between family in-jokes and prophecies: Esau ("hairy") the firstborn, and Jacob (Hebrew *Yakov* – "supplanter" – literally, "heel-grabber"), a few moments his junior. Never were fraternal twins less identical: "So the boys grew. And Esau was a skillful hunter, a man of the field; but Jacob was a mild man, dwelling in tents" (25:27) – on the one hand, the red-headed, blood-stained, gruff he-man; on the other the smooth-faced, smooth-talking mother's boy.

If the boys seem headed for conflict, what about their parents? Will they attend to divine wisdom, following not their own inclinations but the revelation? Will Isaac submit to a divine word from his wife? Will he set aside the patriarchal custom of the country to bestow his blessing and covenant on the younger son? Will Rebekah wait patiently for the prophecy to come true? And will they avoid the trap of favoritism? The answer, sadly, is No, No, No, No, and most definitely No. "And Isaac loved Esau because he ate of his game, but Rebekah loved Jacob" (25:28). Isaac fails to recognize his own case in Jacob's – i.e. the mild-mannered second son who nevertheless by grace inherits the covenant – instead living vicariously through Esau's "macho" derring-do; Rebekah fails to give her maternal love equally, instead treating the prophecy as a license to cosset the one son and despise the other. So even this happily matched couple discovers the means to be unhappy in their own way, joining in their sons' infantile game of one-upmanship. Soon this intra-family competition results in its first full-blown swindle, as the famished Esau one day bargains away his birthright to supplanting brother *Yakov* for a bowl of lentil stew – the famous "mess of pottage" as the King James Version has it. "Thus Esau despised his birthright" – and implicitly the covenant of the LORD (25:29–34).

Isaac compounds this patriarchal favoritism and its damaging consequences with another old family failing. Having avoided Abraham's reproductive mistake of parenthood through a concubine, Isaac repeats one of his father's other discreditable acts: for the third time in Genesis, a patriarch brings his beautiful wife to the land of a heathen king (another Abimelech of Gerar) and presents her there as "my sister," this time without a shred of truth. Yet this time it is not a divine curse on the king that gives them away, but Isaac's romantic desire for his wife. When Abimelech looks through a window, he sees Isaac fondling Rebekah and, as with Abraham and Sarah before, he rather primly professes shock at their dishonesty:

> Then Abimelech called Isaac and said, "Quite obviously she is your wife; so how could you say, 'She is my sister?'" Isaac said to him, "Because I said, 'Lest I die on account of her.'" (26:1–11)

Yet God makes the deceptive couple thrive so much that Abimelech both admires and envies their unique blessedness, until he asks them to leave his country because their prosperity is putting his own people to shame: "And Abimelech said to Isaac, 'Go away from us, for you are much mightier than we'" (26:16).

Still, despite repeating this "sisterly" deception of Abraham's, Isaac mainly repeats and reinforces his father's virtues and successes. Like Abraham generously yielding to Lot in their grazing dispute, Isaac handles squabbles with the bloody-minded Philistines over water rights by withdrawing to another place where, sure enough, God provides even more, as Isaac re-opens the old wells of his father (26:17–22). Thus, Isaac both avoids unnecessary conflict and revives a legacy with new labor. In return – and again, despite the patriarch's manifest flaws – *Yahweh* appears to renew his first Abrahamic promise to bless and to multiply, and Isaac responds by digging a well downward and building an altar upward. He increases so much in wealth and power that Abimelech, having sent Isaac away, now journeys to him with his army, not to attack but to sue in advance for peace. He requests a renewal of the covenant that he – or perhaps his father – had once made with Abraham (26:26–33). The place of their covenant – Beersheba, "the Well of the Oath" or "the Well of the Seven" – will in later generations become the southern outpost of Jewish settlement in the land, still claimed by modern-day Israel. Then, to cap this narrative of rising patriarchal success, comes what the reader should by now be coming to expect – an anticlimax. Isaac's favoritism toward his eldest son begins to bear bitter fruit: "When Esau was forty years old, he took as wives Judith the daughter of Beeri the Hittite, and Basemath the daughter of Elon the Hittite. And they were a grief of mind to Isaac and Rebekah" (26:34–35). Having despised his birthright and the covenant, Esau now marries doubly outside his parents' faith, conforming to the normative polygamy of the land.

In the midst of Isaac's successes and failures, the rivalry between Esau and Jacob heats up – both because Isaac continues to dismiss Rebekah's revelation, and because Rebekah refuses to wait for God to fulfill the prophecy. Esau, the natural heathen, seems an amiable enough dunce, but is completely dead to his parents' covenant; on the other hand Jacob, probably egged on by jealous Rebekah, values the birthright and the covenant, but only as an entitlement and a means of self-advancement. What follows is heartbreaking, family-shattering tragedy. It begins with words that echo a past father–son exchange: "Now it came to pass, when Isaac was old and his eyes were so dim that he could not see, that he called Esau his older son and said to him, 'My son.' And he answered him, 'Here I am'" (27:1). In language reminiscent of God's call to Abraham for the sacrifice of Isaac, Isaac now calls out to his elder son in an effort to circumvent God's call to bless the younger. Isaac's one request? "[T]ake your weapons, your quiver and your bow, and go out to the field and hunt game for me. And make me savory food, such as I love, and bring it to me that I may eat, that my soul may bless you before I die" (27:3–4). In old age, Isaac has been reduced to physical and spiritual blindness, to mere appetite and foolish paternal pride.

But in this family, where espionage begins at home, the wife is not to be outdone. Overhearing Isaac's instructions, Rebekah counterplots with Jacob, telling him to fetch two kids from the flock for slaughter and beat his rival Esau to the culinary punch. Significantly, Jacob objects – not to the idea of deceiving his blind old father, but rather to the danger of Isaac discovering the plot and cursing him instead: "Look, Esau my brother is a hairy man, and I am a smooth-skinned man. Perhaps my father will feel me, and I shall seem to be a deceiver to him; and I shall bring a curse on myself and not a blessing" (27:11–12). Rebekah's reply is forebodingly ironic: "Let your curse be on me, my son," she says, in an unintentional parody of sacrificial motherly love; for soon she will feel a curse indeed. But she hastens to prepare the meal, and she outsmarts blind Isaac further by fitting out Jacob in the goatskins and Esau's clothes to approximate his feel and even his smell.

And at first their clever plan succeeds. Isaac, while initially suspicious that the food has come so quickly, feels and smells his son and becomes convinced that it is Esau:

> And he came near and kissed him; and he smelled the smell of his clothing, and blessed him and said:
>
> "Surely, the smell of my son
> Is like the smell of a field
> Which the LORD has blessed." (27:27)

Isaac moves on to promise "fatness," grain, and "new wine," then turns to the final dynastic blessing:

> "Let peoples serve you,
> And nations bow down to you.
> Be master over your brethren,
> And let your mother's sons bow down to you.
> Cursed be everyone who curses you,
> And blessed be those who bless you!" (27:29)

Jacob, having the blessing that he sought, scuttles away and, almost instantly, comes Esau, ready with freshly cooked game and also asking to be blessed. Though Isaac has behaved foolishly, the narrator nevertheless invites us to feel compassion for the blind old dupe and his slow-witted favorite:

> Then Isaac trembled exceedingly, and said, "Who? Where is the one who hunted game and brought it to me? I ate all of it before you came, and I have blessed him – and indeed he shall be blessed." When Esau heard the words of his father, he cried with an exceedingly great and bitter cry, and said to his father, "Bless me – me also, O my father!"

Isaac knows very well that he has only one such blessing to give, and he realizes with sickening certainty that the blessing rightly was Jacob's by divine revelation, even if Jacob stole it wrongly, but Isaac can't keep his personal bitterness and the touch of a curse out of his words to Esau even as he reluctantly recognizes the fait accompli:

> Behold, your dwelling shall be [away from] the fatness of the earth,
> And [from] the dew of heaven from above.
> By your sword you shall live,
> And you shall serve your brother;
> And it shall come to pass, when you become restless,
> That you shall break his yoke from your neck. (27:39–40)

Esau absorbs the spirit of Isaac's concluding incitement, and, with words that anticipate the Godfather films, vows revenge: "So Esau hated Jacob because of the blessing with which his father blessed him, and Esau said in his heart, 'The days of mourning for my father are at hand; then I will kill my brother Jacob'" (27:41). The favored son eagerly anticipates the death of his father as the occasion to repeat the sin of Cain and kill his brother.

And what of the mother and her favored son? The sweet success of her scheme has a bitter aftertaste: her darling boy must run for his life. "[A]rise, flee to my brother Laban in Haran," Rebekah orders Jacob. "And stay with him a few days, until your brother's fury turns away, until your brother's anger turns away from you, and he forgets what you have done to him" (27:43–45). "[W]hat you have done to him" is rather rich, coming from the woman who conceived the whole plot in the first place and put Jacob up to it. But she will have her own plentiful grief in payment soon, and with interest, for when she and Isaac send Jacob east for a wife, she will never see her son again. Those "few days" that she imagines will stretch to more than twenty years, lengthened both by the love that he finds in Haran, and by the schemes of his Uncle Laban to tie him there. For, true to the biblical pattern of narrative reticence and ironically deferred judgment, Jacob the patriarchal swindler will more than meet his match.

At this juncture, as the story of Isaac draws to an end, the narrative turns up the magnification again, for Jacob is to be a much more major protagonist than his father, and so here we find more formative detail about his journey to the land of Haran. Having been hoodwinked into bestowing his blessing on Jacob, Isaac now consciously renews this blessing, implicitly acknowledging what should have been the case before. He and Rebekah together charge Jacob with finding a wife among her *Yahweh*-worshiping relatives, and then send him on his way, alone. Esau, in a typically tone-deaf misunderstanding of his parents' purposes, imagines that they favor Jacob because he marries within the family, so he contracts marriage with his cousin Mahalath – the daughter of Ishmael! So inadvertently and ironically, the graceless son marries into the family of another graceless son.

Meanwhile, Jacob's journey is beginning – not only as literal travel to his relatives in Haran, but as a spiritual journey of trial and transformation. God will set this supplanter and swindler to a hard school before he can come into the patriarchal blessing of the covenant. And yet Jacob begins this journey with an unexpected and glorious vision. On his way he rests one night near a place called Luz, where he lies down to sleep with a stone for his pillow.

> Then he dreamed, and behold, a ladder was set up on the earth, and its top reached to heaven; and there the angels of God were ascending and descending on it. And behold, the LORD stood above it and said: "I am the LORD God of Abraham your father and the God of Isaac; the land on which you lie I will give to you and your descendants. Also your descendants shall be as the dust of the earth; you shall spread abroad to the west and the east, to the north and the south; and in you and in your seed all the families of the earth shall be blessed. (28:12–14)

Jacob, on the run from a family breakdown resulting from his own scheming and faithlessness, is suddenly given to see that, despite his petty material concerns and his selfish maneuvering for advantage, he is actually part of a much larger story. This God of whom he has heard as a deity of his ancestors and of the past is revealed stunningly to be very much a living God of the present – and the future. Jacob responds with his first recorded act of true reverence: "Then Jacob awoke from his sleep and said, 'Surely the LORD is in this place, and I did not know it.' And he was afraid and said, 'How awesome is this place! This is none other than the house of God, and this is the gate of heaven!'" (28:16–17). "And I did not know it" – these are the words of a changed, or at least a changing, man who is coming to see that there are things in heaven and earth not dreamt of in his self-centered philosophy. The awesomeness of divine presence in this seemingly ordinary place overwhelms him, at least for the moment, and he builds his first stone altar and renames the spot "Bethel," or "The House of God" – vowing that if the LORD will be with him in his present trouble, he will serve Him all his days.

More blessing ensues as Jacob makes his way east, reversing the journey of Father Abraham two generations ago, and recapitulating the journey that brought Abraham's servant to meet his mother Rebekah in chapter 24. Coming providentially to what is probably the same well near Haran and conversing with some locals, whom should they point out to him but the strikingly beautiful Rachel, daughter of Laban, coming to water her flock? Immediately smitten with his lovely cousin, Jacob eagerly waters her sheep and reveals his identity – after which Uncle Laban runs to embrace him with tears and kisses. "And Laban said to him, 'Surely you are my bone and my flesh'" (29:14). And surely this seems like the happiest of endings: the budding young patriarch has a vision, finds God's will for his life, and marries the godly and gorgeous girl. Mission accomplished!

But we have been instructed too long in the turnings of biblical narrative to trust this kind of abrupt and premature happiness, and *Yakov* the underminer will have much to learn in Laban's school before coming into his own. "So Jacob served seven years for Rachel, and they seemed only a few days to him because of the love he had for her" (29:20). This eager service for Rachel's hand finally leads to Jacob's demand for his longed-for reward, described with sharp, almost crude, sexual desire: "Give me my wife, for my days are fulfilled, that I may go in to her" (29:21). Laban sets the honey trap with great care: he provides the wedding feast (no doubt with plenty of wine) and a dark romantic tent, where Jacob heedlessly consummates his pent-up passion – followed by the cruel light of morning: for "Behold, it was Leah!" (29:25).

Only then, with the biter fully bit by the bed-trick, does it dawn on Jacob that he is in the power of a master deceiver: "And Laban said, 'It must not be done so in our country, to give the younger before the firstborn'" (29:26). The scenario would strike Jacob as weirdly familiar, with a sickening twist: impaired vision; the old switcheroo; but in this case the elder preferred before the younger. He is seeing, as in a distorting fun-house mirror, his own swindling of Isaac. Jacob is the LORD's favored son, all right – and now for some disciplinary time "in the woodshed." It's also worth noting that Laban's successful scam, the first of many at Jacob's expense, temporarily restores traditional patriarchal dominance. Not only is the elder first, but the father reigns supreme over all – including over the wives, children, and fortunes of his seemingly hapless son-in-law. In Laban we meet "patriarchy" with a vengeance.

What ensues from Laban's bed-trick and Jacob's marriage-by-deception is a tragicomic – or is it comitragic? – sequence detailing the rivalry of the two sister-wives Leah and Rachel. Leah is jealous of Rachel's apparently superior beauty and her power over the affections of their husband; Rachel bitterly envies Leah's at first effortless fertility, while she seems, as the old saying goes, "barren as a brick." Throughout these two chapters, 29–30, Jacob appears as a comically reluctant, accidental polygamist – eventually squabbled over by competing wives and concubines like a walking inseminator, shuttling wearily between child-hungry women insatiable not so much for his love as for his seed. The adolescent male fantasy of constant copulation with an eager harem is exposed in reality as a relational nightmare, an incubator of lifelong grudges and deadly resentments.

It is a clever device of the narrative to portray the sisters' rivalry through the theme of naming, as the dueling brides Leah and Rachel – and their sexual surrogate maids Zilpah and Bilhah – one-up each other with an escalating baker's dozen of infants, each named to brag or to wound. First comes the initial barrage of baby boys from unloved Leah: Reuben ("'See! A Son!' Now my husband will love me"), Simeon/Shimon ("The LORD 'Heard' me"), Levi ("Now my husband will become 'Attached' to me"), and Judah ("I will 'Praise' the LORD") (29:31–35). Then (shades of Abraham and Sarah) Rachel desperately burdens Jacob with their childlessness – "Give me children or I die!" – and presents her maid Bilhah to him as a surrogate, resulting in two more boys: Dan ("God has 'Judged' my case") and Naphtali ("I have 'Wrestled' with my sister, and prevailed") (30:1–8). The now-infertile Leah retaliates with her own maid/surrogate, Zilpah, who bears Jacob more sons: Gad ("A 'Troop' comes!") and Asher ("I am 'Happy'"), and then Leah buys Jacob's sexual services from Rachel for some supposedly aphrodisiac plants called mandrakes, resulting in two more boys of her own: Issachar ("God has given me my 'Wages'") and Zebulon ("Now my husband will 'Dwell' with me") – and a daughter named Dinah ("Vindicated") (30:9–21). Finally, God hears Rachel's prayer, and for the first time she conceives and bears the much-beloved and much-resented Joseph ("The LORD shall 'Add' to me another son") (30:22–24).

Yet one result of this bitter sisterly rivalry is that, in terms of ancient Near Eastern prosperity, Jacob has been blessed with a conspicuously large family, nearly all of them boys. All that is left is for him to make his fortune – but that promises to be a tall order due to Laban's careful control and slippery dealing. After fourteen years of service to his father-in-law, Jacob has made the old man prosper, but his own accounts are short in the wealth that matters most: livestock. So Jacob makes a proposal – not another fruitless request for a gift or even for his back pay, but simply a request to keep all the speckled and spotted sheep who are born to Laban's flocks. Thus, there will be no doubt about whose are whose: "'So my righteousness will answer for me in time to come, when the subject of my wages comes before you: every one that is not speckled and spotted among the goats, and brown among the lambs, will be considered stolen, if it is with me'" (30:33).

But even here Jacob has underestimated Laban's deviousness. No sooner have they struck hands in the bargain, but Laban instructs his sons to separate out all the speckled and spotted sheep and put three days' journey between them and Jacob. What Jacob does next smacks a bit of heathen sympathetic magic – he peels white stripes in rods from poplar, almond, and chestnut trees and sets them before the watering troughs when the stronger of the flocks come to drink and to breed. Nevertheless, God seems so intent on blessing Jacob that he makes this bit of hocus-pocus pay off, so that "the man became exceedingly prosperous, and had large flocks, female and male servants, and camels and donkeys" (30:43, 31:12).

Now comes a patriarchal moment of truth: since Jacob is entirely disillusioned with Laban's promises and ways, and eager to strike out on his own, after twenty years of waiting he simply decides to pull up stakes and flee Laban without warning, taking his wives, children, and now-abundant livestock. Laban, breathing out threats in hot pursuit, finally catches up with the family group in the mountain country of Gilead. Unbeknownst to Jacob, Rachel has stolen Laban's household gods – a sign of spiritual malaise as well as dishonesty in the matriarch. But Laban's wrath is cooled by a special divine message that he receives in a dream: "Speak to Jacob neither good nor bad" (31:29). Now wanting only "to kiss my daughters and my sons" (note the lingering note of patriarchal possession over Jacob's children, as over his goods) Laban embraces all and agrees to a pact of non-aggression. And, in a humorously ironic final twist, Laban is himself swindled by his own daughter, as Rachel, having hidden the purloined idols in the saddle of her camel, declines to rise and be searched, "for the manner of women is with me" (31:35). Fooled by his superstitious fear of menstrual uncleanness, Laban the would-be omni-patriarch is bested by a woman.

But Jacob has merely jumped from frying pan to fire. For having escaped the largely unjust wrath of his father-in-law, Jacob now must turn and face the largely just wrath of his brother – and the further chastisement of his God. He learns that Esau is coming to meet him with 400 men, and Jacob fearfully halts on the bank of the River Jabbok to prepare for this dreaded encounter with family – only to have it pre-empted by an encounter with "an angel of the LORD."

Theophany

From the Greek for "appearance of God/gods," a biblical theophany is any visible manifestation of the Deity to accommodate the human senses. Old Testament examples include the angel of the LORD's appearances to Abraham and Jacob, the Burning Bush, the Pillars of Cloud and Fire, God's manifestations to Moses and Elijah on Mount Sinai, and Balaam's speaking donkey. These temporary visitations are not to be confused with the Incarnation, the New Testament coming of God the Son to dwell among human beings in the flesh as Jesus Christ. In addition, Christians often regard certain Old Testament Theophanies – such as the LORD's appearances in the Garden of Eden, and the fourth "Man" in the Fiery Furnace of Daniel – as Christophanies, or appearances of the pre-incarnate Christ.

Strangely, this heavenly messenger has little to say, but instead acts out his message, wrestling with Jacob and, stranger still, seeming barely to hold his own in the match. Indeed, we're told that Jacob the "heel-grabber" refuses to release his grip on the divine grappler, clinging for dear life and refusing to let go, as he demands, "unless you bless me." But a single angelic gesture reminds us of both the tremendous divine power and patience that Jacob is being shown in this life-altering moment, for with a mere touch to the hollow of Jacob's thigh, the *Malakh YHWH* puts the patriarch's hip permanently out of joint – neutralizing a crucial source of wrestling power, and giving Jacob a lifelong reminder of their encounter (32:25–26). Furthermore, as with earlier ancestors like Abram and Sarai, God bestows a name change to complete the memorial: "Your name shall no longer be called Jacob [Supplanter] but Israel [Prince with God]; for you have struggled with God and with men and have prevailed" (33:28).

There is compound, complex irony in this passage: crippled yet victorious, the grasping schemer has been transformed into a faithful clinger, while the Almighty seems content to be overpowered by his creature. And indeed it is the Almighty: when Jacob asks his adversary's name in return, the wrestling Spirit answers with a pregnant question, "Why is it that you ask about my name?" Then Jacob provides his own answer, calling the place "Peniel" ("face of God"). "For I have seen God face to face, and my life is preserved" (32:30).

And preservation is what the new-made Israel urgently needs, as he limps from his place of costly blessing across the ford of the Jabbok to meet his brother Esau – and his fate. Yet, even in the wake of his transformative encounter with God, Israel's calculating nature shows itself in a fateful way, as he anticipates Esau's coming onslaught by engaging in a kind of family triage. Sending impressive atoning gifts of whole flocks on before him to Esau, he then divides his children and their mothers into a rank order determined by reverse favor, sending on the maid Zilpah and her brood as the vanguard – and as likely sword-fodder – followed by Bilhah and her children, then Leah and hers, and finally, safest in the rear, the well-favored Rachel and her beloved son Joseph (33:2). It is hard to underestimate the lasting psychological effects that this blatant ranking would have had upon the patriarch's children, particularly on the less favored ones. To be Zilpah's Gad and Asher, or Bilhah's Dan and Naphtali, sent along first to face an armed and angry uncle, would be, in a truly terrible way, to "know your place" – and to carry deep memories that could flower into poisonous resentments in later years. As indeed they did; we learn in the ensuing chapters that a group of the other more expendable sons – Leah's Reuben, Simeon, Levi, and Judah – were the chief instigators of most of the family's mischief and mayhem in years to come.

And Jacob? While he foolishly continues to play favorites, at least he is no coward, going on before all his children, bowing down seven times to Esau, expecting the very worst and hardly daring to hope for any good. Yet what follows is better than what he could have hoped: "But Esau ran to meet him, and embraced him, and fell on his neck and kissed him, and they wept" (33:4). In a sudden tragicomic turn, the vindictive brother becomes kindly welcoming, and Jacob is clearly touched and grateful – if also still wary. Esau looks with wonder on Jacob's large family and on his gift of livestock and demurs: "I have enough, my brother; keep what you have for yourself" (33:9). But Jacob won't be gainsaid; in unspoken atonement for his past deceptions, he insists that Esau keep the gifts, for "I have seen your face as though I had seen the face of God, and you were pleased with me" (33:10). In a kind of happy irony, God uses the unbelieving, "heathen" Esau to model divine grace, his giving of free, unmerited favor.

Yet Jacob has lived too long and seen too much to trust such happiness, and as Esau presses him to travel together and visit, Jacob's slipperiness reasserts itself, as he begs Esau to go on ahead to Seir at his own faster pace, while he follows at a good distance. Jacob then gives Esau the slip entirely, settling instead in Succoth (33:12–17). What are we to think of Jacob's evasive behavior? Is he justified in fearing that Esau's generous mood will break and that he will relapse into bloody-mindedness? Or is Jacob really fearing his own shadow, attributing his own shifty ways to his more cloddish, but also more straightforward brother? Here we see the complications and contradictions of real lived humanity – or of something astonishingly like it.

There are complications aplenty in the episode that follows – the infamous incident of Dinah and Shechem. It serves as a bridge between the account of Jacob's earlier years and the climactic narrative of "Joseph and His Brothers" that ends the Book of Genesis. Here, juxtaposed between the unexpected grace of Esau's mercy and a far greater story of betrayal and forgiveness, chapter 34 shows the chosen family near rock bottom: rootlessly wandering, tempted to assimilation and absorption into the surrounding Gentile world, yet resisting that assimilation in an act that combines cold-hearted treachery, hot-blooded violence, and grotesque sacrilege. And in the midst of it all stands the patriarch Jacob, overwhelmed by the forces of sibling rivalry and tribal zealotry that his own deeds have unwittingly unleashed.

It is first of all the story of a rape: while camped outside the city of Shechem with her family, Dinah, the daughter of Jacob with Leah, catches the eye of the city's prince – also named Shechem and son of the head man Hamor. What happens next makes a brutal kind of sense in the licentious and violent land of Canaan, as the young man lays hold of the young woman, forces her, and deflowers her. But what follows is unexpected: the rapist, "more honorable" than his relatives – probably a dubious distinction – attempts a little romance, coming with his powerful father to his victim's family to ask, after the fact, for her hand in marriage. Remarkably, Jacob says nothing in the exchange that ensues, reacting passively in the face of this tremendous dishonor, and deferring to his sons in managing the affair. Why doesn't he speak directly to Hamor and Shechem? Whatever Jacob's motives for inaction, he demands no punishment for the rape, but rather acquiesces in his sons' offer to the Shechemites of membership in the covenant family (34:20–24).

But the apparently gracious offer is really a cruel ruse, for of course the sign of the covenant is nothing less than circumcision – and the very dark joke will be on the lustful and wily Shechemites once they've had their manhood modified. Because of their greed (they look to have not just intermarriage, but also the wealth of the Hebrews' vast flocks) they find this bloody little bit of surgery surprisingly acceptable, while Simeon and Levi, who are Dinah's full-blood brothers and the low-ranking sons of Israel by Leah, are hungry for vengeance. In executing their plan, these sons of Jacob follow the wisdom of another, much later patriarch – Don Vito Corleone – who advised his son Michael, "Keep your friends close, but keep your enemies closer." That is, the key to effective assassination is to make the victims feel falsely secure – in this case by invoking a sacred ritual of inclusion. To comprehend their gross misuse of the covenant sign of circumcision, imagine, in the context of Christian baptism, bands of feuding Methodist Hatfields and Baptist McCoys up in "them thar hills." Methodists sprinkle, while Baptists dunk, and the Baptists offer peace to all who will go down with them into the sacred waters. So when the Methodists come down to the river to pray, the Baptists take them in their arms and hold them down, and hold them down, and hold them down … and when the bubbles stop rising, there finally is "peace in the valley." Just so, when the men of Shechem had circumcised themselves and "were in pain," Simeon and Levi (ironically, later the father of the sacrificing priesthood) took their swords and slew every last man, taking the women, children, and the livestock too (34:25–29).

Jacob's response is remarkable both for its outrage – he seems genuinely shocked – and for its self-absorption: "You have troubled *me* by making *me* obnoxious [literally 'making me stink'] among the inhabitants of the land, among the Canaanites and the Perizzites; and since *I* am few in number, they will gather themselves together against *me* and kill *me*. *I* shall be destroyed, my household and *I*" (34:30, italics mine). Jacob abhors the action of Simeon and Levi, not because it exploits the covenant sign to commit mass murder, but because it puts him in danger – him and his "household" – by which he seems to mean not these sons of an unfavored mother but his "core family" of Rachel and Joseph. The sons' unrepentant response exudes contempt for their passive and partial father, and reasserts their core family loyalties: "But they said, 'Should he treat our sister like a harlot?'" (34:31). Ironically, neither father nor brothers seem concerned to comfort Dinah herself.

At this grim juncture, into this moral and spiritual vacuum called "the house of Jacob," God speaks. "Then God said to Jacob, 'Arise, go up to Bethel and dwell there; and make an altar there to God, who appeared to you when you fled from the face of Esau your brother'" (35:1). Called to repentance, return, and renewal, the patriarch finally takes the lead, commanding his seriously corrupt and compromised family to join him in a literal and spiritual pilgrimage back to Bethel, "the house of God" – and there to rebuild. They must, in Jacob's words, "Put away the foreign gods that are among you, purify yourselves, and change your garments" (35:2). And Jacob himself must remember his new name, and his true calling: "your name shall not be called Jacob anymore, but Israel shall be your name... I am God Almighty. Be fruitful and multiply; a nation and a company of nations shall proceed from you, and kings shall come from your body. The land which I gave Abraham and Isaac I give to you; and to your descendants after you I give this land" (35:10–12). Name, nation, and land – all eventually will be called "Israel."

And then, as a culmination of shifty Jacob's rededication as princely Israel, God blesses Rachel again with a second pregnancy, and another beloved son comes to be born, near a little town called Ephrath, later to be called Bethlehem. But the Power that gives takes away: the mother for whom achieving pregnancy was life itself now dies in childbirth, and as her life slips away she bequeaths a burdensome name to her lastborn, Ben-Oni, "son of my sorrow." Her bereaved husband countermands her heartbroken last words with a name that speaks both of his revived faith and his persistent favoritism – Ben-Yamin, "son of the right hand," best known as Benjamin. More of this right-hand son soon, whose coming into the world was so laced with sad irony.

Two other losses follow Rachel's death: first, Leah's son Reuben loses whatever status he might have enjoyed as firstborn ("See! A son!") by lying with Bilhah, maid to his mother's rival, Rachel. Whether an act of passion for the "older woman" or of dynastic calculation to assert patriarchal succession, it backfires terribly, earning his father's lasting curse and the disgusted contempt of his younger brothers – which will come into play at a crucial moment in their later history.

The other loss comes as a surprise at this point in the story, for it would seem to have happened long before. We are reminded that, at 180, Isaac still breathes, but just long enough for him "to breathe his last" and be "gathered to his people, old and full of days." Isaac's two divergent sons Esau and Jacob meet again to bury their father, as Isaac and Ishmael before them buried Abraham, and then go their very separate ways (35:27–29). Genesis 36 shows just how separate: for "Esau took his wives, his sons, his daughters, and all the persons of his household, his cattle and all his animals, and all his goods which he had gained in the land of Canaan, and went to a country away from the presence of his brother Jacob. For their possessions were too great for them to dwell together" (36:6–7). In the past, chosen Abram had yielded the land to his nephew Lot, but here it is unchosen Esau who steps aside for his covenant-bearing brother. Whether this is another act of unexpected grace on Esau's part, or simply his admission that God's main purposes are for Jacob, is not made clear, but, in the end, their mother's dream does come true and primogeniture falls away: the older does serve the younger.

6.4 "What Will Become of His Dreams": Joseph and His Brothers

We now come to the final movement in the great story arc of Genesis: the famed account of "Joseph and His Brothers."

Joseph's Literary and Cultural Legacies

A story this ancient and this admired has influenced many imaginative works, from an explicit novelization like Thomas Mann's great tetralogy *Joseph and His Brothers* (1926–1943) to sibling contrast and rivalry in Dostoyevsky's *The Brothers Karamazov* (1880). In the modern musical theater, Andrew Lloyd Webber's *Joseph and the Amazing Technicolor Dreamcoat* (1968, 1973) famously translated Genesis narrative into rock opera, while in Shakespearean drama, the family rivalries and brotherly betrayals of *Hamlet* (1601), *King Lear* (1606), and *The Tempest* (1611) revisit Joseph's family romance, whether with tragic or tragicomic outcomes.

Frequently spoken of as a free-standing narrative and a prose masterpiece in its own right, this unit of fourteen chapters (37–50) nevertheless makes most sense and resonates most deeply when read in context as the culmination of the entire Genesis origin narrative. That is, while these last chapters possess their own inner completeness of form – vividly contrasting and dynamic characters, wide scope over distance and time, rising and falling action, episodic juxtaposition, delayed judgment, and above all powerfully complex irony and thematic grandeur – the effects of these elements are magnified when connected to the forms and themes of the previous thirty-six chapters. If Genesis is about God's good creation, humanity's rebellion, God's punishment, and the beginnings of his plan for redemption, then the Joseph story serves as a crucial turning point. Since *Yahweh's* plan involves a covenant that chooses wanderers, outcasts, and younger sons, Joseph completes the Genesis trajectory by being all of those chosen things and, something much rarer, an almost entirely exemplary man of faith and action. Yet, in a final twist, though Joseph is in one sense the savior of his family and of the covenant, he is not ultimately the standard-bearer of that covenant; instead it is another brother, who first had seemed the villain of the piece. Such are the mysteries of divine choice and grace that the sons of Israel will someday come to be called, not the "Josephites" (or the "Joes"!), but "the Jews" for namesake Judah – the redeemed schemer. For the LORD also chooses reformed rogues.

Yet the story is very much Joseph's. I've referred to him as "almost entirely exemplary" because when we first meet this paragon as a boy, he has one glaring flaw: his towering, and nearly fatal, immodesty. For it's on Joseph that all the accumulated weights of his father's patriarchal malpractice – Jacob's favoritism and his sons' seething resentments, compounded by Joseph's own heedless arrogance – finally come crashing down. It's only a miracle of divine providence, forgiveness, and love that enables him, and his family, to survive and thrive.

To paraphrase Winston Churchill, Joseph is an immodest lad with much to be immodest about. Brilliant, rich, and incorruptibly honest, he is also astonishingly handsome and, more than all that, prophetically gifted as a dreamer and interpreter of dreams. Also – a great driver of the storyline – he is blessed, and cursed, with adoring parents. As chapter 37 opens, we are introduced to seventeen-year-old Joseph, feeding the flock with his brothers.

> And the lad was with the sons of Bilhah and the sons of Zilpah, his father's wives; and Joseph brought a bad report of them to his father.
> Now Israel loved Joseph more than all his children, because he was the son of his old age. Also he made him a tunic of many colors. But when his brothers saw that their father loved him more than all his brothers, they hated him and could not speak peaceably to him. (37:2–4)

Imagine this scenario: it's Christmas, or Hanukkah, or whatever, and the family gathers to exchange gifts. It's a large, wealthy, "blended" family, with a dozen children of multiple mothers by the same father present in the living room – with all of the alliances, discords, and unspoken awkwardness that such a blend can entail. The older children – nearly all boys, many already in their late teens or early adulthood – begin opening their presents, and find the staples of the day: socks, underwear, tangerines, soccer balls, pocket knives, watches, shavers. Then adorable little Joey, five years old, late child by the "trophy wife," unwraps his noticeably bigger box, and pulls out with giggling delight a miniature policeman's uniform! Black shirt, holster belt, toy gun, cop cap, billy club, badge, the works. "Put it on, little soldier!" says his father, a silver fox of a man with a fond glance at the pretty mother. As Joey slips into his gear, brotherly snickers and smirks break out around the room, and the father says, with a wry grin, "Hey! I'm going to need him to keep some of you hoods in line!" "Oh, Daddy, Oh Mommy, thank you!" squeals Joey. "I love you so much! BIIIG HUG!" And after the hug and the snapshots, "Officer Joey" walks up to his burly half-brother Dan – who as it happens has a bit of a police record (aggravated assault) – and points with his plastic billy club, saying glee-fully, "I'm going to keep you in line!" Laughs and groans all around. "Yeah, kid, yeah," says Dan, looking away with a shrug. "Yeah."

Then jump ahead twelve years, and Dan and his half-brother Levi are up to no good with some stolen sound system components in the stockroom of one of the family stores, and in walks seventeen-year-old Joey, catching them in the act. Joey is now a "junior policeman" through his Boy Scout troop, and happens to be wearing his full Police Scout uniform, complete with shoulder radio. That night, the wayward sons will face the wrath of Dad.

If we want to understand Jacob's unhealthy family dynamic in contemporary terms, the above scenario may help; for that "tunic of many colors" – more popularly known as the "Amazing Technicolor Dream Coat" in musical theater or a "Coat of Many Colors" in the country and western song – is not only a sign of fatherly favor, but also a badge of office, and that office is "family informer." Yet Joseph is no mere flattering snitch – he's presented as that rare thing, the straightest of arrows, who looks with genuine shame and disgust on his shyster brothers, and sincerely desires to make things right – for his beloved father, for his family, and for his God. But like many straight arrows, he's maddeningly obtuse about how little the world really cares about truth and justice, and about how much the world is willing to let slide as long as someone else's ox is being gored. Joseph has all the innocence of the dove, but as yet none of the wisdom of the serpent – and his family is a snake-pit.

Still, Joseph is possessed of that awesome – and alarming – gift: the gift of prophetic sight.

> Now Joseph had a dream, and he told it to his brothers; and they hated him even more. So he said to them, "Please hear this dream which I have dreamed: there we were, binding sheaves in the field. Then behold, my sheaf arose and also stood upright; and indeed your sheaves stood all around and bowed down to my sheaf."
>
> And his brothers said to him, "Shall you indeed reign over us? Or shall you indeed have dominion over us?" So they hated him even more for his dreams and for his words. (37:5–8)

With the special tactlessness that only a teenage genius can achieve, Joseph assumes that his brothers will be happy about his bright future as their deserving master; we, who know a little better about human nature, can nearly hear their teeth grinding. Eventually, Joseph's self-glori-fying visions go too far even for his doting father. When Joseph tells the family, "Look, I have dreamed another dream. And this time, the sun, the moon, and the eleven stars bowed down to me," Jacob has had enough:

> [H]is father rebuked him and said to him, "What is this dream that you have dreamed? Shall your mother and I and your brothers indeed come to bow down to the earth before you?" And his brothers envied him, but his father kept the matter in mind. (37:9–11)

To appreciate all that comes later, then, two things must be distinctly understood: first, as repeatedly noted, Joseph's seeming *braggadocio* is fat on the fire of his brothers' jealousy – a fire kindled long ago by Laban's bed-trick in Jacob's wedding tent and spread through the whole family by patriarchal favoritism and the resulting polygamous rivalries. But second, after all, Joseph's declarations, however foolishly impolitic, are not really brag, but fact – he is destined for greatness, and someday his family will know that they owe him all. But though young Joseph is a conduit for divine foreknowledge, he still lacks human wisdom – and that will be very hard-won.

The main outline of Joseph's tragicomic story is so well-known that we needn't belabor all the details; we'll focus on the deployment of distinctively ironic biblical narrative devices to forward the themes of the covenant line, providential grace, and forgiveness, and what I have been calling "anti-patriarchal patriarchy." The narrator, having foreshadowed events to come – the simmering fraternal hatred, Joseph the great ruler and provider of grain, his brothers' eventual homage – sets about rendering Joseph's early downfall with terrible economy. Jacob sends Joseph out on another fraternal surveillance job: "Are not your brothers feeding the flock in Shechem? Come, I will send you to them." Joseph's reply, significantly, echoes Abraham's reply to God when told to go sacrifice his son – "Here I am" (22:1, 37:13). The sacrifice of another son is about to ensue.

Tragicomedy

As the hybrid name suggests, tragicomedy combines elements of tragedy and comedy, but in a particular way. In tragedy, the story begins with the protagonist near the height of prosperity and power, and proceeds toward a terrible reversal of fortune, eventual downfall, and frequently concludes in death. In comedy, the protagonists, usually plural in a romantic context, experience some conflict and trial, but real disaster is averted by some form of comic intervention, often by fools and clowns. Tragicomedy blends both in a distinctive order: usually the story leads with the tragic action, afflicting the protagonist early on with dire suffering that often involves family betrayal and estrangement, great distances traveled, the material ruin or apparent death of principal characters, and the long passage of time. Then, at the point of maximum loss and darkness, "all heaven breaks loose," with miraculous comic returns and discoveries involving repentance and family reconciliation – usually revealing a providential design.

Outside the Bible, great tragicomic works include Homer's *Odyssey* (eighth century BCE), Euripides' *Alcestis* (438 BCE), Dante's *Divine Comedy* (1321), and particularly Shakespeare's last plays (often also called "Romances"), *Pericles*, *Cymbeline*, *The Winter's Tale*, and *The Tempest* (1608–1611). (See also the sidebar on "Joseph and Shakespeare's Prospero.")

While the story of Joseph is the classic Old Testament tragicomedy, other biblical stories fit this description, including the Book of Job, the story of Moses in Exodus, the Davidic narratives of 1 and 2 Samuel, and, above all, the life, death, and resurrection of Jesus Christ in the Gospels. Indeed, one might say that the entire Christian Bible has a tragicomic structure from Genesis to Revelation – with early catastrophic loss and long resulting human suffering being redeemed in the end by providential divine sacrifice leading to comic, and cosmic, reconciliation.

Joseph gets a bit lost on the way, but providentially an unnamed stranger appears to show Joseph the way to his brothers, as if God wants this special appointment kept at Dothan. At the brothers' first distant sight of Joseph – unmistakable in that colorful tunic – their long-suppressed desire forms a plot like lightning: "Look, this dreamer is coming! Come therefore, let us now kill him and cast him into some pit; and we shall say, 'Some wild beast has devoured him.' We shall see what will become of his dreams!" (37:19–20). Oldest brother Reuben seeks to intervene – perhaps out of kindness, perhaps to repair his firstborn favor with the patriarch after his scandalous affair with Bilhah – by simply having Joseph thrown in the pit, planning to return him to Jacob later (37:21–22).

But there's a smarter, rising power among the brothers, who is wily enough to split the difference between rescue and outright murder. That's Judah, and his dealings illustrate the difference between a nominal and a natural leader. The nominal leader – Reuben the oldest – is both ineffectual and disgraced, while the natural leader Judah combines a ruthless eye for the main chance with considerable rhetorical skill. With Joseph languishing in the pit and Reuben temporarily absent on some other business, the brothers look up "and there was a company of Ishmaelites, coming from Gilead with their camels, bearing spices, balm, and myrrh, on their way to carry them down to Egypt" (37:25). These nomadic traders – and distant relatives through Abraham's firstborn son Ishmael – inspire in Judah a "win–win" solution to their dilemma. "So Judah said to his brothers, 'What profit is there if we kill our brother and conceal his blood?'" (37:26) – a troubling echo of Cain and Abel that might suggest the stirrings of conscience. But the operative word in Judah's question is "profit": "shekels of silver" from their slave-trading cousins and the assurance that Joseph's blood would not be on their hands – yet almost certainly on someone else's – plus the quiet satisfaction that the young Police Scout will spend the rest of his short unhappy life in a chain gang.

Ironies abound, and not for the last time. Reuben's attempted good deed only shows up his powerlessness; in a parody of Abraham's attempted sacrifice of Isaac, an animal's blood stands in for the blood of the beloved son; and in an even darker redux, Jacob's youthful deception of Isaac with his brother Esau's clothing is echoed when Joseph's bloodstained "coat of many colors" fools old Jacob himself. Biblical understatement leaves us to imagine what Jacob's sons may have thought or felt in watching his response to the terrible news and the gory garment: "And he recognized it and said, 'It is my son's tunic. A wild beast has devoured him. Without doubt Joseph is torn to pieces.' Jacob tore his clothes, put sackcloth on his waist, and mourned for his son many days. And all his sons and all his daughters arose to comfort him; but he refused to be comforted" (37:33–35).

Might even Judah have felt a twinge of regret in seeing his father paid out so cruelly? Seemingly not, for as the scene changes with the news that Joseph has been sold to Pharaoh's Captain of the Guard in Egypt, we see Judah taking center stage in chapter 38 as a prosperous, self-confident, and apparently remorseless patriarch – and a sexual hypocrite as well. We've already discussed this passage in our previous chapter in terms of both its narrative minimalism and of its ironic juxtaposition with Joseph's resistance to sexual temptation in Genesis 39. As we see the lecherous Judah "hoist on his own petard" by his daughter-in-law Tamar, whose "bed-trick" conceives twin covenant sons – the great "line of Judah!" – we have the satisfaction of seeing the wily patriarch brought low, and by a woman, and we also see the stirrings of spiritual transformation in this natural leader of the family, as he's forced to admit that "she has been more righteous than I" (38:26).

And then the focus shifts wholly to Joseph. Far from being dead, Joseph is, strange to say, on his way to being the most successful slave in the land of Egypt. Sold to Potiphar, the Captain of Pharaoh's Guard and thus the ruler's Head of Palace Security and Chief Warden of Prisons, Joseph ends up in a prosperous and well-connected house, and he draws attention to himself immediately through his diligence and integrity – which are taken as a testimony to Joseph's God. "And his master saw that the LORD was with him and that the LORD made all he did to prosper in his hand" (39:3). Counter to notions of henotheism – allegiance to one god within geographical limits, among many gods of distant lands – *Yahweh* reaches into foreign lands to bless and to protect, displaying his exclusive, monotheistic power.

That monotheistic creed will be vigorously tested in this chapter, though, as it is not only Joseph's master Potiphar who notices his distinctive character, but also his master's wife, who notices his distinctive good looks. The biblical writers rarely comment on the physical beauty of the characters, so when they do, it's important information – Saul's tall handsome stature, David's boyish glory, Bathsheba's naked allure. "Now Joseph was handsome in form and appearance" (39:6), we're told, and instantly we learn why it matters, as "it came to pass after these things that his master's wife cast longing eyes on Joseph, and she said, 'Lie with me'" (39:7). While not precisely a "desperate housewife," she may have been in some sense desperate, since one possible meaning of the Hebrew for her "officer" husband – çariç – is "eunuch." Whether or not Potiphar was a fully equipped man, his wife has a wandering eye, and persists in propositioning her well-favored slave.

The contrast between Judah and Joseph in this "juxtaposition sandwich" is almost perfectly disymmetrical: where the older brother abuses his power and position by seeking out a foreign prostitute, and then hypocritically orders the burning of pregnant Tamar knowing that he has committed the same sin as she, the younger brother resists the overtures of a woman who owns him and possesses the power of life and death over him – and he does so in the name of God. After rebuffing her first entreaties, Joseph asks her, rhetorically, "How then can I do this great wickedness, and sin against God?" (39:9). Rather easily, she might answer, since in her view the writ of the Hebrew God can't possibly extend beyond Canaan into the heart of Egypt, while the local gods Ra, Anubis, Isis, and Osiris are not mainly ethical deities, and are supremely indifferent to mortals' sexual behavior. One can only imagine the lady's incredulity at being told by a foreign slave that his great God cares about his tiny affairs; so she keeps after Joseph in a way that is both comic and pathetic – but ultimately deadly. When after much begging she moves beyond words and grasps his garment, he flees naked – which is the last straw for the lady in all her scorned fury. She concocts a slanderous accusation of attempted rape, and for emphasis repeats it publicly to Potiphar, virtually guaranteeing Joseph's execution.

But strangely, although "his anger was aroused," Potiphar doesn't do the expected and slay Joseph on the spot, but casts him into prison, "a place where the king's prisoners were confined" (39:19, 20). Perhaps this unfulfilled wife of a possibly emasculated "officer" has "vamped" other slaves before, and perhaps Potiphar doubts her now, so that the face-saving punishment imposed on Joseph is relatively light; certainly, we're intended to see the monotheistic hand of *Yahweh* extending to Egypt, protecting and positioning Joseph for future promotion. And however cast down Joseph may be by his unjust imprisonment, he is soon on his way to becoming the most successful *inmate* in the land of Egypt. Growing where he's planted, Joseph quickly becomes as indispensable to the prison-keeper as he had been to Potiphar, so that this warden "committed to Joseph's hand all the prisoners who were in the prison" (39:22).

What then "will become of his dreams"? Trusty prisoner Joseph's great opportunity eventually presents itself, in the form of two sets of doubled dreams. In the first case, two disgraced Pharaonic servants, a butler and a baker, have landed in jail and wake up one morning with parallel dreams, about three grape branches and three bread baskets. Joseph volunteers his abilities – humbly attributed to *Elohim*, not to himself – and interprets both dreams in one of the great "good news–bad news" scenarios. "Now within three days," he tells the butler, "Pharaoh will lift up your head and restore you to your place, and you will put Pharaoh's cup in his hand" (40:13).

The baker, eager to hear his good fortune read out also, asks for his interpretation, and Joseph can't resist a little gallows humor: "Within three days Pharaoh will lift *off* your head from you and hang you on a tree; and the birds will eat your flesh from you." The pun in Hebrew is even stronger, where "lift up the head" is an idiom for "raise or promote", so the baker's "promotion" will be dire indeed. And then the narrator, after noting the almost immediate fulfillment of these doubled dreams, slams the door on Joseph's hopes of deliverance: the chief butler, after his restoration to office, "did not remember Joseph, but forgot him" (40:23).

That is, the butler forgets Joseph until, two full years later, it is in his self-interest to remember him – an opportunity afforded by a second doubled dream. One morning Pharaoh awakes from a troubled sleep talking of seven fat cows consumed by seven gaunt cows, and seven plump heads of grain devoured by seven blighted heads. Neither his wise men nor his magicians can show him the meaning; then the butler clears his throat and speaks:

I remember my faults this day. When Pharaoh was angry with his servants, and put me in custody in the house of the captain of the guard, both me and the chief baker, we each had a dream in one night, he and I... Now there was a young Hebrew man with us there... And we told him, and he interpreted our dreams for us; ... And it came to pass, just as he interpreted for us. (41:9–13)

Within the hour, Joseph is hauled from the dungeon and stands, bathed, clean-shaven, and redressed, in the presence of Pharaoh, listening to the doubled dream. Called to interpret, Joseph again demurs: "It is not in me; God will give Pharaoh an answer of peace" (41:16). He then unfolds the vision as if it were a governmental white paper; seven fat years are coming, followed by seven lean years, when famine shall gnaw all the bellies of the earth. Affirming one of the great structural principles of biblical narrative – that is, doubling for emphasis and confirmation – Joseph also calls for a foresighted food policy: "And the dream was doubled to Pharaoh twice because the thing is established by God, and God will shortly bring it to pass. Now therefore, let Pharaoh select a discerning and wise man, and set him over the land of Egypt" – to collect one fifth of the crop during each bumper year and keep the grain in store cities against the coming hungry years (41:32–36).

And who might that "discerning and wise man" be? It is here that, in the literal sense, Joseph's dreams begin coming true. It is not only Joseph's miraculous discernment and God-fearing humility that recommend him for this dramatic promotion from jailhouse to palace. It is also his logistical skill and his patient diligence, hard-won in managing Potiphar's household affairs and the business of a dungeon. Having begun the day behind bars, so to speak, he ends it clothed in white linen, wearing Pharaoh's signet ring and gold necklace, and riding in a chariot with the command shouted before him, "Bow the knee!" – words with a happily ironic resonance not only for the former slave Joseph but for the liberated Hebrew slaves recalling this story hundreds of years later during the Exodus from Egypt. New wardrobe, new position, new power – these are accompanied by a new name, "*Zaphnath-Paaneah*," meaning something like "the one who reveals mysteries" or "God speaks, and he lives," and a new wife (and only *one* wife) Asenath, daughter of the priest Potiphera – whose name, like that of his old master Potiphar, means "gift of Ra" (41:42–45). Then Pharaoh's new Prime Minister gets to work saving Egypt, and saving the world.

Clearly, God has finally "remembered Joseph," but significantly, Joseph wants to forget – not forget God, but rather forget his very painful past, and invest in his present new life. When Asenath bears him a son, "Joseph called the name of the firstborn Manasseh ["making forgetful"]: 'For God has made me forget all my toil and all my father's house.' And the name of the second he called Ephraim ["fruitfulness"]: 'For God has caused me to be fruitful in the land of my affliction'" (41:51–52). And there is plenty to occupy *Zaphnath-Paaneah*: by his thirty-seventh year, he presides over the greatest food surplus on earth, and is on the cusp of greater power still, as famine spreads and "all countries came to Joseph in Egypt to buy grain" (41:57). For the time being, Joseph is content to "live in the moment" and let his troublesome brothers – and perhaps even his father – slide into oblivion.

But God, we are told, has forgotten neither Joseph's father nor his house, and neither has the narrator. The scene shifts back to Canaan, and old Jacob, still querulous and now quite worried about hunger, has heard that there is grain in Egypt. "'[G]o down to that place and buy for us there, that we may live and not die," he tells his sons. "So Joseph's ten brothers went down to buy grain in Egypt. But Jacob did not send Joseph's brother Benjamin with his brothers, for he said, 'Lest some calamity befall him'" (42:2–4). The wound of Joseph's loss has never healed, and after more than twenty years Jacob may still suspect foul play and wants to protect Rachel's lastborn, "the son of my right hand," from a similar fate at the hands of jealous brothers.

Thus one day, a few weeks later, when *Zaphnath-Paaneah* looks out over the usual crowd of miserable, famished foreigners come for grain, he spies a knot of alarmingly familiar faces – faces "bowed down ... to the earth" in reverence to this great Egyptian lord of bread (42:6). Clearly, Joseph has risen far from that desperate pit in the desert, while his brothers have fallen to their knees, and the posture stirs his memory further: "So Joseph recognized his brothers, but they did not recognize him. Then Joseph remembered the dreams which he had dreamed about them, and said to them, 'You are spies! You have come to see the nakedness of the land!'" (42:8–9).

Joseph and Shakespeare's Prospero

"Thou ... hast put thyself upon this island as a spy," says Prospero to the shipwrecked son of his enemy in *The Tempest* – a play about a Milanese duke overthrown and exiled to a deserted island by his evil brother, Antonio, and by Ferdinand's father, King Alonso of Naples. When Prospero's magic gets Antonio and his conspirators under his power, he tests, torments, yet ultimately, forgives them – at the urging of his spirit-servant Ariel (perhaps significantly, in Isaiah 29:1–2 an alternate name for Jerusalem meaning "Lion of God.") Like Joseph, Prospero struggles with vengeful motives, but in the end, trusting that all his affairs have been ordered "by Providence divine," Prospero concludes that "the rarer action is in virtue than in vengeance" and frees and forgives his enemies, including his brother, and reunites his family.

As we enter into one of the most intensely ironic narrative climaxes ever penned, we see the chosen son confirmed in his divine destiny, and resolving immediately to test his guilty brothers from his position of disproportionate advantage. He knows them instantly, and can understand their Hebrew easily, while they haven't the faintest clue that this Egyptian grandee comprehends their darkest secrets and their every word – and above all that it is Joseph, the last person they'd expect to find either alive or free, let alone the first minister of Pharaoh.

One may be inclined to classify the irony of this scene as the happy sort, as the brothers' alarm takes on a potentially comic tone: "No, my lord, but your servants have come to buy food. We are all one man's sons; we are honest men; your servants are not spies" (42:10–11). "Honest men," indeed! the reader may well exclaim. "No, but you have come to see the nakedness of the land," says the great man – always through an interpreter – with increasing hostility (42:12). The brothers swear that, no, there really are twelve of them – well, eleven really – well, actually, yes twelve, since the youngest is still home with his father, and that the other – "is no more." "It is as I spoke to you, saying, 'You are spies!'" (42:13–14). The brothers are too flustered to count straight, and their every word seems to make the mysterious *Zaphnath-Paaneah* angrier.

Yet there is a strain of deep pathos underscoring the comic irony of this passage. Even after twenty years gone, Joseph still hears himself numbered among the dozen sons of Jacob, and the mention of the youngest brother elicits a test that, despite its harshness, masks a degree of fraternal tenderness: "In this manner you shall be tested: By the life of Pharaoh, you shall not leave this place unless your youngest brother comes here. Send one of you, and let him bring your brother; and you shall be kept in prison, that your words may be tested ..." (42: 15–16). Apparently eager to see Benjamin with his own eyes, Joseph decides to give his brothers a generous taste of the "lock-up," and to see how they respond.

How are we to regard Joseph's motives? Some interpretive traditions emphasize his typological resemblance to God (or Christ) himself, inscrutably testing the hearts and determining the affairs of fallible man. Without denying such typological traditions, though, we should note that the emotions surging through Joseph during his encounters with the other sons of Jacob are also deeply – and dramatically – human. Having thrown the Hebrew "spies" in prison, Joseph lets them stew for three days before offering them a better option:

> Do this and live, for I fear God: If you are honest men, let one of your brothers be confined to your prison house; but you, go and carry grain for the famine of your houses. And bring your youngest brother to me; so your words will be verified, and you shall not die. (42:18–20)

Then the brothers speak guiltily – and unguardedly – to each other about their old crimes against Joseph:

> Then they said to one another, "We are truly guilty concerning our brother, for we saw the anguish of his soul when he pleaded with us, and we would not hear; therefore this distress has come upon us." And Reuben answered them, saying, "Did I not speak to you, saying, 'Do not sin against the boy'; and you would not listen? Therefore behold, his blood is now required of us." But they did not know that Joseph understood them, for he spoke to them through an interpreter. And he turned himself away from them and wept. (42:21–24)

Joseph's suppressed emotional outbursts here and later reveal that he is hardly a dispassionate judge, but rather a man deeply torn between his natural thirst for justice – or is it vengeance? – and his impulses toward forgiveness and grace. If Joseph's years of enslavement and suffering had presented one hard moral test – a test of his patience, endurance, and faith – his new position presents a test even more perilous. After all, what would any of us do if we had in our power the people who had hurt us the most in life? What if that power were practically absolute? Again, biblical narrative minimalism leaves us to guess what thoughts of retribution may run through Joseph's mind during those three days when his brothers wait in his dungeon, or what gloating and glorying play across his imagination.

Still, in the end, it is only one brother (Simeon, the mass murderer of Shechem) whom Joseph holds in prison while the others return home to Jacob, with sacks full of grain and – in a disconcerting discovery – with each brother's bundle of money bound into his sack! The brothers are frightened by this uncanny gift, and Jacob is adamant – at first – that Benjamin shall under no circumstances go down into Egypt, perhaps also never to return. Reuben, with his typical ineptitude, suggests that Jacob kill Reuben's own two sons if he doesn't bring Benjamin home – one can virtually hear Jacob's eyes roll (Oy!) at the stupid and repugnant suggestion, as he refuses more firmly still to let his youngest go (42:35–38).

But fast forward a few months, and hunger has been working its quiet, grinding persuasion. "Go back, buy us a little food" (43:2), Jacob wheedles. When Judah reminds Jacob that without Benjamin there will be no sale of grain, the patriarch can still think only in terms of his own pain and injured dignity: "Why did you deal so wrongfully with me as to tell the man whether you had still another brother?" (43:6). Exasperated, Judah nevertheless controls himself and offers himself as surety for the lad's safety, promising to "bear the blame forever" (43:9) if anything should go amiss. Thus Judah, the future patriarch of "the Jews," establishes the terms for his own climactic test.

Sent back to Egypt with Benjamin and double the money for the grain – Jacob will have his family beholden to no one – the brothers enter a situation even more surreal than before. *Zaphnath-Paaneah* refuses their money, insisting that he's already been paid and that "[y]our God and the God of your father has given you treasure in your sacks" (43:23). As they bow repeatedly before the great man, he inquires with strange earnestness after their father's good health, and when he sees Benjamin, he blesses the lad warmly and then must leave the room suddenly under some strong compulsion; we're told that Joseph's "heart yearned for his brother; so Joseph made haste and sought somewhere to weep" (43:30). Then the eleven brothers are treated to a great feast, with the eerie added feature of being seated according to their birth order, and, for the pièce de résistance, Benjamin receives a portion *five times larger* than his brothers' (43:34). "The older will serve the younger" in a literal act of food service!

Joseph's final test of his brothers begins with his springing a trap. As they depart for Canaan, he has a piece of incriminating evidence – his silver "divining" cup – planted in Benjamin's grain sack, along with his money. Then, when the travelers have barely left the city, he has them run down by his steward, who accuses them of theft, which they fervently deny, offering their goods to be searched, and the steward says that "he with whom it is found shall be my slave, and [the rest of] you shall be blameless" (44:1–10). And in whose bag should the cup be but, of course, Benjamin's?

This discovery offers the brothers a perfectly plausible excuse for repeating their past action of abandoning a half-brother to foreigners, and this time with a sound legal sanction. After all, they might say to Jacob something like this: "the great *Zaphnath-Paaneah* of Egypt, who divines with his mysterious silver cup, has found out Benjamin's crime, and to our great grief our dear brother must answer for it." And while Joseph is the author of this deception, it intensifies his own testing as well, offering him the chance to take sole possession of Benjamin and, once the other brothers have washed their hands of him, to reveal himself and lavish his care and affection on his one full-blooded sibling. But the brothers' deeds here speak more loudly than their words ever could: choosing loyalty and solidarity over abandonment, "they tore their clothes, and each man loaded his donkey and returned to the city" (44:13). They will stand with their brother, come what may.

Thus, the stage is set for the culminating moment in Joseph's story – and also for the moment when the story becomes Judah's. That moment is Judah's speech, which amounts also to a major deed because of what the speech proposes. Judah offers his freedom, and, in effect, the remainder of his life, in exchange for Benjamin's: "Now therefore, please let your servant remain instead of the lad as a slave to my lord, and let the lad go up with his brothers" (44:33). Just as striking as Judah's self-sacrificing offer is his reason for it: "[I]t will happen, when [Jacob] sees that the lad is not with us, that … your servants will bring down the gray hair of … our father with sorrow to the grave. For how shall I go up to my father if the lad is not with me, lest perhaps I see the evil that would come upon my father?" (44:31, 34). Here speaks a man truly different from the jokingly cynical vendor of his own kin from chapter 37 ("What profit is there if we kill our brother?"), and the hypocritical lecher made a fool of by the wronged Tamar in chapter 38. Here is a man who has, somewhere along the way, discovered a heart and a conscience; the "operator" has become a *mensch*.

No doubt, Joseph vividly remembers whose idea it had been to sell him down to Egypt, and it is the sight of the repentant rogue Judah – begging on his knees for the favor of enslavement – that opens the emotional floodgates of this sphinx-like Egyptian, and washes away his disguise. Telling all of his servants to leave him alone with the Hebrews, he turns to the brothers and, with a few short words, upends their world. "I am Joseph," he says, without accent, in their language; "does my father still live?" (45:4). Then silence reigns, as the strange familiarity of Joseph's face sinks in – perhaps he also removes his Pharaonic head dress and the courtier's eyeliner! – and stunned dismay seizes them as they wonder if any of them will be allowed to survive the day, let alone outlive their father. Perceiving their fear, Joseph opens up in a flow of tears and kindness and explanation, repeatedly assuring the brothers that they are not to worry because God has, as the saying goes, been drawing straight with crooked lines.

Suddenly, *Elohim* is the active subject of every statement: "God sent me before you ... to preserve ... and to save... God ... has made me a father to Pharaoh... God has made me lord of all Egypt" (45:5–9). There are plenty of embraces all around, and much weeping on necks, first on Benjamin's, and then everyone on everyone's. And perhaps, just for a moment, Joseph is again that little boy, basking in the affection of that crowd of big brothers whom he had always wanted to admire, but until this day never could.

After this intense emotional climax, the narrator pulls back for a broader focus, and events pick up speed. Pharaoh is pleased to learn that Joseph's brothers have come, and sets in motion a wagon train sent to retrieve Jacob and relocate the entire clan to Egypt's Land of Goshen – ironically, a friendly "pre-Exodus" in reverse. Back in Canaan, Jacob receives the stupendous news: "Joseph is alive, and is governor over all the land of Egypt!" And in a moment of cliffhanger tragicomedy, the old man nearly pegs out on the spot: "And Jacob's heart stood still, because he did not believe them" (45:26). But the spectacle of all those fine draft animals and carts full of merchandise catches his acquisitive eye and revives him, and the stirrings of a father's love move him too: "Then Israel said, 'It is enough. Joseph my son is still alive. I will go and see him before I die'" (45:28). "Then Israel said" – for once, not "Jacob" – invokes his newer, more hopeful name as unexpected happiness breaks through his accustomed pessimism, and he becomes a "prince with God" indeed. The alternation of names continues on the way to Egypt: "So Israel took his journey," we're told, and yet when God appears to him in a dream, He calls out "Jacob! Jacob! Do not be afraid!" (46:1–2). The old schemer will never fully trust happiness, though blessings break forth all around him.

Jacob arrives with quite an entourage – seventy direct descendants from his own body, plus their wives and their many servants, have made his already a great company (46:5–27). Once in Egypt, the tone of tragicomic irony intensifies as Jacob, still full of vinegary complaints, *kvetches* even after this miraculous reunion. "And Israel said to Joseph, 'Now let me die, since I have seen your face'" (46:30) – and then this man with one foot in Sheol proceeds to live another seventeen querulous years (47:28). Gloomily he tells Pharaoh, "The days of the years of my pilgrimage are one hundred and thirty years; few and evil have been the days of the years of my life, and they have not attained to the days of the years of the life of my fathers in the days of their pilgrimage" (47:9); yet he nevertheless blesses Pharaoh – a sign of Hebrew harmony with and spiritual fatherhood to the Egyptians to be remembered in the later days of the Exodus.

Settling in Goshen, the Hebrews treat it as a kind of temporary "promised land" – but only temporary, as Jacob makes his sons vow to lay his bones to rest back in Canaan with his fathers in the field at Machpelah. Though in the darker future, when a Pharaoh will arise who "knew not Joseph," Goshen will become a place of Hebrew enslavement, in the present it is Joseph who is daily gaining mastery over the Egyptians: he helps Pharaoh consolidate his rule as the Egyptians trade their land and freedom for food – perhaps a pleasing irony to Hebrew readers during the Exodus. But it is also a foreboding irony as Joseph builds a system of serfdom that someday will ensnare his own people.

The Hyksos and Habiru?

Many scholars have noted the unusually friendly response given in Egypt to Joseph's family, and also note that the timing of Jacob's and Joseph's lives coincides with the dynasty of the Hyksos. These Semitic invaders of Egypt ruled the land as the Seventeenth Dynasty from 1700 to 1550 BCE, only to be overthrown by an indigenous uprising and replaced by the Eighteenth Dynasty of Pharaohs hostile to foreigners, especially Semitic "cousins" of the Hyksos like the Hebrews, whom these new Pharaohs generally enslaved.

> Furthermore, Egyptian records of the middle Second Millennium BCE make mention of a nomadic shepherding people called the "Habiru" or "Apiru," who seem to have been regarded as a threat under the Pharaohs from Amenhotep I, through Thutmose I, II, and III, to Amenhotep II (that is, from 1545 to 1426 BCE, encompassing the likely times of Moses and the Exodus). These Habiru seem to have at some point been enslaved by the Pharaohs, and the similarity of "Habiru" to "Hebrew" has led some scholars to identify the two groups – though others are more skeptical.

There is more irony yet in Joseph's mishandling of Jacob's blessing. Despite Joseph's glowing general success, he makes a serious error in seeking Jacob's primary blessing on his firstborn son Manasseh. Jacob, of all people, knows God's strange preference for junior brothers – so the dim-sighted patriarch, to avoid being hoodwinked (even by honest Joseph!) as he had fooled his own blind father Isaac, crosses his hands to bless Ephraim first. This displeases Joseph, who for all his hard-won wisdom has forgotten that "the older shall serve the younger" and again places Jacob's right hand on the oldest. But Jacob re-crosses his hands, and for all time he sets "Ephraim before Manasseh" (48:20), upending the patriarchal norm.

This ironic reversal of patriarchal power only increases in chapter 49 as Jacob prepares to be "gathered to his fathers" and proclaims from his deathbed both his blessings and his curses. Firstborn Reuben is again cast aside for his long-ago sin with Bilhah (49:3–4); Simeon and Levi are denounced again for their violence and cruelty (49:5–7); and then there is Judah, the reformed rogue, and the natural leader: he is now a more chastened follower of his father, and of his brothers' good, seeking to do what he knows of God's will.

> The scepter shall not depart from Judah,
> Nor a lawgiver from between his feet,
> Until Shiloh comes;
> And to him shall be the obedience of the people. (49:10)

This prophecy of future rulers and kings – long regarded as a messianic passage by both Jews and Christians – turns the tables yet again. Not the practically flawless Joseph but rather the deeply flawed Judah will father the royal line that leads to "Shiloh," a Prince who will bring peace. Though when read forward, this great narrative is properly called "Joseph and His Brothers," retrospectively it might better be named "The Re-Making of Judah." Irony of ironies, as another Abraham named Lincoln said, "The Almighty has his own purposes."

Nevertheless, once Jacob has dealt with all the other brothers in shorter or longer snippets, he gives special blessing to the two beloved sons of Rachel. Though Joseph is not to be the bearer of the covenant like Judah, he has been the savior of the nation, and during his life, he will bear their father's special love, an almost fatal burden in his youth, but now a rich "crown" of praise in his later fame (49:22–26). Yet with the deliberate anticlimax so typical of biblical last endings, the youngest, Benjamin, like the descendants of his nephews Ephraim and Manasseh, will be a rough and unworthy man, a ravenous wolf devouring the prey and dividing the spoil (49:27) – carrying hardly a single one of Joseph's many virtues.

With Jacob's blessings and cursings done, "he drew his feet up into the bed and breathed his last, and was gathered to his people" (49:33). In the ancient Near Eastern family, the death of the patriarch brought a new order of things, and often the settling of old scores, as the parental authority and his restraints were removed and as a new and younger patriarch arose. Often, as in modern dictatorships or Mafia families, the transition of power led to massive bloodletting. The wisdom of the Corleones is, over the years, to "keep your friends close, but your enemies closer," making it easier to liquidate those enemies (and perhaps those friends) without giving distress to the now-deceased parent. So the final scene in Genesis is both tense with dread and then all the more poignant with deep kindness. Having wept together over their dead father and buried him back in Canaan, Joseph's brothers relapse into fear: "When Joseph's brothers saw that their father was dead, they said, 'Perhaps Joseph will hate us, and may actually repay us for all the evil which we did to him'" (50:15). So they invent last words for Jacob, begging leniency for his erring sons, and then they throw themselves at Joseph's feet as his "servants" – which could easily be translated, "slaves."

Of Joseph's many fine hours, this is probably his finest: moved with sadness that his brothers are still so distrustful and deceitful, he is also moved with *chesed*, steadfast love, as he weeps and embraces these guilt-ridden old men. Not that he minces words, but his words are a paradox for the ages, a classic instance of both/and "thinking like a Hebrew":

> Joseph said to them, "Do not be afraid, for am I in the place of God? But as for you, you meant evil against me; but God meant it for good, in order to bring it about as it is this day, to save many people alive. Now therefore, do not be afraid; I will provide for you and your little ones." And he comforted them and spoke kindly to them. (50:19–21)

Was the brothers' action wrong or right? Evil or good? Cursed or blessed? "YES!"

This speech is a most fitting conclusion to the entire Book of Genesis, which never shrinks from branding and denouncing evil, yet treats evil as neither original nor ultimate, but as always derivative – and, miraculously and tragicomically, as the unwitting servant of God and of good. The patriarch is emphatically not in the place of God; he knows his limitations, and his errors, and in fact knows that his line will someday stand aside for others perhaps less worthy, but even more aware of their need for divine forgiveness and grace. So as in the beginning, here at the book's end we still see God's unexpected graces and unlikely choices, which in equal measure continue to delight and confound the sons of Adam and the daughters of Eve. Yet, as in all tragicomedy, some losses are permanent and terrible, and some scars will endure. Genesis begins as God speaks the stars into their everlasting courses and forms immortals from the earth, but it ends with the great deliverer Joseph, at 110 snuffed out even younger than his father, perishing in exile, and being nailed into "a coffin in Egypt" (50:26). We turn now to the story of how that coffin – and how a whole people – made their way back to the home that they had never known.

Questions for Discussion

1   In what ways is **Genesis** a "**patriarchal**" book? On the other hand, in what ways does it advance an extended critique of "patriarchy" that might appear "**anti-patriarchal**?" How might Genesis distinguish between different kinds of patriarchs and patriarchy?

2   What is a *berith* or a **covenant**? What are the differences between a **bilateral** and a **unilateral** covenant? What might be some examples of such covenants from outside the Bible and from within it?

3   What is meant by the **promises**, **conditions**, and **signs** of a covenant? How do these elements show up in ordinary secular contracts or covenants? How is the appearance of covenant promises especially remarkable in the Bible's unilateral covenants?

4 What are the major distinctions between the **Adamic**, **Noahic**, and **Abrahamic** Covenants in Genesis? What are the **promises**, **conditions**, and **signs** of each? How do we distinguish which of these covenants are **Universal** and which **Particular**?

5 What is the difference between the **hagiographic or "saint's life" tradition** and the portrayals of the Patriarchs? What is the larger narrative and thematic meaning of this "warts and all" treatment?

6 What is **primogeniture**, and how does the Genesis narrative of the patriarchs challenge, undermine, and overthrow this practice? How does this thematic opposition to primogeniture fit with other themes in Genesis of God's creativity, justice, and covenant fidelity?

7 How does the concluding episode of "**Joseph and His Brothers**" consummate the Abrahamic "**arc of the covenant**"? How are the varied elements of biblical narrative style – minimalism, wordplay, doubling, juxtaposition, deferred judgment, and irony – at work in this story-within-a-story?

8 In particular, what great **reversals and surprises** animate and enliven the story of "Joseph and His Brothers"? Who is the hero of the story? Initially? Ultimately? Which character(s) undergo the most change? How do the story's final ironies support or fit into the overall covenant "arc"?

Notes

1 Robert Alter, *The Art of Biblical Narrative, Revised Edition* (New York: Basic Books, 2011), 1.
2 Ibid., 1–2.

7

Biblical Epic I: Making the Nation in the Pentateuch

The previous two chapters have dealt with Genesis as the book of origins *par excellence*: the origins of the heavens and the earth, its varied creatures, and humanity; the origins of sin and death and their expanding effects; the origins of loincloths, murder, polygamy, rainbows, wine, ziggurats, and urban life; and ultimately the origins of a specially chosen patriarch, his chosen family, and their expanding chosen tribes. We also noted the origins of an "anti-patriarchal patriarchy," a strikingly sustained critique of fatherly misbehavior and a favoring of younger brothers, outsiders, and marginalized women. Throughout Genesis we saw also the origin of God's dealing with humanity through covenants, those contracts by which God binds people – and remarkably, himself – with certain promises, conditions, and signs. By the end of Genesis we saw the special blessing of God descending on these younger sons: on the arrow-straight and noble Joseph, but even more – and more surprisingly – on the crooked but repentant Judah. And there the book ended, with the Hebrews taking up an extended but still temporary residence under the special protection of *Yahweh*, Pharaoh, and Joseph in the Egyptian Land of Goshen.

7.1 Mosaic Epic: The Priestly Kingdom

If Genesis ends with the way into Egypt, Exodus tells of the way out – indeed, that is the meaning of the book's Greek title – Ἔξοδος (*Ex-Odos*, "Exit"). It is an epic and heroic story of great testings and fulfillments, for it is in Exodus – and the three books that follow, Leviticus, Numbers, and Deuteronomy – that the twelve sons of Jacob and their seventy pilgrim family members grow into the Twelve Tribes of Israel, a burgeoning nation so numerous and successful as to excite the fear and envy of a great power, and attract its murderous hostility. And in the midst of those terrible trials, a new covenant is given, named for the lawgiver who was himself a man set apart and "drawn out" – Moses. As we will see, this "Mosaic" Covenant established the most exacting divine Law found anywhere in the Bible; also, like the Abrahamic Covenant before, it often is read as applying exclusively to the people specially chosen.

"These are the Names"

As with many Hebrew titles for biblical books, the Hebrew for Exodus, *We'elleh Shemoth*, simply repeats the opening words of the text, "these are the names." This traditional title again highlights the fact that these biblical books are, in essence, extensively augmented genealogies.

Literary Study of the Bible: An Introduction, First Edition. Christopher Hodgkins.
© 2020 John Wiley & Sons Ltd. Published 2020 by John Wiley & Sons Ltd.

Yet this most demanding *Law* is presented as the foundation of true *liberty*. Also, this most *exclusive* and particular Covenant of Moses, like the ones with Abraham before and with David after, also contains within it an ultimate promise of wide *inclusion*. A specific group – Israel – is set apart (and increasingly kept apart) to achieve a mission that will, in the fullness of time, embrace the nations. Abraham's chosen seed will be a blessing to all the earth (Genesis 12:3) and the "son of David" or "root of Jesse" will someday establish justice for the Gentiles (Isaiah 11:10, Psalm 72:1, 8–14); while the LORD promises Moses that the Israelites will be a "kingdom of priests," priests who will mediate his Covenant and his steadfast love to all the peoples (Exodus 19:6).

Love the Stranger

At the heart of the Mosaic Law is a remarkable concern for the stranger, the foreigner, and the sojourner living among the chosen people. In the Pentateuch alone, dozens of passages instruct the Israelites to welcome Gentiles, to refrain from harassing or exploiting them, to set aside provisions for them in time of need, and above all to "love the stranger, for you were strangers in the land of Egypt" (Deuteronomy 10:19). Foreigners who wished to join fully with the congregation were allowed to do so after the circumcision of their males (Exodus 12:48), though this was not to be forced or compelled. Thus, when *Yahweh* declares particular judgments on certain groups – the Amalekites, the Moabites, and the Amorites, for instance – this condemnation must be understood in the context of a larger embrace offered to "the nations."

In literary terms, what we see in the story of Moses and the Israelites is a great ancient **epic**, from the Greek *epos* for a "Song," in this case the song of a **hero**. Like the earlier Near Eastern epic of *Gilgamesh*, and the later European epics of *The Iliad, The Odyssey, The Aeneid, Beowulf, The Divine Comedy, The Faerie Queene,* and *Paradise Lost*, the Mosaic epic displays all the conventions in the Mediterranean tradition of great heroic narrative. It is, as we now say, "EPIC" – that is, very large – in **scope** and **length**; it proclaims its nation-building **epic theme**, in this case liberty through God's Law; it presents us with **heavenly consults** and direct **divine interventions**; it expands its size through **epic catalogues** and **warrior lists**, and advances its narrative through world-altering **epic battles**; it enlivens its story through interactions with **underworld beings**, in this case many of the gods of Egypt; and as a counter to its portraits of evil and violence, it compensates with examples of providential **hospitality**, in this case as, against all odds, Moses and the Hebrews are fed in the desert by the likes of Jethro and finally by *Yahweh* himself.

Above all, at the heart of the story is a single focal **hero** whose trials and triumphs remake history and define the character of his people. If the traditional Near Eastern hero-god acts, in Northrup Frye's phrase, "at the conceivable limits of desire,"[1] displaying his own superhuman powers, instead Moses is heroic mainly in his trust, in his humble patience, and in his obedience to the empowering Creator, *Yahweh*. So Moses as hero not only defines the Israelite nation; he redefines the concept of heroism itself – while the Exodus and its aftermath redefine the meaning of heroic nationhood. The Hebrews are portrayed as so richly human – so complicated by their combinations of humble faith and rebellious unbelief, so quick to complain and to renege on their vows and yet sometimes so sincere in their virtues – that it is impossible to see this chosen people as some epic Master Race, a tribe uniquely endowed by nature to dominate the earth through their own greatness and prowess. No, "you were the least of all peoples; but ... the LORD loves you" (Deuteronomy 7:7–8). It is wonderful to be loved; yet it is also difficult to be loved in spite of oneself.

Clearly, the Book of Exodus does not stand alone. As a continuation of the Genesis narrative, it makes immediate reference back, and then forward: "Joseph died, all his brothers, and all that generation. But the children of Israel were fruitful and increased abundantly, multiplied and grew exceedingly mighty; and the land was filled with them" (Exodus 1:6–7). But good news begets bad: "Now there arose a new king over Egypt, who did not know Joseph. And he said to his people, 'Look, the people of the children of Israel are more and mightier than we; come, let us deal shrewdly with them, lest they multiply, and it happen, in the event of war, that they also join our enemies and fight against us, and so go up out of the land'" (1:8–10).

Who was this Pharaoh who "knew not Joseph"? The narrator declines to name him, but a few possible identities have been proposed, from Eighteenthth-Dynasty rulers Ahmose, or Amenhotep I or II, or Thutmose III, to Nineteenth-Dynasty Pharaoh Ramses II. Egyptian records indicate a dynastic transition in the early part of the sixteenth century BCE, as the invading Semitic Hyksos of the Seventeenth Dynasty were overthrown by indigenous Egyptians under Ahmose.

Egyptian Dynasties and Possible Dates of the Exodus

The Hyksos – Seventeenth Dynasty – 1700–1550 BCE – Semitic invaders of Egypt – Contemporary with Joseph

Ahmose – Eighteenth Dynasty – 1570–1545 BCE – Defeats Hyksos, restores native Egyptians to power

Amenhotep I – 1545–1529 BCE – Enslavement of Hebrews/"Habiru"?

Thutmose I – 1529–1517 BCE – Moses born 1527 BCE?

Thutmose II – 1517–1504 BCE

Thutmose III and Hatshepsut – 1504–1453 BCE – Moses flees 1487 BCE? Further mentions of Habiru "shepherd people" as a threat

Amenhotep II – 1453–1426 BCE – "High" Exodus 1447 BCE?

Akhenaten – 1377–1360 BCE – Priest of Aten/Ra – establishes monotheism

Tutankhamun – 1360–1350 BCE – restores ancient gods

Rameses I – Nineteenth Dynasty – 1306–1290 BCE

Rameses II – 1290–1224 BCE – "Low" Exodus – 1290 BCE?

It is soon after the commencement of the Eighteenth Dynasty that Egyptian records indicate the suppression of a burgeoning nomadic people called the "Habiru" or "Apiru." Could the "Pharaoh of the Oppression," then, have been Amenhotep I, and the "Pharaoh of the Exodus" Thutmose III or Amenhotep II? No Egyptian records mention a successful mass exodus of "Habiru" or Hebrew slaves, nor the catastrophic events that lead up to this exodus in the Bible, but then, one might not expect that Egypt's "official version" would mention such disasters. Indeed, official Egyptian chroniclers are known to have suppressed and even obliterated records of events or religious movements unfavorable to the regimes they served. A now-famous instance is that of Pharaoh Horemheb, last of the Eighteenth Dynasty, who destroyed inscriptions about the decrees and achievements of his predecessors Akhenaten (Amenhotep IV) and Tutankhamun – as it turns out incompletely destroyed them, since twentieth-century archeology was able to recover evidence of Akhenaten's attempts to impose a form of monotheism, and modern archeologists have discovered the long-forgotten tomb of Akhenaten's likely son, Tutankhamun, popularly known as "King Tut."

Archeology of the Exodus

The lack of clear archeological evidence for the Exodus has led some to conclude that there was no such event. However, this argument from silence is itself dubious, for what sorts of evidence would a wandering band of Hebrews leave after thirty-five centuries? Footprints? Tent pegs? Prayer shawls? Latrines? Allowing for some later editing, the distances, landmarks, and even some place names described in the Pentateuch match the actual geography of Egypt, the Sinai, and Canaan to a degree unlikely if the book were purely a pious fiction composed a millennium after the events in the faraway land of Babylon, as some have claimed. And while the excavation of Canaan does not reveal a complete conquest at the end of the fifteenth century BCE, a careful reading of Joshua and Judges indicates a more partial and gradual taking of the land from the Amorites, Amalekites, Midianites, and the Philistines (see Chapter 8).

7.1.1 Moses: A Man Drawn Out

However, one striking convergence of biblical and Egyptian records is the name of the Hebrew Deliverer, *Moses* ("born of/drawn out of"), which resembles Pharaonic names Ah-*mose*, Thut-*mose*, and Ramses/Ra-*mose*, names meaning, respectively, "born of/drawn out of" Ah (the moon god), Thoth (god of justice and death), and Ra (the sun god). This resemblance is indeed fitting if, as Exodus says, Moses had been adopted and named by a Pharaoh's daughter (2:10); and indeed is doubly fitting, since Exodus portrays Moses not only as having been "drawn out" by miraculous rescue from genocide, but also as having been specially called out and set aside for a holy purpose – to draw God's people out of Egypt.

And, whatever his exact origins, Moses remains a heroic figure of towering importance, not only among those Jews who still strive to keep his Law, and among Christians and Muslims who honor his memory, but also in the history of law, ethics, and the arts. Moses is deeply rooted in world religious culture, "high culture," and popular culture in innumerable ways: from Michelangelo's muscular statue in Rome to Rembrandt's famous portrait and the friezes on the gables of the United States Supreme Court; whether as *Moshe* or *Musa* or at Mt. Sinai Hospital in Manhattan; in a black spiritual (and a Faulkner short story) saying "Go Down, Moses" and in folk songs about a "Man Come Into Egypt"; or as an inspiration for Martin Luther King or even for the original comic book Superman – and above all as the traditional author of the Pentateuch. And then there are the "Moses movies": *The Ten Commandments* (1956), *Moses the Lawgiver* (1975), *Moses* (1995), *Prince of Egypt* (1998), and *Exodus: Gods and Kings* (2014). In these films actors as diverse as Charlton Heston, Burt Lancaster, Ben Kingsley, Val Kilmer, and Christian Bale variously re-imagine the Deliverer as a clenched-toothed American patriarch (Heston and Lancaster), a stammering Semitic *mensch* (Kingsley), or a tenderhearted and conflicted American rebel (Kilmer and Bale) – often with subplots of star-crossed romance or sibling rivalry added for good Hollywood measure.

But while some injected glamor and cultural accommodation are inevitable in such films, Moses's story as narrated in Exodus is riveting enough without change. Born as the third child to the Hebrew Amram and his wife Jochebed during a time of oppression, Moses is subject to the same new Pharaonic drowning order as all other infant Hebrew males. However, his mother, with the aid of his older sister Miriam, casts Moses into the river in a way that saves rather than kills him: they "took an ark of bulrushes for him, daubed it with asphalt and pitch, put the child in it, and laid it in the reeds by the river's bank. And his sister stood afar off, to know what would be done to him" (2:3–4). This "ark" – with its reference back to Noah and forward to the "ark of the covenant" – floats providentially into the riverside bathing area of Pharaoh's daughter herself, who, while recognizing the boy as a forbidden Hebrew, compassionately chooses to save the child, and eventually to adopt and raise him herself. Thus, is the child "drawn out" of the water and named as such – "Moses" – then brought up within Pharaoh's court, while still being nursed and instructed by his actual mother (2:7–10).

Moses's double life comes to a head when, as a young man, "he went out to his brethren and looked at their burdens" (2:11). Identifying with his fellow Hebrews, he takes it upon himself to kill an Egyptian overseer who was beating a Hebrew and to hide the body. Then, in an incident foreshadowing his often conflicted relationship with his people, he attempts to stop two Hebrews from fighting, only to have his intervention rejected, and indeed to be accused of murder: "Who made you a prince and a judge over us? Do you intend to kill me as you killed the Egyptian?" (2:14).

With the mixture of weakness and boldness that will mark his heroic career, Moses then flees the wrath of Pharaoh, running to the country of Midian and the Sinai Peninsula, yet bravely rescues some shepherdesses from bullying shepherds at a well in the desert. The father of these women, a God-fearing Gentile named Reuel (also called Jethro), gratefully offers Moses a place in their camp, and the hand of his daughter Zipporah, who soon bears Moses a son called Gershom (whose name means "stranger there"). He seems to be settling into exile and, like Joseph, forgetting his past, when we're told that, just as in Joseph's story, "God remembers" – in this case remembers his suffering people Israel, who are calling out under the oppression of a new Pharaoh (2:24–25).

Thus, the stage is set for what is perhaps the most iconic theophany in the entire Old Testament, the episode of the Burning Bush. What is probably most important about this passage is the trembling, reluctant humility of Moses before the mystery and majesty of God. While Moses is out tending Jethro's flocks near Mount Horeb (Mount Sinai), God appears to him in "a bush [that] was burning with fire, but the bush was not consumed," and tells Moses to remove his sandals, "for the place where you stand is holy ground" (3:2, 5). Then the voice from the bush explains Moses' stunning mission: "Come now, therefore, and I will send you to Pharaoh that you may bring My people, the children of Israel, out of Egypt" (3:10). Later in the Pentateuch, Moses is called "very humble, more than all men who were on the face of the earth" (Numbers 12:3), and that meekness is on display here – apparently to a fault. "Who am I that I should go to Pharaoh?... What is [Your] name?... [S]uppose they do not believe me?... I am slow of speech... Please send by the hand of whomever else You may send" (3:11, 13; 4:1, 10, 13). Never was there a more hesitant Prophet, one less hungry for divine authority, less sure of his own adequacy.

And not without reason – for this is the stuttering, trembling third child of a Hebrew slave sent up against the most powerful ruler on the earth. Yet, however surprising, God's choice of a weak and unlikely instrument fits the pattern already well-established back in Genesis – whether blest younger sons like Isaac, Jacob, Judah, and Joseph; barren wives like Sarah, Rebekah, and Rachel; and favored outcasts like Hagar and Tamar. And God's visible appearance has its surprises too. Of all the manifestations that the Almighty might choose at this juncture – an angel, an earthquake, a whirlwind – a flaming shrubbery might seem unlikely. Yet on fuller reflection this theophany is strangely appropriate: the consuming fire that nevertheless does not destroy, the Deity called by a mysterious name for the unnamable. For when Moses, overwhelmed and puzzled by his mission, asks for God's name, so that he can tell it to the Hebrews, he is asking for more than just a handy label; he is assuming that the Hebrews will see their God (or more correctly, their god) as one among many gods, multiple and competing cosmic forces who need to be invoked by particular "handles" in order to obtain particular favors and functions for which they are best suited. God's answer to Moses both condescends to and rebukes his request. He tells them a name to use that nevertheless explodes the "useful" purpose of divine naming: "I AM WHO I AM" can be rendered as a pronounceable title – יהוה/*YHWH*/*Yahweh*/*JHVH*/ *Jehovah* – but it rejects any limits and any claims to local contingency and particularity, asserting instead God's radical self-existence and self-definition. That self-definition also rejects any easy notions of divine tractability, like some "Genie of the Lamp" conjured by a formulaic call or spell. Finally, the divine "I AM" also claims the precedence of the Creator – this God is always previous – that undergirds the existence of all other beings.

YHWH, the Name of God

It appears, from this passage and from Exodus 6:3 soon after, that the name *YHWH* is new to Moses, and to the people of Israel – who had in the past known the Deity as *El Shaddai* ("God Almighty"). And yet as we have seen, the name *YHWH* appears frequently throughout Genesis from Adam through the Patriarchs. Thus it appears that the name *YHWH* has been read back into the earlier accounts, probably to emphasize the covenant faithfulness of Israel's God from the very beginning of creation. To Orthodox and Conservative Jews, the names of God are so sacred that they are neither spelled out – using "G-d" instead – nor pronounced – He is called *Ha-Shem*, "the Name." In imitation of this Jewish tradition, the King James Version of the Bible generally substitutes "LORD" for *YHWH, Yahweh, JHVH,* or *Jehovah*.

Clearly, *Yahweh's* call is an offer that Moses can't refuse – though not because of overt divine coercion. The LORD meets every one of Moses' objections and questions with concrete solutions and answers – sometimes a bit testy, but never truly wrathful. "Who am I that I should go to Pharaoh?" In answer, God tells Moses that he is chosen specially for this task and as a sign God will return him with the freed Israelites to this same holy mountain of Horeb (3:12). "What is [Your] name?" God gives Moses something to say – "I AM" – while refusing to concede the "god-on-call" premises of Near Eastern divine naming (3:14–15). "[S]uppose they do not believe me?" God gives Moses miraculous signs (a rod transformed to a serpent, a hand afflicted and healed of leprosy, water turned to blood) to demonstrate the message's divine power (4:2–9). "I am slow of speech": God will tell Moses what to say, but also insists, memorably, that Moses' slow tongue – like other common handicaps – is God's own doing for his own mysterious purposes (4:11–12). It's only in response to Moses' final appeal ("Please send by the hand of whomever else You may send") that God loses patience: his "anger is kindled," so God will appoint eloquent older brother Aaron to speak instead! (4:14–16; 6:28–7:2).

So Moses is finally cajoled into becoming the LORD's Prophet in Egypt; yet even as he journeys with his family back to the land of his birth to begin his mission, his continuing unreadiness is made apparent by a strange and rather sensational occurrence on the way: having told Moses that "all the [Egyptian] men who sought your life are dead" (4:19), the LORD meets the Deliverer in an inn on the way and seeks to kill him as well! In one of the Bible's weirdest marital exchanges, Zipporah divines that the root of God's anger is the uncircumcised state of their son, so with "a sharp stone" (!!) she performs the rough-and-ready *bris* herself, throwing the aforesaid foreskin at Moses's feet with the exclamation "Surely you are a bridegroom of blood to me!" (4:25). This moment of domestic discord reminds us that the man appointed to carry the covenant of *Yahweh* forward has failed the keep the most basic sign of the covenant himself – circumcising one's own son into the covenant family. Ironically, it is left to his Gentile wife to fulfill the commandment. Like the Israelites, Moses too has a long journey ahead.

7.1.2 The Exodus: Let My People Go

> When Israel was in Egypt land – *Let My people go*;
> Oppressed so hard they could not stand – *Let My people go*;
> Go down, Moses, way down in Egypt land,
> Tell old Pharaoh: *Let My people go*.
> The Lord told Moses what to do – *Let My people go*;
> To lead the children of Israel through – *Let My people go*.
> Go down, Moses, way down in Egypt land,
> Tell old Pharaoh: *Let My people go*. African-American Spiritual

The steps that begin Moses's intervention in Egypt are clearly faltering ones, but they are, nevertheless, somehow still on a divinely appointed path. The debacle of Gershom's delayed circumcision and of the Prophet's near death is followed immediately by the providentially appointed rendezvous at "the mountain of God" with his brother Aaron, who has been divinely prompted to meet Moses at Mount Sinai. There Moses reveals the full extent of their calling and demonstrates the signs and powers that they will use to rally the Israelites and to confront Pharaoh. Then they head directly to Goshen, where the two brothers, increasingly acting as one, meet with "all the elders and the children of Israel," who initially heed the words and signs of the LORD, bow in worship, and await their deliverance (4:27–31).

Yet part of the divine plan, as already sketched out by *Yahweh* to Moses, is significant delay, because Pharaoh will not cooperate – indeed, in some sense cannot until God's chosen moment. "When you go back to Egypt, see that you do all those wonders before Pharaoh which I have put in your hand. But I will harden his heart, so that he will not let the people go" (4:21). Here commences the epic drama in which the greatest lord of the earth learns to his terrible cost that he also is subject to the LORD of earth and of heaven. As with the providential dramas of Genesis – particularly the reverse-Exodus story of Joseph – the human players in Exodus are frequently unwilling or unable to perceive their place in a larger narrative fraught with ironies both tragic and splendid. And the chief of these ironies is that the powerful actually are powerless, and that, however impossible it may seem, the slave shall be free.

Thus, on the one hand, throughout the Exodus narrative we read that mighty Pharaoh is really God's unwitting tool: variants of "the LORD hardened Pharaoh's heart" occur seven times (4:21; 7:3, 10:1, 20, 27; 11:10; 14:4). Yet interspersed we also read that Pharaoh bears the guilt of his own willfulness: variants of "Pharaoh hardened his heart" (8:15, 32; 9:34) and the more passive "Pharaoh's heart was hardened" (7:13, 14, 22; 8:19) occur seven times. This paradoxical balancing of divine sovereignty with human responsibility is too exact to be anything but deliberate – seven being a number of perfection; and, as we have seen many times before, the Hebraic answer to our inevitable "either/or" question ("Is God responsible or is Pharaoh responsible?") will be "Yes."

But the Israelites also, and sometimes even Moses, lack this constant providential perspective; indeed, the Israelites are presented, if anything, as consistent only in their questioning, their complaints, and in their outright rebellion against the Prophet's leadership. Moses' first encounter with Pharaoh (as *Yahweh* had predicted) goes quite badly, as the hard-hearted monarch responds incredulously to the *chutzpah* of this slave demanding freedom in the name of his god. "Who is the LORD, that I should obey His voice to let Israel go? I do not know the LORD, nor will I let Israel go" (5:2). Then Pharaoh practices a devastatingly effective form of counter-insurgency, commanding that in the brick-yards, the Hebrews now must gather their own straw (a binding agent) to make their bricks, without any decrease in their quota – effectively doubling their labor (5:4–19). The predictable result? The Israelites turn against not their slavemasters but their would-be liberators: "they met Moses and Aaron who stood there to meet them. And they said to them, 'Let the LORD look on you and judge, because you have made us abhorrent in the sight of Pharaoh and in the sight of his servants, to put a sword in their hand to kill us'" (5:20–21). The LORD's response to their lament? That it's all according to plan: "Now you shall see what I will do to Pharaoh. For with a strong hand he will let them go, and with a strong hand he will drive them out of his land" (6:1). The purpose of this protracted Pharaonic delay and the escalation of tensions is to allow God to show his power, not only in his secret decrees and quiet direction of events (as in Joseph's story) but also in spectacular calamities that will be visited upon Egypt.

With the LORD having thrown down the gauntlet, what follows are the famous ten plagues, presented as stages in an escalating showdown with Egypt's many gods – as the nation's deities, and the nation itself, suffer under terrifying judgments (12:12). Even a rudimentary study of ancient Egyptian religion shows that the nation's gods were much less anthropomorphic than the Greco-Roman pantheon; Egypt's deities personified natural and astronomical bodies, and often were pictured with animal and even insect forms. Thus when, in the first plague, *Yahweh* transforms the Nile into blood (7:14–25), it is the Nile-god *Hapi* who comes under attack, as does the underworld god *Osiris*, for ironically the Nile is his bloodstream. So again, the second plague of frogs (8:1–15) both evokes and mocks *Heqt*, the frog-headed goddess of fertility, water, and renewal. (*Heqt* is also the original of *Hecate*, the underworld goddess famously invoked in Shakespeare's *Macbeth*.) The third plague, of lice from the dust of the earth (8:16–19), overpowers the earth-god *Geb*, while the fourth plague, of flies (8:20–32), scorns *Uatchit* and *Khepri*, lords of the flies and of the beetles. And so the plagues unfold, with the fifth plague, on cattle (9:1–7), judging *Apis/Serapis*, the bull-god, and *Hathor*, the cow-goddess; the sixth plague, of boils (9:8–12), defeating *Imhotep* and *Isis*, god and goddess of healing; the seventh plague, of hail (9:13–35), overpowering *Nut* the sky goddess; and the eighth plague, of locusts (10:1–20), humiliating *Serapia*, the goddess who was supposed to protect against such infestations.

There is, no doubt, a certain comic element intertwined with these dramatic confrontations between God and Pharaoh, as the magicians of Egypt reproduce the first and second plagues of the bloody Nile and of the frogs "with their own enchantments" (7:22, 8:7) – like clowns retaliating to slaps in the face by slapping their own faces even harder. These copycat self-afflictions come to a bizarre end with the third plague as "the magicians so worked with their enchantments to bring forth lice, but they could not" (8:18–19) – as if there weren't already enough vermin in Egypt! These useful idiots recognize "the finger of God" only where their own power leaves off, and *Yahweh* increasingly obliges them: from the fourth plague onwards, the LORD tells Pharaoh that He will "make a difference between My people and your people," setting apart the land of Goshen from affliction while the rest of Egypt suffers (8:23).

And in the end the suffering reaches an unbearable pitch: the ninth plague overthrows Egypt's supreme deity, the sun-god Ra (or Amon-Re), as well as the moon-god Thoth, by bringing three days of thick darkness, "darkness which may even be felt" – in effect, six consecutive pitch-black nights – over all the land with the exception of the Hebrew habitation in Goshen (10:21–23). But the cycle, and the LORD's victory, will not be complete until one other Egyptian deity has felt the weight of God's wrath: Pharaoh himself, the son of the gods, whose firstborn heir must die along with all the other firstborn of man and beast (11:4–5).

But more even than this wrath on the gods, the ten plagues present a tragic undoing of Creation itself, as a punishment for Pharaoh's refusal to recognize the power of the Creator over all the earth. In Genesis the first three creative days see the origin of sky, earth, and waters, and the last three creative days see the origin of the beings that fill them; so here in Exodus the original settings of life, and the characters that inhabit them, are infected and undone – at least within the boundaries of Egypt. The sky is filled with loathsome vermin; the earth and its increase are blighted and cursed; and the waters are poisoned, and infested with vile things. Most strikingly, in the final two plagues, the first and the last of God's creatures – that is, the light, and the human race – are put out and put to death, respectively. The God who created light three days before creating the sun, moon, and stars now extinguishes all the lights of Egypt, except within the Hebrew dwellings in Goshen. And all the firstborn of Egypt will die – "from the firstborn of Pharaoh who sits on his throne, even to the firstborn of the female servant who is behind the handmill, and all the firstborn of the animals" (11:5). All classes of this nation that has set itself above the nations will be brought equally low; as in Genesis, the younger again will be preferred to the elder; the king whose father sought the deaths of Israel's sons will lose his own son and heir; and the slaves will live, and go free. Through it all Pharaoh, in the image not only of Egypt but of graceless humanity, mocks, boasts, ignores, bargains, wheedles, whimpers, and betrays – giving anything but obedience to the word of this God, *Yahweh*, and his upstart messengers.

Against the backdrop of all this darkness and death, shining like a diamond on black velvet, is the *Pesach*, the feast of the Passover. In our own day, Passover is still a high point of the Jewish year in the spring month of *Abib*, and the most widely observed of all Jewish festivals. It commemorates the special mercy of the LORD toward the Israelites, and, through the associated Feast of Unleavened Bread, memorializes the haste and hurry of the Hebrews, finally released from bondage. It is a feast still held in private homes, with each family its own congregation; and on the first Passover, Moses commanded each family to sacrifice its own unblemished lamb and apply that lamb's blood to the lintel and sideposts of their doors in Goshen, and to eat the feast in haste with staff in hand – the lamb's meat roasted in fire, along with unraised flatbread and bitter herbs (12:1–11). Yet, while remembering God's special mercy in passing over Israel, and his special wrath on Israel's oppressors, the Law of the Passover ends with a note of inclusion: while no uncircumcised persons may eat of it, Gentile strangers who wish to join the congregation may adopt the covenant sign and join in the feast (12:47–49). This paradoxical relationship of exclusion to inclusion foreshadows the entire practice and purpose of the Mosaic Covenant, as we soon will see.

But before the full Law of Moses can be given at Sinai, *Yahweh* will deal finally with Pharaoh and the Egyptians. Having directed the Israelites to travel, not by the more direct northern "Way of the Philistines" from Goshen east into Canaan, but by the "Wilderness Way" south to Migdol on the western bank of the Red Sea, the LORD now warns Moses and the people that "I will harden Pharaoh's heart, so that he will pursue them; and I will gain honor over Pharaoh and over all his army, that the Egyptians may know that I am the LORD" (14:4). Here we see not only a spectacular instance of divine judgment, but also of divine testing, a test that the Israelites very nearly fail. Despite God's advance warning about the Egyptian attack, when the people see Pharaoh and his hosts sweeping down in their chariots, they turn fiercely (and sarcastically) to blame Moses: "Because there were no graves in Egypt, have you taken us away to die in the wilderness?... Is this not the word that we told you in Egypt, saying, 'Let us alone that we may serve the Egyptians'? For it would have been better for us to serve the Egyptians than that we should die in the wilderness" (14:11–12).

Map of the Exodus

Although significant doubts have been expressed about the historicity of Moses and the Exodus, the places named in the Book of Exodus are historically identifiable in Egypt, the Sinai Peninsula, and Palestine. This map shows the approximate route of the Hebrews, as described in Exodus through Deuteronomy.

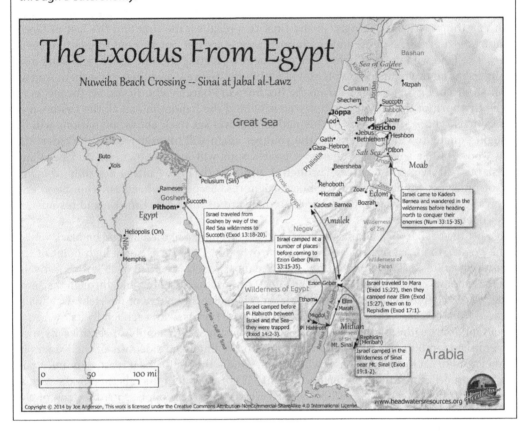

With charging Egyptian chariots at his back, rebellious Hebrews at his side, and the Red Sea straight ahead, Moses stands in the crucible of leadership, and it turns out to be his finest hour. His words are few, calm, and direct: "Do not be afraid. Stand still, and see the salvation of the LORD, which he will accomplish for you today. For the Egyptians whom you see today, you shall see again no more forever. The LORD will fight for you, and you shall hold your peace" (14:13–14). Then, at the LORD's direction, he stretches out his hand over the sea, and the east wind makes a path through the water like dry land, with God's pillar of fire standing guard between the Egyptians and the Israelites as Moses leads his people through the heart of the sea.

What follows is the final act of "hardening" that *Yahweh* inflicts on the Egyptians – final because it is fatal. Despite seeing the miraculous parting of the sea and the pillars of fire and cloud, despite having experienced all of the escalating plagues and the fearsome death of the firstborn, Pharaoh's chariots and cavalry vengefully charge headlong into the watery chasm until the whole force is entirely at the mercy of the waves, and of the God holding them back. But having repeatedly shown no mercy, they receive none:

Then the LORD said to Moses, "Stretch out your hand over the sea, that the waters may come back upon the Egyptians, on their chariots, and on their horsemen." And Moses stretched out his hand over the sea; and when the morning appeared, the sea returned to its full depth, while the Egyptians were fleeing into it. So the LORD overthrew the Egyptians in the midst of the sea. (14:26–27)

As the remains of Pharaoh's army wash up on shore, Moses and the Hebrews burst into a song – indeed a psalm – that fills most of one chapter celebrating "the horse and its rider … thrown into the sea" (15:1), but celebrating this act of fearsome judgment as an act of mercy:

> You stretched out Your right hand;
> The earth swallowed them.
> You in Your mercy have led forth
> The people whom You have redeemed;
> You have guided them in Your strength
> To Your holy habitation. (15:12–13)

And this story is probably best understood from the perspective of those "oppressed so hard they could not stand," in the words of the spiritual. Those who have cried out loud and long in slavery are in the prime position to savor deliverance, and the least likely to puzzle over the ways of the Most High in delivering them, or to grieve for "old Pharaoh." This is especially so if Pharaoh is no mere particular tyrant over one specific tribe, but rather, in the words of Abraham Lincoln, a representative spirit of evil:

> the same spirit that says, "You toil and work and earn bread, and I'll eat it." No matter in what shape it comes, whether from the mouth of a king who seeks to bestride the people of his own nation and live by the fruit of their labor, or from one race of men as an apology for enslaving another race, it is the same tyrannical principle.[2]

So did Louis Armstrong, in his New Orleans-style rendition of the old spiritual, give its refrain a plural, and more universal application: "tell *all pharaoes*, let my people go." Moses' liberation is offered not only for one nation, the Hebrew nation, but as the prototype for all peoples – and this liberty is intrinsically connected to law.

7.1.3   Exodus and Leviticus: Covenant Law and Liberty

In the chapters immediately following the dramatic climax at the Red Sea we repeatedly read of how the Israelites, now freed from Egyptian tyranny, nearly collapse into chaos. The techniques of narrative repetition for emphasis, and of juxtaposition for irony, are much in play. Earlier in Exodus, we've already seen the Hebrews react humanly (which largely means unfaithfully and ungratefully) to God's deliverance and Moses's leadership, so to see and hear them grumbling, backbiting, and generally *kvetching* in the desert is not exactly a surprise. But to witness their complaints and rebellion so soon after such stunning divine intervention is passing strange, like some negative miracle of unbelief in the midst of overflowing heavenly glory. And indeed that appears to be the point: as in Genesis, we witness the stories of people who, if left to their own devices and desires, will use their freedom to return again to spiritual slavery, and abuse their powers of choice to undo all the goods that God and his creation can offer. In short, we're shown that liberation is not enough; only trust in divine goodness and awe of divine rule make truly free. Exodus and Leviticus begin the Israelites' long tutorial in this law of liberty.

"And He Called"

The Hebrew name for the Book of Leviticus, *WaYikra*, reiterates the opening words, "And the LORD called to Moses," thus stressing the Law as the very words of God, calling out to his chosen. The Septuagint title from which "Leviticus" derives, *Leuitikon*, emphasizes the focus pertaining to the priestly family of Levi.

Now, a phrase like "law of liberty" presents an immediate paradox, which can be seen as a contradiction: if law merely limits liberty, and liberty only overthrows law, then the two terms cannot be harmonized, but are in a zero-sum conflict. However, though the Mosaic Covenant greatly ups the ante over previous covenants with God's own plenty of restrictions, we'll see that the *Torah* presents these laws and commandments as harmonized fundamentally with the greater melody of all creation, and also as providing the discipline necessary for a priestly and military order – the nation of Israel – to fulfill what is portrayed as an essentially liberating mission.

These demonstrations of divine provision and protection, despite Israelite grumbling, begin with that greatest of desert needs, water. Before Moses "heals" the poisoned well at Mara – literally "bitter" (Exodus 15:22–26) – before he discovers the twelve wells of Elim (15:27), and before he brings forth water from the rock at Mt. Sinai/Horeb with a blow from his staff (17:1–7), the Prophet in each case faces heavy criticism and opposition from the congregation, some of it life-threatening: the location of the well at Sinai is renamed Massah and Meribah ("tempted" and "contention") and Moses complains to the LORD that "they are almost ready to stone me!" (17:4). As with water, so with food: hungry for their accustomed slave provisions of stew and bread, they pine for the days of bondage and a "free" meal, forgetting even very recent provisions from *Yahweh*. The LORD responds by promising to "rain bread from heaven for you," and Moses makes his merely representative position clear by telling the people that "the LORD hears your complaints which you make against *him*" (17:3–8). This heavenly bread is preceded by airborne meat:

> So it was that quails came up at evening and covered the camp, and in the morning the dew lay all around the camp. And when the layer of dew lifted, there, on the surface of the wilderness, was a small round substance, as fine as frost on the ground. So when the children of Israel saw it, they said to one another, "What is it?" (17:13–15)

"What is it?" – Hebrew *Man hu*? – gives the bread its famous name, "manna," and gives the story a further mysterious twist, as the God whose Name is not a name – "I AM WHO I AM" – feeds his uncannily ungrateful people with a nameless mystery meal.

Significantly, it's almost as an afterthought that, following three full chapters of storm and struggle about desert provisions, a story of divine military protection gets such small space. The unprovoked attack by the Amalekites is the first of many by "people of the land" on the pilgrim Hebrews, and the Israelites' victory is rendered with remarkable brevity (17:8–13). Even more remarkable, though, are the means of victory:

> And so it was, when Moses held up his hand, that Israel prevailed; and when he let down his hand, Amalek prevailed... And Aaron and Hur supported his hands, one on one side, and the other on the other side... So Joshua defeated Amalek and his people with the edge of the sword. (17:11–13)

Clearly, the strange means of victory relate to the story's brevity: it's not by graphically detailed warrior prowess that Joshua defeats Amalek, but by the miraculous intervention of God, as signified by the prayerful, suppliant posture of the Prophet's raised hands. Thus biblical narrative often undercuts expectations of epic violence and battle to focus instead on the deliberate anticlimax of divine deliverance.

War with Amalek

"I will utterly blot out the remembrance of Amalek from under heaven," swears the LORD after Israel's victory at Rephidim (Exodus 17:14). Though the Israelites are portrayed here as the victims of unprovoked aggression, God's declaration of *perpetual* war on Amalek is one of the most disturbing statements in the Bible.

Unlike the more direct divine judgments of Noah's Flood and Sodom's destruction, this curse will require execution not by God's own hand but by the Israelites themselves. Even if we, like the Hebrews, concede the Creator's right to make or unmake his creatures, and acknowledge the past atrocities of the Amalekites, we're likely still to be troubled that God is authorizing his chosen people to execute an extermination order. This curse will appear again in 1 Samuel 15 with Saul's and Samuel's slaughter of this tribe and its leader, and in the Book of Esther, with Haman, an Amalekite, seeking to liquidate the Jews but being outwitted and destroyed by Esther and Mordecai.

Nowhere does the difference between the ancient view of collective, tribal identity and the modern view of individual, personal identity seem so stark. And yet it is also in Exodus and Leviticus that we find deep roots for the idea of God-given personal liberty founded on law.

Far more detailed is Moses's consultation with his father-in-law Jethro (Reuel) in chapter 18. Having sent Moses off to Egypt alone with only his immediate family, Jethro now sees him return as the leader of a great nation on the march (Exodus 38:26 numbers the men eligible for military service at 603,550, suggesting a total number of 2 million or more). But Jethro's joy, and awe at Moses' success is mixed with blunt criticism of his administrative practice. Seeing his son-in-law sitting from morning until evening hearing an endless stream of complaints and cases for judgment, Jethro minces no words:

> The thing that you do is not good. Both you and these people who are with you will surely wear yourselves out. For this thing is too much for you; you are not able to perform it by yourself. Listen now to my voice … you shall teach them the statutes and the laws, and show them the way in which they must walk and the work they must do. Moreover you shall select from all the people able men, such as fear God, men of truth, hating covetousness; and place such over them to be rulers of thousands, rulers of hundreds, rulers of fifties, and rulers of tens. And let them judge the people at all times. (18:17–22)

Even before the details of the Mosaic "statutes and laws" are given, we observe here two related principles that will guide the emerging Hebrew "constitution": *theocentric instruction and worship* joined to *decentralized power*. That is, Moses will teach certain central divine truths to the great congregation, and then largely delegate the interpretation and enforcement of those truths to the "local" levels, the levels of tribes and families. Only the most momentous issues will be brought before the Prophet; power is otherwise devolved (18:22). This approach to statecraft assumes that if from the people and their leaders there emerge "able men, such as fear

God, men of truth, hating covetousness" (18:21), then the apparatus of judgment and coercion can be local and minimal. Above all, this approach assumes the existence of a model "Founding Father" like Moses, meek and modest enough to take criticism, one who "heeded the voice of his father-in-law and did all that he had said" (18:24). Looking ahead – to the era of the Judges, and then of the Kings – as the Israelites vacillate between the polarities of anarchy and absolutism, it is to this ideal of **theocentric decentralization** that the biblical writers appeal: the ideal of law-based liberty.

7.1.3.1 Mosaic Covenant: Moral, Civil, and Ritual Law

We've seen that between the exit from Egypt in Exodus 12 and the giving of the Law in Exodus 19, a series of intervening events demonstrates the need for continuing divine providence and protection as the contexts for divine Law. In particular, the thrust of the narrative is to stress that freedom from slavery is no real liberation unless the people are themselves governed by God. And so we come to Mount Sinai, where the LORD meets Moses and the people in thunder, fire, and smoke, and with a "quaking" that may refer to the people's knees or to the earth itself. Yet despite these fearsome signs and the people's fearful reaction, what's most notable is that *Yahweh's* message through Moses is, fundamentally, one of affection, reconciliation, and outreach.

> Now therefore, if you will indeed obey My voice and keep My covenant, then you shall be a special treasure to Me above all people; for all the earth is Mine. And you shall be to Me a kingdom of priests and a holy nation. These are the words which you shall speak to the children of Israel. (19:5–6)

The unique phrases "kingdom of priests" and "holy nation" speak not only of Israel's special status as "God's chosen," but also of a special mediatory mission, as the Israelites, like priests, stand sacrificially between the Deity and the "laity" – that is, the Gentiles of all the nations. It is the Hebrew's "priestly" calling to preserve and speak God's words to the peoples, and their words to God, and to offer some sacrifice on the world's behalf.

It would be hard to overestimate the impact of these words on the Hebrew self-concept. Significantly, the word used here for "priest" (*koh'n/cohen*) and the name of the priestly tribe (Levi) remain the bases, in all their variant spellings, for two of the most common Jewish family names. Called out from the Gentiles with Father Abraham, the Hebrews are nevertheless called to be a blessing to all the families of the earth (Genesis 12:3); set apart here by Moses as a "holy nation," they are the designated go-betweens to all the nations. Indeed, we find in the Talmud the tradition of the *Lamed-Vav Tzadikim*, "The Thirty-Six Righteous Ones," for whose sake God in every new generation preserves the rest of humanity from destruction. Since, in rabbinical teaching, these humble "hidden saints" don't know who they are, every member of the congregation must strive to live as one of those on whom all human life depends.[3]

7.1.3.1.1 Moral Law: The Ten Commandments

Still, there is no doubt that at Sinai, the Mosaic Covenant is established in a setting more of fear and dread than of divine approachability and tenderness. "And the LORD said to Moses, 'Go down and warn the people, lest they break through to gaze at the LORD, and many of them perish. Also let the priests who come near the LORD consecrate themselves, lest the LORD break out against them'" (Exodus 19:21–22). And so the Covenant commences with the giving of what is often called the **moral law** in Ten Commandments, the first of which lay down the law about the awe that the people owe their God:

> I am the LORD your God, who brought you out of the land of Egypt, out of the house of bondage. You shall have no other gods before Me.
> You shall not make for yourself a carved image – any likeness of anything that is in heaven above, or that is in the earth beneath, or that is in the water under the earth; you shall not bow down to them nor serve them. For I, the LORD your God, am a jealous God …
> You shall not take the name of the LORD your God in vain, for the LORD will not hold him guiltless who takes His name in vain.
> Remember the Sabbath day, to keep it holy. Six days you shall labor and do all your work, but the seventh day is the Sabbath of the LORD your God… For in six days the LORD made the heavens and the earth, the sea, and all that is in them, and rested the seventh day. (20:2–11)

No other gods, no carved or "graven" image (*tselem*), no misuse of God's name (*Ha-Shem*), no *Shabbat* work: *Yahweh* demands, both as the Creator and as the Deliverer from slavery, that all Hebrew morality be rooted in worship – that is, in the recognition and embrace of the Deity's absolute priority and authority. The rest of the commandments, which deal with the most basic human social relations, base these relations on God's metaphysical goodness and thus treat abuses of people as crimes against their Maker:

> Honor your father and your mother, that your days may be long upon the land which the LORD your God is giving you.
> You shall not murder.
> You shall not commit adultery.
> You shall not steal.
> You shall not bear false witness against your neighbor.
> You shall not covet your neighbor's house; you shall not covet your neighbor's wife, nor his male servant, nor his female servant, nor his ox, nor his donkey, nor anything that is your neighbor's. (20:12–17)

The sanctity of parenthood, human life, marriage, property, and honest dealing: all are grounded, beyond social convention or a temporal political regime, in God's will and regarded as intrinsic and inalienable; and with the final command not to covet, the moral law reaches beyond outward behavior to inward motive, as well. Yet for all their absoluteness, none of these Ten Commandments specify particular interpretations or punishments, leaving the application of these few general principles to many local circumstances – but with the assumption that God is the ultimate source and enforcer of the law, who will judge the judges themselves.

Moses and Hammurabi

Much has been written comparing the words from the Code of Hammurabi (c. 1780 BCE) and the later Law of Moses. Hammurabi's code, one of the earliest preserved pieces of legislation on earth, is inscribed on a 7-ft *stele* shaped like a human index finger, now to be found in the Louvre (and in an exact copy in the Oriental Institute of the University of Chicago). Like the detailed Mosaic Civil Law, Hammurabi's code is specific and situational, for instance detailing the making of contracts, the meting out of particular punishments, and the handling of sexual misbehavior.

> However, there is nothing in the Hammurabic Code to compare to Moses's centrally theological focus: Hammurabi names his gods, but claims himself to be the source and author of his Laws. And his code provides nothing to match the Ten Commandments, with their general moral principles intended to guide human behavior in the light of *Yahweh's* character, creative power, and works of deliverance.
>
> Nevertheless, as with comparisons between Babylonian origin stories and the Book of Genesis, both the similarities and differences between Hammurabi and Moses suggest that the later Hebrew text may be written both to echo and to correct the earlier polytheistic writing – and quite possibly within the second millennium BCE, as well.

No doubt, contemporary materialist theories of social construction look askance at such confident divine pronouncements, instead emphasizing that all moral judgments are relative to circumstance, and indeed the idea of ethical contingency is most attractive when we ourselves either dissent from the commandments or stand under their sharp sanction, especially if enforcement is observably corrupt. Yet let our own rights be violated, or even questioned – that is, let our own ox be gored – and it's a rare person who doesn't speak as if those rights are self-evident, inalienable, sacred, even divine; in short, "written in stone." If you have ever used that phrase to describe rules or laws, you have, whether you know it or not, been citing Exodus. We're told that "when [the LORD] had made an end of speaking with [Moses] on Mount Sinai, He gave Moses two tablets of the Testimony, tablets of stone, written with the finger of God" (31:18). In the Talmud, it is stated that this stone was sky-blue sapphire, to remind the people of the firmament, and the celestial throne-room of God (24:10). Thus, for the Israelites, the Law is "written in stone" only after it has been written in the heavens, in the stars, in the wind, and in the human heart.

7.1.3.1.2 Civil Law: The Hebrew Constitution

We turn from the almost telegraphic directness and wide generality of the Ten Commandments, the foundational **moral law**, to the far more numerous and particular conditions of the Mosaic Covenant, often referred to as the **civil law** and the **ritual law**. The rabbinical commentators on the *Torah* have carefully counted all the moral, civil, and ritual laws, discovering fully **613 Mitzvot** (Hebrew for "Commandments"), and their sheer number and specificity may seem both strange and invasive to the contemporary reader. Having delivered the Hebrews from slavery in Egypt, the LORD seems intent on micro-managing them in Sinai and Canaan! Regulations abound about food, travel, clothing, slaves, sex, and festivals; rules multiply about sanctuary, sacrifice, social welfare, tabernacles, arks, marriage, prophets, and kings. Hair length, cud-chewing, household mold, candlesticks, menstruation, earrings, bodily markings, and of course foreskins – nothing seems beyond *Yahweh's* watchful gaze.

For the literary reader of this biblical legislation, two related problems arise: our sympathetic interest (or lack thereof), and the Law's coherence. As to our sympathetic interest, if readers find genealogies tedious, how do they respond to lengthy ordinances governing the sprinkling of blood? And, as to the Law's overall coherence, how does the average reader make sense of all this legal proliferation? First, it's helpful to attempt again, if only briefly, to "read like a Hebrew," and one key to sympathetic engagement is taking a cue from the word *mitzvot* itself, which has traditionally positive connotations in Jewish culture. It is the plural of *mitzvah*, a word familiar even to many Gentiles from the phrase *bar mitzvah*, the coming-of-age ceremony in which a thirteen-year-old boy becomes a "son of the commandment," and thus a man. (In many modern Jewish congregations, a thirteen-year-old girl becomes *bat mitzvah*, a "daughter of the commandment," and a woman.) It's significant that in this rite of passage, as the youth opens the

Torah scroll to read aloud, he or she is given a drop of honey to signify that, in the words of Psalm 19:10, the Law is "sweeter also than honey, and the drippings of the honeycomb," and so among Jews a common expression of praise is that someone "has done a *mitzvah*"; that is, a good deed of loving kindness such as pleases the Almighty. Thus, for the faithful Israelite, the *mitzvot* are no mere negative limits on freedom, but positive calls to active goodness.

Second, as to coherence, one need not be enthralled with the minutiae of the Law to recognize that the *mitzvot* amplify, in their myriad ways, the two great themes of the Israelite national mission: on the one hand priestly holiness and particular separation, and on the other hand general blessing and universal *tikkun olam*, "healing the world." So the following highly condensed discussion of specific Mosaic legislation assumes that, however outmoded, outlandish, or alarming they may seem, the commandments are intended somehow to purify and repair the Hebrews so that they can in turn repair the world.

The foundational assumption of the Hebrew laws about civil society is that, under God, the central governmental unit of the nation is what we now call "the nuclear family." Thus, as discussed in my previous chapters on Genesis, sexual relations are treated as the root of family relations, the seal of life-giving marital covenant love that begins when "a man shall leave his father and mother and be joined to his wife" (the "one flesh" of Genesis 2:24). Sexual relations become immoral and "abominations" when they run counter to this created purpose: Leviticus 18:6–23 condemns varied forms of marital infidelity, including incest (intra-family sex), adultery (extramarital sex), polygamy with two sisters, child sacrifice (destroying the fruits of marital love), homosexuality (sex with a person of the same sex), and bestiality (sex with animals). Forbidden elsewhere are the killing of unborn children (Exodus 21:22–25), premarital sex (Deuteronomy 22:28–29), and prostitution (Leviticus 21:9, Deuteronomy 22:20–21). Polygamy, while tolerated in the periods of the Patriarchs, Judges, and the Kingdoms, was discouraged as inconsistent with the Creation ordinances in Genesis 1–2, portrayed negatively in the biblical narratives, and largely replaced by monogamy among the Jews after the Exile in Babylon.

The family is also treated as the source of day-to-day justice, with the head of the extended family or a near relative named as the **Goel** or "kinsman redeemer." He was charged with prosecuting and punishing crimes both minor and major (Numbers 35:8–34), delivering relatives from oppression and slavery (Leviticus 25:48–49), and, in specific and well-defined cases, "raising up seed" – that is, conceiving children as heirs – for a deceased relative through Levirate marriage (Deuteronomy 25:5–6). (The stories of Tamar and Judah in Genesis, and of Ruth and Boaz in the Book of Ruth, turn on the law of Levirate marriage.) The *Goel*, as police detective, prosecutor, and in some cases executioner, is the main officer of "grass-roots" justice, though strictly limited and governed by laws of evidence (conviction required at least two witnesses – Numbers 35:30) and of jurisdiction (no pursuit or execution within designated "cities of refuge" – Numbers 35:9–11). And the *Goel* is also the chief agent of relief and mercy, aiding widows and orphans and freeing slaves.

Slavery, as a social institution in which family and economic life overlap, is taken for granted in the Law as an evil permeating human culture. Indeed, though in the United States before the Civil War slavery was euphemistically called "the peculiar institution" because it was geographically local to the South, there was nothing "peculiar" about slavery in the world of the ancient Near East and Egypt, being entirely normative. Significantly, although the *Torah* stops short of commanding outright abolition, it is deeply subversive of slavery in all its forms. As we have seen, in Genesis 1–2 all human beings are created equal in the image of God, and earlier in Exodus Israel's national birth is portrayed as a miracle of liberation from Pharaoh; while the Hebrews are strongly warned against selling themselves and their relatives, and commanded to free all Hebrew slaves on a regular seven-year schedule (i.e. the **Sabbath Year**), and to free slaves who have been injured by their masters (Exodus 21:1–27). Furthermore, the unique institution of the **Jubilee Year** (from Hebrew *yoval* for "trumpet blast") commanded universal liberation of all slaves after every forty-ninth year (i.e. after every seventh Sabbath Year) as well as release from all debts and a restoration of all lands to their original owners within their tribes.

> Then you shall cause the trumpet of the Jubilee to sound on the tenth day of the seventh month; on the Day of Atonement you shall make the trumpet to sound throughout all your land. And you shall consecrate the fiftieth year, and proclaim liberty throughout all the land to all its inhabitants. It shall be a Jubilee for you; and each of you shall return to his possession, and each of you shall return to his family. (Leviticus 25:9–10)

This passage provided a well-known inspiration in revolutionary-era Philadelphia, as the words engraved on the famed "Liberty Bell" when it was forged in 1752 read (in the King James Version), "Proclaim LIBERTY throughout all the land unto all the inhabitants thereof." In a more jocular vein, the Civil War tune "The Year of Jubilo" celebrates the Emancipation Proclamation of 1862 and its aftermath by imagining a plantation owner fleeing the advancing Union army and leaving his big house and wine cellar to the jubilant use of his freed slaves.

As with the decentralized handling of criminal justice under the law, so is the doing of "social justice" devolved from the national to the tribal, local, and family levels. Not only is the family *Goel* the chief agent of relief and mercy, and the Sabbath and Jubilee Years required of all, but the law commands every worker of the land to provide for the poor through allowance of **gleaning**.

> When you reap the harvest of your land, you shall not wholly reap the corners of your field when you reap, nor shall you gather any gleaning from your harvest. You shall leave them for the poor and for the stranger: I am the LORD your God. (Leviticus 23:22)

Rather than either ignoring the poor or organizing a state-run, Roman-style dole, the *Torah* assumes that poverty and hunger are best relieved in the context of close family and local community relations under divinely sanctioned law. Thus, the gleaner contributes some work to his upkeep, relief is treated as temporary rather than permanent, and each family and tribe accepts responsibility for its nearest neighbors – including the "stranger" or foreigner. The Mosaic Law resists the common ancient idea of economic dependence on a central state in favor of conditional local relief through family or individual initiative.

Clearly, the *Torah* portrays Israel as a nation born in frank opposition to monarchical and state tyranny, in the person of Pharaoh himself. So we should not be surprised that when the Law considers the eventuality of an Israelite king, it provides for remarkably strict limits on royal and government power:

> When you come to the land which the LORD your God is giving you, and possess it and dwell in it, and say, "I will set a king over me like all the nations that are around me," you shall surely set a king over you whom the LORD your God chooses; one from among your brethren you shall set as king over you… But he shall not multiply horses for himself, nor cause the people to return to Egypt to multiply horses, for the LORD has said to you, "You shall not return that way again." Neither shall he multiply wives for himself, lest his heart turn away; nor shall he greatly multiply silver and gold for himself.

Also it shall be, when he sits on the throne of his kingdom, that he shall write for himself a copy of this law in a book, from the one before the priests, the Levites. And it shall be with him, and he shall read it all the days of his life, ... that his heart may not be lifted above his brethren, that he may not turn aside from the commandment to the right hand or to the left, ... he and his children in the midst of Israel. (Deuteronomy 17:14–20)

These royal limits are so strict that by Near Eastern standards – "a king like all the nations" – this *melech* hardly seems like a monarch at all: no god-king he, but one elected from among the people rather than a mercenary foreigner; no standing cavalry or entangling foreign alliances allowed; no polygamous harem or opulent treasury; and above all no government of personal rule, but rather one of law over ruler, with the king subject to the *Torah* in every particular, and ruling "in the midst of Israel," not "above his brethren."

The Near Eastern God-Kings

Melech, the Semitic word for "king," echoes *Moloch*, the Canaanite deity who was associated most closely with propitiatory child sacrifice, a practice explicitly forbidden in Leviticus 18:21. The traditional title of the Aramean kings of the second and first millennia BCE was Abimelech, "the king is my father" or "father-king" and dictated the state's priority over the family in matters of law and justice. The *Torah* repeatedly and explicitly overthrows any notion of such a god-king, and institutes a decentralized polity that empowers local families, who are nevertheless subject to divine Law themselves. See discussion of 1 Samuel 8 in Chapter 9.

No doubt, passages like this and 1 Samuel 8, along with anti-monarchical writings from the Roman Republic and the English Civil War, influenced the limited-government republicanism of America's founders. It is certainly no accident that Benjamin Franklin recommended to the Continental Congress that the design for the Great Seal of the United States show Pharaoh's army destroyed by pursuing the Israelites into the Red Sea. Around this image were the words, "Rebellion to Tyrants is Obedience to God." Another design prevailed – the eye of divine Providence atop a pyramid with the Latin for "He has approved our designs" (*Annuit Coeptis*) – but it is an interesting historical paradox that books like Leviticus, Numbers, and Deuteronomy, so commonly dismissed by contemporary readers as puzzling, or dull, or frighteningly restrictive, should be among those most explicitly concerned with what we still regard as fundamental civil liberties.

7.1.3.1.3 *Ritual Law: Sacred Space and Time, Life in the Blood*
While certain elements of the *Torah's* civil law offend against modern Western notions of justice (stoning to death, for instance) the most likely reason for the current rather gloomy reputation of the later books in the Pentateuch is their plethora of **ritual law**. Modern societies are not entirely opposed to purity – we like our water clear, our hands sanitized, and our surgery sterile – but as a cultural ideal, *ritual holiness* has largely lost its appeal, as often as not appearing in derogatory phrases like "holier-than-thou," or perhaps the most pejorative of all, "theocracy." But in point of fact, ancient Israel was not a theocracy – which is defined as "political government by priests." As we've already observed, the Levitical priesthood

supervises worship, but the Mosaic Law vests civil power in a decentralized system of elder rule – and eventually in a king. Thus, in a rudimentary way, the Law of Moses separates "Church and State" (that is, the offices of clergy and of ruler) yet still under their covenant God. Israel is not a "kingdom *by* priests," but a "kingdom *of* priests" (Exodus 19:6): every Hebrew participates in the nation's priestly mission to "the nations."

Clean and Unclean

Leviticus 11 elaborates on the Noahic terms (Genesis 7) for clean and unclean creatures. Land animals are clean – and thus can be eaten – if they divide the hoof and chew the cud; water creatures if they have fins and scales; birds if they are not predators or scavengers; and flying insects if they have jointed legs for leaping and hopping. Particularly un-*kosher* are swine, shellfish, catfish, eels, beasts and birds of prey, eaters of carrion, creeping animals, and any flesh that dies of itself.

The rationale for these kosher laws includes symbolism (rejection of things blood-eating, low, creeping, or decaying), guilty association (creatures eaten or worshiped in neighboring pagan cultures), literal hygiene (the removal of disease-bearing agents from the camp), and, above all, divine sovereignty over the food supply, the central source of strength and health.

Rabbinical laws regarding food are part of the larger *halakhah*, or extra-biblical Jewish law, and elaborate extensively on these biblical rules.

So for the modern reader to understand the importance of ritual holiness to the "kingdom of priests," a useful analogy can be made to modern hygiene. Although the Hebrews lacked a germ theory of disease, they had a vivid sense of corruption and contagion, which they understood to come from a contaminating ancestry and from environmental contact; so they sought both cleansing and separation before pursuing their redemptive national mission, rather like surgeons scrubbing before an operation. One Mosaic sacred rite that addresses these concerns is the "Law of the Firstborn":

> you shall set apart to the LORD all that open the womb, that is, every firstborn that comes from an animal which you have; the males shall be the LORD's. But every firstborn of a donkey you shall redeem with a lamb; and if you will not redeem it, then you shall break its neck. And all the firstborn of man among your sons you shall redeem. (Exodus 13:12–13)

As in Genesis, "the firstborn" represents the independent power and wealth to be inherited by a people, and the Egyptians having lost their firstborn by plague, the Israelites have their human firstborn spared by a special sacrifice. Like the Abrahamic sign of circumcision, which marks the male's life-giving organ as *Yahweh's* property, this law reminds the people that the best of their strength is God's.

Many of the *Torah's* ritual laws don't merely command a single action, but mandate richly symbolic zones of space or time. The most sacred space of all was the Tabernacle or Tent of Meeting, described in Exodus 40 as the Hebrews' portable sanctuary from their wilderness wanderings through the time of the Judges, and eventually the pattern for Solomon's Temple and its successors in Jerusalem. In contrast to the decentralized enforcement of the civil law, ritual sacrifice is centralized in the Tabernacle (and later the Temple) to stress the oneness of *Yahweh*; and to pass through the Tabernacle was to engage in a compact figurative pilgrimage toward holiness. Moving from **east to west**, the worshiper and the priest walked through a sequence of objects that symbolized the process and goal of purifying atonement.

The Tabernacle in the Wilderness

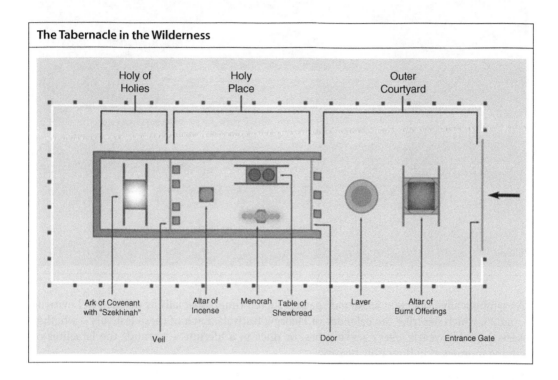

1) Entering the **Outer Court** of the Tabernacle, the worshiper first brought the sacrificial animal to the **Altar of Burnt Offering**, and placed his hand on the animal's head as its throat was cut, symbolizing a substitutionary death for sin.
2) The priest, going on his behalf, then approached the **Basin**, where he washed his hands and feet, symbolizing purification from sin.
3) Passing the **Screen** into the **Holy Place**, the priest passed between the **Showbread** to the north (his right) and the **Golden Lampstand** or *Menorah* to the south (his left), symbolizing the LORD's provision and the LORD's revealing and life-giving light, respectively.
4) Ahead on the **Altar of Incense**, the priest offered up incense as a symbol of the prayer that he raised on the worshiper's behalf.
5) Once a year, on the **Day of Atonement** (*Yom Kippur*), the Aaronic High Priest alone would enter the **Holy of Holies** to offer the nation's prayers of repentance and praise before the **Mercy Seat** on the **Ark of the Covenant** – its cover decorated with two golden *Cherubim* – containing the tablets with the **Ten Commandments**, the pot of **Manna**, and **Aaron's Rod** (symbolizing the LORD's word, his providence, and his power).

The Ark of the Covenant (Reconstructed Model)

As symbolically important as sacred space is sacred time, especially as detailed in Leviticus 23 and 25, which describe the calendar of Hebrew festivals. Each of these festivals – whether observed weekly, yearly, every seven years, or once in a lifetime – reminds the Israelites of "defining moments" in their holy history:

- **Sabbath** (*Shabbat*) – the weekly day of rest based on Genesis 2:2 and Exodus 20:8–11.
- **Passover** (*Pesach*) and **Unleavened Bread** (*Matzot*) – held yearly every March/April commemorating the sparing of the Hebrew firstborn and the "bread eaten in haste" during their deliverance from slavery in Egypt.
- **First Fruits** (*Bikkurim*) and **Weeks** (*Shavuot/Pentecost*) – held yearly every May/June, fifty days – seven weeks plus a day – after Passover, hence Hebrew *shavuot* ("sevens"/"weeks") and Greek *pente*: the "fifty"-day offering of first summer grain to the LORD, also commemorating the giving of the *Torah* at Mount Sinai.
- **Trumpets** (*Zikhron Teru'ah/Rosh Hashanah*) – held yearly every September/October, commemorating the Hebrew New Year (*Rosh Hashanah* means "Head of the Year") and the creation of Adam and Eve; beginning the **High Holy Days** or **Ten Days of Awe** (*Yamim Nora'im*).
- **Day of Atonement** (*Yom Kippur*) – held yearly nine days after Trumpets, the holiest day of the year when the High Priest enters the Holy of Holies.
- **Booths/Tabernacles** (*Succot*) – held yearly five days after the Day of Atonement and lasting seven days, a fall harvest festival when Hebrews build and dine in "booths" (palm-frond tents) to remember their years of wilderness wandering.
- **Year of Release/Sabbatical Year** (*Shmita/Sheviit*) – held every seventh year; all land is to "rest" by lying fallow, all that grows voluntarily is free to all, and all Hebrew debts are released and Hebrew slaves freed, as the LORD freed Israel from Egypt.

- **Year of Jubilee** (*Yovel*) – held after seven cycles of Sabbatical Years, or forty-nine years, it begins on the Day of Atonement in the fiftieth year; all debts are forgiven, all slaves are freed, and all lands revert to their original owners, as when Israel first entered Canaan.

Israelite life is to be lived with a linear, forward-looking mission of blessing the earth, but this life is to be informed by cyclical reminders of its founding covenant. Time's circle and life's arrow somehow combine in a double motion, modeling that there is no advancement without return, no progress without preservation.

Finally, running throughout the *Torah's* ritual law is the expectation of animal blood sacrifice. Here the analogy between ritual holiness and physical sanitation becomes hardest for us to sustain: when Moses sprinkles the congregation using a hyssop branch dipped in a bowl of ox-blood (Exodus 24:6–8), how can a modern Westerner imagine anything but a grisly, gore-spattered mess? This act would hardly look – or smell – like purification to us. Yet we must note that although ritual bloodshed was completely normative across ancient Afro-Eurasian religious cultures, Hebrew sacrifice stands out from the rest for its stated rationale. Blood sacrifice is offered, not because the LORD is hungry and needs to be fed by his people (also denied in Psalm 50:12–14), but rather because "the life of the flesh is in the blood" (Leviticus 17:11) – making atonement for the worshiper's own soul, which is forfeit through sin. In other words, to owe God a life is to owe him a substitutionary sacrifice. Furthermore, in contrast to common Canaanite practice, drinking blood is forbidden under the Law, because it was associated with rituals such as those devoted to "goat-demons" (Leviticus 17:7) where pagan worshipers believed that they magically ingested the life-force of their victims, whether animal or human. So even in their shedding of blood, the Hebrews wear their sacrifice with a difference, seeking purification from sin, and separating themselves from the ways of the neighbor peoples. Like the death-shudder of the sacrificial lamb felt by the penitents, the gore reminds them of the costliness of atonement.

We began this section on covenant law by observing how, in the chapters immediately after their miraculous deliverance through the Red Sea (Exodus 13–18), the Israelites repeatedly rebel in something like a negative miracle of unbelief. Within the world of the narrative, at least, how can the people see the wonders they have seen and yet sin as they do? The next block of chapters (19–31) interrupts this narrative of rebellion by detailing much of the Mosaic Covenant itself: the Ten Commandments; laws concerning the altar, slavery, animals, property, and sex; instructions about observing festivals, and constructing the Tabernacle and its furniture; and rules for ordaining the priests and creating their garments. This segment ends by reporting that *Yahweh* "gave Moses two tablets of the Testimony, tablets of stone, written with the finger of God" (31:18). But those newly engraved stone slabs will not last long; the tablets, like the laws written there, soon will be broken.

7.1.3.1.3.1   Epic Fail: The Golden Calf   The notorious incident of the **Golden Calf** packs more Israelite rebellion into one chapter, Exodus 32, than into all of those previous in the book. Having just sworn to uphold the Covenant in chapter 24, the people, now restless, distrustful, and impatient of Moses' return, enact an "epic fail," rushing to violate a whole raft of commandments at one go. They start at the top: "Come," they demand of Aaron, "make us gods that shall go before us; for as for this Moses, the man who brought us up out of the land of Egypt, we do not know what has become of him" (Exodus 32:1). Denying the LORD's recent intervention, they call out for other gods before him, and for graven images of those gods, slandering God's Prophet into the bargain. Aaron, cravenly obeying the mob, tries to put a pious face on their idolatry: he treats the Golden Calf that he has crafted (a common Egyptian and Canaanite deity) as an image of *Yahweh* himself, and takes the name of God in vain by declaring a "feast to the LORD" for the following day of idolatry and revelry. Then, in a memorable phrase, the worshipers "sat down to eat and drink, and rose up to play" (Exodus 32:2–6) – with the strong implication that not only spiritual but literal adultery may be in that "play."

Meanwhile, up on Mount Sinai, the LORD angrily tells Moses "Go, get down! For *your* people whom *you* brought out of the land of Egypt have corrupted themselves" (32:7, my italics). Sarcastically echoing the rebels' crediting their deliverance to Moses, God threatens to destroy this "stiff-necked people" for their ingratitude, and in the place of Israel, make Moses and his descendants "a great nation" (32:9, 10). Moses' counter-argument appeals to *Yahweh's* reputation and his old promises:

> Why should the Egyptians speak, and say, "He brought them out to harm them, to kill them in the mountains, and to consume them from the face of the earth"?... Remember Abraham, Isaac, and Israel, your servants, to whom you swore by your own self ... (32:12–13)

Yet after the LORD listens to his servant and relents from his rage, the people who have escaped the wrath of God now must face the wrath of Moses. When "he saw the calf and the dancing ... Moses' anger became hot, and he cast the tablets out of his hands and broke them at the foot of the mountain" (32:19). Then he rallies his loyal followers to put down the rebellion and restore order, and in the ensuing violence many of the rebels are killed. This bloodshed is not presented as a mere ideological purge, but as analogous to a general suppressing a troop mutiny in wartime, as the solidarity and discipline of the unit are essential to its mission, and indeed to its survival. After the fight, Moses pleads again with the LORD to forgive the people, even offering his own life as atonement, an offer which *Yahweh* declines, promising Moses special blessing instead, and his people continued protection – though not without future punishments.

This climactic chapter also has its grimly amusing moments. Moses initially punishes the Israelites' idolatry by inflicting poetic justice on their taste for false worship: he "burned [the Golden Calf] in the fire, and ground it to powder; and he scattered it on the water and made the children of Israel drink it." And when Moses confronts his brother Aaron, the first High Priest, over his fashioning of the golden idol, Aaron's reply is a model of spineless executive blame-shifting: "And I said to them, 'Whoever has any gold ... give it to me'... I cast it into the fire, and this calf came out" (32:20, 24). Thus, Aaron explains the golden idol as absurdly self-generating – as if it actually had divine, creative power.

Yet what might have been the end of the Hebrews and their Exodus instead becomes a renewal of their mission in Exodus 33–34, as God meets Moses in his own tent outside the Israelite camp and restores his covenant with Israel, so that Moses fashions two new stone tablets and engraves on them the recently broken Ten Commandments (34:1–4). "So the LORD spoke to Moses face to face, as a man speaks to his friend" (33:11), and then shows the Prophet his *shekinah* glory, yet only, in the memorable phrase of the King James Version, his "back parts," for "You cannot see My face; for no man shall see Me, and live" (33:23, 20). The LORD again promises to "do marvels" for Israel, "driving out from before you the Amorite and the Canaanite and the Hittite and the Perizzite and the Hivite and the Jebusite," yet warning the Israelites that just as these nations finally will be punished for their centuries of idolatry, so Israel itself will suffer the same fate for the same sins (34:10, 11, 12–16).

Just as the chapters (19–31) leading up to the Golden Calf detail the instructions for the Tabernacle, its furniture, and vestments, so the following and final chapters of Exodus (35–40) correspondingly describe how the Hebrews finally construct their sacred Tent of Meeting and craft its accessories. These fine objects are described as specifically as those in any *haute couture* fashion show or the items in any bride's *trousseau*, and as lovingly as the ingredients of a gourmet meal. The craftsmanship is portrayed as painstaking, the materials of the very best, with exquisite tapestries, inlay, engraving, and goldsmithing not only on the outward places seen by the whole congregation, but in the inward spaces known but to God. Exodus 40 ends the book with the final construction of the Meeting Tent, as Moses assembles it exactly according to instruction, and then with the consummation of this construction, as *Yahweh* actually meets Moses there, covering the Tabernacle with mysterious cloud and filling it with revelatory glory. Yet, ironically, God's fullness abounds so much that Moses himself is unable to enter the holy place. The LORD has come to dwell among his people, but the people have far to travel before they can dwell with the LORD.

7.1.4 Numbers: Rebellion and Wandering

The Hebrew title for the Book of Numbers – *BaMidbar*, "In the Wilderness" – could not be more appropriate; for while the book contains some genealogical numbering of the Twelve Tribes, it is above all about a nation lost and wandering in desolate places, both places of the earth and places of the heart. It is a dissertation on the thesis of "a stiff-necked people," rebels with a short memory for blessing and a penchant for ingratitude. In the course of the book, even blessings turn to curses, and even those most loyal to Moses join in mutiny, until Moses himself joins in rebellion – and a whole generation is cast off by the LORD. And yet, in the end, the covenant promises endure for their more hopeful children.

Since the Book of Numbers continues the emphasis in Leviticus on Israel's priestly nationhood and on the Levitical tribe of priests at the heart of national worship, the book begins in Numbers 1–2 by briefly counting eleven of the Twelve Tribes, but not that priestly tribe of Levi. Numbers 3 makes clear that the Levites, rather than possessing their own territory like their brothers and sisters, will be counted separately and spread among the other tribes like leaven, to raise all Israel through teaching and example; and among these Levites, God will separate further the High Priestly family of Aaron and his sons, responsible for overseeing the worship and sacrifice of the Tabernacle. Yet these priests will not hold the reins of civil power, which will be in the hands of tribal and family elders – meaning that while biblical Israel must certainly be understood as *theocentric*, its constitution is not *theocratic*.

These chapters on numbering the people yield to a series (4–10) about the Tabernacle and national purification. Yet, as the reader has by now almost come to expect, these holy preparations become preludes for more rebellion. The people, tired of the now everyday miracle of manna from heaven, pine for the leeks, onions, garlic, and fleshpots of Egypt, a complaint that God answers by sending more meat than they could want, in what amounts to a "plague of quail"; as they gorge on the raw, bloody bird-flesh, even with the meat still "between their teeth," they are struck by terrible pestilence (Numbers 11:33). As popular disenchantment grows against Moses, God makes a further point of decentralization, sharing out Moses' spiritual power to seventy other elders; yet Moses' own siblings Miriam and Aaron still turn against him, on the pretext of Moses' marriage to the dark-skinned "Ethiopian" Zipporah, but really as a challenge to his divinely endorsed leadership. But when God strikes Miriam with leprosy, she and Aaron plead with their younger brother, who mercifully restores her to health and to the camp, after a period of quarantine (12).

Numbers 13–15 portray another cycle of folly, this one with far-reaching consequences. As the Hebrews approach the threshold of Canaanland, Moses appoints a twelve-man reconnaissance party – one from each tribe – to scout out the country, and upon their return, the scouts snatch defeat from the jaws of impending victory by reporting that, though the grapes are huge and the land "flows with milk and honey," nevertheless the inhabitants live in high walled cities, and "they are stronger than we" for there "we saw the descendants of Anak" – a race of giants. Only two scouts – Caleb of Judah and Joshua of Ephraim – give the optimistic minority report: "Let us go up at once and take possession, for we are well able to overcome it" (Numbers 13:27, 31, 28, 30). The congregation responds by murmuring against Moses, crying out melodramatically, wishing they had died in the wilderness, and calling out to replace Moses with "a captain" who will return them to in Egypt (14:1–3). Nostalgic for the security of slavery, the people ignore Joshua and Caleb, kindling the wrath of the LORD, who again threatens to destroy all the Hebrews and replace them with the family of Moses. Again, Moses pleads successfully that they should be spared immediate death, but the consequences are still dire: *Yahweh* says that

> because all these men who have seen My glory and the signs which I did in Egypt and in the wilderness, and have put Me to the test now these ten times, and have not heeded My voice, they certainly shall not see the land of which I swore to their fathers, nor shall any of those who rejected Me see it. (14:22–23)

"Ten times" these people have tested God, and immediately comes the eleventh, as the congregation, in a foolhardy reversal, resolves now to attack the Amalekites and to take the land as originally commanded – though Moses warns them that, having missed their chance at assured victory, they now face certain defeat. The result? "Then the Amalekites and the Canaanites who dwelt in that mountain came down and attacked them, and drove them back as far as Hormah" (14:45).

Numbers 15 provides a brief interlude on punishment and atonement for both "unintentional" and "presumptuous" sins, including a remarkably harsh penalty for a man caught gathering sticks on the Sabbath: stoning to death by the congregation. Chapter 16 brings a showdown over this and other perceived excesses of Moses and Aaron, as Korah the Levite, and Dathan and Abiram the Reubenites, gather 250 of the chief men in Israel to challenge the Prophet and High Priest directly. They make a claim that may ring sympathetically in the modern ear:

> You take too much upon yourselves, for all the congregation is holy, every one of them, and the LORD is among them. Why then do you exalt yourselves above the assembly of the LORD?... Is it a small thing that you have brought us up out of a land flowing with milk and honey, to kill us in the wilderness, that you should keep acting like a prince over us? (16:3, 13)

The accusation takes Moses' own egalitarian covenant words about a "priestly kingdom" and a "holy nation" and turns them against him, charging the Deliverer with arrogance and a lust for power. Yet the accusation rings hollow; we know that Egypt was no Promised Land "flowing with milk and honey," and as Moses and Aaron fall on their faces, they humbly call on God and not the crowd to justify their actions. God answers with one of his more memorable judgments, opening the earth and swallowing the rebel leaders whole in their tents while consuming the 250 rebel elders with heavenly fire. When the congregation still accuses Moses of murder, the LORD sends a plague that kills 14,700 before Aaron can make atonement with holy fire from his censer. Thus Moses is vindicated in his humility: "By this you shall know that the LORD has sent me to do all these works, for I have not done them of my own will" (16:28). In Numbers 17, the LORD further endorses his chosen leaders by causing Aaron's rod to bud miraculously, and in chapters 18 and 19, the LORD gives further instruction on how the Levites are to act as service workers to the Aaronic priests in the Tabernacle, and how the people can be purified from their uncleanness.

Numbers 20 gives especially stark and ironic evidence of God's impartiality; for here Moses himself falls under judgment. The forty years of wilderness wandering have now passed, during which the old generation of Israelites has died and a new one arisen; yet Moses, having led Israel faithfully and humbly despite their frequent provocations, now succumbs to an outburst of pride when the people challenge him yet again, this time to produce water at Kadesh in the Wilderness of Zin. God again reveals his glory to the Prophet, telling him merely to "speak to the rock" to produce a flow of water, but Moses for once claims the glory for Aaron and himself, with lasting consequences:

> [Moses] said to them "Hear now, you rebels! Must we bring water for you out of this rock?" Then Moses lifted his hand and struck the rock twice with his rod; and water came out abundantly, and the congregation and their animals drank.
>
> Then the LORD spoke to Moses and Aaron, "Because you did not believe Me, to hallow Me in the eyes of the children of Israel, therefore you shall not bring this assembly into the land which I have given them." (20:10–12)

The people have their water, but Moses, by joining in their rebellious spirit and claiming to act alone by his own strength, loses his share in the Promised Land. And, adding weight to this judgment, in this same chapter, both Miriam and Aaron die, also without completing the sacred journey to Canaan. Irony of ironies! Again *Yahweh* reaffirms that in Israel no one, not even the chosen Prophet or the High Priest, is above the Law or immune from divine rebuke.

Yet God is not done with Moses – nor, significantly, is Moses done with God. Taking his punishment and his losses in stride, Moses confronts a whole battalion of troubles in Numbers 20–25, in the form of the hostile nations blocking the way to Canaan. First, ancient grudges come into play as Moses petitions the king of Edom for safe passage through his territory, pleading the ancestral brotherhood of Jacob (Israel) and Esau (Edom). But the Edomites apparently remember Jacob's treachery more than their blood-bond, and refuse entry. Yet Moses, for the sake of ancient brotherhood, simply bypasses Edom, rather than offering battle (20:14–21). Second, in chapter 21 comes a series of unprovoked, pre-emptive attacks by Gentile nations against the Hebrew pilgrims, all of which end in Israelite victory – over the Aradites at Hormah, the Amorites under King Sihon, and the Bashanites under the marvelously named King Og.

But third, the Israelites very nearly snatch defeat from victory by succumbing to the spiritual and carnal temptations of Moab, due to the intervention of a strange and compelling character, the Canaanite diviner and sorcerer Balaam. A wicked and greedy man hired by Balak, King of Moab, to curse the Hebrews, Balaam nevertheless repeatedly hears the over-ruling voice of *Yahweh* compelling him to bless them instead in four different prophecies (Numbers 22–24); the last of these divine interventions famously takes the form of Balaam's donkey speaking and correcting the seer (22:28) – a note of sardonic humor. To Balak's increasing alarm, none of his gold can purchase Balaam's binding curse on the Hebrews: for, as Balaam must admit, "there is no sorcery against Jacob, / Nor any divination against Israel… Blessed is he who blesses you, / And cursed is he who curses you" (23:23, 24:9). Indeed, Balak must endure Balaam's prophecies of Moab's future subservience to a coming Israelite king.

However, while Balaam can't directly curse Israel, he advises an indirect stratagem to corrupt them instead: a special army of *femmes fatales* sent to seduce the Israelites into spiritual and literal adultery. We learn that on Balaam's advice, Israel's camp is infiltrated at Peor with Moabite and Midianite cult prostitutes, who induce the people "to be joined to Baal of Peor" in acts of ritual devotion and copulation. The LORD sends a plague on the lecherous Israelites until their ringleaders are caught and hanged in the sun, punished for deeds done in the darkness (31:16, 25:1–4). The lesson for the Hebrews: God can protect you from all your enemies, but even he cannot protect you from the evil desires in your own hearts.

These memorable incidents passed, the remainder of Numbers consists mainly of preparations for Israel's imminent entry into Canaan to take possession. Chapter 26 indeed involves more actual "numbers": a second census of the new generation of men twenty and older, yielding a figure of 601,730 (only a slight net loss from the 603,550 of chapter 1); chapter 27 takes up inheritance laws, and provides for a succession in power, as the LORD chooses the non-Levite Joshua from the tribe of Ephraim to lead the nation after Moses' death; and in Numbers 28–30, Moses reiterates the laws for all daily and yearly ritual offerings and for the keeping of vows, laws that will structure sacred time in the new land.

Numbers 31 establishes laws for conquest and the handling of plunder, recalling God's prophecy to Abram 400 years earlier, that "the iniquity of the Amorites is not yet complete" (Genesis 15:16). Abram's descendants have waited many generations and endured Egyptian slavery before inheriting Canaan. As terrible as God's judgment appears to us, it is presented here as long-delayed and indeed patient, as the Amorites grow complete in their wickedness and ripe for removal. Numbers 32 spells out the rules for dividing the land east of Jordan, and chapter 33 provides a synopsis of the entire Exodus and the wilderness years up to the present threshold moment. Lastly, chapters 34–36 spell out the boundaries of Canaan, specify the officers who will oversee land distribution, establish particular Levite cities among the other eleven tribes, with specially designated cities of refuge, and refine the laws governing female inheritance.

All told, Numbers is a book full of sound and fury, yet one that goes around in wandering circles; a book of stunning divine interventions and yet stupefying human failures; a book in which everyone, including the greatest and best, is tested and found wanting; and yet a book full of second chances and renewed opportunities. If it ends with the fearful threat of coming conquest, it also ends with the hope of promises fulfilled and of future blessing.

7.1.5 Deuteronomy: The Law Renewed

We will move briskly through the last book of the Pentateuch, attending briefly to Deuteronomy as a uniquely repetitive, restorative, and confirmatory book among the five, the "Second Law." In keeping with our literary approach we'll deal mainly with the text as it has existed for millennia, rather than in terms of speculative theories about its composition and about subdivisions and reconstructions for which there is, after all, no actual documentary evidence.

The Rediscovery of Deuteronomy and the Documentary Hypothesis

In 2 Kings 22, during a renovation of the Jerusalem Temple, the High Priest Hilkiah discovers "the Book of the Law" and brings the scroll to young King Josiah, who upon hearing the long-lost book read aloud, "tore his clothes" with grief and commanded Hilkiah to "inquire of the LORD for me … for great is the wrath of the LORD that is aroused against us, because our fathers have not obeyed the words of this book, to do according to all that is written concerning us" (2 Kings 22:8–13). After consulting with the Prophetess Huldah, Josiah institutes a series of reforms closely following the instructions in Deuteronomy, re-instituting the Passover, banning pagan worship, and banishing spiritists.

This story of rediscovery inspired a theory in the late nineteenth and early twentieth century, part of the Documentary Hypothesis (see Chapter 2), that Deuteronomy actually was composed in the reign of Josiah (640–609 BCE) and carried through the fall of Jerusalem (605–587 BCE) – the work of the so-called "Deuteronomic Historian," who, it is suggested, also wrote the Book of Kings to advance a socially progressive universal ethical code. However, the bases for this Higher Critical classification of Deuteronomy as pseudepigraphical pious fiction have been called into question in more recent decades. For instance, Deuteronomy reflects pre-Conquest conditions, neither naming Jerusalem as the capital city nor using the Babylonian or Persian loan-words that might be current in the seventh and sixth centuries BCE. Most strikingly, Deuteronomy follows the form of a covenant or treaty common in the middle of the second millennium BCE – approximately the time of Moses – but no longer current 1000 years later in Josiah's time. Finally, strange to say, Deuteronomy is not uniquely "Deuteronomic" in content; that is, as we will see, in outlook and substance it strongly resembles Exodus, Leviticus, and Numbers, the other legal books of the *Torah*.

From the viewpoint of narrative structure, Deuteronomy completes a thematically rich and coherent "holy history" with a storyline that continues to shape our conceptions of oppression, freedom, transgression, justice, and the role of the state and of law in re-making human behavior.

The book's Hebrew title, *Devarim* ("The [Spoken] Words") captures an essential fact about its form. Deuteronomy presents itself to us as a speech or sermon, as Moses' great valedictory address (actually, addres*ses*) delivered to Israel on the verge of the nation's entry into the Promised Land – from which, the Deliverer stresses with striking candor, the LORD has banned him. But the Greek Septuagint title is significant too; for *Deuteronomion* is, in substance, largely a "Second Law," or rather, as in the Hebrew of Deuteronomy 17:18, *mishneh hatorah hazoth*, a copy or repetition of the Law. The book is, therefore, another prominent instance of Hebraic doubling, a reiteration for the purposes of emphasis and confirmation, yet also usually with a difference.

The repetitions in Deuteronomy of Exodus, Leviticus, and Numbers are many, and easy to itemize briefly. As in Exodus, we find instructions about the Passover (Deuteronomy 16), the Law of the Firstborn (15), a verbatim repetition of the Ten Commandments (5), rules about slavery (15), sex, and marriage (22), and a vivid recounting of the Golden Calf incident and the smashing and replacement of the two tablets of the Law (9–10). As in Leviticus, we revisit legislation about the place and rituals of worship (12), clean and unclean foods (14), the weekly, yearly, and multi-year holidays of the Hebrew calendar (16), and the lands and portions of the Levites (18). And as in Numbers, we hear a rehearsal of Israel's many rebellions, its plagues, punishments, and desert wanderings (1–4, 9), and also of its recent victories over kingdoms on the borders of Canaan (2–3), and of its provisions for tithing (14), the poor (15), and cities of refuge (19). As in all these preceding books of the *Torah*, Deuteronomy places strong emphasis on mercy not only to the Israelite poor and needy, but also on loving the stranger and foreigner in the land (e.g. 10:19).

But despite these many, many resemblances, Deuteronomy presents a number of divergent and unique features that have made it one of the most quoted of biblical books. First, in addition to its overtly sermonic form, there is the *Shema*: the closest thing to an Israelite "Creed," it is called after the Hebrew for its first word, "*Hear*, O Israel: The LORD our God, the LORD is one!" (*Shema Yisrael, Adonai Eloheinu, Adonai echad!*) "You shall love the LORD your God with all your heart, with all your soul, and with all your strength" (6:4–5). This declaration of loyalty to *Yahweh's* emphatic oneness, and of the heart-deep call to active love and faithfulness, is still at the core of Jewish religious identity. Second are the book's predictions and instructions about the coming Hebrew political order: the appointment in Deuteronomy 16–17 of "Judges" (*Shophetim*), not only interpreters of the law, but enforcers, as well as ad hoc commanders-in-chief during military crises. And, as noted above, there are the strictly limiting rules for Kings (17), whose entire mission is defined by reading and obeying *mishneh hatorah hazoth*, "a copy of this law" (17:18), so that Deuteronomy, if not the "Book *of* Kings," is intended as a "Book *for* Kings."

Third, in addition to predicting the coming of Judges and Kings, Moses also predicts in chapter 18 the advent of "a new Prophet" whom the LORD will raise up from among the people and who will speak a new word in God's name. Moses declares an audacious test for the truthfulness of this or any prophet: "when a prophet speaks in the name of the LORD, if the thing does not happen or come to pass, that is the thing which the LORD has not spoken; the prophet has spoken it presumptuously; you shall not be afraid of him" (18:22). We'll revisit this prophecy of the Prophet numerous times as we survey the prophetic literature of Old and New Testaments, and as we trace the development of Jewish and Christian messianic hope.

A fourth unique contribution of Deuteronomy is a set of specific laws concerning divorce (24) and Levirate marriage (25). While divorce, like polygamy and slavery, is tolerated under the Mosaic Law (despite their all contradicting original Creation ideals in Genesis 1–2), the burden of this statute is to protect a woman put away by her husband for some reason other than adultery; the man must give her "a certificate of divorce" ("a bill of divorcement" in the King James Version), which will prevent a ruined reputation and allow for her future remarriage to any but the original husband (24:1–4). Levirate marriage, already an accepted practice since the time of the Patriarchs (see Judah and Tamar in Genesis 38), is here codified as a way of insuring that every widow will receive care and that each house in every tribe will endure complete. In a Near Eastern culture where the security of a woman depended on her husband and her offspring, this decidedly unromantic law gave a woman leverage for compelling a near kinsman to provide needed support and attention.

A fifth and final set of features unique to Deuteronomy is the artfully made cluster of episodes and epilogues that conclude this valedictory book. In Deuteronomy 11, and more fully in chapters 27–28, Moses presents a liturgy for the congregation to recite, once they have crossed over Jordan, in the extraordinarily dramatic setting of Mount Gerazim and Mount Ebal, twin peaks facing each other across a deep ravine. With half of the Twelve Tribes on Ebal warning of curses on the nation, and the other half on Gerazim calling out blessings, the future fate of Israel echoes across the abyss, with the starkest possible divide in view between good and evil. Curses ring out over the valley from Ebal condemning idolatry; contempt of parents; theft of land; cruelty to the blind, the stranger, the orphan, and the widow; incest; bestiality; assault; contract killing; and any other disobedience to God's Law – a remarkably durable list of deadly sins and crimes, each curse answered back with a loud "Amen!" (27:14–26).

From Gerazim come the answering blessings for keeping the Law: blessed in the city and country; blessed in the fruit of their bodies, baskets, and bowls; blessed in coming in and going out; blessed in battle and in barns (28:1–14). Then back from Ebal comes the antiphon of further curses for the wicked – and, forebodingly, the curses outnumber the blessings nearly four-to-one: curses not only on city, country, bodies, baskets, bowls, battle, and barns, but also a crescendo of calamity and that anticipates future horrors. Just a taste of these miseries:

> And you shall become an astonishment, a proverb, and a byword among all nations where the LORD will drive you... They shall besiege you at all your gates until your high and fortified walls, in which you trust, come down throughout all your land... You shall eat the fruit of your own body, the flesh of your sons and your daughters whom the LORD your God has given you... And the LORD will take you back to Egypt in ships, by the way of which I said to you, "You shall never see it again." And there you shall be offered for sale to your enemies as male and female slaves, but no one will buy you. (28:37, 52, 53, 68)

If there's anything more humiliating than being offered to your enemies as slaves, it's their refusing the purchase! Such are the dire warnings attached to the *Torah*; like the Canaanites before them, the Hebrews too can be banished from the land. "Do not think in your heart, after the LORD your God has cast them out before you, saying, 'Because of my righteousness the LORD has brought me in to possess this land'; but it is because of the wickedness of these nations that the LORD is driving them out from before you" (9:4).

This liturgy concludes in Deuteronomy 29 and 30 with a solemn oath to renew the covenant: "I call heaven and earth as witnesses today against you, that I have set before you life and death, blessing and cursing; therefore choose life, that both you and your descendants may live" (30:19). In chapters 31–33, Moses then finishes his farewell: in chapter 31 he inaugurates Joshua as the new Israelite leader, handing over his written scrolls of the Law for safekeeping, and commanding that they be read aloud to the congregation every seven years during the Feast of Tabernacles (*Succot*). In chapter 32, Moses the psalmist teaches a new song to the people, full of reminiscences about God's power and faithfulness, Israel's infidelity, and God's forgiveness and deliverance, with instructions that they will sing the song to keep memory alive; and in chapter 33 Moses, like the patriarch Jacob before him, calls out and blesses each of the Twelve Tribes by name – yet, significantly, without any of Jacob's acerbic criticisms, except (also significantly) for Moses' own tribe of Levi. So Moses' valediction ends with positive reminders of divine love for his people, and a sobering reminder that *Yahweh's* chosen leaders bear a higher responsibility.

Once Moses' words are done, the final reminder of divine impartiality comes in the Prophet's "Pisgah-sight of Palestine":

> Then Moses went up from the plains of Moab to Mount Nebo, to the top of Pisgah, which is across from Jericho. And the LORD showed him all the land… Then the LORD said to him, "This is the land of which I swore to give Abraham, Isaac, and Jacob, saying, 'I will give it to your descendants.' I have caused you to see it with your eyes, but you shall not cross over there." (34:1, 4)

The bitterness of his final exclusion from the Land of Promise is sweetened by the panoramic sight of the land itself – almost cinematic in its reach from north to south and east to west. It is also sweetened by the concluding editorial reminder: that this strange, stuttering Prophet, this prince and outcast of Egypt who led a rabble of slaves into the desert and brought them out a nation, was ordinary yet one-of-a-kind, that "since then there has not arisen in Israel a prophet like Moses, whom the LORD knew face to face" (34:10). The man viewing the Promised Land will never enter it, but he has seen the face of God. In seeing that face and hearing that voice he has redefined heroism as humility; he has learned the greatest leaders' indispensable secret – to insure their own dispensability – and so he passes out of the nation's story, which, as we turn the page to Joshua's book, is only beginning.

Questions for Discussion

1 How does the beginning of the Book of **Exodus** relate back to the concluding episodes of Genesis?

2 How are the elements of the **Mediterranean epic** tradition presented and modified in the Mosaic epic of **Exodus** through **Deuteronomy**? In particular, what does one expect of an **epic hero**, and how does **Moses** meet or modify those expectations?

3   How do **Moses' background, upbringing, and personal characteristics** make him both an unlikely and a uniquely qualified candidate to deliver the Israelites from Egypt?

4   When the LORD appears to Moses, **what aspects of the divine character** are revealed by his appearance, his message, his mission, and his name?

5   How do the **ten plagues** visited on the Egyptians teach varied lessons about the God of Israel and the gods of Egypt?

6   Consider at least **one modern retelling of the Exodus story**. What elements of the original does this version stress? What elements does it ignore or change, and why?

7   In **Exodus** and **Leviticus**, how are **liberty** and **law** defined and portrayed? How are they related to each other? What are the main kinds of law? What do they share in common, and how do they differ?

8   What view does the Book of **Numbers** take of **divine nature** and **human nature**? How are these views exemplified?

9   Compare the Book of **Deuteronomy**, or "The Second Law," to other instances of deliberate doubling or repetition in the Bible. What is being reiterated, and what stated anew?

10   How does the conclusion of Moses' life story in Deuteronomy complete – and modify – the portrayal of an epic hero? How does Deuteronomy prepare the way for the Books of **Joshua** and **Judges** to follow? What does Deuteronomy have to say about **kings**?

Notes

1 Northrop Frye, *Anatomy of Criticism: Four Essays* (Princeton, NJ: Princeton University Press, 1957), 136.
2 Roy P. Basler, ed., *The Collected Works of Abraham Lincoln*, 9 vols. (New Brunswick, NJ: Rutgers University Press, 1953–1955), 3:315. Spoken at Alton, Illinois, October 15, 1858, in reply during the seventh senatorial debate with Stephen Douglas.
3 Tractate Senhedrin 97b; Tractace Succah 45b.

8

Heroic Narrative: Remaking the Hero in Joshua, Judges, and Ruth

We've seen how the Pentateuch works profound changes on the ancient concept of heroism. If a hero is an exemplary figure acting out a culture's highest values, then a clash of cultures will produce a clash of competing heroic models. The patriarchs and prophets of the *Torah* are presented to displace the pattern of the Near Eastern hero-gods who act "at the conceivable limits of desire," displaying their own superhuman powers. Instead, the Hebrew heroes are presented as exemplary mainly in their trust, in their patience, and in their obedience to their empowering Creator God. Remarkably, they also are rendered as richly and complexly human, full of weaknesses, flaws, and contradictions; even the best of them, like Joseph and Moses, make mistakes and often serious misjudgments, and yet even the worst of them – Jacob and Judah spring to mind – prevail through the LORD's power and forgiving, steadfast love.

This reimagining of heroism continues beyond the Pentateuch into the next books about conquests, judges, and kings. Joshua is a prophet, we are told, *not* like the dead hero Moses – now bewept by the Hebrews who had so often cursed him – and so Joshua is unable to match his master in his intimacy with God (Deuteronomy 34:10). And yet, in another sense, Joshua far surpasses Moses in "heroic" success, in seven years leading the Israelites in an astonishing string of victories and conquests, coming closest to the model of Classical warrior heroics. In the sequel to Joshua's book, Judges, heroism comes in for much further revision, with leaders who range from a left-handed assassin, a great woman warrior, and a timid citizen soldier to a friendly *femme fatale*, a foolish father, and a musclebound riddler and lover-boy. Some of these heroes shade over into what in modern times we call anti-heroes – protagonists who defy rather than represent the culture's declared values – and Judges ends with a pitch-black tale of anti-heroism leading to civil chaos. Yet in the midst of those chaotic days of the Judges we meet the local heroes in the Book of Ruth: the title character herself, a foreign woman who chooses to embrace the chosen people inclined to reject her, and the man who loves her and redeems her (and her mother-in-law!) to father a special child – a child whose line will rise from village peasantry to the pinnacle of a great new Kingdom under the rising star of David. This remaking of the hero and this making of the Kingdom are profoundly related.

8.1 Joshua's Conquest: Taking the Promised Land

Joshua is a controversial book, now more than ever.

Literary Study of the Bible: An Introduction, First Edition. Christopher Hodgkins.
© 2020 John Wiley & Sons Ltd. Published 2020 by John Wiley & Sons Ltd.

Joshua's Date and Authorship

Since the Book of Joshua is so clearly a continuation and fulfillment of the Pentateuch – rather like the New Testament Books of Acts is of the Gospels – some scholars have written of a "Hexateuch," or six-volume set. Joshua does not name its author, though it is obviously post-Mosaic, and Joshua 24:26 speaks of how Joshua himself at Shechem "wrote these words [of the renewed Mosaic Covenant] in the Book of the Law of God." Allowing for a possible written contribution from its traditional namesake, the book appears to have been composed in substance early during the time of the Judges, and certainly before the establishment of the monarchy or the conquest of Jerusalem (Joshua 15:8, 18:16). The phrase "to this day," used numerous times throughout the book, often indicates a present time in the fourteenth or thirteenth centuries BCE, as for instance in Joshua 4:9, 6:25, 7:26, 8:28–29, 9:27, 14:14, 15:63, and 16:10. Among its sources is the as-yet-undiscovered "Book of Jashar," also referenced in 2 Samuel 1:18.

Modern archeology has seriously questioned a triumphalist reading of the book, challenging the idea of a wholesale conquest of Canaan in the generation after Moses at the beginning of the fourteenth century BCE. This concern is not hard to answer, since a careful reading of Joshua and Judges discloses a conquest that leaves significant portions and pockets of the land unsubdued (Joshua 13:1) – in ways that match the archeological record of an unfinished conquest.

Archeology and the Conquest of Canaan

Did Canaan fall to the Israelites suddenly or gradually? The archeological evidence, like the Book of Joshua itself, suggests something of both. In one sense, the conquest was strikingly quick: excavations of City IV at Jericho show significant wall collapse at about this time, and the Amarna Letters from the middle fourteenth century BCE speak of the "Apiru" (Hapiru/Habiru) as widespread throughout Canaan, while Joshua 11:23 states that Joshua "took the whole land." Yet archeology reveals the persistence of Canaanite cities and culture in the succeeding centuries, as the Amarna Letters speak of continuing Egyptian alliances with Canaanite kings, while Joshua 13:1 itemizes the many towns, cities, and areas that the elderly Joshua must now leave other Israelite leaders to subdue. Thus, both the Bible and the extra-biblical evidence recovered to date suggest that before the death of Joshua in about 1350 BCE, the Hebrews pervaded the Land of Promise, though with significant pockets of resistance. It is the "push-back" from those pockets, and the invasions of yet other rival peoples, that create most of the action in the succeeding Book of Judges.

But a deeper reservation about the book has grown: conquests and holy conquerors are much out of favor in our day – at least in the West – and as the archetypal biblical conqueror, Joshua's record of military success looks to many like moral failure. How are we to regard the practice of holy war portrayed in this book?

First, there is no evading the textual fact that Joshua is called by the LORD to execute special divine judgment, and his story simply assumes the just character of the longsuffering Creator God whom we first met in Genesis. Much as *Yahweh*, in the story of Noah, had endured many generations of gross human wickedness before sending the Flood, so here in Joshua, six centuries after the promise of the Land to Abram in Genesis 15:16, the "iniquity of the Amorites" [inhabitants of Canaan] is now complete, indeed rotten ripe. As in Genesis, the remarkable thing to the original audience of Joshua would not have been that the LORD is wrathful against his enemies – this was, as we have seen abundantly, an age of angry, blood-thirsty gods – but rather that this peace-loving and holy God had tolerated so long and patiently the bloody, lecherous ways of Canaan: constant warfare, idolatrous worship of god-kings, ritual prostitution of men, women, and children, and common child sacrifice.

Second, the conquest of Canaan is presented as a unique judgment on a particular culture, not as a justification for constant holy wars of conquest and extermination. Indeed, the judg-ments visited on Canaan are hardly different from those threatened to the Hebrews themselves should they violate the Mosaic Covenant by similar practices – including, as we have observed, a failure to "love the stranger" and the alien sojourning in their own land (see Deuteronomy 28). Though many holy warriors have since seen a precedent in Joshua – from Muhammad, Charlemagne, and the Crusaders to Catherine de' Medici, Oliver Cromwell, and Cotton Mather – the book tells the story of a particular providential act, and has more usually been interpreted and applied, both by Jewish and Christian commentators, as a call to faithful spir-itual struggle against spiritual evil – much as modern Muslims seek to define *jihad* inward. Indeed, by the time of Jesus, Joshua's place as an admired spiritual hero had made his name – *Yoshua* ("*Yahweh* saves") – one of the more common among Jewish men, including Jesus (*Y'shua*) himself.

Going forward, then, the narrative leaves no doubt about the divine source of Joshua's mis-sion: he had been set aside by the LORD in Numbers and Deuteronomy, and was always nota-ble for his entire focus on doing the divine will. Lest there be any confusion, in chapters 5–6, Joshua is called by the Commander of the LORD's hosts himself. Actually, we should say "Himself," because Joshua is told, like Moses before the Burning Bush, to remove his sandals on holy ground, while Joshua offers and the Commander receives worship – sure textual indica-tions of a theophany or divine appearance. Joshua's question to the divine Commander reflects common, natural sense: "Are You for us or for our adversaries?" (Joshua 5:13). But the Commander's answer reflects uncommon, supernatural sense: "No, but as Commander of the army of the LORD I have now come" (5:14). This "No" belies Joshua's binary thinking about divine partiality. The question is not whether God is on one side or the other, but whether the Israelites are on his.

And truly sides are being chosen and fatal lines drawn as the book's action begins – with some surprising and ironic outcomes. The first ally that the Hebrews encounter in Canaan seems initially unlikely, yet on reflection makes rough sense: a prostitute, named for the pri-mordial serpent goddess Rahab, who keeps an inn in the wall of Jericho. Two Hebrew spies can enter her place with less question – after all, isn't a brothel a common resort for strange men? – and her sense of alienation from her own community is plausibly higher – for like her namesake, she has been put down and defeated by males all her life. So she tells the spies just what they need to hear:

> For we have heard how the LORD dried up the water of the Red Sea for you when you came out of Egypt, and what you did to the two kings of the Amorites who were on the other side of the Jordan, Sihon and Og, whom you utterly destroyed. And as soon as we heard these things, our hearts melted; neither did there remain any more courage in anyone because of you, for the LORD your God, He is God in heaven above and on earth beneath. (2:10–11)

Behind their high walls, the people of Jericho – who worship power – have already surrendered to fear, but for Rahab her terror is mixed with a newfound awe and fledgling faith in this Hebrew God, mixed with a strange hope:

> Now therefore, I beg you, swear to me by the LORD, since I have shown you kindness, that you also will show kindness to my father's house, and give me a true token, and spare my father, my mother, my brothers, my sisters, and all that they have, and deliver our lives from death. (2:12–13)

As it turns out, this sad woman's hopeless nightly sexual labors have been supporting her entire household, and she glimpses a better future for them among the invading Israelites than she does in the abusive society of her birth. Appropriately, the "true token" of mercy that the spies give her is a "scarlet cord" (2:18) to tie in her window, a precedent (some say) for "red light districts" ever since, but more importantly reminiscent of the lamb's red blood that caused the Angel of Death to pass over during the final Exodus plague on Egypt's firstborn (Exodus 12:7). So the story of Jericho's destruction is tempered with a story of mercy to an outcast – who in her rough way shows more trust in *Yahweh* than many of the Hebrew children, and who, with her family, is on her way to joining the children of Israel herself.

As Rahab's scarlet cord reprises the Passover, so the Israelite entry into Canaan reprises the watery passage of the Exodus itself. The River Jordan is overflowing its banks at harvest time, and when the priests carrying the Ark of the Covenant put their soles in the flood,

> the waters which came down from upstream stood still, and rose in a heap very far away at Adam, the city that is beside Zaretan. So the waters that went down into the Sea of the Arabah, the Salt Sea, failed, and were cut off; and the people crossed over opposite Jericho. Then the priests who bore the Ark of the Covenant of the LORD stood firm on dry ground in the midst of the Jordan; and all Israel crossed over on dry ground, until all the people had crossed completely over the Jordan. (Joshua 3:16–17)

In an added test of faith – and nerve – the priests are portrayed standing "firm" in the middle of the river, trusting only in the power of their "living God … the Lord of all the earth" (3:10, 13) to hold back the torrent.

Placing memorial stones in the midst of the Jordan to commemorate their crossing – stones there "to this day" (4:9) in the writer's own time – the Hebrews revisit another Exodus experience, submitting themselves to circumcision in renewal of the covenant (5:1–9). It may seem a very strange thing to do before a battle – to inflict a temporarily incapacitating wound on all the warriors – but Joshua is shown learning from Moses' nearly fatal mistake in not circumcising Gershom before entering Egypt (Exodus 4:25). Thus, the episode ends with a sign of divine favor, as, for the first time since leaving Egypt, "the children of Israel no longer had manna, but they ate the food of the land of Canaan that year," filling themselves in the Land of Promise (Joshua 5:12). The Exodus is now ended, and the Promise to Abram has been kept. It is now up to the Hebrews to keep their end of the bargain.

The following three chapters (6–8) teach, through positive and negative example, further lessons of obedience before victory: the Israelite conquest of Jericho, followed by congregational sin and their defeat at Ai, followed by the revelation and punishment of that sin and the ensuing Hebrew triumph over Ai. Of course, as the old spiritual famously says, "Joshua fit de battle of Jericho, an' de walls come a-tumblin' down"; but the story makes it clear that the fight – and the victory – are entirely God's. The Hebrews' battle plan is truly weird: their whole army marches silently around the city for six days, led by seven priests blowing seven ram's horns, and on the seventh day marches seven times, followed by a deafening shout. This mode of "attack" certainly would be unnerving to the besieged, but above all it stresses the attackers' complete dependence on the seven-fold perfection of divine timing and power. And, in the midst of the carnage that follows, they are portrayed as scrupulously following Joshua's orders, sparing Rahab's family as promised and taking no personal booty.

They take no personal booty except, as it turns out, for one man of Judah named Achan. His secret crime of looting brings a very public defeat soon after as the Israelites assault the city of Ai and are driven off by its inhabitants in a humiliating slaughter. When a bewildered Joshua complains to the LORD, *Yahweh* rebukes him – "Get up! Why do you lie thus on your face?" – saying that He will not be with them while there is sin in the Hebrew camp (7:10–15). Joshua searches out the culprit, apparently through the casting of lots, which point to Achan, who confesses to stealing "a beautiful Babylonian garment, two hundred shekels of silver, and a wedge of gold weighing fifty shekels" and to hiding them in his tent (7:21). As with looters in times of martial law or horse thieves on the old western frontier, what follows is quick, if very harsh, justice – in this case, stoning to death, followed by burning of the thief, and probably the accomplices in his family, and then the destruction of all their booty. After this dire warning against hypocrisy among the tribes, the Hebrews in the next chapter follow the LORD's strategic instructions by laying an ambush that draws the defenders of Ai out to their doom. Thus, *Yahweh* is portrayed as primarily concerned with the moral purity of his army, while being shown delivering not only through miraculous intervention but also through ordinary military strategy. Yet ethical purity is not equated with ethnic purity: when Joshua culminates the conquests of Jericho and Ai by reconfirming the covenant and reading from the book of the law, note the presence of converts like Rahab and family: "the strangers who were living among them" (8:35).

This counterpoint between exclusion and inclusion continues in the perversely amusing tale of the Gibeonites in Joshua 9. Unlike the other inhabitants of the land – "the Hittite, the Amorite, the Canaanite, the Perizzite, the Hivite, and the Jebusite" (9:1–2) – who rally to fight the invading Hebrews, the Gibeonites decide that the better part of valor is discretion. Instead of resisting, the tribe "worked craftily," sending undercover ambassadors to Joshua decked out with "old sacks on their donkeys, old wineskins torn and mended, old and patched sandals on their feet, and old garments on themselves; and all the bread of their provision was dry and moldy" (9:4–5). Claiming to be "from a very far country," they praise the Hebrew God and ask the Israelites for a covenant treating them as "your servants" – and Joshua, who fails to "ask counsel of the LORD," looks at their convincing props and costumes, trusts his own eyes, and believes them. Having sworn a binding oath to treat the Gibeonites as protected servants, the Hebrews learn only three days later that these wily people are their new neighbors! In a sign of the binding power of a verbal covenant – recall Isaac's binding vow to the deceitful Jacob in Genesis 27 – Joshua shamefacedly insists on honoring the promise, despite the outrage of the Israelite elders. So here we are reminded again of even the prophets' human frailty. We also are reminded that the LORD, while a rewarder of virtue, has a soft spot for *chutzpah*, at least when it is motivated by a prudent fear of his power – and that he is a promise-keeping God, even to the "stranger."

The Gibeonites call on this promise almost immediately, in an incident that precipitates one of the most cosmic of biblical miracles. Adoni-Zedek, king of Jerusalem, still an Amorite city until David's day, rallies four other Amorite kings for a punitive attack against Gibeon for making peace with the Israelites. The Gibeonites send a distress signal to Joshua, and Joshua's immediate rescue involves tremendous divine intervention: as the Hebrew army routs the five kings' armies outside Gibeon, terrible hailstones fall on the Amorites, so that "more who died from the hailstones than the children of Israel killed with the sword" (10:11). But Joshua, to extend the day of battle and to make victory complete, calls on the LORD so that "the sun stood still in the midst of heaven, and did not hasten to go down for about a whole day" (10:13). The idea of the universal Creator God orchestrating the weather and the motions of the planets to aid his covenant people, so absurd to many modern imaginations, would also have seemed bizarre – and terrifying – to the polytheistic Canaanites, so used to worshiping gods with only limited powers confined to particular regions. As in Genesis 1–2 onward, a single transcendent Deity who nevertheless has shockingly local interests is in view here.

Indeed, this account of God's cosmic aid to his chosen people is fittingly the climactic story in the Joshua's brief epic of conquest; for after the execution of the five Amorite kings, the narrative turns to quick "fast forward" summaries of Joshua's southern (10:28–40) and northern (11:1–15) campaigns of conquest, ending with a final overarching summary of all the campaigns (11:16–23). This summary climaxes in a statement reminiscent of *Yahweh's* past judgments in Exodus on Pharaoh: "For it was of the LORD to harden their hearts, that they should come against Israel in battle, that he might utterly destroy them" (Joshua 11:20). Significantly, those who seek mercy from Israel – Rahab and her family, the Gibeonites – receive it, but the great majority of the Canaanites are presented as living only by the sword, so that, driven by their own bloodlust, they die by it. "Those whom the gods would destroy, they first make mad," the ancients said; in Joshua, once this blood-madness is punished and past, "[t]hen the land rested from war" (11:23).

Chapters 12–22 focus on the distribution of the land, in the epic tradition of the catalogue of warriors and tribes, with each of the Israelite tribes and its families specified in relation to each section of Canaan allotted. This segment comprises most of the second half of Joshua's book, and, like all genealogies, makes more interesting reading if you feel an immediate material or spiritual stake in the families named. Special attention is shown to the lot of the Levites, whose inheritance is the priesthood throughout Israel, not any particular territory within Israel (21); and with this concern for ritual righteousness comes a concern for both justice and mercy associated with the cities of refuge, where the accidental shedder of blood can flee from the long arm of family vengeance and vendetta (20) – the dark side of family-administered justice.

As the book draws to an end, the victorious Twelve Tribes seem to be at peace with each other, so that the land will have "rest from war"; yet not all is well as the book closes. Imitating Moses by giving a farewell address before his death, Joshua calls out the secret disobedience of many in Israel, in terms that again recall the notorious secret idolator Achan from chapter 7:

> But Joshua said to the people, "You cannot serve the LORD, for he is a holy God. He is a jealous God; He will not forgive your transgressions nor your sins. If you forsake the LORD and serve foreign gods, then he will turn and do you harm and consume you, after He has done you good."
> And the people said to Joshua, "No, but we will serve the LORD!"
> So Joshua said to the people, "You are witnesses against yourselves that you have chosen the LORD for yourselves, to serve him."
> And they said, "We are witnesses!"
> "Now therefore," he said, "put away the foreign gods which are among you, and incline your heart to the LORD God of Israel."
> And the people said to Joshua, "The LORD our God we will serve, and his voice we will obey!" (24:19–24)

Against the hypocritical protests of the congregation, Joshua brings the hard fact of their continuing infatuation with portable gods in their houses and tents, and challenges them to put away their idols and serve the LORD only. Then, taking them at their word, he erects yet another memorial, a "stone of witness," and then, in the most important memorial of all, on parchment rolls, he "wrote these words in the Book of the Law of God" (24:26). At last, his final exhortations done, Joshua dies and is buried in his new inheritance. Fittingly, in the same passage we're told of the burial of Joseph's old bones centuries after his death in Egypt (24:32). The story has come full circle – the man who began the Hebrews' long sojourn beside the Nile comes to his last rest at the same time as the man who brought that sojourn to its final, and successful, end. Yet there is another, sadder circle in play as well, for, as Joshua's last words attest, there is still "sin in the camp," sin that will return with a vengeance like encroaching perennial weeds throughout the downward cycles in the next book, Judges.

8.2 "When the Judge Was Dead … They Reverted": Cycles of Decay in Judges

The Book of Judges is not a vast epic like the Exodus-through-Deuteronomy story, nor a brief epic like the Book of Joshua, but a more occasional collection of even briefer hero stories. In some sense, this diminished scale in Judges mirrors the book's diminished and diminishing outcomes – for it is, overall, a narrative of decline and fall.

Judges and Ruth: A Matched Set?

Though both the Book of Judges and the Book of Ruth are anonymous, some Hebrew traditions have attributed both to Samuel, the last of the judges and the great transitional figure to the time of kings – writing about 1000 BCE, with possible editing after the Exile around 450 BCE. Thematically, this linkage makes sense, because Judges provides the necessary (and dark) context against which Ruth shines more brightly, and because Ruth ends by announcing the parentage of Israel's greatest king, David.

Yet amidst this overall downward spiral, there are certain peaks and high points: divinely appointed deliverers periodically arise to reverse, or at least delay, the process of decay by acts of faithful courage. The book's name of Judges – from the Latin Vulgate *Judicum* – is misleading to the modern reader, for whom a judge is the presiding official in a court of law, one who weighs evidence, makes legal rulings, and passes sentences to be carried out by other officers. In other words, in most modern societies – as indeed since medieval times in Europe – the judicial function has been separated out from the legislative, executive and military functions of government. But under the loose-knit confederation of Israelite tribes between the Conquest and the Kingdoms, this was not the case. A **Judge** (Hebrew **Shophet** – plural **Shophetim**), while sometimes called upon to adjudicate legal disputes among the Hebrews, was primarily an inspired, ad hoc military Deliverer raised up to answer an immediate threat and who, for the most part, stood down after the crisis was past – rather like a *Dictator* of the Roman Republic (until the Caesars), or a Captain of Militia in Colonial America.

Of the dozen *Shophetim* in this book, many are very briefly described: Othniel and Shamgar (Judges 3), Tola and Jair (10), Ibzon, Elon, and Abdon (12) receive only the barest of mentions. Others, like Ehud (3), get a bit more discussion; while the best known to our ears – Deborah (4–5), Gideon (6–8), Jephthah (11–12), and Samson (13–16) – get two to four chapters each. Among them, they vary a good deal in mission and in method, but all share in common a divine calling to rescue their people, who have fallen under enemy sway – usually as a divine punishment for popular disobedience.

And the cycle of popular disobedience is the dominant recurring theme of the book. In Judges 2, after the death of Joshua is again described, the narrator traces the repeated pattern:

> Nevertheless, the LORD raised up judges who delivered them out of the hand of those who plundered them. Yet they would not listen to their judges, but they played the harlot with other gods, and bowed down to them. They turned quickly from the way in which their fathers walked, in obeying the commandments of the LORD; they did not do so. And when the LORD raised up judges for them, the LORD was with the judge and delivered them out of the hand of their enemies all the days of the judge; for the LORD was moved to pity by their groaning because of those who oppressed them and harassed them. And it came to pass, when the judge was dead, that they reverted and behaved more corruptly than their fathers, by following other gods, to serve them and bow down to them. They did not cease from their own doings nor from their stubborn way. (2:16–19)

As in the LORD's dealings with the people of Israel in the wilderness, *Yahweh* is portrayed as inclined to pity despite their bad behavior, but the difference – and a gloomy difference – is that while the wilderness wanderings in Numbers lasted until the rebellious parents could be replaced by their more faithful children, here in Judges the children "behaved more corruptly than their fathers." So while seasons of loss and oppression alternate with seasons of peace and relative prosperity, the darker seasons are increasingly longer and more frequent, until the book's pitch-black ending.

Yet the book opens with energy and forward thrust:

> Now after the death of Joshua it came to pass that the children of Israel asked the LORD, saying, "Who shall be first to go up for us against the Canaanites to fight against them?" And the LORD said, "Judah shall go up. Indeed I have delivered the land into his hand." So Judah said to Simeon his brother, "Come up with me to my allotted territory, that we may fight against the Canaanites; and I will likewise go with you to your allotted territory." (1:1–3)

The people are on the move, listening for *Yahweh's* guidance, and working together in immediately successful ways: the cruel Canaanite King Adoni-Bezek is brought to heel ("Seventy kings with their thumbs and big toes cut off used to gather scraps under my table; as I have done, so God has repaid me" – 1:7), while Caleb's family takes hold of their inheritance, the sons of Joseph conquer Luz and rename it Bethel, and even Jerusalem is temporarily captured by Israel (1:8, 12, 21, 22).

Yet by the end of this opening chapter, momentum has slowed and action has stalled, as we read about the accumulating failures of Manasseh, Ephraim, Zebulun, Asher, and Naphtali to take full possession, and the Danites are actually in retreat from the resurgent Amorites. The second chapter spells out the pattern of coming acculturation, intermarriage, and idolatry, and by Judges 3, that decline is an ever-increasing reality:

> Thus the children of Israel dwelt among the Canaanites, the Hittites, the Amorites, the Perizzites, the Hivites, and the Jebusites. And they took their daughters to be their wives, and gave their daughters to their sons; and they served their gods. (3:5–6)

In their acts of cultural blending, the unique worship of the God of their fathers seems invariably to be lost. And yet revival and deliverance still arise, and from surprising, unexpected quarters.

8.2.1 Alternative Heroes: Ehud, Deborah, Jael, and Gideon

The first Judge, **Othniel** – who intervenes to lead Israel against the oppressive Cushan-Rishathaim, king of Mesopotamia – seems to fit the more expected heroic mode (3:7–11). The son of Kenaz, Caleb's younger brother, he is linked to a famed leader of the Mosaic era, since Caleb and Joshua were closely partnered during and after the Exodus. Yet when the Israelites backslide after Othniel's deliverance, and God punishes them with servitude to the Moabite King Eglon, God's next *Shophet* **Ehud** comes with a difference: he is left-handed, and, possibly, crippled in his right. Probably because right-handedness is so much more common genetically, in most ancient cultures (and many more recent ones) its opposite has been associated traditionally either with clumsiness or moral evil – witness the French *gauche* or the Latin *sinister*, not to mention the normative uses of "dexterous" and "right" to mean skilled or morally good. And in a way, Ehud is sinister; rather than face Eglon in open combat, he exploits his own otherness – and perhaps a handicap that renders him non-threatening – to engineer a regime decapitation through assassination.

There is a grisly humor about Eglon's death. A grossly fat man, he receives Ehud, who leads the delegation bearing Israelite tribute money, into his cool private palace chambers, and Ehud's improvised weapon goes undetected because it is concealed strapped unexpectedly to his *right* thigh – where a "lefty" can easily grasp it. When all of the other Israelites are dismissed, and Eglon feels most secure, Ehud offers a "secret message," indeed "a message from God" worthy of Vito Corleone: a dagger in the belly! "Even the hilt went in after the blade, and the fat closed over the blade, for he did not draw the dagger out of his belly; and his entrails came out" (3:22). Compounding the irony is the impotence of Eglon's "stone images," which stand mutely by as the king dies, and, in a marvelously deflating detail, Eglon's servants are slow to discover his death because they assume that their mighty lord is enjoying a nice, secluded bowel movement. Meanwhile, Ehud escapes and rallies the Israelites to attack at the fords of the Jordan, sealing off and killing 10,000 Moabite warriors (3:24–30). Typical of *Yahweh's* penchant for favoring younger sons and outcasts, this tale of the left-handed assassin reminds the reader not to underestimate the oddballs – in God's service. The result? Eighty years of Hebrew freedom.

The next "alternative" Judge differs from the norm in a far more consequential way. After a brief mention of the mighty **Shamgar** – who fells 600 Philistines with an ox goad – we meet **Deborah**, "the wife of Lapidoth," and an iconic biblical model of female authority. Two things must be said at once about Deborah's female identity: first, that it is central to her style of leadership and to the meaning of her story; and second, that despite – or rather because of – her being a woman, she is portrayed as the most effective and admirable of all the *Shophetim*. Her courage, her clarity, her dignity, and her battle-ready wisdom are presented as extensions of her being "a mother in Israel" (5:7) nurturing and protecting the children of the nation when the menfolk waver or fail.

From the first, Deborah's femininity makes her an alternative model of power, neither inferior nor questionable in her leadership. She is introduced as already a trusted and established "prophetess," to whom the children of Israel are resorting for judgment as she sits "under the palm tree of Deborah between Ramah and Bethel in the mountains of Ephraim" (4:5) – and what she says comes to pass. In response to the punitive invasions of Jabin, King of Canaan, and of his army commander Sisera, Deborah prophesies to the Israelite commander Barak that he will muster "ten thousand men of the sons of Naphtali and of the sons of Zebulun" and that "against you I … the LORD God of Israel … will deploy Sisera, the commander of Jabin's army, with his chariots and his multitude at the River Kishon; and I will deliver him into your hand." Like the orchestrator of a great pageant, *Yahweh* brings the enemy attacks precisely so that they may be met and defeated. However, Barak – in an implicit indictment of weak Israelite manhood – is a faint-hearted shirker, laying down to Deborah the cowardly condition that "[i]f you will go with me, then I will go; but if you will not go with me, I will not go!" Deborah's riposte to her reluctant general? "I will surely go with you; nevertheless there will be no glory for you in the journey you are taking, for the LORD will sell Sisera into the hand of a woman" (4:6–9). And – as we will learn in another surprise – that woman will not be Deborah, but the story's second alternative hero, Jael.

The narrative gives short shrift to the battle itself – God's intervention through torrential rains makes it a foregone conclusion, despite Jabin's and Sisera's advanced technology in the form of chariots – though Deborah must again rouse the tardy Barak into battle ("Up! For this is the day that the LORD has delivered Sisera into your hand" – 4:14). The Canaanite forces are routed and slaughtered, while Sisera himself abandons his chariot and flees on foot – and here is where the story's truly central action begins, for Deborah's full prophecy and the narrative's full irony come into play. As Sisera runs away, he passes the tent of Heber the Kenite, whose very name suggests Hebrew sympathies but who is nevertheless at peace with the Canaanite King Jabin.

However, Heber's wife **Jael** has less peaceable intentions – yet concealed in the warm words of a welcoming hostess. She calls out to the fleeing, exhausted general, "Turn aside, my lord, turn aside to me; do not fear" (4:18). This phrase "turn aside" is rich in implications: occasionally it can refer to a divinely ordained detour – as when Moses "turn[s] aside" to see the Burning Bush in Exodus 3:3 – but it much more commonly indicates a departure from the "strait and narrow" – as in a turn to false gods and a violation of the law in Deuteronomy 11:28, or when the loose woman would "turn aside" a young man's heart "to her ways" in Proverbs 7:25. Jael's rather suggestive repetition of the phrase, and the added "to *me*," both intensify this implication; so whether or not Sisera actually receives the full range of possible feminine comforts in Jael's tent (and where is Heber?), we're justified in thinking that Sisera enters her tent with carnal expectations, probably as Jael intended. In any case, after her ministrations – which at least include milk and a warm blanket – Sisera is tired enough to lie down for what turns out to be his everlasting rest.

For Jael is a cool hand with a tent-spike and a hammer, fixing Sisera to the ground in a few final well-placed blows and then greeting Barak with news that must have stirred mixed reactions in the victor's breast – for, as Deborah had said, his moment of victory would be his moment of humiliation, as "the LORD will sell Sisera into the hand of a woman." With the typical understatement of the biblical prose style, the narrator leaves us to guess at Barak's chagrin.

As to Jael, whether her actual deeds are sexual or not, she is a fascinating biblical twist on the *femme fatale* tradition, exploiting male yearning for erotic – or here is it maternal? – tenderness in order to bring a man low. The particular twist here, of course, is that as with earlier seductive figures such as Tamar and Rahab in Genesis and Joshua (or Judith in that apocryphal book), her wiles are employed to a good, or at least providential end: Sisera's detour is after all divinely appointed, however lustfully meant, and fulfills a good woman's prophecy.

And it is Deborah who gets the very substantial last word. Deborah's Song in chapter 5 is a masterpiece of its form, the sort of triumph song that, if we don't sympathize with the victors, we might call boastful, but if we do sympathize we call exuberant – like the victory songs of Moses and Miriam in Exodus, and of David in Samuel and Psalms. (And Barak's joining Deborah in singing the song suggests that, whatever his failings, he finally shares in her great gratitude to *Yahweh*.) The song's boasting is above all in the power of the LORD God of Israel, who makes the earth's elements and the heavenly constellations Israel's allies:

> LORD, when You went out from Seir,
> When You marched from the field of Edom,
> The earth trembled and the heavens poured,
> The clouds also poured water;
> The mountains gushed before the LORD,
> This Sinai, before the LORD God of Israel...
>
> They fought from the heavens;
> The stars in their courses fought against Sisera.
> The torrent of Kishon swept them away,
> That ancient torrent, the torrent of Kishon. (5:4–5, 20–21)

Amidst this abundant praise of God, Deborah is more sparing in awarding glory to men, depending on how each tribe responded in the day of battle: Ephraim, Benjamin, Zebulun, Issachar, and Naphtali nobly answered the call, while the no-shows are memorialized and fixed in sarcasm as in amber:

> The divisions of Reuben have great searchings of heart.
> Gilead stayed beyond the Jordan,
> And why did Dan remain on ships?
> Asher continued at the seashore,
> And stayed by his inlets. (5:16–17)

However, in keeping with Deborah's prophecy before battle, the greatest human glory goes, not to the barely mentioned Barak, but to Jael, in lines that virtually crow with sustained irony and reflected feminine pride:

> Most blessed among women is Jael,
> The wife of Heber the Kenite;
> Blessed is she among women in tents.
> He asked for water, she gave milk;
> She brought out cream in a lordly bowl.
> She stretched her hand to the tent peg,
> Her right hand to the workmen's hammer;
> She pounded Sisera, she pierced his head,
> She split and struck through his temple. (5:24–26)

Then the synthetic parallelisms build to a gloating, excruciating, exquisite crescendo:

> At her feet he sank, he fell, he lay still;
> At her feet he sank, he fell;
> Where he sank, there he fell dead. (5:27)

This woman's victory song concludes with a wry coda which adopts another woman's viewpoint – that of the dead Sisera's mother – to remind all Israel, and especially her daughters, what was at stake in the defeat of this cruel, grasping, and lecherous man:

> The mother of Sisera looked through the window,
> And cried out through the lattice,
> "Why is his chariot so long in coming?
> Why tarries the clatter of his chariots?"
> Her wisest ladies answered her,
> Yes, she answered herself,

> "Are they not finding and dividing the spoil:
> To every man a girl or two;
> For Sisera, plunder of dyed garments,
> Plunder of garments embroidered and dyed,
> Two pieces of dyed embroidery for the looter?" (5:28–30)

Like son, like mother; she greedily awaits special spoil that will suit her fancy, while indulgently chuckling over how her thoughtful boy is probably being detained by the pleasant distribution of Hebrew girls for service as sexual slaves – the same son who now lies with his brains oozing out of his ear into the earth, a would-be rapist penetrated by a woman.

> Thus let all Your enemies perish, O LORD!
> But let those who love Him be like the sun
> When it comes out in full strength. (5:31)

One can almost hear the shrill ululation from behind the women's veils. And so, we are told to end Deborah's triumph, "the land had rest for forty years."

If the alternative heroism of Ehud is in his cleverly "sinister" assassination plan, of Deborah in her righteous, firm, and fierce maternal protectiveness, and of Jael in her deadly deployment of feminine nurture, then **Gideon** is an alternate hero in yet another, strikingly different mode. He is initially as reluctant as Barak, but he is nevertheless marked out for glory as an underdog, one who has greatness thrust upon him and discovers his calling only after being forced into answering it. He is the little man chosen as the vessel of divine power, so that he is remembered, not for the greatness, but the smallness of his army, and not for seeking, but declining a crown.

Gideon's story begins in a most unpromising way. The Israelites have again defected to other gods, and the LORD has now sent the Midianites to plague them, so that they have "made for themselves the dens, the caves, and the strongholds which are in the mountains" (6:2). Hiding in holes, the Hebrews are also slowly starving, due to Midian's policy of stealing and destroying their crops, and even forbidding the threshing of grain. So we first see Gideon "threshing wheat in a winepress, in order to hide it from the Midianites" – a process guaranteed to produce terrible bread, since grain was ordinarily threshed on breezy hilltops for the wind to blow the chaff away, while in a sunken winepress, much of the chaff would remain. It is here that the Angel of the LORD first greets Gideon – "The LORD is with you, you mighty man of valor!" – with a greeting that seems like mockery to the dispirited man, who gives the unrecognized visitor a piece of his mind: "O my lord, if the LORD is with us, why then has all this happened to us? And where are all his miracles, which our fathers told us about, saying, 'Did not the LORD bring us up from Egypt?'" As with Moses at the Burning Bush, the LORD looks past the man who is and speaks to the man he will become: "Go in this might of yours, and you shall save Israel from the hand of the Midianites. Have I not sent you?" (6:11–14).

As it dawns on Gideon that he is in the presence of a divine messenger, he fetches a simple food offering and begs a sign – and the angel touches his staff to the offering, which disappears, with the angel himself, in an instant flame. Suddenly terrified at having seen God's face, Gideon fears for his life, until *Yahweh* reassures him and calls him to action against the altar and image of Baal belonging to his own father, Joash. Ironically, despite a divine commission, Gideon's work of destroying the altar and the idol, and raising up a new altar to the LORD, is done at night, "because he feared his father's household and the men of the city too much to do it by day" (6:27).

When his act of holy sacrilege is discovered the next morning, Gideon faces an ad hoc tribunal of angry neighbors, irate that their god has been used as wood for a sacrifice to their God, but his father, inspired by his son's example, defends Gideon, saying that "if [Baal] is a god, let him plead for himself!" (6:31) – leading to Gideon's henceforth being called "Jerubbaal," which means "let Baal plead." Then, in the aftermath of this confrontation, "the Spirit of the LORD came upon Gideon," and in this sudden burst of inspiration he with new boldness "blew the trumpet, and the Abiezrites gathered behind him. And he sent messengers throughout all Manasseh, who also gathered behind him. He also sent messengers to Asher, Zebulun, and Naphtali; and they came up to meet them" (6:34–35).

Yet this suddenly emboldened captain comes down again with cold feet, and needs more divine reassurance – and in one of the most famous instances of "testing God," receives it: the episode of the "fleece." Not once but twice, Gideon puts out a sheepskin under the sky and asks God for a sign, either wet fleece and dry ground, or dry fleece and wet ground. "Do not be angry with me," he begs the LORD, and, surprisingly, God is not angry, but condescends to his servant's faint-hearted request (6:36–40). And also surprisingly, this second answer is finally enough for Gideon and his men: "Then Jerubbaal (that is, Gideon) and all the people who were with him rose early and encamped beside the well of Harod, so that the camp of the Midianites was on the north side of them by the hill of Moreh in the valley" (7:1). They are ready to take the battle to the invaders.

So, to compound these surprises, the LORD insists that this crowd of recruits is too large and too many for his purposes, and sets up a memorable test of his own to winnow them out: down by the riverside, "the number of those who lapped, putting their hand to their mouth, was three hundred men; but all the rest of the people got down on their knees to drink water. Then the LORD said to Gideon, 'By the three hundred men who lapped I will save you, and deliver the Midianites into your hand'" (7:6–7).

Gideon's Famous Few

Gideon's tiny army is one of the chief models in history for the small but noble band who punch far above their weight and triumph against great odds. From Shakespeare's Henry V at Agincourt and George Washington at Trenton to Winston Churchill's Royal Air Force (RAF) during the Blitz, their splendid arithmetic is, in King Henry's words, "the fewer men, the greater share of honor." Indeed, "Harry the King" – who is outnumbered five-to-one and forced to invoke St. Crispin, the patron saint of shoemakers – seems deliberately to echo Gideon in offering to send home anyone "that fears his fellowship to die with us," and then he captures his men's imaginations and their hearts by bluntly embracing their deficiencies:

> We few, we happy few, we band of brothers;
> For he to-day that sheds his blood with me
> Shall be my brother; be he ne'er so vile,
> This day shall gentle his condition:
> And gentlemen in England now a-bed
> Shall think themselves accursed they were not here,
> And hold their manhoods cheap whiles any speaks
> That fought with us upon Saint Crispin's day. (*Henry V* 4.3.23, 41, 60–67)

And we hear echoes of both Gideon and King Harry in Churchill's words of August 20, 1940, on RAF valor against the *Luftwaffe*: "Never in the field of human conflict was so much been owed by so many to so few."

What is it about drinking posture that qualifies or disqualifies a soldier, we may ask? In this case, we might as well ask, what sorts of earlobes, attached or detached? Or, does his navel fold inward or outward? The point is in the apparent arbitrariness of the test, the only criterion being that which will yield the fewest men, and thus the greatest share of glory to God.

The actual battle with the Midianites is a spiritually enhanced masterpiece of psychological warfare. God's first move is to give Gideon his own psychological boost: he enables Gideon to overhear a Midianite soldier describe a terrifying dream predicting a great Israelite victory by "the sword of Gideon," spreading fear throughout their camp. With this knowledge of a demoralized enemy, Gideon issues weapons to his valiant 300: for each, a trumpet, an empty pitcher, and a torch. Though the Midianites are "lying in the valley as numerous as locusts," Gideon positions his men around the valley's edge with their burning torches covered by their pitchers. Then, at the blast of Gideon's trumpet – shades of the battle of Jericho – each warrior blows his horn, smashes his pitcher, and waves his torch, all while shouting "the sword of the LORD, and of Gideon!" (7:9–18). In the night, the already spooked Midianites are suddenly ringed in by trumpets and crashes and shouts and fire.

The result is a bloody rout in which the swords of the Israelites are largely unnecessary because, in the melée of the Midianites' panicked flight, "the LORD set every man's sword against his companion throughout the whole camp" (7:22). Gideon, now the picture of boldness, summons all Asher, Naphtali, Ephraim, and Manasseh to help press their advantage, and they respond by seizing the major watering places and then capturing the Midianite princes Oreb and Zeeb. Obliterating Midianite power and naming rights to the land, "[t]hey killed Oreb at the rock of Oreb, and Zeeb they killed at the winepress of Zeeb. They pursued Midian and brought the heads of Oreb and Zeeb to Gideon on the other side of the Jordan" (7:25). In the following chapter, Gideon's army, led by his chosen 300, surprise, pursue, and capture two other Midianite kings, Zebah and Zalmunna, executing them for the past slaughter of their brothers (8:10–12, 18–21). The Israelites, only a short time after cowering before Baal and starving in hidey-holes, now repossess the Land of Promise in the name of the LORD.

Gideon's finest hour, however, comes at the conclusion of these battles, as his now grateful countrymen make him an offer that is seldom refused: "Then the men of Israel said to Gideon, 'Rule over us, both you and your son, and your grandson also; for you have delivered us from the hand of Midian.'" Yet Gideon, in a true act of alternative heroism, refuses: "But Gideon said to them, 'I will not rule over you, nor shall my son rule over you; the LORD shall rule over you'" (8:22–23). Identifying God as their true King, Gideon implicitly rebukes their idolatrous desire to be like the nations around them, ridden by warlords masquerading as kingly sons of the gods.

Gideon Refuses a Crown

Having noted Gideon as a model for outnumbered underdogs, we can also see him in the company of leaders famed for civic virtue and self-restraint. These include Roman aristocrat Cincinnatus, who in 458 BCE served the Republic as *Dictator* for a mere 16 days, long enough to defeat the Aequi, and then resigned his dictatorship and immediately returned to his farm; Oliver Cromwell, who was offered the vacant British crown in 1657 by Parliamentary flatterers, but rejected it, telling them "[t]his bauble, this worthless trinket, give it to some whore for the price of her bed" (though it must be mentioned, not giving up the powers of Protector); and the victorious George Washington, who was urged by one of his officers in 1782 to make himself King of America, but instead rebuked the man and exhorted his troops to stand down and submit to Congress – these men are remembered as antidotes to the Alexanders, the Caesars, the Tamburlaines, the Bonapartes, not to mention the Hitlers and Mussolinis, the Stalins and Castros, of history.

But, this being the Book of Judges, Gideon's finest hour is really more of a moment, and then the Israelite craving for graven images asserts itself immediately: in the very next verse after rejecting a crown, Gideon solicits the booty of battle, saying

> "I would like to make a request of you, that each of you would give me the earrings from his plunder"... So they answered, "We will gladly give them." And they spread out a garment, and each man threw into it the earrings from his plunder. Now the weight of the gold earrings that he requested was one thousand seven hundred shekels of gold ... (8:24–26)

Gideon departs further from the uncompromising examples of Moses and Joshua, not only asking for this looted gold, but like Aaron with the Golden Calf, transforming the gold into a kind of idol: "Then Gideon made it into an ephod and set it up in his city, Ophrah. And all Israel played the harlot with it there. It became a snare to Gideon and to his house" (8:27). So Gideon, whose simple faith – despite his fear – delivers Israel from political and spiritual servitude, ends by building a bridge back to idolatry, transforming a priestly garment into an object of cultic worship. As we will see, after Gideon sows the wind, in the next generation his family and the nation will reap the whirlwind. For he conceives a sinister son whom he calls Abimelech – ironically, it can mean "my father is king" – who will multiply Gideon's corruption, with none of his restraint.

8.2.2 "Weak ... Like Any Other Man": The Tragedy of Samson

If Gideon's story arc begins with the unlikely hero's inadequacies, builds to a triumph of underdog leadership, climaxes with his self-denying refusal of kingship, and then ends in a sordid coda of greed and idolatry, the story of **Samson** reads rather like a mirror opposite. This hero is divinely announced and specially gifted from birth; despite some early success he increasingly acts alone, squandering his great strength and ability; he is eventually, through his own folly, captured, blinded, and enslaved by his enemies; and yet in the end he manages a final self-sacrifice that brings the enemy down in his own fall. In other words, Gideon's story reads rather like comedy – yet with its happy ending spoiled – while Samson's reads like tragedy – yet with its grim ending redeemed.

Samson's story is often discussed as tragedy, and although the Book of Judges long predates Aristotle's *Poetics* (c. 335 BCE), the later Greek philosopher's theories of what makes for good tragedy can be applied usefully to this mighty judge's fall. According to Aristotle, in the most effective tragedies – like Sophocles' *Oedipus Rex* or Euripides' *Medea* – the play's **protagonist** ("first struggler") is well-born and personally of noble character, yet prone (whether accidentally or deliberately) to **hamartia** ("mistake" or "missing the mark"). This flawed behavior sets in motion a chain of destructive events somehow predetermined by **anagke** ("fate" or "necessity") and often announced by a **nemesis**, such as *Oedipus'* Teiresias. Despite such warnings, the protagonist proceeds on his or her course until being overtaken in a moment of **peripeteia** ("reversal of fortune") that brings a sudden fall from happiness into misery, often leading to death. However, in well-made tragedy, says Aristotle, such peripeteia leads the protagonist to **anagnorisis** ("recognition" or "self-understanding"), and produces in the audience both **phobos** ("fear") and **eleos** ("pity"), resulting in a **catharsis** ("purification" or "purging") of these emotions.[1]

In these terms, then, how tragic are Samson's life and death? Certainly, Samson is no nobleman or king – he is from Dan, one of the less prominent tribes – but his birth and coming are announced by the Angel of the LORD himself, who tells the barren wife of the Danite Manoah:

> Now therefore, please be careful not to drink wine or similar drink, and not to eat anything unclean. For behold, you shall conceive and bear a son. And no razor shall come upon his head, for the child shall be a Nazirite to God from the womb; and he shall begin to deliver Israel out of the hand of the Philistines. (13:3–5)

This *Shophet*-Deliverer is set aside for a special mission under a special Nazirite vow – like his mother's, but for his entire lifetime – to abstain from alcohol and the fruit of the vine, from haircutting, and from touching the dead (see Numbers 6:1–21). Thus, the expectation is that this child will show special virtue, special leadership, and special strength. The last of these qualities indeed manifests in his youth, as "the Spirit of the LORD began to move upon him at Mahaneh Dan between Zorah and Eshtaol" against the Philistines (Judges 13:25).

The Philistines

Although the Philistines appear early on in Judges, it is not until the time of Samson that they become the primary adversaries of Israel. A Phoenician people with a strong seagoing heritage – and worshipers of the fish-god Dagon – they have been identified by modern archeology as one of the "Sea Peoples" opposed and defeated by Pharaoh Ramses III around 1200 BCE, driving them increasingly into Canaan. The possessors of what may have been the world's first true alphabet, their writing system influenced – or perhaps paralleled – Paleo Hebrew and preceded early Greek – and also Latin. Given this ancient literacy, it is perhaps ironic that "philistine" has since Victorian times come to mean someone illiterate, anti-intellectual, and anti-aesthetic – as critics like Matthew Arnold appropriated the name to describe the opponents of the enlightened, cultured, progressive elite. Also ironically, a Latinized variant of "Philistine," "Palestine," long ago replaced "Canaan" as the name of the land still contested by Arabs and Jews.

However, soon this protagonist's weaknesses begin to dominate the action. Though the Nazirite's vow includes no promise of celibacy, he is bound, like all Hebrews, to marry among his people. Samson, on the other hand, sees a Philistine woman in Timnah and immediately demands her for his wife, over his devout parents' objections – for, he says, "she is right in my eyes" (14:3). Then, having bare-handedly killed a lion on his way through a forbidden vineyard to meet his sweetheart, he discovers on a later visit that bees have colonized the lion's carcass, so Samson blithely scoops out the unclean honey and gives some even to his parents. And in further violation of his teetotal vow, Samson entertains his bride's people with a drinking party – the literal meaning of the "feast" in Judges 14:10. Wine, women, and corpses – these are a foreboding set of *hamartia*.

Samson's "missings of the mark" multiply as his story develops. The cocky young judge can't resist boasting about his lion-killing exploit, so he poses this riddle to his drinking companions: "Out of the eater came something to eat, / And out of the strong came something sweet" (14:14). With a large bet at stake – —thirty changes of clothing – these Philistines threaten Samson's fiancée ("we will burn you and your father's house") unless she can coax the secret out of her man. And, in a foreshadowing of disaster to come, she succeeds: "You only hate me! You do not love me!" she whines. "You have posed a riddle to the sons of my people, but you have not explained it to me" (14:15–16). After seven days of wheedling and tears, Samson gives up his weird secret to her – a dead lion full of honey! – only to find himself betrayed to the

Philistines. Taking his revenge, Samson kills thirty Philistines, strips their bodies, and gives their clothes to the wedding party, causing his bride to be given to his erstwhile best man.

Now the violence escalates with the dark humor of a country and western ballad. Denied his conjugal rights, Samson directs his rage at the Philistines in a grand feat of arson by capturing 300 foxes, tying them in pairs with torches between their tails and setting them loose to zigzag through the enemy wheat fields at harvest time. Their crops destroyed, the Philistines retaliate by in fact burning Samson's former bride and her father alive, and Samson strikes back, attacking them "hip and thigh with a great slaughter" (15:8). The survivors demand that the Israelites arrest and hand over their champion, and they quickly oblige, sending 3000 men who might have been fighting the Philistines instead to apprehend their would-be Deliverer at his stronghold, the Rock of Etam. Turned in by his cowardly countrymen, Samson bides his time, allowing himself to be bound and extradited, until, once in enemy hands,

> the Spirit of the LORD came mightily upon him; and the ropes that were on his arms became like flax that is burned with fire, and his bonds broke loose from his hands. He found a fresh jawbone of a donkey, reached out his hand and took it, and killed a thousand men with it. (15:14–15)

So, despite Israel's craven collaboration with their oppressors and Samson's deeply flawed character lacking public spirit, the liberation of the Israelites from Philistine dominion proceeds as if by what the Greeks might call *anagke* or fate, while the author of Judges explains that "it was of the LORD… He was seeking an occasion to move against the Philistines" (14:4). God is found to be using even Samson's weaknesses to spur him in his mission.

Yet as Samson's one-man triumphs multiply, so do his *nemeses*, and occasions seem to conspire against him to bring about his *peripeteia* or downfall. Betrayed by his fiancée and her father in Timnah, by his own people at the Rock of Etam, and by his visit to a harlot in the city gates of Gaza, Samson in each case ups the ante in displays of his supernatural strength – in the last case literally "breaking" out of Gaza, pulling the gates up by their posts and carrying them up a nearby hill for the Philistines to see. Yet no amount of manly brawn can overcome his besetting weakness when he meets perhaps the most famous *femme fatale* of all – Delilah. However much a poet like John Milton, or Hollywood screenwriters, have tried to portray her as torn between some type of romantic attachment and either greed or patriotism, the text of Judges leaves little room for any but her mercenary motives.

Milton's *Samson Agonistes*

Having brilliantly reimagined Genesis 1–3 in his epic *Paradise Lost* (1667, 1674), John Milton in 1671 published *Samson Agonistes* ("Samson the Struggler"), a tragic drama that recasts Samson as not only a strongman, but also as a prophetic intellectual in exile, now defeated and blind, seeking divine guidance amid conflicting voices for a last act of deliverance. Interpreters of Milton's play have long noted his Samson's strong resemblances to the poet himself, the official print champion of the fallen Cromwellian regime, now blind and struggling to find meaning in the collapse of the Puritan Commonwealth at the Restoration of Charles II in 1660. Although Milton's Samson also has been brought low by the feminine wiles of "Dalila," she is presented as more conflicted that the biblical Delilah, at times expressing real passion for her victim. And, true to his Classical models, Milton's Samson is a much more reflective character, achieving a genuine, and patriotic, *anagnorisis* – self-understanding – before exiting to tear down the Temple of Dagon, destroying himself with the Philistine elite.

We are told that Samson "loved a woman in the Valley of Sorek, whose name was Delilah" and that when the lords of the Philistines bribe her with bags of silver to learn the secret of Samson's great strength, she goes to work on him immediately. The narrator, using carefully structured ironic repetition, makes clear her particularly nagging allure:

> So Delilah said to Samson, "Please tell me where your great strength lies, and with what you may be bound to afflict you."
> And Samson said to her, "If they bind me with seven fresh bowstrings, not yet dried, then I shall become weak, and be like any other man." (16:1–7)

Samson lies to her about the bowstrings while perhaps chuckling to himself about how his physical strength has never deserted him, despite all of his broken spiritual vows. To be above the law, and above the lot of common men, is the central conceit of great tragic protagonists like Oedipus, a flaw that the Greeks called **hubris**; and in his folly Samson continues intimate relations even as Delilah's hostile intentions become ever clearer:

> So the lords of the Philistines brought up to her seven fresh bowstrings, not yet dried, and she bound him with them. Now men were lying in wait, staying with her in the room. And she said to him, "The Philistines are upon you, Samson!" But he broke the bowstrings as a strand of yarn breaks when it touches fire. So the secret of his strength was not known. (16:8–9)

More repetitions ensue: "you have mocked me and told me lies," she poutingly says. "Bind me securely with new ropes," he replies, or "weave the seven locks of my head into the web of the loom" (in the second case, clearly he's edging toward the truth), but when the Philistines break in upon him, he breaks free from the ropes and the loom and evades capture (16:10–14).

Finally, worn down by her complaints and with his eyes wide shut to her malicious intent, he commits his supreme folly and reveals his sacred secret. He seems to presume that he is somehow so indispensable to God – or so independently strong – that he will continue to prevail. But, lulled to sleep on her knees and shorn as clean as a sheep, he awakes to his self-made nightmare, betrayed into permanent darkness:

> Then she began to torment him, and his strength left him. And she said, "The Philistines are upon you, Samson!" So he awoke from his sleep, and said, "I will go out as before, at other times, and shake myself free!" But he did not know that the LORD had departed from him. Then the Philistines took him and put out his eyes, and brought him down to Gaza. They bound him with bronze fetters, and he became a grinder in the prison. (16:19–21)

"O dark, dark, dark, amid the blaze of noon," poignantly cries Milton's Samson, "eyeless in Gaza!" (*Samson Agonistes* ll. 80, 41). And clearly the biblical Samson experiences a terrible *peripeteia*, and presents what even Aristotle would call a remarkable **opsis**, or visual spectacle. But does Samson display *anagnorisis* or self-knowledge? In more biblical terms, does he experience repentance, the deep remorse for sin modeled in the Psalms?

The narrator begins to foreshadow some turn for Samson by telling us that "the hair of his head began to grow again after it had been shaven" (16:22). He further builds tension with an account of the gloating Philistine praise of their god Dagon, victorious over *Yahweh* and his now-blind *Shophet*, and when he is summoned to dance in the temple like a blind, chained monkey, Samson – not previously a man much given to prayer – calls out "O Lord GOD, remember me, I pray!" Yet what does he pray? To be forgiven? To deliver his people from slavery? "Strengthen me, I pray, just this once, O God, that I may with one blow take vengeance on the Philistines for my two eyes!" (16:28). It is this merely vindictive and self-referential prayer that God nevertheless answers, as Samson pushes against the temple pillars and Dagon's house comes tumbling down amid great mayhem. But Samson, a very blunt instrument of the LORD, is a far cry from the humble Moses or the patriotic Deborah or the soulful David – in fact, he seems to have little soul at all, especially for one whose birth was announced by an angel. He is the tag-end of the Hebrew heroes, not quite aware enough for full tragedy. Driven by brawn, bravado, and desire, he is a divine bludgeon – rather like the jawbone of an ass – and exists at the border where heroism shades over into villainy.

Samson the Outsider Hero

The "outsider hero" in literature and film is a figure who lives on the edges of society, often as a lone outcast, acting against social norms and rules, and who yet intervenes to save the society that rejects him. Outwardly cool and even apparently hostile, he nevertheless acts with more courage and integrity than the respectable, hypocritical, and cowardly citizenry. A staple of western, mystery, noir, and action genres (and of course of a biblical epic like the film *Samson and Delilah* with Victor Mature and Hedy Lamarr), he is sexually adventurous, overtly self-interested, but nevertheless has a reluctant streak of honesty and compassion, and can be destroyed by female wiles – and sometimes ennobled by female love. Sam Spade and Rick Blaine (Humphrey Bogart) in *The Maltese Falcon* and *Casablanca*; Shane (Alan Ladd) in *Shane*; Tom Doniphon (John Wayne) in *The Man Who Shot Liberty Valance*; Harry Callahan (Clint Eastwood) in *Dirty Harry*; Jake Geddes (Jack Nicholson) in *Chinatown*; Danny Dravot and Peachey Carnehan (Sean Connery and Michael Caine) in *The Man Who Would Be King* – all are Samson's brothers.

8.2.3   The Anti-Hero: "Right in His Own Eyes"

If Samson is a tragic figure, he also rubs elbows in Judges with characters who have something more of the villain about them, yet fall short of full villainy. These characters often are called **anti-heroes** – men who, in one or many ways, rebel against social and cultural norms or against divine laws, generating high interest and varying degrees of sympathy from audiences, but also increasing degrees of condemnation. Since the Book of Judges is organized around progressive spiritual decay, stories of these anti-heroes become more numerous – and more dark – as the book unfolds. If Samson loses his eyes (and his life) in his highly flawed, fatally successful service to the LORD, these anti-heroic stories – of **Abimelech, Jephthah, Micah**, and finally the vicious **"War of the Levite's Concubine"** – exemplify the book's repeated diagnosis of Israelite decadence as a kind of anarchic, willful blindness: "In those days there was no king in Israel; everyone did what was right in his own eyes" (17:6, 18:1, 19:1, 21:5).

   Abimelech's story picks up where the story of his father, Gideon, leaves off. We are told that the Israelites did not "show kindness to the house of Jerubbaal (Gideon) in accordance with the good he had done for Israel" (8:35), and neither does Abimelech. We learn that he is illegitimate, Gideon's son by his "female servant" (9:18), and like the infamous Shakespearean bastard Edmund in *King Lear*, the lesson that Abimelech seems to have learned from his outcast status is to do unto others *before* they do unto you. The "others" in question are his seventy brothers – Gideon had become quite the patriarch – whom Abimelech conspires with the Shechemites to slaughter wholesale, and then accepts from them the crown that his father had rejected. (Ironically, he may have been incited by the pagan Canaanite name Gideon gave him: *Abi-Melech* means, literally, "Father-King" and, besides hinting that Gideon was somehow royal after all, it also echoes the name of the blood-drenched God-King Moloch, demander of child sacrifice.)

Obviously, a "king" alone will not cure what ails Israel: a Godless crown leads only to further disaster. This fratricidal massacre earns the curse of the one escaped brother, Jotham, so that "God sent a spirit of ill will between Abimelech and the men of Shechem" (9:23). Within three years he alienates these king-makers and, in the battles that result, is in the end killed while besieging a city when a woman rather comically drops a millstone on his head. Rather than be remembered as another Sisera, killed by a woman, he orders his armor-bearer to thrust him through – an ignominious end to a man who would be king, who did what was right in his own eyes, but whose civil slaughters undid his father's good work.

The narrator passes over the judgeships of **Tola** and **Jair** with only the briefest mentions, stating merely that Jair "had thirty sons who rode on thirty donkeys; they also had thirty towns" (10:4), suggesting that the office of Judge is becoming one of wealth and influence – perhaps to a fault. And indeed following these judgeships the Israelites reach a new low in religious corruption:

> Then the children of Israel again did evil in the sight of the LORD, and served the Baals and the Ashtoreths, the gods of Syria, the gods of Sidon, the gods of Moab, the gods of the people of Ammon, and the gods of the Philistines; and they forsook the LORD and did not serve him. (10:6)

The sheer variety and multiplicity of their idolatries bespeak their spiritual prostitution. So it is ironically fitting, when again "the anger of the LORD was hot against Israel," and he "sold them into the hands" of the Philistines and the Ammonites (10:7–18), that their next Deliverer should be **Jephthah**, "the son of a harlot" (11:1).

The "whoreson" Jephthah's illegitimacy thus doubles Abimelech's illegitimacy, but also (remember the redeemed harlot Rahab) casts him as a potentially sympathetic underdog. From this lowly beginning, Jephthah develops as an outsider hero, cast out by his family and living in exile away from his people while establishing himself as a powerful bandit leader and guerilla fighter; he is described, like Gideon, as "a mighty man of valor" (11:1), a Hebrew Braveheart. When his fellow Gileadites desperately invite him back to lead the Hebrews in battle against the invading Ammonites and the Amorites, the embittered outcast drives a hard bargain: "If you take me back home to fight against the people of Ammon, and the LORD delivers them to me, shall I be your head?" (11:9), he demands; and the elders swear an oath of obedience to Jephthah before the LORD at Mizpah. Then the newly made *Shophet* issues a bold challenge to the Ammonite king, dismissing their claims to the land by their god Chemosh, and asserting Israelite rights in the name of *Yahweh* (11:12–28).

But the anti-heroic potential in Jephthah's situation and character soon bear bitter fruit. Despite his "God-talk," Jephthah's upbringing in decadent Israel, compounded by his foreign sojourn among heathen bandits, has left him with a semi-pagan understanding of divine intervention: that for services rendered, the gods demands payment in precious blood. So before going to war, Jephthah makes a rash vow: if God gives him victory, then "whatever" – or, significantly, whomever – "comes out of the doors of my house to meet me, when I return in peace from the people of Ammon, shall surely be the LORD's, and I will offer it up as a burnt offering" (11:31).

In the event, he returns triumphant to Mizpah, since with God's aid the campaign is a foregone conclusion, bringing a victory over twenty cities that is described in two short verses (11:32–33). But the cost of victory is supreme, for who should run from his house to greet him but his daughter! She comes out to meet him with timbrels and dancing; and she was his only child. Besides her he had neither son nor daughter. And it came to pass, when he saw her, that he tore his clothes, and said, "Alas, my daughter! You have brought me very low! You are among those who trouble me! For I have given my word to the LORD, and I cannot go back on it." (11:34–35)

What follows, while touching and pathetic, is a species of superstitious vow-keeping that violates the absolute Hebrew prohibition against human sacrifice (Deuteronomy 12:31; 18:9–10). While Jephthah's daughter is allowed some time to wander on the mountains of Israel and bewail her wasted life, no one – least of all Jephthah – ever thinks of putting God's commandment "You shall not kill" before a Canaanite ritual. Doubling the irony, though it seems right in the eyes of the Israelites for Jephthah to treat his vow as ironclad, they soon will break their own solemn oaths to the LORD with easy abandon.

Jephthah's Daughter, Iphigenia, and Ophelia

Jephthah's sacrifice of his unnamed daughter anticipates Agamemnon's tragic sacrifice of Iphigenia, except that the Greek acts in advance, to obtain favorable winds for Troy – as portrayed in Euripides' tragic drama *Iphigenia at Aulis* (408–406 BCE). Significantly, when in *Hamlet* the Prince wants to suggest that Polonius is willing to sacrifice his daughter – "the fair Ophelia" – by using her to spy on her lover, Hamlet compares Polonius not to the heathen Agamemnon but to the Hebrew Jephthah:

> *HAM.*   O Jephthah, judge of Israel, what a treasure hadst thou!
> *POL.*   What a treasure had he, my lord?
> *HAM.*   Why
> 　　　　*One fair daughter and no more,*
> 　　　　*The which he loved passing well.*
> *POL.*   [*Aside.*] Still on my daughter.
> *HAM.*   Am I not i' the right, old Jephthah?
> *POL.*   If you call me Jephthah, my lord, I have a daughter that I love passing well.
> *HAM.*   Nay, that follows not. (*Hamlet* 2.2.285–293)

Jephthah's brief career after the sacrifice of his daughter is marked by renewed division and infighting among the Hebrews, as the Ephraimites object to having been left out of the battle against Ammon. When matters come to blows at the fords of the River Jordan, Jephthah resorts to a famous linguistic test to weed out Ephraimite escapees: any suspicious traveler is told to say "*Shibboleth*" ("stream" or "torrent"), which the Ephraimites – lacking a "sh" phoneme – pronounce "*Sibboleth*," to their immediate doom. "There fell at that time forty-two thousand Ephraimites" (12:1–6). So "Shibboleth" has entered our language as any in-group word or phrase used to exclude those outside the circle of ideology, power, or privilege. And Jephthah, who began his judgeship by uniting the Israelites against common enemies, ends it after only six years having slaughtered thirty Hebrew battalions for mispronunciation.

Jephthah has three immediate successors: **Ibzan** of Bethlehem, **Elon** the Zebulunite, and **Abdon** the Pirathonite. They are unremarkable – or at least unremarked – except for the notable fact that they have many children who make many dynastic marriages and ride many donkeys (12:8–15). It seems right in the eyes of these *Shophetim* that they should above all be heroes to their families; that their closest relatives should flourish and prosper during their service as judges and deliverers – even if no particular services or judgments or deliverances are recorded to counter the anti-heroic trend of their era. These three are followed by **Samson's** famously tragic judgeship (13–16), which we already have discussed as a story that builds our expectations of a heroic revival under a God-anointed leader, only to dash those expectations, but the story nevertheless ends in divine deliverance despite – indeed through – the hero's fall. Significantly, by Samson's time the Israelites have ceased even to "cry out" for deliverance; any help comes through sheer divine grace.

After Samson's flickering light is extinguished, the final five chapters of Judges step back from the chronological succession of *Shophetim* to conclude with a coda about the full consequences of political, spiritual, and moral anarchy. These chapters seem to be set in the time of the earlier judges, during the High Priesthood of Phinehas, grandson of Aaron (20:28). The story of Micah in chapters 17–18 begins on a strange but potentially hopeful note: Micah, who has stolen from his mother, confesses this theft and returns the goods, a heavy cache of silver. The mother is grateful and forgiving, but then what seems to be a touching interlude of domestic reconciliation takes a perverse turn when the mother joyously sets about fulfilling her dream: hiring a silversmith to make an ephod – an idolatrous replica of the priestly garment – and a "molded image."

Time passes, and her son Micah compounds this idolatry by building an entire family shrine with many images, and consecrates his son as its priest. Then Micah completes the sin by hiring a passing young Levite from Bethlehem to "[d]well with me, and be a father and a priest to me, and I will give you ten *shekels* of silver per year, a suit of clothes, and your sustenance." Then, without comment, the narrator quotes Micah's happy reflection, "Now I know that the LORD will be good to me, since I have a Levite as priest!" (17:4, 10, 13). The principles of narrative minimalism and deferred judgment are in play, as the hearers are invited to recall their knowledge of the Levitical law, forbidding this very sort of "magical thinking" by outlawing all idolatry and the prostitution of the priestly office for private gain.

Meanwhile, while this tale of individual idolatry and clerical corruption unfolds, members of the entire tribe of Dan are seeking a more pleasant homeland; so, in what seems to be an extension of Joshua's conquest, they send out spies who discover a quiet town called Laish, unprotected and unallied, and resolve to conquer it for their people. However, as the story develops, we learn that they intend to establish their own syncretistic worship center by hiring away the very Levite whom Micah had hired away from Bethlehem! The spectacle of this rent-a-priest gleefully selling his services to the stronger, higher bidder, and Micah's shocked, shocked complaint about the injustice of it all – "you have taken away my gods!" (18:24) – lend a dark and cynical coloring to what turns out to be an ironic travesty, not a fulfillment, of Joshua's mission.

But the worst and weirdest are to come. Chapter 19 begins with another reminder that "in those days there was no king in Israel" (19:1) and then tells a sordid anti-heroic tale that takes us to the nadir of kingless anarchy, and yet foreshadows the misbegotten reign of Israel's first king, Saul the Benjamite of Gibeah. The story begins with another compromised and worldly Levite, who takes a concubine from the little town of Bethlehem, and then loses her when she "plays the harlot" – as if she weren't already fornicating as his concubine – and then flees to her indulgent father to avoid punishment. When the Levite travels to Bethlehem to "speak kindly to her and to bring her back," the father detains him beyond his planned stay, and when the couple finally depart, the delay puts them outside the Canaanite city of Jebus (later Jerusalem) near nightfall. Building ironic tension, the Levite decides not to "turn aside here into a city of foreigners, who are not of the children of Israel; we will go on to Gibeah" (19:12). Surely, he reasons, the heathen will mistreat them, while their fellow Hebrews will show them hospitality.

What follows in Gibeah is the sort of scenario now common in the lucrative horror film genre: the isolated, inbred town, its darkening streets deserted, its doors bolted and windows shuttered, with wild eyes leering through the cracks and animal-like sounds in the thickening dusk. Neighborliness and hospitality seem dead, replaced by paranoia and a scent of lust in the air. One nervous, well-meaning old-timer approaches and invites them in out of the open square for the night, offering food, wine, fodder for animals, and a wash – the last vestige of old-fashioned decency. The Levite breathes a sigh of relief, and so may we. But indecency is now the order of the day, and of the night – as from all quarters the men of the town gather to pound at the lone host's door and demand that he "[b]ring out the man who came to your house, that we may know him carnally!" (19:22). For this anti-heroic horror story also repeats the worst pagan deeds of Sodom and Gomorrah, "the Cities of the Plain," in this Israelite mountain town – peopled by the descendants of Jacob's favored son Benjamin. The citizens have cast off hospitality, legal limits, sexual restraint, and even natural desire, practicing sheer transgression for its own sake.

In what may be the most unsparingly realistic account found in the entire Bible, we follow the sickening descent into a world of utmost violation, Hobbesean in its total betrayal of all by all: the host betrays his own daughter, offering her to the mob, while the Levite casts his unfaithful concubine out into a scrum of rapists, bolting the door after her. The next day's sun rises on darkness visible:

> Then the woman came as the day was dawning, and fell down at the door of the man's house where her master was, till it was light.
>
> When her master arose in the morning, and opened the doors of the house and went out to go his way, there was his concubine, fallen at the door of the house with her hands on the threshold. And he said to her, "Get up and let us be going." But there was no answer. (19:26–28)

The ravaged woman lies still and cold in the traditional suppliant's posture, with her imploring hands on the threshold. The Levite's response moves from monstrous indifference – no expression of regret, sympathy, or kindness – to monstrous anger, as he loads her onto his beast and carries her the rest of the way home, where "[w]hen he entered his house he took a knife, laid hold of his concubine, and divided her into twelve pieces, limb by limb, and sent her throughout all the territory of Israel" (19:29). With grotesque irony, the Levite's priestly butchering skills with animals are put to use on a human, supposedly his beloved. His bloody action also reminds the first audience for the book – a few centuries later in the Davidic era – of how King Saul had once declared war by dividing an ox in twelve pieces like bloody telegrams to the tribes (I Samuel 11:7). More significantly, though, for later history, this heinous crime against the Levite's concubine was done in Saul's own tribe of Benjamin, and his home town of Gibeah. Even as the storyteller would remember the past evil anarchy before the kings, he also subtly reminds his people of the evils yet to come from bad kings.

The Levite's grisly epistles have exceedingly violent effects, as the shock waves of moral and spiritual chaos in Gibeah radiate outward to all the Hebrews, producing – for the first time in Judges since the opening chapters – a perverse kind of national unity, as the tribes take up arms to punish this outrage in Israel. So the book that began with a unified nation, moving to drive out Canaanite evil, ends with a unified nation turning its violence inward on its own heartland. In the white heat of their righteous wrath, the Israelites very nearly exterminate all of Benjamin:

> And the children of Israel destroyed that day twenty-five thousand one hundred Benjamites ... and struck them down with the edge of the sword – from every city, men and beasts, all who were found. They also set fire to all the cities they came to. (Judges 20:35, 48)

Then, when their bloodlust has passed, a sudden remorse takes hold: "They lifted up their voices and wept bitterly, and said, 'O LORD God of Israel, why has this come to pass in Israel, that today there should be one tribe missing in Israel?'" (21:2–3). To compound the pitch-black comedy of errors, the tribes mandate a holy assembly of mourning for the Benjamites whom they have slaughtered – and then, when one group (Jabesh-Gilead) sends no representatives, the assembly puts aside its peace offerings long enough to attack and exterminate the no-shows! Determined to re-establish the missing Benjamites, they give the female survivors from Jabesh-Gilead to the few surviving men of Benjamin, and then proceed to abduct more wives for their brothers from "the dancing daughters of Shiloh." From berserk vengeance to wailing remorse back to berserk vengeance followed by mass kidnaping and rape, the final verses of Judges portray a nation spiraling downward, led by nameless non-entities, and out of control. And then the final repeated reminder: "In those days there was no king in Israel; everyone did what was right in his own eyes" (21:25). If the foundations are destroyed, what can the righteous do?

8.3 "Famous in Bethlehem": Ruth and Boaz, Local Heroes

In a time of collapsing foundations and libertine chaos, when, as W. B. Yeats put it, "the best lack all conviction / And the worst are full of passionate intensity," what, indeed, can the righteous do? In their small way, a great deal, as it turns out in Ruth, the next book of the Old Testament. "Now it came to pass, in the day when the judges ruled," begins this little book about some decidedly minor and sadly unfortunate people, about outcasts living through hard times against a background of increasingly anarchic tribalism. Like the narrative of Joseph in the Book of Genesis, the Book of Ruth is a kind of tragicomedy, beginning as the tragic action afflicts the protagonist early on with dire suffering that involves family loss, far distances traveled, material ruin or death, and the long passage of time. Then, at the point of maximum loss and darkness, good abruptly triumphs, with comic returns and discoveries involving repentance and family reconciliation – and revealing a providential design.

The Book of Ruth is also a masterpiece of **short narrative**, disarmingly brief and apparently simple in its account of quiet, local heroism, but ramifying outward and upward in its conclusion to embrace national and indeed cosmic destiny. Its heroine and its hero are both exemplars of domestic virtue, and if, as the popular saying goes, "well-behaved women seldom make history," Ruth is certainly an exception. Ruth's book sings the unsung: in her perseverance, her loyalty, her humble servanthood, and her heartfelt affection and kindness, Ruth represents the unobtrusive strengths that seek the shade and the background, and that live to make life livable for others.

And yet, Ruth comes from an unlikely place for a household angel. A daughter of the tribe of Moab, she descends from the original, incestuous sin of Lot and his daughter, and inherits a terrible curse:

> An Ammonite or Moabite shall not enter the assembly of the LORD; even to the tenth generation none of his descendants shall enter the assembly of the LORD forever, because they did not meet you with bread and water on the road when you came out of Egypt, and because they hired against you Balaam the son of Beor … (Deuteronomy 23:3–4)

Illegitimate, inhospitable, implacable, and worshipers of Chemosh – a god who demanded child sacrifice – the Moabites seemed to the Hebrews a thoroughly bad lot, and Ruth was one of them. Indeed, it took terrible disaster to compel Israelites into relations with Moab – the disaster of the famine in Judah that originally drives Elimelech, his wife Naomi, and their sons Mahlon and Chilion out of the ironically named "Bethlehem" ("house of bread") into the forbidden land to the east over the Dead Sea (Ruth 1:1). There a further drumbeat of disaster follows them: during their ten-year sojourn, Elimelech dies, leaving Naomi a widow, and then her sons, after stooping to marry Moabite women, die as well, leaving Naomi desolate, in a cursed and foreign land, and saddled with two childless young Gentile widows.

So the first we hear from Naomi is, not surprisingly, a lament designed to separate the daughters-in-law from her as she turns her face toward Judah again, where she has heard that "the LORD has visited his people by giving them bread" (1:6):

> "Go, return each to her mother's house."... So she kissed them, and they lifted up their voices and wept. And they said to her, "Surely we will return with you to your people." But Naomi said, "Turn back, my daughters; why will you go with me? Are there still sons in my womb, that they may be your husbands? Turn back, my daughters, go – for I am too old to have a husband." (1:9–12)

Naomi's mournful refrain – "return … turn back … turn back" – has a partial effect; or rather, it convinces one of the two, Orpah, to turn back "to her people and her gods," having fulfilled her natural obligations. But Ruth's obligation seems supernatural: "Orpah kissed her mother-in-law, but Ruth clung to her." Ruth's words have come down to us in all of their fine simplicity as a definitive statement of loyalty:

> Entreat me not to leave you,
> Or to turn back from following after you;
> For wherever you go, I will go;
> And wherever you lodge, I will lodge;
> Your people shall be my people,
> And your God, my God. (1:14–16)

Yet, rather than rejoicing at such love for her and her God, Naomi bitterly resigns herself to Ruth's unwanted company, and "stops speaking to her." After what is no doubt a grim journey, their entry into Judah and into Bethlehem compounds her bitterness: the village is astir with their coming; "Is this Naomi?" the local women ask, as if amazed at how life has altered her.

"But she said to them, 'Do not call me *Naomi* [Hebrew for "pleasant"]; call me *Mara* ["bitter"], for the Almighty has dealt very bitterly with me'" (1:19–20). Naomi would rename herself, and not insignificantly her name here for God highlights not his covenant love – *Yahweh* – but his sheer power, and a cruel and arbitrary power it seems. However, this tragic opening chapter ends with the hint of better things ahead: "Now they came to Bethlehem" – now truly a "house of bread" – "at the beginning of barley harvest," in the month of *Aviv* or *Nisan* – this is, the first harvest in the Spring (1:22).

Here enters the account, as yet unnoticed by the mother-in-law and "the Moabitess," "a relative of Naomi's husband, a man of great wealth, of the family of Elimelech. His name was Boaz." How near a relative? We may wonder, for much will hang on that nearness. Regardless, Ruth takes the initiative, asking Naomi's permission to "'go to the field, and glean heads of grain after him in whose sight I may find favor'... And she happened to come to the part of the field belonging to Boaz" (2:1–3). And in the Bible, Chance is God's pen name.

What can be said initially about Boaz? Besides his wealth and his family connection to Elimelech, his name means "swift," and indeed he is a man of action; he is not a young man, but of middle years; and he is cheerfully devout not only in word but in action and thought – the first words out of his mouth are "The LORD be with you!" which inspire "The LORD bless you!" in response from his workers (2:4). He is the sort of man who brings out the best in others, even in bad times, and the times are bad: besides the general context of Judges-era anarchy, there is the recent long famine, and the barely submerged threat of sexual assault even in Bethlehem – "Have I not commanded the young men not to touch you?" (2:9).

But above all, Boaz is a shrewd judge of character, while remaining generous and kind. In biblical narrative, as on stage, action is eloquence, and his actions speak fluently of his unostentatious love of God's Law, and of the widow, the stranger, and the sojourner whom that Law protects. Without fanfare, he acts as the *Goel* or "Kinsman-Redeemer" described in Numbers 35 and Deuteronomy 25. By ever-increasing degrees, he recognizes goodness in Ruth and rewards it: first inquiring who that new young woman gleaner is; then calling her "daughter" and instructing her to glean among his reaping women where the pickings are full, and to drink from their vessels; then praising her loyalty to Naomi and to the LORD, rather than shouldering her aside as a "Moabitess"; then inviting her to share the midday meal with his crew; and finally instructing his workers to let her "glean even among the sheaves" and to "let grain from the bundles fall purposely for her" (2:5–16). Significantly, he shows her increasing favor while nevertheless allowing her the dignity of work to earn her keep. His is the exemplary application of Hebrew "poor law," which seeks to reward the working poor with increasing opportunity rather than encouraging dependency that saps initiative.

Ruth is – a least by the rough agrarian standards and muted romantic expectations of the time – literally swept off her feet by her graying benefactor. "So she fell on her face, bowed down to the ground, and said to him, 'Why have I found favor in your eyes, that you should take notice of me, since I am a foreigner?'" This initial reaction is perhaps simply grateful awe at this important man's strange kindness to strangers. But a suggestion of tenderness and yearning creeps into her words later in the day, as the signs of his interest increase: "Let me find favor in your sight, my lord; for you have comforted me, and have spoken kindly to your maidservant, though I am not like one of your maidservants" (2:10, 13).

If Boaz's intervention sparks warmth in Ruth's heart, it sparks unfamiliar hope in Naomi's. When Ruth tells her from whom she received the overflowing measures of grain which she brings home, the name and the praise of *Yahweh* return to Naomi's lips, and a matchmaker's gleam to her eye: "'Blessed be he of the LORD, who has not forsaken his kindness to the living and the dead!' And Naomi said to her, 'This man is a relation of ours, one of our close relatives'" (2:20). How close? Time will tell.

Ruth 3 begins with Naomi playing the full *yenta* as she instructs Ruth on how to "secure" her future – and her man. Naomi's instructions assume that the reader knows the law of Levirate marriage as found in Deuteronomy 25:5:

> If brothers dwell together, and one of them dies and has no son, the widow of the dead man shall not be married to a stranger outside the family; her husband's brother shall go in to her, take her as his wife, and perform the duty of a husband's brother to her.

Yet Naomi's advice leaves little to chance – humorously, Naomi speaks as if God will help Ruth the more that Ruth helps herself: specifically, by amplifying her own assets and catching Boaz at his most merry. "Therefore wash yourself and anoint yourself, put on your best garment and go down to the threshing floor; but do not make yourself known to the man until he has finished eating and drinking." Then, and not before, "you shall go in, uncover his feet, and lie down; and he will tell you what you should do" (3:3–4).

What, exactly, is it that Naomi is telling Ruth to do? And how, specifically, does she expect Boaz to respond? It's possible that she means literally what she says – that Ruth is to lie at Boaz's actual feet and await his further instructions, like a submissive servant or a good dog. But since the "feet" are not infrequently a Hebrew euphemism for the genitals, Naomi is more likely proposing that Ruth make a sexual overture to Boaz and then wait for the man – who is a little worse, or better, for the wine – to consummate the Levirate marriage on the spot, sealing the deal for good and all.

However we read those "feet," Boaz certainly is in for a surprise. "Now it happened at midnight that the man was startled, and turned himself; and there, a woman was lying at his feet. And he said, 'Who are you?'" Ruth's reply combines a tender plea with a legal claim: "I am Ruth, your maidservant. Take your maidservant under your wing, for you are a close relative" (3:8–9). It's worth noting that Ruth is repeating – and as it turns out, redeeming – past scandalous behavior of her and Boaz's ancestors. Lot's daughters had crept in upon their drunken father to conceive his incestuous sons Ammon and Moab (Genesis 19:30–38); while Tamar had deceived her father-in-law Judah into fulfilling his Levirate duty when she impersonated a prostitute (Genesis 38). But Ruth's behavior – while to our ears sexually *risqué* – is the deed of a fine and chaste widow seeking to provide for her family within God's law, while Boaz is not drunk but "cheerful," and his reply is endearingly delighted, and yet virtuously restrained.

> Blessed are you of the LORD, my daughter! For you have shown more kindness at the end than at the beginning, in that you did not go after young men, whether poor or rich. And now, my daughter, do not fear. I will do for you all that you request… Now it is true that I am a close relative; however, there is a relative closer than I. Stay this night, and in the morning it shall be that if he will perform the duty of a close relative for you – good; let him do it. But if he does not want to perform the duty for you, then I will perform the duty for you, as the LORD lives! (3:10–13)

Here is a man merry with wine, lying at ease literally in the midst of his abundance, and a sweet-smelling young woman offers herself to him in the night for a no-fault "roll in the hay." However, though he is flattered and touched that she has sought him rather than "young men," he will take no advantage of this attractive foreigner. If her heart rises when he promises "I will do for you," perhaps it sinks a bit when he calls her "my daughter" and his integrity compels him to admit that there is a closer relative who may have to "perform the duty" instead. Yet if he won't, Boaz most certainly will, "as the LORD lives!" The mixture of sincere piety and romantic eagerness is especially affecting here.

Boaz shows touching concern for Ruth's welfare and honor. Filling her shawl with six "measures" or *ephahs* of barley (about 60 pounds!), he "laid it on her" and sent her home before morning light so that the town will not know of her visit and gossip. And upon Ruth's return to the house, Naomi knows that Boaz's "swift" and active character will ensure a quick denouement: "Sit still, my daughter, until you know how the matter will turn out; for the man will not rest until he has concluded the matter this day" (3:18).

And he does not rest. The final chapter begins with Boaz going immediately to the council seats in the city gates and pressing the matter with the closer male relative. Amusingly, this potential rival suitor is left nameless, and is called only *peloni almoni* or "so and so" in the text, so that we're invited to see him as a vacillating and selfish foil to the dutiful and ardent Boaz. The narrative creates suspense by raising a previously unmentioned real estate transaction: Boaz invites the man to buy back from Naomi a piece of the late Elimelech's land, and the man jumps at the chance to expand his holdings. But then Boaz discloses the other duties in the bargain: "On the day you buy the field from the hand of Naomi, you must also buy it from Ruth the Moabitess, the wife of the dead, to perpetuate the name of the dead through his inheritance." The "so and so," who knows exactly what "perpetuate" means in this context, abruptly reverses himself, saying "I cannot redeem it for myself, lest I ruin my own inheritance" (4:5–6). Not wanting to father or raise a child in another man's name – and who knows, not wanting to have relations with a "Moabitess" or to displease his wife or wives or children – the fellow begs off, opening the field, in both senses, to Boaz.

In the presence of ten elders in the gate, the two men finalize the transaction with the traditional exchange of sandals (the narrator's explanation of the custom indicates that it had gone out of use by the date of writing) and the elders extend their blessing: "The LORD make the woman who is coming to your house like Rachel and Leah …; and may you prosper in Ephrathah and be famous in Bethlehem." This would seem to be more than enough for the modest Ruth and Boaz: a place in the Israelite line, a devoted spouse and children, a full barn and the admiration of their neighbors, with the approval of God. What more could they expect? What else would such local heroes desire than to be "famous in Bethlehem"? "So Boaz took Ruth and she became his wife; and when he went in to her, the LORD gave her conception, and she bore a son" (4:11, 13).

Significantly, though, the woman of the village imagine and expect even more than do their men, blessing the newborn boy, and his grandmother, whose days of bitterness are past: "Blessed be the LORD, who has not left you this day without a close relative; and may his name be famous in Israel!" And even this national fame undershoots the mark, for "they called his name Obed. He is the father of Jesse, the father of David" (4:17). The infant Obed – whose name means "servant" or "worshiper" – is ancestor to the greatest of Hebrew kings, who will reunite the Twelve Tribes, conquer and establish his capital in nearby Jerusalem, subdue and incorporate the surrounding peoples (including the Moabites) into his empire, and father a royal line that will survive even the division and fall of the Kingdom to await restoration in the messianic "son of David." And when David's son Solomon builds the Temple in Jerusalem, supported by two great front pillars, one of them will be named Boaz for the man "famous in Bethlehem," and the other Jachin, for "foundation" (I Kings 7:13–22, 41–42).

Having glimpsed briefly ahead from the acorn to the oak, the narrator returns finally to this Founding Father, and mother, happy enough in little Bethlehem. The tragicomic reversal is complete: disaster becomes blessing, bitterness is transformed to pleasure, and desolation blooms. Domestic heroes both, Boaz and Ruth personify the mundane, homely virtues on which peoples and nations and civilizations are built, easy to ignore and easier to denigrate, plain as earth and sweat and tears and corn – and without which all grandeur and glory and power eventually tumble. Perhaps well-behaved women – or men – seldom make history; certainly history is filled with memorably ill-behaved actors of both sexes who have sought to make a name for themselves and succeeded at terrible cost. But Ruth and Boaz are the antidotes to that kind of history, quietly overcoming the encroaching chaos with their daily good. The best of human history would not be made without such unknown and local heroes, and like a monument to an unknown soldier, the Book of Ruth represents the nameless, those content to do well and to love mercy, known but to God, and their neighbors – and occasionally, as this story goes, to all the earth.

And what can we say about Ruth herself as specifically a women's hero? The women of Bethlehem have the last word, praising her to Naomi as "better to you than seven sons" (4:15). Considering the bankable value of sons in their world, and the perfect implications of "seven," Ruth is presented as a model second to none for women's work and life. This foreign convert is adopted as the domestic ideal, bearing in mind that this ideal (as in Proverbs 31) blurs the distinction between what we have come to call "domestic" and "civic" virtue; that is, between the life of the family and the life of the city. Ruth, like Rachel and Leah, is a called a "builder of Israel" even in a time when "everyone did what was right in his own eyes": she keeps her vows, cheerfully shoulders her load, provides for herself and for the needy, charms and holds her husband (and her mother-in-law!), wins over a rather bigoted town, and raises a line of world-beaters leading to the Anointed One. The Bible's female heroes include warrior women, poets, beauty queens, redeemed harlots, and entrepreneurs, but none, in the end, can be said to have more long-term effect than Ruth among Israel's founding mothers. Mere words, like beauty, can be vain. "Let her works praise her in the gates."

Questions for Discussion

1 How does a heroic figure like **Joshua** resemble and differ from Classical heroes like Achilles, Odysseus, and Aeneas?

2 What later **historical conquerors** have claimed Joshua as a precedent?

3 Why does the **Book of Judges** begin and end in the way that it does? What is the book's overall narrative arc? What lessons about human nature and human government is it designed to teach?

4 How are the Judges or ***Shophetim*** different from Kings or ***Melechim***? How are they similar?

5 Consider the variety of heroic types in the Book of Judges. How are figures like **Ehud**, **Deborah**, **Jael**, and **Gideon** "alternative" heroes? What difference does gender make in their heroism, if any?

6 What are the tragic elements in the story of **Samson**? How does Samson's story compare to a Classical tragedy like *Oedipus Rex* or a Shakespearean tragedy like *Romeo and Juliet*?

7 Consider the degrees and kinds of "**anti-heroism**" in the stories of **Abimelech**, **Jephthah**, **Micah**, and the "**War of the Levite's Concubine**." What roles do they play in the overall story arc of the Book of Judges?

8 What relation does the **Book of Ruth** have to the world and the themes of the Book of Judges? How are **Ruth** and **Boaz** also alternative heroes? What are the tragicomic elements in their story? How does the Book of Ruth look not only back but forward?

Note

1 Some of these terms – *anagke* and *nemesis* in particular – are not present in the *Poetics*, but have been interpolated from other Aristotelian writings.

9

Biblical Epic II: Making the Kingdom in 1 and 2 Samuel

The Book of Ruth is both a respite from and a correction to the downward spiral of the Book of Judges, reminding us of better things to come, and 1 Samuel both completes the decaying trajectory of Judges and holds out a new hope for Israelite revival. For if the near-anarchy under the *Shophetim* had much to do with the fact that "in those days there was no king in Israel," in Samuel's book the Hebrew monarchy is born. Yet the kingdom almost dies at birth, as the people crown a man who seems every inch a king, but whose tragedy is to be the king whom they want, not the one whom they need.

9.1 Saul's Epic Tragedy: "A King … Like All the Nations" in 1 Samuel

If 1 Samuel contains the fearful and piteous tragedy of King Saul, it also encompasses other literary modes: beginning with the brief tragicomedy of Samuel's mother Hannah, it then presents the adventure-filled **fugitive-hero narrative** of David on the run – a model for the much later English "Robin Hood" tradition – and, above all, it belongs to a great tragicomic epic in the overall arc of 1–2 Samuel, the epic of David's rise, fall, and restoration.

The Whole Book of Samuel

Divided in the Greek Septuagint and in the Christian Old Testament into two parts, the Book of Samuel (Hebrew *Shmuel*, for "heard by God") was originally composed as a literary whole, and still stands as such in the Hebrew Bible. It is probably the work of multiple hands, largely completed toward the end of Solomon's reign in 931 BCE, but it incorporates core material from the transitional period of the judges to the kings (1050–971 BCE), including accounts of the prophet and last *Shophet*, Samuel himself. Much of Samuel is written within the norms of **court history**, with a focus on royal dynasties, but the book also includes perhaps the greatest "underdog" narrative in world literature – the rise of the young David – and unlike the earlier Book of Judges and the later Books of Kings and Chronicles (also single books in the Hebrew Bible), Samuel is built around a few central characters in generous detail. Interpreters often comment on the narrative realism of the book's style, and its sparse – though powerful – incidents of divine and miraculous intervention. In addition to early portions attributable to Samuel (who, after all, is dead before 1 Samuel ends), the book has been credited to the Davidic and Solomonic court prophets Nathan and Gad – and to later unknown editors and redactors. Yet it does not read like "the work of a committee," but as a powerfully integrated whole.

Literary Study of the Bible: An Introduction, First Edition. Christopher Hodgkins.
© 2020 John Wiley & Sons Ltd. Published 2020 by John Wiley & Sons Ltd.

We will look through each of these literary lenses in turn. But first we turn to the tragedy of Saul, and its tragicomic prologue – which includes the original "raiders of the lost ark"!

9.1.1 "The Glory Has Departed": Samuel, the Ark, and Israelite Survival

1 Samuel begins like many a biblical birth narrative: with the grief of a woman who laments her inability to bear children. The woman in question here is Hannah, and in fact, the story of Samuel's conception, birth, and boyhood contains many of the by-now familiar plot elements from Genesis through Judges: the barren wife, the conflicted polygamous marriage, the divine intervention, and the miracle child with a special destiny. Yet despite Hannah's barrenness, her husband Elkanah prefers her to her malicious rival wife, Peninnah, and Hannah proves to be a particularly devoted mother, and also a gifted psalmist. The narrator also makes skillful use of the literary foil in developing the comparison between the next-to-last of the judges, the aged and negligent Eli – with his two wicked sons Hophni and Phinehas – and the sincere and inspired young Samuel. (This comparison anticipates 1 Samuel's eventual controlling contrast between the incompetent and paranoid Saul and the lion-hearted, devout young David.)

As befits a sad story with a happy ending, Hannah's is told with light touches of humor and tenderness. Elkanah, though well-intentioned, is amusingly inept and narcissistic in attempting to comfort his favorite wife: "Hannah, why do you weep? Why do you not eat? And why is your heart grieved? Am I not better to you than ten sons?" (1 Samuel 1:8). Apparently not, as Hannah travels to the Tabernacle at Shiloh to seek the LORD for a miracle, and to escape the needling of Peninnah. Also amusingly, while at Shiloh she is mistaken for a tipsy tippler by Eli: as she fervently but silently mouths her prayers, the ironically myopic seer exhorts her, "How long will you be drunk? Put your wine away from you!" (1:14). This from the man whose priestly sons, we are told, greedily gorged on the sacrificial animals and "lay with the women who assembled at the door of the tabernacle of meeting" (2:13–16, 22).

And lo, God hears Hannah's prayers as she and Elkanah conceive and have a son, whose name (Hebrew *Shmuel*, "heard by God"), memorializes *Yahweh's* answer. True to her promise, she tenderly nurses the boy until he has been weaned, and then brings him to Eli at Shiloh, where "as long as he lives he shall be lent to the LORD" (1:28); and in an especially touching gesture, each year she makes her little priest a new robe for the service of God as yearly he grows "in stature, and in favor both with the LORD and men" (2:18–19, 26). Hannah will be rewarded with other children, and unlike Samson – another judge and Nazirite – Samuel will prove true to his vows. So, like the Book of Ruth just before, 1 Samuel begins with a reminder that, even in difficult times, the faith of ordinary people leads to exponential greatness.

The Psalm of Hannah – 1 Samuel 2:1–10

With memorable phrases like "even the barren has born seven" and "the pillars of the earth are the LORD's," Hannah's poem of praise is of quality equal to the Psalms, and its theme of the proud laid low and the poor raised up makes it a worthy predecessor to Mary's great New Testament Psalm, "The Magnificat":

> He has put down the mighty from their thrones,
> And exalted the lowly.
> He has filled the hungry with good things,
> And the rich He has sent away empty. (Luke 1:52–53)

Furthermore, language like "The LORD kills and makes alive; / He brings down to the grave and brings up" (2:6) clearly inspired lines such as these by the seventeenth-century Metaphysical poet George Herbert:

> These are thy wonders, Lord of power,
> Killing and quickning, bringing down to hell
> And up to heaven in an houre … ("The Flower," ll. 15–17)

Count Hannah among the poets.

Yet even as this opening episode ends brightly, the glory of God seems to be departing from Israel, as the downward spiral of the judges threatens not only the end of an era but of the nation itself. Eli receives a visit from an unnamed "man of God," who prophecies to the erring prophet:

> [T]hose who honor me I will honor, and those who despise me shall be lightly esteemed. Behold, the days are coming that I will cut off your arm and the arm of your father's house, so that there will not be an old man in your house… Now this shall be a sign to you that will come upon your two sons, on Hophni and Phinehas: in one day they shall die, both of them. (2:30–31, 34)

Although, we are told, "the word of the LORD was rare in those days," the man of God's dire prophecy is soon confirmed from the mouth of little Samuel himself, who three times hears a voice calling to him in the night, mistaking the voice for Eli's until his master instructs him to lie still and say, "Speak, LORD, for your servant hears." Ironically, God's words indict Eli yet again: "For I have told him that I will judge his house forever for the iniquity which he knows, because his sons made themselves vile, and he did not restrain them"; also ironically, Eli must solemnly exhort the frightened boy to tell him all; and in a final irony, the exhausted old priest knows better than to object to the verdict: "It is the LORD," he says with resignation. "Let him do what seems good to him" (3:1, 9, 13, 18).

What seems good to *Yahweh* is that Samuel will rise as the nation collapses: "And the word of Samuel came to all Israel" (4:1), while, tragically, the Philistines win a crushing victory over the people at a place called *Ebenezer* (ironically, "stone of help"). More tragically still, the Philistines capture the Ark of the Covenant, which the Israelites had foolishly carried to battle as a kind of good-luck charm ("when it comes among us it may save us from the hand of our enemies" – note the "it" rather than "He" as the "savior"). And the tragedy crescendos when the news comes to Eli as he sits by the Tabernacle gate at Shiloh, "his heart trembl[ing] for the ark of God."

> So the messenger answered and said [to Eli], "Israel has fled before the Philistines, and there has been a great slaughter among the people. Also your two sons, Hophni and Phinehas, are dead; and the ark of God has been captured." Then it happened, *when he made mention of the ark of God*, that Eli fell off the seat backward by the side of the gate; and his neck was broken and he died, for the man was old and heavy. And he had judged Israel forty years. (1 Samuel 4:13, 17–18, emphasis mine)

The slapstick, cartoonish nature of fat old Eli's death deprives it of heroic dignity; yet the narrator does him the justice of noting Eli's grief over the lost Ark, not over his wicked sons, as giving him the fatal stroke. But the tragedy of his failed leadership is great: the people defeated, his worthless sons dishonored and destroyed, the nation's holiest object a trophy of battle, and – to give the defeat a terrible name – Eli's grandson is born to a dead father and a dying mother and called *Ichabod* (Hebrew *I-Khavod*, "inglorious"), for "the glory has departed from Israel" (4:22).

Yet inglorious tragedy shifts toward farce as the Hebrews' seemingly talismanic "god-in-the-box" reasserts himself as God the mighty Deliverer – who strangely enough must begin by delivering himself. A dark comedy of errors ensues as the victorious Philistines carry the Ark of the Covenant to Ashdod and set it up as a tribute in their temple of Dagon – the supreme Philistine deity of fertility, grain, and fish. Yet in the morning Dagon's image is found prostrate on the temple floor before *Yahweh's* Ark, and after being replaced on his pedestal, Dagon is the next morning found with his head and his hands broken across the temple threshold – with only his fish-like torso remaining intact (5:1–5). Clearly, the Hebrew God needs no rescue, but can look out for himself.

Even worse for the Philistines, the wrath of "captive" *Yahweh* breaks out against the people of Ashdod in the form of fatal tumors (the Septuagint and the Vulgate also specify that "rats sprang up," suggesting that these tumors manifested the bubonic plague). Their trophy now a liability, the men of Ashdod fob the Ark off on the five Philistine lords, who send it to the people of Gath, who in return for their hospitality receive severely multiplied judgment, with deadly tumors afflicting "small and great." From Gath to Ekron goes the gift that now no one wants: "They have brought the ark of the God of Israel to us, to kill us and our people! ... let it go back to its own place" (5:6, 9, 10, 11). If the parallels with the plagues of Exodus were not clear enough before, they become explicit as the Philistine priests and diviners ask the people, "Why then do you harden your hearts as the Egyptians and Pharaoh hardened their hearts? When he did mighty things among them, did they not let the people go, that they might depart?" (6:6). So, when the Philistines decide to "let *Yahweh* go," they do so with a tribute manifesting their belief in sympathetic magic: the Ark will be endowed with rich golden images – of tumors and rats! The finest craftsmen of Philistia labor meticulously over these decorative buboes and rodents, and to ensure that the hand of the Hebrew God alone will direct the deadly shrine back to Israel, the Ark is put into a driverless cart drawn by two untrained milk cows who have just been separated from their calves – meaning that the cows' natural inclination will be to return home to their young.

So here we have an exquisitely mad scenario that might have been scripted by Monty Python's Flying Circus:

> they took two milk cows and hitched them to the cart, and shut up their calves at home. And they set the ark of the LORD on the cart, and the chest with the gold rats and the images of their tumors. (6:10–11)

And amidst the madness comes the bovine miracle. The cows, their udders painfully full, nevertheless "headed straight for the road to Beth Shemesh [in Israel], and went along the highway, lowing as they went, and did not turn aside to the right hand or the left" (6:12).

How can the narrator top this strange eventful history? When the cart crosses into Hebrew territory, the men of Beth Shemesh receive their Ark back with great joy. They quite appropriately break up the cart for firewood, slaughter the cows in sacrifice, offer them up as a whole burnt offering – and then, in a fit of killing curiosity, they peek into the holiest of holies, and the LORD "struck seventy men of the people and fifty oxen of a man." Like the terrified Philistines, even God's own people cry out "Who is able to stand before this holy LORD God?" (6:20). Who indeed? For like the Philistines, the terrified Hebrews pass the Ark along until it comes to the town of Kiriath Jearim, and into the priestly hands of Abinadab and his son Eleazar – descendants of Aaron. In retrospect, this judgment on Israel is mixed with greater mercy: for though the faithless Hebrews have earned exile, the Ark has taken their punishment, enduring a temporary banishment, and has worked its own deliverance. Captured and enslaved, dedicated to heathen gods, the Ark brings judgment on both gods and captors, breaking free for return to the land of promise. And yet, as at Sinai, the Ark cannot be tamed even by its own people, any more than its God can be made to serve merely personal or national ends.

Raiding the Lost Ark – For Folklore and Film

The "lost" Ark of the Covenant is one of the great MacGuffins in history. Mentioned in 2 Kings, 2 Chronicles, and Jeremiah as still present in the Temple at the time of Judah's Babylonian Exile in the sixth century BCE, it reappears in the apocryphal/Deutero-Canonical book of 2 Maccabees about 100 years later as rescued by the Hasmoneans. Yet many legends have sprung up about its disappearance and mysterious storage in one exotic locale or another: transported by the Maccabees to Mt. Nebo; by the Abyssinians to Ethiopia or Southern Africa; by the Crusaders to Chartres or Rome, England, or Ireland; by Freemasons to America; even claimed by some to have been found in King Tut's tomb in 1922 (though the "ark" actually found there, while resembling the biblical model, is a good deal smaller and a portable shrine to the god Anubis).

The Ark appears in many reverent film portrayals of biblical times, but perhaps the most famous reimagining takes place in Steven Spielberg's 1981 blockbuster, *Raiders of the Lost Ark*. Spielberg borrows from the Tut story by locating the Ark in an Egyptian tomb, and borrows conceptually from 1 Samuel in the spectacular finale as the Ark wreaks terrible vengeance on those who would desecrate it and use it for their own greedy or wicked ends. An all-American fabulist, Spielberg shows us a parting shot of the Ark confiscated by the US government and secreted in a Nevada warehouse.

Yet Jeremiah, later rabbinic commentators, and the New Testament writer of the Letter to the Hebrews imagine a day when the Ark will be unneeded and forgotten because its holiness will reside in the hearts of all humanity.

If the incident of the lost Ark shows the nation to be near the point of extinction, it also signals the start of a new era under the power of a sovereign God and the leadership of Samuel. In the aftermath of the disastrous days of Eli, with the Philistines pressing in at every side, Samuel calls the tribes together at Mizpah to renew the covenant, telling them to cast out their idols. "So the children of Israel put away the Baals and the Ashtoreths, and served the LORD only... And they fasted that day, and said there, 'We have sinned against the LORD'" (7:4, 6).

The result? A sudden, miraculous and spectacular victory over the Philistines when they gather to crush this Israelite revival: "the LORD thundered with a loud thunder upon the Philistines that day, and so confused them that they were overcome before Israel" (7:10). In a few brief verses – another deliberate narrative anti-climax to stress God's power – generations of Hebrew loss and decline are reversed, true worship is restored, the land taken by the Philistines returns to Israel's control, and peace reigns with the Amorites all the days of Samuel. To sweeten the memory of their defeat under Eli's sons at Ebenezer, "Samuel took a stone and set it up between Mizpah and Shen, and called its name Ebenezer, saying, 'Thus far the LORD has helped us'" (7:12) – this second Ebenezer draining that name of all its ironic bitterness.

But the scene now shifts swiftly, as we're reminded that Samuel's story, however crowned with divine victory, is after all only a transitional prologue to a much greater epic, which begins in earnest in 1 Samuel 8. This epic, like the Mosaic epic discussed previously – and the later

Homeric and Virgilian epics – is also large in scope and length; it also proclaims its nation-building epic theme and presents us with heavenly consults and direct divine interventions; it too expands its size through epic catalogues and warrior lists, and advances its narrative through world-altering epic battles; it also enlivens its story through interactions with under-world beings; and as a counter to its portraits of evil and violence, it compensates with examples of providential kindness and hospitality. And above all, at the heart of the story is a single focal hero whose trials and triumphs remake history and define the character of his people.

Or are there two heroes? For of course the Book of Samuel's great epic hero is David: he will come to dominate the action; his establishment of a godly limited monarchy will emerge as the epic theme; most of its divine visitations, warrior catalogs, and victorious battles will be his; even its scenes of hospitality mainly will display his virtues – and his vices. But David's entrance into the great story is delayed, for he is preceded in the hero's role, and on the throne, by another hero, King Saul, who provides an extended parallel, and an ongoing foil, to his protégé, and his chief victim, the son of Jesse. Yet if David's heroism will be epic, Saul's turns out to be tragic. Significantly, the central issues of David's epic rise, and Saul's tragic fall, are first introduced fully in 1 Samuel 8, from the mouth of the man chosen to anoint them both, and to set them on their paths of cross destinies – Samuel, the last of the Judges.

9.1.2 Cross Destinies: Saul, David, and Chiastic Plot Structure

After the prologue of 1 Samuel 1–7, Samuel's message to the elders of Israel in chapter 8 presents the epic theme of the book, and gives the coming king a standard to fall from – while rather grimly predicting that fall. Many years have now passed, and they have not been kind to the seer or his family, as the elders rather churlishly point out: "Look, you are old, and your sons do not walk in your ways. Now make us a king to judge us like all the nations" (8:5). And indeed it is sadly true, as the narrator notes, that like Eli before him Samuel has failed as a father, with two sons who "turned aside after dishonest gain, took bribes, and perverted justice" (8:2). But just what do the elders want instead? "A king to judge" seems to define monarchy in terms of the *Shophet's* functions: leading in battle, delivering the oppressed, and rendering justice under the Law of Moses. All of these functions are consistent with the definitions and strictures for kings laid out in Deuteronomy 17:14–20, with its ideal of a law-bound limited monarchy dedicated to serving and protecting the people and rejecting royal pomp. However, their added phrase "like all the nations" worrisomely suggests the opposite for the new *melech*: that he will rule as the god-kings of Canaan, Egypt, and Mesopotamia, not under God's law or for the people's good, but as a law unto himself. So Samuel takes offense:

> But the thing displeased Samuel when they said, "Give us a king to judge us." So Samuel prayed to the LORD. And the LORD said to Samuel, "Heed the voice of the people in all that they say to you; for they have not rejected you, but they have rejected Me, that I should not reign over them." (8:6–7)

At *Yahweh's* instruction, Samuel reads out a stern warning to the elders, showing them the behavior of their coming king, and strikingly, it is a warning about what the new king will take for himself:

> He will *take* your sons and appoint them for *his* own chariots and to be *his* horsemen, and some will run before *his* chariots. He will appoint captains over *his* thousands and captains over *his* fifties, will set some to plow *his* ground and reap *his* harvest, and some to make *his* weapons of war and equipment for *his* chariots. He will *take* your daughters

to be perfumers, cooks, and bakers. And he will *take* the best of your fields, your vineyards, and your olive groves, and give them to *his* servants. He will *take* a tenth of your
grain and your vintage, and give it to *his* officers and servants. And he will *take* your male
servants, your female servants, your finest young men, and your donkeys, and put them
to *his* work. He will *take* a tenth of your sheep. And you will be *his* servants. (8:11–17,
emphases mine)

The message is clear: this king "like the kings of the nations" will not serve the LORD, but will
lord it over his people as servants – indeed, practically as slaves conscripted involuntarily to
serve the self-defining state monarchy. Then Samuel, with words steeped in *schadenfreude*,
concludes his anti-absolutist message: "And you will cry out in that day because of your king
whom you have chosen for yourselves, and the LORD will not hear you in that day" (8:18).

But his warnings fall on the deaf ears of a people who fear and envy their enemies and so
aspire to be like them: "Nevertheless the people refused to obey the voice of Samuel; and they
said, 'No, but we will have a king over us, that we also may be like all the nations, and that our
king may judge us and go out before us and fight our battles'" (8:19–20). So God – in a moment
of what one might call deadly permission – tells Samuel to "[h]eed their voice, and make them
a king." And so begins a tragedy whose moral is "be careful what you wish for."

As we commence the story of Saul and David, the first thing to observe is its **chiastic plot
structure**, in which the fall of one character relates to the rise of another. This narrative device,
related to but not identical to juxtaposition, presents one figure who begins in an ascendant
position and then takes a downward trajectory, in extended contrast with another character
who begins in obscurity and then takes an upward trajectory. In the most artful of chiastic plot
structures – as in the Book of Samuel – the contrasting personalities and fates of the "crossed"
characters are intimately intertwined.

X Marks the Spot – Literary Chiasmus

Chiastic plot structure is one type of literary **chiasmus**, so called because it involves a reversal
and inversion of elements that, if pictured in a diagram, resemble the Greek letter "X" or *chi*.

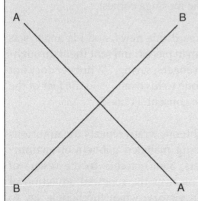

In 1 Samuel, A would represent Saul and B David, as they exchange places: from Saul's introduction
as publicly anointed king in chapter 9 and David's introduction as obscurely anointed shepherd
king-in-waiting in chapter 16, until Saul's defeat and suicide in chapter 31, which leaves David in
possession of Judah's crown as 2 Samuel begins.

The second thing to observe about the story of Saul and David is that Saul's first appearance is already marked paradoxically with signs of both divine blessing toward Saul and divine judgment on and through Saul. As to blessing, 1 Samuel 9 introduces Saul as the son of a Benjamite named Kish, "a mighty man of power. And he had a choice and handsome son whose name was Saul. There was not a more handsome person than he among the children of Israel. From his shoulders upward he was taller than any of the people" (9:1–2). Furthermore, Saul's discovery and anointing by Samuel are providentially designed and ordered, with Saul unknowingly traveling to recover some lost donkeys, seeking out the "seer" Samuel for a little clairvoyant assistance, and instead being told by Samuel – who already knows by special revelation to expect Saul – the stunning news that on this son of Kish rests "all the desire of Israel" in its hope for a new king (9:3–20).

Yet marks of coming weakness and woe also appear from the first. Saul's first response to Samuel's royal commission – "[a]m I not a Benjamite, of the smallest of the tribes of Israel, and my family the least of all the families of the tribe of Benjamin?" – may sound like becoming modesty, but it also may remind the reader of Benjamin's past disgrace in the vicious matter of the Levite's Concubine and the resulting civil war that ended the Book of Judges. And Saul hails from Gibeah itself, the hill town where the horror began – and which will serve as his eventual capital. In addition, the circumstances of Saul's proclamation as king by Samuel are not entirely auspicious. Although upon his anointing by Samuel "the Spirit of God came upon him" (1 Samuel 10:10), that Spirit seems to have left him on the occasion of his proclamation to all Israel soon after at Mizpah. Chosen providentially by lot from among all the tribes, and from all in his own tribe, Saul nevertheless has made himself scarce, and after a vigorous search is found, "hidden among the equipment" (10:22). Modesty or cowardice? Or dangerous instability? Time will tell.

We may indeed forget this gloomy foreshadowing in the flush of Saul's first great success that follows soon after his installation. In chapter 11, we learn that a particularly nasty character named Nahash the Ammonite has besieged the town of Jabesh-Gilead, so that the terrified inhabitants offer to make him their covenantal master – an offer that Nahash accepts on one condition: "that I may put out all your right eyes, and bring reproach on all Israel" (11:2). The men of the town swallow hard and beg off for seven days and send a message to all of the tribes – including the new King Saul – pleading for help. Significantly, far from lording it over his new subjects, Saul is out plowing his own fields when the message comes:

> Then the Spirit of God came upon Saul when he heard this news, and his anger was greatly aroused. So he took a yoke of oxen and cut them in pieces, and sent them throughout all the territory of Israel then by the hands of messengers, saying, "Whoever does not go out with Saul and Samuel to battle, so it shall be done to his oxen." And the fear of the LORD fell on the people, and they came out with one consent. (11:6–7)

One might of course add, "the fear of Saul" – who in his righteous wrath repeats the notorious old Levite's means of messaging from Judges 19 by sending mangled gobbets of anatomy throughout the tribes. But with a great army of volunteers, Saul marches to the rescue of Jabesh-Gilead, routs and slaughters the Ammonites, and receives the renewed adulation of Israel. He is even admirably humble and magnanimous in victory: when the people say to Samuel, "Who is he who said, 'Shall Saul reign over us?' Bring the men, that we may put them to death," Saul replies, "Not a man shall be put to death this day, for today the LORD has accomplished salvation in Israel" (11:12–13). Perhaps this tallest, handsomest of kings will be a good king, too.

However, even in confirming Saul's monarchy in a coronation ceremony at Gilgal, Samuel dampens the celebration with more dark admonitions, exhorting the congregation in a farewell address that repeats the blessings and curses of Moses centuries before at Mount Ebal and Mount Gerazim:

> If you fear the LORD and serve Him and obey His voice, and do not rebel against the commandment of the LORD, then both you and the king who reigns over you will continue following the LORD your God. However, if you do not obey the voice of the LORD, but rebel against the commandment of the LORD, then the hand of the LORD will be against you, as it was against your fathers. (11:14–15)

To dampen the festivities even further, Samuel calls down rain on the very day of the wheat harvest, ruining the prospect of getting the crops in, so that "the people greatly feared the LORD and Samuel" (11:18). Yet despite their wickedness in asking for a king "when the LORD your God was your king," Samuel again promises to pray that, if they will repent in their hearts, God will be merciful. But he ends with a dire warning: "if you still do wickedly, you shall be swept away, both you and your king" (11:18, 12, 17, 25).

Like a rifle hanging over the door in the first act of a play, such warnings are bound to be discharged before the end, and the narrator wastes no time in detailing the steps of Saul's downfall. Chapter 13 begins positively: two years into Saul's reign, he has mustered 3000 permanent troops to fortify strategic points at Michmach and Bethel, and his capital at Gibeah. In a bold move, Saul's son Jonathan – in the first mention of this brave young man – leads an assault on a Philistine garrison at Geba, so that Saul "blows the trumpet" to rally the Israelites and press their advantage. But the Philistines muster in force, with 3000 chariots, 6000 horsemen, and infantry "as the sand which is on the seashore in multitude" – sending the frightened Israelites scurrying to hide "in caves, in thickets, in rocks, in holes, and in pits" (13:1–7).

In the midst of this escalating panic, Saul waits, with the trembling Israelites, for Samuel to arrive and offer a sacrifice and prayer for victory. But Samuel does not arrive at the appointed time; so Saul, in a misguided effort to restore morale, takes Samuel's priestly function into his own hands, offering up the burnt offering. When Samuel comes soon after, he is outraged at Saul's expedient violation of the "separation of powers" between priesthood and crown, and shocks the king by announcing the end of his reign just begun:

> You have done foolishly. You have not kept the commandment of the LORD your God, which He commanded you. For now the LORD would have established your kingdom over Israel forever. But now your kingdom shall not continue. The LORD has sought for Himself a man after His own heart, and the LORD has commanded him to be commander over His people, because you have not kept what the LORD commanded you. (13:13–14)

Who will be this man after God's heart? Could Saul, perhaps, be replaced by his own son Jonathan? That possibility presents itself immediately as Saul, his confidence shattered, holds back from attacking the enemy while Jonathan presses the assault.

Jonathan's attack would seem foolhardy were it not so successful, for it pits precisely two Israelites – the prince and his armor bearer – against an entire Philistine garrison at the rocky pass of Michmash. Jonathan has learned the lesson of Gideon's happy few, and his boldness against the "uncircumcised" is unashamedly devout: as he tells his young comrade, "nothing restrains the LORD from saving by many or by few" (14:6). Exploiting the narrow gap of the mountain pass, Jonathan and the armor bearer dispatch about twenty Philistines one by one in quick succession, spreading terror throughout the enemy camp and emboldening the Israelite garrison across the valley at Gibeah. In the ensuing *melée*, the Philistines turn their swords on each other as the Hebrews make off with a great amount of booty in the form of livestock.

Yet in the next step of Saul's downward slide, his increasingly paranoid style of leadership seriously compromises Israel's victory. Foolishly disregarding the most basic rule of warfare – that an army marches on its stomach – Saul had arrogantly ordered his troops, on pain of death, not to eat a bite "until evening, before I have taken vengeance on my enemies" (14:24). Predictably, his famished soldiers leave off pursuit of the enemy to slaughter their captured sheep and oxen and cattle and to wolf down the raw meat, blood and all – in violation of the Levitical statute (Leviticus 17:10–12). Jonathan also defies his father's order, though not God's law, by eating honey found in the field. When Saul learns of the dietary uncleanness among the troops, he casts lots to establish guilt; ironically, it is Jonathan, one of the few ritually innocent men in the army, who is taken for the offense. Saul, in his wrath, would add insult to the injury of his food policy by stubbornly executing his own son – now a battle hero – until the people rise up and save Jonathan's life (14:24–46). So Saul, in an outworking of Samuel's curse, has done irreparable damage to his own authority and to his army's morale, while driving a wedge between himself and his heir. Meanwhile, the Philistines escape back to their towns. Clearly, as Jonathan himself says, "my father has troubled the land" (14:29). The nation needs new leadership, and in the intrepid son of Saul they seem to have found their man after God's own heart.

The spoils of war are again at issue in Saul's next disastrous misstep, during his campaign against Israel's old enemy, the Amalekites. Though Saul does not scruple to wipe out man, woman, and child, he spares their best livestock and their King Agag – the former of which can be consumed or sold, and the latter ransomed. When confronted by Samuel about his hypocrisy, Saul ignobly blames his troops for his own greedy behavior and promises many atoning sacrifices, but Samuel is not placated, and renews his curse. "Behold," the old prophet says, "to obey is better than sacrifice, and to heed than the fat of rams … you have rejected the word of the LORD, and the LORD has rejected you from being king over Israel" (15:22, 26). Saul's pathetic attempt at pleading for mercy only worsens the damage; grasping at the departing Samuel's robes, he tears them, bringing a final curse: "The LORD has torn the kingdom of Israel from you today, and has given it to a neighbor of yours, who is better than you" (15:28). As if to punctuate this point about terminated kingdoms, Samuel then "hacked Agag in pieces before the LORD at Gilgal" (15:33).

But who is this "neighbor" – significantly, not "son" – to whom God will give Saul's forfeited kingdom? Having feinted toward Jonathan, the narrator now reaches outside the house of Saul and indeed beyond the tribe of Benjamin, to a small border town in Judah.

> Now the LORD said to Samuel, "How long will you mourn for Saul …? Fill your horn with oil, and go; I am sending you to Jesse the Bethlehemite. For I have provided myself a king among his sons." (16:1)

So, as Saul falls, there begins the rise of the most famous underdog hero in the Hebrew Bible, and perhaps in all world literature. The Cinderella tale of David (Hebrew *Daud* or *Dawid*, "beloved") seems predictable to us only because its assumptions have so thoroughly permeated the Western imagination: "For the LORD does not see as man sees; for man looks at the outward appearance, but the LORD looks at the heart" (16:7).

Of course, we know that – at least in the storybooks – "it's what's on the inside that counts." We know, before even our hero knows, that the overlooked, the undergrown, the young, or the outcast will be the Chosen, because of a heart that is good and true and pure. We know that when the old seer comes looking, he will look past the tallest, the most confident, the eldest and the strongest, and persist until he discovers the despised yet Chosen One from the pasture – or the stables, the slums, or the wild. We know that soon the Chosen will face a figure of arrogant evil and punch far above his weight; he will summon unknown, marvelous powers for an upset victory that revives the hopes of his downcast people. We know that success will amaze, delight, and then bedevil our Chosen hero, whose simple virtue will be challenged and beset by an increasing array of devious forces, obstacles, temptations, and failures. We know that after the disappearance or death of the old seer, the powers of darkness will regroup in ways more fearsome than ever before, casting the Chosen One out into a wandering exile, and we know that he will be joined in exile by a ragtag remnant of faithful friends and fellow outcasts. We know that our hero will be sorely tempted to adopt the same evil ways that he has always opposed, but that at great cost he will keep faith with his principles and draw strength from his humble origins and friends. Yet we know that despite his virtue – indeed because of it – he will find himself facing certain annihilation by the overwhelming forces of wickedness that now oppress his homeland. And we know that at the last moment, and against all odds, evil will undo itself and the Chosen One will emerge victorious, inaugurating a new era of peace, justice, and love.

How do we know all this? We know because, whether we call our Chosen One Frodo Baggins, Aragorn son of Arathorn, Luke Skywalker, Harry Potter, Peter Parker, Clark Kent, or Steve Rogers – or Robin Hood or King Arthur – this story that we love to hear in so many retellings is David's. It is, perhaps, a sign of our times that the story of the Chosen One has largely been relegated to the genres of romance, fantasy, and comic book fiction, but in its biblical original it is presented to us as chronicle, not as wishful thinking but as hopeful history.

This history begins with Samuel's anointing of the Chosen One, called as an afterthought from watching Jesse's flocks after his older brothers all prove somehow unsatisfactory – which, as in Joseph's case, will increase their resentment of him. David is only a lad, but a likely one: "he was ruddy, with bright eyes, and good-looking," so not entirely the ugly duckling, and with Samuel's anointing oil, "the Spirit of the LORD came upon David from that day forward" (16:12, 13). "But" – says the very next verse to emphasize the chiastic shift of the scales – "the Spirit of the LORD departed from Saul, and a distressing spirit from the LORD troubled him" (16:14). Furthermore, their crossing narratives are about to become crossed destinies, as Saul's servants seek out a skilled musician to soothe Saul's savage breast and troubled mind. Providentially, one of Saul's courtiers has heard of a boy harpist in Bethlehem of Judah.

So David is doubly chosen: by Saul, to save his sanity and thus his reign, and by God, to overthrow both. Ironically, this handsome and talented youth brought to Saul for music therapy will instead inflame his madness, and this loyal and courageous young shepherd is marked to displace his cowardly king. As usual, the Almighty has his own purposes, and the friction between Saul's evil intent, David's good intent, and God's great intent will generate much of the story's heat and light. So, we are told, David shuttles between Jesse's flocks and Saul's palace – and at first when David played on his harp, "Saul became refreshed and well, and the distressing spirit would depart from him" (16:23).

And in chapter 17, David's next act saves Saul's kingdom, at least for the time being. What to say of the original "David-and-Goliath story"? First, like so many famous old stories, it is the victim of its own success, and after countless retellings can seem banal; for by now we know that in stories like this, armorless fourteen-year-olds casting stones always defeat brutal armored giants wielding javelins. As Oscar Wilde might say, "The good ended happily, and the bad unhappily. That is what *fiction means*."[1] Second, though, the story still has the power to surprise if we read it not as formulaic fiction, but as genre-bending epic chronicle. Compared, for instance, with the *Iliad's* brilliant epic battle of Hector and

Achilles before the walls of Troy, we might say that David vs. Goliath zigs where Homer zags: in other words, where Homer delivers plentiful preparations and extended taunting speeches, gloriously matched warriors, and richly prolonged combat, 1 Samuel presents abbreviated preliminaries, almost comically mismatched warriors, and, most importantly of all, a stunningly brief and anticlimactic fight. It is no insult to the genius of Homer to say that he abundantly fulfills audience expectations: he provides the badinage, the lengthy and teetering blow-by-blow, and in the end the tragic glory that tribal assemblies of warrior males demand of their bards. But the narrator of Samuel doesn't attempt to out-Homer Homer; instead he abbreviates and inverts the form to glorify, not the great Achilles, but the LORD who made heaven and earth. Much as Genesis 1 deliberately disappoints epic Babylonian bloodlust with its account of a soft-spoken, all-powerful Creator, so the story of David's first victory scants high martial eloquence and gory detail to exalt instead the LORD of Hosts.

This is not to say, however, that the author or authors of Samuel seek merely to travesty or deform the epic. Rather, the goal is reform, with an attendant redefinition – not annihilation – of the hero. David may disappoint heroic expectations by arriving at Saul's camp ingloriously bearing provisions, and like a male Cinderella he may endure a storm of contempt from his siblings; he may reject the armor, sword and shield offered him by Saul, and choose instead five smooth stones and a sling; he may cut short Goliath's taunts – and much exciting action – by running right at him and laying him low with a single slingshot; and he may even have to borrow his enemy's sword to finish the kill. But despite all of these departures from the epic norm, at the end of the day, David is still the last man standing, the hero holding the giant's head high as the revived army of Israel sweeps past him to beat down the foe. It is heroism redeemed, not erased – a champion who has boundless confidence in the power of his God, who also knows his own limitations, and so has the humility to stand tall. "You come to me with a sword, with a spear, and with a javelin," David tells the giant.

> But I come to you in the name of the LORD of hosts, the God of the armies of Israel, whom you have defied. This day the LORD will deliver you into my hand, and I will strike you and take your head from you… Then all the assembly shall know that the LORD does not save with sword and spear; for the battle is the LORD's, and he will deliver you into our hands. (17:45–46, 47)

So begins David's lover's quarrel with power and glory. David is certain that God has given him the victory, but the Israelites are inclined to reverse the equation – "Saul has slain his thousands, /And David his ten thousands," chant the daughters of Israel (18:7) – putting him in the paradoxical position of being idolized for his service to *Yahweh*, the scourge of all idols. And this paradox puts him in new danger, for the shift in popular affection is not lost on Saul. He knows that he should have faced the giant – he, the handsome, towering king – but has been bested by a beardless youth, who is now in the eyes of his people far more of a man than he. So David, the slayer of the king's enemies, has made a powerful enemy in the king himself. Goliath never had the chance to target David with his javelin; Saul will have plenty.

As the lionized victor of the Valley of Elah, David finds himself cast into the midst of court and family intrigue. Saul resents and suspects David, more than once casting his spear at the young harpist in his chambers, but Saul's children adore him: "the soul of Jonathan was knit to the soul of David, and Jonathan loved him as his own soul" (18:1), and "Michal, Saul's daughter, loved David" (18:20). Saul deviously resolves to keep his friends close, and his potential enemies closer. He puts David at the head of his troops and sends him into dangerous places – from which, ironically, he returns in ever-increasing triumph. As a public reward for David's service, and to bring him under fuller family control, Saul offers Michal to him as wife, on one crafty condition: "the king does not desire any dowry but one hundred foreskins of the Philistines" (1 Samuel 18:25). Saul presumes that the Philistines will sell this grisly wedding gift dearly – at the cost of David's life. Yet ever the obedient servant, David eagerly slays 200 Philistines for good measure, and gives these unique engagement rings "in full count to the king... Thus Saul saw and knew that the LORD was with David, and that Michal, Saul's daughter, loved him; and Saul was still more afraid of David" (18:27–29).

As Saul's paranoia grows, so does his murderous intent. He seeks to suborn both of his children to destroy David, ordering Jonathan to assassinate his friend, and then sending henchmen to kill David in Michal's bed. Jonathan not only resists the order, but rebukes his father so eloquently as to bring about Saul's temporary repentance. But Saul's hot hate boils over again and again, first in another javelin attack – David's agility is still better than Saul's aim – and then in the bedchamber plot. Yet Michal outsmarts her father, sending David safely through the window while decking out one of the household idols (another symptom of Saul's godlessness) in David's clothes and a goatskin wig as a decoy that buys her husband time to flee (19:1–17). Sadly, the two will never again share the same bed.

Now on the run, David takes refuge first in Ramah with his – and Saul's – old mentor, the seer Samuel. Here he is pursued, first by three successive waves of Saul's men, and then by Saul himself, in a strange episode reminding the reader that behind the apparent chaos and injustice is a divine plan. As each group of king's messengers arrives in turn to capture David, "the Spirit of God came upon the messengers of Saul, and they also prophesied" (19:20), and when Saul himself appears in wrath, "he also stripped off his clothes and prophesied before Samuel in like manner, and lay down naked all that day and all that night" (19:24). Temporarily compelled out of their villainy, David's enemies feel what might be called the unsaving grace of God, a kind of spiritual possession that restrains their evil intentions and allows David again to escape – while leaving their hearts and souls untouched, and soon to relapse.

Jonathan could hardly be a more striking foil to Saul. Having already made a covenant of friendship with David after Goliath's defeat, he reaffirms their bond in even stronger terms, asking David to vow that in the future, he will show favor to Jonathan and his children – a stunning affirmation of David's royal destiny, and a glimpse of what could have been had Saul been willing to stand aside for "God's Anointed":

> And the LORD be with you as he has been with my father. And you shall not only show me the kindness of the LORD while I still live, that I may not die; but you shall not cut off your kindness from my house forever. (20:13–15)

Thus, Jonathan completes David's model of alternative heroism: of equal courage and strength, Jonathan too is a born leader and a devout man, and has many natural gifts for rule, especially as the son of the king. But above all other qualifications for holding power is his willingness to let it go: a humility and a selfless patriotism happy to lead or to follow, depending on the greater good. He is the man who *could* be king, and cheerfully chooses not to be. David, on the other hand, is the man who *will* be king – who will have greatness thrust upon him – but not before a long test of loyalty and faith, and a hard schooling in humiliation and fear. He is on the rise, but by a winding stair.

So begin David's wilderness years. Jonathan reluctantly confirms Saul's intention to kill David, and after a tearful brotherly embrace, he is off, like a prototypical Robin Hood, to wander the hills, the forests, and the border country.

Into the Woods: Young David and Robin Hood

The resemblances between the stories of the young David and of the medieval English folk hero Robin Hood are too many to be entirely coincidental, nor should they surprise us. Fleeing the court of a corrupt and evil king (King Saul, King John), our hero takes refuge in the forest and wilderness (Hereth, Sherwood), gathering to himself a ragtag remnant of resistance fighters from among the dispossessed, the oppressed, and the disgruntled (the Mighty Men, the Merry Men) – including not only mighty warriors but also holy men (Abiathar the Priest, Friar Tuck). Practicing evasion and using guerilla tactics, the hero eludes capture and "lives off the land," supplying protection to the weak and the victims of the regime, sometimes by sharing their plunder taken from the king's rich supporters and from other enemies. Yet given opportunities to act as ruthlessly as his pursuers, he chooses instead the way of mercy – and of tactical patience (David's sparing of Saul and Nabal, Robin's clemency on occasion to Sir Guy and other opponents), and amid his wilderness wanderings wins the heart of a fair lady (Abigail, Maid Marian). Robin's legend is many-layered, but there can be little doubt that at least one of those layers is Davidic.

This is, by all appearances, a terrible setback for David, yet at every turn, David in exile is being tested and proven ready to become David the king. Meanwhile, the more that Saul grasps at maintaining and expanding his power, the further he falls into tyranny and madness. Thus, the "X" of the chiastic contrast marks Saul's tragic undoing.

David's first turning is to a place that reminds us ironically of past blessing and victory: the Tabernacle at Nob, current center of Hebrew worship and also the repository of Goliath's sword. Yet David's return there is marked by his fear and self-protective deception, as he misinforms Ahimelech the High Priest that he has come on Saul's urgent business, asking for bread and for the great sword itself. With a foreshadowing of disaster, we're told that one witness of David's visit is Doeg the Edomite, Saul's chief herdsman, who notes that David takes the offered holy bread and the trophy weapon and hurries off. As it turns out, David runs across the border into Philistia itself, and Goliath's town of Gath, where in a moment of weakness he shockingly offers his services to the Philistine King Achish. But Achish's suspicions are aroused, and David is memorably compelled to quiet the enemy king's distrust by playing mad: "he scratched on the doors of the gate, and let his saliva fall down on his beard," so that Achish asks, sarcastically, "Have I need of madmen, that you have brought this fellow to play the madman in my presence?" (21:13, 15).

While David is prevented providentially from joining the enemy, the consequences of his lies to Ahimelech and the priests are dire. When Saul hears Doeg's twisted version of events – that Ahimelech knowingly aided David in his flight from Saul – Saul summons the priests to Ramah and summarily orders their slaughter. When Ahimelech protests his innocence and even Saul's guards refuse to murder the holy men, the foreigner Doeg redoubles his accusations and volunteers to do the killing himself, striking down eighty-five priests and all that breathes in the sacred village of Nob, grotesquely multiplying Saul's unlawful sacrifice in chapter 13. Only Ahimelech's son Abiathar escapes the massacre and brings the terrible news to David – who by now has re-entered Israel and amassed a band of 400 personal loyalists and malcontents to take refuge in the cave of Adullam and the Forest of Hereth. Yet unlike the blame-shifting Saul, David takes responsibility: "I have caused the death of all the persons of your father's house. Stay with me; do not fear. For he who seeks my life seeks your life, but with me you shall be safe" (22:22–23).

Indeed, David's trust in God returns and emboldens him to step further into the security gap left by the paranoid king. Told that the Philistines are attacking the town of Keilah, David inquires of the LORD who tells him – twice – to go up against the superior force and rescue the town. Then, in a sardonic double irony, Saul (who had neglected Keilah when it was under Philistine assault) now marches to besiege the town until it hands over its hero for execution! Furthermore, David is divinely warned that the people whom he has saved plan to betray him, and so he and his troops – now numbering 600 – escape ahead of Saul's army (23:1–13). A final visit from his loyal friend Jonathan reassures him that eventually he will be king, and the chapter then develops an increasingly absurd account of Saul's pursuit of the ever-elusive David, through the wilds of Ziph, then of Maon, and finally of En Gedi, only to end with Saul receiving the alarm, "Hurry and come, for the Philistines have invaded the land!" (23:14–29).

The next episodes set David's story off even more from typical revenge and action narratives, and also display a high degree of artistic design – specifically, of doubling for emphasis, and of juxtaposition for contrast. They also introduce a whiff of romance into David's otherwise fugitive existence. At the beginning of chapter 24, it appears that David is being run to earth on the "Rocks of the Wild Goats" in the Wilderness of En Gedi, as Saul brings 3000 picked men on the chase. Yet Saul's pursuit provides David with a stunning opportunity to achieve sudden victory – if in the most ignominious way. As Saul takes a break from the manhunt to move his bowels in a cave, his prey becomes the hunter as David creeps up on the intensely occupied king to slice off the corner of his robe. And indeed this incident is a kind of victory for David – a moral victory that demonstrates his self-restraint from taking personal vengeance and validates his coming rule. After Saul exits the cave, David emerges to wave the fragment of the robe, asking plaintively,

> Why do you listen to the words of men who say, "Indeed David seeks your harm"? Look, this day your eyes have seen that the LORD delivered you today into my hand in the cave, and someone urged me to kill you. But my eye spared you, and I said, "I will not stretch out my hand against my lord, for he is the LORD's anointed." (24:9–10)

Even Saul agrees – tearfully – that David is the better man: "You are more righteous than I; for you have rewarded me with good, whereas I have rewarded you with evil... And now I know indeed that you shall surely be king, and that the kingdom of Israel shall be established in your hand" (24:17, 20). Yet while Saul returns home, David returns to his mountain stronghold, knowing better than to trust the unstable king.

David's prudence is confirmed soon after as Saul again sets out in pursuit, and again corners this prey, only to have the tables turned once more. This time David steals into the sleeping king's camp, and his hot-headed nephew Abishai begs for the chance to skewer Saul with his spear; again David refuses to "touch the LORD's anointed," much to his men's consternation – and to Saul's when David calls out, displaying the spear and water jug that he has lifted from next to the monarch's head. "Is that your voice, my son David?" he responds, with the sudden pathos of the paranoid briefly emerging from his irrational fear before descending finally into the darkness. "May you be blessed, my son David! You shall both do great things and also still prevail" (26:17, 25).

These lessons of David's self-restraint – repeated for emphasis – bookend a darkly funny, yet implicitly romantic, incident in chapter 25 that reveals the future king at the breaking point of his patience, and yet also shows another kingly trait: his willingness to accept correction, even – perhaps especially – from a woman. Significantly, juxtaposed with these two accounts of David's reining in his wrath toward Saul, is his near-massacre against a foolish and arrogant land baron. In David's wanderings in the foothills near Mt. Carmel, he has – unlike the English Robin Hood – specifically avoided robbing from the rich, instead actually providing added protection for their large flocks and herds. Now David, short on provisions and knowing that the spring sheep-shearing festival is at hand, sends a friendly reminder to the richest of these herders. "The name of the man was Nabal, and the name of his wife Abigail. And she was a woman of good understanding and beautiful appearance; but the man was harsh and evil in his doings" (25:3). David's request – that Nabal share some of his holiday abundance with the helpful but hungry fugitives – meets with Nabal's insulting refusal, which dismisses David as a thieving rebel. When David receives this insult, he snaps, giving orders for a full assault on Nabal and his household, setting out in the heat of anger. But Nabal's wise wife Abigail hears and intervenes, and clearly she knows how to stir the better angels of David's nature. Packing her donkeys with abundant food, she rushes to meet him, throws herself down before him, and makes an appeal that is part apology, part rebuke, and part proposition:

> Please, let not my lord regard this scoundrel Nabal. For as his name is, so is he: Nabal is his name, and folly is with him! But I, your maidservant, did not see the young men of my lord whom you sent. Now therefore, my lord … since the LORD has held you back from coming to bloodshed and from avenging yourself with your own hand, now then, let your enemies and those who seek harm for my lord be as Nabal … and the lives of your enemies He shall sling out, as from the pocket of a sling… But when the LORD has dealt well with my lord, then remember your maidservant. (25:25–26, 29, 31)

Abigail brings David up short with a pun on her doltish and possibly impotent husband's name – *nabal* means "wilted" or "failed" in Hebrew – then proceeds to express sympathy with his exiled plight and assurance of his eventual victory, alluding admiringly to his famous youthful exploit against Goliath with the slingshot. Yet she also implicitly rebukes him, reminding him of the evils of revenge – a temptation he has recently resisted regarding Saul and will resist again. Finally, she offers him the prospect of God's reward for his virtue, a prospect that may even include herself, should God be willing to send Nabal on a quick journey to Sheol.

Indeed, God is willing. When David gratefully sends Abigail safely home – "blessed are you, because you have kept me this day … from avenging myself" – she scares her drunken husband sober with the account, and he promptly seizes up and dies of a divinely inflicted stroke. Then David sends to the wealthy young widow, and "Abigail rose in haste and rode on a donkey, attended by five of her maidens; and she followed the messengers of David, and became his wife" (25:33, 42). Abigail's "haste" suggests a mutual love match; she knows that the way to David's heart is through his mind, his memory, his moral imagination – not to mention his stomach and his desiring eye for female beauty.

Inserted almost as an afterthought just before the Nabal story is a brief mention (25:1) of a major death – the death of Samuel, the book's namesake and the king-making seer who anointed both the disgraced Saul and his beleaguered young rival. It is in one sense typical of biblical narrative to dismiss the great ones quietly, decentering the human hero to increase the focus on God; yet, as we will see, Samuel will be back for one more unwilling and scathing appearance, as the final voice of Saul's doom.

For Saul's day of reckoning is fast approaching, and with it, seemingly, all Israel's. David, having faithfully restrained himself over and again from imitating Saul's murderous ways, now enters one of the darkest periods in his life. Apparently despairing of divine deliverance, he defects again to Philistia, submitting himself to King Achish of arch-rival Gath, who bestows on him the border town of Ziklag in return for David's promise of regular raids back into his own land of Judah. With David goes the last truly effective force against Philistine invasion – now turned Philistine ally. Or is he? For David is really something of a double agent, outwardly a turncoat, yet actually raiding not against Hebrew towns but against the old Amalekite enemy. And he is ruthlessly effective: when he attacks, he leaves no Amalekite alive – man, woman, or child – to tell any tales. David's double game is squirm-inducing not only for modern readers, but also for ancient ones–what has become of the "man after God's own heart"?

> So Achish believed David, saying, "He has made his people Israel utterly abhor him; therefore he will be my servant forever."... Now it happened in those days that the Philistines gathered their armies together for war, to fight with Israel. And Achish said to David, "You assuredly know that you will go out with me to battle, you and your men." So David said to Achish, "Surely you know what your servant can do." (27:12; 28:1–2)

What *will* David do? How will he respond when called to open battle against his own anointed king and his own chosen people? One senses that even David does not know.

While David enters an ethical netherworld, Saul sinks even lower, peering into Sheol itself. After the LORD refuses to give Saul spiritual guidance about the coming Philistine invasion, the terrified king – who "had put the mediums and the spiritists out of the land" – seeks out a female medium, the infamous "Witch of Endor," to bring back the dead prophet Samuel in a séance. The ironies are many-layered: like a prohibitionist caught in a speakeasy, or an environmentalist on a corporate jet, Saul the scourge of sorcery hypocritically seeks guidance in a den of superstition; he asks to call up the one man who would most abhor mediums, and who has repeatedly predicted his destruction; he arrives in disguise and swears "by the LORD" to the nervous witch that he is not trying to entrap her; and the medium herself is in for the shock of her life, for when she calls Samuel, he actually appears! And he is much displeased.

> When the woman saw Samuel, she cried out with a loud voice. And the woman spoke to Saul, saying, "Why have you deceived me? For you are Saul!"...
>
> Now Samuel said to Saul, "Why have you disturbed me by bringing me up?"
>
> And Saul answered, "I am deeply distressed; for the Philistines make war against me, and God has departed from me and does not answer me anymore, neither by prophets nor by dreams. Therefore I have called you, that you may reveal to me what I should do."
>
> Then Samuel said: "So why do you ask me, seeing the LORD has departed from you and has become your enemy?... For the LORD has torn the kingdom out of your hand and given it to your neighbor, David... Moreover the LORD will also deliver Israel with you into the hand of the Philistines. And tomorrow you and your sons will be with me." (28:12, 15–17, 19)

This is cold comfort, indeed – and Saul collapses like a man unstrung. Two more ironies close the episode: first, as he had done years before to his own hapless army, Saul has deprived himself of food, so that "there was no strength in him"; and second, it is the witch who, in a burst of domestic concern for her king, takes it upon herself to show hospitality – complete with unleavened bread and a fatted calf. It will be Saul's last meal.

We should note here that a visit to the underworld is a standard part of any epic – from Homer to Virgil to Dante to Milton – and thus this biblical epic is not lacking, yet Saul's end is not epic, but tragic, and his chiastic fall is nearly complete. But what of David's corresponding rise? With superb timing, the narrator builds suspense as the Philistine armies rally into place against Israel, with David and his expatriate band among the attackers. The rock and the hard place present themselves: either David will be forced to join the attack against his own people, confirming his treachery to Israel and invalidating his claim to the Hebrew crown; or he will refuse the attack, confirming his treachery to the Philistines, who will turn and destroy him. Yet with these walls closing in on David, the invisible hand of Providence quietly intervenes to point a third way: when the Philistine lords express their suspicion that David will turn coat in the midst of battle, King Achish generously – and naïvely – sends David and his band of brothers to the rear, while all the might of the Sea Peoples marches on Saul at Jezreel (29:1–11).

As it turns out, David is sent away from the front not a moment too soon. When he and his men arrive at their home base of Ziklag, they find a smoking ruin, and their wives and children spirited away by a raiding party of Amalekites. If David has a "rock bottom" in 1 Samuel, this is it: exiled from his old home, rejected by his new masters, and now bereaved of all his goods and relations – and of his men's trust, "for the people spoke of stoning him, because the soul of all the people was grieved, every man for his sons and his daughters." Yet this is the darkness just before dawn, as "David strengthened himself in the LORD his God." Consulting the LORD through the Urim and the Thummim confirms that he will pursue the enemy and prevail (30:6–8). From the worst possible start, all things then fall perfectly into place: a disaffected slave of the Amalekites directs David to the enemy camp, and David and 400 men surprise the raiders in the midst of their victory party, wiping them out and rescuing all the hostages – and all the booty – unharmed. Returning to Ziklag, David may be standing among smoke and ruin, but he has not lost a man, woman, or child, and is richer than when he began. He forgives his critics and distributes the spoil equitably among his men, also sending liberal gifts ahead to the chief towns and elders of Judah. And he is just about to learn that he has outlasted and outlived the worst enemy of his life. Yet it will not be a day of joy, but of grief.

Saul's last day begins in horror and ends in most tragic and shameful death. Saul's always flawed nobility has rotted and collapsed; his fate is writ small and large as a judgment on king and kingdom; his former prophetic mentor has become his tragic nemesis; and Saul's time of *peripeteia* has come. Exhausted and emotionally shattered from his midnight encounter with the damning spirit of Samuel, in the morning he faces an overwhelming force of Philistines, who pursue him and his more valiant sons through the fields of Jezreel to their last stand on Mount Gilboa. Jonathan, Abinadab, and Malchishua all fall around him, and Saul is pierced through with volleys of arrows. His last request of his armorbearer shows not his love for God, but his hatred and fear of the Gentiles: "Draw your sword, and thrust me through with it, lest these uncircumcised men come and thrust me through and abuse me" (31:4). Ironically, the armorbearer, like David before him, refuses to touch the LORD's anointed, so Saul ends his own life, falling on his sword – an act later to be thought noble for a Roman, but here ignominious for a Hebrew.

But worse is to come. The Israelites of the fertile Jezreel Valley and the Trans-Jordan abandon their homes and towns to the invaders, and Saul's mutilated body becomes a trophy of war:

> So it happened the next day, when the Philistines came to strip the slain, that they found Saul and his three sons fallen on Mount Gilboa. And they cut off his head and stripped off his armor, and sent word throughout the land of the Philistines, to proclaim it in the temple of their idols and among the people. Then they put his armor in the temple of the Ashtoreths, and they fastened his body to the wall of Beth Shan. (31:8–10)

The death of Saul is good news in the Asherah temples, but bitter news to the Israelites who had demanded a king "like all the nations" and yet found themselves finally over-run by the nations anyway. He had seemed every inch a king, but now he is a whole head shorter as his decapitated corpse hangs like a scarecrow on the wall of a defeated town. A few "valiant men" from Jabesh-Gilead risk their lives to rescue the bones of Saul and his sons and honor them with cremation, burial and fasting, but Saul's final eulogy will come from the man whose destiny most crossed his own – his chief victim, rival, and mourner, the coming king, David.

9.2   David's Epic Tragicomedy: A Sure House, a Lasting Covenant in 2 Samuel

The second part of Samuel's book begins, a little like the Japanese cinematic classic *Rashomon*, with an alternate account of the first part's conclusion. Into Ziklag staggers a young Amalekite fresh from Saul's camp, who tells of the king's death in terms calculated to win a reward from Saul's enemies:

> As I happened by chance to be on Mount Gilboa, there was Saul, leaning on his spear; and indeed the chariots and horsemen followed hard after him. Now when he looked behind him, he saw me and called to me… And he said to me, … "Please stand over me and kill me, for anguish has come upon me, but my life still remains in me." So I stood over him and killed him… And I took the crown that was on his head and the bracelet that was on his arm, and have brought them here to my lord. (2 Samuel 1:6–10)

However, the Amalekite's calculations are incorrect. David, instead of bestowing a bag of gold on the bringer of this news, responds by rending his garments and mourning, weeping, and fasting for the death of his persecutor. Then, at the end of this day of grief comes a question to chill the man's blood: "How was it you were not afraid to put forth your hand to destroy the LORD's anointed?" (1:14). How was this Amalekite to know that he was talking to the one man who might have had Saul's head multiple times, but chose to spare it on principle? Ironically, the man has no time to correct his tall tale; David's men strike him down, probably the Bible's most dismayed opportunist, at least until Judas Iscariot.

9.2.1   A Biblical Elegy: The Song of the Bow

Following after this opening episode, David's famous **Elegy** for Saul and Jonathan, "The Song of the Bow," displays the rising king's rhetorical skills to remarkable effect.

The Elegy: Structuring Grief

The **Elegy** is an organized, poetic expression of mourning, and as such seeks to impose – or discover – order and meaning in the wake of death. It is a form identified and described by the Greeks but which is much more ancient. Hebrew, Classical, and Christian elegies share certain elements in common: some statement of the speaker's history of relationship to the deceased, with a tribute to happier days of the life now lost; a complaint about the irreplaceable vacancy now left – usually expressed in terms of the **pathetic fallacy** or inanimate nature mourning; the descriptions of varied bereaved persons and their tokens of sadness; and, usually, a concluding consolation recognizing the immortality of the dead, either in a blessed afterlife or in ongoing influence in this world – or both. Some famed English elegies include John Donne's *Anniversaries*, John Milton's "Lycidas," and Thomas Grey's "Elegy Written in a Country Churchyard," all of which adopt and adapt these elements. Notably, David's "Song of the Bow" presents all of these except for the last: David speaks as one inconsolable – at least for the present.

The phrase-making gifts of a great poet meld private and heartfelt grief with a sure-footed sense of public audience: David vents his deep personal feelings while exonerating himself of any guilt in Saul's death, voicing the nation's sorrow while further establishing his moral claim to rule, and paying special tribute to his dearest friend, Jonathan. It is a **eulogy** – Greek for a "good word" or a funeral address – and there was never a better exemplar of the Latin dictum *De mortuis nihil nisi bonum* ("Of the dead speak nothing but good"). Selective without being hypocritical, David's "Song of the Bow" is a masterpiece of magnanimity, remembering the deceased king at his best for those who already know the worst.

> The beauty of Israel is slain on your high places!
> How the mighty have fallen!
> Tell it not in Gath,
> Proclaim it not in the streets of Ashkelon—
> Lest the daughters of the Philistines rejoice,
> Lest the daughters of the uncircumcised triumph.
>
> O mountains of Gilboa,
> Let there be no dew nor rain upon you,
> Nor fields of offerings.
> For the shield of the mighty is cast away there!
> The shield of Saul, not anointed with oil.
> From the blood of the slain,
> From the fat of the mighty,
> The bow of Jonathan did not turn back,
> And the sword of Saul did not return empty.
>
> Saul and Jonathan were beloved and pleasant in their lives,
> And in their death they were not divided;
> They were swifter than eagles,
> They were stronger than lions.
>
> O daughters of Israel, weep over Saul,
> Who clothed you in scarlet, with luxury;
> Who put ornaments of gold on your apparel.
>
> How the mighty have fallen in the midst of the battle!
> Jonathan was slain in your high places.
> I am distressed for you, my brother Jonathan;
> You have been very pleasant to me;
> Your love to me was wonderful,
> Surpassing the love of women.
> How the mighty have fallen,
> And the weapons of war perished! (1:19–27)

Recalling the tall, handsome, and brave king whom he had admired in his boyhood, David saves the warmest and saddest words for Saul's nobler heir, who cheerfully stood aside from the throne for his friend, and whose pure brotherly love outshone the sweetest sexual *eros*.

9.2.2 "From Strength to Strength": King in Hebron, King in Jerusalem

David's highly effective first responses to the disaster of Jezreel and Gilboa set the tone for his entire early reign. Through the first ten chapters of 2 Samuel, despite further divisions, battles, delays, and setbacks, he hardly puts a foot wrong, going from strength to strength to build a sure house and a lasting covenant. Yet the human gravity of sin still applies, and what goes up may come down, raising others in its place. David's ascent to national unity and regional empire is patient and gradual. Initially, it is only his own tribe of Judah who recognize his rule, anointing him at a ceremony in Hebron, while Saul's chief of staff Abner installs Saul's surviving son Ishbosheth over the other eleven tribes of Israel to the north (2:1–11). An early meeting between Abner and David's nephews Joab, Abishai, and Asahel quickly degenerates into a skirmish in which Abner kills Asahel and war breaks out between Judah and Israel (2:12–32).

The United Kingdom of Israel Under Saul and David

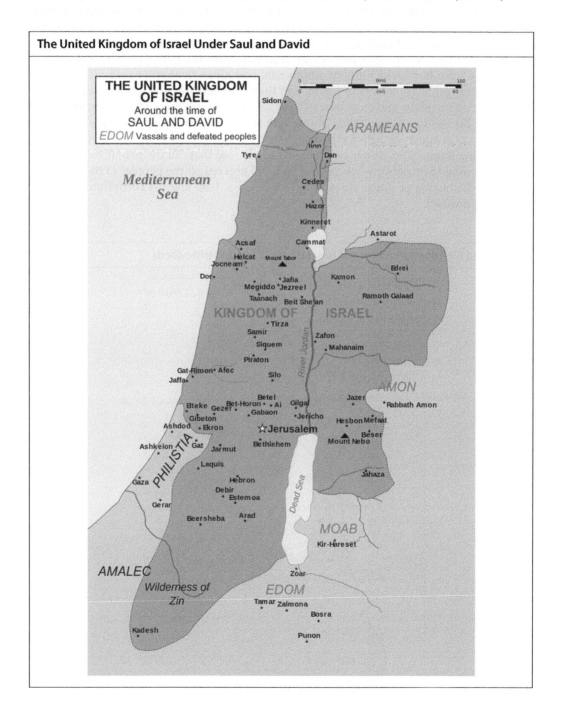

Yet the narrator devotes very little space to this civil war, treating its end as a foregone conclusion: "Now there was a long war between the house of Saul and the house of David. But David grew stronger and stronger, and the house of Saul grew weaker and weaker" (3:1). Instead of pitched battles, almost immediately we're told of the petty and treacherous court intrigues that will, nevertheless, bring about Israel's God-ordained merger with Judah. First Ishbosheth falls out with Abner over Abner's taking Saul's concubine Rizpah for himself. Abner takes his wounded pride to David, offering to hand over Ishbosheth and the northern kingdom in exchange for a major role in the newly united nation. David in turn demands that Ishbosheth and Abner return to him his first wife, Saul's daughter Michal, who once had loved him but whom Saul had given to another man after David's escape. Abner complies, defects to David, and then – to heighten the rather tawdry melodrama – David's nephew and chief of staff Joab murders Abner in cold blood, ostensibly in revenge for his brother Asahel killed in the fight at Gibeon, but more likely to eliminate a rival for power at court. As with Saul's death, David seems genuinely outraged by the murder, mourning publicly for Abner and refusing to eat – so that "all the people took note of it, and it pleased them, since whatever the king did pleased all the people" (3:36). Yet – in a dark foreshadowing of future disaster – David leaves Joab and his conspirator brother Abishai unpunished.

The Divided Kingdoms of Judah and Israel Under David and Ishbosheth

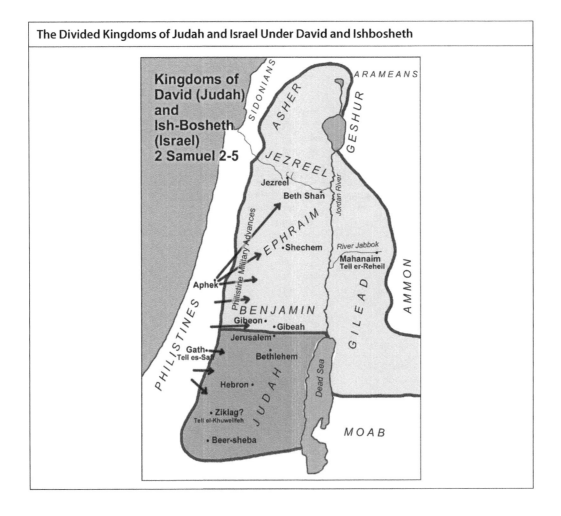

The same cannot be said for the men who perform the final sordid crime in this sequence, perhaps encouraged by David's leniency to Joab. Ishbosheth has lost all hope and gone into hiding, and the brothers Banaah and Rechab, two of Ishbosheth's captains, assassinate their king in his own bed and cheerfully present his head to David at Hebron. David's response takes the smiles from their faces:

> "When someone told me, saying, 'Look, Saul is dead,' thinking to have brought good news, I arrested him and had him executed in Ziklag – the one who thought I would give him a reward for his news. How much more, when wicked men have killed a righteous person in his own house on his bed? Therefore, shall I not now require his blood at your hand and remove you from the earth?" So David commanded his young men, and they executed them, cut off their hands and feet, and hanged them by the pool in Hebron. But they took the head of Ishbosheth and buried it in the tomb of Abner in Hebron. (4:10–12)

David's righteous anger, his swift justice, and his magnanimous piety all confirm his readiness to rule both kingdoms as one.

David's ascent continues as the long-awaited reunification is confirmed in chapter 5, when all Twelve Tribes come to him at Hebron, making a covenant with him, and anointing him king. "David was thirty years old when he began to reign [at Hebron], and he reigned forty years. In Hebron he reigned over Judah seven years and six months, and in Jerusalem he reigned thirty-three years over all Israel and Judah" (5:4–5). It has been a long time since the fourteen-year-old son of Jesse first targeted a rock at Goliath's forehead and felt Samuel's anointing oil on his own. His first unifying act as king of all Israel is to conquer a common capital for the kingdom. The seemingly impregnable Jebus falls in one night to daring Hebrew raiders who enter through the water shaft under the stronghold of Zion, and David restores the city's more ancient and famous name, Jerusalem (5:6–8). David's decisive victory over his former masters the Philistines at Baal Perazim and Rephaim establishes his throne in the eyes of his people and of the surrounding nations (5:17–25). So at 37 David is no longer young but still vital and strong; already the father of six sons by seven wives in Hebron, he soon fathers eleven more in Jerusalem, building a palatial house as a gift from his ally King Hiram of Tyre, and is well on his way to building a dynasty.

Yet it is his first and childless wife – Saul's daughter Michal – who figures prominently in the ironic interlude that follows these triumphs. The previously lost Ark of the Covenant, now found and resident at Baale Judah, is brought up to Jerusalem with great pomp and revelry by the king and 30,000 picked men. The well-intended procession nevertheless runs into disaster because the celebrants have failed to follow the Mosaic Law for handling the Ark, transporting it on an ox-cart rather than carrying it suspended from poles. While nearing the capital, the oxen stumble and a priest named Uzzah reaches out to keep the Ark from falling – as if God cannot care for it himself – only to suffer the same fatal consequences as the presumptuous Philistines of Ashdod, Gath, and Ekron in 1 Samuel 6. This divine rebuke – "God struck [Uzzah dead] there for his error" – dampens the festivities considerably, as David fears to bring this dangerously sacred object into his own house, and leaves it to sojourn in a nearby village.

But after making proper preparations by constructing the Tabernacle in Jerusalem, David's joy can't be contained, and he dances vigorously "before the LORD" and ahead of the Ark, much to the delight of young and old, men and women – except for Michal, who "looked through a window and saw King David leaping and whirling before the LORD; and she despised him in her heart" (6:16). The penalty for her hardness of heart? "Michal the daughter of Saul had no children to the day of her death" (6:23). The incident of the Ark is a reminder that

David's God is still the bountiful yet jealous God of Moses, abundantly blessing his people but sparing neither priest nor royal wife who slight his glory.

It is the new king's passion for the LORD's glory that leads to the culminating covenant in the Hebrew Bible, usually called the Davidic Covenant. As David sits in his new palace made from the cedars of Lebanon, he longs to build a house for his God, and God hears the prayer of his heart. As in the previous covenants with Adam, Noah, Abraham, and Moses, *Yahweh* makes certain specific promises: first, that after his death, David's son "shall build a house for my name" – the Jerusalem Temple – and second, that God will return the compliment, building David's "house" or dynasty so that "your throne shall be established forever" (7:11, 13, 16). If the sign of this Davidic Covenant is the coming Temple itself, perhaps its most striking feature is its conditions – or rather its lack thereof – for David's successor and his descendants:

> I will be his father, and he shall be my son. If he commits iniquity, I will chasten him with the rod of men and with the blows of the sons of men. But my mercy shall not depart from him, as I took it from Saul, whom I removed from before you. And your house and your kingdom shall be established forever before you. (7:14–16)

Under this uniquely unconditional covenant, the LORD's mercy – that is, his *chesed*, or steadfast love – will never depart from David's sons. Thus is planted the seed of Israel's messianic hope in an everlasting and returning "Son of David," who will come to sit on his father's throne and restore his kingdom in the midst of the nations.

As grace notes to this crescendo of divine favor, David continues to thrive both materially and morally. Chapters 8 and 10 describe his continued triumphs over old enemies, the Moabites, the Syrians, the Edomites, and the Ammonites, victories so striking that other nations begin coming to David offering pre-emptive tribute and loyalty, gifts received magnanimously from the rising regional ruler. And juxtaposed between these two chapters of military glory comes the greater glory of David's keeping covenantal faith with his old friend, Jonathan, whose crippled son Mephibosheth David seeks out in order to bless and support. When David asks, "Is there still anyone who is left of the house of Saul, that I may show him kindness for Jonathan's sake?" (9:1), he stands in stark contrast to most Near Eastern kings – including some future kings of Israel – whose usual practice during a transition between dynasties was to exterminate any surviving members of the predecessor's family to remove any rival claimants to the throne. Instead, David kindly embraces Saul's surviving grandson, cherishing him at his own table. Clearly, David is in many ways *not* a king "like the kings of the nations." His line appears to be rising, with no end in sight.

9.2.3 Cross Destinies Times Two: David, Absalom, and Double Chiastic Plot Structure

Yet, also clearly, the opening of chapter 11 reveals that David believes his righteous behavior has earned him a vacation from virtue. Even before his infamous story of adultery and proxy murder unfolds, we're told, "It happened in the spring of the year, at the time when kings go out to battle, that David sent Joab and his servants with him, and all Israel; and they destroyed the people of Ammon and besieged Rabbah. But David remained at Jerusalem" (11:1). One day, after recreation and relaxation in his great palace – perhaps coital recreation, since he's arising from his bed "one evening" – he takes a walk on his high roof for a panoramic view of his city and kingdom. From there he spies "a woman bathing, and the woman was very beautiful to behold" (11:2).

Bathsheba, *Femme Fatale?*

It is worth noting that Bathsheba, while apparently bearing some guilt in her relations with David, is not portrayed in 2 Samuel as the seductress that some have imagined. First, she is bathing in obedience to the Levitical law, cleansing herself from her monthly menstrual uncleanness (Leviticus 15:19–24). Second, whether she is bathing outdoors in a walled garden or in an upper chamber, she is not being deliberately provocative, since it is probably only from the palace roof that she is visible – hardly a common viewpoint. Third, her guilt is lessened by the overwhelming force available to the king should she resist. Nevertheless, unlike David's daughter Tamar in the later episode of palace sexual intrigue (13:12–19), Bathsheba neither protests nor cries out for rescue in the city, thus making herself liable for the death penalty for fornication under Deuteronomy 22:24 – a sentence which, like David's even greater guilt for proposing and coercing her sin, is waived by God's message through Nathan. Yet Bathsheba eventually becomes David's favorite wife, and the mother of the glorious heir Solomon – a sign both of *Yahweh's* grace and of her compensating virtues of discretion and motherly love.

Despite his having many wives and not a few concubines – *like the kings of the nations* – David feels entitled to more – *like the kings of the nations.* Having learned that the bathing woman is Bathsheba, the wife of his brave young officer Uriah, he pushes aside the ninth commandment and summons her to his bedchamber to take her and lie with her. And soon she sends the unwelcome message, "I am with child" (11:5).

The ensuing attempted "cover-up" would be comic were its conclusion not so dark and its long-term consequences not so cursed. Hoping to pin Bathsheba's pregnancy on her husband, David recalls Uriah from the Ammonite front and virtually commands him to make love to his wife, using the coy Hebrew euphemism, "go down to your house and wash your feet" (11:8). The loyal young soldier indeed leaves – followed by a generous food basket from the palace – but gets no farther than the king's own palace door, where he sleeps humbly with the servants. When questioned the next morning by the king, Uriah explains, with very earnest and inconvenient uprightness, "The ark and Israel and Judah are dwelling in tents, and my lord Joab and the servants of my lord are encamped in the open fields. Shall I then go to my house to eat and drink, and to lie with my wife? As you live, and as your soul lives, I will not do this thing" (11:11). Disobeying the king in the king's name, Uriah stands for something above and beyond mere kingly power, and stands in the way of David's plan. Even when the king commands many cups of wine into Uriah, making him drunk, the Hittite is a virtuous drunk: lying down to sleep again among the servants, "he did not go down to his house" (11:13).

So David is at a crossroads. Will he own up to his sin, and face the dire consequences? Or will he conceal his sin, and save face? Facing Uriah, he must deal with a man of true principle, a foreigner (a Hittite) who follows Israel's king and Israel's God out of conviction rather than mere national obligation. Essentially, David is looking into the eyes of his devout, loyal younger self, and he fears and despises what he sees – indeed, wants that self dead. So without apparent hesitation, David sends a note by Uriah's own hand to his clever and unscrupulous nephew Joab besieging Rabbah, ordering him to place Uriah in the thick of the fight and then to pull back. Joab complies and Uriah dies, resulting in a number of other Israelite deaths – a plot worthy of Saul at his worst. When David receives Joab's dispatches, he responds philosophically to Uriah's demise and the collateral damage: "Do not let this thing displease you, for the sword devours one as well as another" (11:25). *C'est la vie! C'est la guerre!* Bathsheba mourns her hapless husband – how deeply or knowingly, we're not told – and then David comforts her by taking her to wife. She bears their son and, and his "perfect crime" is seemingly complete; David, as we say nowadays, is ready to "move on."

"But the thing that David had done displeased the LORD" (11:27). So ends the chapter, and chapter 12 begins as *Yahweh's* messenger, David's court prophet Nathan, takes his life in his hands and enters the king's chambers to tell him a story. It's of a poor man with a single precious ewe lamb and the bad fortune to live next to a rich man with everything except any sense of justice or mercy. The rich man is visited by a traveler, and instead of taking from his own plentiful flocks to feed him, he takes and slaughters the poor man's ewe.

"You are the man": Old Testament Parables

As Prince Hamlet says of his own foray into forensic fiction, "The play's the thing / Wherein I'll catch the conscience of the King" (*Hamlet* 2.2.605–606). Though parables are especially plentiful in the New Testament Gospels (see Chapter 13), the Hebrew Bible has its share of parabolic stories told to catch consciences and illustrate morals by indirection, Nathan's being probably the most famous and successful. Others include Joab's stratagem of the "Wise Woman" and her tale in 2 Samuel 14: 1–24; King Joash's warning fable of "The Thistle and the Cedar Tree" in 2 Chronicles 25: 17–22; and the song of "The Fruitless Vineyard" in Isaiah 5: 1–7. Biblical parables speak to the deeply human love of story, and tell the truth aslant in order to relax listeners' defenses, while engaging their hearts and their emotions where direct accusation or exhortation might fail.

The king responds to the story by rising to the occasion, or one might say to the bait. David, who has spent his youth protecting lambs, and his long exile taking the part of the poor and outcast, suddenly comes to himself, and with a feeling and sincerity that he probably has not known in years, he denounces this sheep-stealer's wickedness with more passion than logic: "As the LORD lives, the man who has done this shall surely die! And he shall restore fourfold for the lamb, because he did this thing and because he had no pity" (12:5–6). Having pronounced the death penalty (followed by a fine!), David appears to have revived his old thirst for justice and mercy.

But ironically, he has been cursing his own image in the mirror of Nathan's parable: "You are the man!" says the prophet, and the most shocking thing about Nathan's blistering rebuke is that Nathan's head remains on his shoulders throughout; that in fact David accepts his pronouncements so meekly. For the prophet foresees troubles coming upon the house of David not as single spies, but in battalions:

> Now therefore, the sword shall never depart from your house, because you have despised me, and have taken the wife of Uriah the Hittite to be your wife. Thus says the LORD: "Behold, I will raise up adversity against you from your own house; and I will take your wives before your eyes and give them to your neighbor, and he shall lie with your wives in the sight of this sun." (12:10–11)

David's only reply: "I have sinned against the LORD." In response, Nathan's final words combine both mercy and deadly judgment: David's own life will be spared, but "the child also who is born to you shall surely die" (12:13–14).

Yahweh is as good, and as fearsome, as his word; David lives, while the child is stricken with mortal illness and lingers for a week, dying on the seventh day. The distraught and prostrate king, in the story's final surprise, hears the evil news, lifts himself from the earth, bathes and anoints himself, worships in the Tabernacle, and "comfort[s] Bathsheba his wife," producing the more fortunate Solomon ("man of peace") in the place of the nameless, ill-fated child of sin. But David will never forget that lost boy: "I shall go to him, but he shall not return to me" (12:23).

Thus, David indeed "moves on" with his life – accepting divine wrath and forgiveness, he returns to the Ammonite front, leading the victorious charge to conquer Rabbah, where he should have been in the first place; yet as David moves on, he lives with the knowledge that more wrath is moving in. His once-secret sin will re-appear in grotesque public scandal, nearly toppling his kingdom, and he will pay with three more sons.

It is David's sin with Bathsheba, and against Uriah, that begins the second, and now doubled, chiastic plot structure found in Samuel. Yet the roles are, at first, reversed from his cross destinies with Saul: now it will be the aging and increasingly ineffectual David whose fall will intersect the rise of a young rival; yet in the final twist, the fallen David will rise again, while the overweening rival falls, sweetening tragedy into tragicomedy. Intensifying these ironies further is the spectacle of the father's sins magnified in his sons', as his own family life generates civil war.

XX Marks the Spot – Chiastic Structure Doubled

2 Samuel displays a doubled chiastic plot structure, this time contrasting the destinies of David and his son and rival, Absalom. Where David is A and Absalom B, their trajectories cross each other fatally twice: first, from David's sin with Bathsheba and the resulting divine curse in 2 Samuel 11–12 and Absalom's appearance as avenging brother of the wronged Tamar in chapter 13, until Absalom's overthrow of David in chapter 15; second, reversing those directions, from Absalom's brief reign of tyranny and folly in chapters 16–17, until David's return from exile and eventual victory – and Absalom's death – in chapters 18–19.

Where David is A and Absalom is B, we see their crossed and competing trajectories from 2 Samuel 13 to 19.

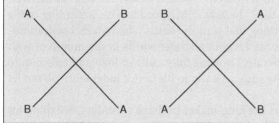

The first piece of rough justice to arise against David from his own household is indeed alarmingly *within* his own household, as David's sexual sin with Bathsheba is compounded by Amnon's sexual sin with Tamar. David's oldest son, like his father, lies abed lusting for a woman, but that woman is Amnon's half-sister and David's beautiful virgin daughter. With the help of a wily relative named Jonadab – shades of Joab – Tamar is maneuvered into Amnon's bedchamber, where the poor girl, despite struggling and resisting, is hotly forced and then coldly cast out, her "robe of many colors" torn, and weeping bitterly. Where David had seduced a neighbor's wife, Amnon rapes a sister; where Bathsheba had silently submitted – perhaps unwillingly – Tamar resists verbally and physically, and then cries out in public. Thus, David's very bad precedent is made much worse, and is about to grow worse still: Tamar's brother is David's second son, Absalom (ironically, "Father of Peace"), and Absalom believes that revenge is a dish best served cold (13:1–22).

Two years pass, time enough to convince Amnon that his rape has been overlooked and forgotten both by David and by Absalom, and Absalom comes to their father asking for his oldest brother's company in a sheep-shearing festival where plenty will be eaten and drunk. Again,

David's past sins come back with interest added: where David had made Uriah drunk and later suborned his murder, Absalom commands his servants to "be courageous and valiant" and to commit proxy murder "when Amnon's heart is merry with wine." Terror falls on all of the king's other sons as they flee on their donkeys, while David is paralyzed with grief, remorse, and confusion, hearing first that Absalom has killed *all* of his brothers, then learning that only Amnon has died – Amnon whose rape had earned the death penalty never carried out by his indulgent father. In a sick combination of guilt and relief (and in a parody of his own flight from King Saul), David allows Absalom to escape into exile, but soon fondly "longs for his son" – not the dead Amnon, but his surviving murderer (13:23–39).

Absalom's plot, which began with avenging his sister Tamar, expands during his exile to something much greater: the overthrow of his father, whom he now holds in contempt, and his establishment as Israel's king. Chapters 13–19 trace the trajectory of his rise, of the coup that brings him to power, of his brief disastrous reign, and of his downfall and death. At first, Absalom has a valuable ally at David's side: Joab, David's nephew, military chief of staff, and main "fixer." Joab is a case study in Machiavellian politics long before Machiavelli: bold, brilliant, ruthless, and indispensable, he has long ago taken the measure of his lord the king and found him shockingly easy to manipulate. Having done multiple murders himself (on Abner and, following David's own orders, on Uriah) and having experienced no consequences, he has come to regard himself as the power and intelligence behind a figurehead monarch.

Thus, in chapter 14, in a dark parody of Nathan's parabolic approach to the guilty David in chapter 12, Joab hires a "wise woman" from Tekoa to tell a tale of two warring brothers to catch the king's conscience. Presenting herself as a widow whose one son has killed the other, she begs David to spare the killer from the death sentence. When David indulgently grants her request, she presses the point, exhorting the king to practice the same clemency in his own family by allowing exiled Absalom's return to Jerusalem. Suddenly David is wise to the wise woman: "Is the hand of Joab with you in all this?" he asks. "[M]y lord is wise, according to the wisdom of the angel of God, to know everything that is in the earth," she flatters back, admitting that "your servant Joab commanded me, and he put all these words in the mouth of your maidservant." Then David, in an act of deliberate, knowing folly, calls in Joab and tells him to allow Absalom's return to Jerusalem. "But," he adds, as a sop to his better judgment, "do not let him see my face" (14:1–24).

Yet Joab's politic support for Absalom – as the king-maker perhaps considers switching his allegiance to the rising power – recoils on Joab when the impatient young man demands more access to his father and, not getting it, sends a message to his sponsor by drastic means, setting Joab's fields on fire. Once burned, Joab is bound to be twice shy of Absalom, but nonetheless engineers an audience with David, and David fondly welcomes his beautiful, tall, lion-maned psychopath back with an embrace and a kiss. But like a Judas-kiss in reverse, this show of lenient paternal affection signals to the designing son that the father is ripe for a fall (14:25–33).

From this point on, events move ahead with all deliberate speed. Soon, Absalom is campaigning in earnest for the throne, building an entourage of fifty runners, with chariots and horses, and embracing supplicants in the city gates, "feeling their pain" while denouncing the out-of-touch regime up in the palace. "Oh, that I were made judge in the land, and everyone who has any suit or cause would come to me; then I would give him justice." And, like many an ambitious politico since, Absalom has truly excellent hair – two hundred shekels' weight per year! "So Absalom stole the hearts of the men of Israel" (15:1–7; 14:26). At the end of four years, the man who would be king has assembled a network of spies and conspirators reaching throughout the realm and up to the very top – including, significantly, *not* Joab, but instead Ahithophel, David's most trusted counselor. The coup begins when David blindly permits Absalom to visit Hebron, the royal city where David's own reign began decades before. Once there, with

Ahithophel and 200 unsuspecting guests, the usurper "sent spies throughout all the tribes of Israel, saying, 'As soon as you hear the sound of the trumpet, then you shall say, "Absalom reigns in Hebron!"'" (15:10).

David receives the terrible news, and something in him seems to snap – snap, that is, back into place. This old soldier and seasoned ruler and veteran of many crises comes to himself and begins decisively to lead again. Ordering the immediate evacuation of Jerusalem to forestall being bottled up in a siege, he gathers his remaining loyalists around him and, even while on the retreat, he lays out the beginnings of a strategy for return: sending the priests Zadok and Abiathar and their sons back into the city with the Ark of the Covenant, he commissions them and his advisor Hushai the Archite to infiltrate the new regime, report on its plans, and, if possible, frustrate them – and especially the wily counsel of Ahithophel. But David's rebound is more than tactical – it is above all spiritual. Faced with the full weight of God's wrath for his past sins – "Behold, I will raise up adversity against you from your own house" – David responds to disaster not only with command but with humble penitence. His head covered and his feet bare, he climbs the Mount of Olives, shedding tears of remorse, and at the mountaintop, looking back on the abandoned city, he bows to worship the LORD (15:13–37).

Perhaps David's greatest humiliation, and show of humility, comes when a Benjamite named Shimei comes forward to curse, throwing dirt and stones and gloating that the man who shed "the blood of the house of Saul" is being run out of his kingdom. David's hot-blooded nephew Abishai bridles at the curse and offers to deprive the "dead dog" Shimei of his head. Instead, David responds by accepting the curse as a kind of rough justice: "What have I to do with you, you sons of Zeruiah? So let him curse, because the LORD has said to him, 'Curse David.' Who then shall say, 'Why have you done so?'" However innocent David is of Saul's blood, he knows that he is guilty of Uriah's. "It may be that the LORD will look on my affliction, and that the LORD will repay me with good for his cursing this day" (16:1–13). Thus, it is at his lowest point that David rediscovers the faith that will raise him up again, and tragedy begins to bloom into tragicomedy.

Yet in the midst of recovery, David still stumbles: he naïvely leaves ten of his concubines behind in the palace to "keep the house" (15:16), and he is taken in by the slander of Ziba the servant of Jonathan's son Mephibosheth, who accuses his crippled master of treason and receives David's hurried gift of his master's lands. And, most perilously, David comes to rest on the near side of the River Jordan, well within striking distance of Absalom's forces. We see some immediate consequences of these mistakes. Back in rebel-occupied Jerusalem, Absalom takes counsel, and the first to speak is Ahithophel, whose devilish wisdom is in the ascendant, advising the young usurper to

> "[g]o into your father's concubines, whom he has left to keep the house; and all Israel will hear that you are abhorred by your father. Then the hands of all who are with you will be strong." So they pitched a tent for Absalom on the top of the house, and Absalom went in to his father's concubines in the sight of all Israel. (16:21–22)

Fulfilling Nathan's prophecy that "I will take your wives before your eyes and give them to your neighbor, and he shall lie with your wives in the sight of this sun" (12:11), Absalom also apes the public couplings of other ancient Near Eastern monarchs, a practice forbidden to Hebrew kings. But Ahithophel's next advice is the *coup de grâce*: since David has camped nearby, "I will come upon him while he is weary and weak, and make him afraid. And all the people who are with him will flee, and I will strike only the king. Then I will bring back all the people to you. When all return except the man whom you seek, all the people will be at peace." Offering to spare the son the trouble of killing his own father, Ahithophel promises a probably literal, and virtually bloodless, regime decapitation. "And the saying pleased Absalom and all the elders of Israel" (17:2–4). And well it should – it appears to be a master-stroke of policy.

But what even the narrator calls Ahithophel's "good advice" is soon frustrated by that unwritten law of committee meetings: it's often not the best word, but the last word, that prevails. As everything hangs in the balance, Hushai rises, and appeals to three motives stronger than Ahithophel's brilliant strategy: Absalom's indolence, his cowardice, and his lust for glory. Hushai counsels delay so that all Israel can be mustered to the fight; he stresses that David and his forces are lion-hearted, "mighty," and "valiant men," and at the moment are "like a bear robbed of her cubs"; and he promises that overwhelming numbers will produce a great and satisfying slaughter in the end. Laziness, fear, and bloodlust prevail: "So Absalom and all the men of Israel said, 'The advice of Hushai the Archite is better than the advice of Ahithophel.'" Ahithophel, a wicked but disciplined man, sees that all is lost and prepares for the coming disaster with an almost humorous efficiency:

> Now when Ahithophel saw that his advice was not followed, he saddled a donkey, and arose and went home to his house, to his city. Then he put his household in order, and hanged himself, and died; and he was buried in his father's tomb. (17:5–14, 23)

Meanwhile, Hushai sends urgent word to David to seek safety across the Jordan, and after a rather thrilling episode in which the messengers are nearly captured, David escapes over the water as far as the fortified city of Mahanaim, and prepares for battle.

As is typical of biblical battles, the fight itself is rather anticlimactic; for by now we know that "the LORD had purposed to ... bring disaster on Absalom" (17:14). The question is not who will win, but rather how Absalom will end, and how David will respond. David wants to lead in battle, but is dissuaded as too valuable – and too old. In a moment of poignant weakness, he pleads with his troops to "[d]eal gently for my sake with the young man Absalom," but Absalom's destiny is determined, ironically, by his own bloodlust, and by the greatest sign of his vanity, his towering *coiffure.* The slaughter that Absalom had desired is visited on him, as 20,000 of his soldiers fall in the woods of Ephraim, while his hair infamously becomes tangled in a terebinth tree, leaving him "hanging between heaven and earth." A messenger tells Joab of the dangling prince, and receives a scolding for leaving him alive. The man tells Joab, "Though I were to receive a thousand shekels of silver in my hand, I would not raise my hand against the king's son." But Joab, never much for scruples, makes quick work of Absalom with three spears to the heart – less for his treason, one suspects, than for burning his fields. Finished by the sword-thrusts of ten men, David's boy is cut down (a final barbering) and tossed into a deep pit under a small mountain of stones. Then the victory trumpet is blown (18:1–18).

The tidings reach David by two different runners, and are broken to him in stages, good news first, perhaps out of fear, but perhaps out of tenderness: "Blessed be the LORD your God, who has delivered up the men who raised their hand against my lord the king!" says one runner. The king demands, "Is the young man Absalom safe?" And the messenger claims ignorance, only to be followed by a Cushite, whom the king again asks, "Is the young man Absalom safe?" So the Cushite answers, with great delicacy, "May the enemies of my lord the king, and all who rise against you to do harm, be like that young man!" (18:19–32). What follows is, in its telegraphic way, one of the great fatherly laments in literature:

> Then the king was deeply moved, and went up to the chamber over the gate, and wept. And as he went, he said thus: "O my son Absalom – my son, my son Absalom – if only I had died in your place! O Absalom my son, my son!" (18:33)

When the sins of the fathers are visited on the children, and the fathers live to see the children dead, grief is great.

Once and Future Kings: David and Arthur

There's no mistaking the many parallels between David's story and that of Arthur, King of Britain: the choice of the "nobody" by the wise prophet Samuel and the wizard Merlin; the hero's youthful exploits displaying strength beyond his years in the slaying of Goliath and pulling the Sword from the Stone; the great sword itself, whether Goliath's or Excalibur; the conflicted relationship with the old king father-figure Saul and Uther Pendragon; the gathering of the Mighty Men and the Round Table Knights; the establishment of a righteous kingdom in Jerusalem and Camelot; the rot at the heart of the kingdom brought by the adultery of David with Bathsheba and either Mordred or Lancelot with Guinevere; the overthrow of the kingdom through the rebellious sons Absalom and Mordred; and the hopes for the "return of the king" in the messianic "Son of David" and the Arthurian *Rex quondamque futurus*, "The Once and Future King." These resemblances can hardly be accidental, since the first full account of Arthur appears in *The History of the Kings of Britain* (1136), the work of the Breton/Welsh monk Geoffrey of Monmouth, who clearly modeled his style on biblical chronicle.

Later additions to and refinements of Arthur's story include the better-known *Morte D'Arthur* (1485) by Sir Thomas Malory; Edmund Spenser's Protestant reimagining in *The Faerie Queene* (1590–1596); Alfred Lord Tennyson's reflection on Victorian aspiration and corruption in *Idylls of the King* (1859–1885); T. H. White's whimsical retelling in *The Once and Future King* (1938–1958); and Mary Stewart's *Crystal Cave* quintet (1970–1985), told from Merlin's point of view. Arthur's tale may have some historical roots in ancient Britain, but it owes much of its story arc, and a good deal of its content, to 1 and 2 Samuel.

But the father in this story is also the king, and he must temper grief with wisdom from an unpalatable source: Joab, Absalom's killer. As David continues to moan in the hearing of his triumphant troops, he is, Joab bluntly points out, seizing defeat from the jaws of victory.

> I perceive that if Absalom had lived and all of us had died today, then it would have pleased you well. Now therefore, arise, go out and speak comfort to your servants. For I swear by the LORD, if you do not go out, not one will stay with you this night. (19:6–7)

Responding to this verbal slap in the face, David pulls himself together and seats himself in the gates of Mahanaim to receive the congratulations of his people. But Joab's harsh words, and especially his necessary ruthlessness in killing the king's son, will briefly cost him his office, and eventually his life.

So, in one of David's first actions after Absalom's fall, the king extends an olive branch to the former rebels by naming their commander Amasa his chief of staff in Joab's place. This is, of course, all in the family, since Amasa and Joab are cousins and both David's nephews by different sisters; it's also a prudent and conciliatory policy to heal the wounds of civil war; but perhaps above all it's a slap back at Joab – who remains a dangerous man to cross, as Amasa soon will feel. Otherwise, David's peace offensive seems to prosper as he makes his progress back to Jerusalem: when re-crossing the Jordan, he is met not only by enthusiastic crowds of Judahites, but also by the trembling Benjamite Shimei, whom David forgives for his curses despite Abishai's renewed offers of extermination. David hears Mephibosheth refute Ziba's slanders and then prudently restores half of Mephibosheth's property – winning his gratitude while keeping Ziba friendly, and the king embraces and rewards Barzillai for his courageous support during the uprising. Indeed, a fierce bidding war breaks out among the Hebrews about who will be first to welcome David back to his throne, as the Israelites of the ten northern tribes protest that the Judahites are monopolizing their near kinsman.

However, this bidding war escalates into renewed civil war when a Benjamite named Sheba convinces the ten tribes that David really does favor Judah over the others:

> [H]e blew a trumpet, and said:
> "We have no share in David,
> Nor do we have inheritance in the son of Jesse;
> Every man to his tents, O Israel!" (20:1)

The fickle Israelites stampede after Sheba, while David orders Amasa (recently a rebel general himself) to muster all of loyal Judah to battle. "Now Sheba the son of Bichri will do us more harm than Absalom," says David, gloomily. When Amasa delays the muster (deliberately?), David turns again to the sons of Zeruiah, Abishai, and the recently demoted Joab, to save the day. While in hot pursuit of Sheba, Joab encounters his cousin and rival, Amasa, takes him aside for an embrace and a conference, and disembowels him, leaving him so that he "wallowed in his blood in the middle of the highway." The chain of command thus clarified, David's army marches on the walled city of Abel where Sheba has holed up, and commences a siege. It looks as if another long bloody season is beginning (20:2–15).

However, we're in for a rough but comic anti-climax. Within Abel's walls is a "wise woman" who calls down to Joab, scolding him for seeking "to destroy a city and a mother in Israel. Why would you swallow up the inheritance of the LORD?" "Far be it, far be it from me, that I should swallow up or destroy!" responds Joab, rather implausibly. But then he offers up a version of Ahithophel's "good" counsel: "Deliver [Sheba] only, and I will depart from the city." And deliver Sheba she does, as the rebel's head soon comes sailing over the wall, no doubt wearing a shocked expression. The insurrection successfully decapitated, Joab "blew a trumpet, and they withdrew from the city, every man to his tent. So Joab returned to the king at Jerusalem" (20:16–22).

9.2.4 Coda: "He Who Rules Over Men"

Although there is more to tell of David in the opening chapters of 1 Kings and in 1 Chronicles (and of course in Psalms), the chronological narrative of this kingly epic is essentially done with Sheba's failed rebellion in 2 Samuel 20. What remains of the book is a kind of coda – or, to put it in cinematic terms, a set of flashbacks to a few pivotal vignettes and statements that appear now, out of time, to epitomize the book's lessons about limited monarchy and just rule. Chapter 21 gives the background for David's kindness to Mephibosheth in chapter 9, as a younger King David seeks to make right Saul's slaughter of his Gibeonite allies by delivering a symbolic seven men of Saul's house to the Gibeonites for expiatory hanging – but sparing Jonathan's crippled son; then a somewhat older David dispatches his Mighty Men to eliminate the threat of the gigantic Philistine relatives of Goliath. Chapter 22 consists entirely of David's celebratory song, virtually identical to Psalm 18, sung "on the day when the LORD had delivered him from the hand of all his enemies, and from the hand of Saul" (22:1), and reminding us that the chosen king was also a choice singer and poet.

Then chapter 23 jumps ahead for the "last words" of "the sweet psalmist of Israel":

> He who rules over men must be just,
> Ruling in the fear of God.
> And he shall be like the light of the morning when the sun rises,
> A morning without clouds,
> Like the tender grass springing out of the earth,
> By clear shining after rain. (23:1, 3–4)

Justice, not brute power and wealth, is the foundation of this throne, and like the ideal king of Deuteronomy 17 he rules under the law of God, rather than claiming to be the law unto himself. This makes his regime as gently refreshing as a dewy dawn, and guarantees "an everlasting covenant" for God's "Anointed" – literally, his *Mashiach*, or Messiah. Following this ideal vision, chapter 23 concludes with an epic catalogue of the Mighty Men who, however imperfectly, fought to put this vision into practice, ending poignantly with the name of "Uriah the Hittite," whose murder signaled the kingdom's loss of innocence, and the beginning of great troubles.

But that is not quite the end. Chapter 24, the last of these final chapters, harkens back to some point relatively early in the reign, when David sought to "number Judah and Israel" in a census which displeases the LORD, perhaps because it indicates David's desire to continue conquest beyond God's allotted boundaries. Intriguingly, a pre-Machiavellian Joab and his fellow officers protest against this hubris, but are over-ruled, and the national head-count proceeds, yielding a number of 1,300,000 "valiant men who drew the sword." Yet David's conscience smites him, followed by a second smite from the prophet Gad, who denounces the sin and offers in *Yahweh's* name a choice of three punishments: seven years' famine, three months' defeat in battle, or three days' plague. Choosing what seems the least dreadful of the three, the king opts for plague, and all hell breaks loose as the angel of the LORD begins to decimate the very fighting force that David had sought to number; 70,000 potential warriors die. David is struck with terrible remorse ("I have done wickedly; but these sheep, what have they done?") and offers up himself in the place of his suffering people. David's offer touches God Almighty: "the LORD relented from the destruction, and said to the angel who was destroying the people, 'It is enough; now restrain your hand.' And the angel of the LORD was by the threshing floor of Araunah (or Ornan) the Jebusite" (24:1–16).

And that hilltop threshing floor? The mortified king, expecting his own death, instead is told by Gad to buy the land, build an altar, and offer sacrifice. And we are told in 2 Chronicles 3:1 that this is none other than the Temple Mount, where Solomon the Son of David will build the House of the LORD. So, fittingly, the Davidic tragicomedy ends, after so many deaths, with a new beginning, and with a reminder that the king remembers his responsibilities and his limitations, he brings life. So Samuel's book concludes by stressing the deadly bounds of royal power and the gracious power of the divine covenant, and it points ahead to the drama of good and bad kings to follow.

Questions for Discussion

1 How does the Hebrew **Book of Samuel** (*Shmuel*) work as a whole? What's the effect of dividing it in half for the Christian Old Testament?

2 What are the **epic characteristics of 1 and 2 Samuel**? How does the narrative action resemble classical epics such as the Babylonian *Enuma Elish*, the Greek *Iliad* and *Odyssey*, and the Latin *Aeneid*? How does it differ? How would we compare David to heroes like Marduk, Achilles, Odysseus, and Aeneas?

3 Why begin the epic story of **Saul** and **David** with the domestic drama of **Hannah**?

4 How does the story of **Samuel** prepare us for the **epic** events to follow – particularly the incident of the "**lost ark**" and the warnings of chapter 8?

5 What are the **tragic elements** in the stories of **Saul** and **Absalom**? How do they compare with classical tragedies like Euripides' *Agamemnon* or Shakespeare's *Richard III* or *Macbeth* – or Samson in the Book of Judges?

6 How is **chiastic plot structure** at work in the interwoven stories of Saul and David, and of David and Absalom?

7 What are the **tragicomic elements** functioning in David's kingly career? How might his story compare with Shakespeare's tragicomic romances *The Winter's Tale* and *The Tempest*?

8 Compare David's story to the medieval British legends of **Robin Hood** and **King Arthur**. What are important resemblances and differences? What influence has David's "**under-dog**" **story** and his "**hero's journey**" had on literature and culture in general?

9 What is the **Davidic Covenant** and what is its role in later Jewish and Christian belief?

10 Why does the Book of Samuel conclude with multiple, "**flashback**" endings?

11 What, overall, is the **epic theme** of the Book of Samuel?

Note

1 *The Importance of Being Earnest*, Act II, Part 2.

10

National Narrative: Chosen Stories of Chosen People in Kings, Chronicles, Ezra-Nehemiah, and Esther

After the epic accounts of Moses, Joshua, and David, interspersed with the anti-heroic and heroic stories in Judges and Ruth, the Old Testament opens out into a series of books that might be described as national narratives: stories chosen mainly out of larger records or documents to exemplify the best and worst acts of the chosen people and their leaders, and to explain their marvelous rise, shameful fall and exile, and strange revival and persistence as a nation. The Book of Kings (like Samuel and Chronicles a single book in the Hebrew Bible) carries on the national themes and threads of Samuel, over four centuries from the start of Solomon's reign through the division and eventual fall of Israel and then Judah; the Book of Chronicles doubles and supplements Samuel and Kings while focusing on Judah; Ezra-Nehemiah (also originally one book) recounts the return from exile to rebuild the Temple, Jerusalem's walls, and the nation; and Esther tells of national survival through one woman's faith and triumph while *in* exile. These are not epics: the many monarchs of Kings and Chronicles are too numerous for single epic heroism, while the hero stories of Ezra, Nehemiah, and Esther are too short for even brief epic scope. Throughout the shifting casts of characters in these books, the clearly central character – though perhaps incognito in Esther's book – is *Yahweh* himself: raising, blessing, warning, judging, cursing, relenting, redeeming, rescuing. Here the common old pun is true: history is presented as "His story."

10.1 Sad Stories of the Death of Kings: Kings and Chronicles

Kings clearly begins by carrying on the deeds and themes of 1 and 2 Samuel, but it also begins on a note of menace.

The Whole Books of Kings and Chronicles

Like Samuel, Kings and Chronicles each comprise one book in the Hebrew Bible. Each was divided in two by the later Greek Septuagint and by Jerome's Latin Vulgate translation, but each functions as a single narrative, drawing from their common sources: the court records of King Solomon, the Books of the Chronicles of the Kings of Judah and of Israel, and the prophetic writings of Isaiah and others. These daily and yearly court records from each reign were carefully selected and excerpted to convey particular theological and political messages about the life – and death – of kings and nations. Though public themes of international relations, war, and domestic policy have their place in Kings and Chronicles, the geopolitical and the governmental often are secondary to the strikingly individual, personal, and spiritual – including the spiritual careers of some great Israelite prophets.

Literary Study of the Bible: An Introduction, First Edition. Christopher Hodgkins.
© 2020 John Wiley & Sons Ltd. Published 2020 by John Wiley & Sons Ltd.

In the Hebrew Bible, the Book of Kings (*Sepher Melechim*) concludes the sequence of "The Former Prophets" beginning with Joshua, while Chronicles (*Divrei Hayyamim*, "Matters of the Days") concludes the *Khetuvim*, and thus ends the entire Jewish canon. This is the canonical order assumed by Jesus in the New Testament when he denounces murderous Israelite hostility to God's prophets, "from the blood of righteous Abel [Genesis 4:8] to the blood of Zechariah son of Berechiah, whom you murdered between the temple and the altar" [2 Chronicles 23:21] (Matthew 23:35) – that is to say, "from the Bible's first murder to the last." The Book of Kings, while traditionally attributed to Jeremiah, does not name its author, who seems to have completed it after the fall of Jerusalem and Judah in 587 BCE, but before the return from exile in 538 BCE. Chronicles mentions that latter return date at its very end, so it seems to have been written primarily not for exiles in a foreign land, but for returnees rebuilding their city and nation. While Chronicles is traditionally grouped with Ezra and Nehemiah as the work of the prophet Ezra, it seems little concerned with the Gentile intermarriage issue so central to Ezra and Nehemiah; thus, Chronicles may precede the other two books by many decades.

Chapter 1 casts us immediately into the intrigues of the elderly King David's court. As the curtain rises on the old monarch's final acts, he lies weak and cold in bed, and he is given the exceptionally beautiful young virgin Abishag the Shunammite to serve him and "lie in [his] bosom" (1 Kings 1:4). The fact that he "did not know her" sexually suggests not so much David's restraint as his incapacity, and this sign of sexual impotence attracts those thirsting for political power – again, from his own family and inner circle.

Specifically, though Amnon and Absalom are dead, the king has yet another handsome, ungrateful, undisciplined, and devious son: Adonijah, the son of Haggith. Like Absalom before him, Adonijah initially has the support of the canny Joab, who looks to make the new king and secure control through him. While David lies abed with Abishag, Adonijah proclaims himself king, assembles his own entourage, and invites his brothers and supporters to a sacrifice-cum-royal-coming-out-party at nearby En Rogel – all of them, that is, except for Solomon and his court-in-waiting. Also pointedly uninvited are "Zadok the priest, Benaiah the son of Jehoiada, Nathan the prophet, Shimei, Rei, and the mighty men who belonged to David" (1:1–10). This is more than a snub, it is a *coup d'etat.*

This time, however, the coup dies aborning. Ironically, it is the prophet Nathan, the man who had pronounced God's judgment on David's and Bathsheba's adultery and on their first son (2 Samuel 12), who raises the alarm to save their second. Going first to Bathsheba, Nathan rouses her to approach the king and remind him of his promise to settle the crown on Solomon; this she does, telling David pointedly that not just the throne, but their lives, are at stake. Reinforced by Nathan, David acts decisively, swearing an oath to crown Solomon, and dispatching the chosen prince on David's own royal mule to the Gihon spring, the living waters at the heart of Jerusalem.

> Then Zadok the priest took a horn of oil from the tabernacle and anointed Solomon. And they blew the horn, and all the people said, "Long live King Solomon!" And all the people went up after him; and the people played the flutes and rejoiced with great joy, so that the earth seemed to split with their sound. (1 Kings 1:39–40)

This master-stroke has the desired results: Adonijah and his party hear the noise all the way from En Rogel outside the city, and their celebration comes to an abrupt end, as they receive word of the coronation and "each went his own way," every man for himself. His support having vaporized, Adonijah himself runs to the Tabernacle to grasp the horns of the altar and plead for clemency.

Meanwhile, Solomon is engulfed by popular affection, while David "bow[s] himself on the bed" and blesses the LORD God of Israel, "who has given one to sit on my throne this day, while my eyes see it!" In contrast to a brother who would steal a throne by guile, a father gives up his throne to see his son and kingdom established, and unlike Adonijah who plots to seal his power in blood, Solomon shows mercy: "If he proves himself a worthy man, not one hair of him shall fall to the earth." Mercy, that is, for the time being: "but if wickedness is found in him, he shall die" (1:44–52). Already, Solomon shows a gift for wisely balanced mercy and justice.

After this action-packed opening, David's life comes to a close in chapter 2. This is in one sense a second ending for David, as we have already encountered his "last words" in 2 Samuel 23; here the son of Jesse gives final fatherly advice to his untried heir that echoes the themes of Samuel, though now there is a sting in the tail. First David exhorts Solomon with Deuteronomic wisdom: "keep the charge of the LORD your God: to walk in His ways, to keep His statutes, His commandments, His judgments, and His testimonies, as it is written in the Law of Moses" (2:3). But then, walking a fine line between justice and vendetta, David maps out for Solomon the deadly obstacle course leading to a truly secure throne.

First, the new king's crowned head will lie uneasy while Joab lives, and breathes, and schemes: "you know also what Joab the son of Zeruiah did to me, and what he did to the two commanders of the armies of Israel, to Abner the son of Ner and Amasa the son of Jether … do not let his gray hair go down to the grave in peace" (2:5–6). Joab's two unpunished murders – unpunished, of course, by *David* – must now be answered, but perhaps above all the necessary yet for David unforgivable blood of Absalom will have blood in return. Second, the loyal Barzillai must be rewarded. But third comes the loathsome Shimei, whose false "malicious curse" on David as Saul's murderer has rankled for years, but to whom David had sworn, "*I* will not put you to death with the sword." However, now comes the shift in pronouns and in generations: "*you* are a wise man and know what you ought to do to him." And then comes the dying king's parting shot: "bring his gray hair down to the grave with blood" (2:9). Unspoken, but implied, is a similar fate for brother Adonijah. David, the chosen one of Samuel, the anointed of God, the sweet psalmist of Israel, the king who yearned to build *Yahweh's* house of praise and who named two of his sons for God's *shalom* – this David ends calling for blood, like a mafia don ordering a death; and then there will be peace. Such an analogy may seem unjust, even shocking: certainly David and his line achieve great goodness and glory, but contrary to the old king's hope, there will be blood, and many will fall far; mainly, this book will tell sad stories of the death of kings.

After David "rested with his fathers," chapter 2 details how Solomon brings each of his adversaries to a sharp, sure end. In a quick, virtually cinematic, montage, first Adonijah, then Joab, and finally Shimei "go down with blood to Sheol," while the devious priest Abiathar goes into exile. The justice is, largely, poetic: Adonijah requests David's beauteous consort Abishag as a wife, treasonously claiming David's "couch" as another way to the throne, but he ends up laid out forever; Joab, the merciless old assassin, is denied mercy while clinging to the horns of the altar; while Shimei is killed by his own contempt – scoffing at the conditions of his house arrest, he runs off to capture two slaves, and is dragged back and cut off in the king's presence. The ironic last words heard by the man who cursed the house of David are that "King Solomon shall be blessed, and the throne of David shall be established before the LORD forever" (2:45).

Chapters 3–10 detail the rise and establishment of Solomon's greatness – but also, as we will see, the seeds of his eventual apostasy. First his rise: as in the Book of Proverbs, Solomon's reverential fear of *Yahweh* is the beginning of his wisdom, and the foundation of his prosperity. The young king has a dream while at Gibeon in which he humbly asks the LORD not for long life, or riches, or military victory, but for a discerning heart of wisdom "to judge this great people of yours." God is pleased by Solomon's seeking first this wisdom: "see, I have given you a wise and understanding heart, so that there has not been anyone like you before you, nor shall any like you arise after you" (3:12). And then the LORD gives Solomon all of the other gifts as well – promising, in a pervasive pun on his name, a reign of unprecedented *shalom*, of peace and prosperity.

This vision is followed by the most famed illustration of Solomon's practical discernment, the great story of "splitting the baby": two harlots come to the king, both having recently given birth, and one complains that the other has stolen her live newborn after the other accidentally smothered her own infant in the night. With each woman claiming the surviving child as her own, and with no witnesses, Solomon seems to face an intractable "she-said-she-said" scenario, until he calls for a sword and makes a modest proposal: "Divide the living child in two, and give half to one, and half to the other"; for surely it's better to have half of a recently living child than none at all? One woman coldly accepts this insanely equal outcome, while the other warmly gives up the living child rather than own part of a dead one. Thus, the verdict declares itself: Solomon, obviously a natural master of "game theory," has built a test to compel the liar to reveal her own lie, and a sordid setting nevertheless discovers a spark of maternal love even in a prostitute (3:16–28).

Having shown this astonishing gift for practical justice, Solomon also displays a knack for building the kind of effective administration that is essential for a sustainable kingdom. First, Solomon attracts and chooses the best talent, all listed in 1 Kings 4:1–19; then he organizes the kingdom in a dozen districts configured differently from the boundaries of the twelve tribes, stressing the central allegiance owed to the crown over the old loose tribal confederacy under the judges. Having removed the devious old head of the army, Joab, he builds a more effective, loyal, and disciplined force under Benaiah, and especially establishes great stables for the horses that will pull his warriors' chariots.

Solomon's glory is founded not only on armed might, but also on the "soft power" of learning and art:

> he was wiser than all men – than Ethan the Ezrahite, and Heman, Chalcol, and Darda, the sons of Mahol; and his fame was in all the surrounding nations. He spoke three thousand proverbs, and his songs were one thousand and five. Also he spoke of trees, from the cedar tree of Lebanon even to the hyssop that springs out of the wall; he spoke also of animals, of birds, of creeping things, and of fish. (4:31–33)

As described in Ecclesiastes 1:13, Solomon seeks out all forms of knowledge, encompassing the prudential, the aesthetic, and the natural, making him a one-man Royal Society. And so Solomon's reign is a time of abundance, of God's promises to Abraham and Moses fulfilled internationally, nationally, and in the safety of home: "Judah and Israel were as numerous as the sand by the sea," "each man under his vine and his fig tree," "from Dan as far as Beersheba" – these are all traditional phrases to warm the Hebrew heart: from east to west, from north to south, Israel has completed his mission, confirmed his borders, grown full and sweet and ripe (1 Kings 4:20–21, 24–25).

The United Kingdom and Greater Israel Under David and Solomon

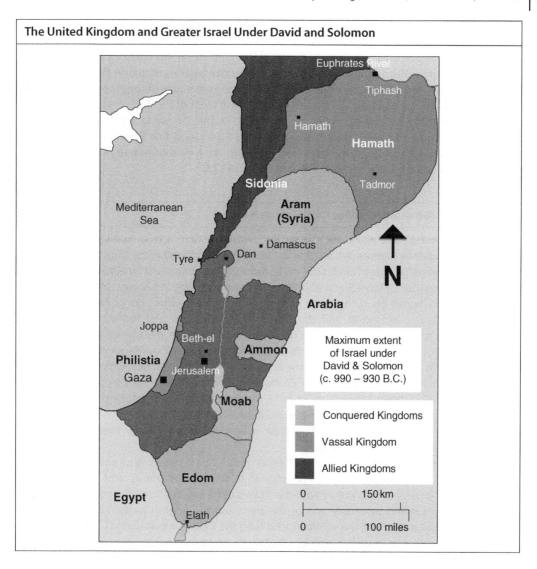

And at the heart of Solomon's vision for Israel is a work that embraces all wisdom, beauty, and truth, and all this abundance, made visible: the "house of the Lord" that will replace the traveling Tabernacle. Chapters 5–7 describe in loving detail the construction and outfitting of the Temple by the architect Huram of Tyre. Like the rare and special parts that make up an auto aficionado's classic car, or the list of lovely gifts in a bride's trousseau, each item is saturated in meaning – gold, silver, and bronze, cedar, cypress, and olive wood. The Temple follows the basic floor plan of the Tabernacle, but on a much grander scale; every piece is rich and fine, engraved and gilded even where human eyes seldom if ever look, within the Holy of Holies. The work begins, we are told, 480 years after the Exodus from Egypt, and the construction takes seven years, from the fourth to the eleventh years of Solomon's reign. He employs Israelites from every tribe, making it a truly national project.

Chapter 7 tells us that the king's own house takes thirteen years to build, even longer than the Temple. Solomon's chief craftsman Huram spares no expense or effort to present a palace to inspire awe in Solomon's friends and subjects, and fear and envy in his enemies. Meanwhile, the last touches on the Temple are described: the great bronze bath standing on the backs of four massive oxen; the carts and lavers and lampstands and other furnishing, most of pure gold (7:23–51); but most prominently the two bronze pillars in front of the Temple that tell the story of Solomon's humble but noble origins: to the right, Jachin ("Foundation"), and to the left, Boaz – named for the rustic Bethlehemite who founded the kingly line by redeeming and wedding a faithful foreign wife; the local hero now stands at the forefront of national glory, a glory that will remain as long as the virtues of Boaz rule (7:15–22).

The Solomonic Renaissance: James I and George Herbert

While many monarchs and many writers have looked back to Solomon for inspiration and precedent, none have done so more deliberately than England's (and Scotland's) King James I (and VI) during the so-called "Jacobean" era (1603–1625). James, like Solomon, was the son of a beautiful and notorious mother – Mary Queen of Scots – and was a scholar in his own right, publishing closely reasoned books on such topics as royal authority (*The True Law of Free Monarchies* and *Basilikon Doron*), witchcraft and the occult (*Daemonologie*), and the evils of smoking (*A Counter-Blast to Tobacco*). He also was a great patron of literature and the arts (he sponsored Shakespeare's troupe of players, The King's Men); he styled himself a bringer of peace to his expanding realms – Virginia was settled in the first years of his reign, and he sought reconciliation with imperial Spain. And of course he is probably best remembered for commissioning the Authorized Version or "King James Bible" of 1611, the most influential scriptural translation ever. Ironically, he also resembled Solomon in rearing a son – Charles I – who governed disastrously and divided the kingdom, and also in his sexual dissipation: in James's case likely homosexual liaisons with handsome male courtiers.

James' contemporary and subject George Herbert (1593–1633) was a poet, Cambridge scholar, parliamentarian, and Church of England priest, who achieved posthumous fame with the 1633 publication of *The Temple*. This poetry collection takes as an organizing metaphor the architecture of Solomon's grand sanctuary and of the more homely English parish church, reading features like the altar, the floor, the windows, and even the locks as representing God's often corrective but still gracious dealings with the believer's heart. In addition, Herbert's foray into Solomonic wisdom literature, *Outlandish Proverbs* (1640, 1651), were frequently quoted on both sides of the Atlantic, along with *The Temple* influencing the writings and speeches of Richard Baxter, Cotton Mather, Benjamin Franklin, Horace Greeley, Winston Churchill, C. S. Lewis, and famed poets from John Wesley, William Blake, and Emily Dickinson to Gerard Manley Hopkins, Elizabeth Bishop, and T. S. Eliot.

In chapter 8 we read of how the storied Ark of the Covenant comes to rest in the new Temple, though we are told that within the Ark there remain only "the two tablets of stone which Moses put there at Horeb" (8:9), the manna and Aaron's rod having disappeared. Then Solomon demonstrates his calling as "the Preacher/Gatherer" (*Qoheleth/Ecclesiastes*) by assembling the people together for a kingly sermon and prayer: explaining to the congregation how the LORD had set him aside, through his father David, "to build a Temple for [God's] name," he then calls on God to fill the House that, paradoxically, cannot hold him. "Behold, the heaven and the heaven of heavens cannot contain You. How much less this Temple which I have built?" (8:27).

The house of God, while serving *exclusively* as the only site of legitimate Hebrew sacrifice, also will serve *inclusively* as a house of prayer for all peoples. Solomon prays:

> [C]oncerning a foreigner, who … has come from a far country for your name's sake … when he comes and prays toward this Temple, hear from heaven your dwelling place, and do according to all for which the foreigner calls to you, that all peoples of the earth may know you and fear you … (8:41–43)

The Temple will stand as a grand visible reminder of *Yahweh's* presence, his justice, and his mercy for all, even for those Hebrews suffering some terrible future exile:

> When [the Israelites] sin against you, and you … deliver them to the enemy, and they take them captive to the land of the enemy, far or near; yet when they come to themselves … and repent, and make supplication to you in the land of those who took them captive … then hear in heaven your dwelling place … and maintain their cause. (8:46–49)

As with Abraham and Moses, separation from the Gentiles has the ultimate purpose of bringing blessing to the Gentiles, and though Israel is chosen for special divine favor, it is also subject to particular divine judgment. Like the Mosaic Law, the Temple is a sign of special blessing and unique responsibility, and like the Law it is inaugurated with a weight of glory and solemnity: the cloud of *Shekinah* glory that guided the Exodus returns to rest on Zion's Holy Place, and for a peace offering Solomon staggers the imagination by sacrificing the livestock from a thousand hills: "twenty-two thousand bulls, and one hundred and twenty thousand sheep" (8:63). Thus, the Temple overflows with abundance and with blood; it is a place of both constant celebration and perpetual atoning admonition.

After the Temple consecration, chapter 9 continues this double-edged theme, as God manifests himself to Solomon again, both to bless the king and to remind and warn him about the disastrous consequences of failure to "keep my statutes." And here the rising tide of Solomonic glory begins to turn. As we cast our minds back over the preceding chapters, we begin to sense that even in the midst of great fulfillment and plenty, Solomon is starting to stray: his multiplying of silver and gold, of horses and chariots, his palace more elaborate and longer-a building than God's own Temple, and the narrator's passing references to continued offerings on the high places – all suggest the coming catastrophe of success. Casting all the way back to the very beginning of Solomon's rise in chapter 3, we now may recall that he had, also counter to the kingly law of Deuteronomy 17, "gone back to Egypt" – for a wife, the daughter of Pharaoh (3:1).

Thus, when chapter 10 tells of the visit from the Queen of Sheba, her visit suggests both the apogee and the turning point of Solomon's reign. A figure of great glamor and passion, the Queen of Sheba comes from Africa to Israel hungry for the life of the mind, but ends up overwhelmed as much by the sensory glories and sensual pleasures of Jerusalem, and especially its king. Solomon tells and shows her all, "and gave her everything that she desired" so that "there was no more spirit in her"; whether some of her desires were sexual, and he gave her his child to bear, is a matter of Ethiopian (and Hollywood) legend, though not of explicit biblical record. Looked at from one angle, Sheba's queen represents the expansion of God's glory among the Gentiles, and foreshadows the ingathering of the nations also predicted by such prophets as Isaiah and Jeremiah. However, from another angle, her visit also represents Solomon's increasing worldliness, and his potential contamination by heathen ways.

Indeed chapter 11 makes clear that as unique as the Queen of Sheba seems, she is actually one of many "foreign women" who came to Jerusalem, these others as wives for Solomon's burgeoning harem, in flagrant violation of the Deuteronomic law against kings multiplying wives, and against intermarriages that will turn the faithful away to worship other gods. In the Song of Solomon, there already are "sixty wives, and eighty concubines, and maidens without number" (Song of Solomon 6:8), while here in Kings we're told that eventually "he had seven hundred wives, princesses, and three hundred concubines; and his wives turned away his heart" (1 Kings 11:3). Quite apart from questions of sexual stamina, Solomon constitutes a one-man Hebrew population explosion – and a solemn warning that intermarriage leads to idolatry.

So while chapters 3–10 foreshadow Solomon's apostasy even during his rise, it's chapter 11 that makes that falling away explicit, along with God's resulting judgment, while still emphasizing the LORD's faithfulness to his covenant.

> So the LORD became angry with Solomon, because his heart had turned from the LORD God of Israel, who had appeared to him twice, and had commanded him concerning this thing, that he should not go after other gods... Therefore the LORD said to Solomon ... "I will surely tear the kingdom away from you and give it to your servant. Nevertheless I will not do it in your days, for the sake of your father David; I will tear it out of the hand of your son. However I will not tear away the whole kingdom; I will give one tribe to your son for the sake of My servant David, and for the sake of Jerusalem which I have chosen." (11:9–13)

In wrath remembering mercy, *Yahweh* mixes punishment with promise, establishing the pattern that will define the Hebrew story for the rest of the kingly era: that of a divided kingdom, with the many northern tribes under a different monarchy, and the southern tribe of Judah constantly governed by a descendant of David. As we have seen before from Genesis through Samuel, future disasters are portrayed as evidence not of divine indifference or caprice, but of divine design and deliberate justice, leavened with *chesed* or lovingkindness.

So it's not merely by divine permission but by divine intervention that increasing unrest troubles Solomon's late years. God raises up a foreign adversary in Hadad the Edomite, and much more seriously a domestic adversary in Solomon's lively young administrator, Jeroboam the son of Nebat, an Ephraimite from the house of Joseph. Hadad has a score to settle with the house of David for its violent subjection of Edom, while the unsuspecting Jeroboam is directly recruited for rebellion by God's own prophet Ahijah. Never in the Bible is a revolt more divinely mandated, or more strictly limited: Ahijah meets Jeroboam while on royal business and informs the surprised official that the LORD plans to tear most of the kingdom from Solomon's heir and give it to him and to his house, perpetually, *if* Jeroboam and his descendants will "heed all that I command you, walk in My ways ... as My servant David did" (11:38). In other words, Jeroboam's reign will be conditioned by the same Levitical and Deuteronomic limits that governed David, and, remarkably, the nation is to be split politically in two but remain religiously one, with the northern tribes still traveling to the Jerusalem Temple for worship.

If Jeroboam's prophetic recruitment resembles Samuel's anointing of the young David, then Solomon's response to news of this prophecy resembles the paranoid jealousy of David's predecessor Saul: Solomon seeks to kill his rival, who flees to the hostile Pharaoh Shishak in Egypt as David did to the Philistines. As portrayed in Ecclesiastes, Solomon ekes out his last days, brooding over his coming doom, and writing bitterly about the curse of incompetent offspring:

> Then I hated all my labor in which I had toiled under the sun, because I must leave it to the man who will come after me. And who knows whether he will be wise or a fool? Yet he will rule over all my labor in which I toiled and in which I have shown myself wise under the sun. This also is vanity. (Ecclesiastes 2:18–19)

That successor is a fool indeed. Rehoboam is Solomon's son by the pagan Naamah the Ammonitess. Ironically, the name Rehoboam means "he who enlarges the people," but he splits the people instead. After Solomon's death, Rehoboam, though already forty-one years old, seems to incarnate youthful folly. He rejects the wise advice of the elders and instead is scripted by the young hotheads in his entourage, as he alienates the fractious northern tribes with delayed adolescent boasting and pompous threats:

> My little finger shall be thicker than my father's waist! And now, whereas my father put a heavy yoke on you, I will add to your yoke; my father chastised you with whips, but I will chastise you with scourges! (1 Kings 12:10–11)

The old King James Bible catches Rehoboam's bravado in language more earthy: "My little finger shall be thicker than my father's *loins*," he says, in an especially odious genital comparison; "but I will chastise you with *scorpions*" (emphases mine). In response, Jeroboam leads a new exodus out of the United Kingdom, as the Israelites raise the old separatist cry of the northern tribes:

> What share have we in David?
> We have no inheritance in the son of Jesse.
> To your tents, O Israel!
> Now, see to your own house, O David! (2 Samuel 20:1; 1 Kings 12:16)

As the secession unfolds with almost tragic inevitability, God intervenes to prevent further Hebrew bloodshed and seal the divide as divine judgment. The bellicose Rehoboam returns to Jerusalem, musters 180,000 men of Judah, and calls for the re-conquest of Israel, but the prophet Shemaiah speaks. "Thus says the LORD: 'You shall not go up nor fight against your brethren the children of Israel. Let every man return to his house, for this thing is from me'" (1 Kings 12:24). And for once, they all obeyed.

But Rehoboam, it turns out, has no monopoly on folly. Jeroboam soon establishes his own disastrous policies, setting his fledgling kingdom on a short route to chaos: reasoning that continuing Israelite religious unity with Judah will undermine his throne's separate status, he deliberately creates a syncretistic, nationalist cult, combining the outward rituals of *Yahweh*-worship with "the ways of the nations." Then he sets up golden calves at Dan and Bethel, echoing Israel's fateful words of apostasy in Exodus: "here are your gods, O Israel, which brought you out of the land of Egypt" (Exodus 32:8; 1 Kings 12:28). In addition to this overt idolatry, Jeroboam also violates the Law by arrogating the separate priestly power to the crown, appointing non-Levitical priests to serve in his state-approved altars and sanctuaries.

Having made Jeroboam the instrument of his judgment, the LORD quickly judges the instrument, as an anonymous "man of God" appears not only to pronounce the quick extinction of Jeroboam's line, but also to predict the name of the far future king of Judah who will destroy Jeroboam's and all other "high places" in the land – Josiah, 300 years hence (1 Kings 13:1–3; 2 Kings 23:15–18). In an episode of dark irony like something late in the Book of Judges, even this "man of God" goes astray from his own message, and is himself struck down by a God-sent lion; and the irony is compounded as the false prophet who tempted him from his mission rescues

The Divided Kingdoms of Judah and Israel Under Rehoboam and Jeroboam – and After

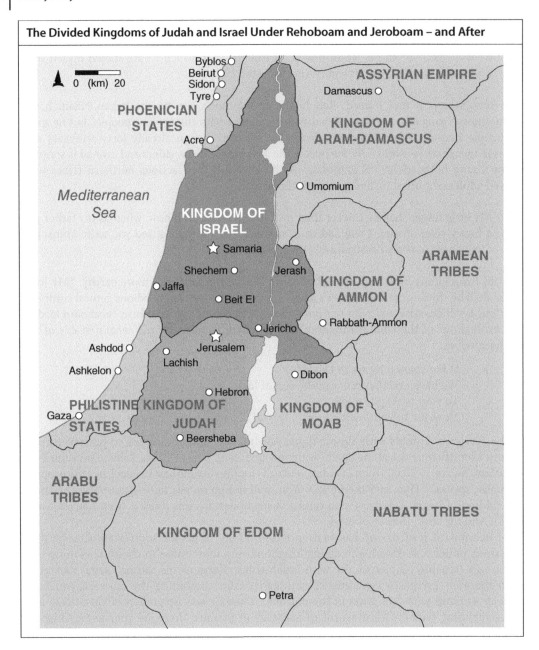

his corpse and mourns his death. The point: even God's prophets aren't exempt from sin and judgment, and conversely even unworthy men have their uses in God's plans (1 Kings 13:11–34).

Jeroboam's first drink from God's bowl of wrath comes when his oldest son and heir is dying, and his wife travels to implore the formerly friendly prophet Ahijah for some good news, but is told that the lad will die more happily that all his kin, because at least he will be mourned and buried, rather than eaten by dogs and wild beasts (14:11–13). Henceforth in Kings "the sin of Jeroboam son of Nebat" will serve as shorthand for any regime that twists the heavenly worship of the Most High to low, idolatrous, and merely political ends. This sin brings, appropriately, almost constant political mayhem, as Israel suffers through nine different short-lived and mainly evil dynasties and almost as many coups before its fall to Assyria in 722 BCE; while Judah, for all of its faults, endures more than a century longer – until 587 BCE – always under the dynasty of David, many of whom are praised as "good kings."

From chapter 14 on, the royal records of 1 Kings and then 2 Kings fall into a fairly regular rhythm: each monarch of the two divided kingdoms is introduced (name, year of accession in the rival kingdom, age at accession, length of reign, often the queen mother's name), followed by a quick judgment on his regime ("he did good/evil in the sight of the LORD"), and a summary of his achievements and/or misdeeds. These summaries vary substantially in length, from a brief paragraph (for a number of truly lackluster or short-lived rulers) to many chapters (usually for rulers of remarkable virtue or wickedness). However, interwoven with this kingly narrative of decline and death, and often superseding it, is a counter-narrative of powerful prophetic intervention, of some minor and even anonymous prophets, but especially of the Israelite master–disciple duo, Elijah and Elisha. Indeed, the kings come and go in often quick succession, demonstrating the failure of the state in matters of the spirit. But as Elijah and Elisha speak truth to power in Israel, Judah, and throughout Canaan, the Book of Kings seems as much a Book of Prophets. While I will note as necessary the prophets' outsized role in the book, I will reserve most discussion of these "forthtelling" prophets for Chapter 12, which takes prophecy as its main topic.

So, while Jeroboam's reign over Israel (931–910 BCE) encompasses the reigns of two kings of Judah (Rehoboam and Abijah), most other monarchs of Judah well outlast their Israelite rivals: Judah's Asa (911–871) reigns during Israel's changing regimes and dynasties from Nadab and Baasha to Elah and Zimri; Judah's Jehoshaphat (871–848) sees the coming of Israel's Omri, Ahab, and Ahaziah; Judah's Uzziah (767–739) outlasts the revolving-door monarchies of Jeroboam II, Zechariah, Shallum, Menahem, and Pekahiah; and Judah's Ahaz (734–728) overlaps the disastrous reigns of Pekah and of Hoshea, who preside over the final collapse of Israel and its destruction by Assyria. Along the way we meet dueling Jehorams (or Jorams – both kings, north and south, die in the year 841), and the closest thing to a successful Israelite king, the relentless Jehu (842–813), who is raised up to destroy the house of Ahab and the prophets of Baal. Ironically, the lethal Jehu reigns during neighboring Judah's darkest hour under the murderous Athaliah (840–835), the Baal-worshiping daughter of Ahab and his infamous wife Jezebel who has married into the house of David on a dark mission of extermination. Athaliah's plot is foiled only at the last possible moment, as the seven-year-old Joash (835–796) is restored to the throne of David and revives his dynasty, which will rule for another 250 years.

With the fall of Israel in 722 BCE, Judah absorbs some of the surviving remnant from the northern tribes into a scaled-down "reunited" kingdom under Hezekiah (728–699), who faithfully outlasts the Assyrian invasion, only to hand off his crown to two unworthy successors, the abhorrent but long-lived Manasseh (699–643), and his only somewhat less wicked son Amon (642–640). However Amon's son, the prophesied Josiah (640–609), is a prodigy of righteousness, the only king of Judah or Israel after David to win the full praise and approval of the book's narrator(s), who say that "he walked in all the ways of his father David." Even from his adolescent days Josiah is careful not only to restore pure Temple worship, but also to destroy all of the "high places" where the backsliding Hebrews worshiped God – or the gods – in their own ways and not *Yahweh's*.

Following Josiah, who dies prematurely and tragically in battle, come the last, evil days of Judah's kingdom, as his ineffectual sons Jehoahaz (609) and Jehoiakim (609–598) lose control of Jerusalem in 605–604 to the invading Babylonians, who allow the Jews to stay as vassals for nearly two decades. Then Jehoiakim's son Jehoiachin (597) rebels against Babylon, which replaces him with his uncle Zedekiah (597–587), who after another decade also rebels, bringing the complete destruction of Jerusalem and the Babylonian captivity of Judah's remnant under Nebuchadnezzar. All told, this roll call of the divided kingdoms names a total of nine rulers who at least partially "did right": King Jehu of Israel, and from Judah, Kings Asa, Jehoshaphat, Joash, Amaziah, Uzziah, Jotham, Hezekiah, and Josiah; the other thirty "did evil."

The Captivity and Exile of the Jews

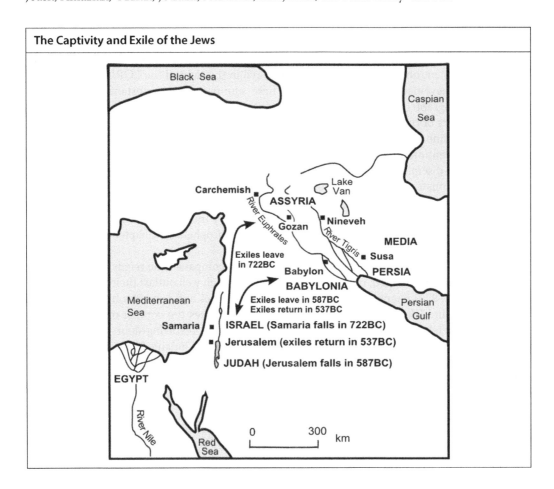

Clearly, the whole Book of Kings, with its "Deuteronomic" outlook (again, from the rules for royalty laid down in Deuteronomy 17:14–20), draws a bright line dividing "good" from "evil" government, and sees a strong causal connection between right worship and righteous state action – that is, between the proper fear of *Yahweh* and the doing of what we today might call social justice. Thus, regularly in Kings (as in Chronicles), rulers who set up and worship false gods, or who adulterate Mosaic religion with pagan practice, also cast aside justice to ignore or oppress the poor. And so we regularly find the narratives of the high and mighty disrupted and even displaced by stories of the common and the lowly; for biblical kings exist to serve the people, and not vice versa. And it is the prophets whom God sends to teach the kings their duty.

10.1.1 "Cast Down the Mighty": Highlights of Misrule and Divine Intervention in Kings

We'll consider a few highlights: we'll see why it's important that the story of Elijah's contest with the prophets of Baal (1 Kings 16–17) precedes the story of his contest with Ahab and Jezebel over their theft of Naboth's vineyard (1 Kings 21–22); for idolators are shown as actively hostile to the God-given rights of ordinary folk. For similar reasons, we see Jehu's termination of Ahab's and Jezebel's merciless line juxtaposed with their daughter Athaliah's nearly successful attempt to exterminate David's more devout and just line (2 Kings 9–11); for while God remembers justice, the wicked still hold their grudges. And when four leprous beggars save the Israelite capital of Samaria from siege after its king and commanders have despaired (2 Kings 6–7), we witness the purposes of God working through the weak and despised, much like God's sudden and miraculous deliverance of besieged Jerusalem under Hezekiah from the seemingly invincible Assyrians (2 Kings 19).

To begin with Elijah and the Baalists: this story follows a bad run of dynastic bloodshed in the new Northern Kingdom of Israel, as Jeroboam's son Nadab (910–909 BCE) is murdered and replaced by an official named Baasha (909–886), whose son Elah (886–885) is murdered and replaced by a chariot commander called Zimri (885), who is immediately overthrown by army commander Omri (885–874) (1 Kings 15–16). When Omri dies and his son Ahab (874–853) takes the throne, the stage is set for further conflict as we're told that

> Ahab the son of Omri did evil in the sight of the LORD, more than all who were before him. And it came to pass, as though it had been a trivial thing for him to walk in the sins of Jeroboam the son of Nebat, that he took as wife Jezebel the daughter of Ethbaal, king of the Sidonians; and he went and served Baal and worshiped him. (1 Kings 16:30–31)

Ahab's adoption of Baal worship brings many other Israelite Baalists out into the open and emboldens Queen Jezebel's 850 prophets of Baal and Baal's consort Asherah, while she sets about slaughtering the prophets of the LORD. In response, Elijah confronts Ahab, condemns his apostasy, and proclaims a drought and then disappears into the wilderness as Israel languishes. Three years pass, and Elijah returns to Ahab's court and challenges all of the rival prophets to meet him at Mt. Carmel to decide the issue: whether *Yahweh*, or Baal, rules. Ahab summons "all Israel" to the showdown, and Elijah sets a suitably divine challenge: that each side set up an altar of sacrifice, slaughter a bull, lay it in pieces on the wood, and "[t]hen you call on the name of your gods, and I will call on the name of the LORD; and the God who answers by fire, He is God" (18:24). The Baalists cut their bull, cry out all day while dancing, cutting themselves, and flinging their own blood to attract the Baal's attention, but no answer by fire.

Elijah mocks the unresponsive Baal – "either he is meditating, or he is busy, or he is on a journey, or perhaps he is sleeping" (1 Kings 18:27) – then he rebuilds the rough-hewn altar of twelve stones for each of the twelve tribes, lays his wood and sacrifice, and raises the level of difficulty even further by soaking altar, wood, and sacrifice three times in water. In the hearing of all, he implores the LORD simply and directly to vindicate his prophet and his own name, and then comes the flaming answer:

> Then the fire of the LORD fell and consumed the burnt sacrifice, and the wood and the stones and the dust, and it licked up the water that was in the trench. Now when all the people saw it, they fell on their faces; and they said, "The LORD, He is God! The LORD, He is God!" (1 Kings 18:38–39)

Though after this great victory Elijah experiences his share of lapses – to be discussed in Chapter 12 – this incident nevertheless establishes the grounds for his climactic faceoff with Ahab and Jezebel over the stolen land of a man named Naboth in 1 Kings 21.

Naboth is the owner of a vineyard adjacent to the royal palace in the lush valley of Jezreel, and is offered payment for the land by the king, but declines because, under Mosaic Law, Naboth is not allowed to sell inherited land out of his family (Leviticus 25:23; Numbers 36:7). Ahab's offer casts the king in an ironical light: he should, of course, know better than to offer money for a sacred inheritance, yet he still shows some residual respect for his subjects' individual rights of property by offering payment at all. Compounding the dark humor of the incident, the king handles the rebuff by returning home and pouting, a strategy that yields immediate results:

> he lay down on his bed, and turned away his face, and would eat no food. But Jezebel his wife came to him, and said to him, "Why is your spirit so sullen that you eat no food?" He said to her, "Because I spoke to Naboth the Jezreelite, and said to him, 'Give me your vineyard for money; or else, if it pleases you, I will give you another vineyard for it.' And he answered, 'I will not give you my vineyard.'" Then Jezebel his wife said to him, "You now exercise authority over Israel! Arise, eat food, and let your heart be cheerful; I will give you the vineyard of Naboth the Jezreelite." (I Kings 21:4–7)

In a few brilliant narrative strokes, we see the high-functioning dysfunction of this royal marriage laid bare: an infantile, spoiled, cowardly husband with the desire to be wicked but neither the will nor the wit, and a manipulative, ruthless, brilliant wife who despises her man and craves his power. And she comes by that craving honestly: as daughter of Ethbaal, King of Sidon, she genuinely believes that the people, their lands, and all their earthly goods exist by the god-king's permission and for his pleasure, a conviction heard in her sarcastic sneer ("You now exercise authority over Israel!") and in her serene certainty of success. She is the patron saint of eminent domain.

Jezebel is all the more effective because she is, also ironically, a careful student of the Hebrew law, as revealed by her chillingly lethal strategy, which uses the letter of the law not only to take Naboth's land and his life, but to destroy his offspring, his name, and his legacy. The queen writes, under Ahab's seal, commanding that the compliant elders of Jezreel

> [p]roclaim a fast, and seat Naboth with high honor among the people; and seat two men, scoundrels, before him to bear witness against him, saying, "You have blasphemed God and the king." Then take him out, and stone him, that he may die. (21:9–10)

Using fasting, a Hebrew religious ordinance betokening repentance for grave collective sin, Jezebel sets up Naboth for public praise that will magnify his public infamy when he is accused by the required minimum of two witnesses (Numbers 35:30) of capital blasphemy and treason: cursing God and the king (Exodus 22:28). Even the punishment is biblically correct: stoning by the whole community outside the city (Leviticus 24:14), a death penalty that includes Naboth's sons (2 Kings 9:26), and the eradication of his name forever out of Israel. It appears to be the perfect crime.

Jezebel!

One of the most enduring figures of glamorous female evil in world literature, Jezebel daughter of Ethbaal, King of Sidon, is a model of feminine intelligence and sexuality in pursuit of power, ironically through controlling powerful men. A villainess in her own right, she is also the mother of Athaliah, a "Manchurian candidate" daughter whom she marries into the royal family of Judah in order to destroy it from within – a time-release plot that very nearly succeeds.

Probably Jezebel's most famous "disciple," however, is Shakespeare's Lady Macbeth, who like her biblical predecessor manipulates her weak-willed husband to share murderous acts despite his more reluctant nature. Jezebel's hideous demise – eaten by dogs who nevertheless refuse to consume her contaminated hands (2 Kings 9:35) – perhaps suggested to Shakespeare Lady

Macbeth's notorious tic of obsessively rubbing and washing her own guilty palms. (Of course, while Lady Macbeth goes mad with remorse, Jezebel shows none – an important difference.) Though some recent feminist interpretations have discovered sympathy for both Lady Macbeth and for Jezebel as strong women using necessarily strong measures to achieve dominance in a vicious patriarchal world, yet to call a woman a "Jezebel" (as in the famed 1938 Bette Davis film of that title) remains a serious insult, with more than a dash of added fear.

However, Jezebel's and Ahab's proxy murder and theft reckon without God and his prophet Elijah. Indeed, despite their careful veneer of legality, they have betrayed the law in deepest consequence, breaking most of the Ten Commandments: committing not only theft and murder, but also coveting, false witness, disrespect of elders, and the active blasphemy of making the LORD's name a means to vain and evil ends. As King Ahab descends on Naboth's vineyard to take possession, Elijah appears as if from thin air with an alarmingly accurate indictment and summary judgment:

> Have you murdered and also taken possession?... Thus says the LORD: "In the place where dogs licked the blood of Naboth, dogs shall lick your blood... Behold, I will bring calamity on you. I will take away your posterity, and will cut off from Ahab every male in Israel, both bond and free"... And concerning Jezebel the LORD also spoke, saying, "The dogs shall eat Jezebel by the wall of Jezreel." (1 Kings 21:19, 21, 23)

Falling from dominion to dog food, Ahab and his queen could hardly expect a more degrading end. Yet in the moment of Elijah's prophecy, as in David's confrontation by Nathan, God remembers mercy in the midst of wrath: as the terrified Ahab rends his garments and fasts in remorse, *Yahweh* gives Elijah a few words of comfort for the king:

> See how Ahab has humbled himself before Me? Because he has humbled himself before Me, I will not bring the calamity in his days. In the days of his son I will bring the calamity on his house. (1 Kings 21:29)

The sins of the greatest against the smallest will not go unpunished, but even great punishment can be softened by repentance.

Still, justice delayed is not necessarily justice denied; almost immediately in 1 Kings 22, and then later in 2 Kings 9, the divine threat is fulfilled to the last gory detail. Though Ahab is more a tool than an initiator of evil, he meets his doom years before the more active Jezebel. Allied with Judah for war against Syria, Ahab hosts Judah's King Jehoshaphat (significantly, his name means "*Yahweh* judges") to plan their attack and hear from Israel's 400 court prophets. All of them predict (predictably) a smashing victory for their patron; all but one, Micaiah, whom Ahab hates ("he does not prophesy good concerning me, but evil"). Yet Ahab commands him to appear anyway. Gallows humor ensues as Micaiah speaks, sarcastically prophesying success until Ahab perversely insists on the truth, and gets it:

> "I saw all Israel scattered on the mountains, as sheep that have no shepherd." And the king of Israel said to Jehoshaphat, "Did I not tell you he would not prophesy good concerning me, but evil?" (1 Kings 22:17–18)

Micaiah reports his heavenly vision of the LORD sending an evil spirit to deceive Ahab into battle through these false prophets, and Ahab rewards Micaiah's frankness by throwing him in prison "until I come in peace." Micaiah zings back: "If you ever return in peace, the LORD has not spoken by me." And when, soon after, the cowardly Ahab goes to battle in disguise, a divinely appointed arrow, fired "at random," nevertheless finds a perfect chink in his armor, and he bleeds out into his chariot and dies. "Then someone washed the chariot at a pool in Samaria, and the dogs licked up his blood while the harlots bathed, according to the word of the LORD which He had spoken" (22:38). An important part of a prophet's message is "I told you so."

Jezebel's demise comes eleven years later, when Elisha sends a young prophet with a flask of anointing oil to Israelite army general Jehu at Ramoth Gilead, with unusual instructions:

> [L]ook there for Jehu the son of Jehoshaphat, the son of Nimshi, and go in and make him rise up from among his associates, and take him to an inner room. Then take the flask of oil, and pour it on his head, and say, "Thus says the LORD: 'I have anointed you king over Israel.'" Then open the door and flee, and do not delay. (2 Kings 9:2–3)

The sprinting prophet does as he is told, leaving behind a puzzled Jehu who rejoins his bantering friends, oil dripping down his forehead. "Why did this madman come to you?" they ask.

> And he said to them, "You know the man and his babble." And they said, "A lie! Tell us now." So he said, "Thus and thus he spoke to me, saying, 'Thus says the LORD: "I have anointed you king over Israel."'" Then each man hastened to take his garment and put it under him on the top of the steps; and they blew trumpets, saying, "Jehu is king!" (9:11–13)

What a difference a little oil makes: going from jocular skepticism to enthusiastic proclamation in the blink of an eye, Jehu's men represent the self-interest and instability of the new regime, but it will last long enough to finish judgment on the house of Ahab – and then some.

Jehu's first target is Ahab's son Jehoram (also called Joram), and Jehu brings God's wrath like a lightning strike, riding furiously down on Ahab's palace that stands, guiltily, on Naboth's stolen land at Jezreel. Each messenger sent by Jehoram switches loyalties and turns in behind Jehu to join the assault, and the new king personally terminates his predecessor with extreme prejudice: "Now Jehu drew his bow with full strength and shot Jehoram between his arms; and the arrow came out at his heart, and he sank down in his chariot" (9:24). The holy terror then rolls on, expanding his mission beyond the house of Ahab (and beyond his divine warrant) to Jehoram's feckless ally Ahaziah, King of Judah, who takes a fatal arrow in the back while fleeing in his chariot and dies at Megiddo (the future Armageddon) (9:27–29). Jehu's apocalypse then pushes into the heart, and the brains, of the old regime, catching up with Jezebel herself high in her palace tower at Jezreel. Appropriately, the vain old woman "put paint on her eyes and adorned her head, and looked through a window. Then, as Jehu entered at the gate, she said, 'Is it peace, Zimri, murderer of your master?'" Her comic and macabre attempts at allure and royal history do no good, as Jehu talks past her to her supposedly loyal eunuchs: "Who is on my side? Who?" Determined to be on the winning side, the neutered servants summarily neutralize their queen, pitching her from the balcony to splatter and thump off the walls to the ground below, where she is finished by Jehu's chariot wheels. With a measure of relish bordering on *schadenfreude*, the narrator reports that Jehu, after pushing into the palace for a restorative meal and a drink, calls to mind the royal corpse outside and commands her burial, "for she was a king's daughter." But too late, for the dogs of Naboth's vineyard have gotten there first: "So they went to bury her, but they found no more of her than the skull and the feet and the palms of her hands." Even the dogs, apparently, have their limits. "This is the word of the LORD, which He spoke by His servant Elijah the Tishbite... '[T]he corpse of Jezebel shall be as refuse on the surface of the field, in the plot at Jezreel, so that they shall not say, "Here lies Jezebel"'" (9:32–37).

From the Valley of Jezreel, Jehu's bowl of wrath overflows the whole of Ahab's line, inundating Ahab's seventy surviving sons at Samaria, and also destroying a full assembly of Baalists who come together at Jehu's invitation assuming that he will join in their worship, but instead are carefully marked out for mass slaughter, and their idols ground to powder and their temples turned to refuse dumps. Jehu proudly surveys his deadly handiwork in his chariot with the visiting Jonadab: "Come with me, and see my zeal for the LORD" (10:1–11, 15–27). But the tide of Jehu's zeal flows over *Yahweh's* appointed bounds, as the Israelite Terminator wipes out all the brothers of Ahaziah, King of Judah (10:12–14); yet Jehu's zeal doesn't extend to Jeroboam's substitute temple in Samaria, which Jehu leaves standing and where he worships. It seems that a scourge, even a divine scourge, can be an imprecise instrument.

However, as in an outer space epic or horror film where the villain, or the villain's agents, escape to rise again in the sequel, so Ahab and Jezebel don't die before placing their evil seed, quite literally, in the heart of rival Judah. Ahab's alliance with the otherwise commendable King Jehoshaphat pays the dark dividend of a marriage between Judah's prince Jehoram (also called Joram) and Israel's princess Athaliah – whose name, ironically, means "The LORD is exalted." Having married their daughter into the royal line of David, Ahab and especially Jezebel have a "sleeper operative" in Judah's court, biding her time, awaiting an opening as she rises from princess to queen consort to queen mother and finally to queen. On the way, Athaliah converts her husband Jehoram, and her son Ahaziah, to Baal worship, but her true opportunity comes in the aftermath of Jehu's purge of Israel. With her parents and husband now dead, and her son Ahaziah killed with them, she steps into the power vacuum on a deadly mission of her own: to wipe out David's house.

There is an ironic chiasmus between the story of the Queen Mother Bathsheba intervening in 1 Kings chapter 1 to save Solomon, the son of David, from his power-hungry brother Adonijah, and of Queen Mother Athaliah intervening in 2 Kings 11 to exterminate (nearly) the entire line of Solomon's heirs and David's sons – that is, her own *grandchildren*. This is as close to extinction as the house of David comes in its more than four centuries on the throne of Judah. While the innocents are being slaughtered at Athaliah's command, her son's sister Jehosheba saves one brand from the burning: the infant Joash, whom Jehosheba's husband Jehoida the priest hides for six long years in the Temple, while Athaliah reigns rampant over Judah. Then, in one shocking day in the queen's seventh year, Jehoiada engineers a restoration, with the palace guards recruited to protect the boy king during his sudden anointing and proclamation as king of Judah, even arming them with the spears and shields that King David had stored in the Temple. By the time that Athaliah discovers the plot, the coronation is a *fait accompli*, with crowds cheering young Joash as he stands beside the great pillar of Boaz holding the *Torah* scroll. The murderous queen cries "Treason! Treason!" but the charge rebounds on her own head as she is taken from the Temple and slain as "she went by way of the horses' entrance into the king's house, and there she was killed" (11:16). Like her mother Jezebel, she dies under horses' feet amidst animal droppings, to no one's regret.

Inserted within this dark story arc of Ahab's wicked and tyrannous house comes an account in 2 Kings 6–7 that emphasizes *Yahweh's* sheer, surprising mercy. Its beginning is grim: "it happened after this that Ben-Hadad king of Syria gathered all his army, and went up and besieged Samaria" (6:24). Starved into desperation, the Israelites are compelled to eat unclean asses' heads and doves' dung, and, in a grotesque parody of Solomon's "splitting the baby," two mothers actually come to the Israelite king squabbling over their cannibal covenant: having slaughtered her own son for a shared meal, one woman demands that the other woman keep her side of the bargain and surrender her boy to the knife. In this context, the unnamed Israelite king despairs of God's help and threatens to behead God's prophet Elisha – who calmly predicts that by this time tomorrow, the starving capital will see cheap flour and barley for sale in its streets, a prediction mocked by one of the king's generals (6:24–7:2).

Into this dire scene, enter the lepers. Four of these infected outcasts sit at the gate of Samaria, and with frank fatalism weigh their options:

> Why are we sitting here until we die? If we say, "We will enter the city," the famine is in the city, and we shall die there. And if we sit here, we die also. Now therefore, come, let us surrender to the army of the Syrians. If they keep us alive, we shall live; and if they kill us, we shall only die. (7:3–4)

Entering the Syrian camp at twilight with nothing left to lose, they find only deserted tents filled with food and booty; for, we are told,

> the LORD had caused the army of the Syrians to hear the noise of chariots and the noise of horses – the noise of a great army;... Therefore they arose and fled at twilight, and left the camp intact – their tents, their horses, and their donkeys ... (7:6–7)

In a "psy-ops" victory of biblical proportions, the entire besieging army has gone AWOL, and the lepers leap to the opportunity, eating to the full and then carrying and burying two loads of loot. But these ragged pariahs have more decency than most of their social betters: "they said to one another, 'We are not doing right. This day is a day of good news, and we remain silent. If we wait until morning light, some punishment will come upon us'" (7:9). Pricked by conscience, they return to tell the king, who is comically slow to believe them, sending a search party using the last few live, uneaten horses in the city. Finding the Syrians genuinely gone, the party confirms the lepers' report, setting off a stampede that crushes the skeptical general underfoot at the gate on the way to the food. "So a seah of fine flour was sold for a shekel, and two seahs of barley for a shekel, according to the word of the LORD" (7:16).

But for sheer divine drama, the centerpiece of 2 Kings, and probably of the entire composite Book of Kings, is the even greater story of deliverance told about Sennacherib's siege of Jerusalem two generations later. As *Yahweh* has rescued besieged Samaria from Syria through the weak and despised lepers in 2 Kings 7, so does he even more stunningly rescue besieged Jerusalem under Hezekiah from the seemingly overwhelming Assyrians in 2 Kings 19 (retold in Isaiah 36–37). We're told that the Assyrians have laid low all resistance along the Fertile Crescent, including the Northern Kingdom of Israel, capturing the last Israelite King Hoshea and deporting his people to far-flung corners of the Assyrian Empire, and bringing in other conquered peoples to repopulate the land and set up their own gods. Judah itself has paid tribute, but to no avail, as the Assyrian King Sennacherib sends his armies from Lachish led by his chief field marshal, the Rabshakeh, to gird Jerusalem with siegeworks and grind it into final submission.

The narrator quickly establishes the machinery of epic confrontation: as at Homer's Troy, great boasts are made outside the city gates as the invading general opens his full word-hoard of intimidation and terror. The Rabshakeh insists on speaking in Hebrew for all the Jews to hear on their city walls, since, in his colorful phrase, it is they who "will have to eat their own excrement and drink their own urine" (18:27). He goes on to repurpose the words of Moses, echoing Deuteronomy 8:7–9 and 30:19, replacing the promises of God with those of his god-king Sennacherib:

> This is what the king of Assyria says: Make peace with me and come out to me. Then each of you will eat fruit from your own vine and fig tree and drink water from your own cistern, until I come and take you to a land like your own – a land of grain and new wine, a land of bread and vineyards, a land of olive trees and honey. Choose life and not death! (2 Kings 18:31–32)

Perversely equating their coming Exile with their former Exodus, the Rabshakeh promises the kind of Providence that only God – and godlike governments – have the confidence to claim, and issues his apocalyptic threats not only against Hezekiah and his people, but also against *Yahweh* himself, dismissing the LORD as another petty local deity:

> Do not listen to Hezekiah, for he is misleading you when he says, "The LORD will deliver us." Has the god of any nation ever delivered his land from the hand of the king of Assyria? Where are the gods of Hamath and Arpad? Where are the gods of Sepharvaim, Hena and Ivvah? Have they rescued Samaria from my hand? Who of all the gods of these countries has been able to save his land from me? How then can the LORD deliver Jerusalem from my hand? (2 Kings 18:32–35)

In the starkest terms, Sennacherib and the Rabshakeh present a divine duel, assured of their easy victory over the Hebrews' invisible deity.

Strangely, though, the people do not cry out with fear or beg for mercy, but instead keep an eerie silence all along the battlements, in obedience to Hezekiah. Hearing the Assyrian taunt from his messengers, Hezekiah tears his garments in mourning, goes into the Temple, and sends word to the prophet Isaiah to call for a word from God, which is not slow in coming, and is as brief as Sennacherib's threats are long:

> Do not be afraid of what you have heard – those words with which the underlings of the king of Assyria have blasphemed me. Listen! When he hears a certain report, I will make him want to return to his own country, and there I will have him cut down with the sword. (19:6–7)

As in the story of David and Goliath, gigantic *braggadocio* is met by understated confidence – followed by stunning action, this time in the form of unmediated divine intervention. After two chapters of grand build-up in 2 Kings 18–19, the siege ends with a sudden and miraculous anti-climax in three laconic verses:

> That night the angel of the LORD went out and put to death a hundred and eighty-five thousand in the Assyrian camp. When the people got up the next morning – there were all the dead bodies! So Sennacherib king of Assyria broke camp and withdrew. He returned to Nineveh and stayed there.
>
> One day, while he was worshiping in the temple of his god Nisrok, his sons Adrammelek and Sharezer killed him with the sword, and they escaped to the land of Ararat. And Esarhaddon his son succeeded him as king. (19:35–37)

Thus, *Yahweh* deprives the Rabshakeh, Sennacherib, and especially their gods of the dignity due an epic "worthy adversary"; that is, the dignity of well-matched single combat. Instead, the extermination of an entire army is the off-handed work of a moment. As the poet Byron would write thousands of years later, "And the might of the Gentile, unsmote by the sword, / Hath melted like snow in the glance of the Lord!" And in the sharpest cut, the Assyrian king who thought the Hebrew God too weak to defend his own city and people finds the reach of the Almighty very long indeed, as he himself is slain in the house of his own god Nisrok by the hands of his own sons.

Each of these highlights – Elijah versus the Baalists and the Jezebel–Ahab regime, the overthrow of their daughter Athaliah in Judah, and the sudden deliverances of Samaria and Jerusalem – assume a world turned upside down by a God who tasks kings and governments with serving rather than dominating their people, who sets strict limits to their laws and ambitions, and will intervene like lightning from a clear sky to cast down the mighty when they worship false gods of state or magic power and ignore the words of his messengers the prophets. This "Deuteronomic" perspective regards "the fear of God" as the foundation of right rule. It reminds rulers that their authority extends only as far as their virtue, and that though they may be given powerful license to scourge the wicked for a time, sooner than they imagine their power will fail, and they will fall with their own victims.

10.1.2 Doubled, with a Difference: The Book of Chronicles

As we've often observed, repetition is a hallmark of Hebrew literature, from the line-by-line parallelisms of the Psalms, to the doubling of Pharaoh's dreams, to the duplication of patriarchal misadventures, divine laws, and entire biblical books. Yet most such duplication also comes with a difference, as if to stress that varied viewpoints are necessary for seeing deep and whole. The Book of Chronicles (see "The Whole Books of Kings and Chronicles" box) fits this description well. While the Book of Kings tells the parallel stories of Israel and Judah in relatively equal ways to account for the fall and destruction of both kingdoms, Chronicles, completed after the return from the Exile, focuses on Judah and the house of David with an eye toward restoration of the nation, and eventually of the Davidic kingdom. While Christian Bibles place Chronicles immediately after Kings among the books of Old Testament history, Chronicles comes last in the Hebrew Bible, among the *Khetuvim* or Writings, associating it with special artfulness, and also concluding the Hebrew canon of scripture. Thus, its deliberate selectivity is heightened over that of Kings. It claims to tell historical truth, citing many other textual sources, but it has no pretensions to exhaustiveness, and the truth that it tells looks not only back to the past but especially forward to the future.

Like the Book of Numbers, Chronicles begins with extensive genealogies. Starting with Adam himself and recapitulating all of the patriarchs of Genesis, the Chronicler traces the line of descent directly to the tribe of Judah (1 Chronicles 1–2), and then to David and his sons up through the Exile and after, down to the present in the time of return and rebuilding (1 Chronicles 3). In keeping with this "once-and-future" beginning, the book's main themes support the post-exilic reconstitution of God's people around the revived Law, the reconstruction of the Temple, and the hoped-for restoration of David's house. Like the Book of Kings, Chronicles treats worship as a bellwether for social justice, blessing, and renewed national prosperity and power. As we observed in Exodus, the first table of the Law begins with obligation to God, in order to increase the believer's duty to his fellow man in the second table of the Law. Yet despite this special focus on Judah and David, the Chronicler takes pains to include genealogies of all twelve tribes (1 Chronicles 4–7), and to stress the glorious wholeness of the United Kingdom under David and Solomon, as well as the reconstitution of this United Kingdom after the fall of Israel under the godly reign of Hezekiah.

So while Chronicles also tells many sad stories of the death of kings, and acknowledges the sinful failings of Judah and its rulers, the Chronicler seeks, as the modern songster puts it, "to accentuate the positive" – without entirely eliminating the negative. As the Jews stream back to Jerusalem and Judah under the more friendly regime of the Persian Emperor Cyrus (1 Chronicles 9:1–2, 2 Chronicles 36:22–23), the Chronicler presents a distinctive re-visioning, though not a direct factual revision, of history as found in the Book of Kings. This re-visioning comes sometimes in the form of addition, and sometimes as omission. For instance, in the midst of the roll call of Judah, the Chronicler adds the benevolent and optimistic Prayer of Jabez, calling on God to "bless me indeed, and enlarge my territory, that your hand would be with me, and that you would keep me from evil, that I may not cause pain!" (1 Chronicles 4:9–10); while in the next chapter we read a bonus anecdote about a coalition of Reubenites, Gadites, and Manassehites who defeat the Hagrites and conquer their territory because they trust in God – encouraging the returned exiles in their hopes of territorial restoration (5:18–22). Similarly, where Kings tells us of Hezekiah's monstrously wicked son Manasseh, Chronicles adds to that sordid account the inspiring coda of Manasseh's late-life repentance following his terrible overthrow and imprisonment (2 Chronicles 33:10–20). On the other hand, the Chronicler assumes that his readers will already know about David's winding and tortured path to the throne in 1–2 Samuel, as well as the dark stories in 2 Samuel 11–12 about David's adultery and proxy murder, and in 1 Kings 11 about Solomon's fall into sensuality and idolatry, so he omits these incidents from his account, providing a portrait of Judah's greatest kings mainly at their triumphant best – while repeatedly gesturing to those other accounts for the fuller story.

Yet Chronicles is no whitewash. For instance, David is still portrayed as angry with the LORD for striking down the priest Uzza who touched the Ark of the Covenant (1 Chronicles 13:11); as being incited by Satan to number the nation of Israel, at terrible cost (1 Chronicles 21:1–30); and, in a phrase not found in the Book of Kings, as being forbidden by God to build the Temple "because you have shed much blood on the earth in my sight" (1 Chronicles 22:8). Solomon is still, as in Kings, shown in his later years laying burdensome labor on his people, persecuting the young Jeroboam, and rearing the disastrously foolish Rehoboam, who still splits the nation with his arrogance (2 Chronicles 10:1–19). Thus, however heroic and wise are these great monarchs, they are nevertheless presented as sinful and fallible men who must rely on divine mercy to fill and cover their faults.

10.2 Return and Rebuild: Ezra and Nehemiah, Restorers of the City

The Book of Chronicles ends on an optimistic note, as God inspires the Persian king to fulfill divine prophecy and call for a Jewish return from exile:

> Now in the first year of Cyrus king of Persia, that the word of the LORD by the mouth of Jeremiah might be fulfilled, the LORD stirred up the spirit of Cyrus king of Persia, so that he made a proclamation throughout all his kingdom, and also put it in writing, saying,
> Thus says Cyrus king of Persia:
> All the kingdoms of the earth the LORD God of heaven has given me. And he has commanded me to build him a house at Jerusalem which is in Judah. Who is among you of all His people? May his God be with him, and let him go up! (2 Chronicles 36:22–23)

These words segue smoothly into the book of Ezra-Nehemiah, which begins with the same decree (Ezra 1:1–4) and proceeds to see it realized, though in fits and starts, in the First and Second Returns, over many decades.

The Whole Book of Ezra-Nehemiah

Though separated in Christian Bibles from the time of Origen in the third century of the Common Era, Ezra and Nehemiah are treated as one book by the Hebrew Bible, by the earliest manuscripts of the Septuagint, by the Talmud, and by Josephus. Clearly a composite book made up of many combined documents, Ezra-Nehemiah was put into its current form between 425 and 400 BCE, incorporating post-exilic genealogies, the memoirs of Ezra and Nehemiah themselves, varied official correspondence (originally in Aramaic), and certain royal decrees of Cyrus, Darius, and Artaxerxes. Jewish tradition has long attributed the book's final composition to Ezra, though it does not name its author.

Paradoxically, throughout this composite book, sovereign divine Providence is shown both working through and prevailing over human failing and disaster. The interplay between failure and triumph is constant: though *Yahweh's* people have endured suffering and exile for their sins, this book abounds in beneficent decrees from heathen kings that are practically dictated by the heavenly LORD; though it tells of brick-and-mortar reconstruction, Ezra-Nehemiah is framed by reminders of the Hebrews' nomadic heritage as sojourners in the earth. "O LORD, you have been our dwelling place in all generations," begins the famous psalm of Moses (Psalm 90:1); the lesson for the returning Israelites is that the only sure and lasting foundation of their city is in the heavens.

Thus, while Ezra-Nehemiah is saturated with specific local and material detail, it is hard to imagine a less "materialist" narrative. Much modern biblical criticism treats the spiritual "superstructure" of holy history as founded on and determined by a political-economic "base"; however, Ezra-Nehemiah seems consciously designed to forestall that treatment by recounting Israel's re-founding of a heavenly regime *before* rebuilding its earthly defenses. Thus, the returning exiles, rather than following common sense and securing the military perimeter of the city before reconstituting cultic sites and reading (or composing) sacred texts, instead reverse this order: the Jews first read the scriptures, then erect an altar, then their Temple, and then finally (decades later) the defensive wall. And although a few leaders figure prominently in the book's events (the Davidic descendant Zerubbabel/Sheshbazzar and the prophets Haggai and Zechariah in the First Return, the eponymous Ezra and Nehemiah in the Second Return, and varied Persian kings throughout), this is a book primarily of God's whole people at work, of ordinary Hebrews doing their small parts to achieve a great end.

Timeline of Return and Restoration for the First Exile – All Dates BCE

539 – Cyrus conquers Babylon.
538 – Cyrus permits Jews to return to Jerusalem to rebuild the Temple.
537 – **First Return** with Zerubbabel/Sheshbazzar.
536 – Temple reconstruction begins.
535 – Temple reconstruction halted amid opposition.
519 – Temple reconstruction renewed under King Darius after preaching of prophets Haggai and Zechariah.
515 – Temple completed and dedicated (four years after work resumed, twenty years after work began, seventy years after Temple destroyed).
458 – **Second Return** with Ezra (fifty-seven years after Temple dedication).
446 – Nehemiah learns of Jerusalem's distress.
445–433 – Nehemiah commissioned by Artaxerxes I for first term as governor of Judah.
445 – Wall completed (April–September) and dedicated.
c. 431–425 – Nehemiah's second term as governor.

As in the Book of Exodus, this book portrays a God who takes the initiative in delivering his people by taking them successfully through trouble rather than sheltering them from it. *Yahweh* hands the great empire of Babylon over to Cyrus the Persian in a stunningly easy conquest in the year 539 BCE, then moves this new emperor's heart with mercy toward the Jewish exiles. "[L]et [them] go up," Cyrus decrees, "to Jerusalem which is in Judah, and build the house of the LORD God of Israel (He is God), which is in Jerusalem."

> King Cyrus also brought out the articles of the house of the LORD, which Nebuchadnezzar had taken from Jerusalem and put in the temple of his gods; and Cyrus king of Persia brought them out by the hand of Mithredath the treasurer, and counted them out to Sheshbazzar the prince of Judah. (Ezra 1:3, 7–8)

In an act of remarkable grace, Cyrus not only ordains a second Exodus, but also commends generosity to the exiles and restores to them the sacred Temple utensils, so long misused and defiled by the Babylonians. The theme of national preservation according to prophetic scripture is amplified further in Ezra 3 upon the expedition's return to Jerusalem in 537 BCE under the leadership of Sheshbazzar (probably David's descendant Zerubbabel, grandson of Judah's next-to-last king, Jehoiachin). In 536 Zerubbabel/Sheshbazzar joins the surviving Levites in rebuilding an altar "as it is written in the law of Moses." Six months later in spring 535, work begins on the Temple itself, and the congregation's reaction is bittersweet: "the people could not discern the noise of the shout of joy from the noise of the weeping of the people" (3:13).

This theme of bittersweetness runs throughout this story of return and reconstruction, for in the Providence of God, Jewish success usually seems to breed resistance and difficulty. The news of this Temple project travels quickly, bringing an immediate response from surrounding "adversaries," who craftily ask to join in the building work, "for we seek your God as you do; and we have sacrificed to him since the days of Esarhaddon king of Assyria, who brought us here" (4:2) – that is, by adding *Yahweh* to the pantheon of their other deities, as if he were another local god to be appeased with occasional burnt offerings. Suspicious of their syncretism and their motives, Zerubbabel declines the offer, and the adversaries' hostility become overt, as they petition the far-off Persian kings Cyrus through Darius I, slowing and often stopping work over the next sixteen years.

Persian Kings During Jewish Return and Rebuilding – All Dates BCE
Cyrus – 559–530
Cambyses – 530–522
Smerdis – 522
Darius I – 522–486
Xerxes I (Ahasuerus) – 486–465
Artaxerxes I – 465–424
Xerxes II – 424
Darius II – 423–404

What follows in Ezra 4 is an interlude describing future opposition, as the narrative jumps ahead from 535 BCE into the next century to document the later work stoppage on the walls and gates of Jerusalem under the Persian kings Ahasuerus (Xerxes I) and Artaxerxes I from the years 486 through 458 – ending with the Second Return. In a master-stroke of bureaucratic obstruction, the local Canaanite enemies of the Jews capitalize on the confusion of a sprawling government, obtaining from Ahasuerus and then Artaxerxes a three-decade "cease and desist" order because the Jews "are building the rebellious and evil city, and are finishing its walls and repairing the foundations" (4:12–23). Just as the narrative reverts to the time of the First Return, we are reminded that the struggle will go on for generations, requiring persistent faith and vigilance.

But return we do in Ezra 5 to the year 519 BCE in the previous century, as the prophets Haggai and Zechariah stiffen the spines of the Temple builders, who resume work while petitioning the new King Darius I, reminding him of Cyrus the Great's decree of 538. This decree Darius duly locates and reaffirms, ordering the Canaanite governor Tattenai to "let the work of this house of God alone," and (in an especially bitter pill for the adversaries) to support the Temple reconstruction with their taxes and tribute or have their own homes torn down (6:8–12). With these generous and fearsome royal protections, the Temple restoration surges forward to completion in only four years.

The Temple rededication in 515 BCE is a study in both continuity and contrasts with the first dedication under King Solomon narrated in 1 Kings 8. The House of *Yahweh* stands again, built according to divine command, under royal protection, blessed by congregational sacrifice and joyful celebration. But what a falling off! Where Israel's own most glorious King Solomon dedicated the first Temple, this second Temple depends on the decrees of a distant Gentile emperor; where the first culminates a splendid building program within great high walls, the second stands vulnerable to outside attack, its walls in ruins; where the former days saw "twenty-two thousand bulls and one hundred and twenty thousand sheep" offered up on the LORD's altar (1 Kings 8:63), the latter days can muster only "one hundred bulls, two hundred rams, four hundred lambs" to the sacrifice (Ezra 6:17). Most tellingly, while God's *Shekinah* glory inhabits and blesses the first Temple, the second Temple is visited by no such pillar of cloud. Indeed, Solomon's prayer to God at the first dedication haunts the restoration with its words of warning:

> When they sin against you (for there is no one who does not sin), and you become angry with them and deliver them to the enemy, and they take them captive to the land of the enemy ... grant them compassion before those who took them captive ... (1 Kings 8:46, 50)

Yet as befitting a people who now have twice been rescued "out of the iron furnace" of exile and restored to their promised land, the returnees again keep their great feast of deliverance, the Passover.

Finally, nearly six decades after this Temple dedication, in 458 BCE, there enters Ezra – in the seventh chapter of a ten-chapter book bearing his name. This is certainly a late appearance if we had conceived of Ezra as the hero of the story, but it's truer to call him an important but secondary player in the action, whose main work was the completion of the book itself, a book whose central protagonist is clearly the Almighty. Thus, we see Artaxerxes I, who earlier had stopped reconstruction work in Jerusalem, strangely moved by the "God of heaven" in the seventh year of his reign to endorse Ezra's request for a Second Return of the Jews to restore more of their languishing city – and to support this return with great numbers of livestock, and even greater sums of Persian gold and silver. "Blessed be the LORD God of our fathers, who has put such a thing as this in the king's heart," writes Ezra, himself wonderstruck at the dramatic reversal of the pagan king's attitudes (Ezra 7:27). Ezra is a descendant of Aaron, and he travels accompanied by "[s]ome of the children of Israel, the priests, the Levites, the singers, the gatekeepers, and the *Nethinim* [Temple servants]" (7:7), leading an expedition to replenish Temple and city supplies, teach the Law of Moses, and to enforce that Law among a people yet again in danger of disappearing by assimilation among the surrounding nations.

Though Ezra is grateful for Artaxerxes' permission and generous support, he is painfully aware that dependence on a pagan government threatens to rob God of his glory. So upon setting out across the Persian river of Avaha, Ezra decides boldly not to ask for protection by Persian troops as they travel the dangerous roads to Jerusalem, but to rely wholly on the LORD (8:22, 31).

Once arrived in Jerusalem, Ezra and his band deliver the king's orders to all the royal satraps and governors of the "region beyond the River" (Euphrates), who snap to action, providing funds, building materials, and additional support for enriching the Temple and Temple worship.

But Ezra finds more shame than joy among the previous generation of returnees; for while they have been rebuilding the physical house of God, they have been allowing the spiritual and familial house of God to decay. Ezra is told that

> [t]he people of Israel and the priests and the Levites have not separated themselves from the peoples of the lands, with respect to the abominations of the Canaanites, the Hittites, the Perizzites, the Jebusites, the Ammonites, the Moabites, the Egyptians, and the Amorites. For they have taken some of their daughters as wives for themselves and their sons, so that the holy seed is mixed with the peoples of those lands. Indeed, the hand of the leaders and rulers has been foremost in this trespass. (9:1–2)

As Ezra's mortified reaction reveals, his alarm is not only about intermarriage, but also about the survival of the Jews as a distinct people, and about the future of God's covenant: "I tore my garment and my robe, and plucked out some of the hair of my head and beard, and sat down astonished" (9:3). After all the deliverance and disaster that has happened to the Jews, the sons and daughters of the covenant have still not lost their taste for corruption. How can *Yahweh's* righteous "remnant" be preserved if they give themselves and their children to unions with the pagans and their many gods?

So Ezra's part of this book of restoration concludes on a note of repentance and mourning, as the people and their leaders gather (evocatively, in the pouring rain) to weep for their sins in having "taken pagan wives" (10:9–11). Like their father Abraham, who put away his concubine Hagar and her son Ishmael while preserving certain provisions (Genesis 21:14) and legal rights (Deuteronomy 21:10–14), the Jews now put away these unlawful sexual partners and their offspring, in language that treats the women more as concubines than as actual spouses. Much of this chapter consists of a soberingly long list of the supposedly good and great in the congregation who have been caught out in their hypocrisy. It is a notably downbeat ending for a story of happy return to the promised land.

But indeed, this is not the end, for as noted before, Ezra-Nehemiah functions as one book, and its second half is focused more centrally on one man's work than is the first half – in fact as a one-man, first-person narrative. We meet that man, Nehemiah the son of Hachaliah, in 446 BCE, a dozen years after Ezra's Second Return – and Nehemiah too is weeping. He is in Shushan (Susa), the Persian capital, and he has just had news from Judah that "[t]he survivors who are left from the captivity in the province are there in great distress and reproach. The wall of Jerusalem is also broken down, and its gates are burned with fire" (Nehemiah 1:3).

Like Joseph, Moses, Daniel, and Esther, Nehemiah is the type of Hebrew providential hero whom God has placed in a position of influence among the *goyim* so as to secure the safety and future of his chosen. In Nehemiah's case, he is cupbearer to King Artaxerxes I, which means that he is trusted with the king's life, since he manages the king's drinks and protects him from poison. Nehemiah also combines the man of prayer and the man of action: his prayers are always practically oriented and matched with deeds. He turns his mourning for the forlorn state of Jerusalem into a prayer for forgiveness and for help, and then resolves to seek that help himself: "let Your servant prosper this day, I pray, and grant him mercy in the sight of this man" (1:11) – "this man" being the king.

While pouring wine for Artaxerxes soon after, Nehemiah inadvertently allows his grief to show, and the king notices. "'Why is your face sad, since you are not sick? This is nothing but sorrow of heart.' So I became dreadfully afraid." As he might well be, since the very same king had forbidden the "rebellious Jews" from rebuilding Jerusalem many years before. But to Nehemiah's credit, he presses forward despite his fear – and with a daring hint of sarcasm: "May the king live forever! Why should my face not be sad, when the city, the place of my fathers' tombs, lies waste, and its gates are burned with fire?" And to the king's credit, his intent is both compassionate and shrewd; used to the ways of courtiers, he cuts to the chase, asking simply, "What is your request?" Nehemiah, the boldest of butlers, grasps the initiative both devoutly and directly – with instant results:

> So I prayed to the God of heaven. And I said to the king, "If it pleases the king, and if your servant has found favor in your sight, I ask that you send me to Judah, to the city of my fathers' tombs, that I may rebuild it." Then the king said to me (the queen also sitting beside him), "How long will your journey be? And when will you return?" So it pleased the king to send me; and I set him a time. (2:2–6)

The king then swiftly reverses his past decree and provides Nehemiah with letters of transit through his territories, and a letter to the king's forester to provide timber for gates and doors. All this in a matter of minutes – for "the king granted them to me according to the good hand of my God upon me" (one of nine repetitions of that phrase in the book). Immediately we're told that Nehemiah is on his way, accompanied by captains of the army and horsemen (2:7–9).

Lest all this seem too magically easy to be true, Nehemiah reminds us here of the hard truth that there is always someone eager to oppose and kill the Jews, and so he introduces the villains of the piece: "When Sanballat the Horonite and Tobiah the Ammonite official heard of it, they were deeply disturbed that a man had come to seek the well-being of the children of Israel" (2:10). Hearing that they have heard, Nehemiah is as canny as he is courageous, and so he arrives quietly in Jerusalem and makes his tour of the city's evocative ruins alone and at night, without telling anyone, not "the Jews, the priests, the nobles, the officials," and certainly not the Canaanite adversaries. From the Valley Gate and the Serpent Well and the Refuse Gate, to the Fountain Gate and the King's Pool and back to the Valley Gate, he surveys the tumbledown damage, and having observed the worst he returns to tell the leaders that the best is to come:

> "You see the distress that we are in, how Jerusalem lies waste, and its gates are burned with fire. Come and let us build the wall of Jerusalem, that we may no longer be a reproach." And I told them of the hand of my God which had been good upon me, and also of the king's words that he had spoken to me. So they said, "Let us rise up and build." Then they set their hands to this good work. (2:17–18)

Yet in what will be a recurring motif, whenever the Jews advance, the anti-Semites ratchet up their rhetoric: "What is this thing that you are doing? Will you rebel against the king?" (2:19), ask Sanballat, Tobiah, and Geshem, implying treason. Yet Nehemiah and the Jews press ahead.

The restoration work develops as a truly shared community effort by "citizen architects," with each family committed to rebuilding that section of the wall nearest to its ancestral home. Chapter 3 provides a roll call of how each family "rose up" to reconstruct a particular segment, making this a strikingly specific account – reaffirming the pervasive biblical theme that "God is in the details," providentially working through local human effort. Sanballat and the other adversaries grow even more contemptuous and threatening:

"What are these feeble Jews doing? Will they fortify themselves? Will they offer sacrifices? Will they complete it in a day? Will they revive the stones from the heaps of rubbish – stones that are burned?" … and all of them conspired together to come and attack Jerusalem and create confusion. (4:2, 8)

Despite the people's growing trepidation, Nehemiah organizes them to work in shifts, some brandishing swords, bows, and spears, others laboring away through all the daylight hours and into the night. Eventually, like pioneers in a Wild West town, the builders work with a tool in hand and a weapon at their sides (4:13–18).

Yet even as the Jews confront opposition from outside, they are weakened by trouble within, as architectural reconstruction exposes their spiritual decay. Much as Ezra had attacked their sexual misdeeds, so Nehemiah rebukes their economic evils: the more powerful people have been abusing their poorer, weaker brethren, while the wealthy are found to be forcing the unfortunate into extortionate mortgages and loans to buy food, and even into slavery (5:1–8). Though Nehemiah faces urgent construction work and violent Gentile threats, he still calls a solemn assembly of the Jews, throwing their crimes back in their faces and demanding immediate restitution to the victims – and setting the example personally by providing no-interest loans and necessary grain for the needy out of his own stores. Shamed by the confrontation, the Jewish leaders promise to do better justice – and Nehemiah demands a solemn vow administered by the priest (5:9–13). Nehemiah assumes that without moral and spiritual reconstruction, new walls will be useless.

This trouble from within the community is matched by a crescendo of danger from without, as the conspirators escalate their intimidation by promulgating more lies about Jewish rebellion and by announcing a plot to assassinate Nehemiah himself. Hoping either to slander him as disloyal to Artaxerxes, or expose him as a coward who flees from danger, the adversaries are cheated of their prey when Nehemiah, told by a Jewish traitor to hide from the threats, instead perceives the treachery and proceeds publicly to the final stages of reconstruction: hanging the great new doors in the city gates (7:1). Sanballat and company must face their failure head-on – their bluff has been called, their disinformation refuted, and the Jews are now safe inside their city gates, united behind dynamic leaders, and revitalized as a spiritually interwoven and self-supporting community beyond intimidation and bribery (7:2–3).

Though the book's central action is now complete, seven more chapters remain, perhaps tiresome to modern readers but dear to the Israelite heart. Chapter 7 lists at majestic length all of the captives who returned to Jerusalem; chapter 8 tells how Ezra read the entire *Torah* aloud to the people, and then led them in celebrating the Feast of Tabernacles; chapter 9 presents a psalm of penitence filled with past misdeeds, present regrets, and future hopes; and chapter 10 presents Ezra's renewed covenant in which the congregation rededicate themselves family by family to the Law, the Sabbath, the festivals, and the offerings, and vow to keep themselves spiritually and sexually separate from "the peoples of the land." With Jerusalem now secure, chapter 11 details the plan to repopulate the other villages of Judah and Benjamin, to re-fill the land and subdue it again for the Hebrew nation, and chapter 12 describes the wall dedication ceremony gate-by-gate and clan-by-clan, with a roll call of the priests and Levites and their responsibilities in the renewed Temple.

To end this crescendo of cleansing, chapter 13 reiterates Nehemiah's labors in purifying Jerusalem of pagan influence, Sabbath violation, and brotherly injustice, as he contends with foe and friend alike in the name of holiness, ending with his watchword, "Remember me, O my God, for good!" (13:31). Like the tedium of someone else's genealogy, this obsession with national mission and restoring sacred stones may not charm our contemporary imaginations, just as the songs of African tribal griots or acres of crosses at the Somme and Normandy may leave cold those who don't know the tribe's troubles or care for dead soldiers' names. So the combined book of Ezra-Nehemiah begins and ends with remembrance – of festivals for wandering pilgrims, of sacred ties that bind, and of holy walls that define and protect.

10.3 "For Such a Time as This": Esther in a Strange Land

The Book of Esther dovetails chronologically into the story told in Ezra-Nehemiah – the events described are usually dated from 482 to 476 BCE – but told from the viewpoint of one who, rather than returning home to rebuild, prospers in exile. The Book of Esther is many things: a Cinderella tale with a memorable villain and a deliciously sardonic twist; a providential story, like Joseph's, of thriving in a foreign land; an account of long-lived grudges, ironic reversals, national survival, and revenge; and an explanation for the origins of a popular Jewish holiday (Purim). It is noted for its high degree of literary art, being shot through with significant repetitions, rich ironies, and memorable phrases, and it has sparked renewed interest for modern readers particularly concerned with the agency and roles of ancient Near Eastern women.

Esther: Canon, Controversy, and History

While enduringly popular among both Jewish and Christian readers over the centuries for its lively account of deliverance, the Book of Esther was the book of the Hebrew Bible slowest to achieve canonicity. Its lack of explicit reference to God or to Jewish religious rituals bothered some – though the addition of the Septuagint's "Rest of Esther" eased the way to acceptance by portraying Mordecai's prophetic dream, and the prayers of both Mordecai and Esther. But the Protestant Reformation rejected this Septuagint passage as apocryphal, and thus reopened the canonicity question for some, to which have been added objections by others to the book's overt nationalism and its violent, vengeful climax. Though there is no clear extra-biblical account of a Queen Esther or Ishtar at the court of Persian King Xerxes I, nevertheless Ahasuerus/Xerxes is undoubtedly historical, as are the king's fear of court intrigue (he eventually died at the hand of a treacherous captain) and the book's portrayal of his exterminating the entire family of a traitor.

An alternate scholarly view is that the Ahasuerus of Esther is not Xerxes I (reigned 486–465 BCE) but rather his son and successor Artaxerxes I (reigned 465–424 BCE) – in other words, the Persian king during the Second Return under Ezra and Nehemiah. In this view, Esther's actions not only prevent the wholesale slaughter of the Jews throughout the Persian Empire, but also dispose the king to favor Ezra and Nehemiah and to sponsor their rebuilding of Jerusalem.

The book's "Cinderella" romance between an outcast commoner and a king has become a staple of its reception over the generations – and also a touchstone for changing attitudes toward women's places and power by contrasting wifely resistance with wifely submission. The book opens by telling us that Ahasuerus has commanded a great seven-day feast, and on the seventh day, while "merry with wine," he further commands seven of his eunuchs "to bring Queen Vashti before the king, wearing her royal crown, in order to show her beauty to the people and the officials, for she was beautiful to behold" (Esther 1:11). But Vashti, who is already rather independently holding a feast for the women of the court, shocks everyone: she "refused to come at the king's command brought by his eunuchs; therefore the king was furious, and his anger burned within him" (1:12). A crisis of male confidence ensues: if Vashti's rebellion goes unanswered, the king's counselors warn, "the queen's behavior will become known to all women, so that they will despise their husbands in their eyes" (1:17).

Vashti!

Interpretive tradition is divided about the stubborn queen of Ahasuerus. Jewish Midrash denounces her as the wicked descendant of Babylonian kings Nebuchadnezzar and Belshazzar, a harridan who forced Jewish women to slave on the Sabbath and who refused to come to her husband not out of modesty, but because of a terrible deformity that she feared to reveal. Other Jewish interpreters increase sympathy for her by portraying the king as demanding that she appear naked, wearing only her crown; while nineteenth-century Christian suffragists like Harriet Beecher Stowe and Elizabeth Cady Stanton held Vashti up as a positive biblical example of resistance to male tyranny. Whether as a vain, untamed shrew or as a heroine of modest dignity, Vashti fascinates.

So Vashti is banished from bed, board, and palace, and Ahasuerus decrees a search for the fairest virgins in the land, who are rounded up and prepared to audition for the prestigious (and dangerous) role of queen. Though this may seem like a fairy-tale premise, it had long been common for Near Eastern kings to bring fresh female flesh to the royal harems each year – and the Persian dragnet pulls in a "lovely and beautiful" Jewess named Hadassah (2:1–4).

In short order in chapter 2, we learn that Hadassah is an orphan raised by her cousin Mordecai; that they are members of the tribe of Benjamin and descended, like old King Saul, from a father named Kish; and that Mordecai lives in the citadel city of Shushan (Susa) the Persian capital, close to the "house of the women" where the bridal candidates, including Hadassah, are being groomed. That they are semi-assimilated Jews is shown by the fact that Mordecai's name means "servant of Marduk" (the chief Sumerian/Babylonian deity); that he counsels Hadassah to hide her Jewish identity while at court; and that he gives her the Persian name Esther, after Isthar, the Babylonian love and fertility goddess (called Astarte by the Canaanites).

This pagan renaming of the heroine heightens the story's suspense, as it highlights her erotic potential, and as readers will wonder naturally when and how the secret of her Jewish identity will be revealed and whether she will be faithful to her people and their ways. Esther's treatment at court leaves no doubt that she is marked for the king's harem: winning the admiration of Hegai the "custodian of the women," she is carefully groomed for a year with extravagant beauty treatments preparing her for a single night's audition in the king's bedchamber – after which she will be remanded to the care of the royal eunuch Shaashgaz, the keeper of the concubines. If "the king delighted in her and called for her by name," she will then return for further sessions (2:8–14).

And true to the Cinderella story arc, that is precisely what happens. Unlike the disgraced Vashti, Esther is characterized by a gentle and submissive spirit toward male authority: she obeys Mordecai's instructions, taking a Persian name and concealing her ancestry; she wins the admiration of Hegai by gratefully following his advice; and on the great night, Ahasuerus is entirely charmed and fully satisfied, so much so that "he set the royal crown upon her head and made her queen instead of Vashti" (2:17). Were it not that this is only the second chapter of a book with nine more to go, one might think that we have reached a happy ending.

But immediately we're reminded of the dangerous world which the new Queen Esther has entered. Two of the king's door-keeping eunuchs, Bigthan and Teresh, are overheard by Mordecai conspiring against the king, and Esther reports Mordecai's alarming news to her husband, winning royal approval for her still secret cousin, whose good deed "was written in the book of the chronicles in the presence of the king" (2:21–23).

Yet this is only a prologue for a far greater peril to be visited, not on the king, but on Mordecai and all the Jews of Persia, including the secret Jew wearing the queen's crown. For into the story enters one of the most durable villains in Hebrew (and indeed world) literature: Haman the son of Hammedatha the Agagite. His singularly ugly patronymic is the key to his villainy, for Haman is a descendant of Agag, king of the Amalekites – the people who had attempted unilaterally to block and exterminate the Israelites during the Exodus (Exodus 17:8–13) – and of the Amalekite king whom Saul had defeated and whom, in delayed divine retaliation, Samuel had "hacked … in pieces before the LORD at Gilgal" (1 Samuel 15:33). A thousand years after the Amalekite assault on Israel, and almost six centuries after the execution of Agag, Haman the Agagite still remembers the ancient grudge. And so does Mordecai: when King Ahasuerus raises Haman above "all the princes of the kingdom" and commands the entire court to bow and pay him homage, Mordecai refuses, standing stiff-necked amid the otherwise prostrate people. So begins the book's defining struggle:

> Haman was filled with wrath. But he disdained to lay hands on Mordecai alone, for they had told him of the people of Mordecai. Instead, Haman sought to destroy all the Jews who were throughout the whole kingdom of Ahasuerus – the people of Mordecai. (Esther 3:5–6)

And, to intensify this struggle, we have the picture of a romantic but also imbecilic Gentile king, exalting the lovely, worthy Esther and the virtuous Jew Mordecai one day, and the poisonously wicked anti-Semite Haman the next.

Stepping back from the more romantic aspects of Esther's story, we also can see its heroine in the position of a feminine Joseph, exiled in a strange land that does not know the ways of her people, and yet through twists of Providence rising to a position of tremendous influence and concealing, but never forgetting, from whom she came. Esther also shares in common with Joseph that quality rarely mentioned in the Bible, but always important when present: striking good looks. Both augment their beauty with diligence and loyalty to their superiors, setting them apart from their peers and winning them favor whatever the circumstances, whether in the fields, the dungeon, the butler's pantry, the seraglio, or the throne room. And both Joseph and Esther are tested in the extreme, in ways that determine not only the fate of their own people, but also the fates of nations.

The particular fate of the Jews, it appears, will be determined by Haman in the casting of the lot, or *Pur*, to set the great day of slaughter. The lot is cast during the first month of Ahasuerus's twelfth year, the month Nisan, and falls on the last month, the month Adar (February–March), and Haman's planned holocaust will be based on all-too-typical charges against the Jews, and other religious or cultural minorities:

> their laws are different from all other people's, and they do not keep the king's laws. Therefore it is not fitting for the king to let them remain. If it pleases the king, let a decree be written that they be destroyed … (3:8–9)

And please the king it does, as Ahasuerus complacently hands his signet ring to Haman, giving a blanket permission to "to do with them as seems good to you" (3:11). And with all the flourishes of legality, like Hitler's Nuremburg Laws leading inexorably to *Kristallnacht*, Haman publishes his decree in letters

> sent by couriers into all the king's provinces, to destroy, to kill, and to annihilate all the Jews, both young and old, little children and women, in one day, on the thirteenth day of the twelfth month, which is the month of Adar, and to plunder their possessions. (3:13)

Yet in Shushan, the royal decree meets with puzzlement, as "the city ... was perplexed" (3:15) and consternation, as Mordecai receives the news with the traditional signs of Semitic grief: "he tore his clothes and put on sackcloth and ashes, and went out into the midst of the city. He cried out with a loud and bitter cry" (4:1).

Mordecai's very public laments soon draw Esther's attention, and when she inquires about the cause, he informs her of the terrible decree and of her responsibility to do all that she can to reverse it. Here comes Esther's great test, which shows her struggling quite humanly with her own mortal fear and her commitment to her people, for her immediate response to Mordecai's call is to point out that for her to approach Ahasuerus without invitation is to risk her life. Mordecai's answer is both blunt and eloquent:

> Do not think in your heart that you will escape in the king's palace any more than all the other Jews. For if you remain completely silent at this time, relief and deliverance will arise for the Jews from another place, but you and your father's house will perish. Yet who knows whether you have come to the kingdom for such a time as this? (4:13–14)

In words that echo powerfully even in our own day, Mordecai reminds his cousin that evil triumphs when the good do nothing, and that silence can become a conspiracy – and that after Haman comes for the rest of the Jews, he will come for her as well. She will not be protected by her pillows, her satins, or her clouds of perfume. To be the last one eaten by the wolf is no deliverance, and to all those who enjoy pleasure and power and influence, the message is clear: you have been given the kingdom "for such a time as this."

After Esther's human hesitation, her decision is brave and sure – and suddenly imperial:

> Go, gather all the Jews who are present in Shushan, and fast for me; neither eat nor drink for three days, night or day. My maids and I will fast likewise. And so I will go to the king, which is against the law; and if I perish, I perish! (4:16)

While showing a kingly resolution, Esther's means of engaging and defeating the evil are notably feminine. First, it is her beauty and past submission, and the desire and affection that they arouse in the king, which she hopes will gain her a hearing. The narrative builds palpable suspense as she approaches the king's throne, unsummoned and unannounced, and it relieves that suspense as the still-smitten king holds out his mighty golden scepter of welcome (5:1–2). Second, her strategy of confrontation is built on feminine skills of indirection and hospitality. When Ahasuerus offers to fulfill any request "up to half my kingdom," Esther, rather than immediately exposing Haman's plot and demanding justice on the spot, invites both the king and Haman to a banquet that same day – where the king repeats his "half my kingdom" offer and where she, in another piece of doubling, invites them both to *another* banquet on the *next* day (5:3–5).

All of this, of course, is rather a tease, building more suspense both for the king and for the readers, as Esther fascinates her husband and cannily deceives the wicked Haman. This suspense ratchets sharply upward as the Agagite, on the night before the flattering banquet with his king and queen, resolves to spring his trap on Mordecai – constructing a gallows to hang his ancestral enemy, this son of Kish (5:14). At this point the silent finger of Providence weighs down the scales of fate, as on the same night an insomniac Ahasuerus turns not to his wife or to a concubine, but to a reading of the court chronicles, which happen to scroll open at the story of Mordecai's timely intervention to save the king from assassination (6:1–4). In a belated fit of gratitude, Ahasuerus orders that something be done for Mordecai, and when the equally nocturnal Haman appears at the palace, the king puts to him the richly ambiguous question, "What shall be done for the man whom the king delights to honor?" (6:6). Ironic amusement increases as the vain Haman presumes that he is the honoree intended, and so recommends a thick slathering of pomp and circumstance, including the king's own robe, horse, and crest, and a great prince of the realm to lead horse and rider while shouting his honors abroad in the streets (6:7–9). Then comes the "big reveal": the honoree is Mordecai, and the crestfallen Haman is just the man to lead the horse!

And Haman's ironic descent has only begun. Returning home from his unwilling parade of Mordecai through Shusan, Haman is met by his erstwhile supporters and his wife Zeresh, who appall him with these words: "If Mordecai, before whom you have begun to fall, is of Jewish descent, you will not prevail against him but will surely fall before him" (6:13). Then the king's eunuchs arrive to take Haman to dinner, and to his doom. At the banquet, Ahasuerus repeats, for the third time, his extravagant offer of "half my kingdom" to Esther, who surprises him by asking not for more power or possessions, but merely that "my life be given me at my petition, and my people at my request. For we have been sold, my people and I, to be destroyed, to be killed, and to be annihilated" (7:3–4).

The brilliance of Esther's strategy is now revealed in the book's climactic moments, for by waiting, she has heightened the king's curiosity and his desire to please, subtly bargaining his expectations upward, only to surprise him with a request that is not grandly expensive but merely negative – kill me not, nor my people! Having raised her own credit with the king, Esther can afford to wait for him to close the circle by demanding to know the villain, and then turn his fury on its proper object, "this wicked Haman." But in a final twist of *schadenfreude*, the narrative reduces Haman to a craven buffoon while topping out the king's rage. Falling across Esther's couch, the merciless Haman begs for mercy, appearing to commit a sexual assault in the presence of a jealous and very powerful husband. The full force of Haman's fall become literally evident as the king orders his vizier hanged immediately from his own gallows, designed to exhibit Mordecai's corpse 50 cubits (75 ft) in the air, but now displaying the shame of his would-be killer (7:1–10).

Following this climax, the book's happy irony seems to be completed when Ahasuerus gives Haman's palace to Esther, and Haman's position and signet ring to Mordecai, who is now revealed to the king as Esther's close relative (8:1–2). Yet, as in many modern thrillers, the resolution of a personal issue with the villain doesn't necessarily defuse the ticking time-bomb of his schemes. In this case, that scheme is the Doomsday Machine of Medo-Persian legal tradition, which does not allow the modification or repeal of a king's decree, even by the king himself. Having set in motion the legal extermination of Persia's Jews, the dead Haman may still destroy his enemies even from the wrong end of a noose.

So Esther rushes again to the king's presence and prostrates herself, begging that she and Mordecai have power to "counteract" Haman's plans, not by repealing the standing order authorizing every Persian subject to slaughter the Jews "on the thirteenth day of the twelfth month of Adar," but by a counter-order allowing the Jews to defend themselves eye-for-eye: "to destroy, kill, and annihilate all the forces of any people or province that would assault them, both little children and women, and to plunder their possessions" (8:11). Mordecai seals this counter-order and posts it throughout the kingdom by swift horse-couriers.

So when the fateful thirteenth of Adar arrives, the tables are turned as any Persian subjects who attack their Jewish neighbors are overpowered, killed, and plundered by the Jews themselves, under royal authority. By the end of this bloody day, the enemies of the Jews are many fewer than before, and there is even a rush on willing conversions to the Jewish way by Persian Gentiles, because "the fear of the Jews" and "the fear of Mordecai" fell on all the peoples. The book's rejoicing over vanquished enemies (however offensive to many modern ears) is unabashed; yet this sharp edge of violence is blunted somewhat by the defensive nature of the action, and by the Jewish embrace of voluntary converts. And, strikingly, as in the time of Moses and Joshua, "they did not lay a hand on the plunder" (9:10, 15, 16). This battle was about self-defense, not booty.

After this second climactic peak to the action, all is done but the nation-wide celebration, and the explanation of how a favorite Jewish holiday came to be, the holiday Purim, which takes its name from Haman's casting of lots for Jewish blood, and celebrates how his blood returned on this own head.

Purim: Celebrating Triumph in Exile

As a holiday celebrating rescue and success while in a strange land, Purim has long been well-loved among the Jews, who after all have spent most of the centuries since Esther's time scattered ever-further around the earth, with no shortage of local Hamans to persecute them. Though based in the Hebrew Bible, Purim, like Hanukkah (which comes from the Apocrypha), has not carried the full sacred weight of Passover or especially the High Holy Days, but rather has added to its scriptural core a carnivalesque aura of costumes, skits, sweet and savory foods, and even parades with floats – a kind of Judaic Mardi Gras, without the Lenten aftermath. Haman, like Guy Fawkes in Britain, is often burned in effigy to great rejoicing, and the few specifically religious duties or *mitzvot* associated with the holiday include the exchange of gifts, the giving of charity, the sharing of the *se'udat Purim* meal, the reading of Esther itself ("the *megillah*"), and the saying of special prayers.

So Esther's book tells of an ancient Cinderella caught up not only into royal romance but ethnic intrigue and villainy; of a latter-day, female Joseph whose beauty, brilliance, and loyalty are providentially used to make the strange land of her exile less strange; and a national narrative of survival, revenge, and triumph. And Esther's book is also like a stone of memory, reminding the people that wandering Israel can and will rise again, whether from seeds scattered abroad in foreign lands, or from walls, gates, and a temple restored in Jerusalem.

We have been discussing national narratives as a subgenre, from the mainly sad stories of Kings and Chronicles, through the reviving, homeward-bound hopes of Ezra and Nehemiah, to the joy-in-exile of Esther. The connecting thread linking these books is the tender and terrifying relationship between *Yahweh* and his covenant people, and they meditate on the infinite costs and blessings of being his chosen. We now turn away from these national narratives to a masterpiece of universal drama; we turn back to a time before the Exile, before the kingdoms, indeed before the Judges or Moses and his Exodus; and we turn from the chosen children of Abraham to a land called Uz, where the name of the LORD is nevertheless known and feared among the Gentiles. And there is a man in the land of Uz whose name is Job, and he too will know God's plenty of fear and testing.

Questions for Discussion

1   How does the Hebrew **Book of Kings** work as a whole? What's the effect of dividing it in half for the Christian Old Testament?

2   What's the effect of beginning **1 Kings** in the midst of a succession crisis surrounding the elderly **David**? How does **Solomon**, like David before him in **2 Samuel**, create a benchmark for kingly virtues and glories? How does the description of Solomon's glorious rise and reign also carry the seeds of Solomon's decline and corruption?

3   What are the issues that lead to the **division of the kingdom** under **Rehoboam**?

4   How does **Jeroboam** son of Nebat, the first Israelite king in the divided kingdom, establish a benchmark for sinful misrule? What specifically is "**the sin of Jeroboam**," and why is it regarded so seriously by the narrator?

5   What are some important effects of alternating back and forth throughout **1 and 2 Kings**, juxtaposing the **leaders of Judah and Israel**? What comparative and contrasting patterns emerge? For what does the narrator praise particular rulers as good, and blame others as evil? Who are the best? The worst?

6   What are some roles of **prophets** in the kingly narrative? What factors preserve Judah longer than Israel? What factors finally bring down each kingdom?

7   How does the Hebrew **Book of Chronicles** work as a whole? What's the effect of dividing it in half for the Christian Old Testament? What are the effects of Chronicles **doubling** many of the accounts of the kings of Judah found in Kings? What kinds of details does Chronicles add to kings, and to what effects? What does Chronicles omit, and to what effects? Why exclude most of the material about the Northern Kingdom of Israel?

8   How does the ending of **2 Chronicles** link it to the beginning of **Ezra**? How do **Ezra** and **Nehemiah** function as a single narrative?

9   How does **restored Jerusalem** in the Book of **Ezra-Nehemiah** resemble Jerusalem under the kings of Judah? How does it differ, and how does life in post-exilic Jerusalem differ?

10 How does Ezra-Nehemiah portray the **relation of the Jews to Gentile authority**?

11 How does Ezra-Nehemiah yet again redefine what it means to be **heroic** – in comparison to past heroic models such as **Abraham, Joseph, Moses, Joshua, Samuel, or David**?

12 How does the national narrative of the **Book of Esther** relate to and fit into the narrative lines of Kings, Chronicles, and especially Ezra-Nehemiah? How does her story resemble that of popular **romance** or **fairy-tale**? Of **Joseph** in the Book of Genesis?

13 How does **Esther's** gender affect her range of action in the Shushan of **Ahasuerus** king of Persia? How does the opening account of **Queen Vashti** establish the conditions for Esther's eventual success? How does Esther further redefine heroism in relation to earlier female heroic models such as **Sarah, Deborah, Ruth**, and **Hannah**?

14 What ethnic and religious backgrounds and contexts define the actions of Mordecai, Esther, and especially **Haman**?

15 How are narrative **doubling** and **irony** at work throughout the Book of Esther? How does the narrative build suspense? How does it achieve its multiple climaxes?

16 What's the relationship between **revenge** and **celebration** in the Book of Esther? What does **Purim** celebrate and memorialize?

11

Drama: The Divine Tragicomedy of Job

"There was a man in the land of Uz, whose name was Job." So begins what England's Victorian poet laureate Alfred Tennyson called "the greatest poem of ancient and modern times"; a story that has permeated the Jewish, Christian, Islamic, and now the world's cultural imagination; a book that may be the Bible's oldest.

As the Sparks Fly Upward: Job's Enduring Influence

The Book of Job is universally acknowledged, on its literary merits, as one of the world's master-pieces. Its influence is so widespread as to defy any list-maker: from ancient Jewish and Christian liturgies, de Lassus's Renaissance motets, Shakespeare's Lear on the heath, and Handel's *Messiah*, to Goethe's *Faust*, Blake's illustrated *Book of Job*, and Capra's *It's a Wonderful Life*, this ancient story of a good man's testing, grief, and reward speaks to an experience so widespread as to be practi-cally universal. Some modern retellings, like Joseph Stein's *Fiddler on the Roof* and Neil Simon's *God's Favorite*, find a good deal of laughter amidst the hero's sufferings and stress the comic outcome; while others, like Archibald MacLeish's *J. B.* and the Coen Brothers' *A Serious Man*, darken the laughter to take a more sardonic and ironic view.

Attributed by Jewish tradition to Moses himself, the book does not name its author but does evoke an era of God-fearing Gentiles like Melchizedek and Moses's father-in-law Jethro; for Job is not an Israelite, but a man of Uz, often identified with the land of Edom in the days of the Patriarchs. Much modern criticism of Job's book has treated its prose narrative frame (chapters 1–2, 42:7–17) as a later addition of the fourth century BCE imposing an explanatory structure and a happy ending on the core of a more ancient tragic poem; however, modern archeology has discovered intact Near Eastern and Egyptian texts of the second millennium BCE in which prose context frames poetry, convincing many other interpreters that Job's multi-layered com-position is largely or entirely original and may date as far back as 1500 BCE – before the earliest possible dates for the Pentateuch.

However we account for its composition, the Book of Job as we have it combines grim human suffering and grand tragic eloquence with a wry comic wit and outbursts of faith, hope, and unexpected happiness. Thus, like the biblical stories of Joseph, Ruth, Hannah, and King David, and like Shakespeare's late plays, Job belongs to the literary mode called **tragicomedy**. As we have seen repeatedly, such stories begin with the tragic action, afflicting the protagonist early on with dire suffering that often involves family betrayal and estrangement, material ruin, and

Literary Study of the Bible: An Introduction, First Edition. Christopher Hodgkins.
© 2020 John Wiley & Sons Ltd. Published 2020 by John Wiley & Sons Ltd.

even apparent death. Then, at the point of maximum loss and darkness, miraculous comic returns and discoveries bring repentance, restoration, and family reconciliation – usually revealing a providential design.

The Book of Job also belongs to the biblical category of **wisdom literature**, and is often compared to Proverbs and Ecclesiastes, offering a bracing contrast to the sunnier prudence of the former and resembling the disillusioned "counterwisdom" of the latter by attacking the misplaced certitude of much traditional wisdom lore, at least as represented by Job's smug and misguided "Comforters." (Please see Chapter 4 for a fuller discussion of wisdom literature.) In particular, Job's book raises perennial questions about the value of **theodicy** – the project of justifying God's ways to man in rationally satisfying terms – versus the value of **theophany** – the direct manifestation and revelation of God to man in personally satisfying terms. It would appear that Job has much in common with Ecclesiastes in their shared emphasis on divine incomprehensibility – that is, on human inability to know why God does what he does. Yet in one particular, Job differs strikingly, for even though Job himself does not know why God permits him to suffer so terribly, the reader does: in order to play out a wager between the LORD and his Adversary, Satan. Or so it would seem. It is this quality of play, of drama, of theatricality that gives the Book of Job much of its distinctive structure and imaginative power.

11.1   Job as Primal Theater

The most immediately notable fact about the Book of Job's construction is that it is composed largely in dramatic dialogue, and that this dialogue is arranged in multiple cycles. Whether or not Job was ever performed in ancient times, as liturgy or as a sort of primal theater, it takes an inherently theatrical form. After the prose introduction in the opening chapters narrating the LORD's confrontation by Satan and leading to Job's sufferings, there begins a series of five sections, rather like "acts" in a play, the first three of which work as rounds in an ongoing debate between Job and the friends – Eliphaz, Bildad, and Zophar – who've come to comfort him. The fourth act introduces a new character, the younger man Elihu, whose celebration of God's majesty in the storm leads into the fifth act entrance of *Yahweh* himself, speaking to Job out of the whirlwind. After the LORD's intervention and the humbling of Job, prose narration returns for the book's conclusion, as Job's fortunes are restored – indeed doubled – and as God endorses Job's behavior over that of his "friends."

In addition to this structure of dialogue acts or cycles, another feature that makes Job's book theatrical is the psychological realism by which character is revealed, developed, and transformed. Although at one level Job and his Comforters repeat themselves in their rounds of argument, these repetitions are not static, but dynamic. We witness increasing levels of irritation and denunciation from the friends as they find their advice and rebukes rejected, and increasing levels of exasperation, anger, and grief from Job as he hears himself accused of crimes about which he knows nothing. Crescendoing shrillness, sarcasm, and contempt culminate in the friends' apoplectic silence, as Job finally despairs of receiving any sympathy from what he calls these "miserable comforters" and takes his complaint directly to the Almighty. Then, after Elihu enters to correct Job and his friends, Job's desire for divine intervention is fulfilled in the book's alarming climax, as the LORD's presence overwhelms – rather than answers – all questions. Along the way, other characters enter the action or are mentioned by the narrator: Job's first children (all dead by the end of chapter 1), a series of ill-news messengers, Job's brothers and sisters, his nameless and embittered wife ("Curse God and die," she advises), his second set of children (who appear marvelously at the end, borne by the same wife), and above all Satan, the LORD's flamboyant critic, who seems to dominate the action at the start, but who vanishes before the book's conclusion.

Indeed it is Satan (Hebrew *Ha-Satan*, "the Adversary" or "the prosecutor") who personifies the mystery of evil at the heart of Job's story: why does a good and almighty Creator allow a man like Job to suffer so extremely? As the varied characters pursue answers to this question, Satan tests the limits of divine justice and patience, and of human knowledge and endurance: first, he accuses God and Job with the same naked, shameless aggression as the serpent shows in Eden; next he incites God to harm Job "without cause"; then he volunteers to inflict that harm, stripping Job of wealth, family, reputation, and health; and finally, as Job lies naked and vulnerable before the world, and as *Yahweh* reveals himself in all his terrific glory, Satan disappears from the tale, without a further word. It is by pressing the boundaries of nakedness and knowledge that Satan serves as a catalyst for discovery, but like many other catalytic agents, he evaporates in the process.

11.1.1 Prologue: Nakedness and Knowledge, Again

As the Book of Job begins, Job is "greatest of all the people of the East." He has seven sons and three daughters, and possesses "seven thousand sheep, three thousand camels, five hundred yoke of oxen, five hundred female donkeys, and a very large household" (Job 1:3). If this drama were a Greek tragedy, one might say that he is in the state of *olbos*, full and arrogant atop Fortune's Wheel and ripe for a fall. But overconfident is just what we are told Job is not: on the contrary, his is "blameless and upright, and one who feared God and shunned evil," a humble man who

> would rise early in the morning and offer burnt offerings according to the number of [all his children]. For Job said, "It may be that my sons have sinned and cursed God in their hearts." Thus Job did regularly. (1:5)

And far from inciting the gods of Olympus to jealousy at his success, Job has won the high praise of the LORD, who points to Job's example among all the "sons of God": "Have you considered My servant Job, that there is none like him on the earth, a blameless and upright man, one who fears God and shuns evil?" (1:8). And if God is for Job, who can be against him?

Yet there is jealousy in the heavenly places – at least when visited by Satan, the Adversary:

> Now there was a day when the sons of God came to present themselves before the LORD, and Satan also came among them. And the LORD said to Satan, "From where do you come?" So Satan answered the LORD and said, "From going to and fro on the earth, and from walking back and forth on it." (1:7–8)

Indeed it's this interloper to whom *Yahweh* is praising the virtues of Job. Who is this wandering gainsayer, and why does he have such heavenly access? We're told almost as little here of his origins as we're told of the Serpent's in Genesis 3, though other Old Testament passages speak of Satan as the spiritual enemy of Israel, tempting and opposing its leaders (1 Chronicles 21:1 and Zechariah 3:1–2), and this passage in Job seems to assume that he is a corrupt angelic being to whom God allows certain powers on the earth.

Satan certainly speaks like the Serpent of Eden; he is blunt and highly provoking. To the LORD's question, "Where have you come from?" he answers airily, "From going to and fro on the earth, and from walking back and forth on it" (Job 1:7) – the cheeky equivalent of saying "Oh, just prowling my turf." When the LORD highlights Job's virtue as a riposte to Satan's impudence, Satan presumes to correct God himself, claiming superior insight and re-casting divine kindness and human loyalty as cynical bribery accepted by toadying hypocrisy.

> Does Job fear God for nothing? Have you not made a hedge around him, around his household, and around all that he has on every side? You have blessed the work of his hands, and his possessions have increased in the land. But now, stretch out your hand and touch all that he has, and he will surely curse you to your face! (1:9–11)

Finding genuine generosity, love, or virtue incomprehensible, Satan dismisses them with a sardonic leer, and proposes a kind of experiment: remove the material supports of Job's godliness, and expose its emptiness. As Berthold Brecht writes in *The Threepenny Opera*, "Even saintly folk will act like sinners / Unless they have their customary dinners."

Surprisingly, rather than casting this naysayer out of his presence, *Yahweh* – with mysterious brevity – overlooks the *lèse-majesté* and accepts the challenge: "Behold, all that he has is in your power; only do not lay a hand on his person" (1:12). What does this act say about God's character? Certainly, that he is almighty, with the power to allow or prevent Job's sufferings, but does his empowerment of the Adversary indicate his deep assurance of Job's loyalty, or his callous disregard for Job's family and fortunes? Or both? With superb suspense, the tale's teller does not say.

What follows is as concise and harrowing a narrative of calamity as any ever penned. Like members of the chorus in a Greek tragedy, four messengers arrive in quick succession with escalating news of offstage destruction: first that Sabean raiders have killed Job's herdsmen and stolen his oxen, then that heavenly fire has consumed Job's sheep and servants, then that Chaldeans have taken his camels and slaughtered their keepers, and finally that

> your sons and daughters were eating and drinking wine in their oldest brother's house, and suddenly a great wind came from across the wilderness and struck the four corners of the house, and it fell on the young people, and they are dead; and I alone have escaped to tell you! (1:18–19)

These strangely choreographed hammer blows fall on the great patriarch, now destitute and childless, and drive him to his knees, but not to cursing:

> Then Job arose, tore his robe, and shaved his head; and he fell to the ground and worshiped. And he said:
>
> > Naked I came from my mother's womb,
> > And naked shall I return there.
> > The LORD gave, and the LORD has taken away;
> > Blessed be the name of the LORD.
>
> In all this Job did not sin nor charge God with wrong. (1:20–22)

Here is biblical "nakedness" at its least erotic and most desolate: the exposure that Job feels is total vulnerability, stripped of any vestige reminding humanity that they once stood unashamed in Eden, clothed in divine love and protection. There also is a crucial struggle implied in Job's blessing of the LORD's name: for it is precisely this act of blessing that refutes Satan's charge that a suffering Job will curse.

But Satan is not the type to stay refuted. In chapter 2 he saunters again into the divine presence, and when challenged by the LORD – "still [Job] holds fast to his integrity, although you incited Me against him, to destroy him without cause" (2:3) – the Adversary doubles down on the wager:

> Skin for skin! Yes, all that a man has he will give for his life. But stretch out Your hand now, and touch his bone and his flesh, and he will surely curse You to Your face! (2:4–5)

Satan's next opportunistic turn of argument is that ultimately, people care less about their family, fortune, and friends than they do about their own "skin," their health and strength, the very castle keep of the self. Breach the inner walls of bodily comfort, he says, and the man will abandon his pretended loyalty to God like a traitor under torture. Remarkably, mysteriously, and disturbingly, *Yahweh* accepts the renewed wager and re-appoints the torturer in the fewest possible words: "Behold, he is in your hand, but spare his life" (2:6). And Satan sets to work.

Job, already crushed and grieving, now receives the sign of this new curse: an outbreak of boils head to toe, marking him as an unclean outcast and forcing him to the refuse dump at the edge of his town, where he wearily scrapes his pustules with a potsherd, his fingernails presumably worn to the nub. The unkindest cut comes when his wife, whether out of despair or venom, counsels that he provoke the LORD to quick-killing wrath: "Do you still hold fast to your integrity? Curse God and die!" (2:9). Clearly, she echoes Satan's bribery–flattery theory of love, and sees Job's loyalty to such a cruel Deity as misplaced. Better to court a kind of divinely assisted suicide, she says, and have it over in a single stroke.

Significantly, Job replies with an observation, and a rhetorical question: first, "You speak as one of the foolish women" (*nevaloth* or "apostates"); second, "Shall we indeed accept good from God, and shall we not accept adversity?" (2:10a). Job defines fidelity to God, like in marriage, as "for richer, for poorer," and implies that love offered to God or to a spouse on the condition of unbroken prosperity and happiness isn't worthy of the name – as in Shakespeare's much later words, "Love is not love / Which alters when it alteration finds / Or bends with the remover to remove" (Sonnet 116, ll. 2–4). And yet Job has now suffered the removal of all but his life. Will the coming tempest shake him? Not yet, but there is a hint of the growing inner struggle: "In all this Job did not sin with his lips" (Job 2:10b). Not with his lips, perhaps, but what about his heart?

Job's heart remains a mystery as word spreads of his calamity, and his friends gather from their countries to sit and grieve with him: Eliphaz the Temanite, Bildad the Shuhite, and Zophar the Naamathite. All of their responses and deeds en route suggest that they are genuinely moved and indeed appalled by his suffering: they make a long, concerted journey "to comfort him"; they are stunned to tears by Job's altered appearance; they rend their garments and sprinkle themselves with dust; and, perhaps most tellingly, "they sat down with him on the ground seven days and seven nights, and no one spoke a word to him, for they saw that his grief was very great" (2:13). That is, to use the literal Hebrew phrase, they "sit *shiva*" (for "seven"), still a mourning custom among the Jews. Far from being eager to lecture and berate their friend, they wait in silent solidarity with him in his plight. And the question remains: will Job curse God?

For Job does indeed want very much to curse. And as chapter 3 opens the main poetic discourse of the book, curse he does – not the LORD himself, but the day of Job's own birth. In a meditation on the relief of oblivion, Job calls down darkness on the light of his birthday, and wonders aloud why he was not stillborn, and why his mother received and nurtured him if all of his life's supposed blessings have in the end amounted to this: that

> ...the thing I greatly feared has come upon me,
> And what I dreaded has happened to me.
> I am not at ease, nor am I quiet;
> I have no rest, for trouble comes. (3:25–26)

We learn that even in the midst of his prosperity, Job had feared a coming day of adversity, and that since disaster finally has arrived, the present pain infects the memory of all past pleasures. And to question the gift of life is indirectly to question its Giver.

11.1.2   Act 1: Debate Begins – Job 4–14

Job's friends now start to intervene. They have endured with him a long time in silence, and they have listened to his opening complaint, with its implicit critique of divine justice. So Eliphaz begins the response, and at first his words are patient and diplomatic, even complimentary:

> If one attempts a word with you, will you become weary?
> But who can withhold himself from speaking?
>
> Surely you have instructed many,
> And you have strengthened weak hands.
> Your words have upheld him who was stumbling,
> And you have strengthened the feeble knees... (4:2–4)

Yet his compliments soon segue into an initially gentle rebuke, and a probing rhetorical question:

> But now it comes upon you, and you are weary;
> It touches you, and you are troubled....
>
> Remember now, whoever perished being innocent?
> Or where were the upright ever cut off? (4:5, 7)

Physician, heal thyself! Eliphaz sees irony in Job's having taught others but being unable to apply life's lessons to his own case – that the innocent are protected, and that the virtuous do not suffer great loss.

Thus, Eliphaz introduces the bone of contention that will stir debate through the next twenty-five chapters:

> Those who plow iniquity
> And sow trouble reap the same.
> By the blast of God they perish,
> And by the breath of His anger they are consumed. (4:8–9)

In other words, says Eliphaz, just as the virtuous do not suffer great loss, so those who suffer greatly must have fallen from virtue. In Eliphaz's view, there is a one-to-one correspondence between human deeds (righteous or wicked) and immediate divine reward or rebuke. But there is a more positive corollary:

> Behold, happy is the man whom God corrects;
> Therefore do not despise the chastening of the Almighty. (5:17)

Eliphaz claims that for those who confess their sins, there can be happy returns of God's blessings; since divine punishment is proportional to human crime, Job need only be spurred by his heavy suffering to admit his great iniquity in order to be restored to God's favor.

Yet confess to great iniquity is just what Job will not do. He admits, indeed insists, that his suffering comes from God – "For the arrows of the Almighty are within me" (6:4) – and he continues to call out to the LORD for annihilation – "That it would please God to crush me" (6:9) – but he rhetorically challenges his friends to "[c]ause me to understand wherein I have erred" and barring that to "concede my righteousness still stands!" (6:24, 29). He then turns again to God, in effect telling him to mind his own blessed business:

> Let me alone,
> For my days are but a breath....
>
> What have I done to You, O watcher of men? (7:16, 20)

Yahweh remains silent for the time being, but now Bildad the Shuhite rises to Job's challenge.

Bildad speaks with less diplomacy than Eliphaz: "How long will ... the words of your mouth be like a strong wind?" (8:2). He bluntly asserts that all of Job's dead children probably deserved punishment, and that if Job were really righteous, God would restore him (8:4–7). Then Bildad ends his opening salvo by holding out hope that Job can indeed be restored to laughter and joy if he will confess and turn away from his gross sins (8:20–22). Job responds to this "consolation" by insisting, in effect, that Bildad is speaking right words to the wrong person. Job concedes universal human sinfulness – "how can a man be righteous before God?" (9:1) – but he nevertheless insists that there's no challenging the judgment of the irresistible power who "shakes the earth out of its place," who "treads on the waves of the sea," and who "made the Bear, Orion, and the Pleiades" (9:6, 8, 9). Then comes his bitter suggestion that God's might makes him inevitably right:

> If it is a matter of strength, indeed he is strong;
> And if of justice, who will appoint my day in court?...
>
> I am blameless, yet I do not know myself;
> I despise my life....
>
> Therefore I say, "He destroys the blameless and the wicked".
> If the scourge slays suddenly,
> He laughs at the plight of the innocent.
>
> The earth is given into the hand of the wicked.
> He covers the faces of its judges.
> If it is not he, who else could it be? (9:19, 21–24)

Ultimately, says Job, "He is not a man...Nor is there any mediator between us" (9:32–33). In the absence of an objective umpire, Job again demands that the LORD "Cease! Leave me alone ..." (10:20).

Job's third visitor, Zophar the Naamathite, is having none of Job's self-defense, and escalates the confrontation.

> And should a man full of talk be vindicated?
> Should your empty talk make men hold their peace?
> And when you mock, should no one rebuke you? (11:2–3)

And what a rebuke! Not only, says Zophar, do Job and his family deserve all of the bitter business that God has dealt them; "Know therefore that God exacts from you / *Less* than your iniquity deserves" (11:6, emphasis mine). Loss of children, home, fortune, wifely sympathy, public reputation, bodily health – what more can the Almighty take from Job, short of the life that he begs to lose? Yet Zophar insists that Job needs even harsher instruction – and yet that

Job will be too stupid to learn from it: "For an empty-headed man will be wise, / When a wild donkey's colt is born a man" (11:12).

Being called an ass brings out the sarcasm in Job, who sums up the Comforters' confidence with withering scorn: "No doubt you are the people, / And wisdom will die with you!" (12:2). Yet Job concedes most of what they say about the power of God. Even the animals sense God's might, he says, and everyone sees how *Yahweh* brings down counselors, judges, kings, priests, elders, and princes; for in Job's jaundiced eye, God is the great humiliator, stripping the haughty and leading them empty away (12:17–25). Tired already of human correction and advice, Job dismisses these self-appointed divine spokesmen and calls again for God to come down and speak for himself: "Though he slay me, yet will I trust him. / Even so, I will defend my own ways before him" (13:15). Job's challenge then ebbs into a despondent prayer, reflecting on the transitory nature of humanity:

> Man who is born of woman
> Is of few days and full of trouble....
>
> But as a mountain falls and crumbles away,
> And as a rock is moved from its place;
> As water wears away stones,
> And as torrents wash away the soil of the earth;
> So you destroy the hope of man. (14:1, 18–19)

Hope in what? Well may we ask, as the Comforters renew their efforts.

11.1.3 Act 2: The Pace Quickens – Job 15–21

The second discourse of Eliphaz presents none of the circumlocutions and niceties of the first; he comes right at Job, charging him with blasphemous arrogance.

> Yes, you cast off fear,
> And restrain prayer before God.
> For your iniquity teaches your mouth ...
>
> Are you the first man who was born?
> Or were you made before the hills?
> Have you heard the counsel of God? (15:4–5, 7–8)

Addressing Job's call for divine attention and intervention, Eliphaz presents an image of a God who is so fastidiously disgusted with the corrupt cosmos that he would never concern himself with a vile mortal:

> If God puts no trust in his saints,
> And the heavens are not pure in his sight,
> How much less man, who is abominable and filthy,
> Who drinks iniquity like water! (15:15–16)

For added impact, Eliphaz itemizes how *Yahweh* makes the wicked man suffer: he writhes in pain, dreads his enemies, wanders in darkness, fears the sword, begs for bread, lives in terror, and dwells in fruitless, ruined desolation (15:20–34). All of this, Eliphaz asserts, the wicked richly deserves, "For he stretches out his hand against God, / And acts defiantly against the Almighty" (15:25). And so, he says, does Job.

As if both to defy and confirm the accusations of these "miserable comforters" (16:2), Job lashes out against God's hostile violence toward him:

> He tears me in His wrath, and hates me;
> He gnashes at me with His teeth;
> My adversary sharpens His gaze on me ...

> He breaks me with wound upon wound;
> He runs at me like a warrior. (16:9–14)

To call God "adversary" (*tsar*) comes perilously close to calling him *ha-satan*. When the LORD is my Satan, where is there to turn?

Job turns to the LORD. Having lodged his complaint against God with the Comforters, he now calls on God himself for relief from those Comforters.

> Now put down a pledge for me with yourself.
> Who is he who will shake hands with me?
> For you have hidden their heart from understanding;
> Therefore you will not exalt them. (17:3–4)

Then he turns again to his "friends," who apparently are rising to leave in disgust, and he taunts them to return and continue the debate:

> But please, come back again, all of you,
> For I shall not find one wise man among you. (17:10)

If there were stage directions in the text, they probably would call for Job to move like a man racked not only with pain, but with angry indecision.

In response to Job's challenge, Bildad returns to the fight, and his weapons are sharper than ever. He probes Job's emotional wounds, dwelling on the sufferings of the wicked that most resemble Job's own.

> His strength is starved,
> And destruction is ready at his side.
> It devours patches of his skin;
> The firstborn of death devours his limbs.
> He is uprooted from the shelter of his tent, ...
> Brimstone is scattered on his dwelling. (18:12–15)

Bildad intimates that if there is perhaps someone nearby whose limbs tremble, whose skin teems with bleeding sores, whose home and fortunes are destroyed, that person – whoever he may be! – had better not set himself up as a preacher of righteousness, but instead get right with God.

Job's answer to this cruel thrust is genuinely poignant, then suddenly transcendent. He cannot but agree with Bildad that God his made him an outcast, for family, friends, guests, his wife, even little children, all "despise me" (19:18). In a spasm of grief and loneliness he reaches out to his tormenters for compassion. "Have pity on me, have pity on me, O you my friends," he cries, "For the hand of God has struck me!" (19:21). Yet in an instant his eyes open on a future and a hope, and he opens his mouth in famous words resonating with certainty:

> For I know that my Redeemer lives,
> And he shall stand at last on the earth;
> And after my skin is destroyed, this I know,
> That in my flesh I shall see God,
> Whom I shall see for myself,
> And my eyes shall behold, and not another.
> How my heart yearns within me! (19:25–27)

Looking beyond his present pain and alienation, he sees a better day – perhaps the Resurrection at the Last Day – when all of his losses in body and soul will be repaired and made right; when God his seeming humiliator, accuser, and adversary will reveal himself fully as God his Redeemer; when, as the libretto of Handel's *Messiah* puts it, "though worms destroy this body, yet in my flesh shall I see God."

Yet Job's hopeful certainty shines only for an instant. Darkness descends again, and Zophar, impressed by neither Job's vision nor his cry for pity, renews the assault. Speaking with a certitude born of dogma rather than observation, Zophar confidently details the deeds of wickedness that presumably attach to Job: he has "oppressed and forsaken the poor, / He has violently seized a house which he did not build," and has fattened himself to bursting at the expense of the weak and starving (20:19, 23). While lodging these grossly unjust accusations, most of Zophar's speech dwells with a relish on the agonies awaiting malefactors like Job, who can look forward to sucking asps' venom, vomiting up their gorgeous feasts, being pierced by flights of bronze arrows, seeing their children reduced to begging, and dwelling in utter darkness lit by God's fiery wrath (20:12–29). Zophar's words leave no doubt that whatever compassion he had felt toward Job has turned to outrage.

Job's riposte takes direct aim at Zophar's central assumption: that the wicked never prosper. Like the litany of complaint in Psalm 73, Job's observations of thriving villainy are addressed primarily to the Almighty himself. Why, he asks, do so many bad men do so well for themselves? The wicked enjoy contented old age, abundant children, plentifully breeding bulls, handsome houses, lovely music, and peaceful deaths; they tell God to mind his own business and apparently are left to theirs. Then Job skewers Zophar's claims about intergenerational judgment:

> They say, "God lays up one's iniquity for his children";
> Let him recompense him, that he may know it.
> Let his eyes see his [own] destruction,
> And let him drink of the wrath of the Almighty.
> For what does he care about his household after him,
> When the number of his months is cut in half? (21:19–21)

A man evil enough to take food from orphans' mouths may well smile with glee to know that his grandchildren, not he himself, will "take the rap." All in all, concludes Job, "How then can you comfort me with empty words, / Since falsehood remains in your answers?" (21:34).

11.1.4   Act 3: Climax, Sullen Silence, and Summation – Job 22–31

Having been accused of "empty words," Eliphaz fills his final round with words of anger and flaming condemnation. Elaborating on Zophar's chain of indictments, he gratuitously charges Job with blatant crimes against the weak and innocent, accusing him of stripping the naked, and stealing from the thirsty, the hungry, the widow, and the orphan (22:6–9). The absurdity of these charges is palpable, since before Job's misfortunes he had been a man noted for his active benevolence, but Eliphaz's moral calculus assures him that only such crimes could have brought such sufferings on Job's head. Like a torturer racking his victim into a guilty plea, Eliphaz tells Job that he has it in his own power to make the pain stop: simply confess "and be at peace" (22:21).

But Job is in no mood to surrender, or even to dignify Eliphaz and company with more answers. Over the next two chapters Job speaks, not to the Comforters, but past them, in a voice somewhere between an overheard soliloquy and an aggrieved prayer: first, of how he longs to confront God – "Would he contend with me in his great power? / No! But he would take note of me" (23:6) – and second, about how the Almighty leaves the weak unprotected and the wicked unpunished (24:4, 7, 14–15). Indeed, it seems that God "gives [the wicked] security" – though in the end, Job asserts, "they are exalted for a little while, / Then they are gone" (24:23, 24). Then Job concludes with the truth-teller's dare flung back to his accusers: "Now if it is not so, who will prove me a liar, / And make my speech worth nothing?" (24:23, 24, 25).

Eliphaz, Bildad, and Zophar have traveled far to sit with Job, and have preached long to correct and chastise him. Nothing frustrates a preacher more than the sense of being ignored, and when the congregation is looking past the preacher to another authority, that can inspire hot or cold fury. The first is powerfully evident in Bildad's last short outburst, which concludes with perhaps the most demeaning imagery yet:

> How then can man be righteous before God?
> Or how can he be pure who is born of a woman?
> If even the moon does not shine,
> And the stars are not pure in [God's] sight,
> How much less man, who is a maggot,
> And a son of man, who is a worm? (25:4–6)

While the accusation is general, the target is specific, effectively shouting at Job, "You vile spawn of a woman! You maggot! You worm!" Bildad's vocabulary of abuse has descended to the pit, and suits the dunghill where Job sits. And if a burst of hot anger is Bildad's final outlet, cold fury is heard in the stony silence that follows. Bildad says no more, his discourse truncated after only a few verses, and Zophar speaks nothing at all, forfeiting his final round in wordlessness that speaks more loudly than words.

Imagine then this small circle of four ancient men seated on a refuse heap, staring balefully and panting with outrage, like hungry old dogs wearied by scrapping for a bone. After the desolate quiet has settled for a while, Job speaks into the vacuum. First he dismisses the Comforters' failed arguments, then sums his case with a paean to divine power and wisdom, finally rising to a grand rhetorical crescendo mourning his lost happiness, and calling down a solemn conditional curse – on himself.

He begins by refuting his visitors: "How have you helped him who is without power? / How have you saved the arm that has no strength?" (26:2). These rhetorical questions have the same implied answer – "Not one bit!" – and indict the false friends' failure to aid either Job himself, or any of the poor and downcast for whom they claim to care. In contrast to their impotence, says Job, the Almighty exercises absolute power over his creatures and inspires awe in all creation, beyond human reckoning:

> The pillars of heaven tremble,
> And are astonished at his rebuke…
>
> Indeed these are the mere edges of his ways,
> And how small a whisper we hear of him!
> But the thunder of his power who can understand? (26:11, 14)

But will *El Shaddai* intervene to take up Job's cause and declare him righteous? Job doubts this, and yet he vows never to yield: though the Almighty "has taken away my justice [and has] made my soul bitter… As long as my breath is in me …[m]y righteousness I hold fast, and will not let it go" (27:2–3, 6). Tenaciously Job insists that he is not among the truly wicked, praying rather darkly that "my enemy" will "be like the wicked," eventually overtaken by the terrors of God – intending, perhaps, the Comforters? (27:7, 9–23). Then, even in the throes of his own troubles, he launches into a lofty interlude about where wisdom is to be found: not in the deep mines, the high mountain haunts of birds and lions, the abyss of the seas, or far Ophir, but only in the mind of God (28:1–28) – and presumably not in the minds of Eliphaz and his ilk, nor even in his own.

Chapters 29–30 present, as if after another long silent pause, Job's retrospective discourse touching in its pathos. Resonating with the nostalgia of every redundant oldster from Shakespeare's Lear to Tennyson's Ulysses, Job remembers when he was a man of respect, when his children prospered, when his reputation went before him like a mighty host and made his words ring among hushed crowds in the city gates – not because he was terrible, but because he was good:

> Because I delivered the poor who cried out,
> The fatherless and the one who had no helper.
> The blessing of a perishing man came upon me,
> And I caused the widow's heart to sing for joy. (29:12–13)

But past happiness only sharpens the tooth of memory; for Job the word "now" conjures a litany of slights and griefs. "But now they mock at me, men younger than I ... now I am their taunting song ... now my soul is poured out because of my plight" (30:1, 9, 18). And, in confirmation, the men who have called themselves his friends and Comforters sit about him in still-hostile accusation.

So to conclude his self-defense and close his case, Job takes an elaborate and solemn oath, calling down more wrath on himself if he has done a fraction of such evil. Chapter 31 amounts to an epic string of "if–then" conditional statements, leading toward a climactic judgment: "*If* I have walked with falsehood... *Then* let me be weighed on honest scales... *If* my heart has been enticed by a woman... *Then* let my wife grind for another... *If* I have raised my hand against the fatherless... *Then* let my arm fall from my shoulder ..." (31:5–6, 9–10, 21–22). If he has despised his servants, left the poor hungry or naked, trusted in gold, worshiped the sun-god, hated his enemy, cursed the foreigner, hidden his own sins, or abused even his own farmland, then – then what? "Then let thistles grow instead of wheat, / And weeds instead of barley" (31:40). That conclusion may seem anti-climactic – mere thistles and weeds as the punishment for such evil? – until the "thorns and thistles" of Genesis 3:18 spring to mind, representing the primal eldest curse on Adam and the earth. In effect, then, Job is calling to be judged as if he had wrought another fall of man.

11.1.5 Act 4: Elihu, Angry Young Man – Job 32–37

This third, and as it turns out, final round of debate among Job, Eliphaz, Bildad, and Zophar presents a hard act to follow. These four men have, it would seem, exhausted every claim and counter-claim, and exhausted their voices in the process. What more can be said that will not be mere repetition? And what argument could possibly reconcile these hardened antagonists to each other, and Job to his God? At this juncture the prose narrator intervenes briefly to introduce not merely a summary of the action, but a new character, and a new turn in the drama:

> So these three men ceased answering Job, because he was righteous in his own eyes. Then the wrath of Elihu, the son of Barachel the Buzite, of the family of Ram, was aroused against Job; his wrath was aroused because he justified himself rather than God. Also against his three friends his wrath was aroused, because they had found no answer, and yet had condemned Job.
>
> Now because they were years older than he, Elihu had waited to speak to Job. When Elihu saw that there was no answer in the mouth of these three men, his wrath was aroused. (32:1–5)

As it turns out, there has been a fourth visitor present at the debate: Elihu, a young man who is respectful enough to defer to his elders, but bold enough to speak up when they have failed. And failed they have, in Elihu's opinion: Job, because he accuses God to justify himself, and the Comforters, because they have condemned Job with baseless charges and found no answers to Job's questions.

Elihu: Redaction, Truth-Teller, or Windbag?

Elihu son of Barachel the Buzite – who can resist such a name? – has drawn a fairly wide range of critical reaction. Many twentieth-century critics, under the influence of Wellhausen's Documentary Hypothesis regarding the Pentateuch, explain Elihu (or explain him away) as a result of imperfect redaction, a later addition to the text who appears rather abruptly and unsuccessfully in an attempt to resolve the impasse between Job and the Comforters. However, more recent discoveries of other intact ancient texts with similar prose frames and interruptions (see this chapter's opening paragraphs) suggest that Elihu may well be integral to the text; and other critics have noted the crucial role that he plays in preparing the way for *Yahweh's* entrance by praising the majesty of God in the whirlwind and storm (36:24–37:24).

But if Elihu is integral to the text, is he right? Many traditional interpreters treat Elihu as a fresh voice of youth and an honest broker, and certainly he does balance his criticisms of both the Comforters and Job, refusing to charge Job with past crimes but blaming him for present arrogance. However, some interpreters have found Elihu arrogant himself, his message of balanced humility spoiled by his apparent youthful self-praise as "one who is perfect in knowledge" (36:4). If thus flawed, Elihu would hardly be the Bible's only instance of a flawed wise man – Solomon being the classic case. Perhaps, then, it is this kind of character complexity that makes this divine Book of Job so profoundly human.

And so Elihu speaks, first to justify his making so bold as a relative youth among elders (32:6–10); second to blame Job's three friends for missing their mark so thoroughly (32:11–22); third, to challenge Job for lapsing from patient, innocent suffering into sinful impiety (33–35); and throughout, to praise the mysterious and impeccable righteousness of the Almighty (36–37). Elihu's discourse is clearly an outburst: "I do not know how to flatter" (32:22) he says, and he certainly doesn't. Fed up and dismayed by the cross-purposes of the Comforters' ill-fitting charges couched in conventional pieties, Elihu admits that "my belly is like wine that has no vent; / It is ready to burst like new wineskins" (32:19). And he talks a bellyful.

Yet Elihu's first approach to Job himself is humble, promising kindness:

> Truly I am as your spokesman before God;
> I also have been formed out of clay.
> Surely no fear of me will terrify you,
> Nor will my hand be heavy on you. (33:6–7)

And Elihu's charge to Job is indeed new. Apparently assuming that Job's past life has been righteous, Elihu blames him for his present rebellion; that is, Job has not necessarily sinned before, but certainly he is sinning now. As Elihu develops his case, Job attempts repeatedly to interrupt but is silenced by the younger man (33:31, 36:2, 37:14), while the other elders sit passively listening. Elihu does bring a fresh perspective, but soon departs from his promised gentleness.

> What man is like Job,
> Who drinks scorn like water,
> Who goes in company with the workers of iniquity,
> And walks with wicked men?
> For he has said, "It profits a man nothing
> That he should delight in God." (34:7–9)

This brief summary of Job's discourse is accurate enough, and Elihu finds him guilty not of specific former crimes warranting severe punishment, but of blasphemously charging God with injustice. As in the psalms of imprecation and complaint, accusing God of wickedness cuts off justice at its source and makes one a brother to the lawless, even if one appears lawful himself.

Elihu increases in bluntness as he elaborates, reminding Job that he is speaking "without knowledge" (34:35), that he is hardly indispensable ("what does [God] receive from your hand?" – 35:7), and that his attitude of ingratitude lumps him with the foolish mass of humanity (35:10–11). Yet as Elihu's critique of Job's self-righteousness mounts, so do his self-congratulatory remarks multiply: "I do not know how to flatter" … "my lips utter pure knowledge" … "I will fetch my knowledge from afar" … "truly my words are not false" … and, climactically, "one who is perfect in knowledge is with you" (32:22; 33:3; 36:3–4). Even allowing for a certain amount of Near Eastern hyperbole and literary doubling, Elihu sounds somewhat like "my lady's eldest son, evermore tattling," and his preening casts a somewhat ironic light back on his exhortations to humility.

And yet, Elihu does in some measure seem, as he claims, to speak for God – or at least to prepare us for God's imminent intervention. As Elihu launches into his peroration about the majesty of divine wisdom and justice, his imagery of God's power turns increasingly to the weather, and to a storm that appears to be brewing on the horizon:

> He draws up drops of water / Which distill as rain… He covers His hands with lightning… His thunder declares it, The cattle also, concerning the rising storm… Hear attentively the thunder of his voice… From the chamber of the south comes the whirlwind, / And cold from the scattering winds of the north. (36:27, 30, 33; 37:2, 9)

As the growing tempest approaches its overwhelming climax, Elihu stresses that his discourse is not merely meteorological, but moral:

> He comes from the north as golden splendor;
> With God is awesome majesty.…
> He does not oppress.
> Therefore men fear him;
> He shows no partiality to any who are wise of heart. (37:22–24)

These are splendid words, and Job, who has been calling out to be visited by the impartial justice of the Almighty, is about to have his answer.

11.1.6   Act 5: The LORD Answers – Job 38–42

Yet *Yahweh's* climactic appearance to Job, while an answer in itself, raises many more questions, and many readers' hackles into the bargain. We may wonder why the LORD answers Job with demands of his own? Why is he so unpleasantly angry? Why does he not tell Job what the reader already knows about his wager with Satan? And what, after all, has become of the Adversary who set Job's trials in motion?

It would be natural to hope that when the LORD finally appears out of the whirlwind, he would speak to Job words of admiration like those in chapters 1 and 2, and words of comfort for what he has suffered since. But the LORD is bracing and stern in his opening challenge:

> Who is this who darkens counsel
> By words without knowledge?…
> Where were you when I laid the foundations of the earth?
> Tell me, if you have understanding. (38:2, 4)

"Gird up now thy loins like a man; for I will demand of thee, and answer thou me" (38:3), reads the old King James Version; like a boxer or a warrior, Job is being told to stand and defend himself; and indeed he is about to be pummeled – not by blows, but by rhetorical questions.

Throughout chapters 38 and 39, *Yahweh* demands that this man who claims to know God's business explain exactly what he knows. By what skill did the Creator measure the earth, found it, shut out the encroaching seas, command the sunrise, snow, and hail, and close the gates of death? Can Job speak thunder, father the rain, bind the Pleiades and loose Orion? Can this man on a dungheap number the clouds, bring life to the dust, slake the thirst of humans, and feed the young lions? Who authored the life and strength of the beasts – mountain goat and newborn fawn, wild ass and ox – and the comic stupidity of the ostrich? Who gave the horse, the hawk, the eagle their special might and beauty? "Shall the one who contends with the Almighty correct him? He who rebukes God, let him answer it" (40:2).

But the humbling answer to every question is either "I don't know" or "You can, I can't." Like a fighter on the ropes, Job is beaten practically speechless:

> Behold, I am vile;
> What shall I answer you?
> I lay my hand over my mouth.
> Once I have spoken, but I will not answer;
> Yes, twice, but I will proceed no further. (40:4–5)

However, the Almighty is neither done, nor satisfied with Job's surrender; he wants another round in the ring with his overmatched opponent to make sure that the lessons sink in. Renewing his challenge to "gird up thy loins," he speaks to Job as if genuinely nettled: "Would you indeed annul my judgment? Would you condemn me that you may be justified?" (40:8). In other words, Job is turning theodicy on its head, justifying his own ways to God by condemning God's ways to man – thus threatening to cut himself off from the only just Judge, and from all justice.

Yet in chapters 40 and 41, the LORD's climactic discourse dwells not on his own ethical perfection in righteousness, but on his surpassing power over creation, as shown in his making and managing two great creatures of land and sea, *Behemoth* and *Leviathan*. Employing another barrage of ironic rhetorical questions, *Yahweh* presses Job to admit the overwhelming might of the One who could call such powerful beings to life. "Look now at the Behemoth" (40:15 – the hippopotamus?), so strong in his loins and belly and feet that even the river's wickedest currents yield to him. Regard Leviathan (the crocodile? the whale?), sinuous and scaly, making the deep boil with his writhing, and invulnerable to puny human weapons. "He is king over all the children of pride" (41:34).

How are we to understand the force of *Yahweh's* argument? Is it that *force majeure* gets the better of reason – in other words, that might makes right? Is Job admitting no more than this in acquiescing to superior power? And what to make of the LORD's seemingly angry, confrontational language to his suffering servant? Clearly, Job's God is not Aristotle's Unmoved Mover, or even James Joyce's artist-God, who "*remains* ...invisible, refined out of existence, indifferent, *paring his fingernails*."[1] As in Genesis, God's creative power is inseparable from his goodness, and therefore highly interactive. So his glorying in the goodness of his own creatures – creatures like the righteous Job in chapter 1 – has its corollary in his anger when that goodness is compromised or mocked, or his own maligned, since his is the foundation of all goodness else. We need not read God's speech to Job as petulant or bullying, nor Job as a browbeaten, broken man who surrenders to a cosmic "Big Brother." On the contrary, Job responds not in terror at divine wrath, but more in wonder and awe at divine mystery:

> You [God] asked, "Who is this who hides counsel without knowledge?"
> Therefore I have uttered what I did not understand,
> Things too wonderful for me, which I did not know...

I have heard of you by the hearing of the ear,
But now my eye sees you.
Therefore I abhor myself,
And repent in dust and ashes. (42:3, 5–6)

The answer that Job needs, as it turns out, is not the answer that he sought; it is not any divine explanation (few are forthcoming) but the divine presence itself – Himself. Better the personal nearness of God, says Job, even an angry God, than any number of words about the just books of a heavenly Accountant, or the refined indifference of a philosopher's or artist's Deity. It's important, then, that when God returns to the story in chapter 38, he returns under the Hebrew covenant name of *YHWH* by which he was called in chapters 1–2, not under the more generic *Elohim* used throughout the dramatic debates of chapters 3–37. The LORD comes to chastise and then restore Job as an adopted son, not to gratify Gentile speculation.

11.1.7 Epilogue: Theodicy vs. Theophany and Satan's Real Absence – Job 42

Yet Gentiles – and not only Gentiles – will speculate nonetheless. Some answers to these speculations are clear enough: first, Job's book seems designed to refute the simplistic *theodicy* of Job's Comforters, their insistence that the Almighty metes out immediate rewards and punishments in this world according to a strict schedule. On the contrary, the world often seems to have been shaved by a drunken barber. Second, the Book of Job seems to celebrate *theophany*, the direct personal manifestation of *Yahweh*, as the deepest answer to the anxiety that attends loss and grief. This lesson seems to be what the LORD has in mind when, having heard Job's humble confession, he turns to rebuke Eliphaz: "My wrath is aroused against you and your two friends, for you have not spoken of me what is right, as my servant Job has" (42:7). (Elihu seems to have taken an early exit.)

What did Eliphaz, Bildad, and Zophar get wrong that Job got right? In retrospect, we realize that throughout their debate with Job *about* God, never once did they speak or call out *to* God – while presuming to speak *for* him. In contrast Job, for all of his emotional gyrations and angry outbursts, was at least complaining in a God-ward direction, demanding that the Almighty appear, as if he actually might. When *Yahweh* does intervene, he sets Job the task of praying for his friends who didn't pray. And a third answer, evident in the LORD's intervening at all, is that he cares for Gentiles like Job – and even the wrong-headed Comforters – as well as Hebrews.

However, there is one answer that Job and his friends do not know, and that the reader does, and this answer raises the book's most persistent final question. That answer? We, the readers, know why the LORD tested Job: in response to a wager from the adversarial spirit Satan. But, we ask, why then doesn't God ever tell Job? Why leave the victim in the dark, and leave Job's family and friends with such a misimpression that "they consoled him and comforted him for all the adversity that the LORD" – not Satan – "had brought upon him" (42:11)? Why does the LORD allow himself to be blamed for, or credited with, all of this calamity?

Yet, on fuller reflection, this may not be a misimpression. Does the reader truly possess even this one answer? We know that the LORD accepted Satan's wager, but do we know why? We do not. Back the inquiry up one step, and it opens out again onto mystery – the Genesis mystery of the evil that God intends for good (Genesis 50:20). To the suffering Job or the restored Job, it seems not really to matter whether *Yahweh* afflicted him directly or by proxy. What wounds – and heals – the patient: the scalpel or the surgeon?

In the end, Satan hardly seems to matter at all, except as a kind of scalpel, an instrument of divine power and purpose. As the book began, Satan claimed superior insight, presuming to correct God himself, but for all of his claims to knowledge, good and holy things remained opaque to him; Satan found Job's genuine generosity, love, and virtue incomprehensible, and dismissed them with a congenitally ignorant leer. In his brief bravura star turn in the LORD's throne room, Satan challenges the notion that humans can love the LORD simply "for himself," rather than for all of his plentiful benefits. Thus, Job's trial reverses the testing of Eden, where a naked lust for "knowledge" led to naked shame. There the first humans, who had everything abundantly but Godhood itself, made a grab for Deity and came to know how exposed, small, and dependent they are. But in the fallen, Gentile land of Uz, nakedness leads to knowledge. A man who has lost everything but God demands that God stand and deliver an answer, and comes to know that God's presence (even in wrath) is enough of an answer – and then receives much more, a double portion of blessing.

So the Satan of Job's book resembles other diminished or vanishing agents of evil: Eden's serpent, slithering off once the curse is proclaimed; Dante's Satan, frozen and gagged in the basement of Hell; Shakespeare's Richard III and Iago, gibbering or stone silent at their last reckonings; Lady Macbeth and Macbeth's witches, suicidally mad or mockingly absent by the play's final act; and Milton's Satan, forced into serpentine, hissing incoherence before vanishing – the eternal loser – from the last two books of *Paradise Lost*. It is this quality of Real Absence, of evil's ultimate Nothingness, that Satan's last vacancy figures forth in the Book of Job.

And what of Job's happy ending? Can we forgive Job his consolation? We may wonder whether God's doubled restoration of Job's fortunes truly compensates for his agonies. When a man has lost seven sons and three daughters, what to him are pieces of silver and rings of gold, or twice as many sheep, camels, oxen, and female donkeys (42:11–12)? Can he be satisfied even if his estranged wife returns to bear him seven more sons, and the three fairest daughters in all the land, and if God grants him twice seventy more years to enjoy these blessings unto the fourth generation (42:13–17)? Won't his memories of disease, disaster, and death sometimes haunt him amidst his joys – like Shakespeare's Prospero returned happily to Milan, where "every third thought shall be my grave" (*The Tempest* 5.1.312)? No doubt, for tragicomedy always involves the bitter-sweetness of enduring loss amidst redemption, of the scars that still ache on their anniversaries. But biblical scars are often certificates of honor, which read us lessons about enduring love. Job's name for endurance has endured through the ages, like so many psalms transforming lament and complaint into hymn.

So perhaps we can forgive Job for being consoled, and reserve judgment about how *Yahweh* afflicts and then consoles him. After all, where were we at the foundation of the earth? Thus, Job's plight implicates and interrogates everyone. Who among us is naked or knowing enough to speak for God? We turn now to that unique and difficult class of men and women who dared.

Questions for Discussion

1   How do the **opening two chapters and the closing chapter** of the **Book of Job** differ from the remainder of the book? How are these opening and closing sections related and linked to the rest of the book? What might these differences and relations mean?

2   What can we infer about the **possible authorship and origins** of the book?

3   What are some **literary and other cultural works** that show the influence of Job's book? Can you think of others? Why, in your opinion, has the book endured in its fame?

4   In what ways does the Book of Job function as a **tragicomedy**? What are its tragic elements? How is it comic?

5   What are **theodicy** and **theophany**, and how do they relate to each other throughout the Book of Job?

6   How does Job's book relate to the tradition of **wisdom literature**? What kind of wisdom does it propose and display? How might it differ from or critique certain wisdom traditions?

7   Why is the Book of Job often spoken of as a work of **drama**? What specifically dramatic or theatrical qualities does the book possess? How does it differ from much of what we might call theater?

8   In particular, how is the book **structured**, and how does this structure relate to its meanings and effects?

9   How would you characterize the dialogues between **the LORD and Satan** at the beginning of the Book of Job? What can we infer about their past histories and relationship? Where do these dialogues take place? How does their debate set the book's main plot in motion?

10   What are we told of **Job's past and present actions**? How do *Yahweh's* and Satan's accounts of Job differ? How does Job respond to the initial waves of calamity that come upon him? What is his condition by the end of chapter 2?

11   Who are **Eliphaz**, **Bildad**, and **Zophar**, and why do they come to Job? How do they treat him at first? How does their actual dialogue with Job begin?

12   How does the dialogue grow into a debate? What is the **essential argument of each "Comforter,"** and how does Job respond to each? How do we see the debate grow in intensity? What are some of its peaks and valleys? What are the effects of both repetitions and interruptions? When and how does the four-way debate end?

13   Who is **Elihu**, and how does his intervention change the terms and the rhythm of the discussion? What are his criticisms of Job's friends? Of Job? What is the essence of his argument? Does it bring anything new to the debate? How does Elihu's discourse prepare us for the LORD's climactic entrance?

14   When *Yahweh* **finally appears**, what are the circumstances? How would you describe his attitude, his tone? In what terms does he address Job? What is his subject matter? What is the gist of his message?

15   How does Job respond to divine **theophany**? How does the LORD respond to Job's response? How does the LORD speak to the Comforters? What becomes of their **theodicy**?

16   What are the **fates of Elihu, and of Satan**? How might these fates contribute to the overall meanings and effects of the book?

17 What is **Job's final status** at the end of the book, after all of his testing? How has he failed? How has he succeeded? What does he know, and what does he not know? What does the reader know that Job doesn't? Why does this matter – or not?

18 What, overall, is the Book of Job's answer to the **problem of evil**?

Note

1 James Joyce, *A Portrait of the Artist as a Young Man* (New York: Huebsch, 1916), p. 252; based on a quotation from Gustave Flaubert's Letter to Mme. Leroyer de Chantepie, 18 March 1857.

12

Prophecy: Who Speaks for God?

"Thus says the LORD." No words capture more clearly the common perception of the biblical prophet: a divine mouthpiece, someone who steps aside and allows God's word to go forth, with little or no personal contribution from the human speaker him- or herself. While this is indeed a common model of biblical prophecy, it is by no means the only one. Prophets throughout the Hebrew Bible are called by God to deliver his message in a remarkable variety of ways: some symbolically brandish bunches of arrows (2 Kings 13:15–19), wear an ox's yoke or cords or sackcloth (Jeremiah 27:2, Ezekiel 4:8, Isaiah 20:2), or go stark naked (Isaiah 20:2–4), while others give bizarre names to their children (Isaiah 8:3–4), weep before an enemy messenger (2 Kings 8:11–12), purchase real estate (Jeremiah 32:8–9), even invite wounds to their own bodies (1 Kings 20:35–38). Balaam is upstaged and rebuked by his own suddenly eloquent donkey (Numbers 22:26–30), while Hosea is told to marry a prostitute in order to model *Yahweh's* steadfast love to adulterous Israel (Hosea 1:2). In the Bible, God not only moves, but also speaks, in mysterious and singular ways.

The diversities of prophecy appear not only in the manner of the message, but in its subject, target, and timing. Some prophets, often called **forthtelling prophets**, speak primarily to the present needs and abuses of the nation, while others, called **foretelling prophets**, mainly predict the future – events near, intermediate, distant, or apocalyptic. So to be "prophetic" in biblical terms can mean a number of things: to cry out against urgent domestic idolatry or injustice, to intervene in great geopolitical affairs, to give comfort to God's afflicted people, or to see far off and into the last things, and declare the end from the beginning. None of these modes excludes any of the others, and most prophets do at least a bit of each; while all communicate in unique and even idiosyncratic ways. Prophets are nobles and laborers, married and monastic, men and women, warriors and conciliators, transcendently eloquent and plain-spoken – and sometimes even silent.

Mothers in Israel: Female Prophets

With surprising frequency, *Yahweh* speaks through feminine voices in the Old Testament. Some women referred to as "prophetesses" either by later rabbis or by the Bible itself include the matriarchs of Genesis and Exodus: Sarah, Rebekah, Rachel, and Miriam; the best of the judges, Deborah (Judges 4–5); the foresighted and poetic mother of the prophet Samuel, Hannah (1 Samuel 1–2); Abigail, the wise, beautiful, and courageous woman who restrained David from murder (1 Samuel 25); Isaiah's wife, called "the prophetess" (Isaiah 8:3); Jeremiah's contemporary, Hulda (2 Kings 22:13–20); and Esther, the lovely, brave, and resourceful Jewish queen of Persia who saved her exiled people from extermination. Significantly, only one woman in the Hebrew Bible, Noadiah, is specifically called a "false prophet" (Nehemiah 6:14) for trying to keep the Jews from restoring Jerusalem. The female prophets, like their male counterparts, speak either to present circumstances (e.g. Miriam, Abigail, and Esther) or to future days (e.g. Rebekah, Deborah, and Hulda), or to both (e.g. Deborah, Hulda).

Literary Study of the Bible: An Introduction, First Edition. Christopher Hodgkins.
© 2020 John Wiley & Sons Ltd. Published 2020 by John Wiley & Sons Ltd.

Yet all claim a common source in the word of a God who is Creator, Redeemer, and Judge.

12.1 *Nevi'im*: Prophets Former and Latter, Major and Minor

This being a chapter on prophecy rather than a commentary on the prophets, it does not pretend to be comprehensive about any or all of these human messengers of the divine. We will begin by overviewing the canonical groupings of these books, then survey major topics and themes common to many, and then attend briefly to individual books and to their distinctives.

In Jewish tradition, the books called *Nevi'im* are differentiated both by antiquity and by length. The **Former Prophets**, Joshua, Judges, Samuel, and Kings (counted as four books in the Hebrew Bible) we have already discussed substantially in the previous chapters on heroic narrative, biblical epic, and national narrative, though there will be more to say below about Elijah and Elisha from the Book of Kings. Besides being traditionally the oldest of the prophetic books, the Former Prophets differ in form from most of their successors by consisting primarily of chronologically linear prose narrative, supplemented by passages of poetry. In contrast, the **Latter Prophets**, Isaiah through Malachi, are traditionally regarded as being composed largely after these oldest four books, and consist substantially or mainly of episodic, often non-chronological poetry, supplemented by some connecting material in prose.

Furthermore, the Latter Prophets are divided by length into **Major Prophets** and **Minor Prophets**. (The designations of "Major" and "Minor" have nothing to do with the comparative importance of each book's message.) In the Hebrew Bible, the Major Prophets Isaiah, Jeremiah, and Ezekiel are three separate books of substantial size (ranging from 66 to 48 chapters per book). The Books of Lamentations and Daniel, included among the Major Prophets in the Christian Old Testament, are found in the *Khetuvim* or Writings of the Hebrew Bible, which treats the dozen Minor Prophets, ranging from one to fourteen chapters in length, as one book called *Trei Asar* ("The Twelve").

Finally, it is worth noting that the individual people called the Former Prophets – Joshua, the Judges, Samuel, and Elijah and Elisha in Kings – are largely forthtelling prophets, speaking deliverance or judgment into the present moment and the very near future, while the Latter Prophets are primarily foretelling prophets – that is, predicting events in the medium or far-off future, or at "the end of the age." Again, these distinctions are not absolute: one finds long-range prediction in Kings (see 1 Kings 13:2 and 2 Kings 23:15), and often what Martin Luther King called "the fierce urgency of Now" shouts from the scrolls of Isaiah, Jeremiah, Ezekiel, Daniel, and the Minor Prophets. Indeed, underlying all biblical prophecy is the notion that while cultures and civilizations may change, rise, and fall, the deep realities of human sin and salvation do not; thus the blessings and broadsides of a Jeremiah or a Jonah to the people of Jerusalem or Babylon or Nineveh are "news that stays news" on the boulevards of Paris, the pavements of London, or the sidewalks of New York.

12.1.1 Forthtelling Prophecy: Elijah, Elisha, and Social Justice

In Chapter 10, we have already discussed at some length the prophetic duel between Elijah and Jezebel's priests of Baal, and the multi-generational judgments brought on Ahab's house by Jezebel's devilishly clever and murderous theft of Naboth's vineyard. What remains to be said in the present context is that, while Elijah and Elisha continue to serve as paradigms of prophetic political and cultural engagement seeking social justice, they nevertheless model the limits of such interventions. For when people speak nowadays of a religious, cultural, or political leader as "prophetic," what this usually means is that he or she voices a sustained, unsparing critique of societal and economic injustice (often called "speaking truth to power") that appeals both to the conscience of the general public, and to the government for redress. But what is to be done when the government – in the persons of the heads of State – are themselves the chief doers of the injustice? And what if the injustice flows directly from a philosophy – like Jezebel's – that government is itself above the law and institutionally accountable to no one, divine or human?

Such are the central problems in the sustained confrontation between Elijah and Elisha, prophets of *Yahweh*, and Ahab and Jezebel, king and queen of Israel. For although these two prophets clearly call for social justice to be done in the sense of ordinary economic and social equity, they do so in the name of an infinite God and a strikingly limited State. Thus, they are not calling for a justice based in the evolutionary materialism of Marxian "class struggle" and enforced by a centralized social bureaucracy. In the Deuteronomist view espoused by the Book of Kings (see the discussions of Deuteronomic thinking in Chapters 7 and 10), Naboth deserves justice not because he belongs to the class of proletarian workers whom history has elected to overthrow their decadent Monarchist oppressors; Naboth deserves justice because he is an Israelite under the protection of Mosaic property Law given by God Almighty, a Law as binding on the government as on all the Israelite people. Further, whether Israelite or not, Naboth is a human bearing the image of God, and God has forbidden any person – man or woman, king or commoner – to violate the divine seal of that image by committing theft and murder, however judicially contrived.

Despite this high Deuteronomic view of human value, one cannot accuse the Book of Kings of being naively optimistic about human nature. The book frankly portrays the resourceful perversion of justice by Jezebel and her willing minions, showing that in the short term even good legal procedure can be exploited by smooth liars and ruthless killers. But because the Book of Kings understands the Law to be written not merely on parchment or clay or stone but in heaven itself, violating the Law of God is ultimately like violating the law of gravity, though with a delay before the inevitable fall. Martin Luther King expressed this view – quoting nineteenth-century New England abolitionist Theodore Parker – when he said that "the arc of the moral universe is long, but it bends toward justice."

But many social justice advocates dissent from this view of divine justice giving law to the world, seeing it as at best a well-meaning human construction and at worst a "false consciousness" enshrining many retrograde evils. Such dissenters insist that if we are to have any justice, we must define and make it ourselves, without reference to imaginary deities and by whatever means necessary. They may admire Elijah's confrontation with Ahab, but could still admire State confiscation of Naboth's vineyards and lands in the name of equality; Marxists may enjoy the spectacle of the working-class prophet condemning a king for killing a worker, but for Marx individual human lives are only as valuable as their economic class, and all individual rights are subordinate to the revolutionary needs of the Collective.

No doubt many historical theocracies and monarchies – and even democratic republics – have invoked God's name to conduct their jihads, crusades, conquests, pogroms, Indian removals and fugitive slave laws, but more recent regimes militantly free of God and king – "atheocracies" and "nonarchies," we might call them – have staged their purges and famines and show trials and cultural revolutions, built their collective farms and gulags, and laid waste their killing fields with at least equal efficiency in the name of the people and workers' justice. Ironically, though humans (whether religious or secular) are the only species capable of recognizing injustice, we also are the only species capable of mass injustice and genocide. It seems that one must be human to commit crimes against humanity, and the biblical prophets "forthtell" that crimes against humanity are first of all sins against God. For these prophets, social justice, to be just at all, must be rooted in divine right – not of kings, or the State, or of any chosen class or caste, but of the Creator.

12.1.2 Foretelling Prophecy: The Scandal of Prediction

If the hallmark of forthtelling prophecy is to speak eternal justice into the present moment, the hallmark of foretelling prophecy is "declaring the end from the beginning" (Isaiah 46:10), predicting the distant – as well as near and intermediate – future. Aside from the many professed miracles of the Old and New Testaments, predictive prophecy is the greatest embarrassment that the Bible offers to the modern, secular mind, a kind of stumbling block or obstacle to serious credibility for biblical teaching, scandalizing reason and relegating these ancient writings for many to the realm of cultural wish-fulfillment or pious fiction. How can ordinary mortals, embedded in everyday material contingency, foresee with any accuracy the rise and fall of distant empires, the dates of exiles and returns and abominations, the names and nativities and deaths of unborn kings – in short, the shape of things to come?

And yet, that last phrase – "the shape of things to come" – suggests just how powerful is the human longing for prediction. It is, for instance, the title first of a 1933 book and then of a 1936 film written by one of the twentieth century's most famed rationalists, H. G. Wells, who despite his anti-religious bent made it his calling to prophesy. Some of his predictions came strikingly true: that a terrible air war would commence in 1940, leaving Britain, Europe, and much of Asia in ruins, and that English nevertheless would become the world's lingua franca. Other predictions fared less well: that this next World War would cause the collapse of all the world's national governments, and that by 1979, a council of Western technocrats would found a new secular World State in the Iraqi city of Basra (the cradle of Sumerian civilization), and engineer the peaceful extinction of Islam – along with Christianity, Buddhism, Judaism, and indeed all the world's religions. Wells' predictions were widely popular through the early 1940s, and after that fell quickly out of fashion as "things to come" came in a rather different shape. This is not to mock H. G. Wells, but simply to note that even secular ages anoint their prophets, yet that the further off the future, the more uncertain the prophecy.

But what if *The Shape of Things to Come* had predicted in 1933 not only the great air war over Britain but also its name, "The Blitz"? What if Wells had foreseen the Nazi-Soviet Non-Aggression Pact of 1939, Hitler's invasion of Russia and the Japanese bombing of Pearl Harbor in 1941, the Allied liberation of Normandy in 1944, and in 1945 the Bulge, Auschwitz, Okinawa, and the atomic blasts that obliterated Hiroshima and Nagasaki? And what if, in 1933, Wells had forecast that a Missouri county "judge" named Harry Truman and a US Army Major named Dwight Eisenhower would by 1946 be the most important men in the world?

This hypothetical case illustrates the actual level of particularity found in biblical prophecies like those of Isaiah, Jeremiah, Ezekiel, and Daniel; for each of them predicts specific event sequences, and sometimes even exact dates and names, not only a decade in advance, but (supposedly) many decades, and even centuries ahead – all to make the point that God rules and false prophets do not:

> Thus says the LORD, your Redeemer,
> And he who formed you from the womb:
> "I am the LORD, who makes all things,
> Who stretches out the heavens all alone,
> Who spreads abroad the earth by myself;
> Who frustrates the signs of the babblers,
> And drives diviners mad;
> Who turns wise men backward,
> And makes their knowledge foolishness;

> Who confirms the word of his servant,
> And performs the counsel of his messengers;
> Who says to Jerusalem, 'You shall be inhabited,'
> To the cities of Judah, 'You shall be built,'
> And I will raise up her waste places;
> Who says to the deep, 'Be dry!
> And I will dry up your rivers';
> Who says of Cyrus, 'He is my shepherd,
> And he shall perform all my pleasure,
> Saying to Jerusalem, "You shall be built,"
> And to the temple, "Your foundation shall be laid."' (Isaiah 44:24–28)

So the LORD – the one who made the heavens and the earth, divided the Red Sea and the Jordan, and decreed the Exile – declares that he will bring the Jews back to Jerusalem to raise up their fallen Temple; and he declares the name of the "shepherd" who will bring it to pass, "Cyrus," the Emperor of Persia, which will overthrow Babylon – two empires not yet born in the days of Isaiah son of Amoz, and a ruler named nearly 200 years before his time.

Similarly, Jeremiah predicts – quite specifically – that the Babylonian Exile will last no less and no more than seventy years (Jeremiah 29:10); Ezekiel's dramatic parables announce the coming destruction of Jerusalem (Ezekiel 4–5); and Daniel describes with remarkable detail and accuracy the rise, fall, and division of the great Eurasian empires for at least four centuries after the Exile (Daniel 2, 10–11). Each of these prophets delineates the shape of things to come with eerie exactness, speaking in the name of the God who can predict all things because, supposedly, he controls them.

Much hangs on that "supposedly." If one supposes an intelligent, almighty, and just Creator like the one introduced in Genesis, it is not difficult to suppose that such a Being can communicate futurity through chosen messengers – and though any particular self-proclaimed prophet might be lying, such predictions so spectacularly fulfilled would seem powerful confirmations of truth. But if one supposes instead a closed, random, material cosmos with no intelligence higher than human reason (or if at least one doubts whether a Supreme Intelligence might exist), then such sensational prophecies must be explained in other ways; that is, as texts actually composed after the fact and presented either as devout myth, noble lie, or lie outright. Thus, many Bible critics have for more than a century posited dates of actual composition much later than the traditional dates: pseudo-Isaiahs of the later sixth century BCE, in the time of Cyrus and the exiles' return (see box "Three Isaiahs?"); multiple "Jeremiahs" with at least one writing after that same "fulfillment"; and a pseudo-Daniel working at about 165 BCE, after the centuries of events "predicted" in the book.

However, the theory of these books as devout poetic myth does not withstand much close scrutiny. Poetic they often are – in Isaiah's case some of the finest poetry in any language – but if by myth we mean legend, folktale, or fable unconcerned with historic truth, then why do these fabulists insist on their own literal prophetic accuracy, as in Isaiah 44:24–28 (quoted above), and embed their predictions in densely referenced historical circumstance, as in the opening chapters of each prophetic book? One does not expect timetables in *Grimms' Fairy Tales*, or precise road maps of the Grail Quest. Surely these books claim accuracy because they are addressed to people – ancient people – for whom historical specifics and fulfillments matter, however much they may be deceived.

More plausible than the mythic hypothesis is that of the "noble lie" – the knowing deception that mimics historical accuracy to exploit religious hope for a benevolent purpose. As Plato's Socrates famously proposes in *The Republic* (3.414e–15c), a *gennaion pseudos* ("virtuous falsehood") will "persuade, in the best case, even the rulers, but if not them, the rest of the city" that the necessary political hierarchy is actually the blessed natural order, sanctioned by the gods. Ideally, says Socrates, the elite guardians of the order will eventually come to believe this lie themselves, but even if they cannot, it is good that inferior, weaker minds and the lower orders should believe the lie, or the social order will collapse.

Yet surely the Hebrew prophets are strange candidates for purveyors of noble lies, since they insist so vigorously that no lie can be noble? Indeed from Isaiah through Malachi, to "prophesy lies" – especially comforting lies that support doomed regimes – is the worst kind of blasphemy, a bearing of false witness against one's neighbor and one's God. (See, for instance, Isaiah 9:15, Jeremiah 14:14, Ezekiel 13:9, Daniel 11:27 – and *ad infinitum*.) Is the light in the prophets such deliberate darkness? Is the whole ideal of divinely sanctioned honesty itself a lie? Yet can rational, modern people consider the possibility that the closed system of material causation can be torn open by "magical thinking" about "imaginary friends"?

Resolving such an impasse is beyond the scope of this literary study. As to hard evidence, skeptics will point out that there are no known Old Testament manuscripts surviving from before the earliest Dead Sea Scrolls (about 150 BCE), making it impossible to demonstrate textually the actual "pre-dated" predictions like Isaiah's of Cyrus, Jeremiah's of the seventy-year Exile, or Daniel's of the imperial wars. Believers will reply that there is no documentary evidence for anything *but* the current forms of the Major and Minor Prophets as whole books, making it impossible to prove textually that their claims of foreknowledge are post-dated fictions or lies – noble or otherwise. Certainly, terms like "skeptic" and "believer" can be misleading, since all parties to this debate both doubt and trust something, whether the mysterious word of an invisible God or the undocumented speculations of human scholars. Perhaps, then, the crucial question is what we desire to believe – or doubt – and why?

12.1.2.1 Messianic Prophecy: The Anointed One

The subspecies of foretelling prophecy that speaks to perhaps the deepest human longing for justice and deliverance predicts a coming Judge or Deliverer. The Hebrew Bible calls him by many names: *Ha Mashiach* ("Messiah"/Anointed One); Wonderful Counselor; Prince of Peace; Root of Jesse; Son of David; Righteous Branch; Suffering Servant; Good Shepherd; Mighty God. The Messiah is the central figure in the unfolding Hebrew prophetic imagination from Moses through Malachi; indeed the Messiah is probably history's greatest instance of a personally focused communal hope, faith, and longing. Other groups and movements have hoped in the restoration of a once-and-future dynasty or doctrine – Caesar/Kaiser/Czarists, Arthurians, Jacobites, Bourbonists, Bonapartists, Mahdists, Peronists, Sandinistas, Kennedys, Bushes, Clintons, Obamas – but judging by the fact that we still refer to such hopes as "messianic," it is the "Son of David" who best qualifies as the archetypal "Desire of all Nations" (Haggai 2:11).

Yet obviously, ironies, schisms, and abysms of disagreement abound regarding this desire. Among the Jews of late antiquity, a debate arose over where Messiah would originate: Bethlehem (as in Micah 5:2) or Galilee (Isaiah 9:1–2)? Would he rule the nations with a rod of iron (Psalm 2:9), or would he be despised and rejected (Isaiah 53:3)? Would he ride to victory (Zechariah 9:9), or die in humiliation (Psalm 22:12–15; Isaiah 53:10)? Would he put the Gentiles under his feet (Psalm 110:1), or bring them as brothers into the house of the LORD (Isaiah 56:6–7)? How could Messiah be the "Son of David" (2 Samuel 7:12–15) and yet greater than David? How can he be "the Mighty God" (Isaiah 9:6)? The life of Jesus of Nazareth as narrated in the New Testament gospels both answered and exacerbated these questions and divisions. For Christians, Jesus is the "Christ" or Messiah, God come in the flesh – and the "either/or" questions above are answered as "both/and," many of the apparent contradictions resolved by the doctrines of his First Coming (in humility) and his Second Coming (in glory). But a majority of Jews would not embrace a crucified carpenter as their Messiah, and over the centuries, as the carpenter's worshipers multiplied beyond all number, many tragically made the Jews suffer for that rejection, even as the gospel of the Suffering Servant spread throughout the earth.

In modern times, even as secular skepticism about any realities beyond the physical has permeated elite and popular culture, the "Desire of Nations" for a Deliverer has not abated, but instead has attached itself religiously to hundreds if not thousands of non-religious objects: scientific theories and technological discoveries, psychoanalytic methods, pharmaceuticals, dietary reforms, political parties and candidates, economic schools, ethnic and gender identity movements, and violent secular religions like Fascism, Marxism, and their variants. We have learned to our great cost that the Mussolinis, the Hitlers, the Lenins, and the Stalins were anti-Christs, false Messiahs, but currently there seems to be less agreement than ever on whether the solution is to embrace Jesus as the true Messiah (he remains adored and admired by billions), seek another Messiah to come (sacred or secular), or despair of anointed Deliverers altogether. But who will cure this "Desire of Nations"? Who shall deliver us from our enduring, dangerous hopes?

12.1.2.2 Apocalyptic Prophecy: Visions of the End, and the Beginning

Perhaps the most dangerous hopes expressed by the foretelling prophets are their revelations of the End Times, the Day of Judgment, the Apocalypse. Though the Greek *apokalypsis* ("revelation") is a neutral term that denotes an unveiling and a bringing to light, whether of good or of evil, nowadays the popular connotations of "apocalypse" are strikingly negative and dystopian. Think of contemporary "apocalyptic" fiction, like Martin Amis's *London Fields*, Cormac McCarthy's *The Road*, and P. D. James' *The Children of Men*, or apocalyptic films such as *2012*, *The Day After Tomorrow*, *I Am Legend*, and *Mad Max*, or apocalyptic television series like *The Walking Dead* and *Falling Skies*. Unlike Tim LaHaye's bestselling *Left Behind* series, none of these books and movies has an explicit religious or biblical focus, but all of them (and many, many more) take off from some cataclysmic, global disaster – an impending nuclear war in the Middle East, the mass infertility of all earth's women, a terrible viral outbreak, or a planetary ecological catastrophe (not to mention space aliens and zombies). In other words, though these entertainments sometimes present moments of beauty and compassion in their dystopian settings, they share in common a profound sense of doom, discovering not a peaceable kingdom but hell on earth, usually without hope of a God in heaven.

So as we speak of "apocalyptic" prophecy in the Old Testament (or the New), we must hear every potential sense of that word: doom and judgment, yes, but also, and finally, repentance, restoration, redemption, and reconciliation. Though there is God's plenty of wrack and wrath in books like Isaiah, Ezekiel, Daniel, Joel, and Zechariah, their ultimate picture of earth's fate features not plagues and smoking ruins, but a renewed, radiant, and blooming land and a new City where righteousness dwells – indeed, where God dwells among his people.

But if biblical apocalyptic is, in the end, surprisingly upbeat, it is also famously offbeat – indeed often phantasmagoric – in picturing Kingdom Come. "Apocalyptic" is not only a subject matter and outlook, but also an unmistakable style:

> In the year that King Uzziah died, I saw the Lord sitting on a throne, high and lifted up, and the train of His robe filled the temple. Above it stood seraphim; each one had six wings: with two he covered his face, with two he covered his feet, and with two he flew. (Isaiah 6:1–2)

> And it will come to pass at the same time, when Gog comes against the land of Israel … that My fury will show in My face… Surely in that day there shall be a great earthquake

in the land of Israel, so that the fish of the sea, the birds of the heavens, the beasts of the field, all creeping things that creep on the earth, and all men who are on the face of the earth shall shake at My presence. (Ezekiel 38:18–20)

After this I saw in the night visions… I watched then because of the sound of the pompous words which the horn was speaking; I watched till the beast was slain, and its body destroyed and given to the burning flame. As for the rest of the beasts, they had their dominion taken away, yet their lives were prolonged for a season and a time. (Daniel 7:7, 11–12)

Six-winged beasts, cosmic earthquakes, talking horns, darkness at noon – these seers look into realms that outstrip language, and their visions share a weird, wondrous imagistic overload, a terrible urgency, breathless awe, symbolic riddling, and, especially, a surreal sense of time and all creation as potter's clay in the hands of the Almighty. The Prophet Moses wrote that God had made the world with a word, and the Latter Prophets predict that God will unmake – and remake – the world with a word, as well.

12.2   The Major Prophets: Isaiah Through Daniel

12.2.1   Isaiah: The Art of Prophesying

The Book of Isaiah is the first and longest of the Latter Prophets, and of the Major Prophets, embracing not only events from the lifetime of Isaiah the son of Amoz (approximately 770–690 BCE), but also later events surrounding Judah's coming destruction, exile, and return (605–500 BCE) – along with visions of the end of the age, and of a new world beyond.

Three Isaiahs?

A corollary of the "Documentary Hypothesis" has been the re-reading of the Prophets as preceding the Law, a view in which varied prophetic figures are imagined devising a Mosaic and kingly past to justify present reform. Related to this "reverse" theory of composition is the idea of post-dated prediction and the dividing of prophetic books according to supposed periods of composition. The most-noted application of this post-dating theory has been to the Book of Isaiah, which, it is proposed, was composed by at least three writers: Isaiah the son of Amoz (also called "Proto-Isaiah"), a member of the Davidic royal family who composed chapters 1–39 from the end of Uzziah's reign through the time of the Assyrian invasions (740–700 BCE); "Second Isaiah" (also called "Deutero-Isaiah"), who composed chapters 40–55 to encourage Jewish exiles in the successive Babylonian and Medo-Persian Empires (600–539 BCE); and "Third Isaiah" (also called "Trito-Isaiah"), who wrote chapters 56–65 to exhort the exiles when they had returned to Judah (539–500 BCE).

Though advocates of this intermittent composition theory refer to the commonness of ancient pseudepigraphical writing and to certain differences in vocabulary, theme, and style among the three putative authors, their main concern is to explain the book's remarkably accurate predictions – Jerusalem's conquest and destruction by Babylon in 605–587, Babylon's eventual overthrow in 539 by Persia, the Persian decree allowing Jewish return to Judah in 538, the exact name of the Persian Emperor Cyrus (Isaiah 44:28) – as predictions "after the fact."

(Another theory of non-holistic composition sees the book as falling into two parts: chapters 1–33, supposedly predicting judgment to come, and 34–66, reflecting on judgment already accomplished.)

Advocates of traditional holistic composition by Isaiah son of Amoz argue, first of all, that the forty years of his ministry allow sufficient time for transformations in the author's vocabulary and style; second, that the book's main themes (the universal holiness of *Yahweh*, the coming destruction and Exile of Judah, the overthrow of Babylon and Jewish return) are repeated in cycles throughout the book; and that, as with the Pentateuchal Documentary Hypothesis, these speculative divisions are so far unsupported by any actual separate documents. (The Isaiah Scroll found among the Dead Sea Scrolls at Qumran in 1947 dates to about 125 BCE and is essentially identical to the Masoretic text of Isaiah from 1000 years later – and both present the complete text in a unitary book.) Given that the book's naming of Cyrus comes in the context denouncing the pagan gods' false predictions (Isaiah 44:24–28), these advocates of "holistic composition" find it strange that Isaiah's book, with such lofty ethical content, would rely so emphatically on deceiving the reader with fabricated, post-dated predictions of its own.

Structurally, Isaiah is episodic and cyclical, displaying a remarkable juxtaposition of varied times and eras, often out of chronological order – sweeping forward, circling back, and repeating. For instance, in the course of the first fourteen of the book's sixty-six chapters, the prophet holds forth against the sins of Judah and Israel in the later eighth century BCE (Isaiah 1; 2:4–4:1); jumps far ahead to a vision of a future age when "all the nations" will stream into Zion to worship *Yahweh* under the leadership of the messianic "Branch of the LORD" (2:1–4; 4:2-6); returns to the eighth-century present as Isaiah is called and sent with a message to the current King Ahaz (6–7); predicts the imminent overthrow of Israel by Assyria (8:1–21; 9:8–10:4); celebrates the distant future birth and reign of the messianic "Prince of Peace" and "Root of Jesse" (9:1–7; 11:1–10); foretells the LORD's wrath to come on his wrathful instruments Assyria and Babylon, as well as on Philistia (10:3–19; 13:1–22; 14:3–32); and foresees the return of God's people to their homeland from two future exiles (10:20–27; 11:11–16; 14:1–2). Time is telescoped, flashbacks and flash-forwards abound, two verses can juxtapose two separate millennia, and the Almighty often speaks in an eternal present tense.

Yet for all of its kaleidoscopic variation in time and theme, there is art in Isaiah's seemingly mad visionary fluidity. If the book is cyclical, like Ecclesiastes and Job (see discussions in Chapters 4 and 11), its cycles are not merely going around in circles, but spiraling upwards through recurring glimpses of the catastrophic and the sublime, rising toward a heavenly climax. Reiterations disclose patterns, as further judgments on Israel's pagan neighbors and coming conquerors in Isaiah 14–23 yield to an oracle of the last days in 24–27 and a vision of final judgment and salvation in 28–35. A brief narrative interlude (Isaiah 36–39, repeating the events of 2 Kings 18–20 and 2 Chronicles 32) brings this cosmic conflict down to the local level, recounting Assyria's siege of Jerusalem, the arrogant rantings of Sennacherib's general the Rabshakeh, and the LORD's sudden obliteration of the enemy and his deliverance of faithful King Hezekiah and his people – and an anti-climactic reminder of Hezekiah's late folly. This particular story told, there begins the volume of the "comfort of Israel" (40–48) promising a return from the threatened exile, the redemption of Israel, the benevolence of Persian King Cyrus, and the judgment of wicked Babylon; followed by the renewal of the covenant under a divinely empowered messianic Servant-King (49–55) who will suffer on behalf of Israel and the nations in order to gather all peoples to himself; and the final call (56–66) for Israel to act in their present earthly circumstances in the light of this predicted heavenly destiny – with a coda reminding them of eternal punishment for unrepentant transgressors.

Questions of prediction and structure aside, Isaiah is famed for an astonishing verbal style, rich in juxtaposition and paradox, that places it in the first rank of the world's greatest poetry. Isaiah is among the most-quoted books in the Hebrew Bible – the New Testament's Pauline epistles alone quote Isaiah twenty-seven times – and its words have been invoked with special frequency in the context of war and the hope for lasting peace:

> They shall beat their swords into plowshares,
> And their spears into pruning hooks;
> Nation shall not lift up sword against nation,
> Neither shall they learn war anymore. (2:4)

Isaiah's renowned vision of "the Peaceable Kingdom" also inspires many with his paradoxical picture of natural enemies reconciled in a new age of childlike innocence and restored Edenic harmony:

> The wolf also shall dwell with the lamb,
> The leopard shall lie down with the young goat,
> The calf and the young lion and the fatling together;
> And a little child shall lead them....They shall not hurt nor destroy in
> all My holy mountain,
> For the earth shall be full of the knowledge of the LORD
> As the waters cover the sea. (11:6, 9)

Isaiah speaks of Jewish return from Babylonian Exile in words that have stirred hope among all the world's outcasts, encouraging them to see the hand of God in their suffering:

> "Comfort, yes, comfort My people!"
> Says your God.
> "Speak comfort to Jerusalem, and cry out to her,
> That her warfare is ended,
> That her iniquity is pardoned;
> For she has received from the LORD's hand
> Double for all her sins." (40:1–2)

At the heart of Isaiah's hope for a bright future is the prediction – repeated in many ways and forms – of a coming Messiah who will combine the powers of the mightiest king, the compassion of a humble shepherd, and the sacrificial courage of the kindest lover with the eternal reign of the Deity himself:

> For unto us a Child is born,
> Unto us a Son is given;
> And the government will be upon his shoulder.
> And his name will be called
> Wonderful, Counselor, Mighty God,
> Everlasting Father, Prince of Peace. (9:6)

Here Isaiah gives names usually reserved only for the Deity (*Peleh, Yoetz, El Gibbor, Avi Ad, Sar Shalom*) to this coming king "upon the throne of David" (9:7); this "Prince of Peace" is wise and tender, yet fearsome in his protection of the weak:

> His delight is in the fear of the LORD,
> And he shall not judge by the sight of his eyes,
> Nor decide by the hearing of his ears;
> But with righteousness he shall judge the poor …And with the breath
> of his lips he shall slay the wicked. (11:3–4)

Called to bring the house of Jacob back to God, this Servant is nevertheless sent to the Gentiles as well: "And now the LORD says, … I will also give you as a light to the Gentiles, That you should be my salvation to the ends of the earth" (49:6). Called from among his people to rescue them, they will nevertheless cast him out, a Servant who somehow saves by his suffering, the Shepherd slaughtered like an atoning lamb:

> [H]e was wounded for our transgressions,
> He was bruised for our iniquities;
> The chastisement for our peace was upon him,
> And by his stripes we are healed.
> All we like sheep have gone astray;
> We have turned, every one, to his own way;
> And the LORD has laid on him the iniquity of us all. (53:5–6)

Yet brought to the lowest, crushed with the worst, he will rise above the best, dispensing salvation like conquerors' booty:

> He shall see the labor of his soul, and be satisfied.
> By his knowledge my righteous Servant shall justify many,
> For he shall bear their iniquities.
> Therefore I will divide him a portion with the great,
> And he shall divide the spoil with the strong … (53:11–12)

Death is new life; defeat is victory; weakness is strength; and down is up. These most violent paradoxes lie at the heart of Isaiah's assault on violence; here is the soul of non-violence, quietly assured of triumph because a Power above all human powers will see it done, the Power that calmly spoke the world into being. It is the cosmic *eucatastrophe*.

Isaiah, with his eagle eye, sees farther and in more directions (both chronologically and spatially) than perhaps any prophet until John the Divine. According to Jewish tradition, Isaiah paid a terrible price for his visions: as an old man sawn in two by command of the wicked King Manasseh. But his words live and thrive, beloved of Jews and Christians (who call him the "evangelical prophet"), and inspiring the world's hopes for beating swords to plowshares.

12.2.2 Jeremiah and Lamentations: The Weeping Prophet of Hope

The Book of Jeremiah, the second of the Major Prophets, strikes a more even balance than Isaiah between forthtelling and foretelling, and its many excursions into the messianic and apocalyptic future are nevertheless embedded in a roughly chronological narrative of the prophet's ministry in the last decades before and the first years after Jerusalem's fall. Jeremiah is called from the womb to be a particularly contrarian prophet, and his name has given us a word – "jeremiad" – for a sermon or tract predicting societal doom.

Jeremiads

"Woe Unto Ye!" "The End Is Near!" "Prepare to Meet Thy God!" These and similar statements, now the stock-in-trade of cartoonists portraying doomsayers wearing sandwich boards, are at the heart of an ancient prophetic tradition that has come to bear the name of the "weeping prophet" of Judah, Jeremiah the son of Hilkiah. Although in popular usage a "jeremiad" often refers to an excessively or even insanely pessimistic message, the Book of Jeremiah portrays a prophet whose message is all too true. As a voice of doom doomed to be ignored, Jeremiah resembles the prophetess Cassandra of classical epic and tragedy, the daughter of Troy's King Priam cursed by Apollo to predict truly but never to be believed. Like Jeremiah, Cassandra predicts the overthrow of her city, is thought to be insane and a traitor, and is imprisoned to prevent her message spreading. But Jeremiah, unlike Cassandra, not only survives the foretold disaster but also lives to restore "a future and a hope."

Practitioners of the jeremiad have been many, from the other Hebrew prophets, and from John the Baptist and Jesus, to Augustine in his *City of God*, Savonarola's reformist sermons in Florence, John Donne's *Lamentations of Jeremy*, George Herbert's *Church Militant*, and Michael Wigglesworth's *Day of Doom* in colonial New England. More recently, environmentalists and more secular voices have taken up the jeremiad, predicting disastrous climate change, and calling for far-reaching racial and gender revolution, and an end to unjust economic systems – though unlike Jeremiah in his day, many of these more modern prophets have been embraced and institutionalized by their governments and by wealthy and powerful leaders. Resembling the apocalyptic (see Section 12.1.2.2), the jeremiad is nevertheless most urgently concerned with present ills and wrongs, rather than foretelling far-off events.

But it is Jeremiah's tragedy, and his great gift, to have within his uncompromising "pillar of iron" a "heart of flesh," which has earned him the tenderer sobriquet of "the weeping prophet" – as shown in his profoundly elegiac Book of Lamentations, mourning Jerusalem's destruction. A patriot sent to order his nation's surrender, he must witness the last heedless years of Jerusalem's prosperity and the crushing humiliations of her defeat, bearing the violent scorn of her rulers and then pitying their overthrow. And yet, ever against the grain, the pessimist Jeremiah predicts return and restoration in the face of despair, and reaffirms his lasting portion in the land of his fathers. That his darkest predictions are portrayed as having come true provides, paradoxically, the assurance that his prophecies of restoration and happier days will come to pass as well.

The book's opening verses ascribe its prophetic words to Jeremiah, a priest from Anathoth who ministered during the years of Judah's last kings (640–586 BCE), though they also state that his assistant Baruch often served as an amanuensis (Jeremiah 36:4–6), and it seems likely that Baruch composed the third person account (37–45) of the prophet's persecution and imprisonment during the last days of Jerusalem – and perhaps the final appendix (Isaiah 52) detailing the Babylonian destruction of the city. Completed after the Exile had begun, Jeremiah's book reminds the exiles of the reasons for God's wrath against his chosen people, and also promises that the Exile will end in seventy years (25:11–12, 29:10).

After describing his call in Jeremiah 1, the prophet moves directly into an extensive set of conditional oracles (2–18) against still-prosperous Judah; conditional because they exhort the people and their rulers to repent and avert God's judgment. After Judah's continuing rejection of Jeremiah and his warnings, chapter 19 announces that the time for mercy has passed, and inaugurates a series of increasingly dire predictions (19–24) that David's dynasty will fall, Solomon's Temple will be destroyed, and the Jews carried away to captivity in Babylon – indeed that only those who surrender and submit to exile will be saved from the burning. Jeremiah 25–29 announce that two generations of exile lie ahead: seventy years of submission to the LORD's Babylonian scourge, who then will feel God's scourge themselves as the Almighty "will repay them according to their deeds" (25:14) and tear their empire from their hands.

Chapters 30–33 reverse the book's emotional polarity by picturing the coming years of joyous return and revival, then by portraying a messianic age under a New Covenant that will replace the broken Mosaic Covenant, and finally by culminating in Jeremiah's hopeful, seemingly foolish act of buying at full price a piece of family land now worthless in the wake of Jerusalem's fall. Chapters 34–39 backtrack to the last days before Judah's overthrow, as the wicked kings Jehoiakim and then Zedekiah suppress Jeremiah's message of downfall and lock the prophet away in a dungeon – where soon Zedekiah comes to beg his advice and prayers as Babylon besieges the holy city. Refusing this advice ("Surrender!") Zedekiah is captured, and sees his sons killed before being blinded; while Jeremiah is freed on the orders of Nebuchadnezzar himself. Chapters 40–45 conclude this destruction narrative, describing the machinations that lead to the assassination of Governor Gedaliah and Jeremiah's journey to Egypt, where he prophecies to Jews who have fled there, and to the exiles taken to Babylon. Chapters 46–51 look forward to God's successive judgments on Israel's historic enemies (Egypt, Philistia, Moab, Ammon, Edom, Syria, the Arabs, Elam, and Babylon), but the book ends with chapter 52's harrowing account of God's wrath against Jerusalem.

Thus, Jeremiah is both tragic and tragicomic: it begins with increasingly certain predictions of doom, and ends with destruction fulfilled; yet folded into this envelope of disaster is a letter of hope and even more certain joy. Its five main themes are grim and great. First, no biblical book has a sterner sense of the individual's call to face down collective evil; that, as Frederick Douglass said, "One and God make a majority":

> "[B]ehold, I have made you this day
> A fortified city and an iron pillar,
> And bronze walls against the whole land –
> Against the kings of Judah,
> Against its princes,
> Against its priests,
> And against the people of the land.
> They will fight against you,
> But they shall not prevail against you.
> For I am with you," says the LORD, "to deliver you." (1:18–19)

Second, as these words suggest, Jeremiah combines concern for the oppressed, "the stranger, the fatherless, and the widow" (7:6), with equal judgment on the entire nation. God commands the prophet:

> Therefore do not pray for this people, nor lift up a cry or prayer for them, nor make intercession to Me; for I will not hear you… The children gather wood, the fathers kindle the fire, and the women knead dough, to make cakes for the queen of heaven; and they pour out drink offerings to other gods, that they may provoke Me to anger. (7:16, 18)

"Do not pray for this people": a fearsome command from the merciful God whose mercy is nearly exhausted, the God who has saved and re-saved the people but, having been cast off by them, is threatening to cast them off.

In addition to these themes of the lone prophet's authority and the egalitarian judgment of *Yahweh*, a third great theme is God's sovereignty over all the nations, and their answering responsibility for their deeds. Though Babylon has been a sword of judgment in the LORD's hand, yet

> it will come to pass, when seventy years are completed, that I will punish the king of Babylon and that nation, the land of the Chaldeans, for their iniquity, ... and I will make it a perpetual desolation. (25:12)

Though other nations and empires will rise in Babylon's place, all eventually will reel like drunken men under the anger of God:

> Take this wine cup of fury from my hand, and cause all the nations, to whom I send you, to drink it. And they will drink and stagger and go mad because of the sword that I will send among them. (25:15–16)

Fourth, Jeremiah voices a special doom for the false prophets, who claim a word from God but have none, and who preach a false security that misleads the people to their destruction:

> And from the prophet even to the priest,
> Everyone deals falsely.
> They have also healed the hurt of my people slightly,
> Saying, "Peace, peace!"
> When there is no peace. (6:13–14)

> Do not listen to the words of the prophets who prophesy to you.
> They make you worthless;
> They speak a vision of their own heart,
> Not from the mouth of the LORD. (23:16)

Like Isaiah, Jeremiah distinguishes between a true divine revelation and the dream of one's own evil heart, with the spiritually blind leading the blind.

Yet, while Jeremiah is second to none in dreadful oracles, his fifth great theme, also like Isaiah, is the hopeful promise of return from exile, and of a New Covenant under the Son of David:

> Behold, the days are coming,...
> That I will raise to David a Branch of righteousness;
> A King shall reign and prosper,
> And execute judgment and righteousness in the earth.
> In his days Judah will be saved,
> And Israel will dwell safely ... they shall no longer say, "As the LORD lives who brought up the children of Israel from the land of Egypt," but, "As the LORD lives who brought up and led the descendants of the house of Israel from the north country and from all the countries where I had driven them." And they shall dwell in their own land. (23:5–8)

Envisioning a second Exodus greater than the deliverance under Moses, Jeremiah also foresees a New Covenant greater than the Old Covenant given at Sinai:

> Behold, the days are coming, says the LORD, when I will make a new covenant with the house of Israel and with the house of Judah... I will put my law in their minds, and write

it on their hearts; and I will be their God, and they shall be my people. No more shall every man teach his neighbor, and every man his brother, saying, "Know the LORD," for they all shall know me, from the least of them to the greatest of them, says the LORD. (31:31, 33–34)

The written Law, now broken by Israel, will be replaced with an inner scripture, a direct knowledge of God's mind, written on the willing heart. This returned, regenerated nation will fulfill the Abrahamic and Mosaic destiny of the Jews by acting as a blessing to all the earth, and as a kingdom of priests, and, in the meantime, Jeremiah writes to the exiles in Babylon telling them that their calling is to pursue not only their own welfare, but also the welfare of the Gentiles:

> Build houses and dwell in them; plant gardens and eat their fruit. Take wives and beget sons and daughters; and take wives for your sons and give your daughters to husbands, so that they may bear sons and daughters – that you may be increased there, and not diminished. And seek the peace of the city where I have caused you to be carried away captive, and pray to the LORD for it; for in its peace you will have peace. (29:5–7)

Jeremiah's letter to the exiles is extraordinarily important in a Jewish history made up of far more wandering and exile than peaceful settlement in the homeland. Taking care of one's own and then of one's neighbor becomes the guiding social ideal governing Jewish relations with the surrounding world.

Perhaps the most vividly tragicomic moment in Jeremiah comes in chapter 32. It is 586 BCE, the tenth year of King Zedekiah's ten-year reign; Nebuchadnezzar is besieging Jerusalem; and Judah's last king has imprisoned the prophet – for predicting that he will be the last king of Judah. With siege works gaining on the city's walls each day, Jeremiah's cousin Hanamel from their village of Anathoth manages to visit the prison, and proposes the strangest of real estate transactions: will the prisoner, in a besieged city in a conquered country, claim his right of redemption and purchase Hanamel's ancestral field back home? He proposes the full price of seventeen silver shekels – approximately seventeen shekels greater than its current market value. In the prison courtyard, with the sound of battering rams in the background, Jeremiah signs and seals the contract:

> Then I knew that this was the word of the LORD. So I bought the field from Hanamel, the son of my uncle who was in Anathoth, and weighed out to him the money – seventeen shekels of silver. And I signed the deed and sealed it, took witnesses, and weighed the money on the scales ... before all the Jews who sat in the court of the prison. (32:8–10, 12)

But, being Jeremiah, he points out the obvious ironies to the Almighty:

> Look, the siege mounds!... And you have said to me, O Lord GOD, "Buy the field for money, and take witnesses"! – yet the city has been given into the hand of the Chaldeans. (32:24–25)

Answering a query with a question, the LORD replies,

> Behold, I am the LORD, the God of all flesh. Is there anything too hard for me?... Just as I have brought all this great calamity on this people, so I will bring on them all the good that I have promised them. And fields will be bought in this land of which you say, "It is desolate, without man or beast; it has been given into the hand of the Chaldeans" ... for I will cause their captives to return. (32:17, 42–44)

It is the principle of the literary "foil" that brilliant things show brightest against the darkest backgrounds. The weeping prophet's hopeful deed at his nation's midnight glitters across the millennia. Thus Jeremiah 31–32, which prophesy the New Covenant of the heart and put the prophet's money on his predictions, form the confident heart of this often heart-breaking book.

The Book of Lamentations does not name its author, though traditionally it is attributed to Jeremiah, and like the Book of Jeremiah dates to a time between the fall of Jerusalem in 586 BCE and the return of the first exiles in 538. Also like the Jeremiah's book, the structure of Lamentations folds a message of hope into a larger envelope of loss and grief. In addition, Lamentations has much in common with the Psalms: it is Hebrew poetry of a high order; it is composed in an intricate acrostic form, like Psalm 119; and it mourns the fall of Jerusalem, like Psalms 88 and 89, and the Exile, like Psalm 137. Finally, Lamentations resembles David's great funeral elegy for Saul and Jonathan, "The Song of the Bow" (2 Samuel 1:17–27) by meditating on greatness overthrown, and the Book of Job, dumbfounded at devastation wrought by the hand of a good God.

"How lonely sits the city / That was full of people!" the book famously begins. "How like a widow is she, / Who was great among the nations! / The princess among the provinces / Has become a slave!" (Lamentations 1:1). Punning seriously on the name of Father Abraham's wife – the Hebrew for "princess" is *sarai*, the original name of Sarah – the poet then imagines the great lady's grief, and proceeds through each of the book's five chapters to elaborate on related themes of devastation, divine wrath, popular mourning, national humiliation, and, in the end, a plea for mercy. The poetry has not only its acrostic pattern (each stanza in each chapter beginning in sequence with one of the twenty-two letters of the Hebrew alphabet) but also a unique meter, called *qinah*, with five beats per line in the original language. Thus, this outpouring of anguish and horror is expressed in a highly structured form, paradoxically suggesting that the apparent chaos of national collapse is somehow following a predetermined divine pattern.

> And at the heart of this lament we find expectation springing like a desert oasis.

> Through the LORD's mercies we are not consumed,
> Because His compassions fail not.
> They are new every morning;
> Great is Your faithfulness.
> "The LORD is my portion," says my soul,
> "Therefore I hope in Him!" (3:22–24)

This sudden burst of trust and faith counsels that "The LORD is good to those who wait for him" and that "It is good for a man to bear / The yoke in his youth" (3:25, 27). Yet, with this brief reminder that that divine Sun still shines beyond the clouds, darkness rolls in again, threatening through the book's very end to quench the bright promise:

> Turn us back to You, O LORD, and we will be restored;
> Renew our days as of old,
> Unless You have utterly rejected us,
> And are very angry with us! (5:21–22)

So these lamentations end by voicing the alarming possibility of divine oblivion: not that God is powerless or unjust, but that he has willed to forget, and has finally turned his back.

12.2.3   Ezekiel: "Son of Man, Can These Bones Live?"

Ezekiel, the third of the Major Prophets, also inhabits this spiritual space between hope and fear. Like Jeremiah, Ezekiel writes to the exiles, warning against false assurance and even falser despair, counseling the Jews to settle into their distant places of banishment while expecting eventual deliverance, return, and reconstruction. Ezekiel's book divides four ways: an opening account of the prophet's apocalyptic call in exile and his initial behavior; then extensive allegorical oracles against the past and continuing sins of Israel and Judah; pronouncements against the wicked Gentile nations that have served as God's scourge on his chosen; and a section on future revival, including its famous vision of dry bones in the valley and its final, richly figurative revelation of Jerusalem restored, vast and foursquare.

In many ways, Ezekiel can be read as a doubling of Jeremiah and a tripling of Isaiah, a confirming reiteration of the older prophets' judgments on Israel and the nations, and of their exhortations and assurances for the exiles. Significantly, Ezekiel repeats Jeremiah's insistence that divine judgment, while inherited, is nevertheless also earned by each new generation: that "every one shall die for his own iniquity" (Jeremiah 31:30), or "the soul who sins shall die" (Ezekiel 18:4) – rather than blaming God's wrath solely on the sins of the fathers. Ezekiel also reiterates Jeremiah's promise of a "new heart," which he in turn voices twice:

> I will give them one heart, and I will put a new spirit within them, and take the stony heart out of their flesh, and give them a heart of flesh, that they may walk in my statutes and keep my judgments and do them; and they shall be my people, and I will be their God. (11:19–20, 36:26–28)

But despite the strong similarity of message to these two earlier seers, Ezekiel has a story, a style, and a visual repertoire all his own. Like Jeremiah also a Levitical priest, he is among the first exiles marched away in 597 BCE after Nebuchadnezzar's first capture of Jerusalem under King Jehoiachin. Carried to the River Chebar, he settles, as Psalm 137 famously puts it, "by the rivers of Babylon," and is challenged immediately there by that psalm's poignant question: "How shall we sing the LORD's song in a foreign land?" (Psalm 137:1, 4). The answer comes to him in a vision "in the fifth year of Jehoiachin's captivity" (593 BCE), and in his own "thirtieth year," the year in which priests normally assumed full Temple responsibilities, but with the Temple 700 miles away, and less than a decade from destruction, the LORD calls this priest to a different kind of service.

The call is powerfully, even bewilderingly, apocalyptic, like the prophet's call in Isaiah chapter 6. In images that will be echoed in the books of Daniel and Revelation, out of a whirlwind bursts a theophany of God and the beings who inhabit his presence in the throne room of heaven. Or rather, as Ezekiel repeatedly insists, he beholds something "like" these heavenly beings and places, for he is aware of how inadequate are all words and pictures for rendering divine realities. He sees great winged beasts, their wingtips touching like those of the cherubim over the Ark of the Covenant, each beast with the four faces of a man, a lion, an ox, and an eagle. These beings rule four creaturely realms: human, wild, domestic, and airborne; they face the four corners of heaven, and the spirit of each beast inhabits its own self-propelled "wheel within a wheel" that is "full of eyes" and moves in the directions of all the four winds. Above these beasts is a crystal dome, surrounded by flames and a rainbow glow, and over this dome, on "the likeness of a throne," sits "the likeness of a man," speaking with a voice "like the voice of the Almighty." All of these likenesses together the prophet calls "the appearance of the likeness of the glory of the LORD" (1:4–28).

The appearance of this divine–human Being in heaven is matched by an answering name that the divine voice gives to Ezekiel: "And he said to me, 'Son of man, stand on your feet, and I will speak to you'" (2:1). In this context, God's oft-repeated term for his messenger – "Son of man"/*ben adam* – is a humbling reminder of his earthiness, his human ordinariness, his descent from the *Adam* who fell, but also a reminder of the heavenly treasure that God will trust to his earthen vessel.

Son of Man: Ordinary Mortal or Divine Messiah?

Ezekiel and Daniel use the phrase "Son of Man" in ways that are strikingly different, though not necessarily opposed. Throughout Ezekiel the Hebrew phrase *ben adam*, applied by God to the prophet himself, means "average human being," while in Daniel, the "one like the son of man" (Aramaic *bar enosh*) is seen "coming with the clouds of heaven" to "the Ancient of Days," who gives him "dominion" on earth (Daniel 7:13–14). This double-edged signification – ordinary mortal or divine Messiah? – is adopted in the New Testament by Jesus, who embraces the ambiguous "Son of Man" as his favored self-descriptor over the more explicit "Messiah," an inflammatory title that he generally chooses to keep secret until an opportune time.

Indeed, earthiness and corporeality remain important in Ezekiel's mission, as he is called to make frequent symbolic actions and gestures that communicate his message. Chapters 4–24 are rich in dramatized parables: *Yahweh* commands Ezekiel to make a clay replica of Jerusalem, ring it with iron, and batter it down (chapter 4); shave his head and beard with a sword, and burn the hair in mourning (chapter 5); bear his belongings through the city, eating in haste like an exile (chapter 12); and, most drastically, the LORD takes from the prophet his beloved wife, but commands him not to weep or grieve her death, signifying the coming of God's remorseless judgment on "the desire of your eyes," Judah (chapter 24). Ezekiel's sermons also abound in verbal figures, his most vivid being allegories of human relations: chapter 16 casts Israel as a foundling baby girl, rescued and affectionately raised by the LORD into a beautiful nubile woman, who nevertheless wantonly turns away from her divine Guardian to prostitution and infanticide; while chapter 23 doubles the lesson, portraying the defunct Northern Kingdom of Israel ("Samaria") as the harlot Oholah, and the dying Southern Kingdom of Judah ("Jerusalem") as her sister harlot Oholibah – both defiled and then betrayed by their heathen suitors.

But probably the most famous of Ezekiel's figures for the Jewish nation is his vision, both chilling and hopeful, of "the Valley of the Dry Bones" in chapter 37.

> The hand of the LORD came upon me and brought me out in the Spirit of the LORD, and set me down in the midst of the valley; and it was full of bones. Then he caused me to pass by them all around, and behold, there were very many in the open valley; and indeed they were very dry. And he said to me, "Son of man, can these bones live?" (37:1–3)

Imagining Israel as a vast killing field of corpses picked clean by the birds of the air, Ezekiel taps deep into the well of human horror: the fear of final decay as oblivion, with the rattling bones and grinning skull as its icons. But the vision then looks deeper, into divine hope, and the primal eldest blessing of man's creation, when the LORD "breathed into his nostrils the breath of life" (Genesis 2:7):

> Again he said to me, "Prophesy to these bones, and say to them, 'O dry bones, hear the word of the LORD! Thus says the Lord GOD to these bones: "Surely I will cause breath to enter into you, and you shall live. I will put sinews on you and bring flesh upon you, cover you with skin and put breath in you; and you shall live."'" (37:4–6)

No longer seen as simply a return or revival, the restoration of Israel is imagined as a second creation to match the promised new "covenant of peace," which "shall be an everlasting covenant with them; I will establish them and multiply them, and I will set My sanctuary in their midst forevermore" (37:26).

That renewed sanctuary and city receive nine chapters of special attention at the end of Ezekiel's book, in a description that outstrips the size and glory of any known Hebrew Temple, whether of Solomon, of Zerubbabel and Ezra, or even of Herod the Great. Though Ezekiel's Temple shares the floorplan of Moses' Tabernacle and the First Temple planned by David, Ezekiel's whole sanctuary complex dwarfs all others, covering 150,000 square feet, if read literally. Ezekiel's Temple combines Solomonic architectural features with images reminiscent of the Garden of Eden (a river runs through it) and Mount Sinai (law goes forth from it), and his description comes immediately after the destruction of the cosmically evil Gog, prince of Rosh, from the land of Magog (chapters 38–39). Thus, Ezekiel's final vision seems to represent a culmination of holy history in a time of rule by the messianic king, when God will dwell among his people, and when God's capital no longer will be called *Yeru Shalayim* (Jerusalem), but *Yahweh Shammah*, or "The LORD is there" (48:35). Though this vision of the renewed Holy Temple, City, Garden and Mount comes to Ezekiel in the twenty-fifth year of the Babylonian captivity, it seems to look beyond the return from that captivity under Ezra and Nehemiah to a great ingathering of all nations at the very end of time.

12.2.4 Daniel: "Man Greatly Beloved"

Daniel, the last and briefest of the Major Prophets, is also the most apocalyptic. Daniel's book divides evenly between the first six chapters narrating the prophet's life and ministry among the Jewish exiles in Babylon (interspersed with Daniel's Joseph-like interpretation of kingly dreams) and the latter six chapters of apocalyptic prophecies concerning the coming of cosmic judgment, redemption, and the end of the world. Like Joseph, Moses, and Esther, Daniel is a stranger in a strange land: deported to Babylon as an adolescent in 605 BCE, he is made a eunuch and inducted into an elite "de-Judification" cohort intended to assimilate bright young Hebrews fully into the mainstream of Babylonian culture and religion; thus, he and his comrades Hananiah, Mishael, and Azariah are renamed Belteshazzar, Meshach, Shadrach, and Abed-Nego. Yet while Daniel and his friends emerge as exemplary imperial administrators, they nevertheless remain loyal to the God of their fathers, refusing the king's rich but ritually unclean food in favor of plain vegetables, while outshining "all the magicians and astrologers who were in all his realm" (Daniel 1:20). Thus, Daniel, the "man greatly beloved," outlasts the Babylonian Empire that captured and gelded him, living well into the reigns of the Medo-Persians Darius and Cyrus.

Daniel's book is neither a history of the Jews in Babylon nor a detailed biography of the man; instead, it is a theologically selective narrative in which the prophet's long life is represented by narrative bursts of a few pivotal events that establish his character, define his mission, and illustrate the over-ruling providence of God. Like Joseph with Pharaoh, Daniel accurately interprets two of Nebuchadnezzar's dreams, and Joseph-like he rises to the peak of imperial administration. But unlike Joseph's success, Daniel's excites poisonous jealousy among incompetent and inferior Gentile rivals, who conspire to destroy "Belteshazzar" and his friends – first, by throwing Meshach, Shadrach, and Abed-Nego into a "fiery furnace" (Daniel 3) and decades later by throwing the elderly Daniel into a den of lions (Daniel 6). In both cases the lives of the faithful are miraculously preserved, bringing destruction on their enemies and drawing reverent praise of the LORD from the Gentile kings Nebuchaznezzar and Darius. In between these terrible tests, Daniel dares to confront the arrogance of Nebuchadnezzar and his successor Belshazzar, in both cases rebuking them and predicting the humbling (and restoration) of the former and the overthrow of the latter.

Thus, Daniel's undulating career, alternating repeatedly between supreme counselor and persecuted pariah, is no mere picture of a political survivor but of a man of true principle, who knows that he is – as Thomas More said at the chopping block – "the king's good servant, but God's first." Indeed, Daniel's friends put the matter well in telling the outraged Nebuchadnezzar that they will not worship the king's golden idol come what may:

> [O]ur God whom we serve is able to deliver us from the burning fiery furnace, and he will deliver us from your hand, O king. But if not, let it be known to you, O king, that we do not serve your gods, nor will we worship the gold image which you have set up. (3:17–18)

And Daniel voices something beyond mere defiance when criticizing the Babylonian regime, exhorting Nebuchadnezzar to "break off your sins by being righteous, and your iniquities by showing mercy to the poor" (4:27). What he voices is a "forthtelling" prophet's passion for mercy and justice, coupled with a "foretelling" prophet's sight of future judgment.

Daniel's climactic confrontation comes with the indolent, hedonistic, and cowardly Belshazzar, last of the Babylonian line, whose bacchanalian drinking party abuses the sacred vessels of the LORD's looted Temple, but is interrupted by the famous "handwriting on the wall" spelling out the telegraphic threat "MENE, MENE, TEKEL, UPHARSIN" (5:5, 25). Daniel, offered treasure and third place in the kingdom by Belshazzar for a favorable interpretation, instead answers in words as direct as a body blow:

> Let your gifts be for yourself, and give your rewards to another... This is the interpretation of each word. MENE: God has numbered your kingdom, and finished it; TEKEL: You have been weighed in the balances, and found wanting; PERES: Your kingdom has been divided, and given to the Medes and Persians. (5:17, 26–28)

And the account then concludes with devastating brevity: "That very night Belshazzar, king of the Chaldeans, was slain. And Darius the Mede received the kingdom, being about sixty-two years old" (5:30–31).

Daniel's book shifts midway from mainly narrative to mainly apocalyptic discourse, and these visions of chapters 7–12 have inspired and provoked as much interpretive debate as any prophetic passages in Old Testament or New, including the Book of Revelation to which it is often compared. It is Daniel who foretells, in one of the most-quoted of messianic passages, "one like a son of man ... coming with the clouds of heaven ... to the Ancient of Days" to be given "glory and a kingdom" and "everlasting dominion" (7:13–14). But even more compelling to interpreters has been the Daniel 9 timetable of the Anointed One's appearance and death, and its aftermath:

> I have come to tell you [says the angel Gabriel to Daniel], for you are greatly beloved; therefore consider the matter, and understand the vision:
>
>> ... Know therefore and understand,
>> That from the going forth of the command
>> To restore and build Jerusalem
>> Until Messiah the Prince,
>> There shall be seven weeks and sixty-two weeks;
>> The street shall be built again, and the wall,
>> Even in troublesome times.

> And after the sixty-two weeks
> Messiah shall be cut off, but not for himself;
> And the people of the prince who is to come
> Shall destroy the city and the sanctuary.
> The end of it shall be with a flood,
> And till the end of the war desolations are determined. (9:23, 25–26)

How to read this prophetic schedule? Those so inclined have assumed, with good traditional warrant, that a "week" (*shiva* – literally "seven") in this context refers to a seven-year period, so that "seven weeks and sixty-two weeks" translates to 483 total years. But beginning when? If the "command to restore and build Jerusalem" is read as Cyrus the Great's decree of 538 BCE allowing Jews to return and rebuild the Temple, then Messiah's advent can be expected in 55 BCE. If the decree is that of Artaxerxes I in 458 BCE allowing Nehemiah to restore public Temple worship, then Messiah appears on the scene in the year 25 CE. And if the decree is that of Artaxerxes in 444 BCE to rebuild the walls and gates of Jerusalem, then (using the 360-day lunar year of the Jewish calendar), the "Anointed prince" may be "cut off" in 33 CE.

If the years 25 and 33 CE ring bells – they approximately bracket the public life and ministry of Jesus – then it is clear why these seemingly arcane speculations matter, not only to religious believers of many sorts, but also to historians of the ancient Near East. One of the earliest of these, the Romano-Jewish scholar Flavius Josephus (37–c. 100 CE), writes in *The Jewish War* (75 CE) that the Judeans of the early first century CE were obsessed with the imminent coming of their Messiah. "[W]hat most stirred them up to war was an ambiguous oracle that was found also in their sacred writings, that about that time one from their country should become ruler of the world" (vi.5.4). Whatever one may believe regarding the Christian teaching of Jesus as that Messiah, it is clear from Josephus and other extra-biblical sources that when Jesus appeared in the third decade of the first century, he stepped into an atmosphere of heated messianic expectation – a fact also acknowledged by the New Testament writers, who speak of many other potential "Christs" on the Hebrews' minds. And it is likely that Daniel's prophecy of the "Anointed Prince," with its timetable interpreted as above, added much of the fire to this apocalyptic fervor. Thus, Daniel's messianic prophecy, dating between two and five centuries before the days of Jesus and Josephus, contributes in part to the conditions of its own fulfillment by generating among the Jews a small troop of would-be Christs and their followers.

The same cannot precisely be said for Daniel's visions in chapters 10 and 11, which foresee geopolitical events among Gentile nations that had little or no access to Hebrew scripture. Daniel 11:2–35 predicts the succession of four more Persian kings after Cyrus, followed by a great Greek conqueror whose empire will absorb Persia's and spread even further to the east; then his vision details the breakup of that Greek Empire into four parts under four kings, with the kings of the north and south struggling for supremacy – and the northern king eventually prevailing and forcing abomination and idolatry on the Jews and their sanctuary.

Remarkably, these prophecies map on to Eurasian geopolitical history in scores and scores of specific ways – from the reigns of Persian emperors Cambyses, Gautama, Darius the Great, and Xerxes I (529–464 BCE); through the conquests of the Greek Alexander the Great (333–323 BCE); to the division of his empire among four generals Cassander (Greece), Lysimachus (Asia Minor), Seleucis (Babylon and Persia), and Ptolemy (Egypt) (303 BCE); leading to the multiple back-and-forth wars for possession of Syria and Palestine between the northern (Seleucid) and southern (Ptolemaic) dynasties (303–164 BCE). Virtually all interpreters see the blasphemous "king of the north" (11:31) as Antiochus IV Epiphanes (175–164 BCE), who in 168 BCE insisted on being worshiped by the Jews as a living god, forbade circumcision and the reading of the *Torah*, banned sacrifices in the Hebrew Temple, and built an altar there to Zeus Olympias. Daniel 11:36–45 breaks off from this outline of history, describing a continued tyrannical reign of a sacrilegious king, leading some commentators to see a reference to the reign of Herod the Great (c. 40–4 BCE), and many others to an apocalyptic End Times regime of an "Anti-Messiah" or "Antichrist," whose crescendo of abomination will provoke God's climactic intervention.

So, after all of this geopolitical mayhem, Daniel's final chapter invokes the Last Judgment, when

> .... at that time your people shall be delivered,
> Everyone who is found written in the book.
> And many of those who sleep in the dust of the earth shall awake,
> Some to everlasting life,
> Some to shame and everlasting contempt. (12:1–2)

In the meantime, Daniel is told to preserve his book and get on with his daily life, for until the End Time, "many shall run to and fro, and knowledge shall increase."

> Go your way, Daniel, for the words are closed up and sealed till the time of the end. Many shall be purified, made white, and refined, but the wicked shall do wickedly; and none of the wicked shall understand, but the wise shall understand. (12:4, 9–10)

Daniel's message, here and throughout, is that there will be no ultimate resolution to human tribulation in the battle between good and evil until God brings an end and a new beginning.

12.3 The Minor Prophets: "The Day of Small Things"

As we've already noted, the difference between Major and Minor Prophets is not the importance or professed truth of the message, but the length of the book. The Minor Prophets run the gamut from lyric poetry to prose midrash, from acted parables and present-tense oracles to apocalyptic and messianic visions. In some, the LORD speaks through the prophet's daily experiences and deeds, while in most he speaks through the seer's mouth – and always in his written words. What follow are very brief accounts of these twelve prophets' main themes, each book's structure, its style, and its place in the overall prophetic arc.

12.3.1 Hosea: "Take Unto Thee a Wife of Whoredoms"

"Whoredom" – the King James Bible's seventeenth-century word for prostitution – still has the power to shock, and shock is what *Yahweh's* order to the prophet Hosea seems intended to provoke. Never was there a stranger command from a holy God to a devout man: "Go, take unto thee a wife of whoredoms and children of whoredoms: for the land hath committed great whoredom, departing from the LORD" (Hosea 1:2, KJV). The prophet obeys, marrying a known harlot named Gomer, making his life, his wife, and his dubiously conceived children a continuously lived object lesson about the infidelities of Israel. Writing in Israel's last decades of relative prosperity and moral decay before its final downfall in 722 BCE, Hosea sees the nation's specific "adultery" as its syncretism, its combining the worship of *Yahweh* with that of pagan gods. Hosea's whole life becomes allegory, even the names of his children Jezreel (a beautiful fertile valley plagued by bloodshed), Lo-Ruhamah ("No-Mercy"), and Lo-Ammi ("Not-My-People"). Chapters 1–3 tell the story of how their foreboding names and destinies are overthrown as Hosea shows them mercy and reconciliation.

In the book's nine remaining chapters, the LORD speaks as a jealous husband, threatening to put his wanton national "spouse" away – "They are all adulterers, like an oven heated by a baker" (Hosea 7:4) – but like Hosea, he tenderly overcomes his anger, saying that Jezreel and "No-Mercy" shall receive mercy, and that "Not-My-People" shall be re-adopted as his people. It is possible to read Gomer's actions with some human sympathy, as a woman looking for love in all the wrong places, but it would be a mistake to sentimentalize her "whoredom" as hiding a stereotypical "heart of gold" that makes her somehow worthy of redemption. Instead, Gomer's hardened infidelity is a picture of human betrayal and folly, and Hosea's ultimate treatment of her illustrates *Yahweh's* unconditional *chesed*, steadfast and loving, redeeming the unworthy in spite of every offense.

12.3.2 Joel: "The Day of the Locust"

It is hard to date Joel's book with certainty, because its prophecies of disaster are stated generally enough that they might apply to a variety of particular military and natural calamities in the history of Israel and Judah. Central to its message is "the day of the LORD" as the day of the locust:

> What the chewing locust left, the swarming locust has eaten;
> What the swarming locust left, the crawling locust has eaten;
> And what the crawling locust left, the consuming locust has eaten. (Joel 1:4)

These inexorable devouring swarms have been interpreted over the millennia as either figurative, representing foraging armies from Egypt, Assyria, Babylon, Greece, or Rome, or as literal grasshoppers, denuding the trees and vines and grain, darkening the sky in their clouds. But if the day of the LORD is "a day of clouds and darkness" and grim judgment, it is also a day of ultimate hope for those who recognize the finger of God in their disaster and respond with repentance. These humble people will weather God's wrath on the sins of Jew and Gentile alike in "the valley of decision" (Joel 3:14), but afterwards they will witness the refreshing and revival of the land, when

> the mountains shall drip with new wine,
> The hills shall flow with milk,
> And all the brooks of Judah shall be flooded with water;
> A fountain shall flow from the house of the LORD. (Joel 3:18)

Plague, famine, sword, fire – and blessing for those who trust and abide: that is the bracing essence of Joel.

12.3.3 Amos: "Let Justice Run Down Like Water"

Though a southerner from Judah, Amos, like Hosea, prophesied in the Northern Kingdom of Israel during a period of relative peace and prosperity, yet only a few decades before the kingdom's complete overthrow by the Assyrians in 722 BCE. Amos is the model of the forthtelling prophet: a rural laboring man from the village of Tekoa in Judah, he speaks unstintingly and with rough-hewn eloquence against current idolatry and social injustice, seeing mistreatment of the poor as a consequence of false worship and contempt for God. First attacking the godless brutality of Israel's traditional enemies – Syria, Egypt, Tyre, Edom, and Ammon – he turns soon to target the wickedness of the godly, both in Judah and Israel, predicting eventual destruction for each and all. Mincing no words, Amos calls the hard-drinking, self-indulgent rich women of Samaria "you cows of Bashan" (Amos 4:1), warning them and their husbands that

> As a shepherd takes from the mouth of a lion
> Two legs or a piece of an ear,
> So shall the children of Israel be taken out
> Who dwell in Samaria. (Amos 3:12)

Judah too will suffer "because they have despised the law of the LORD" (Amos 2:4). Facing a future of smoking ruins and mangled remains for their present sins, the Hebrews nevertheless piously offer up sacrifices in the temples of Jerusalem and Samaria, devoutly praying that "the day of the LORD" will fall on their enemies. This hypocrisy provokes Amos's most stinging rebuke:

> Woe to you who desire the day of the LORD!
> For what good is the day of the LORD to you?
> It will be darkness, and not light.....
> Though you offer me burnt offerings and your grain offerings,
> I will not accept them,
> Nor will I regard your fattened peace offerings.....
> But let justice run down like water,
> And righteousness like a mighty stream. (Amos 5:18, 22, 24)

Echoing Isaiah's attack on religious "lip-service" (Isaiah 29:13), Amos envisions locusts like Joel's and cities aflame like Jeremiah's, but also in the end predicts the restoration of David's throne in an era of flowing messianic prosperity (Amos 9:11–15). The sycamore-trimmer from Tekoa knows the benefits of radical pruning.

12.3.4   Obadiah: "Concerning Edom"

While most of the prophets spread their chastisements over many peoples, Jewish and Gentile, Obadiah focuses his reproaches on one target, Edom, with pinpoint intensity. Israel's Edomite cousins were consistently hostile throughout Hebrew history in Canaan. However, the resemblances of Obadiah 1–9 to Jeremiah 49:7–22, as well as to the scorching imprecation of Psalm 137:7 (both of which recall Edom's enthusiastic partnership in Jerusalem's Babylonian destruction) suggest to many interpreters a post-exilic date in the sixth century BCE. Obadiah's single message in its very brief space is that God knows and feels the sufferings of his people, both with compassion and with an outrage that will burn like a consuming flame until all of the nation's unrepentant oppressors have been reduced to ash, and Israel is restored to supremacy.

12.3.5   Jonah: "Should I Not Pity Nineveh?"

In marked contrast, though not necessarily opposition, to Obadiah's single-minded poetic oracle against the Edomites, the Book of Jonah presents a witty prose object lesson satirizing self-righteous calls for nationalist vengeance. The book makes the Assyrian capital of Nineveh the object not of deserved divine wrath but of an amazing grace. Interpreters disagree about whether the story is intended as chronicle or fable: the prophet Jonah son of Amittai is mentioned in 2 Kings 14:25, suggesting historicity, but other commentators on Jonah detect a strong flavor of fish story in its whimsical narrative. Whether meant as history or parable, it is that deeply Jewish thing, a seriously funny tale. Rich and wry, it also has a heart.

For someone whose name means "dove," Jonah is hawkishly inclined toward the Ninevites – and why not? These Assyrians practiced pitiless siege warfare that reduced walled cities first to famine-stricken chaos and then to rubble, with hills of the defenders' severed heads erected as monuments to their resistance. Masters of bronze-age *blitzkrieg* and perpetrators of ancient holocausts, the Assyrians were the *Herrenvolk* of their day, and Nineveh their Berlin. So when the LORD calls Jonah to "[a]rise, go to Nineveh, that great city, and cry out against it" (Jonah 1:2), imagine God calling a rabbi from the Warsaw Ghetto in 1942 to travel across the bloodlands of central Europe into the heart of Nazidom, there to confront the *Führer* and the whole Reichstag with a blunt yet merciful command: repent of conquest and death camps and Zyklon B gas and cremation ovens – or perish. This analogy may help us to sympathize with Jonah: he fears not for his life, but for the mercy of his God, who may be so softhearted as to forgive this nest of murderers. Thus, he heads out in the opposite direction to Tarshish (1:3), probably the coast of Spain.

The reluctant prophet's misadventures are the stuff of Hebrew and Sunday Schools and catechism classes the world over, and have given the name "a Jonah" to any jinxed sailor on any ship: trying to flee the presence of the LORD, he instead meets God's special attention in the form of a tempest. The heathen seamen around him cry out to their gods, but Jonah resignedly tells them not to bother – instead, just "[p]ick me up and throw me into the sea" (1:12). When they reluctantly do so, the sea grows calm, the infidel mariners worship *Yahweh*, and Jonah continues his unintentionally successful missionary journey in the belly of a "great fish" (1:17–2:10) back toward the place where he least wants to preach: Nineveh. Once there, he declares the city's imminent downfall, a sermon doomed to succeed, for the city repents, "from the greatest to the least of them" (3:5). If such a message from such a messenger strikes us as improbable or bizarre, then (back to our Fascist example) imagine a conscience-stricken Hitler and a troop of heartbroken SS men rending their garments and rushing to open the gates of Auschwitz and Dachau.

If we receive this strange message of Jonah easily, then probably we are not receiving it. If I am black and volunteer to help elderly members of the Ku Klux Klan, an Armenian concerned for the welfare of the Turks, a Cuban-American who prays for the soul of Fidel Castro, or a holocaust survivor who supports a fund for Nazi widows, then I have grasped what Jonah is about. However, if I love my friends and hate my enemies, or would rather see history's monsters destroyed and not redeemed, then I am in Jonah's target audience. "And should I not pity Nineveh," the LORD asks Jonah, still angered by God's mercy on the wicked, "that great city, in which there are more than one hundred and twenty thousand persons who cannot discern between their right hand and their left – and much livestock?" (4:11). *Yahweh* forgives his enemies because, in some sense, they know not what they do; but also because, in a world full of greater or lesser sinners, he has no one else to work with. Perhaps the best way to understand stories of divine grace is to read them from the villain's point of view.

12.3.6 Micah: Birth Pangs of the Kingdom

"Who is like the LORD?" asks the very name of the prophet Micah (Hebrew *Michayahu*). Like Amos a rural laborer, Micah of Moresheth is a contemporary of Isaiah son of Amoz, and like him is sent to Jerusalem in the days of kings Jotham, Ahaz, and Hezekiah (740–700 BCE) to answer that no one is like *Yahweh*, and that none perfectly keeps his word. The book alternates between successive sections itemizing the nation's sins, and others threatening divine wrath and promising messianic redemption. Micah sees the "Daughter of Zion" as a mother in her birthpangs (Micah 4:9–10), bringing to life a new kingdom that will banish theft, false prophecy, and exploitation of the weak, establishing the reign of the messianic shepherd king to be born in David's city:

> But you, Bethlehem Ephrathah
> Though you are little among the thousands of Judah,
> Yet out of you shall come forth to me
> The One to be Ruler in Israel
> Whose goings forth are from of old,
> From everlasting. (Micah 5:2)

Then, having predicted that God will remember his kingly promises to Israel, Micah concludes by celebrating divine forgetfulness:

> He does not retain his anger forever...
> You will cast all our sins
> Into the depths of the sea. (Micah 7:18, 19)

Unlike the pagan gods whose wrath is unquenchable and whose thirst for blood insatiable, Micah sees *Yahweh* as uniquely soft of heart – the God who will visit his people to comfort them.

12.3.7 Nahum: "Woe to the Bloody City!"

There is no known extra-biblical record of an eighth-century BCE mass repentance in the Assyrian capital of Nineveh like the one described in the Book of Jonah, though we might not expect that there would be a record, since subsequent regimes probably would have expunged accounts of such a spiritually humiliating interlude. But there is plenty of evidence outside the Bible for Nineveh's late seventh-century downfall and obliteration as described in the Book of Nahum. The prophet's name means "comfort," but the consolation here is that of vengeance enjoyed by Assyria's victims who will observe what happens when the longsuffering of the LORD, extended even to pagans, is finally exhausted and his full fury descends, in this case by the hand of another cruel conqueror, Babylon. The language is vivid, even graphic: not only majestic images of "his fury ... poured out like fire, And the rocks ... thrown down by him" (Nahum 1:6), but also excruciating portrayals of human debasement to haunt one's sleep. "Woe to the bloody city! ... the mistress of sorceries ... I will lift your skirts over your face, I will show the nations your nakedness" (Nahum 2:1, 4–5). Whips and clattering chariots and piled corpses, lions tearing the slain to ribbons, children's heads smashed on every street corner – eye for eye, tooth for tooth, blood for blood, hell for hell. "All who hear news of you will clap their hands over you" – and sing a song of *schadenfreude*.

12.3.8 Habakkuk: "On the Day of Wrath, the Just Shall Live by His Faith"

The *danse macabre* of Nahum is followed and answered immediately by "the burden which the prophet Habakkuk saw" (Habakkuk 1:1); for the same Babylonians who bring a heavy reckoning on Assyria bring it on the Jews as well. The book begins with the prophet's first question, about pervasive violence in Judah – violence that is at its heart violation, both of the bodies and souls of its victims, both of law and life. How long can it go on? Habakkuk asks. God answers that he will end the violence by ending the violent. He is raising up a new and sharper scourge in the Chaldeans, "a bitter and hasty nation": they are swift and unstoppable, lawless, boundless, merciless, and they mock kings and princes as they descend like eagles to rip open their prey and feast. Habakkuk imagines himself standing high upon a rampart (Habakkuk 2:1) as he asks his second question: will Babylon run rampant forever? God's answer is that, even in the worst of times, "the just shall live by his faith" (Habakkuk 2:4), waiting patiently for blessing, and for the woe that will descend on all the wicked, heathen or Hebrew. The book's burden ends with a song, not this time of *schadenfreude*, but of steadfast love among the ruins:

> Though the fig tree may not blossom,
> Nor fruit be on the vines;
> Though the labor of the olive may fail,
> And the fields yield no food...
> Yet I will rejoice in the LORD,
> I will joy in the God of my salvation. (Habakkuk 3:17–18)

This resolute song illustrates the principle of the literary foil: the darker the background, the brighter the contrast. For Habakkuk, though the whole world turns to coal, the diamond of faith shines all the brighter.

12.3.9 Zephaniah: "I Will Gather Those Who Sorrow"

Zephaniah's name means "*Yahweh* has hidden," and may suggest that the prophet, born during the reign of Judah's evil King Manasseh (699–643 BCE), was somehow sheltered from the idolatry and violence of that regime. Zephaniah prophesies during the time of Manasseh's grandson Josiah (640–609 BCE), an era of zealous reform – the book of Deuteronomy discovered and implemented, the Temple repaired and cleansed of syncretistic worship, the "high places" removed, the laws of economic and social justice enforced. But Zephaniah looks beyond the hopeful moment to a grimmer future, for however sincere the boy-king's heart may be, the people's repentance is too shallow and their sins too deep to avert the coming *Dies Irae*:

> [A] day of wrath,
> A day of trouble and distress,
> A day of devastation and desolation,
> A day of darkness and gloominess,
> A day of clouds and thick darkness,
> A day of trumpet and alarm
> Against the fortified cities
> And against the high towers. (Zephaniah 1:15–16)

Along with judgment on Judah's enemies Philistia, Ammon, Moab, Ethiopia, and Assyria will come doom on Judah herself, and for the same crimes, for the child who knew better has done as badly, or worse. Yet, echoing Isaiah, Zephaniah looks beyond doom to restoration, and brokenness will yield to joy: "I will gather those who sorrow... At that time I will bring you back" (Zephaniah 3:18, 20). Judah's bones cannot rejoice until they have been duly broken.

12.3.10 Haggai: "The Desire of All Nations"

If Zephaniah looks ahead to the day of doom and then to the restoration that will follow, Haggai writes in the moment of rebuilding. It is the second year of Persia's Darius the Great (519 BCE), and Judah has been back from the Exile and in Jerusalem for seventeen years; Haggai addresses a series of brief, sharp-edged homilies to the people and their leaders, who have stalled in their efforts at rebuilding the Temple, while looking to their own comforts: "Is it time for you yourselves to dwell in your paneled houses, and this Temple to lie in ruins?" he demands – noting how terrible have been their recent harvests, a token of divine disfavor (Haggai 1:4, 6). Significantly, the sitting governor over Jerusalem is Zerubbabel, descended from David and all the kings of Judah, and he, along with the High Priest Joshua, is stirred by Haggai's call to raise the funds and labor force to renew the work. About two months later, after work has recommenced, Haggai encourages them with another message looking past their own day, and even past the Temple itself, to a time of ultimate messianic fulfillment, when the LORD "shall shake all nations, and they shall come to the Desire of All Nations, and I will fill this Temple with glory … the glory of this latter Temple shall be greater than the former … and in this place shall I give peace" (Haggai 2:7–8). In serving their God in his renewed house, they are renewing not only their own prosperity, but bringing future blessing on all peoples.

12.3.11 Zechariah: "Behold, Your King"

When one hears the word "apocalypse," the word "encouraging" is probably not the first that leaps to mind. Yet Zechariah (appropriately, the name means "*Yahweh* remembers") is indeed a book of apocalyptic encouragement, looking forward into different windows of future time to remind the Jews just restored from Babylonian Exile that their work in rebuilding their Temple and their city will not be forgotten, and indeed is part of a much greater cosmic plan. Contemporary with the more confrontational prophecies of Haggai, Zechariah's visions show spots of time alive with representative images: a perpetually burning lampstand and a fruitful olive tree, a flying scroll, a mysterious woman in a basket, four chariots rushing to the corners of the earth, three evil shepherds and one faithful. Perhaps the most vivid images are those of Messiah, paradoxically humble yet omnipotent:

> Behold, your king is coming to you;
> He is just and having salvation,
> Lowly and riding on a donkey,
> A colt, the foal of a donkey…His dominion shall be from sea to sea,
> And from the River to the ends of the earth. (Zechariah 9:9–10)

As in Isaiah, this humble universal Lord is portrayed as a wounded healer, one who is "pierced" for the people (Zechariah 12:10), and as a good shepherd destined for an agonizing death that will try and purify his sheep:

> "Strike the shepherd,
> And the sheep will be scattered;
> Then I will turn my hand against the little ones.
> And it shall come to pass in all the land,"
> Says the LORD, ….
> "I will bring the one–third [of the sheep] through the fire,
> Will refine them as silver is refined,
> And test them as gold is tested." (Zechariah 13:7–9)

While the reconstruction of the Temple enters into these prophecies, they treat the Temple, like everything else in creation, as pointing ahead to a great fulfillment "on that Day" when all things "shall be holiness to the LORD of hosts" (Zechariah 14:21).

12.3.12 Malachi: "Who Can Endure the Day of His Coming?"

The brief Book of Malachi combines in almost equal measure the strands of forthtelling and foretelling prophecy that interweave throughout the Former and Latter Prophets. Thus, the book is a fitting end not only to the twelve Minor Prophets but also to the writings of all the

Nevi'im – a distinction made perhaps even more striking by the fact that Malachi (Hebrew *malakh*) means "messenger," about as simple a description of the prophet's calling as can be given. In addition, Malachi appears at the very end of the Christian Old Testament (Chronicles ends the Hebrew Bible), as if to stress that all the Law and the prophets stand on a threshold, looking both backwards and forwards. Malachi indeed does look back at the LORD's past love to Israel, only to denounce Israel's own present sinful ingratitude; writing at the time of Nehemiah's restorationist governorship of Judah (446–425 BCE), Malachi excoriates the people for falling into the same sins that led to their Babylonian captivity in the first place – priestly corruption, sorcery, perjury, sexual infidelity, and the exploitation of widows, orphans, and foreigners. Referring to Israel's widespread hope in the coming Messiah, Malachi tells them, in effect, to be careful what (and whom) they wish for.

> And the Lord, whom you seek,
> Will suddenly come to his temple,
> Even the Messenger of the covenant,
> In whom you delight…
>
> But who can endure the day of his coming?
> And who can stand when he appears? (Malachi 3:1–2)

The Jews, who have longed for the day of the Deliverer coming down in wrath upon their many oppressors, are thus warned that judgment will begin not with the *goyim* but with the household of God, and that the LORD will burn among them "like a refiner's fire": "For behold, the day is coming, burning like an oven, and all the proud, yes, all who do wickedly will be stubble. And the day which is coming shall burn them up" (Malachi 4:1). In the end – and this is in fact how Malachi ends – only Moses and Elijah can prepare the way for the Anointed One:

> Remember the Law of Moses, My servant,…
>
> Behold, I will send you Elijah the prophet
> Before the coming of the great and dreadful day of the LORD.
> And he will turn
> The hearts of the fathers to the children,
> And the hearts of the children to their fathers,
> Lest I come and strike the earth with a curse. (Malachi 4:4–6)

Those who have attended to Moses and Elijah – the Law and the prophets – will experience "the Sun of Righteousness" arising "with healing in His wings" (Malachi 4:2); those who have not will know only a scorching heat that turns their world to ash. So end the prophets; their visions put the hearer in hope and in fear.

"Where there is no vision, the people perish," says the proverb. It is a fundamental human urge to rise above and look ahead. Even the most anti-metaphysical of us seek transcendence as the sparks fly upward – if not through the oracles of some Supreme Being, then through supreme courts or astrology or demographics, economic theory or phrenology, climate projections or cybernetics. Whether the words of the prophets are written in the scriptures, the stars, or statistics, or merely written on the subway walls, we will continue to seek out seers and visionaries to divine our destinies and the desires of our hearts. Are these prophets true or false? Is the light in them darkness? And how to tell? These remain the most important questions on earth – and beyond.

Questions for Discussion

1 When people today use the word "**prophetic**," what are some of the possible meanings?

2 What are some different ways – **verbal and non-verbal** – in which the Hebrew prophets delivered their messages?

3 To what do the traditional Jewish terms **the Former Prophets** and **the Latter Prophets** refer, and what understanding of prophetic chronology underlies these terms?

4 What does it mean to distinguish between **forthtelling prophets** and **foretelling prophets**? Who are some primary examples of each type? How absolute or relative are these distinctions?

5 What distinguishes the **Major Prophets** from the **Minor Prophets**? How does the "Major/Minor" distinction relate to or cut across the "forthtelling/foretelling" distinction and the "Former/Latter" distinction?

6 What do the **forthtelling** prophecies of the Hebrew Bible have in common with modern views of **social justice**? In what ways, both theoretically and practically, might biblically prophetic and "social" conceptions of justice diverge or disagree? Consider some justice and reform movements of the past few centuries – abolition of slavery, civil rights, children's rights, women's rights, prohibition, minority rights, right to life/reproductive rights, economic rights, sexual rights, animal rights, criminal/victims' rights – in the light of these commonalities and divergences.

7 What are some of the most notable **foretelling** prophecies discussed in this chapter? What are the major ways of explaining the remarkable predictive accuracy of many foretelling prophecies? What **metaphysical and philosophical assumptions** underlie these varying explanations?

8 Who are some major practitioners of **messianic prophecy** in the Hebrew Bible, and what are its hallmarks? How does the figure of a "Messiah" function in Jewish traditions? In Christian belief? As a more general cultural and imaginative symbol?

9 Who are some major practitioners of "**apocalyptic prophecy**" in the Hebrew Bible, and what are its hallmarks? How does Old Testament apocalypticism inform and influence modern ideas of "the Apocalypse"? How do contemporary versions of the Apocalypse revise or depart from these biblical models?

10 What are some **literary and other cultural works** that show the influence of biblical prophecy? Why, in your opinion, have these biblical books endured in their fame?

11 How are other **literary features and forms** – narrative, poetic structures, irony, satire, drama, sermon – at work in various prophetic books to increase their impact?

12 How are the themes of **divine justice and divine mercy** interwoven and juxtaposed within and among the prophetic writings? Are there moments when you hear these state-

ments of the LORD's judgment as alarmingly harsh? As bothersomely lenient? As "just right"? How might the original hearers of these prophecies have responded?

13   Relatedly, how are the themes of **divine rebuke and divine comfort** interwoven and juxtaposed within and among the prophetic writings? For what does *Yahweh* most often chastise his people? By what means does he most often seek to encourage them?

14   In what varying ways do the prophets address the problem of **collective/intergenerational vs. individual responsibility**?

Part III

The New Testament/New Covenant

13

Gospel Narrative: Kingdom Coming

13.1 Make It New: Another Covenant

When Ezra Pound, an American poet with a prophetic streak and an Old Testament name, burst on the literary scene a century ago, he gave the world what amounted to a revolutionary aesthetic creed: "Make it new." Cultural critics and interpreters have debated ever since what, for Pound and his fellow self-proclaimed "Modernists," this newness meant. Was it something schismatic, an explosive break with the past? After all, Pound did call the first Modernist magazine *Blast* – hardly a title to attract traditionalists. Or was Modernist "newness" to mean progress along a continuum, the constant rediscovery and refreshment of the "news that stays news" – another Poundian definition of poetry? Were the Modernists making a literary "revolution" in the sense of demolishing old forms to make something radically different? Or was theirs a "revolution" in the original sense, a "re-volving" and return to some first principle, some primary truth, or beauty?

Such questions we inevitably ask about the newness of the New Covenant – more commonly called by its synonym, "The New Testament." On the side of continuity, the gospels report that Jesus came "not to destroy the Law and the Prophets ... but to fulfil" (Matthew 5:17) and that "it is easier for heaven and earth to pass away than for one tittle of the Law to fail" (Luke 16:17). All four gospels quote, often extensively, from the Hebrew Bible to demonstrate that Jesus not only kept all the expectations of the Mosaic Covenant, but also accomplished the acts of the coming Messiah, from Bethlehem birthplace to "despised and rejected" death throes – and resurrection, with promised return "in judgment." Indeed, the books of Matthew, Mark, and Luke portray Jesus as endorsed by Moses and Elijah, the great Lawgiver and the archetypal Prophet themselves, as they return to speak with him on the mount of Transfiguration (Matthew 17:3, Mark 9:2–8, Luke 8:28–36). Clearly, the New Testament writers present Jesus himself as a Jew among Jews, a keeper of the *Torah*, and the fulfillment of the house of David.

Yet for all of this stress on continuity, the New Covenant's fulfillment of the Old is necessarily a disruption, indeed an abolition. It is no light thing for Jesus to announce, as he does almost offhandedly in Mark's gospel, that the dietary laws that had defined the Israelites for more than 1400 years were now obsolete, since "whatever enters a man from outside cannot defile him, because it does not enter his heart but his stomach, and is eliminated, thus purifying all foods" (Mark 7:18–19). Jesus repeatedly claims to possess this abolishing power, punctuating that claim with the even more alarming prediction that the days of the holy Temple and its ritual laws are numbered, that soon "not one stone shall be left upon another" (Matthew 24:2, Mark 13:2, Luke 19:44). Thus, while the New Testament reads itself as the devoutly wished consummation of the Hebrew Bible, most Jews, like the Pharisees within the New Testament story itself, have seen the New Covenant, and often Jesus himself, as violating rather than fulfilling the "Old."

Perhaps the greatest irony in this ancient Jewish–Christian divide is that Judaism has always acknowledged the incompleteness of the Hebrew Bible, and its need of fulfillment. As we observed

Literary Study of the Bible: An Introduction, First Edition. Christopher Hodgkins.
© 2020 John Wiley & Sons Ltd. Published 2020 by John Wiley & Sons Ltd.

in the previous chapter, long before the advent of Christianity, the prophets looked forward to a day when the Anointed One, the Son of David, will return to restore his people and speak peace to the nations, and as Jeremiah famously puts it, a "New Covenant" will be written on the hearts of all (Jeremiah 31:31). Furthermore, after the advent of Jesus, and the subsequent destruction of the Temple by Rome, the newly exiled Jews completed what is in essence another scriptural "testament" of their own, the Talmud: an extra-biblical compilation of Jewish Law in the form of the binding precepts of the Elders – the Mishnah (200 CE) – and a further rabbinic commentary on the Mishnah – the Gamara (400–500 CE). It is by Talmudic study and commentary, along with ritual, dietary, and ethical practice, that Judaism has largely defined itself for the past two millennia in the absence of its holiest site for the offering of Mosaic sacrifice. Thus, Jews and Christians agree that the Hebrew Bible requires both messianic and scriptural completion; they disagree simply – and much ado about that "simply"! – on the who and the how of completion.

Our literary study of the two Testaments does not require us to resolve this great division, but it does bring light to the question of New Testament comparisons with the Hebrew scriptures in style, form, and substance. We need not agree with Elizabethan playwright (and atheist) Christopher Marlowe that the New Testament is "filthily written" to note that the Old Testament possesses much more in the way of great poetry, epic narrative, and high drama than the New. Even the styles of Old Testament and New Testament languages differ: "classical" Hebrew vs. *koiné* or "common" Greek. The Hebrew Bible is written in an elevated, literary tongue; the New Testament in a workaday *lingua franca*.

Yet the New Testament contains some very fine literary art. The few New Testament psalms embedded in Luke (often called by their Latin titles the *Magnificat*, the *Benedictus*, and the *Nunc Dimittis*) hold their own with the greatest songs of Moses or Deborah or David; the parables of Jesus are among the most exquisite little stories ever told; his sermons and sayings have pierced a hundred generations to the heart; the simple reportorial style of the Gospels and Acts sometimes rises to the understated grandeur of Genesis or Samuel; and Revelation is the most lurid and gorgeous and ecstatic "apocalypse" of all – and the one that gives that Greek name to all others. Even the New Testament letters of Paul, Peter, James, John, and Jude, plain earthen vessels of doctrine that they are, often run with new wine and fine spirits, and sometimes even these epistles sing, quite literally, a new song.

Still, searching out such acknowledged veins of imaginative ore risks missing what is perhaps the New Testament's most encompassing stylistic fulfillment of the Old: in its relative brevity and plainness, it serves as the ultimate example of the climactic anti-climax, a trope that often punctuates Hebrew narrative. Like David's sudden slaying of Goliath, or the LORD's overnight destruction of the Assyrians at the gates of Jerusalem, the lightning ministry of the New Testament Christ leaves the Hebraically informed reader gaping at a pathway strewn with miracles, at an empty cross and at an empty tomb. Anticipated in epic oracles spanning at least ten centuries, the long-expected Son of Man is come and gone in a three-year flash, leaving in his wake puzzlement, shocked hostility, and reverent, hopeful awe. Never has "less is more" meant so much to so many.

13.2 "A House Divided": Intertestamental Developments and Religious/Political Parties in Jesus' Day

While literary analysis alone cannot resolve the historically intractable dispute between Jews and Christians over the natures of the Messiah and the New Covenant, it is necessary that we know something of the divisions among the Jews themselves at the time of Jesus if we are to understand the first-century Hebrew imagination that gave rise to the Christian story, and to its detractors. For the Jewish–Christian divide began as a split among Jews over what *kind* of Messiah to expect. As we saw in the previous chapter, the prophetic oracles and histories that conclude the Hebrew

Bible portray a return from Babylonian Exile that is both fulfillment and prologue. The restored Jerusalem Sanctuary, as foreseen by prophets from Jeremiah, Ezekiel, and Daniel, to Haggai, Zechariah, and Malachi, is not an end in itself but rather a place-holder and staging ground for something, indeed someone, much greater, as "the Lord, whom you seek, will suddenly come to his Temple" (Malachi 3:1) – a Lord who is anointed King, yet is somehow Priest as well.

In the 450 years between Malachi and John the Baptist, the Jews and their priests had been ruled by Persian emperors (450–330 BCE) and Greek Seleucid kings (330–166 BCE), and had seen priests of Levi's tribe, the Hasmoneans, throw off Gentile rule to reign as kings in their own right (166–63 BCE). Then they had seen their nation fall again to foreign dominion as the expanding empire of Rome took possession of their land, first under Pompey the Great and succeeding Procurators (63–37 BCE), next under the half-Edomite vassal King Herod the Great (37–4 BCE), and finally under Herod's offspring, and the Roman Governors of Judea (4 BCE–27 CE). Yet not even the Hasmoneans, priests that they were, could claim descent from the anointed royal house of David.

And the Son of David was eagerly awaited. As we have seen in the preceding chapter, the timetable of Daniel 9:23–26 could be read as yielding an appearance of the Anointed One in the third decade of the first century CE; thus, when John the Baptist came on the scene at just that time, messianic expectation appears to have been at its height. And yet, while hope for a Deliverer was widespread among the Jews, they frequently fell out over how they should live until his coming, and about what he would do when he came. The **Pharisees** (or "devout ones") saw themselves as the promoters of spiritual reform through social engagement, affirming obedience to the entire Tenakh (i.e. the whole Hebrew Bible) plus the "traditions of the elders" that eventually would form the core of the Talmud. The ancestors of later "Judaism," they were believers in the dietary and ritual law, in an eternal heaven, a hell, and the resurrection of all Jewish believers from the dead. While opposed in principle to Roman rule, they believed that spiritual righteousness would bring about the coming of Messiah, who would smash the Gentile yoke and rule the nations with a rod of iron; thus, they reluctantly complied with much Roman policy while hoping for a day of deliverance – and building their own "fences" of commentary and interpretive narrative around the precious texts of the *Torah*.

The **Sadducees** ("Sons of Zadoc," a former High Priest) were the religious party most compliant with Rome, and who benefited most from that compliance. They were a priestly caste whose wealth derived from their Temple tithes and their cooperation with the Roman rulers; they regarded only the *Torah* – the five books of Moses – as truly authoritative, and found their identity (and fortune) in Temple ritual and sacrifice, putting aside the socially demanding words of the prophets, along with any clear belief in a blessed or cursed afterlife or bodily resurrection – or a Messiah. Their rejection of these beliefs often put them at odds with the Pharisees, with whom they nevertheless shared most governing functions as Elders on the Council of the Sanhedrin.

The **Zealots**, as their name suggests, were the radicals and revolutionaries of the era, seeking the violent overthrow of Rome and the restoration of the Jewish kingdom under Messiah, who would crown their efforts at resistance to Gentile tyranny by slaying all the kings of the *goyim* and setting the Jews over the affairs of the world. Entirely opposed to the materialism of the Sadducees, they also often were at odds with the Pharisees, whose gradualism through spiritual reform they found weak and inadequate.

The **Essenes** were Jewish ascetics and mystics who, having despaired of societal reform or violent resistance, withdrew to monastic communities in the desert caves at and around Qumran by the Dead Sea. They copied and preserved their own copies of the Tanakh along with their own sacred and ritual texts, many of which were quite famously discovered in the Qumran caves in 1947, preserved in clay jars by the extremely dry climate. Their scriptural scrolls are now the oldest of all copies of the Hebrew Bible, including a complete Isaiah scroll.

Finally, the **Herodians** identified themselves wholly with the Roman tributary regimes of Herod and his descendants, abandoning even many of the religious and ritual attachments of the

Sadducees in favor of fuller accommodation with Gentile ways, and especially with Roman polit-ical goals. Loathed as apostates by the Pharisees, as sacrilegious by the Sadducees, as traitorous collaborators by the Zealots, and as completely worldly by the Essenes, the Herodians generally lived well on the benefits of their political masters, and considered that the best revenge.

First-Century Palestine

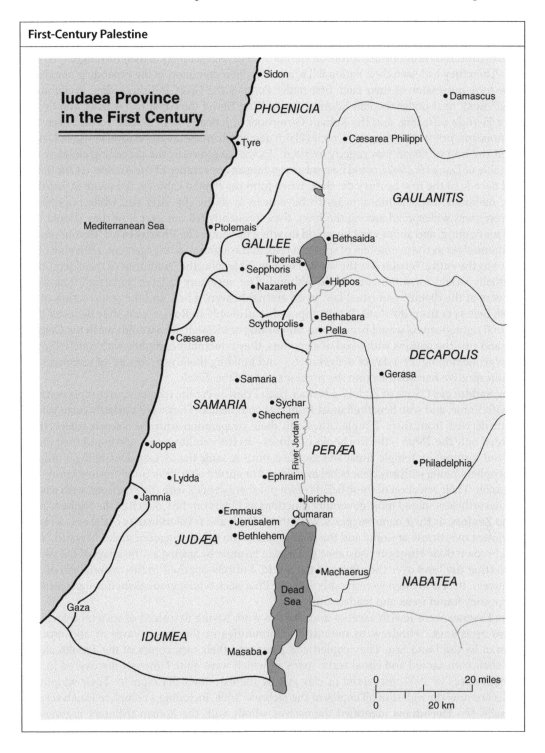

Iudaea Province in the First Century

Sidon
Damascus
PHOENICIA
Cæsarea Philippi
Tyre
GAULANITIS
Mediterranean Sea
Ptolemais
Bethsaida
GALILEE
Tiberias
Sepphoris
Hippos
Nazareth
Bethabara
Scythopolis
Pella
Cæsarea
DECAPOLIS
Gerasa
Samaria
SAMARIA
Sychar
Shechem
Joppa
River Jordan
PERÆA
Philadelphia
Lydda
Ephraim
Jamnia
Jericho
Emmaus
Qumaran
Jerusalem
Bethlehem
JUDÆA
Machaerus
NABATEA
Dead Sea
Gaza
IDUMEA
Masaba

0 — 20 miles
0 — 20 km

According to the gospels, Jesus crossed paths with these groups, often extensively, and his teachings intersected with many of theirs, though often he was at odds with each. With the Herodians he is portrayed as sharing the least, speaking dismissively of Herod Antipas (son of Herod the Great) as "that fox" (Luke 13:32), a name warranted by Herod's overt flattery of the Emperor Tiberius, his incestuous marriage to his sister-in-law/niece Herodias, and his cowardly execution of John the Baptist at her demand (Matthew 14:3–12; Mark 6:14–24; Luke 3:19, 20). In the end, though Jesus attracts some Herodians as disciples, Herod acquiesces in Pontius Pilate's crucifixion of Jesus. About as incompatible as the Herodians with Jesus are the Sadducees, against whose sharp dealings in the Temple marketplace Jesus speaks and acts with great sternness and some striking violence, overthrowing the tables of the merchants and money-changers and driving them out with a whip; furthermore, Jesus' embrace of both the Law and the Prophets, and of heaven, hell, and the resurrection, contradicts the Sadducees' severely restricted, quasi-materialist spirituality.

The Essenes are not mentioned by that name in the New Testament, but since the 1947 discovery of their documents at Qumran, many scholars have pointed out strong resemblances between their recorded practices and those of Jesus' cousin and herald, John the Baptist. Withdrawing to the desert, practicing ritual washing, living in spare simplicity, and preaching a heart-deep repentance, both the Essenes and John recall Elijah, whose return to announce Messiah is predicted at the end of Malachi's prophetic book. They come to call Israel out of its worldly, material corruption and to "prepare the way of the LORD" as proclaimed in Isaiah. Yet, unlike the Essenes, John is not building a monastic order; instead, he calls himself "a voice crying in the wilderness" (Mark 1:3) to identify "the one who will baptize you with the Holy Spirit and with fire" (Matthew 3:11) – and once he identifies Jesus as that one, he disappears from the scene, to Herod's dungeon and a headless death. It is possible that Jesus – who praised John as greatest among all the prophets (Matthew 11:11, Luke 7:28) – attracted not only many of John's baptized disciples but also some full-fledged Essenes as well, but he would have had to attract them out of their Dead Sea caves, back onto the roads and into the villages and cities of the land to preach his gospel. For Jesus' disciples, though commanded not to be "of the world," are called to be very much in it.

The fiery baptism promised by John would have appealed more literally to the Zealots, at least one of whom, "Simon the Zealot," is numbered among Jesus' original twelve "**apostles**" ("sent ones," from Greek *apostello* for "I send"). Yet to join Jesus' band, any Zealot would have to abandon his cherished hatred of the Gentiles in general and of Romans in particular; for the Master is portrayed as blessing and healing the *goyim*, including a slave at the request of a Roman centurion, and recommending going "the second mile" with Roman overlords in order to overcome evil with good. While Jesus responds to Rome's Procurator Pontius Pilate with royal dignity rather than submissiveness or craven fear, his teaching of love for enemies would have scandalized Zealots marinated in holy contempt for heathen peoples and rulers.

The Pharisees present the most extensive and ironic interactions with Jesus. They might have been expected to become fellows, or at least fellow travelers, with the Nazarene: scripturally saturated, socially engaged reformers thoroughly committed to godly living, they looked for the resurrection life of the world to come, and warned against the loss of body and soul in hell. They even proselytized among the Gentiles to win them to Israel's God – with some success. And indeed, a few of the Pious Ones (most famously Nicodemus, Joseph of Arimathea, and Saul of Tarsus) eventually joined Jesus' disciples, Joseph even providing the Master with a tomb.

But it was the Pharisees, more than any other Jewish group, who, according to the gospel narratives, laid him in that tomb. As geographical proximity often makes natural enemies, so doctrinal nearness often sparks the sharpest dissensions over difference. And as noted above, the first wedge issue was tradition: the elders' additions to the Law, the Prophets, and the Writings, additions for which Jesus reserved his most scalding scorn:

> But woe to you, Scribes and Pharisees, hypocrites! For you shut up the kingdom of heaven against men; for you neither go in yourselves, nor do you allow those who are entering to go in. Woe to you, Scribes and Pharisees, hypocrites! For you devour widows' houses, and for a pretense make long prayers. Therefore you will receive greater condemnation. Woe to you, Scribes and Pharisees, hypocrites! For you travel land and sea to win one proselyte, and when he is won, you make him twice as much a son of hell as yourselves. (Matthew 23:13–15)

Crucial to Jesus' increasing dissent from the Scribes and Pharisees, and to their finally murderous hatred for him, is their insistence on, and his refusal of, small points of non-scriptural tradition as necessary for salvation – and what he condemns as a double standard that imposes on others what they cannot keep themselves.

But underlying Jesus' many challenges to pharisaical authority is an underlying claim – implicit through most of the gospel narratives but finally explicit at each climax – about his messianic identity. We will discuss the oft-noted "Messianic Secret" motif in Section 13.4, but the central narrative irony of the larger gospel story is the irony of mistaken identity, of the "prophet … without honor … in his own country": "He was in the world, and the world was made through Him, and the world did not know Him. He came to His own, and His own did not receive Him" (Matthew 13:57, Mark 6:4, John 1:10–11). This irony assumes that this anointed prophet's "own country" includes not only Judea, or Galilee, or all of Palestine, but all the world, the "end of the earth" (Acts 1:8). So the gospels' tragic drama of incomprehension among Jewish sects at the eastern edge of the Roman Empire becomes the microcosm for all guilty human blindness in their day of visitation – but also history's greatest tragicomedy of divine love.

13.3 Synoptic and Johannine: Stereoscopic Vision Revisited

I have been speaking of the gospels as a unit, which in some sense they are, but they are by no means unitary or identical. If the Four Evangelists are Hebraic in their messianic focus, their Old Testament reference, their climactic anti-climax, and their tragicomic irony, they also enact that most Hebrew of structural devices: literary repetition. As in the Hebrew Bible, such repetition can take the form of emphatic refrain, of synonymous doubling or tripling, and of contrasting and even antithetical perspective. But are these repeating sources and their many differences to be seen as fundamentally harmonious or discordant? As clashing or stereoscopic? Clearly, the gospel writers present their diversity of viewpoint as if it were complementary rather than contradictory: Luke begins by noting that "many have taken in hand to set in order a narrative of those things which have been fulfilled among us," and offers to supplement, not to correct or refute, those accounts based on his own fuller research (Luke 1:1). Similarly, John's gospel ends by acknowledging that "Jesus did many other signs in the presence of His disciples, which are not written in this book … which if they were written one by one, I suppose that even the world itself could not contain the books that would be written" (John 20:30, 21:35). To the Old Testament stereoscopic imagination, such textual diversity would suggest rich correspondences and intentional variety in rendering from many angles the irreducible complexity of Jesus's astonishing life.

However, in Chapters 1 and 2 we discussed the reactions of nineteenth- and twentieth-century scholarship to this textual multiplicity in both Testaments. We noted the frequent modern assumption that the Bible's enumeration and variety reveal accident, not design; political and dogmatic rupture, not organic harmony; and a collision of intractable opposites, not a *discordia concors*. Greco-Roman and Anglo-Saxon ideals of non-contradiction, more recently amplified by Darwinian and Marxist theories of material and dialectic determinism, spurred a fundamentally deconstructive approach to sacred texts, and these assumptions and theories have fostered disintegrative documentary hypotheses – "JEDPR" for the Old Testament, "Q" theory and demythologization for the New.

The most obvious form of textual difference among the gospels appears among the first three – Matthew, Mark, and Luke – which seem to share a common, or **Synoptic**, viewpoint and structure, and John, the **Johannine** gospel, with its strikingly different form, vocabulary, and register of events in the life of Jesus. Thus, the Synoptics appear to follow a similar outline, while the Johannine gospel departs notably from that outline, and much New Testament scholarship since the turn of the twentieth century has sought to explain these similarities and departures. The Synoptic chronology proceeds from the baptism and temptation of Jesus and the call of his disciples, through his hometown rejection, his increasingly frequent miracles, sermons, and parables, and his Transfiguration and predictions of his death, to the events of the Passion Week: his triumphal entry, cleansing of the Temple, denunciation of the Pharisees, apocalyptic prophecies, Last Supper, arrest, trial, crucifixion, and resurrection.

While chronology plays a role in the Gospel of John, this gospel consciously stands aside from the timeline (and the parables) of the earlier gospels to reflect more pervasively on the divine identity of Jesus. John omits most of the Synoptics' incidents, and structures itself instead around the "signs" worked by Jesus, and around his "I am" sayings. Certain famous stories appear in John only: the water changed to wine (John 2), the Samaritan woman at the well (John 4), the woman caught in adultery (John 8), the healing of the man born blind (John 9), and the raising of Lazarus from the dead (John 11). Nevertheless, like the Synoptics, John's gospel tells of Jesus's baptism, the calling of his disciples, a cleansing of the Temple (though earlier in his ministry), varied miracles and healings including the feeding of the 5000, increasing confrontation with the Pharisees, and the events of the Passion Week, including his resurrection appearances.

13.3.1 Mark, "Q," and Synoptic Composition

What can we make of these clear textual similarities among the Synoptics, and the differences distinguishing John's gospel from the rest? As we noted in Chapter 2, an early twentieth-century theory of German critic Johannes Weiss sees behind Matthew and Luke a common source – German *Quelle* or "**wellspring**," thus "**Q**." Q is said to have been based on the Church's earliest oral traditions written down in the 50s and 60s CE, and to have contained the rough outline of Jesus's ministry, possibly omitting the resurrection. This outline supposedly served as a minimal framework for the additions and adornments of Matthew and Luke, who were also thought to have consulted a separately sourced Mark. John's gospel, on the other hand, has been seen by much modern scholarship as arising from a "Johannine Community" devoted to the Apostle John's legacy and memories and to have been composed a bit later, in the 90s CE.

Once the **Q hypothesis** is broached, other natural questions arise: Why are certain details included in some Synoptic Gospels and omitted in others – the birth narratives, for instance? Did Q record the minimal and mundane details of an itinerant Palestinian rabbi before the insertion of the fictional embellishments and factional struggles that are reflected in later competing gospel accounts? Some modern scholars of this "demythologization" school have written of Q as if it were something like Thomas Jefferson's famous *Life and Morals of Jesus of Nazareth*, his personally expurgated New Testament, which razored out all mentions of the miraculous, including the resurrection, retaining only the mortal deeds and the rational and ethical sayings of Jesus, which Jefferson is said to have revered above all other wisdom. But who in the first century would have valued a completely non-miraculous, disenchanted gospel narrative? The anti-supernatural Sadducees? Admirers of Lucretius? A readership of Greek Epicurean philosophers? No doubt small pockets of something like naturalist materialism existed in late antiquity, but amid the supernaturally saturated Jewish and Gentile communities at large it would have been most strange for a new religion to advertise its Messiah as a mere man sporting a scroll of wise sayings.

And, if Q actually existed, why is there no fifth gospel contained in the New Testament? That is, why would the early Church not have recorded and canonized it along with the other gospels? It does not seem likely that such an important source would be deliberately left in oblivion – especially when its inclusion would have fulfilled a famous biblical precedent: five books of Moses, five books of Psalms, and five books of Jesus. Or if such a bare-bones Q had no demonstrable separate existence, perhaps the original *Quelle* was the Gospel of Mark itself? Here, intriguingly, Mark does present one textual fact of special interest to a more secular age: its resurrection account is missing from the earliest known manuscripts, leading many twentieth-century demythologizers to suggest that this greatest of miracles was not part of original Church teaching and was added in the second century to slake the metaphysical thirst of the new faith's adherents.

But while prompted by a real manuscript absence, this larger assertion about Marcan omission makes no narrative sense: though the oldest versions leave off after Mark 16:8, before the risen Jesus appears to his disciples, they don't break off before an angelic appearance at the tomb announcing "He is risen!" Indeed, to read from Mark 1:1 through 16:8 is to read a book built increasingly around the promised death and resurrection of its protagonist, however truncated; three times Jesus predicts his demise and return (Mark 8:31, 9:31, 10:33–34), not to mention the angel's "he-told-you-so" in 16:6–7. Furthermore, the earliest manuscripts of the other gospels include the resurrection, and the other New Testament writings from Acts through Revelation assume and celebrate Jesus's rising as essential to the faith. (The very likely though mundane explanation of Mark's missing conclusion? As with many ancient books, the ends of the affected scrolls doubled as covers and eventually wore off.)

Above all, as we noted in the chapters above, by the later twentieth century these influential Old and New Testament documentary hypotheses began to run up against certain empirical limits: after more than 100 years of concerted archeological and archival search, the lack of any actual J, E, D, P, or Q documents to confirm the hypothetical ones. As with the *Torah*, there were multiple oral and textual sources preceding the known manuscripts – for those same manuscripts tell us as much. But the *Torah* tells us of the ten *Toledoth*, not J, E, D, and P, and the gospels tell us of eyewitness testimony and of many earlier accounts, not a sanitarily secular Jeffersonian "Q." None of this is to assert that because the Bible says so it must be so; only that, apart from the *Jefferson Bible* in the Library of Congress, there is no gospel text (including the Gnostic Gospels) that knows anything but a wonder-working Christ. The search for a "Jesus of history" apart from a "Christ of faith" in the extant gospels is an almost entirely speculative enterprise, though a persistent one.

13.3.2 Jesus of History, Christ of Faith?

The impossibility of separating the "historical Jesus" from the "religious Christ" *textually* is a fact that can cut multiple ways. It can be taken to mean either that the whole gospel record must be taken as entirely factual, or as fully fictional. It is beyond the scope of this book to adjudicate such a divide; a literary approach like ours takes a mediating and admittedly provisional view by asking what kinds of stories (factual or fictional) the gospels seem to be telling, in order to communicate what kinds of truth? The answer is that the four gospels as we have them, for all their many differences, tell the story of the divine Messiah entering earthly history wearing human flesh in order to serve, suffer, die, and rise. And they tell it not merely to entertain, divert, or amuse, but "that you may believe that Jesus is the Christ, the Son of God, and that believing you may have life in His name" (John 20:31).

Yet the gospels' overtly evangelical purpose does not mean that records of extra-biblical history know nothing about Jesus. The gospels' Jesus story may or may not be interwoven with fiction, but Jesus is not a figure from the mysterious mists of antiquity. He is born at a very distinct moment in a highly particular place in a careful record-keeping bureaucratic empire and among a people, the Jews, with probably the highest per capita literacy rate in the ancient world. The Jesus of the gospels walks amid historical places among actual figures, quotes carefully preserved scriptures, practices well-attested religious rituals and eats well-known meals, speaks a known tongue (Aramaic), and dies by the most brutal, and commonly feared, means that his imperial masters could devise. None of this proves that Jesus was born of a virgin or walked the waves or rose from among the dead, but these many miracles jostle cheek-by-jowl with the most ordinary details that a life in first-century Palestine could offer.

Historically, then, did Jesus exist? In a word, yes. There are enough specific textual mentions of Jesus outside the New Testament to warrant the strong conclusion that Jesus lived, spoke, and acted as a person of the first century in many of the ways described in the New Testament. In fact, if we are to reject the historicity of Jesus entirely, then to be consistent we must also reject other ancient figures who are in some ways less well-attested and yet whose existence very few doubt: figures like Socrates, Siddartha, and even Muhammad. One needn't be a Christian believer to affirm the historicity of Jesus, any more than one need be a Platonist to believe there was a Socrates, a Buddhist to believe that Gautama lived, or a Muslim to believe that Muhammad once walked the earth.

What are the evidences? First, in the initial centuries of the Common Era there are the references to Jesus in such Roman and classical writers as Pliny the Younger, Suetonius, Tacitus, and Celsus; then there are the mentions of Jesus or *Y'shua* in the Jewish writings of Josephus and the Talmud; and then there are other early mentions of Jesus in Greco-Roman writers like Thallos, Serapion, and Lucian of Samosata. Some of these references are admiring, others criticize Jesus for inspiring disobedience to Rome, and the Jewish writings typically treat Jesus as a blasphemer, a bastard, or a satanically inspired sorcerer. Second, there are the references to Jesus in the so-called "Gnostic Gospels," most of which come a good deal later than this first group and therefore reflect less on actual contact with those who knew Jesus, but rather are bent on repurposing certain early Christian teachings to fit with the mystical Neoplatonism that was widespread during the later eras of the Roman Empire.[1]

And then there are the New Testament documents themselves. The first thing to note is that, whatever we may believe about their claims, these are by far the best-attested books of any that have survived from ancient times, anywhere in the world. Compare the most famous work ascribed to Julius Caesar, *The Gallic Wars*; there is only one known manuscript of that book, dating from 900 CE, nearly 1000 years after its composition. In contrast, there are over 4000 extant manuscripts containing most or all of the canonical New Testament, many dating back to less than 100 years after the events described; indeed the earliest known fragment of John's gospel dates back to only thirty-five years after its original composition in about 90 CE. If antiquity and multiplicity count for anything, then these documents need to be taken seriously.

Furthermore, the account given of Jesus in the New Testament strikingly corresponds with the non-biblical accounts mentioned above, if we take into account that the New Testament describes sympathetically what many of these others describe with hostility. The Jesus of the gospels is born of strange and contested parentage; his teachings and actions put him afoul of both the Jewish and Roman authorities; he acquires a reputation as a miracle-worker; he makes strange claims of his own divinity (very strange for a monotheistic Jew); and finally he is put to death on a cross by the Romans with Jewish cooperation, and then disappears from his tomb a few days later. In other words, the basic outline of Jesus's life as described in the New Testament is corroborated by non-biblical sources.

Finally, and this is crucially important, the New Testament documents do not present themselves to us as legend or myth (two very popular forms in the ancient world) but as eyewitness testimony. They are not tales of "once upon a time," but accounts of specific places and times. Most of the New Testament writers claim to be retelling either what they have to some degree seen themselves (like Matthew, Mark, Luke, John, Paul, and Peter) or what others have seen and told them (like the writer of the letter to the Hebrews). We may doubt their claims, or emphasize discrepancies between their accounts. But we shouldn't doubt that these writers intended to be taken literally and historically when they describe Jesus's words and deeds, including miraculous deeds like healings and resurrections.

Thus, we come to a strange conclusion: either the New Testament writers single-handedly invented realistic fantasy fiction about 2000 years before its time, passed it off as fact, and then in many cases died by torture to defend their fantasies and lies; or they were in some measure telling the truth as they saw it, corroborated by the testimonies of many contemporaries. They didn't see everything Jesus said or did, nor do they claim to. But they do claim to have seen and known someone who said and did the most astounding things, who undid, and remade, their world, and whom they believed to be the great Jehovah in the flesh. Such an idea may fill us with puzzlement, disdain, outrage, or wonder, but when something this big, important, and strange intrudes on the historical record, we should pay close attention.

In the present book, our preferred way of paying close attention is literary analysis. The purpose of our discussion is neither religious apologetic nor anti-religious refutation, but full imaginative and interpretive engagement with the known biblical texts in context. So going forward we'll join the many biblical critics who have turned their attentions from speculative source criticism to the literary and artistic study of these texts, not as they may or even should have been, but as they now exist. We will ask of the New Testament what we did of the Old: questions about poetic form and figure, plot, characterization, repetition, and irony, and about persistent themes and narrative form. And one of the most persistent themes uniting at least the Synoptic Gospels is that of the so-called Messianic Secret, and the closely related storytelling form of the parable.

13.4   "Tell No Man": The Messianic Secret

Though the gospels begin and end with open proclamations that Jesus is the divine Messiah, they generally proceed in between more like mystery stories, but of a unique sort: stories in which the reader already has plucked out the heart of the mystery, while all the actors, save Jesus himself, discover the whole truth only at the climax. Thus, the gospel reader is treated to a perspective rather like that of God "who knows the end from the beginning": at the start we hear immediately of "Jesus Christ, the Son of David" (Matthew 1:1), "the Son of God" (Mark 1:1, Luke 1:35), and "the Word [who] was God" (John 1:1), but once the story begins we hear the great Secret-Bearer himself assiduously avoid the name of "Messiah" or "Christ" or "King," commanding the awestruck few who guess to "tell no man" (Mark 7:36).

To trace this theme of Christ Incognito through the gospels is to catalogue a series of Jesus's deliberate understatements, verbal ambiguities, and clever evasions as he sidesteps the title of "Christ" itself, while we note an increasingly marvelous string of wonders, miracles, and signs that speak in deed what he declines to say in word. For instance, Mark, though the shortest gospel, records a remarkable number of "undercover" moments in Jesus's ministry: forbidding ejected demons to reveal his identity (Mark 1:25); giving the "secret of the kingdom of God" in parables (Mark 4:11); explaining these parables to his disciples only privately (Mark 4:34); commanding the family of a girl raised from death that no one should know (Mark 5:43); healing the deaf and blind and then, ironically, ordering silence about the healer (Mark 7:36, 8:26); affirming Peter's recognition – "You are the Christ" – and "strictly warn[ing] them that they should tell no one" (Mark 8:29–30); appearing in transfigured glory to Peter, James, and John, and then forbidding them to mention it "till the Son of Man had risen from the dead" (Mark 9:9); and, after entering Jerusalem triumphantly and cleansing the Temple, refusing to tell the priests, Scribes and elders "by what authority I do these things" (Mark 11:33). Nearly all of these secret-keeping incidents appear also in Matthew, Luke, or both, and John presents an "Undercover Christ" of sorts, though differently detailed than in the Synoptics.

Christ's "Open Secret" in John?

The Gospel of John presents the Messianic Secret, though in keeping with other themes that it shares with the Synoptics, the point is made with largely different examples, and on the whole presented less emphatically. As in the Synoptics, Jesus is portrayed early in John's gospel as the divine Word unrecognized by "his own"; as one who did not trust or "commit himself" to some would-be followers because "he knew what was in man" (John 2:24–25); as a man of action letting his increasingly dramatic signs and wonders speak for themselves; as the true divine King nevertheless reluctant to be recognized too soon as such (John 6:15); and as a careful speaker generally avoiding the title of "Christ" or "Messiah," preferring the more ambiguous "Son of Man." Yet early in John's gospel, Jesus reveals his messianic identity clearly to the Samaritan woman at the well of Sychar (John 4:25–26); by John 5 he is sailing close to the wind with the Pharisees, referring to God as his "Father" (John 5:19–23); and by chapter 8 stopping just short of calling himself "Christ" by telling them that "before Abraham was, I am" (John 8:58).

Yet, throughout the gospels, and in a kind of chiastic inversion, Jesus's deeds speak louder the more that he exhorts to silence. Exorcisms, resurrections, healings of the handicapped, transfiguration, casting out the money-changers from "my Father's house" – not to mention forgiving sins, raising up cripples, walking the waves, and feeding the multitudes – this crescendo of wonders cries out that "one greater than Moses" and "before Abraham" is here, exercising God-like power. And throughout the gospels, Jesus applies to himself the richly ambiguous title "Son of Man." As we observed in Chapter 12, this phrase can mean Ezekiel's "ordinary human being" (as in Ezekiel 2:1), or Daniel's anointed Deliverer coming to receive "glory and a kingdom" and "everlasting dominion" from the "Ancient of Days" (Daniel 7:13–14).

But why a Messianic Secret at all? If Jesus came "to bear witness to the truth," why hide it? Multiple reasons suggest themselves. First, from a storytelling point of view, every narrative needs some sort of tension, some issue hanging in suspense and requiring resolution, and one of the best and most durable narrative hooks is that of the undercover investigation by a god or king in exile or disguise, whether Zeus and Hermes testing the kindness of Baucis and Philemon, or Odysseus returning incognito to Ithaca.

But a more potent factor than any narrative hook is the historic wave of messianic fervor that swept the Jews of Palestine in the first decades of the Common Era; that, as Josephus writes in

The Jewish War, "one from their country should become ruler of the world" (vi.5.4). In such an atmosphere of expectation, early identification as the Messiah would put even heavier demands on Jesus's freedom of movement, as we see illustrated in the gospels when "great multitudes" follow the healer and preacher, pressing on Jesus who repeatedly "withdraws himself" to pray in solitude (Matthew 14:23, Mark 6:46, Luke 5:16, John 6:2). Some interpreters even have seen an element of "reverse psychology" in Jesus's exhortations to secrecy, as often his very orders to "tell no man" inspire the opposite result: "Then he commanded them that they should tell no one; but the more he commanded them, the more widely they proclaimed it" (Mark 7:36).

However, the most likely reason is a testing of people's motives; Jesus asks some potential disciples whether they follow him simply "because you ate of the loaves" (John 6:26), and rebukes James and John for wanting to sit at his right and left hands in glory (Mark 10:37, 41), and to "call down fire from heaven" on the heathen (Luke 9:54–56). In Chapter 12 we have already discussed the complex messianic vision of the Hebrew prophets – Ruler or Rejected? Rod of God or Prince of Peace? Supreme Son of David or Suffering Servant? – but apparently most first-century Jews preferred the more triumphant side of the paradox, expecting the LORD's promised anointed to come and dash the nations in pieces like a potter's vessel. The gospels, on the other hand, without denying the coming Wrath of the Lamb, put the Lamb's own blood first – and thus, in storytelling terms, Jesus's whole ministry amounts to a long, painstaking redefinition of his messianic role before revealing his "true identity."

And what a moment of self-revelation! For Jesus, having brilliantly evaded charges of actionable blasphemy for three years under ever-increasing surveillance, hands his mortal enemies the perfect form of words with which to condemn him. And why would he do so at his moment of maximum vulnerability? For that is what he does: betrayed to arrest under cover of darkness by a troop of soldiers, spirited away from any friendly public to a rigged midnight tribunal intent on his death, Jesus "kept silent and answered nothing" until the High Priest asks the overwhelming question:

> "Are You the Christ, the Son of the Blessed?"
>
> Jesus said, "I am. And you will see the Son of Man sitting at the right hand of the Power, and coming with the clouds of heaven."
>
> Then the high priest tore his clothes and said, "What further need do we have of witnesses? You have heard the blasphemy! What do you think?"
>
> And they all condemned Him to be deserving of death. (Mark 14:61–64)

Strange enough for this wise and wily teacher to give up so much so quickly after so long. Stranger still to give it up with the briefest of phrases – "I am" – which echoes *Ha Shem*, *YHWH*, the name of God himself. And perhaps strangest of all, the very confession that condemns Jesus to death as a suffering sacrifice is followed by the triumphal words defining Daniel's vision of coming judgment: "And you will see the Son of Man sitting at the right hand of the Power, and coming with the clouds of heaven" (Mark 14:62, following Daniel 7:13). Thus, the bleating of the sacrificial Lamb anticipates the roar of Judah's Lion.

The most obvious effect of this Messianic Secret motif, and of Jesus's climactic unveiling, is to highlight the error of the Pharisees, who do not grasp the mystery before them, a mystery that, as Paul writes to the Corinthians, "none of the rulers of this age knew; for had they known, they would not have crucified the Lord of glory" (1 Corinthians 2:8). But the gospels portray Jesus's family, friends, and disciples as doing little better. Jesus's own brothers do not believe in him (Matthew 12:46–50, Mark 3:31, John 7:5); one disciple betrays him (Matthew 26:47–50, Mark 14:43–45, and Luke 22:47–48); his own mother Mary comes to take him home because they all said "he is out of his mind" (Mark 3:21); and all of the disciples are rendered as "slow of heart to believe in all that the prophets have spoken" (Luke 24:25). Even those who grasp the Messianic Secret early either misunderstand it – expecting the Apocalypse now – or they back-slide from the knowledge, like Peter denying "he ever knew him" (Matthew 26:72; Mark 14:69–70; Luke 22:54–57; John 18:13–27). Finally even the reader, who knows Jesus's messianic identity from the start, must absorb the shock of his shameful defeat as the prelude to his resurrection victory.

13.4.1 Parables: Kingdom Secrets, "Ears to Hear"

We have seen that each gospel narrative lives mostly in the mysterious space between the reader's opening notice that Messiah has come, and the characters' halting and varied recognitions of their visitation, and within this framing narrative strategy of suspense and deferral, no literary form thrives more fully than the parable. Parables provide that artful slant, or more correctly, the necessary curve, to slip truth past the twin sentries of popular nationalist fervor and jealous pharisaical inquisition. From Greek *parabolé* ("curve" – hence *parabola* in geometry), the typical New Testament parable is an indirect, very short story, usually with an explicit moral point, though sometimes the point is more implicit. Jesus's parables are distinct from proverbs and figurative sayings because they possess some kind of narrative plot; they also are distinct from fables or fairy tales, seldom containing elements of fantasy (Luke's parable of Lazarus being the exception). Though fictional rather than historical, Jesus's parables draw heavily upon common daily experience to present universal truths about earthly and heavenly life.

Parables are found in all four gospels, though given their close thematic association with the Messianic Secret motif, they are most frequent throughout the Synoptics, while rare in John.

Parables: By the Numbers

The exact number of New Testament parables depends somewhat on definitions. If certain brief figurative teachings or *pericopes* (from Greek "cutting-out" or "extract") are treated as parables – The Mustard Seed (Matthew 13:31–32, Mark 4:30–32, Luke 13:18–19), The Vine and the Vinedresser (John 15:1–8), the Good Shepherd (John 10:1–16) – then as many as sixty parables can be counted in the four gospels; while reckoning only with Jesus's stories, however brief, the total is closer to thirty-three in the Synoptics. Of these latter Synoptic parables, Luke contains the most (twenty-four) with eighteen of them unique to Luke; Matthew contains twenty-three, eleven of which are unique; and Mark presents eight, of which two are unique.

Relatively early in Matthew, Mark, and Luke, Jesus ties his use of parables explicitly to the "hiddenness" of his Kingdom and Kingship:

> To you it has been given to know the mystery of the kingdom of God; but to those who are outside, all things come in parables, so that
>
> "Seeing they may see and not perceive,
> And hearing they may hear and not understand;
> Lest they should turn,
> And their sins be forgiven them." (Mark 4:11–12, quoting Isaiah 6:9–10; cf. Matthew 13:11–17 and Luke 8:10)

Thus, Jesus's parables are intended strategically to be unclear, at least temporarily; yet they are not coded tests of Gnostic illumination, but rather tests of the hearer's spiritual intent. Jesus claims that those who resist his message do so not due to ignorance but to sinful pride that refuses to hear words of truth and rebuke. Yet his parables bring good news to the willing – all under the plausibly deniable cover of fiction. As in Nathan's Old Testament parable of the Ewe Lamb to adulterous King David (2 Samuel 12:1–7), parables are the serious play to "catch the conscience" of king or commoner when its guard is down, baiting the hook of faithful virtue with the delights of story.

And Jesus's stories continue to delight, and to engage the world's imagination. If you've ever described someone as "a Good Samaritan," or "a prodigal son," or simply "talented," you'll know that these parables' titles and phrases have spread past the walls of the church and even beyond the old boundaries of Christendom out into the stream of shared world culture; like the psalms, these little gems offer facets for every eye, though sometimes they bring unpleasant rebuke along with their intimations of amazing grace.

How then to read a parable? If they are for those with eyes to see and ears to hear, for what do we look and listen? Their elements are in one sense similar to those of any short story, and their demonstrated power and popularity over millennia and around the world suggest that they can float effectively free of their original settings. Yet their textual and historical contexts matter, and knowing something of these is bound to enrich our experience of the parables themselves, and of the gospel narratives that they amplify. So, in encountering a parable, it's helpful to ask the following questions: (i) What is the story's **context**? (Where and when does Jesus choose to tell the tale?) (ii) What is its immediate **audience**? (What can we know about its first hearers in its particular setting?) (iii) What is its **mode**? (Would you describe the story's details as more realistic and ordinary, or as more fabulous and fantastic from the start?) (iv) Who are the parable's **characters**, and what are they called or named? (v) How is the parable **structured**? (What patterns or repetitions appear?) (vi) What is the story's **plot**? (What expectations does it create from the start and what surprises does it deliver by the end? Is the outcome **ironic**?) (vii) What is the **point** or the "moral" of the story, and is this point explicitly stated or implicitly understated? (viii) How does the parable **advance the larger narrative** of the gospel in which it appears?

Most of these questions would be valuable when interpreting any story, but they are particularly useful when approaching tales as deeply involved in larger accounts – and in the character of the storyteller – as are Jesus's parables. Take, for instance, the Good Samaritan, which appears in Luke 10. In terms of context, by this point in Luke's gospel Jesus and his disciples are riding the crest of increasing glory and excitement. Jesus has preached throughout the country around his base at Capernaum on Galilee's north shore, healing many sick, casting out demons, raising a girl from death, feeding 5000 at a sitting, and even being gloriously transfigured in the sight of Peter, James, and John. Returning to Capernaum, he has sent "the twelve" apostles, and then seventy more disciples, out to evangelize the Galilean, Samaritan, and Judean towns, and they have returned flush with success, joyfully proclaiming that "Lord, even the demons are subject to us in Your name" (Luke 10:17).

It is in this context of public adulation that a member of Jesus's audience who is a "lawyer" (a pharisaical expert in *Torah* and tradition) steps out of the crowd and begins to examine him, asking "Teacher, what shall I do to inherit eternal life?" Jesus, quick on his feet and playing things close in the face of inquisition, simply reverses the question, asking the questioner how he reads the scripture on this point. The lawyer's answer – "'You shall love the LORD your God with all your heart, with all your soul, with all your strength, and with all your mind', and 'your neighbor as yourself'" (Deuteronomy 6:5; Leviticus 19:18) – wins Jesus's straightforward approval. But praise from the rabbi is not enough; the lawyer, we're told, wants to "justify himself" and counters with the famous question, "who is my neighbor?" (Luke 10:25–29). So Jesus tells a story.

So much for the initial questions of **context** (in Capernaum, after early evangelistic success) and **audience** (a potential religious adversary in a larger crowd of supporters and interested hearers). The **mode** of the now-famous story of "a certain man [who] went down from Jerusalem to Jericho, and fell among thieves" (Luke 10:30) seems straightforwardly realistic, as travelers along the mountain trails between the Jewish capital and the Jordan Valley would share a common fear of violent bandits in their path. As is typical in Jesus's parables, the **characters** are unnamed, and yet designated by a specific behavior or social status or other identity – ordinary Jewish traveler, thieves, priest, Levite, Samaritan, innkeeper. Also typically, the characters appear in an order that suggests a classic three-part **structure**. (In today's terms, Jesus might have begun, "three guys walk into a back alley – a priest, a Levite, and a Samaritan...") An increasingly ironic **plot** quickly emerges, as Jesus first satirizes clerical hypocrisy, with the holy men callously giving their suffering Jewish brother nothing but a wide berth – a jab likely to tweak the pious lawyer and to please the less devout Jewish laypeople in the crowd. But then Jesus turns the **irony** on the Jewish crowd's general ethnic pride, introducing the hero of the tale, a despised Samaritan. And he compounds the irony by making the Samaritan, not the beneficiary of Hebrew kindness, but the giver of kindness and a wordless rebuke to Hebrew indifference.

Thus, the **point** or moral of the story isn't only the classic Sunday School lesson that Jesus's followers should show active goodness to others, however unworthy, but also the more radical point that everyone really is "my neighbor," including the people that I naturally despise, and who may put me to shame by their more active virtue. The point is not that Samaritans are naturally good and helpful people, but that a good neighbor is any person who acts like one, and that, however nasty or benighted his background, he may be better than you or I. To get the full impact, replace "Samaritan" with some more contemporary type of person that you loathe, and then imagine him or her doing you a very good turn – even saving your life.

So "The Good Samaritan" **advances the larger narrative** of Luke by answering first the lawyer's implicit denial of universal "neighborhood" among the Jews; and second the popular Jewish denial of neighborly status to Gentiles; and third by further preparing Jesus's followers to receive a kingdom, and a king, that embrace not only the lawyers, priests, Levites, and Hebrews, but all among the nations who faithfully "show mercy" and will "go and do likewise" (Luke 10:37).

To glance more briefly at another example: the parable of the Prodigal Son appears in the **context** of increasing tension between Jesus and the Pharisees over the place of Law and grace in salvation. The mood of Luke's narrative has darkened considerably, with Jesus lamenting over hard-hearted Jerusalem in chapter 13, and issuing ever-more-pointed warnings against pharisaical self-righteousness, self-exaltation, and hypocrisy throughout chapter 14. Luke 15 begins by announcing that "all the tax collectors and the sinners drew near to him to hear him. And the Pharisees and Scribes complained, saying, 'This man receives sinners and eats with them'" (Luke 15:1–2). In this setting, in a series of three related parables, Jesus addresses this **audience** of his critics and adversaries poignantly, appealing to their better angels. In his usual realistic **mode**, Jesus resorts to the most mundane of objects (a lost sheep, a lost coin, and a runaway son) to proclaim the joy that should break out when the lost are found. The **characters** in the third and most complex of these parables are a father and his two disgruntled sons, each unhappy in his own way; indeed, the parable might more accurately be called "The Prodigal Son and his Embittered Brother."

As to **structure**, the parable takes part in what we might call "multiple multiplicity" – first, externally because it is the climactic and fullest story in a three-part sequence of "lost-and-found" tales, and second, internally because in it the younger, fugitive son repeats his penitential speech, and his case is contrasted antithetically with that of the older, grudgingly compliant brother. The parable's **plot** serves up a series of increasing surprises: first that the younger boy so flagrantly disrespects his father by demanding his inheritance, as if the father were dead; second that the father, unlike a typical Near Eastern patriarch, actually gives him the money rather than disowning him for the insult; third, that the returning wastrel is met, not by a curse, or even by a demotion to the servant's quarters, but by his father running to embrace him, giving him a ring and a robe and a banquet featuring a fatted calf; and fourth, that the apparently more reliable older son is revealed as motivated not by love or loyalty, but by anger, pride, jealousy, and greed.

Fifth, and perhaps most surprisingly, the story lacks an ending, turning outward on its pharisaical audience with the father's unresolved invitation, and implicitly challenges all the officially pious to repent of their virtues and finish the action of grace with their own lives. What will the older brothers do – the one in the story and the Pharisees listening to it? Will they turn away from the welcoming feast or join it? Will they quench their self-righteous anger and embrace joy? Thus, the **point** of the story is that, ultimately, the story points back at the hearers, **advancing the larger narrative** that the heart of the law is mercy.

Another example of Jesus's parabolic art tells of a certain rich man and a beggar named Lazarus. This parable appears to be delivered in roughly the same **context** and to the same **audience** as "The Prodigal Son"; for soon after Jesus has confronted the Scribes and Pharisees in Luke 15 with his triple call to mercy and joy, they nevertheless "derided him" because "they were lovers of money" (Luke 16:14). So Jesus tells them a story that illustrates the connections between wealth, self-righteousness, and ethnic pride, and this time its **mode** is more that of a fable, with a degree of metaphysical whimsy and bone-dry wit. The **characters**, besides the rich man (traditionally called "Dives") and the beggar Lazarus (a rare instance of a proper name in a parable), there are God's angels, Father Abraham, and (offstage) the rich man's five brothers – and Lazarus's only earthly friends, the dogs. The story is **structured** around a series of increasingly ironic reversals of fortune, and its **plot**, surprisingly, begins at the end – Death – which turns out to be a new beginning. More ironically still, the victim-hero of the piece has no lines, while the villain won't shut up, and ends foolishly debating the Father of the Faithful himself.

More specifically, Jesus begins by introducing his hearers to a wealthy Hebrew who feasts while his countryman Lazarus starves and languishes outside his door, his sores licked by dogs. Scarcely having met the cast, we're told that "the beggar died, and was carried by the angels to Abraham's bosom. The rich man also died and was buried." The latter's destination? "Torments in Hades" (Luke 16:19–23). So immediately Jesus's wealth-loving audience receives two surprises besides the narrative shock of a story that seems over before it starts: first, that a man like Lazarus who appeared cursed on earth can be blessed in the bosom of Abraham; second, that a prosperous covenant child of Abraham can nonetheless be damned. In a further rather fabulous surprise, the damned dead can somehow talk with the blessed, as the (formerly) rich man calls up across the cosmic abyss to Abraham, and in a wry twist, "Dives" in Hades still regards the beggar as his natural servant, despite their radically reversed positions: "send Lazarus that he may dip the tip of his finger in water and cool my tongue" (Luke 16:24). With a semi-compassionate shrug, Father Abraham sends his ironic regrets: the last are first now, he reminds his "son," and anyway, the damned are in a regrettably no-go zone, where "there is a great gulf fixed" (Luke 16:26).

But the dead man's never-say-die attitude persists, as he begs Abraham to send Lazarus back from bliss to visit the rich man's five heedless brothers and warn them to escape the wrath to come. "They have Moses and the prophets; let them hear them," Abraham demurs. Unwilling to take no for an answer, Dives contradicts, claiming that "if one goes to them from the dead, they will repent." Abraham closes discussion, and the lost man's fate, by pointing out that "If they do not hear Moses and the prophets, neither will they be persuaded though one rise from the dead" (Luke 16:27–31) – concluding the story and pointing back to the Pharisees by foreshadowing their hostile unbelief, even after Jesus's resurrection.

It seems likely that Charles Dickens took some inspiration from this parable for his own famous tale of a ghost warning a covetous old sinner to avoid a hellish fate by remembering that mankind is his business. Yet Jesus's story is not *A Christmas Carol* (or "A Hanukkah Hymn"!), nor does Lazarus play Jacob Marley to Dives's Scrooge. For the **point** or moral of the parable is not only that the rich man should have been his brother's keeper; it is that returning ghosts and even resurrection miracles are of no avail for Abraham's sons who will not listen to the scriptures that they claim to know and love so well. Thus, "The Rich Man and Lazarus" **advances Luke's narrative** by raising the stakes in Jesus's critique of pharisaical hypocrisy and willful blindness. Indeed the parable segues into further and more open denunciations of pious spiritual pride – such as the story of "The Pharisee and the Tax Collector" (Luke 18:9–14) – denunciations that one might call reckless, were it not for Jesus's repeated and sober certainty that his ministry is indeed reckoned to end with his death and resurrection (Luke 9:22, 13:32, 18:33).

We could continue analyzing the parables' narrative art almost infinitely and with great reward. But this book not being a commentary, we have neither time nor space to explore their riches: how the parable of "The Wheat and the Tares" (Matthew 13:24–30, 36–43) belongs to a suite of "ingathering" parables told in a **context** of increasing opposition and counsels patience as God works out his plan; how the **audience** for "The Unforgiving Servant" (Matthew 18:21–35) is a group of disciples and answers Peter's perhaps self-serving question, "How often shall … I forgive? Up to seven times?"; how the **characters** for "The Persistent Widow" (Luke 18:1–8) include an "unjust judge" who strangely presents a hostile and unsympathetic view of God by portraying him as a corrupt magistrate, yet the parable tells us to pray anyway; how "The Wedding Feast" (Matthew 22:1–14) is **structured** around repeated and increasingly violent insults to a great king seeking guests for his son's marriage banquet; how "The Unjust Steward" (Luke 16:1–15) surprises us with the **plot** twist of a dishonest manager rewarded by his master for his shrewd dealings; and how the **point** of "The Rich Fool" (Luke 12:13–21) is the vanity of "he who lays up treasure for himself, and is not rich toward God." From the first of the parables to the last, these masterpieces of indirection push Jesus's Messianic Secret about as close to full disclosure as possible without straightforward confession. The time for truth told slant has almost passed; soon all parties will prove piercing earnest, and each book of Jesus's life will recount his death.

13.5 Gospel vs. Biography: Chosen Stories of the Chosen One

Can we then call these written lives of Jesus biographies? Yes and no. On the affirmative side, whatever we may believe about the gospels' truth claims, they do present themselves as either eyewitness or secondhand accounts of a man who lived in space and time and died in particularly fraught historic circumstances with world-historical importance. They present not only a selection of his deeds, but also of his words, displaying astonishing samplings of his mind, and of the often stunned responses of family, friends, followers, countrymen, enemies, and outsiders.

Yet, on the other hand, the gospels stake no claim to the ideal modern biographer's exhaustive detail or unmoved objectivity; all of them are cheerfully partial, both in the sense of being accounts by convinced believers, as well as unapologetically selective about the stories they tell and the details they repeat. All four gospels have been described as extended Passion narratives, providing just enough background detail to make sense of the crucifixion and resurrection story at the end of each. Still, their selectivity keeps close company with their claimed truthfulness; indeed, the putative eyewitness author of John's gospel asserts his principle of inclusion and supports it with added testimony of truth: "these [things] are written that you may believe that Jesus is the Christ, the Son of God, and that believing you may have life in His name" (John 20:31); and "this is the disciple who testifies of these things, and wrote these things; and we know that his testimony is true" (John 21:24). So, with their common purpose in mind, we will turn to consider how the gospels select and arrange their frequently similar but often divergent materials for particular audiences and distinct, though closely related, purposes. As the Old Testament books of Samuel, Kings, and Chronicles choose specific stories from the massive lore of the Chosen People, so the Four Evangelists choose remarkable and often peculiar accounts from the abundant and uncontainable life of the Chosen One.

13.5.1 Matthew: Jesus, Son of Abraham

As the gospel that opens the New Testament, Matthew is emphatically written by a Jew for Jews about the Jewish *Mashiach*, "Jesus Christ, the Son of David, the Son of Abraham" (Matthew 1:1).

Matthew: Origins and Authorship

Originally composed between 60 and 80 CE, this book has from its earliest known manuscripts been called by its Greek title *Kata Matthaion*, "According to Matthew," and, though anonymous, has traditionally been associated with one of Jesus's twelve apostles, the reformed tax collector Matthew (Matthew 9:9), also known as Levi the son of Alphaeus (Mark 2:14, Luke 5:27). The book's original title suggests that at the time of composition there already were other known accounts of Jesus's life, with the author of Matthew providing a distinctly Judaic perspective for a primarily Jewish readership – indeed some ancient commentators speculated (without surviving manuscript evidence) that its original language was Hebrew or Aramaic, translated into Greek. As a tax collector Matthew/Levi would have been literate not only in Hebrew but also in Aramaic, Greek, and possibly Latin, yet he would have belonged to a despised class of economic collaborators with Rome, a factor in the accounts of his conversion in the Synoptic Gospels.

In later Christian iconography, Matthew is the first of the Four Evangelists, represented symbolically by a winged man or angel personifying the exalted humanity of Jesus Christ. (These icons of the Four Evangelists are derived from the visions of Ezekiel 1 and Revelation 4:6–9.)

Yet while deeply Jewish, Matthew is not narrowly ethnocentric, displaying along with its Jewish focus a robust prophetic attack on Jewish sin, and it points finally to the fulfilled Abrahamic promise that the Chosen People will bring a blessing to all the earth (Genesis 12:1–2), and that their Anointed One is come to be the whole world's Christ. Still, for most of its length, Matthew is notable for its particularly Semitic flavor, using more Hebrew and Aramaic loan-words than the other gospels, and employing more Hebrew euphemisms: for instance, "Kingdom of Heaven" rather than the more direct "Kingdom of God," and, at the moment of Jesus's "Great Confession" before the Sanhedrin, "You say so," an idiom for Mark's "I am" (Matthew 26:64).

13.5.1.1 *Toledoth Y'shua*: The Generations of Jesus
Like many a Hebrew chronicle, Matthew starts with a genealogy. Matthew 1:2–16 recites the ancestry of Jesus, beginning, significantly, with Father Abraham and arranged into three groups of fourteen (doubled sevens, thrice perfecting the number of perfection): the first group from the patriarchs to the first kings of Judah, the second to the fall of Jerusalem, and the third

through the exile and return to the birth of "Jesus who is called Christ." All of these ancestors, and indeed the entire book, are described in Greek as *Biblos genéseos Iesou Xristou* – "the book of the generations of Jesus Christ" – *genéseos* translating the Hebrew word *toledoth* so central, as we have seen in Chapter 6, to organizing the Book of Genesis (e.g. Genesis 2:4, 5:1). Thus, the first book of the New Testament revisits the primal structures in the first book of the Old, and going forward, the *genéseos* of Matthew are organized into five extended discourses, like a new five-part *Torah* with Jesus as the new Moses – with first the "Sermon on the Mount" (Matthew 5–7) revisiting the memory of Sinai, and each beginning with a gathering of his disciples (also 10–13, 18–20, 21–22, and 23–25).

Furthermore, though all the gospels cite the Old Testament, Matthew does so most often, and always to demonstrate Jesus' fulfillment of Hebrew national destiny and messianic prophecy. This pattern is apparent from its famous birth narrative onward: as an angel of the Lord assures Joseph of Jesus's miraculous conception, prophetic confirmation comes from Isaiah 7:14, "Behold, the virgin shall be with child, and bear a Son, and they shall call His name Immanuel," which is translated, "God with us" (Matthew 1:23); "wise men from the East" come looking specifically for the "King of the Jews" as described by Micah 5:2, which promises his birth in Bethlehem (Matthew 2:1–6); after his birth his parents escape King Herod's wrath by taking him to Egypt, so that Jesus can represent all Israel by re-enacting the Exodus – "out of Egypt I called my son" as in Hosea 11:1 (2:13–15); and Herod's "slaughter of the innocents" is presented as a terrible fulfillment of the mournful prophet's lament (Jeremiah 31:15), "a voice heard in Ramah ... Rachel weeping for her children" (Matthew 2:16–19). After John the Baptist appears as the "voice crying in the wilderness" of Isaiah 40:3 (Matthew 3:3), Jesus's baptism presents him as determined to "fulfill all righteousness" (Matthew 3:15), that is as a *mitzvah* (a righteous deed) done in a *mikvah*, or ritual bath.

Jesus soon emerges as the better Moses, going up onto the mountain to present the fulfillment of the *Torah*, fleshing out the old Commandments written in stone with new Beatitudes to be written on the heart – and distinguishing between "what was said" (mere human tradition to be corrected), what Moses has said (to be fulfilled and completed), and what "I say," the final word (e.g. Matthew 5:21–22, 27–28, 31–34). He heals a leper and requires that he go to a Levitical priest to offer a gift of Thanksgiving and keep the Mosaic command (8:1–4). He sets aside twelve apostles, a tribute to the Twelve Tribes of Israel, and sends them first only to "the lost sheep of the house of Israel" and not (yet) to the Gentiles or Samaritans (10:5–6).

But while keeping within the boundaries of Israel, he denounces the complacency and sin of Jewish towns like Chorazin and Bethsaida (11:20–24), and attacks the laxity of traditional divorce laws that exploit women (19:1–10), while he boldly steps outside the borders of tradition, announcing that "the Son of Man is Lord even of the Sabbath" as he harvests and heals on a Saturday (12:1–14). Rejected in his home town of Nazareth (13:53–58), he soon reaches out to mixed Jewish–Gentile–Samaritan multitudes in border country, praising the humble faith of a Canaanite woman whose daughter he delivers from a demon (15:21–28). As he reveals his messianic identity explicitly to his disciples, he begins to stress not his coming reign over the nations, but his death at Roman hands on a Roman cross (16:13–23). And in the midst of "transgressing" human borders and traditions, he receives the divine endorsement of transfiguration on another mountain in the supremely Jewish company of Moses and Elijah, who personify the Law and the Prophets (17:1–13).

After this moment of messianic glory, he intensifies his exhortations to service and humility, repeating his prediction of coming death in Jerusalem (Matthew 18–20). Finally, he enters David's capital in a flurry of Old Testament references and fulfillments: riding on Zechariah's donkey, hosanna'd as the Son of David, cleansing the Temple with the words of Jeremiah (Jeremiah 7:11) on his lips, citing the Psalms (Psalm 110:1) to delay or silence his critics, lamenting over the holy city like all the Hebrew prophets at once, and announcing like Daniel (Daniel 11:31, 12:11) the great destruction and tribulation to come (Matthew 21:1–8, 9–11, 12–13, 22:41–45, 23:37–39, 24:1–51).

Once captured and condemned by the leaders of his own people, and handed over to Gentiles for execution, Jesus is even shown speaking Aramaic on the cross – *Eli, Eli, lama sabachthani?* ("My God, my God, why have you forsaken me?") – as the Son of David quotes his kingly ancestor (Matthew 27:46 quoting Psalm 22:1), and his death rips open the curtain to the Holy of Holies in the Temple (Matthew 27:51), while he "fulfills all righteousness" even in burial, wrapped in clean linen and laid in a tomb on the Day of Preparation (Matthew 27:59–62). But he rises as King of Kings, "in heaven and on earth," over "all the nations" (Matthew 28:18–19).

Thus, the most Jewish of the gospels, with the greatest focus on the Old Covenant, carefully and gradually manages a transition into the New. Matthew honors Hebrew identity and uniqueness, yet incrementally shades over into universal inclusion and embrace; the book celebrates the glory of Israelite life and tradition, including that very Jewish trait of harsh self-criticism, nowhere harsher or more prophetic than in chapter 23 when Jesus sears the Scribes and Pharisees with a litany of woes that are as hot to the touch today as they were in Herod's Temple. And a book that begins by tracing the *Toledoth Y'shua* back to Abraham ends by claiming the fulfillment of the LORD's promise to the Father of the Faithful: "in you all the families of the earth shall be blessed" (Genesis 12:3). Matthew's specifically Jewish Messiah is *Yahweh's* blessing to all the earth.

13.5.2   Mark: Jesus, Son of God

Mark is the gospel written most for the Roman or Romanized reader. From its opening phrases echoing an imperial formula, through its muscular, action-oriented narrative, to its special awareness of Gentile puzzlement at Jewish phrases and ways, Mark speaks to the assumptions and values of readers who are at home with the *Pax Romana*. Yet, as Matthew honors Jewishness while challenging its failings, so Mark's fluency in *Romanitas* makes its confrontations with central Roman beliefs and practices that much more telling and remarkable. For while it overgoes even the most arrogant Roman claims about Caesar as "Son of God," this heavenly Christ born to supplant Caesar comes "not ... to be served, but to serve, and to give His life a ransom for many" (Mark 10:45).

13.5.2.1   "Render Unto Caesar": Mark and *Romanitas*

The briefest and briskest of the gospels, Mark also may be the earliest and in some sense the template for its fellow Synoptics Matthew and Luke (see box on "Mark: Origins and Authorship" and discussions of gospel source criticism, pp. 23, 337-8).

Mark: Origins and Authorship

Originally composed between 60 and 70 CE, this book has from its earliest known manuscripts been called by its Greek title *Kata Markon*, "According to Mark." Though strictly speaking the book is anonymous, it has from earliest times traditionally been associated with John Mark (*Johanan Marcus*), the half-Hebrew half-Roman missionary companion of Simon Peter, Saul/Paul, and Joseph/Barnabas – and cousin of the latter (1 Peter 5:13, Acts 12:12, 25; 13:5, 13; Colossians 4:10; Philemon 24). Though he was not an apostle, Mark's close apostolic associations have bolstered the traditional authority of the book, which is probably the earliest of the known gospels and regarded by many as a source or template for the other two Synoptic Gospels Matthew and Luke. (See discussions of Mark in relation to source criticism and "Q" theory, pp. 23, 337-8.)

As part Roman, John Mark is said to have served as Peter's Latin interpreter, and Mark's gospel certainly shows significant engagement with Roman ideas and attitudes. It is famed for its Roman directness and conciseness; indeed it may include an oblique and unflattering reference to the evangelist himself in Mark 14:51–52 as the "certain young man" who, at the time of Jesus's arrest, eluded capture by leaving his linen garment and running away naked. Similarly, if Peter is indeed the main source for many of the recorded deeds of Jesus, Peter's flaws and failings are on remarkably frank display in this gospel, as in the later Synoptics. Acts 15:36–41 also records a falling out between Paul and Barnabas over Mark's fitness to serve – though 2 Timothy 4:11 shows that division eventually healed. Thus, Mark and the gospel bearing his name are presented to us as simple, unvarnished sources of actionable truth.

In later Christian iconography, Mark is the second of the Four Evangelists, represented symbolically by a winged lion portraying the royal courage and power of the risen Christ.

Its action begins, as the Romans would say, *in medias res*, "in the midst of things," with John the Baptist dressed like Elijah and announcing the "one" who will bring the long-awaited Way and Day of the LORD (Mark 1:2-8, citing Isaiah 40:3 and Malachi 4:5). But as we have noted, this action is prefaced by a single verse, Mark 1:1: "The beginning of the good news of Jesus Christ, the Son of God." This apparently straightforward statement is more layered than it sounds: it not only announces a beginning, but appropriates and repurposes a formula of Roman emperor-worship. Most Mediterranean peoples at the beginning of the Common Era, even at the Far Eastern end of Rome's empire, would recognize a Greek phrase like this: *arché tou euaggeliou tou Augoústou Kaísarou huiou tou theou*; "the beginning of good news of Augustus Caesar the son of the god." Statues and monuments were engraved with words like these honoring Augustus's "descent" from his adopted father, the "divine Julius"; the Emperor's birthday was celebrated as "the beginning of good news" brought by the imperial "savior"; and imperial decrees from the "divine Tiberius," the current emperor, began by proclaiming the heavenly source of their *euaggelion*/evangelion/gospel. So when Mark's narrative begins by announcing its world-altering "good news" emanating not from a divine Roman Caesar but from a divine Jewish Messiah, its statement is not only theological but unavoidably political. Theologically, it is a shock to the profoundly monotheistic Hebrew imagination that the Most High could lower himself to become human, but politically, this message puts the Roman world on notice that their Lord Caesar has a rival in the Lord Jesus.

Probably the most striking quality of the narrative that follows is how constantly it "cuts to the chase," describing the succession of Jesus's deeds with as little elaboration as possible. We already have seen above that Mark's account of Jesus's ministry, while thoroughly interwoven with the miraculous and supernatural, reads rather like a "bare-bones" account in comparison to Matthew, Luke, and especially John. Mark's signature word is "immediately" (Greek *euthus*), which occurs thirty-six times from chapter 1 to the start of chapter 15, when the Sanhedrin hands Jesus over to Pilate to suffer during the last two chapters in somewhat slower time – as if this "extended Passion narrative" were especially eager to get the Son of God up on the cross for all the world to see.

Thus, in Mark, Jesus is a kind of young man in a hurry, with a focus more on deeds than words. Whether being led out "immediately" to be tempted, or "immediately" calling disciples or healing the sick or casting out demons or walking the waves, Jesus is constantly "on task" in a manner that would be admired by any Roman soldier or official with orders to execute. In Mark the wicked also are especially purpose-driven, with villains from Herodias, Herod, and the Pharisees to Judas and the Sanhedrin doing their evils "immediately," serving up severed heads, murder plots, traitor's kisses, and crucifixion with dispatch. Thus, the world-shattering story of God's Son come in common flesh and nailed to a pair of cross-poles in the sun is delivered with the lightning directness of a javelin's throw or a legion's charge, as an act of Providence so certain that it feels over almost as soon as it's begun.

If Mark's economy of effort speaks to *Romanitas*, so does its accommodation of Roman ways and Latin terms. While treating the Old Testament with scriptural respect, Mark relies much less on quoting it than does the Hebraically themed Matthew. Though writing in the Greek *lingua franca* inherited from Alexander's empire, Mark (part Roman himself, and a translator) uses Latin phrases and interprets the ways of the East, and of the Jews, for the empire of the West. He explains Jewish ceremonial washing customs (Mark 7:2–4); he translates certain Greek terms to Latin and uses Latin terms without comment (5:9; 6:27; 12:15, 42; 15:16); he interprets Hebrew and Aramaic phrases (5:41; 7:11, 34; 14:36); and he uses Roman rather than Hebrew ways of telling time (6:48; 13:35). In short, a cultural amphibian like Mark can anticipate points of Roman confusion, and smooth the way for understanding.

But what, after all, does Mark most want his Romanized reader to understand? It is one thing to honor Rome's laconic efficiency and forestall inter-cultural confusion, but it is quite another to begin the book by appropriating an imperial formula about the divine Son and then end that Son's life with execution on a Roman cross. For the cross was, along with the republican *fasces* and the imperial eagle, among the most potent of Roman emblems. The cross is now so familiar to many of us as a Christian symbol of mercy and redemption that we easily forget how to Mark's first readers it was a sign of the ultimate sanction brought by *Romanitas*, and the threat of terror that supported its laws – perhaps even more so than Rome's great roads, aqueducts, theaters, baths, and sewers. As with the revelation of the Messianic Secret in the Synoptics, it is strange enough to declare that the divine Caesar has a cosmic rival in a Jewish "Son of God" (a claim bolstered in 1:1, 11; 3:11; 5:7; 9:7; 13:32; and 14:36, 61–62); it is stranger still to portray for a Romanized audience that rival tortured and killed *by Romans* at the insistence of his own people; and it is strangest of all that this murdered Son of God should have said that his divine purpose was in fact not to be served, but to serve and to die as a ransom, and then to rise (10:33–34, 45). The way of the world, including the Roman world, is that God-Kings rule, and the people serve; this Servant-God-King would invert that natural order.

How then is the Roman reader to take Mark's message? On the one hand, this Suffering Servant presents no direct threat to Caesar, especially since he has told his followers to "render unto Caesar" (12:17), and even Pilate can find no fault in him until an angry mob intimidates him into ordering the crucifixion (15:13–15). Yet on the other hand, what greater threat to the divine Caesar could there be than this Son of God's assertion that the State is not ultimate, but accountable in this world and beyond to a higher Law; that in the end even Caesar must render unto God? Thus, Mark's servant Son of God foments the greatest of all political revolutions: by refusing an earthly kingdom, he models that all earth's states and kingdoms and politics ought not to be served, but instead serve.

13.5.3 Luke-Acts: Jesus, Son of Adam

As Mark's gospel reaches out to Romanized Gentiles, Luke's gospel and its companion, the Acts of the Apostles, looks past the military boundaries and political institutions of Rome's empire to the greater cultural empire of the Greek, or Hellenistic, world, a much broader Gentile realm dating back four centuries to the time of Alexander the Great. Alexander's military conquests had stretched south from Macedonia in Greece to Egypt and eastward to India, and his Greek language all the way to the "Pillars of Hercules" in the western Mediterranean; and while his empire's political unity had collapsed after Alexander's death in 323 BCE, Hellenistic language, aesthetics, religion, and philosophy still bound this loose-knit sphere with innumerable imaginative ties as important as the coercive sway of Rome. By using common, or *koiné*, Greek, all of the New Testament writers participate in this greater **Hellenosphere**, but Luke-Acts does so most thoroughly and eloquently. If Matthew addresses specifically Jewish interests and Mark particularly Roman ones, Luke-Acts speaks to humanity in its broadest sense, and on the most expansive scale among the five New Testament histories. Without in any way denying Jesus's identities as Son of Abraham and Son of God, Luke writes of a deeply human Son of Adam. Yet this new Adam comes to reverse the effects of the first Adam's sin, and to bring redemption to every tribe and tongue under heaven.

Luke-Acts: Origins and Authorship

This matched set of two books has from its earliest known manuscripts been attributed to Luke, a Greek physician from Antioch and traveling companion of Saul/Paul on his later missionary journeys. Luke's gospel, the longest of the four, may draw on Mark's, and Acts ends with Paul still alive and under house arrest in Rome (tradition says that Paul died in Nero's great persecution of 64 CE). If taken at face value, these details yield a plausible composition window of 61–64 CE, well before the destruction of the Temple in 70 CE – which Luke does not mention except as prophecy. The gospel always has been called by its Greek title *Kata Loukon*, "According to Luke," and the Book of the Acts of the Apostles (*Praxeis ton Apostolon*) comes from the same fine Greek stylist and is addressed to the same reader, Theophilus, and its title imitates accounts of the *Praxeis* or "Deeds" of other great men in Greek antiquity. Circumstantial evidence for Lucan authorship seems very strong, because in Acts 16:6 the author joins Paul's missionary band and from then on the narrative shifts mainly to the first person plural "we"; and in Colossians 4:14, 2 Timothy 4:11, and Philemon 24 Paul writes specifically of Luke, "the beloved physician," as present with him.

Nevertheless, much contemporary source criticism of Luke has tended to discount this internal textual evidence and propose a somewhat later date of 80–90 CE, while emphasizing the supposedly frequent contradictions between Luke-Acts and Paul's letters, especially in the multiple retellings of Paul's conversion in each. Though Luke knew Paul, he probably had not read all of his letters, and Luke and Paul would be expected to tell and retell certain stories each in his own way. We will take up the question of Paul's epistles in Chapter 14, but suffice it to say that, as in our earlier discussions of Old Testament textual doubling, one person's "contradiction" is frequently another person's "complementarity." Insisting on absolute unanimity among substantially similar accounts presents a standard unique to modern biblical scholarship; courts of law and ordinary historical studies willingly tolerate reasonable degrees of variability based on point of view and intended audience, without asserting actual contradiction or fabrication – which at this historical distance are often as difficult to prove as any religious doctrine of textual infallibility.

As a Greek, Luke comes by his Hellenistic Gentile focus naturally, and as a physician, he shows special attention to medical conditions, and particularly to female concerns, suggesting that he may have had a practice among women, or at least in what we would now call "family medicine." As a recounter of Jesus's deeds, he acknowledges that he is not the first, but affirms that he has done his own original research, interviewing "those who from the beginning were eyewitnesses and ministers of the word" and promising his reader "an orderly account … that you may know the certainty of those things in which you were instructed" (Luke 1:1–4). Although Luke records some of the greatest parables and fables ever told, neither Luke nor Acts presents itself to us as fable or myth, but as "certainty" with "infallible proofs" (Acts 1:3).

In later Christian iconography, Luke is the third of the Four Evangelists, represented symbolically by a winged ox or bull, portraying the strength, service and sacrifice of Jesus Christ. And in Luke-Acts the perfect humanity of the Son of Adam declares salvation to every human "in Jerusalem, and in all Judea and Samaria, and to the end of the earth" (Acts 1:8).

13.5.3.1 "Most Excellent Theophilus": Luke's Testimony

Of the four gospels, Luke begins with the most specific statement of its intended audience: *kratiste Theophile*, "most excellent Theophilus" (Luke 1:3). And yet this specificity brings its own mysteries. A minority of interpreters see Theophilus ("friend of God") as an honorific title complimenting either an unnamed or generic reader for his fair-minded spiritual interest. However, the other honorific, *kratiste*, is applied elsewhere in Luke-Acts, and in other non-biblical literature, to specific powerful officials: "most excellent Felix" (Acts 24:2) and "most excellent Festus" (Acts 26:25), leading many other commentators to suggest that this Theophilus was an important Roman, the name or nickname "Theophilus" being fairly common in the first-century world. Was he Paul's lawyer in Rome? Was he perhaps Titus Flavius Sabinus, the brother of the future Emperor Vespasian and a Prefect of Rome under Claudius and Nero? Or was he perhaps a powerful Jew – the former High Priest Theophilus ben Ananus (reigned 37–41 CE), or the future High Priest Mattathias ben Theophilus (65–66 CE)? Or was he some now-forgotten officer of the empire reviewing the new movement's testimony to the life of Jesus and the acts and travels of his disciples? In any case, he seems to have been someone whose good opinion, and perhaps financial support, Luke thought very much worth having, since he is the dedicatee not only of Luke but of Acts (Acts 1:1).

What then would Theophilus expect to be told, and what would Luke want him to know? Luke writes as to a practical, open-minded, and potentially sympathetic reader, one who will be interested in an "orderly account" based on the testimony of "eyewitnesses" that will establish "the certainty of those things in which you were instructed" (Luke 1:2–4). Luke thus mixes modesty with confidence: his is not the first or only account of Jesus's life and deeds, but it is the longest of the four gospels, and it will add further reliable information to what others already have spoken and written. And, as the graceful Greek style of the dedication promises, Luke will deliver this narrative with an eye toward wonder and beauty.

13.5.3.2 Discoursing Wonders: Luke and the Marvelous

And from the beginning, Luke discourses wonders. If "immediately" is a key word in Mark, "marvel" in its varied forms is a key to Luke-Acts. While miracles abound in all the gospels, Luke records the awestruck response of witnesses about twice as often as do Matthew or Mark or John, and this is especially true in Luke's nativity story. He sets the stage for the coming universal "Son of Adam" and "Son of God" with a background story about a locally Jewish son of Aaron, the elderly, childless priest Zacharias, who leaves his barren old wife Elizabeth to minister according to his appointed rounds by burning incense in the Jerusalem Temple. While mediating for the people before God, Zacharias is shocked and skeptical when an angel from the Ancient of Days speaks into the present moment with news too good to be trusted.

The news would be strangely familiar to a devout Jew: like Abraham's Sarah, infertile Elizabeth will bear him a son in her old age; like the Nazirite Deliverer Samson the boy will "drink no wine nor strong drink"; like Malachi's returning Elijah he will "turn the hearts of the fathers to the children"; and like Isaiah's great herald he will "make ready a people prepared for the Lord" (Luke 1:13–17; Genesis 21:2, Judges 13:7, Malachi 4:6, Isaiah 40:3). The note of fulfillment is unmistakable, but Zacharias seems deaf to it, instead demanding confirmation. The angel's reply sounds quietly affronted: "I am Gabriel, who stands in the presence of God," and the messenger confirms his "glad tidings" with a sign by striking the soon-to-be father temporarily dumb. Yet even with this impediment, Zacharias manages to find his way home and get his Elizabeth with the prophesied, prophetic child.

Meanwhile, compounding this marvel, six months later Gabriel is posted to Nazareth in Galilee, to Mary, a young unmarried cousin of Elizabeth's from the house of David. He announces to this astonished adolescent that surpassing even Elizabeth's barren-born John, she will conceive and carry the virgin-born Jesus, without the seed of her betrothed Joseph. The maiden's child will be named for the great conqueror Y'shua/Joshua; the boy is destined to rule from the throne of David over the house of Jacob, begotten and filled by the Holy Spirit, and he will be called "the Son of God"; "for nothing will be impossible with God." Mary's response contrasts sharply with Zacharias's: "Behold the maidservant of the Lord! Let it be to me according to your word" (Luke 1:26–38).

Narrative intensity builds as these two expectant women on the opposite ends of life come together, like planets aligning to announce the dawn of a new age. Mary travels to Judah, and is scarcely in at Elizabeth's door before the unborn John "leap[s] in her womb"; then Elizabeth is inspired to announce the divine identity of Mary's child, and to praise "the mother of my Lord" as "she who believed" (unlike her doubtful and now speechless husband). Marvels multiply in living paradox: the blossoming crone, the conceiving virgin, the prophetic fetus, the silenced patriarch, and women triumphant.

A New Song: Christian Psalms

Luke's gospel, the most literary in its Greek style, collects not only the largest number of Jesus's parables, but also a number of what we might call "New Testament psalms." Even when not composed in Hebrew, the parallelistic psalm form translates well into other languages, and Luke's beloved songs are now often known by their opening words from the old Latin Vulgate translation: the *Magnificat* of Mary ("My soul magnifies the Lord," Luke 1:46–55), the *Benedictus* of Zacharias ("Blessed is the Lord God of Israel," Luke 1:68–79), the *Gloria in Excelsis* of the nativity angels ("Glory to God in the highest," Luke 2:14), and the *Nunc Dimittis* of Simeon ("Lord, dismiss now your servant in peace," Luke 2:29–32). In particular, the *Magnificat*, like the Old Testament songs of Hannah (1 Samuel 2:1–10) and Deborah (Judges 5) celebrates the world-altering power of God intervening in the lives of downtrodden people, and especially women (Luke 1:46–52). Set to music countless times, from ancient chants and medieval plainsong through Renaissance motets and protestant psalters to baroque oratorios and popular choruses, the sounds of these first Christian hymns have gone out to all the earth, and their words to the end of the world.

This birth narrative achieves its semi-climax with the delivery and circumcision of Elizabeth's son. There is a hint of humor in the misunderstanding that breaks out over the boy's name: the well-meaning but meddling neighbors and relatives would overrule Elizabeth and insist on patriarchal tradition in favoring "Zacharias," but the voiceless father comes to his wife's aid, writing "His name is John" on a tablet, and he receives his voice, and his only son, as his reward. A disagreement dissolves into awe and celebration, and happy irony reigns.

The gospel's opening mood of marvel reaches its climax, though, in the birth of Jesus. How will a child conceived in Nazareth of Galilee come to be born in Bethlehem of Judea? What will be the setting of his birth? Who will attend the Christ at his delivery? How will his coming be announced to the world? The answers to these questions may seem obvious or cliché to us, who even in a more secular age know the story time out of mind. Of course Messiahs are born in mangers, we think; of course the common people see what the mighty can't understand; of course God chooses the lowly to shame the proud. That's his job.

But what's most striking about Luke's birth narrative is not its humble situation (there are, as we have seen, plenty of Old Testament precedents for neglected, ignored, outsider heroes), but the sheer, grinding degradation of the circumstances juxtaposed with such an astonishing burst of heavenly glory. Luke's "Son of Adam" comes into a world that, as the poet Gerard Manley Hopkins puts it, is "bleared, smeared with toil," one that "wears man's smudge and shares man's smell" to the highest and lowest degree (see "God's Grandeur," ll. 5–8). First, Jesus enters life in the toils of a heartless, far-flung bureaucratic empire – which nevertheless serves God's purposes to the letter. It is a "decree ... from Caesar Augustus" that uproots Mary and Joseph from their Galilean town and forces them on a difficult journey to their ancestral home of Bethlehem, all in order to be registered for greater taxation; yet this coerced relocation, adding insult to injury, fulfills the ancient prophecy of Micah 5:2 (Luke 2:1–6). Second, this traveling couple scrape rock bottom in their accommodations, walking a kind of *Via Dolorosa* through Bethlehem, apparently rejected by the local inn and compelled by Mary's labor pains to take shelter in some barn or cave or outbuilding with no place but a feeding trough to lay the child. Yet this girl on the ground in the dark, alone except for her husband (who is not the father) is "the maidservant of the Lord" (Luke 2:7).

Third, the first witnesses to the birth are the lowest of society's low: stinking, itinerant, marginal men, shepherds on the night shift. Yet it is they who are visited by the great angel band, the "multitude of the heavenly host" announcing glory and peace and "goodwill toward men" – toward all humanity, starting at the bottom with them. They are in a holy terror, and yet are told to seek out a baby in a manger and meet their long-expected Savior (Luke 2:8–14). They do as they are told, without question, and find the results more than satisfactory. Finally, this news from an angelic choir is then passed on not by Temple cantors or palace heralds, but by word of mouth from wandering shepherds, entering into local lore and waiting three decades for the re-appearance of Elizabeth's and Mary's sons, grown to manhood. "And all those who heard it marveled" (2:15–20). Among those who marveled the most, when the child is presented at the Temple, are an old man and woman named Simeon and Anna, who represent all ancient Israel waiting for its coming King, and now are able to "depart in peace" – but not before Simeon summarizes the entire topsy-turvy nativity by telling Mary that "this Child is destined for the fall and rising of many in Israel," and that "yes, a sword will pierce through your own soul also, that the thoughts of many hearts may be revealed." The child brings a new order of things, not only upside down, but inside-out (2:21–35).

As a kind of coda to this wondrous birth story, and as a preface to the arrival of the grown Messiah, Luke delivers one more account from Jesus's youth, when at twelve years old, on his family's annual Passover visit to Jerusalem, he is separated from his party and is found three days later at the Temple, conversing with the old teachers as with his peers, amazing all by his wisdom and comprehension. He has a brief but fraught exchange with Mary, who sounds like any mother scolding her son for giving her such a fright. But his response is coolly preternatural, especially coming from a boy a year shy of his *bar mitzvah*: "Why did you seek me? Did you not know that I must be about my father's business?" Certainly not Joseph's carpentry business; and Mary, of all people, should have known – but in a kind of reverse wonder, she and Joseph who were more than present at his wondrous birth "did not understand the statement which he spoke to them." Yet, after their return to Nazareth, Jesus "was subject to them, but his mother kept all these things in her heart" (2:41–51).

After these wonders, twenty years roll by, and as Jesus's adult cousin John returns to the scene, Luke again locates events not in Wonderland, but in a particular place at a specific moment in history:

> in the fifteenth year of the reign of Tiberius Caesar, Pontius Pilate being governor of Judea, Herod being tetrarch of Galilee, his brother Philip tetrarch of Iturea and the region of Trachonitis, and Lysanias tetrarch of Abilene, while Annas and Caiaphas were high priests ... (3:1–2)

That is to say, it is not only what we now call the year 28–29 of the Common Era, but in a land under the discordant rule of a depraved libertine emperor, a feckless hack of a colonial governor, an incestuous princeling and his jealous brother, and two rival high priests. The ancient kingdom of David and Solomon has been farmed out and subdivided between jobbing tetrarchs, imperial apparatchiks, and local collaborators.

And John's message is perfectly tailored to the moment: "Brood of vipers! Who warned you to flee from the wrath to come? Therefore bear fruits worthy of repentance, and do not begin to say to yourselves, 'We have Abraham as our father'. For I say to you that God is able to raise up children to Abraham from these stones" (3:7–8). John gives no more indulgence to Jews than to Gentiles: each in his station must repent and do what comes unnaturally, such as giving one's extra coat to a needy neighbor, or collecting only a fair tax, or laying off the soldier's extortion racket (3:10–14). Surprisingly, this scathing message attracts multitudes, and even more surprisingly, the preacher refuses to capitalize on the demagogic opportunity, dismissing out of hand any claim to be the Christ, and pointing instead to one "whose sandal strap I am not worthy to loose. He will baptize you with the Holy Spirit and fire" (3:16). But some things never change: the speaker of these bold words soon will be cast into prison by the powers that be, in this case King Herod called out for his liaison with his rival brother's wife.

Yet before John disappears into the dungeon, his mission culminates when his cousin Jesus comes down to the waters with the multitude: "When all the people were baptized, it came to pass that Jesus also was baptized; and while He prayed, the heaven was opened. And the Holy Spirit descended in bodily form like a dove upon Him, and a voice came from heaven which said, 'You are my beloved Son; in you I am well pleased'" (3:21–22). Including himself with the common mass of ordinary sinners, Jesus is nevertheless highlighted by a heavenly sign. As we have already observed about the Messianic Secret throughout the gospels, it appears as a kind of chiastic inversion: the more Jesus seeks the modesty of the crowd, the more he stands out.

Of the many miracles narrated by Luke, seven are unique to this gospel – and significantly, since recounted by a Greek medical man, six are miracles of healing performed for marginal or downtrodden folk or Gentiles: the first miraculous catch of fish (5:1–11), the centurion's servant healed (7:1–10), the widow of Nain's son raised from the dead (7:11–16), the crippled woman and the man with dropsy both cured on the Sabbath (13:10–17, 14:1–6), ten lepers made whole (17:11–19), and a man's ear restored, even during Jesus's arrest (22:49–51). The lowly objects of Jesus's mercy add significantly to the wonder involved, and ironically Jesus himself wonders – both times at Gentiles: first at the faith of a Roman centurion, and second at the Samaritan leper, the only one of ten to return and offer thanks.

Indeed, from its opening angelic promise of "peace on earth, good will toward men" (2:14) to Jesus's final command that "repentance and remission of sins should be preached in his name to all nations" (24:47), this gospel of the "Son of Adam" makes it exceptionally clear that the Jewish Christ has come for all peoples and to burst all boundaries "beginning at Jerusalem" but expanding to Judea and Samaria and to the end of the earth. And Luke shows Jesus bursting bonds as well, for while his deepest concern is with the sinful captivity of the heart and the oppressions of the soul, like Isaiah he also proclaims "liberty to the captives and … those who are oppressed" (4:18), countering the wealth-worshiping spirit of the times by blessing the poor and calling woe on the rich (6:20, 24). Perhaps foremost among those to be liberated by the Son of Adam are the daughters of Eve, to whom Luke devotes an unusual amount of attention: from Elizabeth, Mary, and Anna in the birth narratives of chapters 1–2 and the bereaved widow and repentant prostitute in chapter 7, through Jesus's female disciples in chapter 8, his friends Mary and Martha in chapter 10, and the crippled woman in chapter 13, to the women wailing Jesus to the crucifixion in chapter 23 and then running with joy to bring news of the empty tomb in chapter 24. It is women's faith and women's love that often drive the narrative, and frequently despite male folly and failure. In cultures as frequently misogynist as the Greco-Roman and the first-century Judaic, Luke's exceptional concern for the female is a marvel in itself.

Luke's concluding wonder, following the resurrection, is the tragicomic story of two disciples on the road to Emmaus, a village about a day's walk west of Jerusalem (Luke 24:13–35; cf. Mark 16:12–13). A perfect encapsulation of the Messianic Secret motif, it also resembles the stories of Abraham and the angel of the LORD in Genesis 18, or the Greek myth of Baucis and Philemon encountering Zeus and Hermes. Like these accounts, the Emmaus story depends for its effects on a deity or prince (and Jesus is both) going incognito questing for truth and testing his people. As with other tragicomedies, the narrative assumes a context of grief, in this case the recent grisly death of Jesus in Jerusalem, and plays mortal ignorance off against divine comprehension, with the reader pleasantly in on the secret as happy ironies multiply. A playful tone is established immediately as Jesus, miraculously unrecognizable to the two disciples on the road, asks with apparent innocence why they are so sad, and receives an incredulous scolding for not knowing the biggest news of the year, and then a schooling in the doings and death of this tragically disappointing prophet. In such tragicomic tellings, the delight lies in wondering how long the blessed ruse will last, and the dullness of the disciple Cleopas and his friend makes for a long, slow reveal – until "their eyes were opened and they knew *him*, and he vanished from their sight" (24:25–31).

So the crescendo of wonder that characterizes Luke climaxes with sudden revelation and disappearance – two of the most stunning effects in a magician's repertoire – to be topped at the very end by a doubling of both marvels. First Jesus, having vanished from Emmaus, reappears as abruptly in Jerusalem, standing "in the midst" of the disconsolate disciples. But far from being faithfully joyful, instead "they were terrified and frightened, and supposed they had seen a spirit," which is a misconception only corrected when Jesus invites them to look at his wounds, embrace his body, and give him a snack of "broiled fish and some honeycomb" (24:36–43). (Throughout the New Testament, and nowhere more than in Luke, the risen Son of Adam is portrayed as robustly human and physical, yet also miraculously spiritual: on the one hand bearing scars, touching friends, eating and drinking, while on the other hand immortally strong and able to come and go instantly through material obstacles and over large distances.)

Jesus's last disappearance, like the one just previous, takes place among, and to benefit, his disciples, though in a much larger group. After a last Bible lesson that "all things must be fulfilled which were written in the Law of Moses and the Prophets and the Psalms," he tells them to wait in Jerusalem "until you are endued with power from on high" by the Holy Spirit. Then he "was parted from them and carried up into heaven," leaving the story literally "in the air" as his followers return to the capital to wait (24:44–53). If ever a book called out for a sequel, Luke does.

13.5.3.3 Acts of the Holy Spirit: "The World Turned Upside Down"

That sequel, as its title "the Acts of the Apostles" suggests, is a book of action, and its action begins, literally, where the Gospel of Luke leaves off, with Jesus's heavenly Ascension. What the third gospel leaves implicit in Christ's leave-taking last words, Acts makes explicit. When the disciples ask about when he will "restore the kingdom to Israel," he answers that theirs is, as usual, the wrong question: "It is not for you to know times or seasons which the Father has put in his own authority." But then he answers the question that they should have asked, one not about ethnic political power, but about the spiritual power to advance a new universal realm of mercy: "you shall receive power when the Holy Spirit has come upon you; and you shall be witnesses to me in Jerusalem, and in all Judea and Samaria, and to the end of the earth." Then he is taken up into a cloud, leaving them gaping until two angels nudge them back to their present duty with a promise about the future: "This same Jesus, who was taken up from you into heaven, will so come in like manner as you saw him go into heaven" (Acts 1:6–11).

Thus does the risen Jesus deliver the working outline for the Acts of the Apostles: its opening chapters 1–7 focuses on the expansion of the new movement in Jerusalem; then in chapters 8–12 the outbreak of a great persecution scatters most of the Church throughout the provinces of Judea and Samaria; followed by the explosion in chapters 13–28 of missionary "witnesses" first through the eastern Mediterranean, then to Asia Minor and Greece, and finally to Italy – sending the gospel on its way toward Ethiopia to the south, the Pillars of Hercules to the west, and in all directions to "the end of the earth." Jesus's farewell speech provides not only the centrifugal storyline but also the sacrificial, bottom-up ethos of the mission; significantly, the word "witnesses" is the Greek *martyres*, so that by the middle of the Book of Acts, the Jews and Greeks of Thessalonica are calling Paul and Silas "[t]hese who have turned the world upside down," and are either joining the Christian witnesses or seeking to "martyr" them (17:6). Finally, Jesus lays out not only a mission and a method, but also promises the necessary *dynamis* or "power" in the coming of the Holy Spirit, spoken of throughout Acts as a self-effacing divine person who carries on all that "Jesus began to do and teach" (1:1–2).

So over and again in Acts, as in the gospels, the marginality, calamity, and chaos that afflict Jesus and his followers turn out to advance a serene divine plan, as the unlikeliest and indeed most hostile events and persons become instruments to serve God's ends. There is paradox aplenty: the book begins with an ending (the Ascension), and ends with a beginning (an apostle entering yet another city to preach). Its action, initially set in Jerusalem at the eastern edge of Caesar's empire, has by its conclusion arrived in Rome, the center of the Western world. The Church, at first an obscure Jewish sect made up of a few bereaved disciples, grows to a majority-Gentile faith spreading to hundreds of thousands around the Mediterranean. Persecution and martyrdom (again, the latter concept has its origins in Acts) do not crush the new religion, but instead empower and spread it.

And as to God's mortal instruments, at first it may seem that the protagonist will be Peter, or then Stephen, or even Philip, while the emerging villain of the piece appears clearly to be Saul of Tarsus, but before the book is half-done, this lethal super-Pharisee is converted and transformed into the apostolic protagonist, renamed Paul, who in chapters 13–28 is sent on inspired and dangerous journeys to ever-farther places and peoples. Yet as the story develops around this protagonist, its true hero emerges above, before, and yet after all: the most intimate and pervasive and active of the book's many actors, that same "Holy Spirit." Along the way, Theophilus (and we) will read much, as in Luke's gospel, about the sick healed and the dead raised, about the word proclaimed, a new martyr made, and Jerusalem again in an uproar, but we also will read of the gospel's outward movement: of cities from Damascus to Ephesus set abuzz, and of places like the Areopagus and Rhodes, Malta, and the Aventine Hill echoing with the names of Jesus and the resurrection. Councils, governors, synagogues, and academies are all confounded, while itinerant evangelists, spontaneous gatherings of women, the poor, and the outcast model a new, inverted order that is breaking in on Caesar's realm.

Interpreters of Acts tend to find one of two arguments driving this Lucan account of the early Church for Theophilus. The first of these readings sees a collision between the dominant Greco-Roman pagan culture and an in-breaking, apocalyptic gospel message that challenges all established practices and threatens to redefine all relations by creating a new kind of people called "*he ekklesia*": "the called-out assembly" or "the church." This reading focuses on how the gospel message unsettles and transforms cities like Lystra, Philippi, Athens, and Ephesus (Acts 14, 16, 17, 19). The second main way of reading Acts notes the author's constant efforts to exonerate the "Christians" of any seditious or revolutionary intent toward Rome, by portraying disciples and apostles repeatedly being tried and found innocent by Roman authorities. This latter reading points to trials before imperial officials like Gallio, Claudius Lysias, Felix, and Festus (Acts 18, 21–23, 23–24, and 25–26), all of which end either in outright acquittal of the Christians, or in the officers' personal expressions of sympathy.

Since both of these readings reflect important and solid textual evidence, other interpreters ask how the "apocalyptic" narrative of Acts can be reconciled with its "reassurance" narrative. An integrative answer appears rather obvious once it is broached: that the "upside down" character of the gospel is only a matter of perspective; that, in Luke's view, those are the words of an already-inverted world judging those who have come to set it right, as if a civilization standing on its collective head were to object when people arrive suddenly saying that the sky is up. Just as importantly, says this integrative reading, those come to set the world upright seek to do so not through seditious violence or coercion, but through their own transformed and transformational living. They model a life based on the confession of Jesus Christ as *Kyrios* or "Lord"; on the mission to spread his saving message "to the end of the earth"; and on the assembly of these believers together in local worshiping and acting communities, *hai ekklesiai,* "the churches."[2] If there is to be any violence, it will be done (as it is done throughout Acts) only against the new "Christians" by those who experience their alternative way of mercy and forgiveness as a threat; that is, by those who prefer life in a capsized world.

13.5.3.4 Preacher, Martyr, Evangelist, and Convert: Peter, Stephen, Philip, and Saul/Paul

Some pivotal moments in the text will serve to illustrate this integrative reading: from Peter's first sermon and first arrest, to the stoning of the first "martyr" Stephen, to the roadside evangelism of Philip, to the conversion of Saul, and then Peter's opening to the Gentiles and the expanding circles of Saul/Paul's missionary journeys. The first pivot comes when in Acts 4 Peter and the apostles are captured and called before the Sanhedrin on charges of improper healing. Peter's response is not defiant but humble, yet with a humility that sounds effectively like defiance to the hostile elders: "Whether it is right in the sight of God to listen to you more than to God, you judge. For we cannot but speak the things which we have seen and heard" (4:19–20). Speaking to the Sanhedrin not as wicked men, but as merely mistaken for their killing of Jesus (3:17), Peter speaks of himself and his comrades not as rebels, but as men bound to obey a higher authority, and offers them God's disconcerting mercy.

The narrative's second pivot comes in Acts 7, when the deacon Stephen stands trial on charges of blasphemy. His defense consists entirely of reminding the court that the Tanakh speaks throughout of Messiah's coming to restore the true meaning and practice of *Torah* – an argument that earns him the supreme Deuteronomic penalty of stoning at the court's own hands, under the leadership of the young Saul of Tarsus.

Stephen and Saul: Archetypal Martyr and Convert

Our English word "martyr" – "a person who undergoes death or great suffering for a faith, belief, or cause" (*Oxford English Dictionary* def. 2.a) – derives directly from the story of Stephen in the Book of Acts. Yet the original Greek word *martyros* means not one who dies or suffers but one who gives testimony (*martyrion*), one who tells honestly what he or she has seen, as in a courtroom, and in the sense that we still use "witness" legally today. It is in this original sense that the departing Jesus uses the plural *martyres* to commission his disciples in Acts 1:8: "you shall be witnesses to me in Jerusalem, and in all Judea and Samaria, and to the end of the earth," for it is their calling to go and say what their eyes have shown them. It is an intrinsic irony of the gospel that bringing "good news" should be fatal; that simply by bearing witness, Stephen converts *martyros* to "martyr," and *martyrion* to "martyrdom"; so that by Acts 22:20 a man can confess in prayer to Christ that "when the blood of your martyr Stephen was shed, I also was standing by consenting to his death." And it is a supreme irony that this archetypal Christian martyr should have been martyred by this archetypal Christian convert, Rabbi Saul of Tarsus, alias Paul the Apostle. From Latin *convertere,* "to turn with," a "convert" like Saul turns to be with his victim Stephen as Stephen is with Christ, becoming a new man named Paul in the process.

The martyrdom of Stephen ends the opening section of Acts 1–7, and inaugurates a period of persecution that drives the Church (though not its leaders) out of Jerusalem and into all of Palestine and indeed along the eastern shore of the Mediterranean. But this apparent disaster quickly emerges as a providential dispersion and a third pivot, as the Apostle Philip takes to the road in Acts 8 and encounters an Ethiopian court eunuch traveling to the Temple and primed to hear the gospel, who eagerly believes. While he travels, the Ethiopian reads in the Old Covenant Book of Isaiah, with its prediction of a Suffering Servant "led like a sheep to the slaughter" (Isaiah 53:7); thus this Gentile becomes a bridge to the New Covenant news from a missionary God to the world.

The narrative's fourth pivot, in what is probably one of the two most consequential episodes in Acts, occurs when the lead persecutor Saul encounters the risen Jesus while on his way to Damascus with a warrant to root out the new movement. Significantly, even this zealous rabbi, who is "still breathing threats and murder against the disciples of the Lord" (9:1) immediately recognizes the rightful call of God in the voice that speaks to him from a burst of light, and with a tone more in sorrow than in anger:

> Then he fell to the ground, and heard a voice saying to him, "Saul, Saul, why are you persecuting me?"
>
> And he said, "Who are you, Lord?"
>
> Then the Lord said, "I am Jesus, whom you are persecuting. It is hard for you to kick against the goads." (9:1, 4–5)

Responding to the compassion behind these words – divine compassion, remarkably, for a man trying vainly to exterminate the immortal – Saul's conversion is instant; his next words offer only his humble service, and though temporarily blinded, when he arrives in Damascus he is baptized and adopted immediately by the Christians whom he had sought to destroy (9:6–19). Thus, the gospel appears not as the radically new or alien, but as the restoration of former sight, and as the recognition of a love and truth somehow known and resisted for too long.

This fourth pivot point of Saul's conversion in Acts 9 is a crucial event repeatedly described for varied other audiences in Acts 22 and 26, and also in 1 Corinthians 15 and Galatians 1. This conversion is followed in Acts 10 by the book's fifth turning point, and the second great consequential episode in as many chapters. Chapter 10 presents Peter as initially reluctant to embrace Gentiles; it begins when a God-fearing Italian centurion named Cornelius is called in a dream to look in Joppa for a man called Simon Peter; and Cornelius soon arrives to fulfill Peter's dream, a dream sent to shock him out of his Hebraic exclusiveness with a vision commanding him to "arise …, kill, and eat" a whole array of Levitically unclean animals let down for him in a sheet. With a flash of the old impulsive Peter from the gospels, given to correcting God himself, the apostle responds "Not so, Lord! For I have never eaten anything common or unclean."

> And a voice spoke to him again the second time, "What God has cleansed you must not call common." This was done three times. And the object was taken up into heaven again. (10:14–16)

At this very moment Cornelius's men stand at Peter's door, inviting him to meet the centurion in Caesarea, and when Peter travels there they confirm, to their mutual astonishment, the divine origin of their appointment: they determine that their two visions come from the same Lord, who now commands the unimaginable. "In truth I perceive that God shows no partiality," says Peter to Cornelius and his household. "But in every nation whoever fears him and works righteousness is accepted by him" (10:34–35). And then, in confirmation of Peter's Great Inclusion,

> the Holy Spirit fell upon all those who heard the word. And those of the circumcision who believed were astonished, as many as came with Peter, because the gift of the Holy Spirit had been poured out on the Gentiles also. (10:44–45)

And then Cornelius and his household, already baptized in the Holy Spirit, are baptized with water as well.

Having embraced Gentiles – and Romans! – as spiritual equals, Peter is called immediately to defend his actions among the rest of the Church leadership in Jerusalem, who for a moment sound like the Sanhedrin reacting in horror: "You went in to uncircumcised men and ate with them!" (11:3). But hearing Peter's account of the tandem visions, the divinely appointed meeting, and especially the descent of the Spirit, their objections melt into awe: "When they heard these things they became silent; and they glorified God, saying, 'Then God has also granted to the Gentiles repentance to life'" (11:18). In a further contrast to the hard-hearted Sanhedrin, again following the Jerusalem Council's judgment, Rabbi Saul of Tarsus is again waiting in the wings, but this time not as an engineer of death, but as a now-seasoned convert eager to assist Barnabas in Antioch, the place where "the disciples were first called Christians" (11:19–26). With a new breadth of mission and a new name, the "Christian" movement is about to push further outward under dynamic and surprising new leadership.

But as is usually the case in Acts, the next great leap forward is precipitated by further opposition, now, in chapter 12, from King Herod Agrippa, who was the namesake of his grandfather, the Idumean client King Herod the Great, and also of Augustus Caesar's great lieutenant Marcus Agrippa. During his brief reign (39–44 CE) Herod Agrippa pleased both the Romans and the leading Jews with his demonstrated loyalty to the Caesars and hostility to the Christians. Yet Acts portrays him as rather amusingly hapless: though his soldiers manage to execute the Apostle James and to imprison Simon Peter (12:1–4), Peter's miraculous escape shows the ease with which God overrules kings (12:5–19); and Herod Agrippa's darkly funny death – "eaten by worms" after accepting blasphemous worship – shows the extent of divine power over the powerful (12:20–23). So this outbreak of persecution, like its predecessors in the Passion narratives and in Acts 7–8, serves to demonstrate the Lord's timing even in allowing some temporary scope to wicked men, and the exponential results for the gospel as "the word of God grew and multiplied" (12:24).

That lesson is amplified in Acts 13–14, as Herod's fall segues into Saul's rise – Saul of Tarsus, the arch-persecutor now converted and humbled, his zeal not quenched but redirected.

Paul's Missionary Journeys

From chapter 13 on, the Book of Acts consists mostly of the Apostle Paul's evangelistic travels, telling of four distinct, though overlapping, missionary journeys by Paul and his associates; early Church and local traditions tell of a possible fifth. On his **First Missionary Journey, narrated in Acts 13–14 (46–48** CE**)**, Paul teams up with Barnabas and Mark, beginning and ending in Syrian Antioch and visiting Cyprus and the cities of south-central Galatia (now Turkey), first preaching in the local synagogues, and then in public venues. On Paul's **Second Missionary Journey, described in Acts 15:39–18:22 (49–52** CE**)**, he teams up with Silas in Jerusalem, later joined by Timothy at Lystra, and by the author Luke himself at Troas, as he revisits the new Galatian churches before passing over to the Greek lands of Macedonia and Achaia, climaxing with his famous Areopagus/Mars Hill sermon in Athens, before returning to Jerusalem by way of Corinth and

Ephesus. On Paul's **Third Missionary Journey, found in Acts 18:23–21:16 (53–57** CE**)**, he starts from Antioch accompanied mainly by Luke, joining others on varied legs of his travels to many of the now-familiar Galatian churches (with a two-year stay in Ephesus), the new churches in Greece, and the Greek islands of Samos and Rhodes – meanwhile writing his letters to the Corinthians and Romans before ending in Jerusalem. Luke's account in Acts climaxes with Paul's **Fourth Missionary Journey in Acts 27:1–28:16 (59–62** CE**)**, a very different kind of passage, taken mostly in chains; for Paul has been arrested upon return to Jerusalem in 57 CE and is tried multiple times on charges of blasphemy and sedition there and in Caesarea. Having appealed his case to Caesar, Paul is sent under guard on a voyage to Rome, with landfalls in Galatia and Crete before a Mediterranean tempest and shipwreck on Malta; after three months' delay he arrives in the imperial capital, yet despite house arrest he is still as the book ends "teaching the things which concern the Lord Jesus Christ with all confidence, no one forbidding him" (28:31).

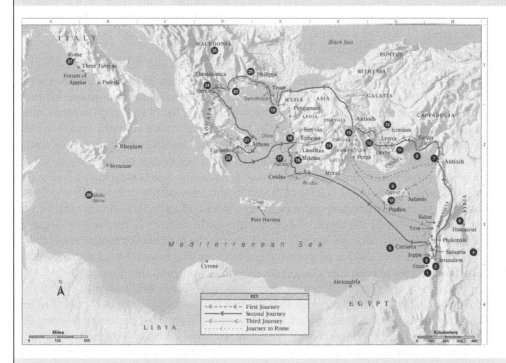

This optimistic ending to Acts has inspired early Church and local traditions of Paul's **possible Fifth Missionary Journey (62–64** CE**?)**, in which, after acquittal by Caesar, Paul fulfilled his ambition expressed in Romans 15:24 and 28 by traveling to Spain, as claimed in later accounts by the early Church fathers Clement of Rome and Eusebius. But whether the Caesar in question (the infamous Nero) released Paul or not in 62 CE, by 64 Paul again became Nero's prisoner, and eventually his victim in the arena, finishing his many journeys as a martyr.

The missionary call of the convert Saul presents the sixth and final major narrative pivot in Acts, for though only half-done, the book now follows a pattern of ever-wider evangelistic dispersion and growth of the Church among the Gentiles. Further turns of plot regarding Saul's personal trials and triumphs do nothing to alter this grand arc of exponential expansion among "the nations" and toward "the end of the earth"; rather, these plot twists enable this expansion.

As the gospel thus hatches out of its Hebraic shell into the much larger Gentile world, the twin themes that will govern the remainder of Acts are those of, on the one hand, the increased unsettling of Greco-Roman cultural norms by this "Christian" movement, and on the other hand, the exoneration of the Christians of sedition or violence. The book seeks to demonstrate that God's new order is coming not as a crashing and destructive wave, but as an inevitably yet gently rising tide, accompanied by the strong but merciful power of the Holy Spirit. So it is the Spirit who declares at this sixth and last pivot point, "Now separate to me Barnabas and Saul for the work to which I have called them" (13:2).

Thus, at their very first missionary landfall at Paphos on Cyprus, we are told that Saul and Barnabas are immediately opposed by Elymas, the Jewish court sorcerer to the island's Roman Proconsul Sergius Paulus, Elymas regarding their message as a threat to his metaphysical hold on the proconsul's mind. And so Saul, without any violent action or verbal attack on Rome, calls down temporary blindness on the false prophet – the same temporary blindness that Christ had used to convert Saul to Paul. For it is at this moment, in the presence of the "intelligent" Roman Sergius Paulus (13:7), that Saul is first called by the latinate "Paul" (13:9), as if to emphasize that his divinely empowered message is consistent with his peaceful intentions toward Rome. The result? "Then the proconsul believed, when he saw what had been done, being astonished at the teaching of the Lord" (13:12).

This first outing by "Barnabas and Saul" (hereafter usually "Paul and Barnabas") presents the pattern of Paul's typical future missionary encounters, in which the successful proclamation of the Good News in the synagogues usually raises first Jewish and then Gentile opposition, followed eventually by official vindication, if not full endorsement. In chapter 14 Paul and Barnabas, after healing a lame man, are first worshiped as gods by the local multitudes at Lystra, and then only days later Paul is stoned nearly to death by the same mob after Jewish rivals from nearby towns turn the crowds against him. In chapter 16, at Philippi, Paul casts a demon out of a fortune-telling slave girl, whose owners have him beaten and jailed; when a miraculous earthquake breaks the jail's bars and chains, Paul stops the suicide of the jailer, who immediately embraces Paul's Christ, and the apostles are publicly released and honored by the local magistrates, who are mortified to learn that they have allowed the abuse of Roman citizens. In chapter 17 on the Areopagus at Athens, Paul is heard more patiently but still mainly rejected by the philosophers; while in chapter 18 at Corinth, Paul, Silas, and Timothy are dragged by angry Jews before the Achaian proconsul Gallio, who flatly refuses to hear their charges about a private religious dispute because he "took no notice of these things" (18:17). When in chapter 19, Paul's successful two-year ministry in Ephesus damages the idol-makers' business so badly that the silversmiths riot in the name of the divine "Diana of the Ephesians," the city clerk comes to quiet the crowded theater by assuring the public that "these men … are neither robbers of temples nor blasphemers of your goddess" (19:37).

The abortive trial before Gallio and the interrupted riot at Ephesus provide a template for a number of such proceedings in chapters 21–26 in between Paul's Third and Fourth Missionary Journeys, as over and over the civil authorities refuse to condemn Paul's doctrine, and sometimes even admire it. For instance when Paul's return to Jerusalem in 57 CE stirs rumors that he plans to bring a Gentile into the Temple courts, the resulting riot is broken up by Roman Garrison Commander Claudius Lysias, who first allows Paul to quiet the crowd with the story of his conversion, and then, discovering Paul's Roman citizenship, calls the Sanhedrin to question him (21:26 – 22:30). When the Pharisees and Saducees of the Sanhedrin split over Paul's doctrine of the resurrection, Claudius Lysias sends Paul to Governor Felix in Caesarea, accompanied by 200 soldiers and a note saying that the issues involved "questions of their law," but "nothing … deserving of death or chains" (23:29). When the Jerusalem leaders fail in their plot to assassinate Paul, they try slander, hiring an orator named Tertullus to accuse Paul before Felix of sedition as "a creator of dissension among all the Jews throughout the world" (24:5). Even the obviously corrupt Felix refuses to condemn Paul – we're told that he listens to him repeatedly, hoping for a bribe (24:26) – but also refuses for two years to release Paul; wishing "to do the Jews a favor," he passes the case on to his successor, Porcius Festus.

In this same vein, Festus, motivated less by justice than by political aggrandizement, hears Paul's defense: "Neither against the law of the Jews, nor against the temple, nor against Caesar have I offended in anything at all" (25:8). But despite the lack of any evidence for either blasphemy or sedition, Festus announces his plan to re-try Paul in Jerusalem, (perhaps) unaware that the chief priests and elders will again attempt assassination in transit. Then Paul, perceiving this plot, publicly plays his trump card: he appeals to Caesar, invoking his right as a Roman citizen to argue his case before the emperor himself. Paul's passport thus made for Rome, Luke nevertheless describes one last hearing in Caesarea, this one before the last of the Herodians, King Agrippa II and his sister Bernice. In briefing the king, Festus makes clear that the Jews' charges involve not serious crimes but instead "some questions against him about their own religion and about a certain Jesus, who had died, whom Paul affirmed to be alive" (25:19).

When Paul stands forth, he compliments the king for being "expert in all customs and questions which have to do with the Jews" (26:3), and launches into an account of his own life before and after conversion – which amounts to a summary of the entire Book of Acts. Thus, with Agrippa we review in Acts 26:4–23 the whole history of the Church from a tiny cluster of marginal, bereaved disciples threatened by a relentless persecutor – Saul/Paul himself – to a movement spreading around the Mediterranean and approaching the capital's gates. Paul's rhetoric, disarmingly humble yet supremely confident, is throughout both welcoming and challenging. When Festus tries to dismiss Paul's testimony as madness brought on by "much learning," Paul boldly deflects the comment to the part-Jewish Agrippa, inviting him to testify also: "King Agrippa, do you believe the prophets? I know that you do believe." And then comes the king's stunning admission: "You almost persuade me to become a Christian" (26:27–28). This near-confession is topped immediately by the apostle's fearless, yet touching, evangelistic appeal to everyone present: "I would to God that not only you, but also all who hear me today, might become both almost and altogether such as I am, except for these chains" (26:29).

When a man on trial for his life cordially invites a king, a princess, and an imperial governor to share in his happiness, the world has fully turned upside down, and there is wonder and fear as the great ones admit among themselves, "This man is doing nothing deserving of death or chains," and, with perhaps some genuine regret, "This man might have been set free if he had not appealed to Caesar" (26:31–32). So readers are reminded yet again of the providential design overruling rulers and laws and mobs and murderers: that though Paul is essentially declared innocent by Agrippa, he is nevertheless compelled on his way to Rome because he has appealed to Caesar, and because sooner or later the Caesars too have a rendezvous with Christ. Remarkably, Luke does not know that future emperors will take the sign of the cross, but he writes as if he does.

After this narrative climax and last judicial endorsement, the remaining two chapters of Acts move Paul toward his final destination by the usual means of calamitous opposition, but in this case, the opposition is not human – not another mob of outraged Jews or rioting Gentiles – but natural, an uprising of the elements themselves in a great storm at sea. It is a story which seems inspired in its telling by that of Jonah, and which has influenced many miraculous shipwrecks in Shakespeare, from *The Comedy of Errors* and *Twelfth Night* to *Pericles* and *The Tempest*. Troubles and trials come thick and fast: Paul's prediction of catastrophe ignored at Crete; the terrible two-week gale that drives them toward destruction; Paul's dream of deliverance and his practical, courageous instructions; their running aground on Malta with the loss of the ship and the rescue of all souls; even Paul's survival of a Maltese snake-bite – all reveal Chance to be God's pen-name and disaster to be blessing in disguise, as means to a happy end.

Given the special stress in Luke-Acts on eyewitness testimony, it's important that the author narrates these last adventures of the years 61–62 CE (Acts 27–28) in the first person plural, as indeed Luke had first joined Paul about 50 CE in Troas (16:10–26) and rejoined him periodically over more than a decade in Greece and Asia (see the explicit "we" and "us" language in

Acts 20:6–16 and 21:1–25; for Luke seems to have been Paul's most constant companion from Acts 16 through 28). Luke writes as one having witnessed and shared in Paul's disasters and in his miraculous deliverances from the worst natural and human slings and arrows.

Yet while dramatic and climactic, these last chapters also appear to end the narrative with a fresh start: arrived in Rome, Paul as in the past again visits a synagogue, again gets a hearing among his Hebrew brethren, again wins some Jews but is rejected by many others, and again takes the gospel to the Gentiles – an outcome in keeping with the Holy Spirit's prophecy quoted from Isaiah 6:9–10. The concluding words of Luke-Acts make two things clear: that the Spirit is breaking out now among the nations; and that the leaders of the *goyim* have nothing to fear from the Christians, and will be wise to let Paul's word go forth "with all confidence, with no one forbidding him" (28:31). These last words of Acts also bridge forward: into Paul's Letter to the Romans, which proclaims the Kingdom at the heart of empire, and to the Gospel According to John, which begins with the first Word of all.

13.5.4   John: Jesus, Son of the Father, Word Made Flesh

The decades between the completion of Luke-Acts in about 62 CE, and the composition of John's gospel about thirty years later, were cataclysmic for the Jews, and pivotal for the Romans and the religious culture of their empire.

John: Origins and Authorship

This book dates to 85–90 CE, after the Roman destruction of Jerusalem and during the time of the Emperor Domitian's persecution of the Christians. The author of the fourth gospel is not named explicitly in the text, but its earliest complete manuscripts are entitled *Kata Ioannen* and its author has been identified since the early second century as the Apostle John, son of Zebedee and brother of James. The writer seems to have been a Jew, for he displays clear knowledge of Hebrew terms, customs, rituals, and beliefs, as well as of Judean and Palestinian geography; and he claims to have been an eyewitness to many incidents recorded in his book (John 19:35). Furthermore, the author speaks repeatedly of "the disciple whom Jesus loved" (John 13:23) as this eyewitness (John 21:24), and the fact that John son of Zebedee is never mentioned in the book as he is in the first three gospels strongly suggests to many that the narrator was John, modestly declining to identify himself.

Though the Apostle John probably lived no longer and wrote no later than the late first century, early twentieth-century critics proposed other authors and dates of composition in the mid-to-late second century and even later, until the 1920 discovery in Egypt of Rylands Papyrus 52 and its identification in 1934 as an authentic piece of John 18 (verses 31–33 on the front and 37–38 on the back). This papyrus, dated by handwriting style to about 125 CE, demonstrates that by early in the second century this gospel was in use at a point along the Nile fairly distant from Jerusalem, indicating already wide and established circulation. Thus, most scholars now date John at about 85–90 CE.

As noted above, the eyewitness testimony of John claims not to correct or in most cases even to duplicate that of the Synoptics, but rather to supplement earlier accounts from the life of Jesus so full of incidents that "if they were written one by one, I suppose that even the world itself could not contain the books that would be written" (John 21:25). Organized around "signs" and "I am" sayings of Jesus, John's gospel is structured as much thematically as chronologically, and provides accumulating evidence that the doer of these wondrous signs is indeed the great "I AM" himself, the Word made Flesh. Yet while providing eyewitness testimony, the book also endorses faith that does not depend on sight: "Thomas, because you have seen me, you have believed. Blessed are those who have not seen and yet have believed" (John 20:29).

In later Christian iconography, John is the fourth of the Four Evangelists, represented symbolically by an eagle, portraying a soaring and far-sighted vision of Jesus the *Logos* in his eternal divine glory.

Between 66 and 70 CE, any remaining Jewish cooperation with Rome collapsed as the messianic hopes of the Zealot movement sought open war to drive out the Gentile invaders, bringing the full wrath of the Caesars down on Jerusalem, its priests, and Sanhedrin, and even its holy Temple. General Vespasian, a veteran of Claudius Caesar's conquest of Britain, combined forces with Vespasian's son Titus and achieved the subjugation of Judea, Titus finally taking Jerusalem and leveling the Temple – as described in *The Jewish Wars* by Flavius Josephus, a captured Jewish rebel turned imperial advocate.

This time of Judaic disaster (the Temple has never been rebuilt) was also a time of Roman turmoil as the death of the singularly incompetent, cruel, and corrupt Nero commenced the tumultuous "Year of the Four Emperors" (69 CE), when in bloody sequence ruled first Galba, then Otho, then Vitellius, and finally Vespasian himself, whose legions declared him emperor while he was still in the East. As founder of the Flavian dynasty, Vespasian restored stable rule and built Rome's famed Colosseum with the spoils from the Jerusalem Temple before dying in 79 CE. His son Titus reigned briefly until 81 CE, and was honored by his brother and successor, Domitian, with the great triumphal arch that still stands in Rome's Via Sacra, celebrating the downfall of Jerusalem. The political and religious upheaval wrought by these events brought in an era of tremendous religious innovation, as the old Olympian deities of Greece and the ancestral gods of Rome increasingly gave way to Eastern mystery religions blended with Platonic philosophies – and with certain borrowings from the rising Christian movement. At this crossroads between Jewish collapse, Roman religious syncretism, and Greek metaphysical teaching, John's gospel intervenes.

13.5.4.1 "And Dwelt Among Us": Gnosticism Refuted by the Word Made Flesh

If Matthew speaks strongly to Jewish cultural assumptions, Mark to the action-oriented Roman imagination, and Luke-Acts to the sprawling cultural sphere of the Greek-speaking world, John's gospel seeks to reconcile all of these qualities – Jewish particularity, Roman directness, and Hellenistic universal metaphysics – in the unique person of Jesus, the divine Word (Greek **Logos**) made historical, physical Flesh (Greek **Sarx**). The growing spiritual movement that we now call **Gnosticism** (from Greek *gnosis*, or "knowledge") had increasingly popularized centuries-old teachings from Plato of Athens (428–347 BCE) – particularly Plato's idea that a great divine *Logos* was the ultimate source of all human souls, which have nevertheless fallen from spiritual purity to be trapped in the corrupt, illusory, ignorant prison of fleshly bodies and material substance. Thus, for Plato the only true happiness consists in escaping from the realm of Flesh, and reuniting with the oneness of the true Word. This popular **Platonism** promised deliverance through great spiritual teachers who came to impart secret words of knowledge that enabled a few chosen initiates to break free from evil materiality and rejoin the true divine One.

By the late first century CE, this "Middle Platonic" movement had absorbed a good deal of Christian language as the new Judaic faith spread around the empire, despite vigorous and ongoing attempts at its eradication by the emperors and other local authorities. Thus is "Gnosticism" born as a kind of Christian heresy, as Jesus had come to be seen by many Gnostics as a great divine manifestation, a teacher arrived to impart a saving *gnosis* passed on secretly from initiate to initiate in mystical formulations. Gnosticism was generally hostile to Jewish ideas of sacrificial atonement and spiritual humility. It also usually promoted **Docetism** (from Greek *dokein*, "to seem"), the doctrine that Jesus was a purely spiritual manifestation who only "seemed" to be born in a human, Hebrew body, and who never suffered pain or crucifixion. Indeed in Gnostic thinking, the material world is the work not of the divine *Logos*, but of the *Demiurge* (Greek *Demiourgos* for "Craftman" or "Artisan"), a subcreator who lacks a divine nature but only works in imitation of divine patterns. Thus, the material world is a vastly inferior copy of a heavenly original (as explained in Plato's *Timeaus*, 360 BCE).

When read in this context, the prologue to John's gospel turns the tables on the Gnostics' Christian borrowings, counter-borrowing and then strikingly redefining Platonic terminology, much as the Book of Genesis imitates and then overthrows the polytheistic creation narrative of the *Enuma Elish*. And indeed Genesis is an especially appropriate analogy, for John's opening words clearly echo the opening of great Hebrew *Barashit:* "In the beginning" (Genesis 1:1).

The Gnostic Gospels

Often called the New Testament Apocrypha, these accounts of Jesus's life were written under Gnostic influence from 150 to 400 CE, though they clearly include some earlier material found in the canonical New Testament gospels themselves. The Gnostic Gospels generally deny Jesus's incarnation, death and physical resurrection; portray Jesus as a wonder-worker and mystic; reject the Old Testament as false and misleading, and dismiss Christ's sacrificial atonement as unnecessary; and often deny that women can experience spiritual enlightenment. Many of these documents are found in the Nag Hammadi Library discovered in 1945 in Egypt, but copies of some have been known for many centuries. The Gnostic Gospels have for most of their history been condemned by historic Christian Churches, Catholic, Orthodox, and Protestant, but are now easily available in modern editions. They include the following:

Apocalypse of Peter	Gospel of Thomas
Barnabas	Hermas
Gospel of the Ebionites	Logia Jesu (Words of Jesus)
Gospel according to the Egyptians	Preaching of Peter
Gospel according to the Hebrews	Gospel of the Lord
Gospel of the Naassenes	Gospel of Truth
Gospel of Nicodemus	Gospel of Mary
Gospel of Peter	Gospel of Judas

So we read "In the beginning was the Word, and the Word was with God, and the Word was God" (John 1:1). The deliberate echo of the Genesis creation leads immediately into a clear evocation of Platonic language; like Hellenistic Jewish philosopher Philo of Alexandria (25 BCE–50 CE), John seems to promise a harmony of Hebraic and Greek concepts of deity. Such a harmony would see the *Logos* as before all and the source of all; indeed the reversed syntax of "the Word was God" in Greek, *Theos en ho Logos* ("God was the Word"), makes it categorically clear that the pre-existent Word was wholly divine. "He was in the beginning with God," the book continues. "All things were made through him, and without him nothing was made that was made" (1:2–3). Perhaps, the first-century reader might think, this divine Word is identical to Plato's *Logos*, the source of all the Forms copied by the subdivine Demiurge in manufacturing our lowly mortal world. Reading further, it appears that this Word is the only source of enlightenment for an otherwise ignorant and uncomprehending humanity: "In him was life, and the life was the light of men. And the light shines in the darkness, and the darkness did not comprehend it" (1:4–5). Thus, so far, the gospel seems congruent with Gnostic language and ideas.

This congruence appears to continue as the prologue further unfolds:

> There was a man sent from God, whose name was John. This man came for a witness, to bear witness of the Light, that all through him might believe. He was not that Light, but

was sent to bear witness of that Light. That was the true Light which gives light to every man coming into the world. (1:6–9)

Here, it would seem, a Gnostic spiritual teacher is being introduced, a man named John who has come to enlighten all worldlings shrouded in the fleshly veil of ignorance by pointing toward the true "Light" of divine knowledge about to shine into the world. The following verses intensify this perception, confirming that the coming Light from the originating Word has been misunderstood and rejected by the foolish multitudes.

> He was in the world, and the world was made through him, and the world did not know him. He came to his own, and his own did not receive him. But as many as received him, to them he gave the right to become children of God, to those who believe in his name: who were born, not of blood, nor of the will of the flesh, nor of the will of man, but of God. (1:10–13)

Read Gnostically, this fleshly realm is entirely obscure and inscrutable, except to the chosen initiates whose enlightenment depends not on physical birth or body, nor on carnal or mortal will.

How then does one become enlightened? What initiation, what special formula of words is required? What is the secret that will decipher the mysteries of the world and the Word? Here any reader expecting a Gnostic answer – some sort of arcane code for mystic acolytes – receives a jolt of surprise: "*And the Word became flesh, and dwelt among us*" (1:14). The answer, it turns out, is that we may be asking the wrong question: it should not be, "what is the esoteric escape from fleshly ignorance?" but rather, "how will God bring grace into our fleshly existence?" And the further answer is that far from abhorring the material world, the divine Creator comes to call it his home. For the Gnostic, *Logos* and *Sarx*, "Word" and "Flesh," are incompatible opposites – like "light" and "darkness," "good" and "evil," "oil" and "vinegar", but for this gospel writer, the ethic of Genesis applies after all, as the God who "in the beginning" made the world is somehow willing to come down among his human creatures and inhabit it with them.

The shock of this conceptual explosion sends its waves back through the preceding passage, recasting all of the supposedly Platonic language in decidedly Hebraic ways. The creating Word is not an abstract giver of divine Forms for some subordinate Demiurge to copy badly, but instead is *Elohim* himself, who spoke all things into being by the power of his Word, who pronounced them "very good" (Genesis 1:31), and who now has fashioned Flesh for himself to wear in his new earthly habitation. And yet this *Yahweh* in human form is rejected on earth not because the world he made was originally evil or dark, but because the world's people have knowingly and willfully chosen evil and can no longer stand the light. Yet this Word made Flesh now reaches out to any who will return and receive him – not some esoteric elite, but anyone from low station to high who is willing to face the Light.

This narrator claims to have faced the Light – and lived: "[W]e beheld his glory, the glory as of the only begotten of the Father, full of grace and truth" (John 1:14). Being "begotten," in ancient physiology, meant a son receiving the essence of his father, his full nature – and in this case a divine Father's fully divine nature. And the "man sent from God whose name was John" turns out to be no mystic master imparting secret words, but John the Baptist, who pointed to the "only begotten," "bore witness of him and cried out, saying, 'This was he of whom I said, "He who comes after me is preferred before me, for he was before me"'" (1:15).

Finally, having appropriated and redefined Platonic language, the narrator turns to one specific name, as to the one Word of power: "And of his fullness we have all received, and grace for grace. For the law was given through Moses, but grace and truth came through Jesus Christ"

(1:16–17). Correcting both Platonic elitism and Jewish exclusivity, the narrator asserts that all can be saved by speaking and trusting this one name, this one Word. "No one has seen God at any time. The only begotten Son, who is in the bosom of the Father, he has declared him" (1:18). The utter uniqueness of the divine Word, now for the first time called God's "Son" (as in Matthew, Mark, and Luke), somehow guarantees to "as many as received him" the open offer of divine adoption for all as "children of God" (1:12).

We have spent so much space on this prologue not only because it is one of the most famous passages in the Bible and in the world, but also because it crystallizes both the style and the substance of John throughout. For in John, the relation between style and substance is unmistakably paradoxical: on the one hand, the book speaks an eerily sublime and simple metaphysical language, and on the other hand, it tells the story of how the metaphysical descends into and inhabits the physical, of the Word's power demonstrated *through*, rather than *against*, the Flesh. The book's hero, the divine Word and God's Son, Jesus Christ, comes down from heaven to die in the flesh, nailed by his hands and feet to cross-trees under the sky; he returns to life not as a spirit but in a renewed body that steps through walls and enjoys broiled fish for supper. Many religions tell stories of divine visitors to earth, others of a divine Creator, and some even tell of dying gods; this Christian religion, born out of a transcendently monotheistic Judaism, is the only one in which God the Creator becomes a mortal man and remains a divine man even after he rises, immortal, from death.

13.5.4.2 "What Sign Do You Show Us?": The *Semeia* of John

John's prologue thus creates a template for the action of his entire book. Jesus Christ, Word made Flesh, has come to make the Father known, and he will do so in a series of "signs" (Greek *semeia*) and "I am" sayings intended to demonstrate his divine power and assert his claim to full divine nature. This account of signs and sayings is given as supplementary to those of the other gospels, and is representative rather than exhaustive, for "truly Jesus did many other signs in the presence of His disciples, which are not written in this book" (20:30). Significantly, there are seven signs chosen by the author to illustrate the meaningful range of Jesus's power during his life, and progressively to reveal his divine identity; this perfect number is then "topped" by the climactic sign of his crucifixion and resurrection, which is confirmed to his disciples by a final sign when he meets them as they return to their fishing nets. Each sign is not only a show of power, but also a kind of acted parable, displaying through the physical creation Jesus's control over spiritual realms and realities.

The first of the signs "manifesting his glory," the changing of water to wine in Cana (2:1–11), has a kind of droll humor about it, as Jesus, his disciples, and his mother attend a wedding feast where the wine runs out. Like many a proud mother, Mary turns confidently to her son for help, who demurs, saying, "Woman, what does your concern have to do with me? My hour has not yet come" (2:4). Nothing daunted, Mary gives him an implicit command, simply telling the servants, "Whatever he says to you, do it" (2:5), and he obediently commands them to fill six large pots with water and then draw some out for a taste. The caterer and the bridegroom, unaware of the source, are both shocked that wine so fine would be brought out so late in the feast, when most people "have well drunk" and wouldn't notice. Here is pictured Jesus's creative power to bring one of life's chief blessings – "wine that makes glad the heart of man" (Psalm 104:15) – and a major signifier of God's Spirit, and to do so with delightful quality, at a marriage, traditionally representing *Yahweh's* love to Israel. And he loves his mother.

Jesus's second sign at Cana reaches into the palace of nearby Capernaum, as he heals the son of a royal official (John 4:46–54). His reputation having traveled, he is sought out by the nobleman, whose son is dying, and Jesus takes his plea as an opportunity, first, to call out against the Jewish appetite for marvels, but second, to reward a father's faith – and third, to show his power not only over mortality but over space and time. "Unless you people see signs and wonders, you will by no means believe" (4:48), Jesus exclaims, as if testing the father's persistence. The suitor simply intensifies his suit – "Sir, come down before my child dies!" (4:49) – only to have his expectations exceeded when Jesus pronounces the boy healed, from many miles and a day's journey away. When the father rushes home to receive the good news, he confirms that the fever had left his son on the day before, "at the seventh hour," precisely the time when Jesus had spoken the word (4:53). Thus, in a happy irony, what begins as a stern correction from Jesus turns out to be a mighty blessing.

The third sign, healing the paralytic at the pool of Bethesda (5:1–8), involves somewhat darker ironies than the Cana miracles. At a Jerusalem bath with supposed (but ineffective) curative powers, Jesus addresses a man lying paralyzed for thirty-eight years and no better for his proximity to the water. Jesus bypasses the traditional healing practice, commanding the man instead simply to "[r]ise, take up your bed and walk" (5:8), which he does immediately – and on the Sabbath. When the "Jews" (by whom John generally means the Pharisees) catch the man carrying his bed on the day of rest, they respond, not by rejoicing at the miracle, but by seeking to harass the miracle-worker. The sign's lessons? Not only does Jesus have God-like power over bodily paralysis, but he also raises the spiritually paralyzed to active life – and has the divine authority to overrule the Sabbath laws: "Jesus answered them, 'My Father has been working until now, and I have been working'" (5:17). But in response to healing, the opposition is hardening: "Therefore the Jews sought all the more to kill him, because he not only broke the Sabbath, but also said that God was his Father, making himself equal with God" (5:18).

Jesus's fourth sign, the feeding of the 5000 (6:5–14), is one of the few miracles described in all four gospels. Having crossed the Sea of Galilee, he is met by "a great multitude" who have seen his many "signs which he performed on those who were diseased" (6:1–2), and withdraws to a mountain with his disciples. But being told that the crowds are hungry, his compassion is stirred, and he nonpluses his followers by asking Philip where they can buy bread to feed the throng – "[b]ut this he said to test him, for he himself knew what he would do" (6:6). When Andrew mentions a boy with "five barley loaves and two small fish," Jesus has them seat the thousands on the grass, gives thanks, and distributes the bits of food until, somehow, everyone is fed and full, with twelve baskets to spare. This miracle of increase resonates with the Old Testament story of manna in the wilderness, a physical sustenance that is also spiritual food, leading to Jesus's self-description, "I am the bread of life" (6:35). And the multitudes only grow to follow this giver of breath and bread.

The fifth sign, walking on water (6:16–24), follows immediately from the fourth. As the recently fed 5000 seek out Jesus "to take him by force to make him king," instead he seeks solitude in the mountains while his disciples depart across the Sea of Galilee, rowing into an increasingly stiff storm toward Capernaum. Then, in the night as their difficulty increases, Jesus appears, "walking on the sea and drawing near the boat." Initially terrified, disciples are reassured when he speaks ("It is I") and welcome him into the boat, "and immediately the boat was at the land where they were going." This sign stresses Jesus's divine power over the mighty elements – there are few things more God-like than controlling the wind and waves – yet this Deity uses his power not to seek earthly rule (which he evades), but to aid his struggling friends.

Jesus's sixth sign, restoring sight on the Sabbath to the man born blind (9:1–41), raises the stakes as he comes into greater conflict with the Jewish leaders, while introducing one of the most engaging cameo characters in the New Testament, the sightless man himself. When Jesus's followers see the blind beggar in Jerusalem, they ask the loaded theological question, "Rabbi, who sinned, this man or his parents, that he was born blind?" (9:2). Jesus recasts their question, asserting that "[n]either this man nor his parents sinned, but [this happened] that the works of God should be revealed in him" (9:3), then proceeds to demonstrate that "I am the light of the world" (9:5) by spitting on the ground, rubbing the man's eyes with the clay, and telling him to go wash in the Pool of Siloam. "So he went and washed, and came back seeing" (9:7). But this happy ending is only the beginning of a darker story about willful blindness.

With the healed man walking the streets as living testimony to Jesus's power, debate breaks out about whether it is really the same formerly blind person, while some demand an explanation from the fortunate, but suddenly beleaguered, man (9:9). His dialogue is notable for being straightforward, factual, and increasingly puzzled by the level of suspicion and hostility aroused by his blessing. He confirms that Jesus healed him, but admits that he doesn't know where his benefactor has gone. But instead of being left alone, the man is haled before the Pharisees, who appear to be more interested in refuting than interrogating him. "This man is not from God, because he does not keep the Sabbath," they insist, to which the undaunted fellow replies with an inconveniently reasonable question, "How can a man who is a sinner do such signs?" and calls Jesus "a prophet" (9:14–17). Seeking to discredit the troublesome eyewitness, the Pharisees summon his parents, who cravenly refuse to substantiate their son's healing claims: "He is of age; ask him" (9:23).

Called back for a further harangue, the healed man confronts the intransigence of the authorities with growing pluck, refusing to change his story, and pushing back with infuriating wit: "I told you already, and you did not listen. Why do you want to hear it again? Do you also want to become His disciples?" (9:27). Then he turns piercingly earnest:

> Why, this is a marvelous thing, that you do not know where he is from; yet he has opened my eyes! Now we know that God does not hear sinners; but if anyone is a worshiper of God and does his will, he hears him. Since the world began it has been unheard of that anyone opened the eyes of one who was born blind. If this man were not from God, he could do nothing. (9:30–33)

This is too much for the Pharisees, who invoke the same neat doctrine of deserved suffering assumed by the disciples: "'You were completely born in sins, and are you teaching us?' And they cast him out" (9:34).

In a touching coda, Jesus finds the excommunicated man, consoles him, and drives home the point of the sign: "For judgment I have come into this world, that those who do not see may see, and that those who see may be made blind" (9:39). Now afflicted by the miracle of sight, this man chooses to trust his eyes and the man who healed them, exclaiming "Lord, I believe!" Then Jesus turns to the eavesdropping Pharisees: "If you were blind, you would have no sin; but now you say, 'We see'. Therefore your sin remains" (9:41). Their refusal of the light is about to turn lethal.

The seventh, perfecting sign of Jesus's earthly ministry undoes not blindness but death itself in the raising of his friend Lazarus (11:1–45). So much can be said about this famed episode that to comment further is daunting. Yet at root Jesus's emptying of Lazarus's tomb signals that the man whose word can generate the best wine and most plentiful bread, who can raise the cripple and quench the fever and renew the eyes, and who can both walk the waves and still them, is above all "the resurrection and the life" (11:25). And for all of its hefty theological freight, this story is rich in human drama: the friend deathly ill, the rabbi deliberately delayed in coming, the bereft sisters distraught and reproachful, the Resurrectionist weeping moments before turning grief to joy, the warning about "a stench," the stone rolled away, the dead man walking back into life – and the plot to bring the life-giver death:

> Then the chief priests and the Pharisees gathered a council and said, "What shall we do? For this man works many signs. If we let him alone like this, everyone will believe in him, and the Romans will come and take away both our place and nation." And one of them,

Caiaphas, being high priest that year, said to them, "You know nothing at all, nor do you consider that it is expedient for us that one man should die for the people, and not that the whole nation should perish." (11:47–50)

The greatest paradox of Jesus's story, here as in the other gospels, is that a man who can raise the dead does not choose to keep himself alive; and it is matched by the irony that those who have most earnestly sought the Christ hate him with a perfect hatred when he arrives. They had all demanded a sign, and when they get their signs seven-fold – when *Yahweh* stands living and breathing at their gates – they scheme to get their God hung on a scaffold, believing that by some anti-miracle he will stay dead.

For there is never any question in John (nor in Matthew, Mark, or Luke) of whether Jesus will rise. "I lay down my life that I may take it again," he has already announced (10:18); "You could have no power at all against me unless it had been given you from above," he tells the Roman governor Pilate, who is nonplussed by the uncanny dignity and confidence of this imprisoned "King of the Jews" (19:11, 19); and throughout his arrest and execution, we are reminded regularly that "these things were done that the Scripture should be fulfilled" (19:36). He is held to the cross as if by an act of will; the Word has been made Flesh, and he is determined to go the way of all flesh from full earthly life through to death. He even chooses the moment of his departure: "It is finished," he declares (19:30). His agony is presented as real – he is scourged and crowned with thorns, he carries his cross and he cries out "I thirst!" (19:1–3, 17, 28) – but yet he dies with sovereign dignity, to take up his life three days later as if it were a dropped garment.

The divine sign of John's crucified Christ – this sign of the cross and the dying, rising God – compels a look back at the divine "I am" sayings interwoven with the signs which led to that crucifixion. Seven of these **eight "I am" sayings** (*Ego eimi* in Greek) are important as metaphors in themselves: "**I am the bread of life**" (after feeding the 5000 – John 6:35, 48); "**I am the light of the world**" (just before and after healing the blind man – John 8:12, 9:5); "**I am the door**" and "**I am the good shepherd**" (distinguishing himself from the wrongly exclusive and abusive Pharisees – John 10:9, 11); "**I am the resurrection and the life**" (about to call Lazarus from the tomb – John 11:25); "**I am the way, the truth, and the life**" (at the Last Supper, telling his disciples the road "to my Father's house" – John 14:6); and "**I am the true vine**" (explaining how he will give his disciples abiding life and fruit as "the branches" – John 15:1, 5, 7). The most literal, explicit, and shocking of these "I am" sayings – **before Abraham was, I am**" (8:58) – plays not with metaphor but with verb tense to make the central proclamation that Jesus is eternally *YHWH*, the great "I AM" existing "before Abraham" and revealed to Moses in Exodus 3:14 as the covenant-making Creator and Deliverer. Yet when he thus identifies himself to the chief disciples of Moses in the Temple, "they took up stones to throw at him" (8:59).

In his first letter to the Corinthians, Paul writes that "Jews request a sign, and Greeks seek after wisdom" (1 Corinthians 1:22), and, especially in John's gospel, when Jew and Greek receive what they've demanded, neither can stand it. "The Lord whom you seek will suddenly come to his Temple" (Malachi 3:1), and when he does "come to his own," he is trussed up and slaughtered as the sacrifice. Thus, continues Paul, "I preach Christ crucified." And the Greco-Roman mind is shown, uncomprehending, as blindest when it sees the Light in person. "'What is truth?' said jesting Pilate, and would not stay for an answer," wrote Francis Bacon of that encounter, the answer standing incarnate in Pilate's Praetorium, and at a scourging post, brutalized by Roman soldiers (John 18:38, 19:1–2). Yet as hostile and blind as these representative Jews and Gentiles appear, the "good shepherd" still has sheep of both folds, and a few other episodes of John's climactic gospel hold out the hope that "as many as received him, to them he gave the right to become children of God" (1:12).

The stories of Nicodemus and the Samaritan "woman at the well" are juxtaposed in chapters 3 and 4 to demonstrate that both Hebrew piety and Gentile profaneness, though each oblivious in its own way, can be redeemed by meeting Jesus. Nicodemus, the eminently respectable Pharisee and Sanhedrin member, comes secretly to Jesus by night, anxious to avoid being seen with the controversial rabbi, but equally anxious to hear a man whose many "signs" have convinced him to seek out "a teacher come from God" (3:2). But Jesus disregards the ruler's opening compliments and thrusts instantly to the heart: "Most assuredly, I say to you, unless one is born again, he cannot see the kingdom of God" (3:3). And when the eminently disreputable Samaritan woman – five times married and divorced – offers Jesus a midday drink and a debate over possible places of worship, Jesus disregards these arguments and presses home: "Woman, believe me, the hour is coming when you will neither on this mountain, nor in Jerusalem, worship the Father… God is Spirit, and those who worship him must worship in spirit and truth" (4:21, 24). Likewise Nicodemus is astonished to hear, in John's most famous verse, that all of his conscientious works are irrelevant without faith: "For God so loved the world that he gave his only begotten Son, that whoever believes in him should not perish but have everlasting life" (3:16). The Samaritan woman is, if possible, even more astonished to hear that she has been disputing with the long-expected Messiah: "I who speak to you am he" (4:29, 26).

These two cameos are completed by a third: another Jew, this one an even more sordid woman, caught in the act of adultery. Dragged by the Pharisees hot from coitus into the street – significantly, they don't bring her male partner in sin – she is cast before Jesus to test him with a theological Hobson's choice: either excuse her and disobey the Mosaic command "that such should be stoned," or condemn her, and lose the love of the sympathetic crowds. As usual, Jesus maneuvers brilliantly, saving both the woman's life and her soul: he calls down the letter of the Mosaic Law – that those bringing charges must do the stoning – and enlists her accusers as executioners, on one condition: "He who is without sin among you, let him cast the first stone" (8:7). Even for the most hardened hypocrites, this is too much:

> Then those who heard it, being convicted by their conscience, went out one by one, beginning with the oldest even to the last. And Jesus was left alone, and the woman standing in the midst. When Jesus had raised himself up and saw no one but the woman, he said to her, "Woman, where are those accusers of yours? Has no one condemned you?" She said, "No one, Lord." And Jesus said to her, "Neither do I condemn you; go and sin no more." (8:9–11)

Yet however engaging these characters – Nicodemus, the Samaritan and adulterous women, the man born blind, Lazarus in his tomb – and however consistently Jesus outsmarts his enemies, no amount of maneuvering will spare him the cross, for he refuses to evade it.

13.5.5   Ordinary Splendor: The Miracle of the Everyday

Yet if the crucifixion and resurrection constitute the climactic sign of John's gospel, one more remains, as a kind of coda to complete the portrait of "the Word made Flesh." In John 21, the disciples have returned unsuccessfully to fishing, and Jesus appears, mysteriously disguised, and suggests one more cast of the net. When they "were not able to draw it in because of the multitude of fish," they suddenly recognize their Lord, who proceeds to cook and share fish and bread with them. This episode echoes previous events – an earlier miraculous catch when Peter had told Jesus, "leave me, for I am a sinful man" (Luke 5:1–11); Jesus teaching by the sea (Mark 4:1); the feedings of the 5000 and 4000 with fishes and loaves; Jesus's disguised appearance on the Emmaus road (Luke 24:13–32) – and concludes as Jesus forgives Peter's past betrayal, narrated by all Four Evangelists. Thus, this final chapter of the last gospel presents a summing up, and a reminder that after the agonies of crucifixion and the ecstasies of resurrection come daily feeding and fellowship. Fleshly life, even redeemed life, is the day-to-day of small things adding up to great ones, as ordinary and miraculous as a fish dinner with God by the lake.

Thus, the newness of these four Testaments lies in the renewal of old ways, old promises kept and covenants completed, ancient prophecies fulfilled in ways stunning in the moment but treated as inevitable in retrospect. John's gospel ends by pointing back to the other, earlier gospel accounts, and pointing beyond them to the incalculable life of Jesus, which they have all tried, in inevitably finite ways, to sum up.

> And truly Jesus did many other signs in the presence of His disciples, which are not written in this book; but these are written that you may believe that Jesus is the Christ, the Son of God, and that believing you may have life in His name... And there are also many other things that Jesus did, which if they were written one by one, I suppose that even the world itself could not contain the books that would be written. Amen. (John 20:30–31, 21:25)

What is most striking about these claims is their modest infinitude; careful to highlight their own human limits, they nevertheless insist that those very limits point to divine immensity. Word has been made Flesh, so that now, despite and indeed through all of its shortcomings, Flesh can speak the Word. We turn now to that most everyday of literary forms employed by the first disciples to spread that Word, the epistle.

Questions for Discussion

1   What are some ways in which the "newness" of the **New Covenant** can be understood? How, in particular, does Jesus speak in the gospels about his message in relation to the "old" Mosaic covenant?

2   How does the history of the so-called **Intertestamental Period** lead to the varied **religious/political parties** of Jesus's day? What were those parties? How did they relate to each other? To the Roman authorities? To Jesus in the varied gospel accounts?

3   What are the main commonalities – and differences – among the so-called **Synoptic Gospels**? What are the chief differences – and commonalities – between the Synoptics as a group and the **Gospel of John**?

4   What are the main assumptions, insights, and limits of the New Testament **Documentary Hypothesis** related to the so-called **Q Source**? What textual facts does the "Q" hypothesis seek to explain? What are the more recent modifications and alternatives to the "Q" hypothesis?

5   What are the main assumptions, insights, and limits of source criticism that distinguishes between the **Jesus of history** and the **Christ of faith**? What is meant by "history" and "faith" in this formulation? What can be known about Jesus of Nazareth from sources outside the New Testament?

6   What is the **Messianic Secret**? By whom is this secret kept, and from whom? For what reasons? How does this motif relate to the distinctions between the Synoptics and John?

7   What is a **parable**, and how does this literary form relate to the Messianic Secret motif? How do Jesus's parables relate to the particular contexts in which he is portrayed as telling them? What are the usual elements of a parable, and how do they work together?

8   What are the differences and similarities between a **gospel narrative** and a **modern biography**? By what principles do the gospel writers claim to choose their material? What claims do they make to historical and spiritual truth?

9   How does the **Gospel of Matthew** speak to the particular interests of a presumably **Jewish readership**? How does the gospel nevertheless push back against certain common assumptions of first-century Judaism?

10 How does the **Gospel of Mark** anticipate **Roman attitudes** and concerns? How does Mark nevertheless undermine and overthrow certain central elements of *Romanitas*?

11 How does the **Gospel of Luke** speak to certain abiding interests not only of **Theophilus**, but also of the larger **Hellenistic culture** of the first century? How does it press the case for Jesus's universal mission? How do the wonders and miracles figure in Luke's account?

12 How does the **Book of Acts** extend Luke's gospel account with strategies of both reassurance and of confrontation directed at the Gentile reader? To whom is the gospel message a threat, and to whom is it not? Who are the **multiple protagonists** of Acts, and who, finally, is the **hero** of the story? Why does it end as it does?

13 How does the **Gospel of John** adopt and **echo the language of** late first-century Greek "gnosis" or "**Gnosticism**"? How does the gospel redefine and repurpose that language? How does the distinctive structure of John's gospel – around "**signs**" and "**I am**" sayings – shape its message? How does the gospel's distinctive verbal style relate to its substance? How, in the end, does John relate to and reflect back on the earlier gospels?

Notes

1   See Robert E. Van Voorst, *Jesus Outside the New Testament: An Introduction to the Ancient Evidence* (Grand Rapids, MI: Eerdmans, 2000).

2   See particularly C. Kavin Rowe, *World Upside Down: Reading Acts in the Graeco-Roman Age* (Oxford and New York: Oxford University Press, 2009).

14

Epistle: Divine–Human Correspondence

In concluding our discussion of the four gospels and the Book of Acts, we noted that at the heart of the Christian message is the idea of divine incarnation, of the Word becoming Flesh, taking on the ordinary human lot, and embracing the commonplace in order to raise the common to glory. And of all the literary forms represented in the Bible, the most ordinary, the least apparently artful, is the letter, or epistle. The point of a letter, like the purpose of a human messenger, is to communicate information or news or affection as transparently as possible, without calling undue attention to itself either by its style or mode of presentation. The Apostle Paul, the New Testament's most famed letter-writer, describes his messenger's role in the most workaday terms available: "But we have this treasure in earthen vessels, that the excellence of the power may be of God and not of us" (2 Corinthians 4:7). Thus, the New Testament epistles generally follow a standard form common for ancient correspondence in order to convey as plainly as possible truths that the authors believe to be utterly extraordinary.

Stylistically, letters are therefore somewhat opposite to poems (which deliberately embellish, ornament, amplify) or parables (which tell their truth slantingly, circuitously, through a veil), and generally they lack the storytelling drive of narratives. Furthermore, in an era before cheap paper or practically infinite electronic space, ancient letters were often constrained by the physical limits of available parchment or papyrus – and dependent on the skills of specialists called **amanuenses** or scribes. Letters ordinarily were, and are, addressed directly to specific groups or individuals and speak particularly of mundane, often earthy things. Yet what happens when a letter tells of one particular divine Person who has come to inhabit the earth in human form? What kinds of pressures and changes will that content work on the humble letter form? This chapter explores how the treasure sometimes adapted to the vessel, and sometimes reshaped it.

What ancient factors had shaped that vessel? Much as internet technologies originally were created for military and government communication, the most ancient surviving epistles from Egypt are Pharaonic communiques of the Fifth and Sixth Dynasties (2494–2181 BCE) to troops and officials, written in rarified hieroglyphic script and delivered by special messengers. By the Eleventh Dynasty (2134–1991 BCE), epistles were being put to educational use, and standardized formulas had developed for composing letters, eventually in Demotic script. These formulas were adopted and adapted by later Greek and Roman correspondents composing in their alphabetical scripts. By the Hellenistic Age (323–31 BCE), letter writers had established the standard three-part structure employed throughout the Greeklands and the Roman Republic, a structure still in use during the early Roman Empire when the New Testament epistles were composed.

The **first** of these three parts of the Hellenistic epistle was an **Introduction**, with its opening Salutation naming the sender first and the receiver second, followed by a greeting (*chairein*) wishing the reader grace (*charis*); after this Salutation, the Introduction is often completed by

Literary Study of the Bible: An Introduction, First Edition. Christopher Hodgkins.
© 2020 John Wiley & Sons Ltd. Published 2020 by John Wiley & Sons Ltd.

a generic wish for the reader's health and a brief prayer to a god or the gods. The **second** of the letter's three parts was its **Main Body**, conveying the writer's information, instructions, ideas, and/or affections. **Third** and finally comes the formal **Conclusion**, sending both greetings from family and mutual acquaintances, and a farewell (*erroso/erosthai*) to the reader and those with him. Here, from the second or third century CE, is a brief letter (*Oxyrhynchus Papyri* CXVII) following this form:

> Chaerus to his brother Dionysius, greeting (*cheirein*). I have already urged you in person to have the horoscope in the archives prepared and also for the sale of the slaves' children, and to sell the wine that comes from both the near and the far vineyard, keeping the money in a safe place until I come. I send you some good melon seeds through Diogenes the friend of Chaereas the citizen, and two strips of cloth sealed with my seal, one of which please give to your children. Greet your sister and Cyrilla. Rhodope and Arsinous greet you. I pray that you would fare well (*errosthai*).

A plain earthen vessel indeed! The basic rhythms of this letter are those of Paul's New Testament epistles from Romans to Philemon; yet Paul and his fellow Christian correspondents vary and transform these rhythms to follow a different beat.

The most immediately obvious differences may seem cosmetic: though Paul follows convention in his Introductions by naming first himself and then his readers, yet his identity is bound up with his apostolic role, and his Salutation formula includes not only the *charis* or "grace" of the Greeks, but also the "peace" or *shalom* of the Jews (Greek *eirene*). And the conventional Health Wish is often subsumed by Paul in a Prayer or a Thanksgiving offered not to the healing god Asclepius but to *Iesou Christou tou kuriou hemon*, "Jesus Christ our Lord." Similarly, while Paul's Conclusions offer the kinds of greetings typical of Hellenistic form, he frequently transforms the closing farewell into a benediction, calling down God's blessing on the heads of his readers.

Yet what may seem cosmetic changes are truly cosmic; rather than invoking the gods as an occasional pro forma afterthought, Paul brings the divine near from beginning to end, and makes God central throughout. Thus, the most striking change is to the Main Body of the letter: from a catchall of commonplaces and mundane details, the letter's Body comes to incarnate the Word made Text. While letters to individuals like Timothy, Titus, and Philemon mention quotidian details and express personal concern, their main substance is theologically and morally weighty, and Paul's letters to particular churches are complex treatises developing many layers of argument, the Letter to the Romans most of all. Also, letters to whole churches represent a revolution in thought and communication: for while other contemporary letters are addressed to particular individuals on either personal or official business, Paul writes to an entire assembly of people with a message for all, and yet (unlike imperial proclamations or public orations) he writes not on state business but on something both higher and lower – a divine message for ordinary people. Thus, Paul creates a rhetorical space that implicitly challenges the public sovereignty of Caesar, building alternative communities dependent not upon the earthly state, but upon a heavenly Lord.

In addition to these **Pauline Epistles**, the **General Epistles** – Hebrews through Jude, sometimes called "Catholic" or "Universal" – carry Paul's implicit imperial challenge a step further, since they are addressed to even larger bodies of believers, whether to "the twelve tribes which are scattered abroad" (James 1:1), or to an even more widespread "elect," all those "called out" by and for Jesus (1 Peter 1:2, 2 John 1:1, Jude 1:1). And some General Epistles – Hebrews, 1 John – dispense with the opening Salutation entirely, moving immediately into argument and exposition. Nevertheless, even Hebrews ends with some more particular and individual references, for the New Testament letters never lose sight of their correspondence among specific personalities – even if the persons corresponding include the Father, Son, and Holy Spirit.

14.1   Sent to the Nations: Pauline Epistles

The first thing to be noted about Paul's epistles is that they should not exist. They are doubly impossible: first as letters to churches from a man who once sought to exterminate the Church, and second as coming from a former "Pharisee of Pharisees" who now works almost entirely out among the Gentiles. As we observed in our discussion of Acts, the very fact that there is a rabbi named Saul, now called Paul, writing "to the Jew first and also to the Greek" (Romans 2:10), constitutes a double revolution in itself, both within Judaism and in the wider world of the *goyim*. And considering that this apostle to the nations planted most of the seeds that sprouted and grew into Christian Europe, and eventually the Christian Americas, the man, his message, and these letters are of not only religious and spiritual but world-historical importance.

The second thing to note about the Pauline Epistles, and then about the General Epistles, is that like the Major and Minor Prophets of the Old Testament, they are arranged by length, not by date of composition or by supposed importance: first come the longest (Romans) through the shortest (Philemon) of Paul's letters; and second come the longest (Hebrews) through the shortest (Jude) of the General Epistles. And a third note about the numbering of the letters: unlike Old Testament books such as 1 and 2 Samuel, which actually constitute a single text divided by early Christian scribes for reasons of convenience, books like 1 and 2 Corinthians and 1 and 2 Timothy are separate, discrete letters – though written to the same audiences.

"With my own hand": Pauline Authorship

All of the letters traditionally attributed to Paul the Apostle begin explicitly with Paul's name as sender, with the exception of Hebrews, for which very few now would claim Pauline authorship. Composed probably between 49 and 64 CE, these letters vary somewhat in length, style, and content, leading to significant modern debate over which can be regarded as genuinely Pauline, and which as pseudonymous. There is little modern disagreement over the authenticity of Romans, the Corinthian letters, Galatians, Philippians, 1 Thessalonians, and Philemon; while many modern critics have attributed all or parts of Ephesians, Colossians, 2 Thessalonians, and the Pastoral Epistles (1 and 2 Timothy and Titus) to other hands. The reasons given include variations in vocabulary (between the Pastorals and the rest); clear duplication of content (between Colossians and Ephesians); and differences in eschatology (between 1 and 2 Thessalonians).

No doubt, Paul actually "wrote" little of any letter, since he dictated them to amanuenses such as Tertius (Romans 16:22), with the apostle occasionally inserting personal messages in his own distinctive handwriting (1 Corinthians 16:21, Galatians 6:11, Colossians 4:18) – which may in itself account for some variations in diction and style as scribes varied. The obvious re-use of language from Colossians in Ephesians could indicate a disciple borrowing Paul's name and imitating Paul's structure while expanding and innovating on his content, though this overlap might also be explained as Paul's creation of circulating letters with similar content, but with his own locally appropriate variations. Altered vocabulary, phrasing, and even ideas may indicate pseudepigraphical writers – or, more simply, the ordinary variety of one man's expressions addressed to different audiences over many years. In the absence of any original autographs of the letters (almost always the case with ancient writings) it is impossible to assert authorship with absolute certainty. But neither is there any compelling reason to deny Pauline authorship to any of these letters. Phony until proven genuine? Or authentic until proven pseudonymous? Who benefits from the doubt?

Finally, we should note that these impossible letters of Paul, which exist in spite of themselves, make it their equally impossible business to reconcile natural enemies: not only God with humanity and Jew with Greek, but also conqueror with conquered, Greek with barbarian, and master with slave, all under the sign of the most despised weapon in the Roman arsenal of fear, the cross. Paul writes as one well aware of his preposterous calling, and he embraces it: "because the foolishness of God is wiser than men, and the weakness of God is stronger than men" (1 Corinthians 1:25). No one could say that Paul's message to the churches succeeded perfectly; yet it succeeded beyond his world's wildest imaginings.

14.1.1 Paul's Letters to Churches

When Paul wrote to the various churches, he wrote not to strangers, but, usually, to people he knew, because his letters follow on and extend his four missionary journeys stretching from Judea and Syria through Asia Minor and Greece and eventually to Italy. He wrote mainly to churches that he had founded, or co-founded; to friends and devoted disciples – though sometimes to adversaries and critics as well. His church letters generally assume a reading aloud to the whole congregation, as an addition to the kind of public presentation of "the Law and the Prophets" common in the synagogues. Yet Paul writes not as to the ancient and ethnically homogenous Jewish communities, but to new assemblies as diverse as the populations of their home cities – and as potentially fractile. Certainly the Roman Empire (like many previous) had corralled an astonishing array of disharmonious peoples together in relative peace under Caesar's eagle, but the binding agent was bloody constraint by legions, not general citizenship or common consent – let alone shared brotherly or divine love.

We are so accustomed to thinking of historic and modern churches in national or ethno-cultural terms – Armenian or Greek Orthodox, Irish Catholic or Southern Baptist, African Methodist Episcopal or Church of England – that we easily forget the radically transnational and interethnic mandate and makeup of the churches first spawned by Paul and the other apostles. These variegated congregants had little or nothing worldly in common besides their coerced *Romanitas* and the accident of location. So Paul grasps at a mosaic of metaphors to describe their new spiritual union: as a divinely chosen and a freely choosing fellowship; as members of a family or a flock; as bondsmen to the same kind Master; as heirs of a King, stewards of treasure, and as organs in a body, the very hands and feet and mouth of their newfound Christ. Paul proclaims an *e pluribus unum* not of birth or the sword, but of rebirth and heart and spirit. It is, as he admits, folly – but only, he says, to those who lack the uncommon sense of faith.

14.1.1.1 At the Center of Power: Romans

Paul's Letter to the Romans comes first among the epistles because of its length (at sixteen chapters the longest of all), but historically it is arguably also the most influential, having played a central role in the conversions of such crucial figures as Augustine of Hippo, Martin Luther, and John Wesley. Laying out his understanding of the gospel for Roman believers whom he had never met (it is probably his only letter to strangers), Paul introduces himself to a church located at the very center of imperial power and based in a city that attracts a bewildering multiplicity of nations, including not only the native Latins, but also people from every corner of the empire – among them a large synagogue of the Jews. Yet in writing to the inhabitants of the capital, Paul's concern is not, as in contemporary Washington or Westminster or Brussels, seeking government connections to obtain special treatment or favorable policies; instead, he writes to offer Rome something that no state or even god-emperor can give: eternal grace and everlasting life.

Paul's Roman Road

Probably written from Corinth between 54 and 57 CE, the Letter to the Romans introduces and expands Paul's understanding of the gospel to a blended congregation of Jewish and Gentile Christians whom he had never met but whom he someday hoped to visit. Apparently the faith had already come to the imperial capital at least a decade earlier, perhaps soon after Pentecost, not through apostolic preaching but through the circulation of new religious ideas along trade and military routes. Thus, one of the empire's greatest material achievements, its network of roads and ports, hastened its spiritual transformation.

In making this offer, Paul is aware that he is presenting a paradox: a gift that no one naturally wants but that everyone desperately needs. Though he speaks to the church as "all who are in Rome, beloved of God, called to be saints" (Romans 1:7), he also addresses the Jews and Gentiles outside it, opening his argument by stating the human predicament that transcends the Hebrew–Greek divide: that everyone knows enough of God to be damned by. For the Gentile, lacking special scriptural revelation, the natural revelation in the surrounding world still calls him rebel and ingrate: "For since the creation of the world [God's] invisible attributes are clearly seen, being understood by the things that are made, even his eternal power and Godhead, so that they are without excuse, because although they knew God, they did not glorify him as God" (1:20–21). It is human nature to suppress this truth; for the Gentile, whether Greek or Roman or barbarian,

> became futile in their thoughts, and their foolish hearts were darkened. Professing to be wise, they became fools, and changed the glory of the incorruptible God into an image made like corruptible man – and birds and four-footed animals and creeping things. (1:21–23)

As bad as matters are for the Gentile, for the Jew, scriptural revelation raises the stakes further, as the knowledge of God's Holy Law only increases responsibility: "For circumcision is indeed profitable if you keep the law; but if you are a breaker of the law, your circumcision has become uncircumcision" (2:25). The outcome? "What then? Are we [Jews] better than they? Not at all. For we have previously charged both Jews and Greeks that they are all under sin" (3:9).

"What then?" is typical of Paul's method – his style throughout the letter being relentlessly interrogative and dialectic as he presents one, then another side in his developing argument. His skills in legal debate and persuasive rhetoric are evident right through the epistle, as he seeks to demonstrate that every one – Jew or Greek – shares the same essential sin problem, and shares an infinite interest in his proposed solution: since "there is none righteous," and no one is justified by works of the law, then "a man is justified by faith apart from deeds of the law" (3:10, 28). Depending on perspective, this is a wondrous, or an alarming, proposition, and in any case a seismic one, shaking as it does the foundations of both Greco-Roman natural virtue, and of the Judaic system in which Saul/Paul had been trained. And so, to make his case to his fellow Jews, the erstwhile master of the Law commences to reread the entire *Torah* through the person and teachings of *Mashiach Y'shua* – Christ Jesus – enlisting even Father Abraham as a hero of faith.

Paul's argument is ingeniously chronological. In order to show the primacy of faith over the Law, he notes that long before Moses received the *Torah* with its 613 *mitzvot* (Exodus 19–20), even before Abram became Abraham and received the covenant sign of circumcision (Genesis 17), the Patriarch had been justified by faith: "And he believed in the LORD, and he accounted it to him for righteousness" (Genesis 15:6, Romans 4:22). Paul's focus on faith also reaches out to Gentiles by going back even further in time beyond Moses and Abraham to Adam, the father of all living – and the author of the death that plagues all humanity. "For if by the one man's offense death reigned through the one, much more those who receive abundance of grace and of the gift of righteousness will reign in life through the One, Jesus Christ" (Romans 5:17). Furthermore, faith also puts Gentiles on an equal footing with Jews, freeing them from any obligation to keep the Mosaic ritual Law, and removing a major barrier to full non-Israelite participation in the growing Church.

But more important for Paul than the legal "justification" that comes by grace through faith is the newfound power that faith brings to overcome the power of evil in one's own life. "What shall we say then? Shall we continue in sin that grace may abound? Certainly not! How shall we who died to sin live any longer in it?" (6:1–2). Paul uses the metaphor of baptismal immersion to redefine the believer's life as now "dead to sin" and "alive to God" (6:11). He also turns to imagery of slavery and freedom – with the natural man in bondage and unable to choose goodness, while the saving grace of God frees the will and enables the "new man" to love and embrace righteousness (6:20–22). In other words, the believer receives not only a pardon for sins past, but a new nature with a new life that tends toward God and his goodness.

Yet Paul also recognizes that this lively new tendency is not the same as easy victory. In fact, he devotes all of Romans 7 to the current predicament of the believer who finds two natures at war within himself: a new "inward man" who "delight[s] in the law of God," and "another law in my members, warring against the law of my mind, and bringing me into captivity to the law of sin which is in my members" (7:22–23). Worse yet, attempting to live according to God's Law by mere willpower only magnifies the problem: "Now if I do what I will not to do, it is no longer I who do it, but sin that dwells in me.... O wretched man that I am! Who will deliver me from this body of death?" (7:20, 24). Paul's back-and-forth method seems to have landed him in a stalemate.

However, as it turns out, according to Paul this day-to-day impasse between sin and goodness is only a passing phase, because, in the long run, God's Spirit not only overcomes the sins of the flesh, but gives new life to the redeemed body. "There is therefore now no condemnation to those who are in Christ Jesus, who do not walk according to the flesh, but according to the Spirit... [I]f the Spirit of him who raised Jesus from the dead dwells in you, he who raised Christ from the dead will also give life to your mortal bodies through his Spirit who dwells in you" (8:1, 11). Far from a Platonic dualism in which physicality and spirituality are perennially at war, Paul (like John in his gospel) sees body and spirit as eventually redeemed and finally transformed by the divine power of the dead and risen Christ. Though sin will persist, in any given moment the Christian can choose the good, and eventually will become good.

The most striking fact about Paul's view of the Christian struggle is that, like the good news of regeneration, it crosses all of the religious, ethnic, and class boundaries dividing Roman life, and takes little notice of matters that might occupy the inhabitants of this city so central to imperial power. Paul portrays this struggle as almost entirely internal, within the self: the believer's truest enemy is not the physical body, or a persecuting Caesar, or even the Devil, but his or her own evil inclinations, powerful still even in their death throes. Thus, all other physical, social, political, and material circumstances are seen as incidental to this central conflict, indeed negligible:

> For I consider that the sufferings of this present time are not worthy to be compared with the glory which shall be revealed in us. For the earnest expectation of the creation eagerly waits for the revealing of the sons of God.... For we know that the whole creation groans and labors with birth pangs together until now. (8:18–19, 22)

Resorting to images of childbirth, Paul repurposes the pagan image of Mother Earth to portray all creation in hard labor to bring forth a glory that presently can only be imagined, revealed not merely "*to* us" or "*for* us" but "*in* us." The heavenly Father is bringing a new humanity to birth, and nothing can stop the delivery; in retrospect, even the worst afflictions will appear as blessings, shedding their tragicomic disguise:

> And we know that all things work together for good to those who love God, to those who are the called according to his purpose. (8:28)

Revisiting Joseph's forgiveness of his brothers – "you meant evil against me; but God meant it for good" (Genesis 50:20) – Paul reiterates the central Judeo-Christian hope in a good and sovereign God, while pushing forward into waters that trouble even while comforting:

> For whom he foreknew, he also predestined to be conformed to the image of his Son, that he might be the firstborn among many brethren. Moreover whom he predestined, these he also called; whom he called, these he also justified; and whom he justified, these he also glorified. (Romans 8:29–30)

God's children – foreknown, predestined, called, justified, and glorified, those who are marked out "according to his purpose" – have nothing to fear and everything to hope for.

But what about the others? Boldly, Paul devotes all of chapter 9 to questions of predestination and election that have long divided Catholics from Protestants, and Protestants among themselves. Though couched as a hypothetical condition, his teaching echoes the books of Exodus, Isaiah, and Hosea in crediting God with absolute control in electing the saved and the damned:

> What if God, wanting to show his wrath and to make his power known, endured with much longsuffering the vessels of wrath prepared for destruction, and that he might make known the riches of his glory on the vessels of mercy, which he had prepared beforehand for glory, even us whom he called, not of the Jews only, but also of the Gentiles? (9:22–24)

Whether God is choosing Jacob over Esau in the womb, hardening Pharaoh's heart, preserving a remnant of Israel's exiles, or redeeming godless *goyim*, he exercises the potter's say over the clay, the creative artist's total rights over his creations, making and unmaking as he sees fit. In the apostle's view, what is remarkable is not that the Lord would judge some and spare others, but that he would spare anyone at all.

Though Paul's doctrine of election tends to fall harshly on modern ears, he is not uncompassionate in presenting it: grieved in heart that so many of his fellow Jews have rejected the gospel, he continues in chapters 10 and 11 to hold out assurance that someday God will gather more of his chosen people out of Israel – now doubly chosen – and join them to the redeemed Gentiles; indeed he's willing to admit that Israel's temporary refusal is providential because it enables the Gentiles' inclusion or "grafting" of their wild stock into the domestic Hebrew olive tree (11:23–24). And underlying Paul's discussion of predestinarian mysteries is his humbling assertion that God's ways are incomprehensible to limited, mortal minds: "Oh, the depth of the riches both of the wisdom and knowledge of God! How unsearchable are his judgments and his ways past finding out!" (11:33). Paul (like Moses, David, Isaiah, and the other prophets) knows that if he were God, dividing the sheep from the goats, he would choose unjustly, but above all Paul knows that he is not God.

Having gazed into the unfathomable depths of what God knows and humans do not, Paul turns from discussing salvation by grace through faith – *not* works – to discussing faith *that* works. That is, having explained how Jew and Gentile, from different starting points, come to new life equally through trust in Christ, he proceeds in chapters 12–16 to describe how that new life should show itself in increasingly practical and specific ways. Assuming that true regeneration reveals itself in fruitful growth, he invites believers to give free rein to their new natures.

> I beseech you therefore, brethren, by the mercies of God, that you present your bodies a living sacrifice, holy, acceptable to God, which is your reasonable service. And do not be conformed to this world, but be transformed by the renewing of your mind, that you may prove what is that good and acceptable and perfect will of God. (12:1–2)

This exhortation is remarkably mild: rather than commanding them as subjects by the coming wrath of God to act out of fear and constraint, he begs them as brothers by God's mercies to act willingly out of gratitude, to return love as the "reasonable" response to the love they have received. He calls on them to break out of the world's confining patterns, freeing their minds and transforming their deeds.

What follows, then, in the letter's final chapters is something gently subversive of all coercive and obligatory systems, whether familial, religious, or governmental. Because Paul conceives of the Holy Spirit as powerful enough to remake and move the soul, his urgings present not a checklist of qualifying behaviors fulfilling a conditional covenant, but instead a call to allow the new life within to reveal itself in the many varied actions of unconditional love. The Mosaic Law, no longer a ladder of achievement, is fulfilled and displaced by a law of liberty. The will, freed by the Spirit from making inevitably self-interested choices, reaches outward to love enemies (12:14, 17), give to the needy (12:8, 13, 20), obey the governing authorities (13:1–7), love neighbors (13:8–10), and put off sinful patterns of action in favor of Christ-like generosity and kindness (13:11–14).

So the "Christian liberty" of which Paul writes is defined, not by how much it can do in *spite* of others, but instead how much it can do in *service* of others. Indeed, chapter 14 deals in detail with contentious matters of opinion in terms that seem bracingly relativistic: though the "strong" Christian knows that all foods are clean and that he can eat anything he likes (14:14), he nevertheless refrains from eating foods that offend the conscience of the "weaker brother" while in his presence (14:21). Similarly, though the mature Christian knows that all days can be equally holy (14:5), she doesn't engage in fruitless disputes with someone who observes special holy days as part of his Christian worship (14:6). Thus, love of the brethren should take on the specific form of deferring to each other in "indifferent" matters (and according to Paul, most matters are indifferent), eager to maintain unity in the few truly essential matters of love and faithful action. Though Paul's later letters will take up the question of discipline for certain sinful behaviors, the most severe sanction is exclusion from communion and fellowship; for violent coercion has no place in the Pauline or indeed in any New Testament system of Church government. Rather than burdening each other with additional rules, regulations, prohibitions, and penalties, Christians are told to bear each other's burdens and scruples, so that they can glorify God together (15:1).

Remarkably, Paul's picture of Christian community anticipates and combines elements of libertarian and collectivist thinking – yet without the anarchic and self-indulgent spirit of some libertarianism, and without collectivism's too-frequent resort to high fines and taxes, minute regulation, and even violent compulsion and torture. Instead, Paul assures believers that because their eternal blessings are secure, they can afford to be patient, tolerant, even celebratory of Christian diversity, and that because their lives and fortunes are now under-written by the Spirit of God, they can afford to give and to do voluntarily and sacrificially for the good of the Church and the secular community. In other words, in writing to the denizens of Rome, the most powerful city on earth, Paul promises them something that their Caesars and legions lack: the strength to love.

14.1.1.2   At the Center of Trade: 1 and 2 Corinthians

Paul's confident and optimistic teachings, written to a body of Roman Christians whom he had never met, are put to a sterner test when addressed to the believers in Corinth, whom he knew all too well.

Corinth: A Troublesome and Beloved Church

Paul seems to have written his surviving letters to the Corinthians not many months apart, and probably in the year 55 CE. The first canonical letter was written during Paul's stay in Ephesus, and the second while he was traveling in Macedonia en route from Ephesus to Corinth. (Scholars note that a now-lost letter seems to have preceded 1 Corinthians – see 1 Corinthians 5:9 – and that another lost letter may have preceded 2 Corinthians – see 2 Corinthians 2:4.) The Corinthian church grew up at the crossroads of Rome's Mediterranean Sea trade, on the northwestern shore of the narrow isthmus that joined the Peloponnesus to the Greek mainland and divided the west-ern, Ionian waters of the Corinthian Gulf from the Aegean waters of the Saronic Gulf to the south-east. Long before the cutting of the Corinthian Canal in the late nineteenth century, the 4 miles (6.3 km) across the isthmus were traversed by a portage of ramps and logs over the narrow neck.

The Corinth of Paul's day was the most important city in Greece, in fact the Roman provincial capital. It had a relatively recent re-foundation in 44 BCE, honoring Julius Caesar a century after its total destruction during Rome's conquest of Greece in 146 BCE by Lucius Mummius. The new city was thriving, and as such was a site of recently acquired mercantile wealth, of a transient and ethnically varied free and slave workforce, and of all the pleasures, vices, gods, and passions usu-ally found among the populations of port cities. The church, drawn by Paul's preaching out of this swirling stew of multicultural commerce, seems to have struggled with the complicated bless-ings of diversity: with little in common in worldly terms, the congregation of cosmopolitan Jew and polyglot Gentile, rich and poor, free and slave, men and women, stoic and ecstatic threat-ened to fracture along many partisan lines. Jewish moralism jostled against pagan license, and Paul strives to point out the errors of both, while pointing beyond petty divisions over non-essentials to the transcendent, sustaining powers of love, interdependence, and resurrection life.

Since ancient times, the "Corinthian" has been proverbial for fine dress, fancy decoration, and licentious living, and indeed the word has entered the English language to describe elaborate architecture, ornate literary style, dandified clothes, and libertine ways. Much of what Paul writes in his two letters bears out this reputation, for clearly this Corinthian church has, in his words to the Romans, been "conformed to this world" (Romans 12:2) – or perhaps has never really left it: he speaks to issues that show human passions to be rampant, including party spirit, sexual laxity, and unwise leniency toward some with excessive harshness toward others. Some Christians are even dragging others into the secular courts, and the visible signs of super-natural unity – the Lord's Supper and the gifts of prophecy and tongues – have become occa-sions for disputes and divisions.

As founder of the Corinthian church (Acts 18:1–17), Paul takes these problems very seriously, and in fact quite personally; for, as becomes clear from 2 Corinthians, the exhortations of 1 Corinthians had been met not only with remorse and repentance, but also with defiance and derision directed at himself. With no legions of soldiers or coercive powers at his disposal, how will this former persecutor reconcile this congregation's divisions and face his detractors?

14.1.1.2.1 *From Many, One: The Unity and Diversity of the Body in 1 Corinthians*
The answer is: directly yet positively – and with bursts of poetic eloquence and even a dash of self-deprecating humor. After his brief salutation, thanking God for endowing them with the gifts of the Spirit, he launches immediately into the heart of the matter:

> Now I plead with you, brethren, by the name of our Lord Jesus Christ, that you all speak the same thing, and that there be no divisions among you, but that you be perfectly joined together in the same mind and in the same judgment. (1 Corinthians 1:10)

As he did with the Romans, he chooses to entreat rather than command, and announces the spiritual ideal toward which they should strive: humble unity of mind and judgment. Putting his finger on the natural tendency to split into factions over personalities, he holds their sectarianism up to unsparing light, sardonically dismissing any possibility that he might hanker for cult-leader status:

> Is Christ divided? Was Paul crucified for you? Or were you baptized in the name of Paul? I thank God that I baptized none of you except Crispus and Gaius, lest anyone should say that I had baptized in my own name. (1:13–15)

Just as he has no iron fist, he also reminds them that they have not joined an elite coterie of the clever, affluent, and powerful, but rather that "I determined not to know anything among you except Jesus Christ and him crucified. I was with you in weakness, in fear, and in much trembling" (2:2–3). And yet, he continues, the Spirit is paradoxically more mighty than any human power, and wiser than any human wisdom, and the Spirit's sign is modest love, not proud division.

Thus, Paul's opening appeal sets the terms for everything that is to come in these two letters: if the Corinthians have the Holy Spirit, as he hopes and as they loudly claim, they will show it by submitting to each other and to Christ. And in fact everything in the first letter follows directly from this template: his portrayal of himself and the other apostles as unprepossessing "fools for Christ's sake"; his exhortation to sexual self-control and to showing the blatantly immoral the door; his call to bear with being cheated rather than suing each other in pagan courts; his counsel of mutual yielding and fidelity in marriage; his encouragement to defer one's own "liberty" to the scruples of "the weaker brother"; his entreaty to put the needs of others before one's own rights; his appeal to women (newly welcomed into the mixed messianic assembly) to continue covering their heads to show submission; and his injunctions to observe the Lord's Supper in good order and to exercise spiritual gifts not for personal glory but for the good of all (4:10, 5:1–8, 6:7, 7:3–5, 8:9–13, 9:19, 11:2–26, and 12:7, 12). The climactic image of these twelve chapters is, significantly, that of the church as a body – that wonderfully symmetrical organism that we all experience from the inside out, astonishingly diverse and complex in its constituent parts, yet (except in unusually ill persons) amazingly harmonious in shared purpose and action, a walking *e pluribus unum*.

In contrast, to satirize the Corinthians' communal chaos Paul resorts to some sharp parody. What if, he asks, their physical bodies acted like their church body?

> If the foot should say, "Because I am not a hand, I am not of the body," is it therefore not of the body? And if the ear should say, "Because I am not an eye, I am not of the body," is it therefore not of the body? If the whole body were an eye, where would be the hearing? If the whole were hearing, where would be the smelling? (12:15–17)

The images of an enormous disembodied eye rolling about, or of a foot hopping free, or an ear fluttering like half a butterfly appeal to a sense of the absurd, reminding us that a sense of humor is a sense of proportion. Will these quarreling Christians laugh themselves into harmony?

In answer, Paul segues from the ridiculous to the sublime. While satire may catch the conscience, nothing can move the feelings and the will like beauty and love, and what follows in 1 Corinthians 13 is almost certainly the most beautiful "love song" ever penned – if by "love" we mean not only the familial, romantic, or friendly affections, but the steadfast and unconditioned *chesed* and the sacrificial *agapé* by which the Hebrew Bible and the Greek New Testament define the character of God, who undergirds all other loves. This divine love is difficult to distinguish from mercy and grace, because they are all so similar in action: unmerited and unsought by the self-righteous and self-sufficient; offered by Christ with blood and tears and often rejected by sinners as in insult; yet finally irresistible to the poor in spirit, embraced by the heartbroken like a buoy in a storm and enjoyed like a feast in a famine. And, by some miracle, says Paul, this love can be theirs not only to receive but to give.

To grasp the fuller meaning of the "Love Chapter," so much a staple at weddings and funerals, we must read it as both embedded in its context of a fractious, self-saturated church, and yet as oriented to eternity, as if one were to catch a glimpse of Bunyan's Delectable Mountains through a chink in the walls of some filthy lockup – and then to discover that this gap is the way out to the High Country. The chapter is exquisite in itself, yet far more so when seen in poignant contrast to its setting. Having just discussed the congregation's sordid squabble over spiritual gifts, Paul promises "a more excellent way," and delivers a description splendid beyond all hope.

So much has been, and can be, said to explain this text that I will confine myself to one further observation: though famed for its heart-melting tenderness of expression, its main point is love's durability, its survival when all other things have passed away – for "Love never fails" (1 Corinthians 13:8). Love prevails primarily because it is indestructible while everything else wears out, because prophecies, tongues, knowledge, and also agonies and evils, will all become obsolete. The exact opposite of wishful thinking, Pauline love is too good to be false, an immortal diamond glittering in the dross.

---

1 Corinthians 13: The Great Love Psalm

Famed even among those with little biblical knowledge, Paul's "Love Chapter" nevertheless usually escapes notice as what it is, both formally and poetically: a Hebraic psalm, albeit composed in Greek. Rich in simile and metaphor, the passage is structured around parallel repetition – often tripled, for special emphasis; it makes use of refrain ("love is … love is … love is") and a kind of litany of what love is not (envious, puffed-up, rude, angry, vindictive); and its insertion in an extended discussion of unlovely strife marks a dramatic instance of juxtaposition. It even has the ebb and flow of deep internal rhythms, evident in English and even more so in the original. Perhaps it is time to begin printing it in Bibles as verse!

The influence of this chapter on literature, from Augustine to Dante to Herbert to Dostoyevsky, is immeasurable, but one prominent example will do: Shakespeare's Sonnet 116, "Let me not to the marriage of true minds," follows Paul's lead by defining both what love is not and what it is, dismissing that which "alters when it alteration finds, / Or bends with the remover to remove." Instead, positive images of permanence, endurance, and quiet triumph climax the poem: the "ever-fixéd mark," the "star to every wand'ring bark," which "bears it out, even to the edge of doom." Though later the Sonnets seem to fall away from this lofty conception of sacrificial of love, back into self-accusing confusion, they never repudiate this moment of heavenly clarity and aspiration toward something eternal, beyond self-love, self-contempt, and lust. In the words of Shakespeare's Cleopatra, his Sonnets express "immortal longings," caught from St. Paul.

After this climactic love-hymn, Paul turns to practical applications – much in keeping with a heavenly love that expresses itself in earthly good. The true exercise of spiritual gifts, he says, reveals itself in ways that are consistent with spiritual humility and good order. Rather than making ecstatic prophecies and tongues ends in themselves, these *charismata* are intended by God for the encouragement of the church, and as a testimony to visiting non-believers. Thus, tongues and revelations, while welcome in the congregation, must be interpreted: "[b]ut if there is no interpreter, let him keep silent in church, and let him speak to himself and to God" (114:28). Women, now welcome in mixed Christian worship (they were traditionally excluded or segregated both in the pagan temples and in Jewish synagogues), are themselves welcome to pray and prophecy aloud, as long as they continue to cover their heads and refrain from disrupting the service by curious chattering (11:5, 14:34–35).

Having driven home his practical point about mutually submissive love, Paul builds to a second and final inspirational climax in chapter 15 about the evidence for and the meaning of Christ's resurrection. In Paul's doctrine, Christian faith produces not only ecstatic states and cooperative minds, but also the sober certainty of waking bliss. Like Luke's and John's gospels claiming to present eyewitness testimony of miraculous healings and life from the dead, Paul stresses that the physical resurrection of Jesus is central, indeed essential, to the believer's life of hope; thus

> if Christ is not risen, your faith is futile; you are still in your sins! Then also those who have fallen asleep in Christ have perished. If in this life only we have hope in Christ, we are of all men the most pitiable. (15:17–19)

According to Paul, Jesus's resurrection guarantees not only the historic reality of God the Son's earthly intervention, but also the acceptance of his atoning sacrifice by God the Father. Far from teaching a doctrine of positive thinking in which pleasant fictions overrule the world's realities, Paul insists that any sustainable source of metaphysical hope must actually be physically true. He even numbers himself among the over 500 eyewitnesses of the risen Christ (15:6–7), though, he insists, an unworthy one.

Having stated his case for certainty of the resurrection, he shifts from reason to celebration. Frequently set to music over the centuries (most famously in Handel's *Messiah*) his paean rises to a high pitch of chiastic eloquence:

> But now Christ is risen from the dead… For since by man came death, by Man also came the resurrection of the dead. For as in Adam all die, even so in Christ all shall be made alive… The last enemy that will be destroyed is death…
>
> Behold, I tell you a mystery: We shall not all sleep, but we shall all be changed – in a moment, in the twinkling of an eye, at the last trumpet. For the trumpet will sound, and the dead will be raised incorruptible, and we shall be changed. (15:20–22, 26, 51–52)

"Death, thou shalt die!" gloats John Donne at the end of his Holy Sonnet 10, "Death, be not proud" (l. 14) – a most succinct statement of the paradox at the heart of Christian belief, in which the Last Enemy becomes the greatest friend by ushering the faithful into everlasting life. Yet Paul, even at his most heavenly minded, concludes with an immediate earthly application: "Therefore, my beloved brethren, be steadfast, immovable, always abounding in the work of the Lord, knowing that your labor is not in vain in the Lord" (15:58). So it is fitting that 1 Corinthians 16 draws the letter to an end with practical messages, instructions about money, and future travel plans, and then concludes with an exhortation to await Paul's coming and, in the meantime, to act out of love, not rivalry.

14.1.1.2.2 *"Talking Like a Madman": Paul's Self-Defense in 2 Corinthians*
One might hope that such an epistolary masterpiece might have moved the Corinthians to peace, but that does not seem to have been its shorter-term effect. Written eloquence was not enough; instead, it is evident from the letter that we call 2 Corinthians (actually probably the fourth in a string of Pauline letters to this church) that the church's immediate response was further conflict, intensified by blistering attacks from some in the congregation on Paul's character and apostolic authority. So, in between these two canonical letters, Paul appears to have popped across the Aegean from Ephesus for a brief and unsuccessful personal visit, followed by a rather severe letter (now lost) calling them again to repentance. This stern letter, carried by Titus, had a much better effect, giving Paul joy of their spiritual restoration (2 Corinthians 2:1, 3–4, 7:6–16). Yet in this final letter to Corinth, Paul writes as a man with unfinished business, concerned lest attacks against him personally will somehow hinder the work of the gospel collectively. Thus, he delivers one of the least defensive self-defenses in all literature, presented with wry, disarming humor as well as open-handed emotional candor.

The main subject of Paul's candor is Paul himself. He had already admitted his unworthiness of apostolic office (1 Corinthians 15:9) and his lack of personal "presence": "I was with you in weakness, in fear, and in much trembling" (1 Corinthians 2:3) – a point which he repeats in 2 Corinthians 11:6, conceding his lack of fine oratorical training. He is, if anything, even more candid about his deep, paternal attachment to the Corinthians themselves:

> You are our epistle written in our hearts, known and read by all men; clearly you are an epistle of Christ, ministered by us, written not with ink but by the Spirit of the living God, not on tablets of stone but on tablets of flesh, that is, of the heart. (2 Corinthians 3:2–3)

Again "pleading with you by the meekness and gentleness of Christ" (10:1), he reminds the skeptics and opponents among them that authority flows not from domineering behavior or boastful claims of wealth and worldly power, but rather from being marked out by the Suffering Servant for more suffering service. About that, indeed, he will "boast," and compare himself with his self-proclaimed rivals and critics. He adopts the demeanor of the jester or licensed fool, bragging about that which the world finds shameful in order to shame the world:

> Are they ministers of Christ? – I am talking like a madman – I am more: in labors more abundant, in stripes above measure, in prisons more frequently, in deaths often. From the Jews five times I received forty stripes minus one. Three times I was beaten with rods; once I was stoned; three times I was shipwrecked; a night and a day I have been in the deep; in journeys often, in perils of waters, in perils of robbers, in perils of my own countrymen, in perils of the Gentiles, in perils in the city, in perils in the wilderness, in perils in the sea, in perils among false brethren; in weariness and toil, in sleeplessness often, in hunger and thirst, in fastings often, in cold and nakedness … (11:23–27)

Then, summing up these impressive statistics, he doffs his madcap and speaks straight to the purpose: "If I must boast, I will boast in the things which concern my infirmity" (11:30). If his detractors are so eager to push into his apostolic office, they must be eager to share *all* of its perquisites.

Yes, there is glory, he admits: "I know a man in Christ" (he means himself) "who ... was caught up into Paradise and heard inexpressible words, which it is not lawful for a man to utter." Yet this awe is tempered with agony: "And lest I should be exalted above measure by the abundance of the revelations, a thorn in the flesh was given to me... For when I am weak, then I am strong" (12:2, 4, 7, 10). What then, Paul concludes, are the "signs of an apostle"? "Signs and wonders and mighty deeds" (12:12), certainly, but the scars of ministry, too. Thus, Paul's self-abnegating satire comes to an earnest point: even his enemies must realize that they can't humiliate a humbled man.

14.1.1.3   The Law of Grace: Galatians, Ephesians, Philippians, Colossians

The four briefer letters that follow Romans and 1 and 2 Corinthians share in common those first three letters' basic structure of explaining doctrine and then applying it, as the gospel's theory is all about practice. Yet these latter four epistles, for all their evident practicality, share with the former three a stress on the primacy of grace and faith over works as the starting point of salvation. In Paul's view, the Mosaic Law, though good and just, can only convict and condemn; only God's saving grace can bring a new nature to the believer. This new creation, like the first creation in Genesis, is a divine gift, not a human effort; yet similar to the natural laws set in motion by God at the foundation of the world, the law of grace results in growth and action, like the biological laws of life itself.

14.1.1.3.1   *Proclaim Liberty: The Damascus Road to Spiritual Freedom in Galatians*

Galatians is unique among the Pauline Epistles for the type of its intended audience – for Galatia was not a city, but a larger province of Rome's empire in central Asia Minor, where Paul had traveled during his first three missionary journeys.

Galatians: Letter to a Region

One theory places the letter's composition in 49 CE, and assumes that Paul addresses the churches of the southern Galatian region visited during his First and Second Missionary Journeys: Pisidian Antioch, Iconium, Lystra, and Derbe, at about the time of the Second Jerusalem Council (Acts 15), which dealt with issues of law and gospel.

Another theory favors a date half a decade later, in 54–55 CE, and an audience of the north Galatians, after his Third Missionary Journey there and not long before Paul's Letter to the Romans and his multiple letters to the Corinthians, which similarly deal with matters of faith and works in diverse and potentially fractile congregations.

In either case, though, Paul addresses this letter to the churches in a Roman administrative province in central Anatolia (modern Turkey) called "Galatia" after the Celtic invaders from southern Gaul (modern France) via Macedonia early in the third century BCE. The Galatian capital Ancyra (the modern Turkish capital Ankara), and the smaller cities Pessinus and Tavium, had become Hellenized before incorporation into the Roman Empire in 25 BCE under Augustus, though in addition to Greek the Galatians still spoke a Celtic language similar to that of Gaul and of the Treveri in the Rhineland. Galatia had ancient connections to Israel: Josephus links its pre-Celtic inhabitants with the biblical figure Gomer, son of Japheth (Genesis 10:2), and more recent archeology connects them to the Hittites of Abraham's day (Genesis 23). And Galatia, like Paul's boyhood province of Cilicia immediately to the south, boasted well-established Jewish communities, which may help to account for the continuing influence of "Judaizing" teachers in the region's churches.

Yet despite this wider audience, Paul's gospel is deeply personal, focused as it is on the redemption of particular individuals, so it makes sense that he begins his letter to the Galatians with a piece of autobiography.

Paul's Confessions: The Birth of a Genre in Acts and Galatians

Confessio is Latin for "speaking along with" or "acknowledgment," yet it is not to Latin literature but to Old Testament poetry, and to the New Testament figure of St. Paul, that the world most owes the genre usually called "Confessional." Paul's template – candor about a sinful past as context for a dramatic conversion story – receives its popular name at the end of the fourth century CE in Augustine's *Confessions*, the north African bishop's account of his own arrogant, hedonistic young heart which, to paraphrase the book's famous opening words, was "restless until it found rest in Thee."

This personal narrative of his turn on the Damascus Road, however, has an important collective purpose: to confirm the divine source of Paul's message, in order to overthrow the influence of legalistic doctrines on the impressionable Galatians.

And Paul's address to the Galatians is, if anything, even more blunt than his multiple rebukes of the Corinthians. Scarcely has he finished his greeting – stressing his apostleship "not from men nor through man, but through Jesus Christ and God the Father" (Galatians 1:1) – but he launches into a pained, and painful, reprimand to frame his own story:

> I marvel that you are turning away so soon from Him who called you in the grace of Christ, to a different gospel... But I make known to you, brethren, that the gospel which was preached by me is not according to man. For I neither received it from man, nor was I taught it, but it came through the revelation of Jesus Christ. (1:6, 11–12)

Insisting that his message is not man-made or even man-taught, he proceeds to give his oft-repeated account of his past zealous persecution of the Church, his Damascus Road encounter with the risen Savior, the blinding insight that it brought him, his three years of Arabian desert wandering, his meeting with Peter and the apostles, and – another eleven years later – his eventual calling as an apostle. The old Saul is gone, the new Paul lives: "I have been crucified with Christ; it is no longer I who live, but Christ lives in me; and the life which I now live in the flesh I live by faith in the Son of God" (2:20).

Paul's purpose in giving his testimony at this point and in this way is twofold: to establish that, however cruel and wicked his past acts, his word now is directly from God; and to show that no one could know better the ways of the Law, its lofty demands, and its crushing disappointments. For, given his Pharisaical history, he claims to see most clearly the stakes in the debate over Law and grace. "O foolish Galatians! Who has bewitched you ...? Did you receive the Spirit by the works of the law, or by the hearing of faith? Are you so foolish?" (3:1–3). And indeed, seeking works righteousness, he says, is a fool's errand: the Law, though good and true, can only bring a curse to sinners, for "[c]ursed is everyone who does not continue in all things which are written in the book of the law, to do them" (Deuteronomy 27:26, Galatians 3:10). Even by Old Testament warrant, he argues, legal obedience can save only the sinless; and the sinless need no salvation. Christ is the only way out, the only way to freedom, because in crucifixion Christ has "become a curse for us (for it is written, 'Cursed is everyone who hangs on a tree')" (Deuteronomy 21:23, Galatians 3:13). Switching metaphors, Paul compares the Law to a virtuous, stern tutor whose purpose was to prepare a child for grown inheritance; "[b]ut after faith has come, we are no longer under a tutor" (Galatians 3:25).

Thus, Paul's gospel is a proclamation of full adult emancipation; for whatever the constraining or confining circumstances pressing on the believer, they no longer define his – or, significantly, her – identity: "There is neither Jew nor Greek, there is neither slave nor free, there is neither male nor female; for you are all one in Christ Jesus" (3:28). Remarkably, Paul anticipates in this one laconic statement the postmodern trinity of race, class, and gender, announcing not their abolition but their spiritual irrelevance in a kind of declaration that in Christ, all men – indeed all people – are re-created equal. But more importantly for Paul than his converts' naturalization as equal citizens of the heavenly city is their adoption as equal children and heirs of the heavenly Father. For this reason Paul fears that the Galatians will slide back from free sonship, acting out of gratitude and love, into laborious slavery, acting out of calculation and dread. He warns against teachers who wish to add Mosaic compliance to faith in Jesus as further conditions for God's acceptance. He even pulls in a typological allegory to persuade them: referring back to Genesis, he warns that Abraham's son Ishmael, despite being the oldest, was not the covenantal heir because he was the son of Hagar, the slave woman, while Isaac, the younger, was nevertheless the "son of the promise" because the son of the freewoman, Sarah (Genesis 16, 21; Galatians 4:31).

The rest of Galatians repeats Paul's exhortations to reject slavery and to remain free – and to walk freely in love and in the Spirit. "Stand fast therefore in the liberty by which Christ has made us free, and do not be entangled again with a yoke of bondage" (Galatians 5:1). He warns that such reliance on fleshly circumcision will yield "the works of the flesh" – a toxic mix of deadly sins from adultery to drunkenness to murder (5:19–21) – while "the fruit of the Spirit is love, joy, peace, longsuffering, kindness, goodness, faithfulness, gentleness, self-control. Against such there is no law" (5:22–23). Yet this litany of sweet divine fruits is countered somewhat by Paul's flash of very bitter human outrage against the teachers whom he sees as moving in to cut out and cut up vulnerable members of his flock: "I could wish that those who trouble you would even cut themselves off!" (5:12) – a phrase which plays on the Judaizers' insistence that only circumcision can complete salvation. In essence, Paul is telling them to take their wisdom to its logical conclusion and emasculate themselves.

But except for this glimpse of the old angry Saul of Tarsus, Galatians ends, like Paul's preceding doctrinal letters, on a practical and personal note. Christians will use their liberty to bear others' burdens and share their own goods, he says; they also will remember that God's eternal mercy will not always exempt people from the temporal consequences of their folly, "for whatever a man sows, that he will also reap" (6:7). His final words, written for emphasis in his own handwriting, repeat one last time his warning not to mark themselves unnecessarily by circumcision, but to glory in Christ's wounds on the cross. To those eager to cut their flesh to save their souls, he concludes, poignantly, "let no one trouble me, for I bear in my body the marks of the Lord Jesus" (6:17).

14.1.1.3.2 Cure the Walking Dead: Spiritual Rot and Resurrection in Ephesians

Paul's epistle to the Ephesians takes up the doctrine of divine grace elaborated in Romans, and defended in Galatians, and asks probingly how this heavenly grace can remake everyday lives. How do expansive concepts like sin, grace, faith, law, and predestination work out in marriages, families, and in labor? How, Paul asks, does the Church discover the mystery of divine love at the heart of ordinary things? To answer these questions Paul begins from the loftiest perspective – indeed, "in the heavenlies" – and then descends dramatically to the darkest abyss of human nature, confronting the worst of the bad news before embracing the best of the good. Grimmer than a death's head, and yet brighter than an optimist's smile, Ephesians exceeds cynical gloom, outstrips hope, and seeks to make drudgery divine.

Ephesians: A Circular Letter?

Paul probably wrote Ephesians in the year 60 or 61 CE from house arrest in Rome, at about the same time that he wrote both Philippians and Colossians. In fact, although the letter is specifically addressed "to the saints who are in Ephesus" (though only in some manuscripts) it makes no other personal references to particular local names or details. This has seemed strange to some interpreters, given Paul's past years in Ephesus, as described in Acts 19 and 20. Located in western Asia Minor, Ephesus was the gateway to Roman Anatolia, and the principal city of the region boasting one of the empire's greatest temples, dedicated to the goddess Artemis, or Diana; and the Ephesian church seems to have been the largest in Roman Asia. So the letter may have begun as the first stage in an encyclical, a set of general doctrinal epistles based on the same theological outline and then simply addressed to particular congregations. In fact, as we will see below, Colossians follows much the same lineaments as Ephesians, only more briefly.

Ephesians divides rather neatly into two main and equal parts: chapters 1–3, laying down principles about who Christians are, and chapters 4–6, specifying practical actions by which Christians walk. The first chapter begins the opening section by explaining the earthly good of being heavenly minded: believers who are "predestined … to adoption as sons" (Ephesians 1:5), heirs of eternal life, and secure in the spiritual power that raised Christ from the dead can afford to overflow with grace and kindness in this present world. Chapter 2 contrasts this blessed redeemed state with the naturally sinful state of humanity, and Paul's dominant metaphor is that of the "revenant," the bogy of the rotting "walking dead" feared by many ancient cultures, including the Greeks – and revived in modern times as the "zombie":

> And you [Christ] made alive, who were dead in trespasses and sins, in which you once walked according to the course of this world, according to the prince of the power of the air, the spirit who now works in the sons of disobedience, among whom also we all once conducted ourselves in the lusts of our flesh, fulfilling the desires of the flesh and of the mind, and were by nature children of wrath, just as the others. (2:1–3)

Human in appearance but corpses at heart, the unregenerate – whether Gentile or Jew – move about in a miasma of doom, propelled by demonic inspiration and their own corrupt impulses as they stumble toward the wrath that their deeds deserve. It is hard to imagine a gloomier picture of human potential.

As in the antediluvian horror of Genesis 6:5 – "every intent of the thoughts of [man's] heart was only evil continually" – the sinner's spiritual inability is vividly imagined. With less hope of spiritual self-improvement than a cadaver has of self-healing, the only cure for the walking dead is resurrection, a gracious divine infusion of new life: "For by grace you have been saved through faith, and that not of yourselves; it is the gift of God, not of works, lest anyone should boast" (Ephesians 2:8–9). This resurrection, says Paul, amounts to being remade, "For we are his workmanship, created in Christ Jesus for good works, which God prepared beforehand that we should walk in them" (2:10). Shifting metaphors to architecture, Paul integrates this individual salvation into collective redemption, speaking of Christ as the "chief cornerstone" and Christ's people as stones "being fitted together, grow[ing] into a holy temple in the Lord" (2:21).

Chapter 3 makes clear that since one of the natural man's besetting crimes is ethnic and religious hatred, one of the signal fruits of regeneration is love of former enemies: the wonderful mystery, now revealed, is that "the Gentiles should be fellow heirs [with the Jews], of the same body, and partakers of His promise in Christ through the gospel" (3:6). According to Paul, humanity is now beginning an age not only of spiritual regeneration, but also of new revelation, as things hidden "from the beginning of the ages" (3:9) become plain and obvious – starting with the conversion of Paul, the persecuting Pharisee and "less than the least of all the saints" (3:8), into a messenger of grace and reconciliation.

Having described the new shared resurrected identity of these once-hostile adversaries, Paul turns in chapter 4 to the second and final section detailing how such born-again beings should behave. As with the Corinthians, he knows that kindness to people of other kinds will not come naturally: "I, therefore, the prisoner of the Lord, beseech you to walk worthy of the calling with which you were called, with all lowliness and gentleness, with longsuffering, bearing with one another in love, endeavoring to keep the unity of the Spirit in the bond of peace" (Ephesians 4:1–3). As in Romans 12:1 begging rather than commanding, and as in 2 Corinthians 11:23 boasting only in the humiliation of his jail cell, Paul calls his hearers to live what they are – or at least what they should be.

Yet in Paul's gospel, the word "should" has a different force than that of mere moral effort; it is not mainly the "should" of obligation, but rather the "should" of probability and likelihood, as a living seed should sprout and a bud should bloom. Success in this case is the only sign of life; failure is the sign, not of weakness, but of death. As in his Roman and Corinthian letters, Paul enumerates spiritual gifts that are given for harmony, not rivalry, and he reminds his audience of their new mind in Christ. Four times in six sentences he uses a paradoxically passive construction to recommend inaction as action: "Let him who stole steal no longer… Let not the sun go down on your wrath… Let no corrupt word proceed out of your mouth… Let all bitterness … be put away from you" (Ephesians 4:25–31). In other words, they must allow their evil deeds to stop, and believers must allow themselves to perform what somehow they already are: "be kind to one another, tenderhearted, forgiving one another, even as God in Christ forgave you" (4:32).

Chapter 5 expands on this language of the spiritual "walk" – walking in love, walking in light, walking in wisdom (5:1–21). Then, at the end of this chapter and on into chapter 6, Paul arrives at the epistle's most practical destination, the often conflicted crossroads of marriage, family life, and employment. Calling for mutual submission among all believers, he particularizes this calling for wives toward their husbands, then raises the stakes for the husbands, telling the men to give up their lives for their wives as Christ did on the cross. Reminding children to obey their parents, he turns the tables by exhorting fathers not to "provoke your children to wrath"; prompting servants and slaves to obey their masters, he makes the exhortation mutual, calling masters to "give up threatening" and to recall that their heavenly Master will call them to account for any harsh words and deeds (5:21–6:9).

The World Turned Inside Out: Paul and Social Hierarchy

We've seen how the Book of Acts portrays a "world turned upside down" (Acts 17:6) in which everything about the first-century world order – its obsessions with power and knowledge and self – was to be displaced by an inverted ethic of service and love. And in Galatians Paul assumes an essential spiritual equality among all believers of whatever race or sex or rank (Galatians 3:28). Paul's treatment of social hierarchies in Ephesians and Colossians partakes of this same spirit, seeking to right a capsized system, and to model an order in which the foolish things of this world will shame the wise. Modern Western readers are likely to miss the real shock administered to Paul's contemporaries by his teachings (Ephesians 5:21–6:9, Colossians 3:18–25) on marriage, family, and work.

In a Roman world where the *paterfamilias* could legally put his wife, children, and slaves to death, no one would have found anything strange in Paul's statements about their submission, yet many if not most in Paul's day would have boggled at his doctrines of mutual submission, and of leadership as humble sacrifice. By telling husbands to lay down their lives for their wives, fathers gently to nurture their children, and masters to cherish their servants, Paul is turning the world not only upside down but inside out. He bypasses the question of "who is in charge" by charging authority with its obligations rather than its privileges, focusing on inner duties and affections rather than outward compliance. Ancient authoritarians and some modern egalitarians would object that Paul is naïvely ignoring the realities of power and the need for coercion; Paul would likely respond that he has known the greater power of divine love.

Having called the spiritually dead to rise (chapters 1–3) and walk (chapters 4–6), Paul concludes Ephesians by warning them to stand and prepare to fight – not "against flesh and blood," but "against principalities, against powers, against the rulers of the darkness of this age, against spiritual hosts of wickedness in the heavenly places." As if believers were living in two dimensions at once, they are told to present a peaceful face toward their fellow humans, but to prepare for war against the demonic realm, donning "the whole armor of God so that you may be able to stand against the wiles of devil" (6:11–12). Itemizing this spiritual armor in a brief allegorical passage (6:13–19) – the chief inspiration in John Bunyan's *Pilgrim's Progress* for Christian's armor worn during the fight against Apollyon – Paul leaves his readers encouraged, exhorted, armed, and ready for battle. He closes by reminding them that he too inhabits both realms as "an ambassador in chains": a prisoner of an earthly regime in Rome, he nevertheless represents the Emperor of Emperors.

14.1.1.3.3 *"Let This Mind Be in You": The Springs of Joy in Philippians*

The counter-cultural living called for by Paul's gospel would be hard, dry work – indeed as unsustainable as sweat-labor in the desert unless the workers have learned to draw from an invisible source of refreshment. So in his letter to the Philippians, Paul keeps returning to that source – which, paradoxically, is not drilled deep like a well in dry country, but is a kind of heavenly spring, unstoppably flowing from above with hope and joy that cheerfully defy circumstances. Paul's circumstances at the time of writing were indeed grim: probably from prison, whether in Caesarea or Rome, Paul addresses a church that he planted, so to speak, from the Philippian jail. As narrated in Acts 16, he and Silas had offended at Philippi by liberating a slave girl from a demon, for which they were beaten by a mob and tossed into a dungeon, where they proceeded to sing happily in their chains until a midnight earthquake opened the cells, and brought the terrified and suicidal jailer on his knees to his captives for spiritual deliverance (Acts 16:16–34).

Philippi: Soldier's Colony, Gentile Church

Paul's "prison letter" probably was written, along with Ephesians and Colossians, from Rome in 61 CE during his house arrest there (Acts 28), though some scholars place the writing a few years earlier, during a previous, unrecorded imprisonment at Ephesus, or months earlier, while in Caesarea toward the end of his two-year imprisonment there en route to Rome (Acts 23–26). Paul addresses a unique, largely Gentile church in the Roman *colonia* (colony) of Philippi, named in the fourth century BCE by Alexander the Great for his father Philip. This prosperous Macedonian city stood on the Egnation Way from Rome to its eastern provinces, and had been the site of the decisive battle in 42 BCE when the armies of Rome's Second Triumvirate defeated Brutus and Cassius, the assassins of Julius Caesar. Settled by retired soldiers of the imperial legions, the city had no synagogue – the convert Lydia is portrayed in Acts 16:13–15 keeping her Sabbath worship down by the riverside – and Paul warns its mainly Gentile congregation against Jewish proselytizers who teach that circumcision is necessary for salvation (Philippians 3:2–6).

Thus, Philippi's church had been founded in a literal shaking of foundations and in the reversal of an unjust hierarchy. Such a paradox presages Paul's claims in Philippians that the way up is down: that Christ models the true nature of things by beginning on high and, like the light and the rain, seeking the dark and low places of the earth.

So Paul, though a ruling apostle, begins his letter not by telling the Philippians what they owe him, but what he owes them. Opening with a paean of thanksgiving, he extols their God-given fullness overflowing to him in generosity. This humble and joyful start segues into what might seem to be bad news, his reminder that currently he is in "chains"; yet the ebullient Paul celebrates these bonds as opportunities for gospel witness "to the whole palace guard" (whether in Caesarea or Rome) and as making the brethren in Judea "much more bold to speak the word without fear" (Philippians 1: 13–14).

Thus, Paul overflows with happiness – forms of the Greek *chará* (joy) appear sixteen times in the short book – but the caged bird sings most eloquently in the second chapter, as he praises the deliberate downward trajectory of the Most High:

> Let this mind be in you which was also in Christ Jesus, who, being in the form of God, did not consider it robbery to be equal with God, but made himself of no reputation, taking the form of a bondservant, and coming in the likeness of men. And being found in appearance as a man, he humbled himself and became obedient to the point of death, even the death of the cross. (2:5–8)

This jailhouse hymn to the incarnation traces Christ's great "emptying" – Greek *kenosis* – through its descending stages, as each new bottom opens out onto further abysses below: from being fully "equal with God," to obscure earthly manhood, to despised slavery, to a death sentence, to the most excruciating of Roman executions. But this descent rebounds in re-ascent: "Therefore God also has highly exalted him and given him the name which is above every name, that at the name of Jesus every knee should bow" (2:9–10). The most telling word here is "therefore"; it is as if some law of metaphysics dictates that, logically, an intentional plunge to the rescue requires an equal and opposite rising – that somehow the fall furthers the flight.

For, as it happens, this hymn-like passage is embedded in Paul's larger discussion of relations among believers; as in the previous letters, he confronts the naturally fragile unity of a diverse body, and seeks to inspire a cohesive humility among them. Yet in this case he appeals not only to the self-humbling model of Christ; he also relies on the Philippians' affection for himself, asking them to "fulfill my joy by being like-minded," as if their making him happy would be their own reward (2:2). This confidence springs from a deep familiarity – the Philippians are not only "saints" and "brethren" throughout, but also "my beloved" and "my joy and crown" (4:1) – and the letter is sprinkled with warm and feeling personal references, to his disciples and traveling co-workers Timothy and Epaphroditus (both favorites with the congregation), to Euodia and Syntyche (two quarreling friends whom Paul implores to make peace), and to Clement ("a fellow-worker in the gospel") (2:19–30, 4:2–3). Over and again, Paul's prescription for congregational ills and divisions is simply joy – "Rejoice in the Lord always. Again I will say, rejoice!" (4:4) – as if it were silly to waste time worrying and bickering when they might simply be drinking deep of God's everyday glory. Thus, Paul signs off by noting the gospel's inroads in the heart of the enemy's camp: "All the saints greet you, but especially those who are of Caesar's household" (4:22).

14.1.1.3.4 *"Firstborn Over All Creation": Christ Almighty in Colossians*
If Philippians celebrates the power of joy, then Colossians extols the joy of power – not one's personal power, or any coercive secular power in the State or for the Church (for the Church would have none for centuries) but the joy of contemplating Christ's perfect power

wedded to his perfect goodness in the service of perfect love. As Genesis inverts the natural order of ancient Near Eastern cosmology by imagining an omnipotent Deity who exalts the lowly, so Colossians upends first-century cosmology and social order by asserting that love, justice, and mercy command creation's heights, and also the deepest heart of reality. If, as many scholars believe, Colossians presents a condensed version of Ephesians' teachings on marriage, family, and work as part of a "circular letter" distributed in varied forms throughout Asia Minor, this epistle nevertheless places a new focus on the divine *dunamis* (Greek "power").

Colossians: Once More for Emphasis

Paul probably wrote Colossians in the year 60 CE from house arrest in Rome, at about the same time that he wrote Philippians, Ephesians, and Philemon. (See boxes on those three letters.) Colosse, an important wool-trading city in the Phrygian region of Asia Minor, was home to large Greek and Jewish populations, and at the time of Paul's letter had an established Christian congregation – apparently not founded by Paul himself – which was being influenced by the Gnostic and syncretistic religious teachings against which he warns in this epistle.

This focus enables ordinary mortals to live according to everlasting truth in a corrupted age: Paul's opening prayer is that the congregation in Colosse be "strengthened with all might, according to His glorious *power*, for all patience and longsuffering with joy" because God "has delivered us from the *power* of darkness and conveyed us into the kingdom of the Son of his love" (Colossians 1:11, 13, emphases mine). Thus, Colossians is concerned not so much with the power to be great, but with the power to be good, like *Christos Pantocrator* – Christ Almighty – himself.

Paul praises Christ's almighty goodness in a hymnic passage immediately following this prayer, clearly referencing not only the creation account of Genesis 1 but also the paean to creative divine Wisdom in Proverbs 8:22–31:

> He is the image of the invisible God, the firstborn over all creation. For by him all things were created that are in heaven and that are on earth, visible and invisible, whether thrones or dominions or principalities or powers. All things were created through him and for him. And he is before all things, and in him all things consist. (Colossians 1:15–17)

Like Adam, Jesus Christ bears the divine image (Greek *ikon*, translating Hebrew *tselem*), but he is more than Adam, indeed Christ is the true "firstborn," the oldest Son carrying not only his Father's image but his very essence, and he is the inheritor of all the Father's realms. And with double reason – for Christ is not only the heir, but himself the agent of creation, the one who made heaven and earth and all of their subsidiary powers, and the one who holds all this creation together still. Paul could hardly have expressed a more robust view of Christ's deity.

Having praised the omnipotent Christ, Paul immediately applies that omnipotence to the practical cases of Church and social life:

> And he is the head of the body, the church, who is the beginning, the firstborn from the dead, that in all things he may have the preeminence. For it pleased the Father that in him all the fullness should dwell, and by him to reconcile all things to himself, by him,

whether things on earth or things in heaven, having made peace through the blood of his cross. (1:18–20)

Because, Paul argues, Christ is pre-eminent in all things, he has the power to decree peace in the Church and in the world, and because he became lower than all things on the cross, he gives an example of how that peace is to be made: through sacrifice. Contrary to the unnatural doings on earth, it is in the true nature of the most powerful to serve the least. Thus, Paul redefines nature itself.

Paul is well aware that the breathtaking ambition of these words will strike most of his contemporaries, and perhaps many of his fellow Jews and even some professing Christians, as the purest nonsense. So in chapter 2 he warns his readers against inroads by certain kinds of syncretic Gnostic "philosophy": "Beware lest anyone cheat you through philosophy and empty deceit, according to the tradition of men, according to the basic principles of the world, and not according to Christ" (2:8). Such Hellenistic philosophies based their views of reality on a split between the spiritual realms of the Forms and "the basic [or 'elemental'] principles of the world" (Greek *stoicheia*), probably a reference to the four elements of earth, air, fire, and water. These philosophies sought to explain all health and behavior in terms of proper balances among these four elements, and between them and the corresponding four humors of black bile, blood, yellow bile, and phlegm – often with a mystical overlay of extra-biblical Jewish lore about angelic messengers and ascetic purification. Against this radical division between spiritual and material realms, Paul proposes a radical integration in the person of Christ himself: "For in him dwells all the fullness of the Godhead bodily; and you are complete in him, who is the head of all principality and power" (2:9). It is on this basis of a reconciled cosmos under an omnipotent, incarnate Christ that Paul then expounds the principles of Christian living in marriage, family, and the workplace.

Arguing that the heavenly-minded Christian now has the power to do some earthly good, Paul repeats, more briefly, his advice from Ephesians: on wifely submission and husbandly cherishing, on children's obedience and paternal kindness, and on servants' wholeheartedness and masterly fairness (3:18–4:1). Then he concludes, sending greetings to and from particular people, including, significantly, "Luke the beloved physician" (4:14), his traveling companion in his later years and his eventual chronicler in the Book of Acts. Finally, as in Ephesians and Philippians, he reminds them – twice – of his "chains," and bids farewell in his own handwriting. He has taught them that "your life is hidden with Christ in God"; hidden in a Roman prison, he awaits with the far-off Colossians deliverance by an all-powerful Savior, for "[w]hen Christ who is our life appears, then you also will appear with him in glory" (3:3–4).

14.1.1.4 Paul's Apocalypse: 1 and 2 Thessalonians

The reappearance of the glorified Christ – the *Parousia* or "Second Coming" – is a teaching more often associated in the popular imagination with certain predictions in the gospels, and with the Book of Revelation. But it is a central concern of two Pauline Epistles as well: his letters to the Thessalonians. As with Paul's letters to the Corinthians, we can trace here an increasingly intense interaction between the apostle and a cherished congregation on matters of controversial "false teaching"; however, in this case that teaching has primarily to do with the timing of Christ's return, a topic touched on in only one chapter of the Corinthian letters, 1 Corinthians 15. Paul's concern for the Thessalonians is that a doctrine intended as a source of profound hope for the next world, and a motivation for good works in this world, is being converted into a cause of crippling anxiety, or debilitating fatalism.

---

1 and 2 Thessalonians and the Apocalypse: The World's Last Night in Stereoscope

Probably written from Corinth in 50 or 51 CE, Paul's correspondence with the church at Thessalonica may be the oldest of his surviving letters, at least if a later date of composition (i.e. 55–56 rather than 49 CE) is accepted for Galatians. Paul's brief preaching visit in 49 CE to Thessalonica's synagogue (Acts 17:1–9), while initially well received, had eventually occasioned violent reprisals led by some Jews. They were dismayed at the success of Paul's message, which, the rioters famously complained, had "turned the world upside down" (Acts 17:6). Thus, while much of the space in the first three chapters is devoted to somewhat disconnected personal matters (to which Paul's companions Silvanus [Silas] and Timothy may have contributed material) 1 Thessalonians hits its stride in chapter 4 when Paul takes up that ultimate inversion at the end of time, "the coming of the Lord" (1 Thessalonians 4:15).

While the same trio of Paul, Silvanus, and Timothy are named as composing and sending 2 Thessalonians (see 1:1), modern challenges have been leveled against Paul's authorship of this second letter on varied grounds, though these are rather hard to reconcile: while some have claimed that the doctrine of the two letters is so similar that the second is a mere copied imitation of the first, others have argued that they teach contradictory eschatologies (theories of the Last Days) and thus cannot have come from the same mind(s) and pen(s). As noted previously, in the absence of any autographs of the originals, it is impossible to "prove" authorship. However, reasonable comparison of 1 and 2 Thessalonians suggests more than enough difference to make the second a sequel to, rather than a copy of, the first, and enough resemblance in ideas to suggest complementarity. Thus, those seeking either perfect identity or clear contradiction of outlook are all likely to be disappointed.

The two letters read as if composed in fairly close sequence: the first mentions the End Times as a consolation to a persecuted and suffering church, while the second elaborates on that teaching, and attempts to correct misunderstandings arising from the first.

Even Paul's first salutation to the Thessalonians declares the centrality of the *Parousia* to their new faith, remarking on "how you turned to God from idols to serve the living and true God, and to wait for his Son from heaven, whom he raised from the dead" (1 Thessalonians 1:9–10). But the new converts seem to have expressed anxiety about those who have died since Paul's departure, so Paul reassures them that Christ's resurrection will someday belong to all the faithful, whether dead or alive:

> For if we believe that Jesus died and rose again, even so God will bring with him those who sleep in Jesus… For the Lord himself will descend from heaven with a shout, with the voice of an archangel, and with the trumpet of God. And the dead in Christ will rise first. Then we who are alive and remain shall be caught up together with them in the clouds to meet the Lord in the air. (1 Thessalonians 4:14, 16–17)

Yet, continues Paul, the "times and seasons" of Christ's return remain mysterious, for "the day of the Lord so comes as a thief in the night" – as a complete surprise, with sudden destruction, even as the world calls out "Peace and safety!" (1 Thessalonians 5:2, 3). "Therefore," Paul warns, "let us not sleep, as others do, but let us watch and be sober" and also "comfort each other and edify one another" (1 Thessalonians 5:6, 11).

However much Paul intended a message of sobriety and comfort in this first letter, it appears from his second to the new church that his words were misunderstood, or perhaps deliberately misrepresented, in ways that produced both apathy and anxiety. To those anxious that Jesus has already returned and they have been "left behind," he writes reassuringly that they are "not to be soon shaken in mind or troubled, either by spirit or by word or by letter, as if from us, as though the day of Christ had come" (2 Thessalonians 2:2). Apparently a false epistle had troubled their hope (he signs this letter "with my own hand" to guarantee authenticity – 2 Thessalonians 3:17), so Paul reminds the church that though Christ's return will come as a surprise, it will be unmistakable, being associated with the appearance of "the son of perdition … the lawless one," a figure of such unprecedented human evil and deceptive power that he will demand universal worship "so that he sits as God in the temple of God" (2 Thessalonians 2:4).

But in addition to the metaphysically distressed are their opposites, the spiritually idle. In these indolent brethren, the thought of an imminent "Second Coming" has bred not worry but fatalism, and with it laziness and gossip. So Paul warns the church that "[i]f anyone will not work, neither shall he eat. For we hear that there are some who walk among you in a disorderly manner, not working at all, but are busybodies" (2 Thessalonians 3:10–11). For these Paul recommends the church's ultimate punishment: "note that person and do not keep company with him, that he may be ashamed." Yet even this shunning is more redemptive than punitive: "do not count him as an enemy," Paul concludes, "but admonish him as a brother." As in 1 Thessalonians, the apostle's main point is that the church must "not grow weary in well-doing," but instead be found in active, loving service whenever the Master returns (2 Thessalonians 3:13–15).

14.1.2   Paul's Letters to Individuals

As often as Paul expresses personal affection and concern in his letters to entire churches, a few of his letters address individuals alone. Yet, however rich these four individual letters may be in personal reference, they nevertheless concern themselves with weighty matters in the life of not only the particular believer but also of the whole congregation. The first three of these letters – 1 and 2 Timothy and Titus – are usually called the "Pastoral Epistles" because they speak to two young pastors about the specific blessings and trials of leading a local *ekklesia* or church assembly; the fourth deals with one man, Philemon, about the fate of another – an escaped slave named Onesimus. Like all of Paul's letters, these final four treat singular circumstances and particular situations as doorways into general practices and universal truths.

14.1.2.1   Pastoral Epistles: 1 and 2 Timothy, Titus

One of Paul's chief concerns in his missionary travels was to cultivate leadership for the new church bodies that he left scattered around the Mediterranean's northeastern rim and its island archipelagos. He attracted many disciples and traveling co-workers over the years: Aquilla, Aristarchus, Barnabas, Epaphras, Gaius, John Mark, Justus, Luke, Priscilla, Secundus, Silas, Sopater, Tertius, Trophimus, and Tychicus – to name many but not all of those who appear in his letters and alongside him in the Book of Acts. But a special few of these beloved companions became his pastoral protégés and emissaries, trained and trusted not only to evangelize but also to care for specific church bodies in all their idiosyncratic complexity, and to raise up local leaders for them. Two of these happy few, each of whom Paul called his "true son in the faith," were Timothy and Titus.

To Timothy, Paul writes two surviving letters and to Titus one, though 1 Timothy more closely resembles the epistle to Titus than it does 2 Timothy. For while all three Pastoral Epistles concern themselves substantially with the problem of "false teachers" in the church, it is in 1 Timothy and Titus that Paul spells out more clearly than anywhere else the specific qualifications and duties of the church's main officers, the *episcopos* (overseer or bishop) and the *diaconos* (deacon). For this and other reasons (see box on "1 and 2 Timothy and Titus") it appears that 1 Timothy and Titus were written at around the same time during Paul's last missionary journey, while 2 Timothy belongs to the time of Paul's final imprisonment at Rome, just before his execution.

---

1 and 2 Timothy and Titus: Servant Leaders and Famous Last Words

All three of the "Pastoral Epistles" claim in their opening verses to come from "Paul, an apostle of Jesus Christ," and all speak to their young pastoral addressees with great personal affection and specific biographical knowledge. (For instance, Paul writes of Timothy's mother and grandmother Eunice and Lois in 2 Timothy 1:5, and of Titus's travel plans in Titus 3:12–13.) Furthermore, both Timothy and Titus are mentioned repeatedly elsewhere in the New Testament as Paul's traveling companions – for example, Timothy in Acts 16:2–3 and 1 Corinthians 16:10, and Titus in 2 Corinthians 2:13 and Galatians 2:1–3. Some scholars have noted differences between the vocabulary in the Pastorals and that of Paul's earlier epistles as grounds for questioning Pauline authorship, yet these differences can reasonably be ascribed to different amanuenses, and most likely, to the simple passage of time.

For the Pastorals are the latest of Paul's letters, written probably, in the cases of 1 Timothy and Titus, around 62–63 CE, during Paul's final missionary journey, and in the case of 2 Timothy, between 64 and 68 CE, from a Roman prison where he awaited martyrdom. Samuel Johnson said that "when a man knows he is to be hanged in a fortnight, it concentrates his mind wonderfully," and Paul's already well-focused mind was concentrated to a gem-like clarity toward the end. He underscores to his young disciples the urgency of preaching the word "in season and out of season" (2 Timothy 4:2), and of devolving leadership only on those with the proven faith and character to treat leadership as service, and he concludes his swan-song epistle with some of the most famous last words ever penned: "I have fought the good fight, I have finished the race, I have kept the faith" (2 Timothy 4:7).

Indeed, much as the longer letter to the Ephesians may have provided an outline for the shorter to the Colossians, the longer 1 Timothy seems to provide a template for the briefer Titus. Both letters open with personal endearments – to Paul's half-Jewish, fully circumcised "son in the faith" Timothy in Ephesus, and to his fully Greek, uncircumcised "son in the faith" Titus on Crete – and then move briskly to give instructions on the choosing of leaders in the context of false teachers making inroads with their young churches. As also addressed in the letter to the Colossians, these teachings seem to have consisted of some Jewishly inflected version of emergent Gnosticism, claiming a cult of secret enlightenment and contempt for the body as grounds for hedonistic excess and a denial of Christ's resurrected authority (1 Timothy 1:8–11, Titus 1:10–16). Thus, says Paul, it is urgent that Timothy and Titus put the right kind of shepherds in charge of their flocks:

> appoint elders in every city as I commanded you – if a man is blameless, the husband of one wife, having faithful children not accused of dissipation or insubordination. For a bishop must be blameless, as a steward of God, not self-willed, not quick-tempered, not given to wine, not violent, not greedy for money, but hospitable, a lover of what is good, sober-minded, just, holy, self-controlled, holding fast the faithful word as he has been taught, that he may be able, by sound doctrine, both to exhort and convict those who contradict. (Titus 1:5–9, closely resembling 1 Timothy 3:2–7)

Using the word *episcopos* (overseer or bishop) interchangeably with *presbyteros* (elder), Paul mines the bedrock on which the church will be built: men respected in the community, loyal and effective husbands and fathers, kind, unflappable, courageous, generous, intelligent, reasonable – leaders by example, and not in word only. Also, Paul invokes similar criteria for the church's deacons, its ministers of mercy and down-to-earth heavenly help (1 Timothy 3:8–13). And where are Timothy and Titus to find such paragons? Look not among the elite, but down among the faithful, says Paul; despite a history of turmoil in Ephesus (Acts 19), and the generally bad reputation of Cretan men (Titus 1:12), the well-traveled apostle is sure that God will raise up tried and true servants in every place, and that it will be their calling to raise up more.

Thus, while the Pastoral Epistles are not deeply reflective theological treatises like Romans, Ephesians, or Colossians, they affirm those theological teachings by being what we might call "theopractical" – describing a plan and a structure for implementing the gospel vision, for fighting what Paul calls "the good fight of faith" (1 Timothy 6:12). And that plan mainly depends not on elaborate governmental hierarchies or detailed systems of regulation, but on the character and wisdom of individuals, working together not as cogs in a machine but as living organs in a well-knit body, animated by the Spirit and moved by Christ, the Head.

14.1.2.2 "More Than a Slave": Philemon

Paul's final letter to an individual is also his shortest, and therefore last in his section of the New Testament canon. Philemon, we learn from this epistle's mere twenty-five verses, is a longtime friend and gospel "fellow laborer" living in Colosse.

Onesimus: The Man Who Stole Himself

Written from house arrest in Rome with Timothy's help, and probably sent at the same time as Colossians in 60 CE, Paul's letter to Philemon addresses a good friend on a literally personal issue: the return of stolen property in the person of the letter-bearer, the runaway slave Onesimus. In a modern world that rightly regards slavery as one of the chief crimes against humanity, it may be hard for the reader to understand why Paul doesn't simply order Philemon to free Onesimus and have done with it – or why Paul would send Onesimus back; or, for that matter, why Onesimus would turn self-courier and go. But the Roman Empire, for all its devotion to order and legality, lacked any concept of God-given individual dignity and rights, which after all have a Judeo-Christian basis. Thus, Paul's letter is quietly revolutionary in its gentle but firm subversion of the slave culture, not because such revolution is his primary purpose, but because he sees liberty and dignity as naturally flowing from Christian love and brotherhood.

The letter breathes with personal affection, expressed in warm greetings to Philemon, his family, and "the church in your house." Yet something is not quite right; someone has gone missing from Philemon's household, someone who strangely enough is now with Paul in Rome, the someone who is both the subject of the letter and the letter's deliverer: Philemon's escaped slave Onesimus. The epistle asks a great deal of both its bearer and its receiver, for Paul requests that Onesimus return valuable stolen property – himself – and that Philemon give up his rights to this valuable property in return for receiving a Christian brother.

It may be hard for us to imagine how Paul could say such complimentary things to a slave-owner, or why Onesimus would go back to Philemon who, under Roman law, had the right to kill him, both as a slave and as a runaway. But Paul makes clear that his goal for these two men is something even greater than freedom for one and submission for the other:

> Therefore, though I might be very bold in Christ to command you what is fitting, yet for love's sake I rather appeal to you … for my son Onesimus, whom I have begotten while in my chains, who once was unprofitable to you, but now is profitable to you and to me. I am sending him back. You therefore receive him, that is, my own heart, whom I wished to keep with me, that on your behalf he might minister to me in my chains for the gospel. But without your consent I wanted to do nothing, that your good deed might not be by compulsion, as it were, but voluntary. For perhaps he departed for a while for this purpose, that you might receive him forever, no longer as a slave but more than a slave – a beloved brother … (Philemon 8–16)

Mixing personal pathos (for the last time we hear Paul rhetorically rattle his chains), a pun (Onesimus means "useful" or "profitable"), veiled authority ("I might … command"), and a calling in of past favors, Paul appeals beyond mere manumission to actual brotherly reconciliation, confident that Philemon's better angels will prevail, and compulsion will give way to voluntary love. That we can read this letter twenty centuries on suggests that they did.

14.2 General Epistles: Hebrews, James, 1 and 2 Peter, Jude

We've observed how hard it is to overstate the strangeness of the Pauline Epistles – their very existence is singular (letters to churches from the one man who most sought to destroy churches), and though their author is beset by violent controversy all his life, their burden is peace and reconciliation through love. As we turn now to the last, non-Pauline Epistles in the New Testament, the strangeness continues, from an anonymous letter to Jews about how their Jewish Messiah is also the Gentiles' Christ (Hebrews), through letters, from the man who denied Jesus, about courage under trial (1 and 2 Peter), to letters from two brothers about the Savior who probably came from their own mother's womb (James and Jude). (We will consider the three letters of John separately.)

These five letters are usually described together as "General" or "Catholic" Epistles, because they share in common a general or universal (hence "catholic") address beyond the boundaries of specific local churches. The anonymous Letter to the Hebrews addresses Jewish followers of Jesus in general, and the letter partakes strongly of its readers' ethnic identity; the rest of these epistles address all believers, regardless of nation, people, or city, and are marked by the unique personalities of their authors. Thus, generality meets specificity in these letters.

14.2.1 Better Than Moses: The Letter to the Hebrews

The four gospels and the Book of Acts portray a Church born out of the synagogues and Temple worship of Israel, and thus at first as an overwhelmingly Jewish movement. Jesus, the apostles, and all the earliest disciples were Jews, and the earliest waves of mass conversion at Pentecost were of Jews as well, albeit "from every nation under heaven" (Acts 2:5). Yet the gospels and Acts make clear that this Hebrew messianic flowering is intended to bear miraculous Gentile fruit. Thirty years after Pentecost, the second great wave of Gentile conversion had left many of the initial Jewish converts feeling isolated, puzzled, and even abandoned. Cast out of synagogues, still oppressed by Rome's crescendo of hostility to Jews, and increasingly outnumbered by *goyim* in the burgeoning churches, many were tempted to return to the ancestral fold. It is to answer these anxieties that this special and anonymous epistle was written.

Hebrews: Anonymous Letter to a Nation

The Letter to the Hebrews begins with a mystery: it lacks the opening "from–to" salutation usual in the Hellenistic epistolary form, so that, while its audience of diasporic, messianic Jews can be very clearly inferred from its content, its authorship remains unknown. Though by the middle second century CE Clement and Origen attributed the letter to Paul, most scholars from the sixteenth century on have denied Pauline authorship – its writer denies apostolic rank to himself (Hebrews 2:3), and in any case, it would be the only Pauline epistle not to begin with an explicitly Pauline greeting. The author is master of a fine Greek style and a deep knowledge of the Septuagint, and was probably a Hebrew himself, had suffered imprisonment for his faith, and was personally known to many in his audience, as well as to Paul's protégé Timothy. Many candidates have been proposed, none decisively: Pauline companions including Barnabas, Luke the evangelist (though a Gentile), Apollos, Priscilla (though a Greek participle identifies the writer as male – 11:32), Epaphras, and Silas, as well as Clement of Rome. Significantly, the letter combines a Pauline doctrine of justification by faith with Johannine language of Christ the divine Word.

Of the letter's date we can be more sure. It addresses a rising tide of Roman persecution (10:32–34), which probably locates it at least a decade after Claudius's expulsion of the Jews from Rome in 49 CE, most likely at the time of Nero's escalating attacks on Christians in 64 CE, but at latest the letter comes a few years before Jerusalem's destruction in 70 CE, because it speaks of Temple worship as still active and functioning – if now spiritually obsolete.

Rich in reference to the Old Testament and to Jewish custom, the letter reminds its readers that the way out of their predicament is not returning to the now obsolete rituals of earthly Temple worship, but moving forward with the true High Priest himself – Jesus who is also the promised Prophet and messianic King, and the fulfillment of centuries-long ritual typology and scriptural hope. Clearly written while the Temple still stood in about 64 CE, the letter anticipates the day – the terribly close day coming in 70 CE – when not one of the Temple's stones would be left upon another. Thus, says the anonymous author, God's chosen people will choose to embrace the substance of Christ, rather than retreat to the shadow of past, and passing, tradition.

The epistle falls into two main sections: in chapters 1–10, an extended argument for the superiority of God's Son, Jesus Christ, over Hebrew Law and ritual, and in chapters 10–12, a briefer case for the practical implications of that superiority. More specifically, chapters 1 and 2 present God's Son as pre-eminent over the angels; chapters 3 and 4 show Christ to be greater than Moses and his Law; chapters 4 through 7 proclaim Christ's priesthood over Aaron's; and chapters 8–10 illustrate Christ's supremacy in his new covenant, in his spiritual tabernacle, and his final sacrifice. In the second, shorter section of chapters 10 through 12, Christ's new covenant demonstrates its primacy through greater responsibility, empowering faith, and the promise of a heavenly Jerusalem. But this superiority neither dismisses nor denigrates the Hebraic past; instead, in keeping with how the gospels and Acts handle Hebrew practice, it fulfills and completes that practice.

At the heart of the letter's argument about the Mosaic Law is the metaphor of the "shadow" versus the "substance," or what in later interpretation has been called the "type" versus the "fulfillment." In this "typological" view, the main purpose of the Old Testament's myriad characters, stories, and laws is to point ahead, like lived parables, to the coming reality of Jesus Christ; thus the Aaronic priests still ministering (for a few more short years) in the Jerusalem Temple according to the Mosaic instructions serve the copy and shadow of the heavenly things, as Moses was divinely instructed when he was about to make the tabernacle. For [God] said, "See that you make all things according to the pattern shown you on the mountain"... But now [Christ] has obtained a more excellent ministry, inasmuch as he is also Mediator of a better covenant. (Hebrews 8:5–6)

While literally and historically important in their own right, the prophet Moses and the High Priest Aaron represent the coming completion of God's "new covenant" in the divine Son and Messiah, as also predicted in Jeremiah 31:31.

Having argued that Christ is better than Moses as the substance is better than the shadow, the writer of Hebrews in chapter 11 employs this idea powerfully in his reading of the entire salvation history of the Jews. Figures from Abel and Abraham through Samuel and David are said to prefigure the coming Messiah, particularly in their reliance on faith to receive God's blessings. "Now faith is the substance of things hoped for, the evidence of things not seen" (Hebrews 11:1), the author famously writes, as if faith itself were the substantial and indeed material down-payment on the coming wealth of heaven: for it is through faith that they all

> subdued kingdoms, worked righteousness, obtained promises, stopped the mouths of lions, quenched the violence of fire, escaped the edge of the sword, out of weakness were made strong, became valiant in battle, turned to flight the armies of the aliens. Women received their dead raised to life again. (11:33–35)

This "cloud of witnesses," including the lawgiver Moses himself, all look forward to Jesus, "the author and finisher of our faith, who for the joy that was set before him endured the cross, despising the shame, and has sat down at the right hand of the throne of God" (12:2). Thus, the present generation of suffering Hebrews can embrace their own trials, confident that, like their fathers and mothers before them, they are traveling not to Mount Sinai, with its terrible fires and thunders, but "to Mount Zion and to the city of the living God, the heavenly Jerusalem, to an innumerable company of angels" (12:18, 22). Like John Bunyan's Pilgrim named "Christian" – whom this passage no doubt inspired – the wandering Hebrew believer is off on a great quest to discover "the city which has foundations, whose builder and maker is God" (11:10).

14.2.2 Trials of the Faith that Works: James

As the Letter to the Hebrews addresses the Israelites who have trusted in Jesus, so the Letter of James addresses all whose faith in Jesus has made them spiritual Israelites. "To the twelve tribes which are scattered abroad" (James 1:1), he begins, bestowing full Abrahamic identity on Gentiles as well as Jews – and holding them to the same moral standards as the Law and the Prophets.

James: Letter from "the Brother of the Lord" to the New Israel

Though some have taken the "twelve tribes" mentioned in James' salutation to mean a mainly Jewish audience like that of the Epistle to the Hebrews, the reality long before the first century CE was that only three of the original twelve tribes of Israel survived with any tribal integrity after the fall of the Northern Kingdom in 722 BCE: Judah, Benjamin, and Levi. Thus, James seems to intend the new spiritual Israel, the Church, spreading out from the diasporic synagogues from which it grew throughout the Roman Empire, but now made up increasingly of Gentile converts, as well as "completed Jews."

Though there was more than one important James in the early Church (the others being the apostle "James the Greater," brother of John and son of Zebedee, and another "James the Less," son of Alphaeus), tradition has attributed this letter to "James the Just," "the brother of the Lord" (Matthew 13:55, 25:56; Mark 15:40, 16:1; Acts 15:13, 21:18; Galatians 1:18), whom many Protestants believe to have been the son of Joseph and Mary and brother of Jesus, Joses, Jude, and Simon, while believers in the perpetual virginity of Mary (Roman Catholics, Orthodox, and some Protestants) believe this James actually to have been Jesus' cousin, though figuratively called his "brother" in the New Testament.

Though the authenticity of James was challenged during the Reformation era by Martin Luther, the early Church historian Hegesippus regarded the letter as genuinely the work of "James the Just" written sometime between 44 CE – when concerted persecution of diasporic Christians began – and 62 CE, the year of James's death.

Profoundly ethical and bracingly practical, James most resembles one of the Old Testament's "forthtelling" oracles like Elijah or Amos; thus, his is the New Testament book that most famously – even notoriously – insists on good works of justice and mercy as the only true evidence of living faith. Like Jesus's blistering gospel denunciations of the Sadducees' greed and the Pharisees' hypocrisy (see Matthew 22–23), James's moral outrage flows directly from his compassion for the suffering and his sense of every person's God-given dignity. Both Jesus and James speak as direct heirs of Mary, whose "Magnificat" fiercely "magnifies the Lord" who "has scattered the proud in the imagination of their hearts," "put down the mighty from their thrones," and "exalted the lowly" (Luke 1:51–52), and who will reward suffering with glory.

Thus, James begins by reminding his readers that suffering is the likely lot of every believer – and that it is a good thing, too. "My brethren, count it all joy when you fall into various trials" (certainly a counter-intuitive kind of joy) "knowing that the testing of your faith produces patience" (James 1:2–3). Suffering, says James, separates the genuine from the false, the faithful from the "double-minded" or opportunistic; it also differentiates the "rich" and fair-weather brother from the poor but bona fide true believer who weathers the storm. Indeed, James puts a phrase like "true believer" in a different perspective; consistent with his roots in *Torah*, James says that the infidel is exposed not only by his or her misbelief, but by *infidelity* – that is, by the distance between profession and practice. "Be doers of the word, and not hearers only, deceiving yourselves," he writes (1:22), and his operant understanding of "true belief" is not in an opposition of "faith vs. works," but rather "faith *that* works" – through trial, loss, and temptation, come ruin or rapture.

Clearly, James is writing to correct a notion of "faith" (Greek *pistis*) as mere intellectual assent to a creed or a set of propositions, rather than as the active, transformative outworking of divine grace which, according to Paul in Ephesians 2:10, remakes the Christian as "[God's] workmanship, created in Christ Jesus for good works, which God prepared beforehand that we should walk in them." Thus, while Paul and James have often been set at odds by commentators as the opposing advocates of salvation by "faith" vs. "works," James's most famed passage on the topic seems to be saying much the same as Paul in Ephesians:

> But someone will say, "You have faith, and I have works." Show me your faith without your works, and I will show you my faith by my works. You believe that there is one God. You do well. Even the demons believe – and tremble! (James 2:18–19)

Laying his axe to the root of "faith" as propositional assent, James paints the stunning scenario of the demons' damning "belief" in a God whom they hate, dreading their inevitable doom. "Thus," says James, "faith by itself, if it does not have works, is dead" (2:17).

For James, a "lively" faith is shown as much by what it won't or can't do, as by what it does. Not only does faith endure "various trials"; it tolerates no prejudice or favoritism (2:1–13), it refuses to curse or slander (3:1–12), it refrains from exalting oneself, condemning one's brother, and boasting about the future (4:1–10, 11–12, 13–17). Celebrating these spiritual disabilities, James instead casts a vision that echoes with prophetic urgency, proverbial compression, and psalmic power:

> Come now, you rich, weep and howl for your miseries that are coming upon you! Your riches are corrupted, and your garments are moth-eaten. Your gold and silver are corroded, and their corrosion will be a witness against you and will eat your flesh like fire. You have heaped up treasure in the last days... You have condemned, you have murdered the just; he does not resist you. Therefore be patient, brethren, until the coming of the Lord. See how the farmer waits for the precious fruit of the earth, waiting patiently for it until it receives the early and latter rain. You also be patient. (5:1–3, 7–8)

No fire sermon of Isaiah or Amos ever seared with a sharper, bluer flame, or turned more quickly to words of comfort and patience. The very pithiness of James's message is part of its meaning – it is adamant, glittering in its cutting conciseness, immortal diamond; yet suddenly kind, tender, compassionate, as in the letter's very last words: "Brethren, if anyone among you wanders from the truth, and someone turns him back, let him know that he who turns a sinner from the error of his way will save a soul from death and cover a multitude of sins" (5:19–20). The fire of James is a consuming flame, purifying the dross from a working faith.

14.2.3 The Forge of Persecution and the Cancer of Corruption: 1 and 2 Peter

"To the pilgrims," begins the First Epistle of Peter, and one of the letter's main themes is the interplay between wandering and permanence – indeed, paradoxically, the pilgrims' deliberate wandering in search of permanence.

---

1 Peter: Letter to the Dispersion

As with the Letter of James, some have taken 1 Peter's audience of "the pilgrims of the Dispersion in Pontus, Galatia, Cappadocia, Asia, and Bithynia" (1 Peter 1:1) as referring exclusively to Jewish converts from the Diaspora. However, while such Jews would certainly be among those addressed, it is more likely that, like James, Peter is applying Hebrew terminology to a newly Christian context and thus is writing to all believers "dispersed" about Asia Minor – as 1 Peter 1:18 and 4:3 fairly clearly indicate a substantially Gentile readership.

Since the earliest times the letter has been attributed to Simon Peter, the apostle known both for his spiritual perception ("You are the Christ!" – Matthew 16:16) and his fearful denial ("I do not know him!" – Luke 22:57) regarding Jesus. Some modern scholars have questioned his authorship due to the letter's fine Greek style thought unlikely to have come from a humble Hebrew fisherman, but Simon Peter was likely literate and (at least) bilingual all his life, and might well have perfected his Greek over the thirty years since the crucifixion, especially with the help of an amanuensis such as Silvanus (1 Peter 5:12). The other main objection to Petrine authorship has been that the persecutions described by the letter supposedly did not occur until the time of Domitian in the 90s CE; however, this objection ignores the very real persecutions under Nero during the 60s that took Paul's life, and according to ancient tradition Peter's, between 65 and 68 CE. Both apostles very likely died in Rome, Peter's location when he wrote this letter (1 Peter 5:13, interpreting "Babylon" as Rome). Thus, the letter most probably was composed by Peter and Silvanus at Rome between 65 and 68 CE.

In an irony perhaps not lost on the author, Peter (Greek *Petros*, Aramaic *Cephas*, "The Rock") writes to these wayfaring strangers, wandering through a transient world of woe, about "the word of the LORD [that] endures forever" (1 Peter 1:25, quoting Isaiah 40:8), and also about Christ, "the chief cornerstone" – who is also "A stone of stumbling / And a rock of offense" (1 Peter 2:7, 8, quoting Psalm 118:22 and Isaiah 8:14). In other words, the "Rock" who rolled (Peter, the one who denied Christ three times) commends the immovable "Rock" of Jesus Christ, who is both the foundation of a whole new order and the overthrow of the old.

Yet, as in the "upside down" world of the Book of Acts, this revolutionary overthrow comes not through violent rebellion, but through humble well-doing as "sojourners" in the midst of worldly corruption and "fleshly lusts," and above all through submission to even highly flawed human authorities: whether as subjects to the emperor and local rulers, or as servants to masters, or as wives to husbands (1 Peter 2:13–3:6) – husbands being told reciprocally to honor their wives "as heirs together of the grace of life" (1 Peter 3:7). In this temporarily inverted world, persecution and suffering are the frequent unjust rewards for good living – just as they were for Jesus's life – and yet rewards indeed, because shared with the Savior (1 Peter 4:12–13).

It is in this context that Peter exhorts these spiritual "shepherds" (Greek *poimenoi*, often translated with the Latin word *pastores* or "pastors") to keep watch over their poor wandering flocks according to the model of Jesus the "Chief Shepherd" himself, "not by compulsion but willingly, not for dishonest gain but eagerly; nor as being lords over those entrusted to you, but being examples to the flock" (1 Peter 5:2–3). The apostle's charge to these elders may sound as impossible as shepherding frightened lambs through a wildfire, yet he promises that the flame will not hurt them, and the wayfarer's reward is "the crown of glory that does not fade away" as if purified on persecution's forge (1 Peter 5:4).

If 1 Peter warns against searing outward trials, 2 Peter warns of trials from within – both within the self and within the Church. Its theme is false teachers: those who peddle brands of esoteric *gnosis* like those denounced by Paul in Colossians and Titus, and who twist or mock the doctrine of the *Parousia* or "Second Coming" of Christ. No doubt, a diatribe against "false teaching" may be uncongenial to many contemporary readers. We live in an era that often celebrates heterodoxy, heresy, and rebellion against convention, an age when, as Pink Floyd memorably sang, "we don't need no thought control." In fact many modern readers are likely to dismiss any religion characterized by a corrupt "false consciousness," a hypocritical system of metaphysical fantasy and speculation designed to justify the believer's lust and greed as somehow divinely ordained and blessed. Perhaps ironically, then, it is against just such bogus religion that 2 Peter directs its dire warnings – that is, warnings against the cancer of self-serving spirituality.

---

2 Peter: Eyewitness on the Edge of Glory

This letter, like 1 Peter, claims to come from the Apostle "Simon Peter" (2 Peter 1:1), and accentuates that claim with an account of standing among the "eyewitnesses of his majesty" on the Mount of Transfiguration with Jesus when "he received from God the Father honor and glory when such a voice came to him from the Excellent Glory" (2 Peter 1:16–17; cf. Matthew 17:1–8). Nevertheless, while 2 Peter was endorsed as canonical by later Church Fathers such as Athanasius, Cyril, Ambrose, and Augustine, the epistle lacks the early attestation of most New Testament letters, and many modern scholars have classed it as pseudonymous because its Greek style is less refined than that of 1 Peter.

Those scholars who regard 2 Peter as genuine note the claims of authenticity that it makes for itself; they also point out that it is hardly consistent to use the differing Greek styles of 1 and 2 Peter to invalidate the authenticity of *each other*, when the likelihood of different amanuenses with varying Greek vocabularies offers a thoroughly plausible explanation. The letter's defenders also highlight an overlap between the letter's vocabulary and Peter's speeches in the Book of Acts. If regarded as genuine, 2 Peter is certainly among the last messages from the apostle before his martyrdom under Nero: "shortly I must put off my tent," he writes, "just as our Lord Jesus Christ showed me" (2 Peter 1:14) – a possible reference to Christ's warning in John 21:18–19. The letter presents the voluble eyewitness apostle, doomed to glory, and delivering his last testament.

As we observed above in our discussions of John's Gospel and Paul's letters to the Colossians and to Titus, the "Gnosticism" of the mid-to-late first century was an amalgam of Platonic and Neoplatonic doctrine and newly absorbed Christian language, and at its core expressed contempt for the corrupt, illusory prison of fleshly bodies and material substance as the "world" of ignorant darkness. The twin-born children of this doctrine were an asceticism that condemned all earthly pleasure, and a hedonism that made sensual pleasure life's chief pursuit – both justified by the supposed "worthlessness" of bodily existence, and both condemned, as we've seen, throughout the New Testament (Galatians 5:19–21, Colossians 2:20–23, 1 Timothy 4:4, Titus 3:3). It is against the teachers of the latter hedonistic variant that 2 Peter directs its warnings, and they are strident:

> They are spots and blemishes, carousing in their own deceptions while they feast with you, having eyes full of adultery and that cannot cease from sin, enticing unstable souls. They have a heart trained in covetous practices, and are accursed children. (2 Peter 2:13–14)

Sins verbal, dietary, sexual, intellectual, financial – practically all areas of human inner and outer life have been permeated by this doctrine of perpetual indulgence, founded on a belief that in a cosmos where only the spirit matters, no deed done in the flesh can have any weight or consequence. In rebuttal, the letter draws analogies to some of the Bible's most notorious architects of self-destruction: the fallen angels, the drowned generation of Noah, the incinerated citizens of Sodom and Gomorrah, the false prophet Balaam (2 Peter 2:4–11, 15–16), all of whom are "wells without water, clouds carried by a tempest, for whom is reserved the blackness of darkness forever" (2 Peter 2:17). Never does Peter recommend any physical violence against these charlatans; rather, the wise will simply separate themselves from these plague carriers and leave them to their own ends.

And regarding ends, the letter concludes by noting the false teachers' contempt for Christ's promised return, and also by answering their jibes about a "Second Coming" that never comes:

> scoffers will come in the last days, walking according to their own lusts, and saying, "Where is the promise of His coming? For since the fathers fell asleep, all things continue as they were from the beginning of creation." (2 Peter 3:3–4)

The response? These scoffers "willfully ignore" that once before the world was suddenly destroyed by water, and that the last judgment will bring (in the words of the old spiritual) "no more water but the fire next time" – and at a time of God's mysterious choosing; for "the day of the Lord will come as a thief in the night, in which the heavens will pass away with a great noise, and the elements will melt with fervent heat" (2 Peter 3:10). Only those faithful ones who have not melted before temptation will, in the end, be fireproof.

14.2.4 Fire and Hope: Jude

The brief letter of Jude, the last of the non-Johannine "General Epistles," presents a watchful and dire vision: he's clear in denouncing those women and men who have "given themselves over to sexual immorality and gone after strange flesh" (Jude 7), and like 2 Peter he too predicts the fire next time.

Jude: "Covering" 2 Peter?

This short epistle presents itself as the work of Jude (Greek *Ioudas* or "Judah"), "the brother of James." If this James is "the brother of the Lord" (see the box on the Letter of James), then this Jude also would be Jesus's brother (Matthew 13:55, Mark 6:3, 1 Corinthians 9:5) – though if that is the case Jude, like James, declines to make this relationship explicit, preferring to call himself "a bondservant of Jesus Christ."

Besides the intriguing family identity of the author, the two most arresting aspects of this letter are, first, its close resemblance to parts of 2 Peter, and second, its citation of the non-canonical Jewish books, *The Assumption of Moses* (Jude 9) and *1 Enoch* (Jude 14). To address the last issue first, it is rare but not otherwise unknown for the New Testament to reference other than canonical Old Testament authors: Paul cites certain apocryphal Jewish writings in 2 Timothy 3:8, and some Gentile poets in Acts 17:28, 1 Corinthians 15:33, and Titus 1:12, in each case because of their apt phrasing. As to the strong correspondence (but not exact identity) between 2 Peter 2:1–18 and Jude 4–16, many scholars assume that Jude, being likely the first written and thus widely established among the early churches, was duplicated in 2 Peter for strong and familiar effect; while others argue that Jude borrows from Peter's farewell letter for similar effect. In either case, like a modern musician "covering" another's popular song, one epistle writer repurposes the words of another, making them his own and perhaps tailoring them for a different moment.

But Jude's burden, while largely negative, is not exclusively or finally so. Having compared the former apostates of Old Testament times with those corrupt "spots" in their latter-day churches, he calls believers everywhere to counteract the counterfeit with the genuine, "building yourselves up on your most holy faith, praying in the Holy Spirit, keep[ing] yourselves in the love of God, looking for the mercy of our Lord Jesus Christ unto eternal life" (Jude 20–21). Authentic faith, Jude says, builds rather than destroys, prays rather than preys, loves rather than lusts, delivers rather than damns: "And on some have compassion, making a distinction; but others save with fear, pulling them out of the fire" (22–23). Then, having begun with a dark warning, he concludes with a heavenly hymn:

> Now to him who is able to keep you from stumbling,
> And to present you faultless
> Before the presence of his glory with exceeding joy,
> To God our Savior,
> Who alone is wise,
> Be glory and majesty,
> Dominion and power,
> Both now and forever.
> Amen. (24–25)

Like the great Apocalypse of John, Jude's miniature prophecy ends with a tragicomic turn, surprising us with a hopeful sunrise after the fiery end of days.

14.3   Johannine Epistles: "God is Love"

Coming between the very similar 2 Peter and Jude, the unique epistles of 1, 2, and 3 John form a spiritual triptych in which we are invited to view not only varied angles on the face of Jesus Christ, but our own faces and (for John writes as if this is possible) our own hearts. Generally attributed to the author of John's gospel, and often to the author of the Apocalypse, these three epistles bridge the gap in the so-called "Johannine Corpus" (i.e. the works traditionally ascribed to John the Apostle) between narrative and prophecy; that is, between a mainly sequential retelling of chosen local events in Jesus's earthly life and an immense, trans-temporal Revelation of life beyond life.

John's epistles complicate the usual categories of general, particular, or personal letters. Though 1 John seems quite "catholic" in its universal outlook, and is addressed to a grammatically plural audience of "little children," it might be written to one great individual soul; though 2 John addresses itself to "the elect lady," interpreters debate whether this is a particular woman, a particular church, or Christ's immortal, invisible bride; and while the "Gaius" to whom John writes in 3 John seems specific enough – as do the petty disputes which John "the Elder" seeks to resolve – there is always the sense of the cosmic about to break into the very smallest quotidian details. Certain English poets of the seventeenth century (John Donne, George Herbert, and their disciples) have come to be called "Metaphysicals" because, in Donne's words, they "make one little room an everywhere," and we might as well call John's epistles "Metaphysical Letters" because, both in their substance and style, they are somehow vastly larger inside than out.

1, 2, and 3 John: "Which … Our Hands Have Handled"

Like the fourth gospel, these three letters are technically anonymous, none explicitly naming its author, and indeed in the first and longest of the three even foregoing the traditional Hellenistic salutation. Nevertheless, in their vocabulary, their style, and their themes they clearly track the "voiceprint" of that fourth gospel and thus share in its strong and early attribution to John the son of Zebedee, the apostle and "beloved disciple" – who like the writer of 1 John also claims eyewitness experience of Jesus Christ. A likely reference to 1 John by Polycarp about 110 CE places its composition (like 2 and 3 John) before that date, and probably not long after the time of John's gospel in 85–90 CE, during the last decade of John's life. (Speculative attempts to attribute these letters to the gospel writer John Mark or to an otherwise unknown "John the Elder" have not met with wide acceptance.)

Thematically, 1 and 2 John share with the Gospel of John their concern for the earthly, fleshly "manifestation" of "God's Son," in contradiction to the developing Gnostic doctrine of "Docetism," the belief that Jesus was a purely spiritual apparition who only *seemed* to be bodily human. Thus, 1 John stresses the concreteness of Christ, that "which we have heard, which we have seen with our eyes, which we have looked upon, and our hands have handled" (1 John 1:1). 3 John, leaving these assertions of the Word made Flesh, concerns itself with reconciling the petty and fleshly divisions caused by one brother's refusal to extend hospitality to traveling Christians. From their doctrine of God's incarnate love to their insistence on generously "incarnational" living, the three Johannine epistles, like John's gospel, insist on glory and goodness "manifested" in the everyday.

The first and longest of these letters gives us one of the most succinct, powerful, and admired phrases found in the entire Bible: "God is love" (1 John 4:8). Whether sublimely echoed by William Blake ("Love, the human form divine") and Leo Tolstoy ("Where Love Is, God Is"), or ironically emblazoned over a squalid workhouse by Charles Dickens in *Oliver Twist*, these words, like Jesus's Great Commandment in Mark 12:30–31 and Paul's "Love Chapter" of 1 Corinthians 13, have great popular appeal because they seem to bypass all of the gnarled complexities of religion and restate the essentials in language direct and beautiful. Yet, as with Jesus's and Paul's pronouncements on love, John's arrives relatively late in its book, and all come embedded amidst darker surroundings: hostile questioning of Jesus by the scribes and Pharisees, rancorous dissension in the Corinthian church, and, in John's case, concluding a severe warning about the coming of false prophets and the Antichrist. Thus, if John presents "God is love" as the compressed essence of "true religion" – and he does – then it remains necessary to understand the contexts and teachings that this verbal gem epitomizes so brilliantly.

Indeed, before reaching its great conclusion that "God is love" in chapter 4, 1 John spends most of its space defining what else God is, and is not, as well as defining love itself, before naming Love Himself. The letter begins by declaring that God is *life* – "the life," as we have observed, that was "from the beginning" and "was manifested to us" in "his Son Jesus Christ." This life, we are told, can be enjoyed "in fellowship with us" and with the Father and the Son – an astonishing brotherhood of man and God (1 John 1:1–5). Then, almost immediately, we are told more good news, "the message which we have heard from him and declare to you, that God is light and in him is no darkness at all." "God is *light*," a sweet and beautiful thought for those walking in darkness, except for the sting in the tail: "If we say that we have fellowship with him, and walk in darkness, we lie and do not practice the truth."

Yet there's more good news to counteract that bad news: "But if we walk in the light as he is in the light, we have fellowship with one another, and the blood of Jesus Christ his Son cleanses us from all sin." Oh, joy! the believer may think, until being reminded instantly, "[i]f we say that we have no sin, we deceive ourselves, and the truth is not in us." And then comes further relief, for "[i]f we confess our sins, he is faithful and just to forgive us our sins and to cleanse us from all unrighteousness." But beware! "If we say that we have not sinned, we make him a liar, and his word is not in us" (1 John 1:6–10). After being whipsawed back and forth like this, the reader may well wonder, Why? In terms of literary form, this antiphon of sin and forgiveness, this call-and-response of grievance and grace, resembles the antithetical parallelisms of the psalms. Thus, if a reader feels insulted by the repetition, it is not his intelligence, but his integrity, that John means to question.

This opening pattern thus provides a key for reading the rest of the letter. John presents the objects of our deepest desire – Life! Light! Love! – and draws us to them, only to expose the self-made barriers that separate us from full possession; then he points the way in to the desired object, only to remind us (to our dismayed delight) that this object is a Person whose love will cost us, as T. S. Eliot writes in "Little Gidding," "not less than everything." Thus, following this pattern, chapter 2 takes up definitions of that most desired object, love. Some of these definitions are negative: not breaking God's commandments, not hating the brethren, not loving the world ("the lust of the flesh, the lust of the eyes, the pride of life"), not believing the "antichrist … who denies that Jesus is the Christ" (1 John 2:16, 22). Other definitions are correspondingly and antithetically positive: keeping God's commandments, loving the brethren by doing good and caring for them, loving the Father more than the world, abiding in the truth about the Father by acknowledging his Son (1 John 2:3–29). Chapter 3 augments these definitions by declaring God's active, seeking goodness – "Behold what manner of love the Father has bestowed on us, that we should be called children of God!" – and by promising a radical, enabling transformation in all believers who someday "shall be like [God], for we shall see him as he is" (1 John 3:1–2). Having contrasted sin, which is either active evil or passive non-good, with the love of active good, John then asserts the imperative for the "child" to act like the Father. God's outgoing, sacrificial love, John says, both enables and demands a like response in his true children: "By this we know love, because he laid down his life for us. And we also ought to lay down our lives for the brethren" (1 John 3:16).

It is only here, after substantiating the word "love" with these varied definitions and examples of what love does, that John tells us Whom love is: not the denying, dividing "spirit of the Antichrist," but God himself. "Beloved, let us love one another, for love is of God; and everyone who loves is born of God and knows God. He who does not love does not know God, for God is love" (1 John 4:7–8). Having established that love is not mainly a feeling, but rather a constant practice revealing a depth of being, John again reminds us that this good news implies potentially bad news: that true love for God is shown only by consistent loving action, exposing the pretense of mere love-words. Yet in another hopeful rebound, John comforts the fearful with a reminder that God is always previous: "There is no fear in love; but perfect love casts out fear… We love him because he first loved us" (1 John 4:18–19). But still a last turnabout brings a final un-sweetener, and a warning to the hypocrite: "If someone says, 'I love God,' and hates his brother, he is a liar; for he who does not love his brother whom he has seen, how can he love God whom he has not seen?" (1 John 4:20).

This unanswerable question segues into a final chapter expressed now almost entirely in the affirmative: the believer's trust begets new life which enables obedience (1 John 5:1–5); the witnesses of heavenly revelation and of Christ's atoning death confirm the certainty of salvation (1 John 5:6–13); God's sympathetic ear guarantees that prayers will be heard (1 John 5:14–17); and knowing the genuine means recognizing the false – ending with a stern yet tender warning: "Little children, keep yourselves from idols" (1 John 5:18–21). Thus, by adopting a psalm-like pattern of significant repetition – some antithetical, some synonymous and synthetic – John's first letter schools his "little children" with its reiterative yet beautifully incantatory lessons: that the God who is life, light, and love practices not just what he preaches but Whom he is, and that his "only begotten Son" begets all God's children anew.

The epistle of 2 John bears a relationship to 1 John analogous to that between Colossians and Ephesians, Titus and 1 Timothy, and Jude and 2 Peter; that is, as a briefer repetition of a longer message. Rehearsing 1 John's admonitions to "walk in the truth" and to beware the teachings of "antichrist" who denies "Jesus Christ as coming in the flesh" (2 John 4, 7), John's second letter is otherwise of interest because of its salutation, unique among all New Testament epistles: "The Elder, to the elect lady and her children" (2 John 1). While some have interpreted this greeting as indicating the entire "church universal" (i.e. the "elect lady" as "the Bride of Christ"), and others as a particular woman in a sister church (see box, p. 411), the most likely reading is that the audience is the "sister church" herself. This reading is preferable because of how the letter ends:

> Having many things to write to you, I did not wish to do so with paper and ink; but I hope to come to you and speak face to face, that our joy may be full.
>
> The children of your elect sister greet you. (2 John 12–13)

Clearly, John would not be promising to leave one "church universal" and visit another down the road for a "face to face" reunion; and, given that John generally uses "children" metaphorically for "Christian disciples," it seems most likely that he intends this final greeting not as from a set of nieces and nephews to their aunt, but as from one congregation to another – "elect" meaning those whom God has "called out" and saved. These elect ones are counseled to keep the faith, and not to keep company with teachers who undermine it, or welcome them into their homes – likely the same proto-Gnostic sybarites warned against in 1 John, Jude, 2 Peter, and elsewhere.

John's third epistle addresses a similar issue of hospitality, but with the problem reversed. Whereas in 2 John "the Elder" warns his "children" against encouraging and endorsing false teachers by playing host to them, in 3 John the same Elder warns a friend in another congregation against the tight-fisted sin of inhospitality to traveling brethren. In this letter we have some actual names: "The Elder, to the beloved Gaius, whom I love in truth," it begins; and in its few remaining verses we read of Gaius complimented for his kindness to journeying teachers and strangers, but another man named Diotrephes criticized for an attitude of sour opposition to traveling preachers. This itinerant group might include the Elder himself, but more immediately John means a certain Demetrius whom he commends to Gaius's care, adding a threat to come himself and dress down the officious Diotrephes; not content with shutting his own door on itinerant evangelists, this local Scrooge insists on ejecting from the congregation anyone more generously inclined. John ends with a promise that "I hope to see you shortly, and we shall speak face to face" (3 John 14) – a promise that Diotrephes might well regard as a threat.

The rest is silence – we have no record of the Demetrius's visit, or the Elder's, or of Diotrophes's likely discomfiture. It may seem strange to some that the great "Johannine Corpus" includes such petty matters; that the man who wrote "In the beginning was the Word" and "God is love" ends his last letter with a tiff over room and board. Yet it is right to recall that this is likely the same writer whose gospel follows the stupendous climax of the Resurrection with the homely coda of a fish-fry on the beach. It was, appropriately, a Minor Prophet who warned us not to despise the day of small things (Zechariah 4:10), so no doubt John would extend that to include the day of small spites. "For," as the Elder might repeat, "he who does not love his brother whom he has seen, how can he love God whom he has not seen?"

We began this chapter on the New Testament letters by noting that, in literary terms, the epistle is the humblest, least prepossessing of biblical genres, a kind of earthen vessel made to carry divine–human correspondence far beyond its station, even beyond its ken. Yet we have seen this earthy form reshaped to strange and beautiful ends, sometimes pressed to gem-like brilliance and transmuted even into gold. In that very paradox the epistles thus reflect and correspond to the transformational message that they carry. We turn now, and finally, to the other end of the literary spectrum: the fantastic angelical canvas, the concert hall of the heavenly hosts, the grand theater of cosmic tragicomedy, the sum of all horrors and hopes, and yet a letter, too – the Apocalypse.

Questions for Discussion

1 What are the probable origins of the ancient **epistolary form**, and what were the standard Hellenistic letter-writing conventions in place by the first century CE?

2 What sorts of **changes** did New Testament letter writers frequently make **to these inherited conventions**? How might the specific content of these early Christian writings actually have influenced these formal changes?

3 What is an **amanuensis**, and what are some examples of such persons' contributions to the New Testament letters?

4 What are the main distinctions among the so-called **Pauline Epistles**? Besides Paul's presumed authorship, what are the main differences between these Pauline Epistles and the so-called General or **Catholic Epistles**?

5   What are some of the factors involved in determining the **authorship, audience, and date** of particular letters?

6   According to what **organizational principle(s)** are the Pauline and General Epistles arranged?

7   What might be surprising or unlikely about the very existence of Paul's New Testament writings? What factors influenced **Paul's choice of destinations** for his letters?

8   What were the chief **characteristics of the church at Rome** to which Paul wrote? How might those characteristics have shaped his exposition of his gospel message to them? How has the Letter to the Romans influenced later generations and eras in Christian history?

9   What were the chief **characteristics of the church at Corinth** to which Paul wrote? How might these characteristics have shaped his two surviving letters to them? What metaphors and images does Paul use to picture and promote Christian unity? How does 1 Corinthians 13, the famous "**Love Chapter**," fit into the argument of the letter? Into psalmic tradition? How does Paul go about defending himself against his detractors in 2 Corinthians?

10   How do the **particular characteristics and circumstances of the churches in Galatia, Ephesus, Philippi, and Colosse** shape how Paul presents questions of grace, faith, and good works to those congregations? What roles do Paul's confessional autobiography and personal predicament play in all of these letters? How does Paul address questions of familial, social, and political hierarchy in Ephesians and Colossians, and what are some theories of how these two letters were composed? Against what competing doctrines does Paul write in Galatians and Colossians? What grounds does he give for his joy in Philippians?

11   What is **eschatology**, and how might **1 and 2 Thessalonians** differ from – and complement – each other in this regard?

12   In the so-called "**Pastoral Epistles**" to **Timothy** and **Titus**, how does Paul employ and define terms for church office like "overseer/bishop" (*episcopos*), "elder" (*presbyteros*), and "deacon" (*diaconos*)? What are the apparent overlaps and distinctions among these offices? How do Paul's personal relationships and circumstances enter into these letters? Into his letter to **Philemon**? How does this latter letter address the issue of slavery?

13   Among the **General Epistles**, how does the anonymous **Letter to the Hebrews** address the predicament of **Jewish Christians** doubly persecuted for their messianic faith? How does James complicate and/or complement Paul's doctrine of salvation by grace through faith? How do **1 and 2 Peter** confront the twin problems of external persecution and internal church corruption? Against what competing doctrines is 2 Peter aimed? How does **Jude** relate to 2 Peter's apocalyptic message?

14   What do **1, 2, and 3 John** contribute to the so-called "**Johannine Corpus**"? How do these letters resemble the Gospel of John and each other? How does 1 John use strategic repetition to school the audience and cumulative definition to render the character of God more intelligible as the personification of life, light, and love? Who or what is "antichrist"? How do the brief messages of 2 and 3 John relate to 1 John's teaching?

15

New Testament Apocalypse: Kingdom Come

Never was there a stranger letter, or a more mysterious correspondence: "The Revelation of Jesus Christ, which God gave him to show his servants – things which must shortly take place… Blessed is he who reads and those who hear the words of this prophecy, and keep those things which are written in it; for the time is near" (Revelation 1:1, 3). And never has there been (in the word's original sense) a more *terrific* correspondent, who appears to his amanuensis, a man named John on the isle of Patmos, in a vision as terrible as an army with banners, so that John falls "at his feet as dead":

> I saw… One like the Son of Man, clothed with a garment down to the feet and girded about the chest with a golden band. His head and hair were white like wool, as white as snow, and his eyes like a flame of fire; his feet were like fine brass, as if refined in a furnace, and his voice as the sound of many waters; he had in his right hand seven stars, out of his mouth went a sharp two-edged sword, and his countenance was like the sun shining in its strength. (Revelation 1:12–16)

Thus begins the world's most famous account of The End; and yet, coming as the last book in the Christian Bible, the Revelation reverberates with myriad echoes of the Hebrew books that went before, from Genesis, Exodus, Numbers, Joshua, Kings, and Job, to Psalms, Isaiah, Jeremiah, Ezekiel, Daniel, and most of the Minor Prophets – echoes, not direct quotations, for everything in the Revelation has been changed into something rich and strange.

We have already discussed in Chapter 12 the Old Testament prophets and their apocalyptic subgenre, and there we observed that the Greek *apokalypsis* ("revelation") is a neutral term that denotes an unveiling and a bringing to light, whether of good or of evil, so that in reading apocalyptic literature we should listen for every potential sense of "apocalypse": doom, wrack, and wrath, certainly, but also, and finally, repentance, restoration, redemption, and reconciliation. Indeed, we observed that while the modern use of "apocalyptic" strongly stresses horror, disaster, and destruction, biblical apocalypses often end tragicomically in joy and wonder, with God dwelling among his people in a New Jerusalem on a New Earth, and with every tear wiped away. And finally, we observed that the apocalyptic possesses its own distinctive language and style, combining fantastic yet systematic symbols, numerical patterns, ecstatic hymns, stern judgments, uncanny horrors, upwellings of hope, and outbreaks of heart-melting beauty.

All of these elements appear in the Book of Revelation, and yet the book is far more than the sum of these inherited parts; though indebted to the biblical and extra-biblical traditions of the past, its unique shaping of things to come has penetrated more deeply into the world's imagination than any other prophecy. The book's influence has been profound on cultures ancient and modern, sacred and secular, high and low: from Byzantine mosaics and the Sistine Chapel

Literary Study of the Bible: An Introduction, First Edition. Christopher Hodgkins.
© 2020 John Wiley & Sons Ltd. Published 2020 by John Wiley & Sons Ltd.

ceiling to Bosch's and Breugel's frog-demons and Holman Hunt's *Light of the World*; from the medieval Dies Irae (*Day of Wrath*) and Handel's "Hallelujah Chorus" to Stowe's "Battle Hymn of the Republic" and Simon and Garfunkel's "Sound of Silence"; from the epic visions of Dante's many-leveled Hell and Spenser's Una and Duessa to Milton's great War in Heaven and Bunyan's Apollyon – as well as Blake's "Jerusalem" and Tolkien's Smaug and Sauron. The Revelation lives in titles like Yeats's "Second Coming," Steinbeck's *Grapes of Wrath*, and Bergman's *Seventh Seal* – not to mention O'Connor's "Revelation"; and it echoes in Tennyson's Victorian longings for the Millennial "thousand years of peace" and in *Jane Eyre's* concluding "Come, Lord Jesus!" And we hear the language of Revelation in every fear of nuclear "Armageddon" and every call for "a man on a white horse," every reference to "the Book of Life" and "the Alpha and the Omega," every jibe about "the Whore of Babylon," a "scarlet woman," or "the pearly gates," and in every tabloid speculation about "the Mark of the Beast" and calculation of "666." In each of these and countless other allusions, we are inspired and haunted by John's Apocalypse – and by the other apocalypses, great and small, that preceded his.

15.1 Little Apocalypses: The Gospels and Epistles

In his essay "The World's Last Night," C. S. Lewis writes that perhaps the greatest embarrassment to the modern Christian is the New Testament writers' strong and imminent sense of Christ's return, or *Parousia*. And strong it is; in little apocalypses sprinkled throughout the gospels and the epistles, the Second Coming of Jesus Christ as Divine Judge is eagerly predicted and warmly anticipated. As we have seen in Chapter 14, the *Parousia* is earnestly awaited by Paul in 1 Corinthians and in 1 and 2 Thessalonians, by Peter's second epistle and John's first two, and by Jude. Furthermore, it was most famously predicted in Jesus's "Olivet Discourse" recounted variously in Matthew 24–25, Mark 13, and Luke 21. This Second Coming is the "blessed hope" that faith may tomorrow become sight, that all wrongs will be righted, that the sufferings and martyrdoms will be rewarded with a divine "Well done!"; and it is clear that all of these writers, like John on Patmos, hope that Christ is "coming quickly" (Revelation 22:20), which, as Lewis points out, Christ did not – at least as far as the lifespans of the earliest Christians, and all the succeeding centuries, were concerned. "These all died in faith," writes the author of Hebrews about the Old Testament heroes of faith (Hebrews 11:13); but so did all of the New Testament authors and heroes as well.

And yet, while there can be no doubt that Christ's "coming quickly" was central to the belief of the early Church, a closer look at the apocalyptic passages in these epistles and gospels shows that these messengers distinguished between their own fervent desires for instant deliverance and the more unpredictable timing of God's actual purposes, so that "quickly" also can be understood as "suddenly" or "abruptly," its emphasis being on unexpected surprise and unpredictability as well as on strict chronological immediacy. Since it is not our purpose to engage either in religious apologetics or in skeptical demythologization, but only to discern how these first-century writers imagined their relation to "Kingdom Come," we do not need to resolve the tension between the "Already" and the "Not Yet" inherent in their statements. But we need to begin by recognizing that these early Christians, no less than a twentieth-century Christian writer like Lewis, were fully aware of the tension inherent in a phrase like "unpredictable prophecy."

In fact, we have already noted in the previous chapter that the letters of Paul and Peter register the anxiety and derision provoked by their apocalyptic teachings. While in 1 Thessalonians Paul had warned that the Lord could return at any time "as a thief in the night"

(1 Thessalonians 5:3), in Paul's following letter he seeks to calm fears that Christ has already come *secretly*, arguing that though sudden, his coming will be manifest to all as the universal overthrow of a supremely evil regime (2 Thessalonians 2:2–4). Similarly, 2 Peter speaks of a sudden "thief in the night" and of an inescapable cosmic conflagration (2 Peter 3:10), but he first addresses mocking dismissals of Christ's unfulfilled promise:

> beloved, do not forget this one thing, that with the Lord one day is as a thousand years, and a thousand years as one day. The Lord is not slack concerning his promise, as some count slackness, but is longsuffering toward us, not willing that any should perish but that all should come to repentance. (2 Peter 3:8–9)

Remarkably, the seventeenth-century metaphysical poet John Donne dramatizes the point of these passages in his seventh sonnet, which begins with urgent longing for an overdue Doomsday, relishing the thought of the wicked in their suffering, but reverses course at the ninth-line *volta* when he reconsiders that if this were truly the world's last night, he might find himself not among the sheep but with the goats:

> But let them sleep, Lord, and me mourn a space;
> For, if above all these, my sins abound,
> 'Tis late to ask abundance of thy grace,
> When we are there. Here on this lowly ground,
> Teach me how to repent; for that's as good
> As if thou'hadst seal'd my pardon with thy blood. (ll. 9–14)

In Donne's view, a humble and sensible person will not be too eager for final judgment, lest he find himself condemned with the other deserving parties. Indeed, the consistent stress of Paul's and Peter's references to Judgment Day is not on carefully setting a "Doomsday Clock" or gloating over the damned, but on readying himself lest he share in the wrath to come.

Nowhere is this attack on spiritual presumption more pointed than in the gospel accounts of Jesus's discourse on Mount Olivet, where he not only shows awareness of the believer's paradoxically unfulfilled eagerness, but makes that paradoxical state the point of his message, and of his warning. In each of the first three gospels, this discourse begins with a provocative claim from the Master that sparks an urgent question from his disciples:

> [A]s some spoke of the temple, how it was adorned with beautiful stones and donations, [Jesus] said, "These things which you see – the days will come in which not one stone shall be left upon another that shall not be thrown down." So they asked him, saying, "Teacher, but when will these things be? And what sign will there be when these things are about to take place?" (Luke 21:5–7)

In response to his prediction of total destruction for their Most Holy Place, the disciples naturally want a timetable.

But a timetable is precisely what Jesus refuses to give, stressing instead the protracted delays, false alarms, and false prophets to come before the Temple's fall, and again before "the end of the age" – which seems to be a quite separate event. Before the world's end, says Jesus, "the gospel must first be preached to all the nations" (Mark 13:10) – a time-consuming process – and "Jerusalem will be trampled by Gentiles until the times of the Gentiles are fulfilled" (Luke 21:24) – perhaps a significantly long era.

Which "Generation"?

Mark's gospel records the following saying of Jesus just before his warnings against calculating "that day and hour": "Assuredly, I say to you, this generation [Greek *genea*] will by no means pass away till all these things take place" (Mark 13:30). What might this "generation" mean? Some have taken this phrase to refer directly to the generation of Jews in Jesus's own day, making this a promise of an imminent destruction of Jerusalem – accomplished indeed within that "generation" in 70 CE; others have read it as promising the "end of the age" following immediately on Jerusalem's fall (still within about forty years and obviously never fulfilled); and still others read "generation" not as a thirty-year span but as the present "Church Age," an era of the fallen, sinful human "generation of Adam" who are nevertheless coming increasingly under the gospel's influence and redemptive power. Thus, the phrase has been read as referring either to relatively immediate fulfillment, to far-off fulfillment, or perhaps to both – that is, "the end of *your* world soon, the end of *the* world much later."

In the meantime, Jesus says, the persecutions and sufferings of the faithful will be many and terrible as they long for the Coming that does not come. Thus, under worldly pressure to conform, their chief temptation will be an unholy blend of overconfident speculation about Christ's arrival time and jaded indifference to the event itself:

> But of that day and hour no one knows, not even the angels of heaven, but my Father only. But as the days of Noah were, so also will the coming of the Son of Man be. For as in the days before the flood, they were eating and drinking, marrying and giving in marriage, until the day that Noah entered the ark, and did not know until the flood came and took them all away, so also will the coming of the Son of Man be. (Matthew 24:36–39)

Jesus's twin targets are a false assurance about "that day and hour" of "the Son of Man," and the riotous living of the mice who play while the cat's away – or in Jesus's terms, the "evil servant [who] says in his heart, 'My master is delaying his coming,' and begins to beat his fellow servants, and to eat and drink with the drunkards" (Matthew 24:48–49). All of the other details in these three passages – including the repeated references back to Daniel's "Son of Man" and his "abomination of desolation" (Daniel 7:13–14 and 9:27) and Matthew's parables of the Faithful and Evil Servant, the Wise and Foolish Virgins, and the Talents (Matthew 24:45–25:30) – reinforce the double lesson that the Church will be tested by a harrowing wait and that, however short or long, this wait will end suddenly at a time of God's mysterious choosing.

15.2 "An Angel Standing in the Sun": The Brilliant Difficulties of Revelation

If the gospels and epistles look ahead eagerly but rather glancingly to the Last Days, John's Apocalypse stares full-eyed into the blazing light of revelation, and the result involves both blindness and insight. Much as in the gospels Jesus warns his disciples that no one (remarkably, not even he himself) can know "that day and hour" (Matthew 24:36, Mark 13:32), so the Revelation conceals The End while disclosing it, conveying its message about the Last Days with an uncanny combination of urgent confidence and riddling ambiguity. Even the book's authorship and date are difficult to know clearly: a majority of modern scholars favor an otherwise unknown "John of Patmos" writing during the persecutions of the Emperor Domitian (81–96 CE), though many others maintain the traditional attribution to John the Apostle, evangelist, and epistolist, and some see either one or the other John writing about thirty years earlier, during the last days of Nero (54–68 CE).

Other readers have wished Revelation away entirely as all too difficult and even incendiary –

Author of the Revelation: Who Was John the Divine, and When Did He Write?

Penning their opinions only a few decades after Revelation's composition, the Church Fathers of the early second century CE – Justin Martyr, Irenaeus, and Clement of Alexandria among them – attribute the book to John the Apostle, son of Zebedee, the "beloved disciple" and traditional author of the Johannine gospel and epistles. Yet by the third century, Dionysius, the bishop of Alexandria, was arguing against the Apostle John's authorship of Revelation on the grounds of stylistic and thematic differences from the Johannine books, and more modern critics have noted that these books decline to name their author, while the Apocalypse speaks straightforwardly in the first person "I, John" (Revelation 1:9). As with the stylistic differences between Paul's earlier and later epistles, and between 1 and 2 Peter, some scholars propose differing amanuenses to distinguish the other Johannine books from Revelation, also noting that both the Johannine epistles and Revelation are addressed by a beloved "elder" to persecuted churches, personifying the true Church as a blessed and chosen woman, and that John's gospel and the Revelation (unique among New Testament books) describe Jesus as "the Lamb" and "the Word."

The authorship question relates to different schemes for dating the book. Although a very ancient tradition portrays the Apostle John as living to an old age and surviving well into the 90s CE, exiled to the island of Patmos during the persecution of Domitian, others doubt that he could have lived into his 80s or 90s. These critics conclude either that another "John of Patmos" wrote the book around 95 CE, or that John the Apostle (or some other "John the Divine") wrote the book during Nero's persecutions of 67–68 CE. It is difficult to be certain about either exact dates or author, but most scholars favor a later Domitian-era date, whether the Revelation is given to the son of Zebedee or to an otherwise unknown elder named "John" on Patmos.

---

from Protestant Reformer Martin Luther, who denied its canonicity, to modern post-Christians like D. H. Lawrence, who denounced what he saw as the vulgar bloody-mindedness abetted by "Patmossers" who thirsted for divine revenge on their enemies. But despite being an ongoing font of controversy, and of kaleidoscopically varied interpretations, Revelation's visions of bane and blessing partake deeply of literary pattern and metaphysical method, so before we survey the range of interpretive traditions that the book has generated, we will analyze the actual structure and language of its oracles, observing the "how" of its order and the "what" of its vocabulary before we address the "why" of its possible meanings.

15.2.1 Fearful Symmetry: Structuring the Vision

The main structural characteristics of the book can be described in four words: **epistolary**, **numerological**, **embedded**, and **chiastic**. The first set of characteristics, as we began by noting, are **epistolary**, those of the ancient letter. Revelation 1–3 constitutes what is certainly the longest salutation of any New Testament epistle, and perhaps of any know letter of its era: the opening greeting that announces "The Revelation of Jesus Christ" from "John, to the seven churches which are in Asia" (Revelation 1:1, 4), receives spectacular elaboration in the initial vision of the blazing "Son of Man," and then in Christ's distinctly personalized salutes to each of those seven churches – Ephesus, Smyrna, Pergamos, Thyatira, Sardis, Philadelphia, and Laodicea – combining welcome, praise, diagnosis, and rebuke. Then, at Revelation's end, this epistolary form reasserts itself, closing the scroll with a warning not to add to or subtract from its message; and it finally concludes with a divine testimonial to its truth, with Jesus's promise to come "quickly," and with an answering call from John for that return.

This epistolary frame, with its perfect seven-fold complement of imperfect churches, introduces the book's most evident organizing device: a cascade of **numerology**, with proliferating multiples of two, three, six, and twelve – and especially seven. Not only are seven churches addressed; we meet seven visionary cycles from chapters 4 through 22, then within the first cycle (4:1–8:1) seven seals, the seventh of which opens into the second cycle (8:2–11:19) with its seven angels and trumpets, the seventh of which announces the third cycle (12–14) with its seven symbolic histories, with its concluding History of the Son of Man commencing the fourth cycle (15–16), which begins cosmic judgment in its seven bowls of wrath. In addition, Revelation presents other things in sevens: golden candlesticks, stars, lampstands, horns, eyes, thunderclaps, heads, crowns, last plagues, golden vials, mountains, and kings. Along these seven-fold ways (indicating fullness or completion) we also encounter other signifying numbers: two prophetic witnesses (doubled for confirmation); three angelic messengers, along with the blessed trinity of Father, Son, and Spirit, and the cursed trinity of Dragon, Beast, and False Prophet (three for divine perfection – or perfect evil); the four winds (the whole earth or creation); the cursed number 666 for the Beast (the number of human sin – six – perfected three-fold); the New Jerusalem's twelve foundations, twelve gates, and twelve thousand furlongs, and its Tree of Life yielding twelve fruits twelve times yearly (the number of civic or social perfection); Heaven's twenty-four elders (twelve times two – social perfection doubled) and its 144,000 sealed saints (twelve times twelve thousand – a number of election). Numerophobes may recoil from all of this metaphysical math, but all should admit that, far from being some sort of amorphous pipe dream, this revelation exhibits deep design.

Evident within this epistolary frame and this numerological scaffolding is the **embedding** of ever-greater detail in a Matryoshka-like nesting-doll structure – except that in this case, each nested layer opens into something greater than the previous one, so that the accumulating revelation appears increasingly larger inside than out. Thus, the seventh seal opens (eventually) onto the seventh trumpet, which in due course announces the seventh symbolic history, which leads ultimately to outpouring the seventh bowl of cosmic wrath – all in succession forming a telescoping vision, like the measureless replicating depths of an infinity mirror (or a modern computer menu of branching links). Furthermore, each of these embedded seventh openings is preceded by a dramatic pause; thus, the entire heavenly vision that commences in God's throne room in Revelation 4 amounts to one great universal *fermata* seventeen chapters long as scrolls and visions unseal, cosmic time stands still, and all things wait on God's decrees.

A signal feature of this embedding and mirroring is literary **chiasmus**, in which characters, events, and themes of one section of the text are repeated in reverse order in a later section, as the rise and fall of one figure or group relates to the fall and rise of another. Thus, in Revelation 12–22, we find a classic chiastic structure portraying the temporary reign and final destruction of ultimate evil as it intersects with the trial and victory of ultimate good:

God's People – the Woman Clothed with the Sun – in Distress (Revelation 12:1–2)
    The Dragon – Satan – Attacks (12:3–6)
        The Beast and the False Prophet (Second Beast) Reign (13:1–18)
            The Bride – God's People Represented by Virgin Purity (14:1–5)
                Babylon the Whore – The Wicked Represented by Defilement (17:1–14)
                Babylon Destroyed – The Wicked of the Earth Mourn (17:15–18:24)
            The Bride – God's People Represented by Marriage – Consummated (19:1–10)
        The Beast and the False Prophet Destroyed by Christ's Return (19:11–21)
    The Dragon – Satan – Destroyed in the Lake of Fire (20:1–10)
God's People – Shining Like the Sun – in the New Jerusalem (21:1–22:5)

As in the Old Testament books of 1 and 2 Samuel – where David's downs and ups are contrasted with the ups and downs of Saul and Absalom – Revelation plays out these royal chiastic dramas in a theater symbolically more vast, indeed truly cosmic.

15.2.2 *Theatrum Mundi*: Staging the Vision

So these epistolary, numerological, embedded, and chiastic structuring devices heighten the book's essentially theatrical and symbolic effects – or, to put it more simply, they construct an epic stage on which the Revelation's sweeping symbolic tragicomedy can be performed. Who are the *dramatis personae* in this *theatrum mundi* – the cast of characters in this great theater of the world? In order of appearance, they are as follows:

John: A "brother" exiled to the island of Patmos "for the testimony of Jesus Christ" (1:4, 9).

Jesus Christ: The Dead and Risen Messiah (1:1), also appearing as the Alpha and Omega, the Beginning and the End (1:8), the Son of Man (1:12–16), the Lion of the tribe of Judah and the Root of David (5:5), the Lamb (5:8–13), the Woman's Child (12:2–13), the Bridegroom (19:7–9), the Man on a White Horse (19:11), King of Kings and Lord of Lords (19:16), and the Bright and Morning Star (22:16).

The Seven Churches of Asia: Ephesus, Smyrna, Pergamos, Thyatira, Sardis, Philadelphia, and Laodicea (2:1–3:22), each represented by its own "angel" or messenger.

The One Who Sat Upon the Throne Set in Heaven: Almighty God in Glory (4:2–3).

The Four Living Creatures: Winged Lion, Ox, Man, Eagle before God's Throne (4:6–11, 5:8–14).

The Twenty-Four Elders: Representing all the Redeemed, Twelve Tribes plus Twelve Apostles (4:4, 5:8–14).

The Four Horsemen: Plague Riders on horses – White (Conquest), Red (War), Black (Famine), and Pale (Death) (6:1–8).

The 144,000: A Chorus of Israelites "sealed by God" (7:3–8).

The Great Multitude: A Chorus of the faithful who have survived "the Great Tribulation" (7:9–14).

The Army of 200 Million: Crosses the River Euphrates River to attack the Beast (9:16).

The Angel Standing on the Sea and on the Earth: Gives John a Little Book to eat (10:5, 8–9).

The Seven Angels: Blowing Seven Trumpets announcing Seven Last Plagues (8 and 9; 11:15).

The Two Witnesses: A Pair of Prophets performing miracles for three and a half years in Jerusalem (11:3–6), killed and resurrected (11:7–14).

The Woman Clothed with the Sun: Gives birth while pursued by the Dragon (12:1–17).

The Woman's Child: Born on the run, destined to rule the earth, caught up to heaven (12:2–13).

The Dragon: The Serpent of old, also called the Devil and Satan, enemy of the Woman and Child (12:3–10, 13:2–4, 16:13, 20:2).

The Beast: A Wicked Creature from the Sea with seven heads and ten horns (11:7, 13;1–4, 14:9–11, 15:2, 17:1–13).

The False Prophet: The Second Beast, a Wicked Creature from the Land who exalts the Beast (13:11–18, 16:13, 19:20, 20:10).

The Whore of Babylon: The Scarlet Woman who rides the Beast (17:1–16, 19:2).

The Angel Standing in the Sun: Calls birds of midheaven to eat the flesh of kings (19:17).

A couple of these characters (John and Christ) appear throughout the entire book; some (the Seven Angels, the Dragon, the Beast, the False Prophet, the Whore) have recurring roles; while most make brief but usually spectacular cameo appearances, as if to affirm that all roles, however fleeting the stage time, are cosmically important. But, whether a character's time on stage is brief or long, it always requires words; and the language of Revelation is extraordinary.

15.2.3 "The Words of This Book": Speaking the Vision

For those whose only exposure to apocalyptic prophecy is the Book of Revelation itself, its vocabulary may seem uniquely bizarre, a kind of wild, phantasmagoric image-stream more psychedelic than propositional – indeed, as a few have suggested in modern times, the out-pourings of a psychotic mind, perhaps under the influence of psychoactive substances. However, as we observed in Chapter 12, the apocalyptic style and structure were already well-established literary conventions by John's time, modeled many centuries earlier by Hebrew prophets such as Isaiah, Ezekiel, Daniel, Joel, Zephaniah, and Zechariah. Thus, if Revelation is psychotic, it is an exceedingly strange instance of a transgenerational mass psychosis. No, whatever altered consciousness that John may have experienced on Patmos – and clearly, he does claim to have been "in the Spirit" (Revelation 1:10) while composing – it is far more likely that the book deliberately shares in the organizational norms and the language of its literary genre – characteristics that, many would claim, reflect not only a common generic history but also varied glimpses into a shared metaphysical reality.

In our earlier discussion of Old Testament apocalyptic structure and language, we saw that the episodic nature of books like Isaiah and Zephaniah displays a remarkable juxtaposition of varied times and eras, often out of chronological order – sweeping forward, circling back, and repeating. Time is parsed and rearranged with flashbacks and flash-forwards, and God seems to speak in an eternal present tense – or even in the past tense about future events. This portrayal of prophetic time as flexible – expanding or contracting at the divine will – carries over into Revelation as the already-noted *fermata* that seems to frame most of the book's action from Revelation 4 through 19, with all of heaven and earth suspended in anticipation as successive scrolls disclose the future as if it were past. The book's distinctive way of speaking derives partly from this mind-bending sense of temporal and spatial flexibility, serving up a world in which one divine–human person incarnates "the beginning and the end" (1:8), where the opening of a sealed scroll brings "silence in heaven for about half an hour" (8:1), where "bowls of wrath" are poured out over all the earth (16:1–21), where a Beast has "two horns like a lamb and spoke like a dragon" (13:11), or speaks not words but frogs (16:13), and where the "Tree of Life" somehow straddles a river that is also a street (22:2).

But Revelation's unique phrasing also depends on a symbolic system certainly more legible to its original readers than to us. Just as a modern American can be expected to recognize a Democratic donkey or a Republican elephant, or a modern Briton a Scottish thistle or a London Transit logo (none of these being self-evidently meaningful to an uninformed outsider), many ancient readers of Revelation would have found its imagery more self-explanatory than do we. For instance, the throne room of God, with its crystal sea and its exotic creatures like a lion, calf, man, and eagle (Revelation 4:1–11), speaks much the same symbolic language of serene power and comprehensive sway over creation as Isaiah 6 and Ezekiel 1:10. Similarly, the weird multi-horned Beasts (Revelation 13:1, 11) evoke already familiar monsters of tyrannous rule from Daniel 7:8; the "horn" itself in these passages also appears as a symbol of power in the Psalms (92:10); and John's composite beast of leopard, bear, and lion (Revelation 13:2) replicates the same national symbols of Greece, Medo-Persia, and Babylon invoked in Daniel 7:4–6. So the Seven Plagues in Revelation 16:1–21 repeat and compress the famed Ten Plagues of

Egypt from Exodus 7–12; the Bride (Revelation 21:2) references the *Yahweh*-to-Israel marriage tradition of Ezekiel 23, Hosea, and the Song of Solomon; and the Seven Trumpets and Darkness at Noon (Revelation 8–12, 16:10) reprise in slower time the trumpet of doom and darkness in Joel 2:1–3, 31. Some of Revelation's symbolic entities and objects remain fairly obvious signifiers for us even today – scales of justice, rulers' crowns, bread, purifying and punishing fire, scrolls of knowledge, foreheads of intellect, and hands of labor. Other symbols will make at least intuitive sense – a lampstand for a church, a sword for the truth, a prostitute for worldly temptation, Babylon for human evil, Jerusalem for redeemed goodness, a Lamb for sacrifice, a Lion for strength, and a man on a white horse as Savior.

Thus, for instance, when "the Beast ... causes all, both small and great, rich and poor, free and slave, to receive a mark on their right hand or on their foreheads" (Revelation 13:16), then we can reasonably discern that a monstrous and blasphemous ruler and his regime will claim godlike ownership of all the labor and all the thoughts of their subject peoples; and when we read further that this mark will be "the name of the Beast, or the number of his name," and that this number is "666," we can conclude, numerologically, that this Beast somehow incarnates the sum of all human evil (six, the "number of man" created on the sixth day, tripled). Likewise, when we read about the New Jerusalem "descending out of heaven from God" and measuring "twelve thousand furlongs ... [i]ts length, breadth, and height are equal" (21:16), we are asked to imagine a perfect cube (about 15,000 miles square!) laid out entirely in multiples of twelve, completely symmetrical in all its proportions, and stupendously enormous. Symbolically speaking, then, this passage signifies that redeemed humanity will live together in one great harmonious space, a "City Foursquare" built on the spiritual foundations of the Twelve Tribes and the Twelve Apostles, under the Son of David in a restoration of David's city, but now bursting beyond all tribal and national boundaries When we read in terms of these inherited symbol-systems and its structural and stylistic design, Revelation emerges not as a patched-up metaphysical horror tale full of psychotic sound and fury, but as an intricately crafted and majestically unfolding spectacle about how, despite wicked angels and men doing their damnedest, "all manner of thing shall be well."

15.2.4 "If Anyone Adds ... and Takes Away": Interpreting the Vision

But if carefully unpacking such symbols, phrases, and structures seems to unveil a spiritual drama about the terrifying schemes of evil and the splendid triumph of good, most interpreters of Revelation over the past two millennia have not been satisfied with a "merely" spiritual interpretation. It would be wrong to dismiss this dissatisfaction as idle curiosity, or mere sensationalism, or sheer fanaticism; for though Revelation has attracted plenty of bad attention (most beautiful and powerful things do) we can hardly blame either the Church or the world for seeking over the centuries for answers to the main question normally asked of foretelling prophecy, including Old Testament prophecy: When will all this happen? Or, as the disciples asked Jesus before the Temple walls, "What will be the sign when all these things will be fulfilled?" (Mark 13:4). To break this main question down further into sub-questions: Has this perhaps already happened? Is it happening in my time? If so, what should I do? If not, how far off is it, and how to live now? How will the world know that it *is* happening? How will we tell the evil from the good? And what does it all *mean*?

Throughout its interpretive history, answers to these questions about the Book of Revelation have generated a bewildering variety of approaches, but when one sifts through them, they sort out into four main schools: the **Preterist** (reference back to the first-century past and the early Roman Empire); the **Historicist** (reference back and forward to the entire history of the "Church Age" from the first century until the end of the world); the **Futurist** (reference forward to specific coming events – probably imminent events – just before the return of Christ); and the **Spiritual/Symbolist** (reference now to the eternal present, with spiritual hope for the future). When taken in the context of biblical prophetic interpretation overall, none of these approaches necessarily excludes any or all of the others; yet most interpretive practitioners tend to behave either as if they are all mutually exclusive, or as if one can borrow from other views because they are superseded by one's own. We will consider each interpretive school in the above order, examining its claims to represent Revelation's intent, and its impact on biblical scholarship and on the popular imagination.

15.2.4.1 Preterist: Apocalypse Then

As "preterit" is a grammatical term meaning "past tense" – an action that has already occurred – so **"Preterist"** means the "past" in prophetic interpretation – events that have already taken place. Technically, Preterist readings of Revelation argue that its events are past to *us* in modern times, but were still in the very near future for John at the time of writing. Thus, in Preterist terms, the central drama of the Apocalypse is the Great Tribulation that descends upon the world when Babylon (Rome and its imperial legions) under the corrupt leadership of the Beast (the Emperor Nero) sets about usurping God's throne while systematically exterminating both historical Israel (the Jews) and spiritual Israel (the Church), setting in motion terrible destruction that descends on Jerusalem and her inhabitants.

The Number of His Name: The Neronic Beast

This Preterist past-tense reading is bolstered not only by Nero's historical notoriety for grotesque and blasphemous arrogance, but also by a calculation of the Beast's numerical name, "666" (the Greek number *hexakosiai hexekonta hex* of most New Testament manuscripts), as code for the evil Emperor himself: *Neron Kaisar* rendered in Hebrew (קסר נרון) and then transliterated into Greek (Νρον Κσρ – *Nron Ksr*). (An alternative version is "616" – the Greek number *hexakosioi deka hex* of a very early manuscript called the *Codex Ephraemi Rescriptus* – and is still rendered as *Nero Kaisar* by transliterating the Hebrew קסר נרו as Greek Νρο Κσρ – *Nro Ksr*). Preterists also note that after Nero's suicide in 68 CE – followed by 69 CE, the bloody and chaotic "Year of the Four Emperors" – a legend grew up of *Nero redivivus*, "Nero revived from the dead," which Preterists claim to appear in Revelation as the Beast's death and revival (13:3). And they read Christ's concluding promise – or threat – that he is "coming quickly" (22:20) as meaning that he is coming immediately.

Thus, for the Preterist, the myriad dramatic scene changes of Revelation – all of its seven-fold structures and its embedded unfoldings – exist to encourage first-century Christians to see the terrible tribulations of their time as ordained by God, the "One Upon the Throne," in order to reveal the Root of David at the proper moment, and then to usher in the New Jerusalem at Christ's coming conquest of "Babylonian" Rome. Though some secular Preterists see the book as a kind of fantastic wishful thinking foisted by manipulative leaders on a suffering people, or as a post-dated imposture from the time of Domitian thirty years after Nero, many others see it as genuinely prophetic of actual first-century events and the eventual and remarkable triumph of Christianity over the empire and the transfer of sovereignty from the Caesars to the Church of Rome. (Significantly, the first Preterist to develop an extensive system was the Spanish Jesuit Luis de Alcasar, who wrote in the early seventeenth century to refute Protestant "Historicist" readings of Revelation that identified the Beast with the Pope himself.) But some more recent Protestant Preterists, while reading most of Revelation in reference to the time of Nero, Vespasian, and the destruction of Herod's Temple, allow that the book's final chapters do indeed look ahead into a distant future at the end of the age.

15.2.4.2 Historicist: Apocalypse Then to Now

If prophecy is the history of the future, then the **Historicist** reading of Revelation offers a past and future history of the world. While the Preterist focuses largely on correspondences between the details of Revelation 4–19 and first-century history, the Historicist focuses on two of the earliest chapters, addressed to the Seven Churches of Revelation 2–3, in order to extend its discussion from the first century through the present moment, and beyond. In this interpretation, each of the Seven Churches of Asia represents a particular era in Church history, culminating in the Second Coming – which is usually treated as imminent. Thus, practitioners of this approach tend to see themselves at the culmination of history, with all past times climaxing in their own. The first Historicist readers of Revelation appear to have been inspired by Joachim de Fiore (1135–1202), the Sicilian mystic who saw his world on the verge of a new age when evil would be defeated, religious divisions swept away, and Christ would reign directly from Jerusalem. Certain thirteenth-century Franciscans took Joachim a step further, identifying as Antichrist the Holy Roman Emperor and papal enemy Frederick II (1194–1250), who claimed absolute rule over his empire and was rumored to keep a dragon and many other wicked beasts at his Sicilian palace. Two-and-a-half centuries later, Christopher Columbus seems to have been inspired by Joachim's prediction that the Last Days would be ushered in when the gospel was preached to "all nations, and kindreds, and people, and tongues" (Revelation 7:9), including those in "the coastlands of the sea" (Isaiah 24:15), giving his transatlantic quest for the Indies a spiritual as well as a material motive.

But it was not until the Reformation that Historicism came fully to the fore. Most of the first reformers – John Calvin and Theodore Beza in France and Switzerland, Thomas Cranmer in England, John Knox in Scotland – subscribed to some Historicist account of the "Church Age," generally along the following lines:

1) **Ephesus**: The Church at the end of the apostolic age, having lost its "first love," 95 CE.
2) **Smyrna**: Period of the great persecutions, ending with Constantine's conversion, 95–312.
3) **Pergamos**: The compromised Church under imperial favor and imperial collapse, 312–500.
4) **Thyatira**: Rise of the oppressive imperial Papacy, with a believing remnant, 500–1500.
5) **Sardis**: A believing remnant within a dead Church, leading to Reformation, 1500–1560.
6) **Philadelphia**: A true evangelistic, professing Church, yet not fully pure, 1560–1660.
7) **Laodicea**: The final state of Apostasy, revival of the Papal Beast, defeated by Christ's return.

It is this outline of past and future history that we find underlying George Herbert's apocalyptic vision of the gospel's westward movement in *The Church Militant* (1633); firing the Millenarian hopes of the Puritans during the English Civil Wars and Cromwellian Commonwealth (1642–1660); informing the archangel Michael's account to Adam of the Last Days late in John Milton's *Paradise Lost* (1667); and inspiring Cotton Mather's celebration of "the great works of Christ in America" in *Magnalia Christi Americana* (1702).

But the Protestant Historicists could not entirely escape history, which kept happening, sometimes to their consternation. As each generation passed without either the fall of the Papal Antichrist or his obvious triumph, and especially as the Protestant Anglosphere expanded into history's largest and most dominant cultural and commercial empires, British and then American Christians found themselves far more at home in the world than they could have hoped or feared, and by the nineteenth and early twentieth centuries, respectively, their empires had become something much vaster, mightier, and potentially more wonderful or terrible than old Rome itself. While academic and cultural elites began to distance themselves from biblical laws and hopes and visions, those keeping the flame of Protestant apocalypticism returned to Revelation with an expanded timetable in mind, attempting to fit more and more eras of the recent past into the Seven Churches' representations of the future – a future in which, these interpreters trembled to think, their own Western Zions might be overwhelmed by new Babylons, or birth Babylon itself.

As the United States, following the Puritan dream, declared itself "a city on a hill," as progressive British governments sought to "buil[d] Jerusalem in England's green and pleasant land," and while ancient "Holy Roman" and Ottoman Empires collapsed, new Beasts emerged from the earth and the sea, first in Lenin's and Stalin's Soviet Union, then in Mussolini's Italy, Hirohito's and Tojo's Japan, and Hitler's Third Reich. And something new was born along with these Beasts: a truly global and secular sense that the Apocalypse was upon us, that reality was outstripping our collective religious nightmares, and that the Beast of Beasts, as the great post-Protestant poet Yeats put it in "The Second Coming," "slouches towards Bethlehem to be born." So with a baleful tomorrow thundering on the close horizon, Historicism among the Protestant faithful gave way to Futurism.

15.2.4.3 Futurist: Apocalypse Soon

In our day, **Futurism** has become the default reading of Revelation. It is likely that the average reader who knows anything of prophetic interpretation – especially if that knowledge comes from the internet, popular press, or mass media – understands, admires, dreads, mocks, or loathes the Revelation in Futurist terms. Indeed, it is often a commonplace held by skeptics in secular societies that the Apocalypse, whatever its origins, has devolved into a deep well of ignorance, drawn on by charlatans, demagogues, and fools to sway weak minds already prone to xenophobia, psychosis, and an allegiance to dying social hierarchies. Nothing, in this view, could be farther from the dispassionate and objective world of scholarly inquiry.

However, it was not always so. Indeed, Futurism was born in the bookish studies of nineteenth-century Protestant British and American scholars, who sought to reconcile their Historicist inheritance with the unprecedented transformations and upheavals of their era. A man or woman born in 1810 came into a world in which news still spread at the speed of a horse, sea travel yet depended on the vagaries of the wind, Antarctica, the Arctic, and much of the Americas, Africa, and Australia remained unknown to Europeans, and the slave trade had only just been abolished under the influence of evangelical reformers. Departing this life in 1900 – having lived in North America, Britain, or western Europe – he or she left a world in which news traveled in a flash by wire across continents and under oceans, steam and diesel engines powered global fleets and railroads, Antarctica and the Arctic alone remained unexplored and unsettled, two Ohio bicycle-makers were about to conquer the air, and slavery itself had been legally abolished around the world.

Yet this tide of almost Utopian progress came at a high cost: men, women, and children labored in deep mines and dangerous factories, huddled urban masses breathed foul air, colonized and conquered peoples were exploited and pushed to the edge of extinction, and mechanized warfare raised casualty lists and death tolls to staggering heights. And material progress itself, in the Futurists' view, was a spiritual danger, breeding worldly presumption, idleness, spiritual complacency, and hedonism – indeed all the vices and spoils of Babylon. Not since the days of the Caesars had Revelation's warning against the "merchants of the earth" and their lust for merchandise seemed so urgent: lust to buy and sell not only "gold and silver, precious stones and pearls, fine linen and purple, silk and scarlet," and not only "cinnamon and incense, fragrant oil and frankincense, wine and oil, fine flour and wheat, cattle and sheep, horses and chariots," but also "bodies and souls of men" (18:12–13).

Apparently modernity was creating a discordant convergence of conditions favorable to totalitarian regimes, with an increasingly post-Christian elite ready to exploit popular ethnic and economic passions in order to create new secular religions that would combine military and industrial forces under mass cults of personality. Against this background, Anglo-American Bible scholars who had been trained to regard the Pope as Antichrist began to entertain other candidates for that bad eminence, speculating that times were ripe for the rise of the ultimate Beast, who would be not only a religious cult figure (like the Pope), but a political or military figure with pretensions to deity. In Britain, Anglo-Irish lawyer, translator, and linguist John Nelson Darby (1800–1882) – who viewed the invention of the telegraph as a work of

Satan – developed a system of prophetic interpretation that incorporated the Seven Church Ages of the older Historicist view, but which saw them culminating soon in a far more fearsome "Beast," combining the abominations of the ancient Caesars and Renaissance Popes with the brutal powers of heavy industry and technology, all flowing into a vast sea of Apostasy. American lawyer and Bible scholar Cyrus Scofield (1843–1921) (who regarded biblical "Higher Criticism" as evidence of the coming Great Apostasy) expanded Darby's "Dispensationalist" system into a fully annotated reference Bible (1909), complete with introductions, charts, tables, timelines, and detailed notes explaining how all of scripture (not only Revelation and other apocalyptic passages, but the entire Old and New Testaments) fit into their eschatological system.

Dispensationalism: Dividing the Word, Charting the Ages

Dispensationalism takes its name from the seven Dispensations, or historical ages, each of which is governed by a distinct set of divine expectations to which God holds humanity responsible.

- The **Dispensation of Innocence**, from Creation to Fall, during which a sinless Adam and Eve lived under probation subject to the one law of the Tree of Knowledge, ends with their expulsion from Eden.
- The **Dispensation of Conscience**, from Fall to Flood, during which humans do what is right in their own eyes, ends with the earth "full of violence" extinguished by universal drowning, Noah's Ark excepted.
- The **Dispensation of Human Government**, from Flood to Babel, during which human rulers are responsible under Noah's Law to enforce capital punishment, ends with the tyranny of Babel and the dispersion of humanity.
- The **Dispensation of Promise**, from Abraham to Moses, during which the Hebrews are to walk by faith, ends when they refuse to enter Canaan and are punished with forty years of wilderness wandering.
- The **Dispensation of Law**, from Moses to Jesus Christ's Crucifixion, during which the Hebrews are under the full Mosaic Law, ends when Christ's death fulfills the Law.
- The **Dispensation of Grace**, from the Crucifixion to the Rapture of the Church, during which salvation is freely given to all by grace through faith, ends when Christ Raptures all true believers, setting off the Great Tribulation.
- The **Millennial Kingdom**, from the Return of Christ to the Last Rebellion and Final Judgment, during which Christ reigns from Jerusalem for 1000 years, ends when Christ judges Satan and establishes New Jerusalem.

Though incorporating many traditional elements of Protestant apocalypticism, Dispensationalism emphasizes the differences brought by "rightly dividing the Word of Truth." Dispensationalists depart from the Reformation's covenant theology by stressing, first, that Old Testament Jews lived distinctly under Law and not under Grace; second, that the Jews and a coming restored nation of Israel would retain a special and separate role in the present and future plan of God rather than simply being absorbed into the Church; third, that the Antichrist is a supremely evil figure of the future rather than the papacy in the present; fourth, that the Tribulation is also a uniquely monstrous future era under Antichrist rather than the common lot of Christians until the Last Judgment; fifth, that the Rapture of the Church is a separate event before the Second Coming of Christ; and sixth, that after his Second Coming, Christ will reign on earth for 1000 years before the final rebellion and punishment of the Dragon (Satan) and the establishment of New Jerusalem. And the Dispensationalists continually update their End Times chart of the Seven Church Ages, with late Victorian interpreters (for instance) bringing the Reformation Church of Sardis up to 1750, the evangelical Church of Philadelphia up to 1900, and the apostate Church of Laodicea into the era of biblical "Higher Criticism" with the Tribulation about to begin with the new twentieth century.

From a literary standpoint, the most striking feature of Dispensationalism is its historical-grammatical **literalism**, which insists that to be true, every image or figure in Revelation – and in other biblical prophecies – must correspond to some specific past or future event or person. Thus, for instance, biblical numerology is not to be read as primarily symbolic, with the Dragon's "seven heads and ten horns" (12:3) representing a general perfection of evil power, but rather as literally enumerating seven different rulers over ten future kingdoms. Similarly, Revelation's unfolding cycles of disaster and divine intervention are not to be read as deepening symbolic reiterations of one primal good-over-evil drama, but rather read sequentially as a series of discrete future events unspooling one after another. Neither Darby nor Scofield went so far as to speculate about the exact true identities of these coming literal Beasts and abominations, but the Scofield Reference Bible arrived just in time for the collapse of Victorian optimism and the all-too-literal beastliness of two world wars, which produced enough "antichrists" and atrocities to fulfill the direst nightmares.

Thus, we should not too easily discount the rather exuberant pessimism of modern Dispensationalist interpretation, which eagerly seeks evidence for its Last Days hypothesis. Should we be surprised that hundreds of millions read something like Babylonian woe into the Somme, the global Influenza Pandemic, *Il Duce*, the worldwide Depression, Soviet terror-famines, Stuka dive-bombers, the Blitz, the Holocaust, Dresden, and Hiroshima? Indeed more recent bestselling Dispensationalists – Hal Lindsay and Tim La Haye among them – have continued to see Revelation fulfilled in the headlines, treating the modern State of Israel as fulfilling predictions of Israelite revival, while reading Soviet helicopters as biblical plagues of locusts, and microchips as the latest Mark of the Beast to be implanted in the head and hand.

Ironically, metaphysics and materialism sometimes coincide, for certain fundamentalist Christians' loathing of credit cards and ATMs resembles Marxist hatred of banks and money. Such an example of convergence between religious Right and atheist Left reminds us that Marxism is itself a kind of apocalyptic secular religion, a materialist Futurism conjuring up persistent hopes for the Last Days of capitalism, a Great Tribulation of final class struggle, the Messianic triumph of the proletarian dictatorship, and the Millennium of a classless and cashless society. The persistent question remains who is worthy – indeed who is able – to bring in the Peaceable Kingdom, and by the shedding of whose blood? Given such commonalities across the political and metaphysical divide, can we really blame the Dispensationalists for wanting to see in the symbols of the past the material fulfillments of the future? However over-ingenious, forced, or contrived we may find such exegesis of the daily news, they participate in our general human yearning for a look ahead to an Eden restored, and our universal dread of some Armageddon.

15.2.4.4 Spiritual/Symbolist: Apocalypse Now – and Always

It is this quest for the universal that drives the least prescriptive and most flexible interpretive school, the **Spiritual** or **Symbolist**. "Spiritual" readings of Revelation began by the third century, as Church Fathers like Origen of Alexandria (185–254 CE) and Augustine of Hippo (354–430 CE) came to terms with the facts that not only had the world not ended, but that Christians were moving from persecuted minority to tolerated and preferred majority in the Roman Empire. In such a transformed religious and political landscape, constant apocalyptic dread seemed out of place – though by Augustine's time the empire itself was teetering, which he regards in *The City of God* (426 CE) as divine justice for its past crimes. Yet for all of its indefiniteness, the Symbolist reading of Revelation definitely knows what it is not: namely, it is not Preterist, Historicist, or Futurist. Resisting what most modern Symbolists see as the divisive tendency to turn the Apocalypse into a metaphysical sideshow and numbers game, or into an echo chamber for sectarian animus and partisan politics, Symbolists (many of them within the

Roman Catholic and Orthodox traditions) instead read the Apocalypse as eternally present and yet always becoming.

Thus, Symbolist interpreters frequently warn against playing what one might call "pin-the-tail-on-the-Antichrist," that is, speculating on a string of marginally plausible but (now) demonstrably unsatisfactory candidates for a starring or supporting role in the Day of Doom. In the case of the Antichrist, these candidates have included – each in his own era – Nero, Domitian, Muhammad, Frederick II, the Borgia Pope Alexander VI, all the popes, Napoleon Bonaparte, Benito Mussolini, Adolph Hitler, Joseph Stalin, Henry Kissinger, the Ayatollah Khomeini, Mikhail Gorbachev, Saddam Hussein, and just about every American president from Franklin Roosevelt through Donald Trump. Yet, some Symbolists note, the word "Antichrist" does not even appear in Revelation, and that where it does in 1 and 2 John, we read that "even now many antichrists have come" (1 John 2:18), as if to suggest that the term can apply to multiple villains, or perhaps even the villain under our own hat.

And, the Symbolists also reasonably ask, why didn't the world end in 365 CE (as predicted by Hilary of Poitiers), 1000 (Pope Sylvester II), 1260 (Joachim de Fiore), 1600 (Martin Luther), 1656 (Christopher Columbus), 1736 (Cotton Mather), 1844 (William Miller), 1967 (Jim Jones), 1982 (Pat Robertson), or 2000 (Isaac Newton and Jerry Falwell)? These are only a small fraction of the past-due speculations about The End of Days. Symbolists attempt to remove the Apocalypse from a supposedly dead Preterist past or a dire and speculative future and instead treat its spiritual drama as constantly present; thus, they try to draw attention away from what they see as sensationalized evil and toward spiritual self-examination. Many also complain that by focusing on the more spectacular figures of villainy and vice or on a timetable for their arrival, we frustrate the central purpose of the book: as its opening verse says, "The revelation of Jesus Christ," the glorification of the Lamb himself.

Yet if Symbolists respond understandably to the excesses and demonstrable failures of literalist Futurism, their "spiritual" readings can fall into excesses of their own by encouraging or at least abetting interpretations of the Apocalypse as "merely symbolic." Even if one regards the idea of actual divine revelation as imaginary, one need not share the view that somehow symbols and symbolism can be safely dismissed and ignored, or divorced from history. On the contrary, symbols matter precisely *because* they are "imaginary" – that is, because human beings think primarily in images, speak in languages founded on condensed imagery, and respond with deep and often passionate feeling to images and symbols that time and tradition and special conditioning have invested with great associative power. No doubt there are few, if any, truly "universal" symbols guaranteed to move all equally; nevertheless virtually all people will be inspired, spurred, or incited by some set of symbols, and great masses of people by certain common symbols.

Thus, though it is clearly true that symbols cherished by some – a flag, an emblem, a religious icon, a logo – will be despised by others, generally this does not mean, as some are carelessly inclined to say, that such symbols "mean nothing" to those who despise them. Indeed, it is only because of a common substrate of meaning that this despising can take place at all. For the D-Day veteran overcome with awe by US flags and crosses stretching to the horizon at a Normandy graveyard, and the flag-burning protester wearing an inverted crucifix, agree that these flags and crosses "mean" the United States and the Christian religion – two entities either loved or hated, but their symbols far from meaningless. Similarly, if a hostile passerby defaces a "peace sign" in a front yard and a "mirror of Venus" on a car bumper, it is usually because he or she agrees that these shapes symbolize disarmament and feminism, not because they are unintelligible.

Furthermore, while many symbols, like forgotten languages, wear out and become unintelligible over time, or are misread in later ages, this decay does not make them "meaningless" any more than the Rosetta Stone was meaningless for the 2000 years during which it lay buried in

Egypt awaiting its rediscovery in 1799 by those with eyes to see. Likewise, the myriad symbols in the Book of Revelation, while perhaps defaced and partly buried under two millennia of cultural forgetting, well-intended misreading, and willful abuse, may preserve authentic information about how it is to be read and appreciated, if only we know what to ask.

15.2.5 The Three-Fold Answer: A Symbolic Drama of Past, Present, and Future

And what do we ask of Revelation? More importantly, what does Revelation ask of us? How does it demand to be understood? We began the above section on Revelation's four main interpretive schools by noting that, within the traditions of prophetic interpretation overall, these approaches – the Preterist, the Historicist, the Futurist, and the Symbolist – need not be mutually exclusive, whatever some of their practitioners might say. So how does the Apocalypse seek to be read? The answer, to use an appropriate biblical number, is three-fold: as the Son of Man commands John from the start, "Write the things which you have seen, and the things which are, and the things which will take place after this" (1:19). That is, Christ the Lord "who was and is and is to come" (4:8) instructs John to record past, present, and future – past history, present event, and future prediction. From this perspective, all three approaches to the book's chronology – Preterist, Historicist, and Futurist – contribute to its overarching symbolic drama, and to its total meaning.

Thus, from John's viewpoint, it is his task to register (and ours to read) past, present, and future as distinct yet interpenetrating. Old Testament echoes affirm the typological reading of the biblical past as lived prophecy for the present and future; allusions to the present suffering of the Church under beasts like Nero and Domitian are subsumed into the eternal present of the three-fold God who knows the end from the beginning; and future fulfillments are predicted (as in much Old Testament prophecy) in the "prophetic past tense," that is, as being so certain that we can speak of them as already done. And, notably, each of John's present-day Seven Churches is described as having a past, present, and future. Combining all these days of future past with past futures and the prophetic present can boggle the mind, and when we see the prophetic drama enlivened with such an astounding cast of characters, our eyes may dazzle, as with the sight of that angel standing in the sun.

But to recognize that, in literary terms, Revelation asks to be read eclectically is not fully to understand what it is saying, nor necessarily to believe it. Indeed, acknowledging these kaleidoscopic qualities is likely to make us less certain of specific referents, of particular timetables, of symmetric historical charts, and yet, no literary reading can by itself rule out the possibility of future consummations. For however much some Symbolists might disagree, it remains true that the Bible's prophecies, especially the numerical prophecies, are intended to be read, if not entirely literally, at least with literal future referents and numbers in mind. When in Genesis 40 and 41 Joseph interprets the dreams of his fellow prisoners and then of Pharaoh, the imagery of those dreams – grape clusters, bread baskets, gaunt cows devouring fat cows, blighted grain eating up good grain – turns out to mean something quite specific for the future. In the latter case, Joseph declares that

> [t]he dreams of Pharaoh are one; God has shown Pharaoh what he is about to do: the seven good cows are seven years, and the seven good heads are seven years; the dreams are one. And the seven thin and ugly cows which came up after them are seven years, and the seven empty heads blighted by the east wind are seven years of famine. (Genesis 41:25–27)

This miniature burst of prophecy from the time of the patriarchs is "apocalyptic" not only in its revelation of alarming pictures – carnivorous, cannibal cattle! self-consuming grain! – but also in the particular meanings of these stylized figures, which are indeed symbolic (they represent good and lean years), but not "merely symbolic": their total is counted not only figuratively as a seven-fold perfection of suffering, but literally as actual periods of time. Yet interpretation is still required: the butler's and baker's three bunches and three baskets mean three days, not three weeks or years, and Pharaoh's doubled dream indicates not twenty-eight years total, but fourteen, because "the doubling of Pharaoh's dream means that the thing is fixed by God, and God will shortly bring it to pass" (Gen. 41:32). In other words, we are being told that these richly symbolic "little apocalypses" will yield up their literal meanings – remember the "weeks of years" in Daniel 9:24–27 – but only to the proper interpreter at the right time.

Joseph's predictions come about "shortly"; but what of longer-term prophecy? What about the many, many apocalyptic passages and books from Isaiah and Ezekiel to Joel and Malachi – and from Matthew to Revelation – which speak of "latter days" and indeed the Last Days? Are we to read these, as some Preterists do, as referring only to their original places and times, with The End Times proclamations understood as literary hyperbole for dramatic effect? What should be said is that, first, these passages and books themselves seem to distinguish between their short-term and long-term predictions: predicting some things as imminent (Jeremiah 21:3–7, Daniel 9:1–2) and some things as apparently at The End of Days (Jeremiah 23:5–8, Daniel 7:13–14). That is, these prophets often claim to tell the difference between "forthtelling" words spoken for the present moment and "foretelling" words seeing afar off into the great "forever and ever." Second, as we have observed above and in our previous two chapters about the New Testament outside the Revelation, the gospels and epistles speak not only to immediate circumstances but quite consciously of a future era when ultimate evil will be fully manifested (2 Thessalonians 2:1–3), Christ will destroy it upon his return (1 Corinthians 15:23–25), the world will be consumed with fervent heat (2 Peter 3:10), and then will commence a "new heavens and a new earth in which righteousness dwells" (2 Peter 3:13). "How far off?" is, of course, the question, but all of these writers seem sure that there is an answer, even if no one living has ears to hear or eyes to see it.

15.3 Full Circle: A Tree in a Garden

Here we confront the limits of what a literary approach to Revelation can achieve. We have observed the book's remarkable coherence as a symbolic and cosmic drama, the systematic nature of its imagery, and its distinct interpenetration of chronological time and eternity, and we have seen how the four main interpretive schools can complement, correct, or contradict each other. But having seen so much, we must admit that we still stand on the outside of Revelation's fullest meanings. Perhaps, as with other imaginative writing, it is only a willing suspension of disbelief that can put us inside the structure, much as architects may admire from the outside the glories of a great temple, but not obtain access to its inner chambers unless they enter in faith.

But if literary study cannot pronounce finally on the past, present, and future mysteries of the Apocalypse, it certainly can admire fine poetry and prose, and that even rarer thing, fine prose poetry – and Revelation's last chapters contain some of the best ever penned:

> Now I saw a new heaven and a new earth, for the first heaven and the first earth had passed away. Also there was no more sea. Then I, John, saw the holy city, New Jerusalem, coming down out of heaven from God, prepared as a bride adorned for her husband. And I heard a loud voice from heaven saying, "Behold, the tabernacle of God is with men, and he will dwell with them, and they shall be his people. God himself will be with them and be their God. And God will wipe away every tear from their eyes; there shall

> be no more death, nor sorrow, nor crying. There shall be no more pain, for the former things have passed away." (21:1–4)
>
> But I saw no temple in it, for the Lord God Almighty and the Lamb are its temple. The city had no need of the sun or of the moon to shine in it, for the glory of God illuminated it. The Lamb is its light. (21:22–23)

If the earth and the sky could speak, this is how they might sound. So many writers – from Augustine's *City of God* and Dante's *Paradiso* to Bunyan's Celestial City and Bradbury's *Fahrenheit 451* – echo this passage's blissful assurance. Whatever we may make of its theology or eschatology, this is great writing: as spare, muscular, and elemental as the best of Modernism, yet as joyous as first love or a spring dawn.

And literary study certainly can appreciate grand designs, with the Christian Bible's being perhaps the grandest. This book of books begins in Genesis with two trees in a rivered garden, a paradise soon lost by exiles cast out to wander, or to dwell in the cities of men, and it ends in these last chapters of Revelation by coming full circle to a renewed garden, and a greater tree, and a river running through it:

> And he showed me a pure river of water of life, clear as crystal, proceeding from the throne of God and of the Lamb. In the middle of its street, and on either side of the river, was the tree of life, which bore twelve fruits, each tree yielding its fruit every month. The leaves of the tree were for the healing of the nations. And there shall be no more curse, but the throne of God and of the Lamb shall be in it, and his servants shall serve him. They shall see his face, and his name shall be on their foreheads. There shall be no night there: They need no lamp nor light of the sun, for the Lord God gives them light. And they shall reign forever and ever. (22:1–5)

Just as God's first creation of light and his last re-creation of heaven and earth needed no sun, so here we find again, as for the first time, a River and Tree of Life, closing the circle on both the Word and the Works of God. And Leviticus had promised that God would pitch his tabernacle among the people, and we have seen the New Heavens and New Earth before, at the end of Isaiah's vision, and the City Foursquare before, at the end of Ezekiel's.

Yet this final revelation of Kingdom Come presents us not only with a returning circle, but with a progressive line from Eden to Apocalypse: for the new garden and river and tree now form the heart of that great City, as if all the Tree's leaves had healed the wandering nations, and their often-deadly cities can somehow be re-purposed, reconciled, "made new." That City needs no Temple besides the now-intimate Almighty, nor any Tree of Knowledge but the face of God, and no sun but the Light. And because there is no more curse, there can be no more sin; for where all are pleased to love, all are free to do as they please.

What, then, does all of this mean? To some it will mean everything, to some a great deal, to some little or nothing, and to some – perhaps many – it could mean anything. We have seen that the book asks to be read in past, present, and future tenses, and in the end it warns its readers against adding to or subtracting from its words (22:18–19); yet it also warns against anyone presuming to open its scroll and interpreting hastily.

> Then I saw a strong angel proclaiming with a loud voice, "Who is worthy to open the scroll and to loose its seals?" And no one in heaven or on the earth or under the earth was able to open the scroll, or to look at it.
>
> So I wept much, because no one was found worthy to open and read the scroll, or to look at it. (5:2–4)

While plenty of the faithful, and some no doubt less faithful, have stepped forward to provide more than enough answers, according to Revelation itself there is only one person worthy or capable of interpreting these things fully, of opening the great scroll and loosing all seven of its seals. And however faithful or skeptical we are, and regardless of religion or creed, we must agree that this person – "the Lion of the tribe of Judah, the Root of David" (5:5) – has not set foot on earth since John laid down his pen.

While a thousand millions of the faithful wait for that arrival, millions more are embarrassed or amused or disheartened by the protracted delay – and billions of others hope at least for some renewal of the earth. In the meantime John's Patmos vision provides a theater for viewing our past and future histories in the light of something beyond time. It judges former Beasts; it helps us to identify Beasts in our own day, and in ourselves; and it both threatens and promises final judgment on all beastliness, and predicts the outbreak of everlasting peace. For those expecting only apocalyptic agony from John's vision, his final chapters may leave us surprised by joy, as old Eden and the New Jerusalem embrace each other, and the often tragic drama of the Bible turns fully tragicomic. But after this sublimely happy climax comes an anticlimactic reminder for what we might call the return to secular time: "He that is unjust let him be unjust still; and he which is filthy, let him be filthy still; and he that is righteous, let him be righteous still; and he that is holy, let him be holy still" (22:11–12).

So, while Christendom listens for that final knock on the cosmic door, all the world is warned, lest we think that human means can bring fully divine ends – for that is what the Beasts have generally promised, often troubling the earth with cures worse than the disease. And as in true tragicomedy, John's vision of blessing and reconciliation is tempered by an awareness of lasting alienation for some souls, as the blessed gates close on "whosoever loves and practices a lie" (22:15). Having staged the ultimate Conclusion, Revelation ends inconclusively; whatever one believes about Kingdom Come, we might agree that to keep from practicing lies we should at least avoid premature conclusions about the truth.

Questions for Discussion

1 What elements of **epistolary form** help to open the **Book of Revelation**?

2 Can you recall some examples of how the **Revelation has influenced cultures** ancient and modern, sacred and secular, high and low?

3 How do the "**little apocalypses**" of the **gospels** and the **epistles** imagine and portray the *Parousia*, Christ's "Second Coming"? How "soon" or "quickly" is it expected? How do these writers anticipate believers' disappointment with Christ's perceived delay, and how do they address that delay?

4 What are the different theories of **who wrote Revelation and when**? Why, according to these varied views, was the book written at all? What, if anything, do these competing theories share in common?

5 What are the **main interpretive difficulties** of Revelation? Why have some readers, both religious and secular, attacked and condemned the book?

6 What are the **main structural principles** around which Revelation is organized? Can you give an example of each principle at work?

7   What are the **theatrical qualities** of the Revelation? How might recognizing its dramatic qualities prepare us for addressing certain perennial interpretive questions? Who are some of the crucial characters acting in the drama?

8   What features characterize the **language and the imagery** of Revelation? What relation does this language show back to the apocalyptic books and passages of the Hebrew Bible, and how might this relationship help in opening up some of Revelation's meanings?

9   For each of the four main interpretive traditions that address Revelation – **Preterist**, **Historicist**, **Futurist**, and **Symbolist** – what is its central defining idea? How does this central idea influence or determine which textual details receive more attention or less? What are the interpretive strengths and weaknesses of each approach, as far as the book's text is concerned? What influence has each tradition shown, over whom, and when? What are some of the larger theological, social, and cultural implications of each interpretive school?

10 What light can a literary approach throw on the **differences and similarities** among the four main interpretive traditions? How far might these four schools be in some measure **reconciled**? What are the limits to what a literary approach can accomplish in explaining and resolving the book's interpretive difficulties?

11 How does Revelation **close not only the New Testament but the entire Christian Bible**? What references do Revelation's chapters – especially its concluding chapters – make back to the Hebrew Bible/Old Testament, particularly to its many prophetic books and to its opening Book of Genesis? How is Revelation's conclusion "**fully tragicomic**"?

Appendix 1

Suggestions for Further Reading

Ackerman, J.S. and Warshaw, T.S. (1976). *The Bible as/in Literature*. Glenview, IL: Scott, Foresman, and Company.

Alter, R. (2011). *The Art of Biblical Narrative*. Revised Edition. New York, NY: Basic Books.

Alter, R. and Kermode, F. (1987). *The Literary Guide to the Bible*. Cambridge, MA: The Belknap Press of Harvard University.

Bright, J. (1972). *A History of Israel*, 2e. Philadelphia, PA: The Westminster Press.

Carroll, R. and Prickett, S. (eds.) (1997). *The Bible. Authorized King James Version with Apocrypha*. Oxford: Oxford University Press.

Cassuto, U. (2005). *The Documentary Hypothesis and the Composition of the Pentateuch. Eight Lectures*. Philadelphia, PA: Jewish Publication Society of America/Varda Books.

Dinsmore, C.A. (1931). *The English Bible as Literature*. New York, NY: Allen and Unwin.

Gabel, J.B., Wheeler, C.B., York, A.D., and Citino, D. (eds.) (2006). *The Bible as Literature: An Introduction*, 5e. Oxford: Oxford University Press.

Harris, S.L. (2010). *Exploring the Bible*. New York, NY: McGraw Hill.

Hoerth, A.J. (2009). *Archaeology and the Old Testament*. Grand Rapids, MI: Baker Books.

Hyers, M.C. (1984). *The Meaning of Creation: Genesis and Modern Science*. Philadelphia, PA: Westminster John Knox Press.

Jack, A.M. (2012). *The Bible and Literature*. London: SCM Press.

Jasper, D. and Prickett, S. (2007). *The Bible and Literature*. Hoboken, NJ and Oxford: Wiley-Blackwell Publishers.

Keller, W. (1981). *The Bible as History*. Trans. William Neil. New York, NY: William Morrow and Company.

Kurz, W.S. (2007). *Reading the Bible as God's Own Story: A Catholic Approach for Bringing Scripture to Life*. Frederick, MD: The Word Among Us Press.

Miles, J. (1996). *God: A Biography*. New York, NY: Vintage Books.

Moore, H. and Reid, J. (eds.) (2011). *Manifold Greatness: The Making of the King James Bible*. Oxford: Bodleian Library.

Moulton, R.G. (1938). *The Modern Reader's Bible*. New York, NY: Macmillan.

Norton, D. (2000). *A History of the English Bible as Literature*. Cambridge: Cambridge University Press.

Prickett, S. (ed.) (2014). *The Edinburgh Companion to the Bible and the Arts*. Edinburgh: Edinburgh University Press.

Ryken, L. (1992). *Words of Delight: A Literary Introduction to the Bible*. Grand Rapids, MI: Baker Academic.

Ryken, L. (2014). *A Complete Handbook to Literary Forms in the Bible*. Wheaton, IL: Crossway Books.

Ryken, L. and Ryken, P. (2009). *The Literary Study Bible*. Wheaton, IL: Crossway Books.

Literary Study of the Bible: An Introduction, First Edition. Christopher Hodgkins.
© 2020 John Wiley & Sons Ltd. Published 2020 by John Wiley & Sons Ltd.

(1982). *The Holy Bible. New King James Version*. Nashville, TN: Thomas Nelson Publishers.

Thomas, D.W. (1961). *Documents from Old Testament Times*. New York, NY: Harper and Row.

Wangerin, W. (1996). *The Book of God: The Bible as a Novel*. Grand Rapids, MI: Zondervan.

Whybray, R.N. (1994). *The Making of the Pentateuch: A Methodological Study*. Sheffield: JSOT Press.

Wieder, L. (ed.) (1994). *King Solomon's Garden: Poems and Art Inspired by the Old Testament*. New York, NY: Harry N. Abrams/Times Mirror.

Wright, G.E. (1960). *Biblical Archaeology*. Philadelphia, PA: The Westminster Press.

Appendix 2

Boxes and Illustrations

Literary Study of the Bible: An Introduction, First Edition. Christopher Hodgkins.
© 2020 John Wiley & Sons Ltd. Published 2020 by John Wiley & Sons Ltd.

Index

a

Aaron   150, 151, 153, 156, 167–171, 191, 198, 211, 264

Aaronic priesthood   165, 198, 211, 354–355, 404–405

Aaron's rod   165, 170, 246

Abdon   197

Abel, city of   238

Abel, son of Adam   80, 81, 104–105, 115, 135, 242, 405

Abiathar   220, 235, 243

Abigail   220, 222, 297

Abijah, King of Judah   251

Abimelech, King of Gerar (title of multiple Canaanite rulers)   17, 104, **118, 119, 123**, 163

Abimelech, son of Gideon   191, **195–196**

Abinadab, Aaronic priest   211

Abinadab, son of Saul   224

Abishag the Shunammite   242–243

Abishai   221, 227, 235, 238

Abner   **227–229**, 234, 243

Abraham   20, 22, 37
   and "anti-patriarchal patriarchy"   **114–120**
   and deferred narrative judgment   81, 118
   and Eliezer   121, 126
   and Hagar   80–82, 115, 119, 265, 392
   and the Hittites   19, 121, 390
   and Ibrahim in Qur'an, compared   115
   and Ishmael   82, 115, 119, 265, 392
   and Melchizedek   80, 114
   and narrative doubling   80
   and narrative irony   83
   and Sarah as his "sister"   17, 114, 118
   and second wife Keturah   122

   and theophany   128
   as father of the Jews   357
   as hero of faith in Romans   381
   as father to Gentiles in James   405
   bargaining for Sodom and Gomorrah   **116–117**, 358
   birth of Isaac   83, 116, 118
   blessing to "all the families of the earth"   113, 146, 247, 311
   called out of Ur in Chaldea   **112–113**, 126, 158
   circumcision of   **113**, 164, 381–382
   compared with Jesus   341, 373
   cutting the covenant   **113**
   death of   122, 131
   in parable of rich man and Lazarus   346–347
   in Protestant Dispensationalist theology   429
   Jesus as son of, in Matthew   348–350, 353
   marriage of Isaac   121
   multiple misdeeds of   82
   name change from Abram to Abraham   **114**, 115, 381–382
   rescue of Lot with Sodom and Gomorrah   114
   sacrifice of Isaac   82–83, **119–120**, 135
   yielding to Lot   114

Abrahamic Covenant *see* Covenants

Abram *see* Abraham

Absalom
   alliance with Ahithophel   234–235
   alliance with Joab   234
   attempted coup, **233–236**
   as avenging brother of Tamar   233–234
   beauty of   234
   and chiastic plot structure   **230–238**, 422
   compared to Amnon and Adonijah   242
   compared to David   233–234

Literary Study of the Bible: An Introduction, First Edition. Christopher Hodgkins.
© 2020 John Wiley & Sons Ltd. Published 2020 by John Wiley & Sons Ltd.